Durham's

Place-Names
of
Greater
Los Angeles

Durham's Place-Names of California Series

- Fourteen volumes cover the state of California by region
- The most complete California place-name series

• *Durham's Place-Names of California's Gold Country Including Yosemite National Park:* **Includes Madera, Mariposa, Tuolumne, Calaveras, Amador, El Dorado, Placer, Sierra & Nevada Counties** ISBN 1-884995-25-X

• *Durham's Place-Names of the California North Coast:* **Includes Del Norte, Humbolt, Lake, Mendocino & Trinity Counties** ISBN 1-884995-26-8

• *Durham's Place-Names of California's Old Wine Country:* **Includes Napa & Sonoma Counties** ISBN 1-884995-27-6

• *Durham's Place-Names of Greater Los Angeles:* **Includes Los Angeles, Orange & Ventura Counties** ISBN 1-884995-28-4

• *Durham's Place-Names of California's Central Coast:* **Includes Santa Barbara, San Luis Obispo, San Benito, Monterey & Santa Cruz Counties** ISBN 1-884995-29-2

• *Durham's Place-Names of California's Eastern Sierra:* **Includes Alpine, Inyo & Mono Counties** ISBN 1-884995-30-6

• *Durham's Place-Names of California's Desert Counties:* **Includes Imperial, Riverside & San Bernadino Counties** ISBN 1-884995-31-4

• *Durham's Place-Names of* **San Diego County** ISBN 1-884995-32-2

• *Durham's Place-Names of Central California:* **Includes Madera, Fresno, Tulare, Kings & Kern Counties** ISBN 1-884995-33-0

• *Durham's Place-Names of California's North Sacramento Valley:* **Includes Butte, Glenn, Shasta, Siskiyou & Tehama Counties** ISBN 1-884995-34-9

• *Durham's Place-Names of The San Francisco Bay Area:* **Includes Marin, San Francisco, San Mateo, Contra Costa, Alameda , Solano & Santa Clara Counties** ISBN 1-884995-35-7

• *Durham's Place-Names of California's South Sacramento Valley:* **Includes Colusa, Sacramento, Sutter, Yuba & Yolo Counties** ISBN 1-884995-36-5

• *Durham's Place-Names of California's North San Joaquin Valley:* **Includes San Joaquin, Stanislaus & Merced Counties** ISBN 1-884995-37-3

• *Durham's Place-Names of Northeastern California:* **Includes Lassen, Modoc & Plumas Counties** ISBN 1-884995-38-1

The above titles are available at better bookstores, on-line bookstores or by calling 1-800-497-4909

Durham's

Place-Names
of
Greater Los Angeles

Includes Los Angeles, Orange
and Ventura Counties

David L. Durham

Clovis, California

Word Dancer Press books may be purchased at special prices for educational, fund-raising, business or promotional use. Please contact Special Markets, Quill Driver Books/Word Dancer Press, Inc. at the above address or phone number.

To order another copy of this book or another book in the Durham's Place-Names of California series, please call 1-800-497-4909.

Quill Driver Books/Word Dancer Press, Inc. project cadre:
Doris Hall, Dave Marion, Stephen Blake Mettee

ISBN 1-884995-28-4

Library of Congress Cataloging-in-Publication Data

Durham, David L., 1925-
    Durham's place names of Greater Los Angeles : includes Los Angeles, Orange and Ventura counties / David L. Durham.
    p. cm. -- (Durham's California place-names series)
    Includes bibliographical references.
    ISBN 1-884995-28-4 (trade pbk.)
    1. Names, Geographical--California--Los Angeles Region. 2. Los Angeles Region (Calif.)--History, Local. 3. Los Angeles County (Calif.)--History, Local. 4. Orange County (Calif.)--History, Local. 5. Ventura County (Calif.)--History, Local. I. Title: Place names of Greater Los Angeles. II. Title.

F869.L83 D87 2001
917.94'9'003--dc21

                                                            00-054634

Cover photograph, "Los Angeles, California, Downtown Skyline with San Gabriel Mountains," by Michelle & Tom Grimm, courtesy of the Los Angeles Convention and Visitors Bureau, Los Angeles, California.

CONTENTS

GAZETTEER

CALIFORNIA
GREATER LOS ANGELES
AREA COUNTIES SHADED

Introduction

Purpose, organization and scope

This gazetteer, which lists geographic features of Los Angeles, Orange and Ventura counties, California, is one of a series of fourteen books that cover the whole state. This series is derived from *California's Geographic Names: A Gazetteer of Historic and Modern Names of the State,* David L. Durham's definitive gazetteer of California. Each book contains all the entries for the counties covered that are included in the larger volume.United States government quadrangle maps, which are detailed, somewhat authoritative, and generally available, are the primary source of information. Included are features that are named on quadrangle maps, or that can be related to features named on the maps. The books list relief features, water features, and most kinds of cultural features, but omit names of streets, parks, schools, churches, cemeteries, dams and the like. Some names simply identify a person or family living at a site because such places are landmarks in sparsely settled parts of the state.

The listing of names is alphabetical, and multiword names are alphabetized as one word. Terms abbreviated on maps are given in full in the alphabetical list, and numerals in names are listed in alphabetical order rather than in numerical order. In addition to the principal entries, the list includes cross references to variant names, obsolete names and key words in multiword English-language names. For each principal entry, the name is followed by the name of the county or counties in which the feature lies, a classifying term, general and specific locations, identification of one or more quadrangle maps that show the name and other information. All features named in an entry generally belong to the same county. The classifying terms are defined under the heading "Geographic Terms" beginning on page *xi*.

Locations and measurements are from quadrangle maps, distances and directions are approximate, and latitude and longitude generally are to the nearest five seconds. Distances between post offices are measured by road, as the mail would be carried. Other distances are measured in a straight line unless the measurement is given with a qualifying expression such as "downstream" or "by road." For streams, the location given generally is the place that the stream joins another stream, enters the sea or a lake, or debouches into a canyon or valley. For features of considerable areal extent, the location given ordinarily is near the center, except for cities and towns, for which the location given is near the center of the downtown part, or at the city hall or civic center. Measurements to or from areal features usually are to or from the center. Specific locations are omitted for some very large or poorly defined places. Books, articles, and miscellaneous maps are listed under "References Cited." The references identify sources of data and provide leads to additional information. If a name applies to more than one feature in a county, the features are numbered and identified elsewhere in the list by that number in parentheses following the name.

SETTING

General.—This book concerns geographic features in three counties—Los Angeles, Orange, and Ventura—that front on the southern coast of California. The map on page *vi* shows the location of the counties. Townships (T) and Ranges (R) refer to San Bernardino Base and Meridian. Although the region is highly urbanized and industrialized, all of the counties include some remote and unsettled parts. The region generally has a moderate climate near the coast and a somewhat harsher climate farther inland. Most of the inhabitants depend on water brought from outside.

Los Angeles County.—Los Angeles County lies along the coast between Orange County and Ventura County, and includes highlands to the north and east. The east part of Los Angeles County is at the southwest tip of Mojave Desert—the name "Mojave" for the desert is from the designation of Indians that lived farther east near Colorado River (Gudde, 1949, p. 219); United States Board on Geographic Names (1934, p. 11) rejected the form "Mohave Desert" for the name, and cited local usage for the decision. San Clemente Island and Santa Catalina Island offshore belong to Los Angeles County. The first state legislature created the county in 1850, and in 1851 the county boundaries were changed so that it included the territory of present San Bernardino County; in 1853 the east part of this huge area was lost when San Bernardino County itself was organized, and more territory was lost in 1889 with the formation of Orange County; the Los Angeles-Ventura County line was uncertain from the beginning, and it was not until 1923 that all of the Los Angeles County boundaries were finally defined (Coy, p. 140-156). Los Angeles has been the county seat from the beginning (Hoover, Rensch, and Rensch, p. 146).

Orange County.—Orange County includes lowlands adjacent to Los Angeles County and highlands farther south. The state legislature created Orange County in 1889 from part of Los Angeles County, and the county boundaries have not changed (Coy, p. 196). Santa Ana is and always has been the county seat (Hoover, Rensch, and Rensch, p. 259).

Ventura County.—Ventura County extends from the coast inland to include the lower part of the valley of Santa Clara River and highlands adjacent to the river. The county includes Anacapa Island and San Nicolas Island offshore. The state legislature created Ventura County in 1872 from the east part of Santa Barbara County; some territory was added to the east by a resurvey of Los Angeles-Ventura County line in 1881, a boundary made official in 1923 (Coy, p. 291-293). Ventura has been the the seat of county government from the beginning; the county name is derived from San Buenaventura mission (Hoover, Rensch, and Rensch, p. 576).

GEOGRAPHIC TERMS

Anchorage —A somewhat protected place where ships anchor.

Area —A tract of land, either precisely or indefinitely defined.

Bay —A body of water connected to a larger body of water and nearly surrounded by land.

Beach —An expanse of sandy or pebbly material that borders a body of water.

Bend —A pronounced curve in the course of a stream, and the land partly enclosed therein.

Canyon —A narrow elongate depression in the land surface, generally confined between steep sides and usually drained by a stream.

Cave —A naturally formed subterranean chamber.

City —An inhabited place that has a population greater than about 25,000 in an urban setting.

District —Part of an inhabited place, either precisely or indefinitely defined.

Dry lake —A lake bed that normally lacks water.

Dry wash —A normally dry watercourse that on a map is shown without a stream.

Embayment —An indentation in the shoreline of a body of water.

Escarpment —A cliff or a nearly continuous line of steep slopes.

Gully —A small canyon-like depression in the land surface.

Hill —A prominent elevation on the land surface that has a well-defined outline on a map, and that rises less than 1000 feet above its surroundings.

Intermittent lake —A lake that ordinarily contains water only part of the time.

Island —A tract of normally dry land, or of marsh, that is surrounded by water.

Lake —A body of standing water, either natural or artificial.

Land grant —A gift of land made by Spanish or Mexican authority and eventually confirmed by the United States government.

Locality —A place that has past or present cultural associations.

Military installation —Land or facility used for military purposes.

Mountain —A prominent elevation on the land surface that has a well-defined outline on a map, and that rises more than 1000 feet above its surroundings.

Narrows —The constricted part of a channel, river, canyon, valley, or pass.

Pass —A saddle or natural depression that affords passage across a range or between peaks.

Peak —A prominent high point on a larger elevated land surface.

Peninsula —An elongate tract of land nearly surrounded by water.

Promontory —A conspicuous, but not necessarily high, elevation of the land surface that protrudes into a body of water or into a lowland.

Range —An elevated land surface of ridges and peaks.

Relief feature —A general term for a recognizable form of the land surface produced by natural causes.

Ridge —A prominent elongate elevation on the land surface; occurs either independently or as part of a larger elevation.

Rock —A rocky mass that lies near or projects above the surface of a body of water.

Settlement —An informal inhabited place.

Spring —A natural flow of water from the ground.

Stream —A body of water that moves under gravity in a depression on the land surface; includes watercourses that have intermittent flow and watercourses that are modified by man.

Town —An inhabited place that has a population of about 500 to 25,000 in an urban setting.

Valley —A broad depression in the land surface, or a wide place in an otherwise narrow depression.

Village —An inhabited place that has a compact cluster of buildings and a population less than about 500.

Waterfall —A perpendicular or very steep descent of the water in a stream.

Water feature —A general term for something or some place involving water.

– A –

Abadi Creek [VENTURA]: *stream,* flows 5.25 miles to Sespe Creek 6 miles west-southwest of Reyes Peak (lat. 34°36'30" N, long. 119° 23' W; near W line sec. 13, T 6 N, R 24 W). Named on Old Man Mountain (1943) 7.5' quadrangle.

Abalone Cove [LOS ANGELES]: *embayment,* 7 miles south of Redondo Beach city hall along the coast (lat. 33°44'30" N, long. 118°22'50" W). Named on Redondo Beach (1951) 7.5' quadrangle.

Abalone Point [LOS ANGELES]: *promontory,* 0.5 mile east of Avalon on the northeast side of Santa Catalina Island (lat. 33°20'35" N, long. 118°19' W). Named on Santa Catalina East (1950) 7.5' quadrangle.

Abalone Point [ORANGE]: *promontory,* 2.25 miles west-northwest of Laguna Beach city hall along the coast (lat. 33°33'15" N, long. 117°49'10" W). Named on Laguna Beach (1965) 7.5' quadrangle. Meadows (p. 102) listed a small cove called Morro Bay that is located on the east side of Abalone Point.

Abbott's Landing: see **Balboa** [ORANGE].

Aberdeen Canyon [LOS ANGELES]: *canyon,* less than 1 mile long, 5.25 miles north-northwest of Los Angeles city hall (lat. 34°07'15" N, long. 118°17'15" W). Named on Hollywood (1953) 7.5' quadrangle.

Abrams Canyon [LOS ANGELES]: *canyon,* drained by a stream that flows 1.5 miles to Pine Canyon (3) 1 mile west of the village of Lake Hughes (lat. 34°40'40" N, long. 118°27'30" W; sec. 22, T 7 N, R 15 W). Named on Lake Hughes (1957) 7.5' quadrangle.

Absco: see **Ventura** [VENTURA].

Acelga: see **Santa Ana** [ORANGE].

Acton [LOS ANGELES]: *town,* 20 miles northeast of downtown San Fernando in Soledad Canyon (lat. 34°28'10" N, long. 118°11'45" W; mainly in sec. 36, T 5 N, R 13 W). Named on Acton (1959) 7.5' quadrangle. Postal authorities established Acton post office in 1887 (Frickstad, p. 69). According to local residents, the name is from Acton, Massachusetts (Hanna, p. 2).

Acton Camp [LOS ANGELES]: *locality,* 1.25 miles south of Acton in Soledad Canyon (lat. 34°26'55" N, long. 118°11'50" W; near NW cor. sec. 12, T 4 N, R 13 W). Named on Acton (1959) 7.5' quadrangle. Acton (1939) 6' quadrangle has the label "CCC Camp" at the place.

Los Angeles County (1935) map shows a feature called Chitwood Canyon that opens into Soledad Canyon from the north opposite the site of Acton Camp.

Acton Canyon [LOS ANGELES]: *canyon,* drained by a stream that flows 2.5 miles to lowlands 1.5 miles north-east of Acton (lat. 34°29'15" N, long. 118°11'20" W; sec. 25, T 5 N, R 13 W). Named on Acton (1959) and Ritter Ridge (1958) 7.5' quadrangles.

Adams Barranca [VENTURA]: *gully,* extends for 2 miles from the mouth of Adams Canyon to Santa Clara River 2.5 miles south-southwest of Santa Paula (lat. 34°19'30" N, long. 119°05'10" W). Named on Santa Paula (1951) 7.5' quadrangle.

Adams Canyon [LOS ANGELES]: *canyon,* 2 miles long, opens into lowlands 17 miles east-southeast of Gorman (lat. 34°45'35" N, long. 118°33'30" W; at N line sec. 27, T 8 N, R 16 W). Named on Burnt Peak (1958) and Neenach School (1965) 7.5' quadrangles.

Adams Canyon [VENTURA]: *canyon,* drained by a stream that flows 6.25 miles to the valley of Santa Clara River 2.5 miles west of Santa Paula (lat. 34°20'45" N, long. 119°06'10" W). Named on Santa Paula (1951) and Santa Paula Peak (1951) 7.5' quadrangles. The name commemorates William G. Adams, who started digging a well for oil in a branch of the canyon in 1872 (Ricard).

Adams Hill [LOS ANGELES]: *peak,* 5.5 miles west-southwest of Pasadena city hall (lat. 34°07'45" N, long. 118°14'05" W). Named on Pasadena (1953) 7.5' quadrangle.

Adams Square [LOS ANGELES]: *locality,* 5.5 miles west of Pasadena city hall (lat. 34°08' N, long. 118°14'30" W); the place is northwest of Adams Hill. Named on Pasadena (1953) 7.5' quadrangle.

Adobe Creek [VENTURA]: *stream,* flows 3.5 miles to Sespe Creek 8 miles north-northwest of Wheeler Springs (lat. 34°36'20" N, long. 119°21'50" W; near SW cor. sec. 18, T 6 N, R 23 W). Named on Reyes Peak (1943) and Wheeler Springs (1943) 7.5' quadrangles.

Adobe Mountain [LOS ANGELES]: *hill,* 11 miles north-northeast of Black Butte on Los Angeles-San Bernardino county line (lat. 34° 42'15" N, long. 117°40'15" W; around SE cor. sec. 12, T 7 N, R 8 W). Named on Adobe Mountain (1955) 7.5' quadrangle.

Agoura [LOS ANGELES]: *town,* 29 miles west-northwest of Los Angeles city hall (lat. 34°08'35" N, long. 118°44'20" W). Named on Calabasas (1952) 7.5' quadrangle. Seminole (1932) 6' quadrangle has both the names "Picture City" and "Agoura P.O." at the place. Postal authorities established Agoura post office in 1927 and moved it 0.5 mile west in 1937 (Salley, p. 2). When they established the post office at the community of Picture City, they requested a one-word designation for the facility; the name "Agoura" was chosen because the site was on Agoura ranch (Gudde, 1949, p. 4). According to Hanna (p. 2), the name "Agoura" is a corruption of the surname "Lagoura" of an early settler.

Agua Amarga Canyon [LOS ANGELES]: *canyon,* drained by a stream that flows 2.5 miles to the sea 5.25 miles southwest of Redondo Beach city hall at Lunada Bay (lat. 33°46'10" N, long. 118°25'15" W). Named on Redondo Beach (1951) 7.5' quadrangle.

Agua Blanca Creek [VENTURA]: *stream,* flows 16 miles to Piru Creek 7.5 miles southeast of Cobblestone Mountain (lat. 34°32'25" N, long. 118°45'40" W; at S line sec. 3, T 5 N, R 18 W). Named on Cobblestone Mountain (1958), Devils Heart Peak (1943), and McDonald Peak (1958) 7.5' quadrangles.

Agua Caliente de San Juan: see **San Juan Hot Springs** [ORANGE].

Agua Canyon [LOS ANGELES]: *canyon,* drained by a stream that flows less than 1 mile to Arroyo Seco 5.5 miles north-northwest of Pasadena city hall (lat. 34°13'25" N, long. 118°10'45" W). Named on Pasadena (1966) 7.5' quadrangle.

Agua Chinon Wash [ORANGE]: *stream,* flows 7.5 miles to San Diego Creek 9 miles southeast of Santa Ana city hall (lat. 33°39'05" N, long. 117°45'20" W). Named on El Toro (1968) and Tustin (1965) 7.5' quadrangles. The canyon of the upper part of the stream is called Tomato Spring Canyon on Corona (1902) 30' quadrangle. The name "Agua Chinon" is from Cañada de Agua Chinon, an early name for present Limestone Canyon (Stephenson, p. 124).

Agua del Palo Verde: see **Laguna Reservoir** [ORANGE].

Agua del Toro: see **Serrano Creek** [ORANGE].

Agua Dulce [LOS ANGELES]: *village,* 9 miles northeast of Solemint in Sierra Pelona Valley (lat. 34°29'45" N, long. 118°19'30" W; at NW cor. sec. 26, T 5 N, R 14 W). Named on Agua Dulce (1960) 7.5' quadrangle. Postal authorities established Agua Dulce post office in 1955 (Salley, p. 2).

Agua Dulce: see **Palmdale** [LOS ANGELES].

Agua Dulce Canyon [LOS ANGELES]: *canyon,* 8 miles long, opens into Soledad Canyon 7.5 miles east-northeast of Solemint (lat. 34° 26'20" N, long. 118°19'25" W; near S line sec. 10, T 4 N, R 14 W). Named on Agua Dulce (1960) and Sleepy Valley (1958) 7.5' quadrangles. Los Angeles County (1935) map shows several canyons near Agua Dulce Canyon: Decker Canyon, which opens into

Soledad Canyon from the north less than 1 mile east of the mouth of Agua Dulce Canyon (near W line sec. 11, T 4 N, R 14 W); Burke Canyon, which opens into Soledad Canyon from the north 1.25 miles east of the mouth of Agua Dulce Canyon (sec. 11, T 4 N, R 14 W); Johns Canyon, which opens into Soledad Canyon from the north 1.5 miles east of the mouth of Agua Dulce Canyon (near W line sec. 12, T 4 N, R 14 W); Alpine Canyon, which opens into Soledad Canyon from the south opposite the mouth of Agua Dulce Canyon; and Paso Canyon, which opens into Agua Dulce Canyon from the northwest about 1.5 miles north of the mouth of Agua Dulce Canyon (sec. 3, T 4 N, R 14 W).

Aguage del Padre Gomez: see **Tomato Spring** [ORANGE].

Aguagito: see **San Juan Capistrano** [ORANGE].

Aguaje de la Centinela [LOS ANGELES]: *land grant,* at Inglewood. Named on Inglewood (1964) and Venice (1950) 7.5' quadrangles. Ignacio Machado received the land in 1844; Bruno Avila claimed 2219 acres patented in 1872 (Cowan, p. 13).

Aguaje del Cuate: see **Gavilan** [ORANGE].

Aguaje Lodoso: see **Mud Spring** [LOS ANGELES].

Agua Magna Canyon [LOS ANGELES]: *canyon,* 1.5 miles long, 4.5 miles south of Torrance city hall (lat. 33°46'20" N, long. 118°21'15" W). Named on Torrance (1964) 7.5' quadrangle.

Agua Negra Canyon [LOS ANGELES]: *canyon,* 1.25 miles long, 4.5 miles south-southwest of Torrance city hall (lat. 33°46'30" N, long. 118°21'30" W). Named on Torrance (1964) 7.5' quadrangle. The name is from adobe-blackened water in the canyon (Fink, p. 22).

Ah-DA-HI: see **Camp Ah-DA-HI** [LOS ANGELES].

Airplane Flat [LOS ANGELES]: *area,* nearly 6 miles west of Mount San Antonio (lat. 34°17'10" N, long. 117°44'50" W). Named on Mount San Antonio (1955) 7.5' quadrangle.

Akens Canyon [LOS ANGELES]: *canyon,* drained by a stream that flows 1 mile to Big Tujunga Canyon 1.25 miles north of Sunland (lat. 34°16'40" N, long. 118°18'30" W). Named on Sunland (1953) 7.5' quadrangle.

Alamitos Bay [LOS ANGELES]: *bay,* opens to the sea 5 miles east-southeast of Long Beach city hall by the mouth of San Gabriel River (lat. 33°44'35" N, long. 118°07' W). Named on Long Beach (1949), Los Alamitos (1950), and Seal Beach (1950) 7.5' quadrangles. Early maps show marsh at the place fed by water of San Gabriel River; in 1934 officials of Long Beach ordered that the course of San Gabriel River be separated from the bay (Gleason p. 101-102).

Alamitos Beach [LOS ANGELES]: *locality,* less than 1 mile east-southeast of present Long Beach city hall along Los Angeles Terminal Railroad (lat. 33°46' N, long. 118°10'45" W). Named on Downey (1902) 15' quadrangle.

Alamo Camp [VENTURA]: *locality,* 1.5 miles northwest of McDonald Peak (lat. 34°39'05" N, long. 118°56'30" W; near SW cor. sec. 36, T 7 N, R 20 W); the place is along Alamo Creek (1). Named on McDonald Peak (1958) 7.5' quadrangle.

Alamo Creek [VENTURA]:

(1) *stream,* flows 5.25 miles to Mutau Creek 15 miles east-northeast of Reyes Peak (lat. 34°40'20" N, long. 119°00'55" W; near W line sec. 29, T 7 N, R 20 W); the stream heads at Alamo Mountain. Named on Lockwood Valley (1943) and McDonald Peak (1958) 7.5' quadrangles.

(2) *stream,* flows 9 miles to join Beartrap Creek and form Cuyama River 4 miles south of Reyes Peak (lat. 34°41'25" N, long. 119°17'30" W; sec. 23, T 7 N, R 23 W). Named on Reyes Peak (1943) and San Guillermo (1943) 7.5' quadrangles.

Alamo Mountain [VENTURA]: *ridge,* northwest-trending, 2 miles long, 2.25 miles north-northwest of McDonald Peak (lat. 34°39'55" N, long. 118°57'15" W). Named on McDonald Peak (1958) 7.5' quadrangle.

Alamos Canyon [VENTURA]: *canyon,* drained by a stream that flows 6 miles to Arroyo Simi 3.5 miles east of Moorpark (lat. 34° 17' N, long. 118°49' W; sec. 1, T 2 N, R 19 W). Named on Simi (1951) 7.5' quadrangle.

Alder Creek [LOS ANGELES]:

(1) *stream,* flows 2.25 miles to Gold Creek 4.25 miles north-northwest of Sunland (lat. 34°19'10" N, long. 118°19'50" W; sec. 27, T 3 N, R 14 W). Named on Sunland (1953) 7.5' quadrangle.

(2) *stream,* formed by the confluence of North Fork and West Fork, flows 4.25 miles to Big Tujunga Canyon 5.5 miles south-southwest of Pacifico Mountain (lat. 34°18'25" N, long. 118°04'20" W; sec. 31, T 3 N, R 11 W). Named on Chilao Flat (1959) 7.5' quadrangle. North Fork is 2 miles long and is named on Chilao Flat (1959) 7.5' quadrangle. West Fork is 2.25 miles long and is named on Chilao Flat (1959) and Pacifico Mountain (1959) 7.5' quadrangles. Present West Fork is called North Fork on Alder Creek (1941) 6' quadrangle. East Fork enters from the east 2.5 miles upstream from the mouth of the main creek and is nearly 4 miles long. Middle Fork enters 3.5 miles upstream from the mouth of the main creek and is 3 miles long. East Fork and Middle Fork are named on Chilao Flat (1959) 7.5' quadrangle.

Alder Creek [VENTURA]: *stream,* flows nearly 7 miles to Sespe Creek 2 miles northeast of Devils Heart Peak (lat. 34°33'50" N, long. 118°57'10" W; sec. 36, T 6 N, R 20 W).

Named on Devils Heart Peak (1943) and McDonald Peak (1958) 7.5' quadrangles. East Fork enters from the east 1.5 miles above the mouth of the main stream; it is nearly 3 miles long and is named on Devils Heart Peak (1943) 7.5' quadrangle.

Alder Gulch [LOS ANGELES]: *canyon,* drained by a stream that flows 1.5 miles to San Gabriel River 5 miles west-northwest of Mount San Antonio (lat. 34°19'10" N, long. 117°43'40" W; at E line sec. 29, T 3 N, R 8 W). Named on Mount San Antonio (1955) 7.5' quadrangle.

Alder Saddle [LOS ANGELES]: *pass,* nearly 2 miles southeast of Pacifico Mountain (lat. 34°21'50" N, long. 118°00'45" W; near E line sec. 10, T 3 N, R 11 W); the pass is at the head of Middle Fork Alder Creek (2). Named on Chilao Flat (1959) 7.5' quadrangle.

Alder Spring [ORANGE]: *spring,* 2.5 miles south-southeast of Santiago Peak in Trabuco Canyon (lat. 33°40'45" N, long. 117°30'45" W; near NW cor. sec. 4, T 6 S, R 6 W). Named on Santiago Peak (1954) 7.5' quadrangle.

Alexander Spring [LOS ANGELES]: *spring,* 1.25 miles northeast of Crystal Lake (lat. 34°19'45" N, long. 117°49'30" W). Named on Crystal Lake (1958) 7.5' quadrangle.

Alhambra [LOS ANGELES]: *city,* 7.25 miles east-northeast of Los Angeles city hall (lat. 34°05'35" N, long. 118°07'35" W). Named on El Monte (1953) and Los Angeles (1953) 7.5' quadrangles. Postal authorities established Alhambra post office in 1885 (Frickstad, p. 70), and the city incorporated in 1903.

Alhambra: see **North Alhambra** [LOS ANGELES]; **West Alhambra**, under **Shorb** [LOS ANGELES].

Alhambra Wash [LOS ANGELES]: *stream,* flows 6.5 miles to Rio Hondo 3 miles southwest of El Monte city hall (lat. 34°02'45" N, long. 118°04'25" W). Named on El Monte (1953) and Los Angeles (1953) 7.5' quadrangles.

Alimony Ridge [LOS ANGELES]: *ridge,* north-trending, 1 mile long, 8 miles west of Valyermo (lat. 34°27'15" N, long. 117°59'30" W). Named on Juniper Hills (1959) 7.5' quadrangle.

Aliso [ORANGE]: *locality,* about 3 miles southeast of present Santa Ana city hall along a railroad (lat. 33°43'30" N, long. 117°50" W). Named on Santa Ana (1901) 15' quadrangle.

Aliso Beach [ORANGE]: *beach,* 2 miles southeast of Laguna Beach city hall along the coast (lat. 33°30'35" N, long. 117°45'05" W; sec. 6, T 8 S, R 8 W); the feature is at the mouth of Aliso Creek. Named on Laguna Beach (1965, photorevised 1981) 7.5' quadrangle.

Aliso Canyon [LOS ANGELES]:

(1) *canyon,* drained by a stream that flows 8.5 miles to Soledad Canyon 2 miles east of Acton (lat. 34°28'15" N, long. 118°09'45" W; sec. 32, T 5 N, R 12 E). Named on Acton (1959)

and Pacifico Mountain (1959) 7.5' quadrangles.

(2) *canyon,* nearly 3 miles long, opens into lowlands 4.5 miles east-northeast of Chatsworth (lat. 34°16'40" N, long. 118°31'35" W). Named on Oat Mountain (1952) 7.5' quadrangle.

Aliso Canyon [ORANGE]: *canyon,* drained by a stream that heads in Riverside County and flows 2.5 miles to Lucas Canyon 10 miles east-northeast of San Juan Capistrano (lat. 33°34'10" N, long. 117° 30'30" W; at W line sec. 10, T 7 S, R 6 W). Named on Cañada Gobernadora (1968) and Sitton Peak (1954) 7.5' quadrangles. Called Verdugo Canyon on Lake Elsinore (1942) 15' quadrangle, where present Verdugo Canyon is unnamed.

Aliso Canyon [VENTURA]: *canyon,* drained by a stream that flows 8 miles to the valley of Santa Clara River 2.5 miles north of Saticoy (lat. 34°19'10" N, long. 119°08'40" W). Named on Ojai (1952) and Saticoy (1951) 7.5' quadrangles.

Aliso Canyon: see **Deer Canyon** [LOS ANGELES] (1); **Devil Canyon** [LOS ANGELES].

Aliso Canyon Wash [LOS ANGELES]: *stream,* heads at the mouth of Aliso Canyon (2) and flows 7 miles to Los Angeles River 3.5 miles east-southeast of the center of Canoga Park (lat. 34°11'25" N, long. 118°32'25" W). Named on Canoga Park (1952) and Oat Mountain (1952) 7.5' quadrangles.

Aliso City: see **El Toro** [ORANGE].

Aliso Creek [ORANGE]: *stream,* flows 18 miles to the sea 3 miles southeast of Laguna Beach city hall (lat. 33°30'40" N, long. 117° 45'10" W; sec. 6, T 8 S, R 8 W). Named on El Toro (1968), Laguna Beach (1965, photorevised 1981), and San Juan Capistrano (1968) 7.5' quadrangles. Called Alisos Creek on El Toro (1950) and Santiago Peak (1954) 7.5' quadrangles.

Aliso Point [ORANGE]: *promontory,* 3.25 miles southeast of Laguna Beach city hall along the coast (lat. 33°30'20" N, long. 117°45' W; sec. 6, T 8 S, R 8 W); the feature is southeast of Aliso Beach. Named on Laguna Beach (1965, photorevised 1981) 7.5' quadrangle.

Alisos Creek: see **Aliso Creek** [ORANGE].

Aliso Spring [LOS ANGELES]: *spring,* 2.5 miles west-northwest of Pacifico Mountain (lat. 34°23'45" N, long. 122°04'25" W); the spring is in the upper part of Aliso Canyon (1). Named on Pacifico Mountain (1959) 7.5' quadrangle.

Alla [LOS ANGELES]: *locality,* 6.5 miles north of Manhattan Beach city hall along Pacific Electric Railroad (lat. 33°58'50" N, long. 118°25'40" W). Named on Venice (1950) 7.5' quadrangle.

Allison Gulch [LOS ANGELES]: *canyon,* drained by a stream that flows 2.5 miles to San Gabriel River 6 miles west-southwest of Mount San Antonio (lat. 34°15'45" N, long.

117°44'45" W). Named on Mount San Antonio (1955) 7.5' quadrangle.

All Nations Camp [LOS ANGELES]: *locality,* 3.5 miles west-northwest of Big Pines (lat. 34°23'50" N, long. 117°44'45" W). Named on Mescal Creek (1956) 7.5' quadrangle.

Almond [ORANGE]: *locality,* less than 1 mile east-southeast of present Buena Park civic center along Southern Pacific Railroad (lat. 33°51'35" N, long. 117°59'05" W; at S line sec. 36, T 3 S, R 11 W). Named on Anaheim (1950) 7.5' quadrangle.

Almondale: see **Pearblossom** [LOS ANGELES].

Alolia: see **Saugus** [LOS ANGELES].

Alosta: see **Glendora** [LOS ANGELES].

Alpine [LOS ANGELES]:

(1) *locality,* nearly 3 miles south-southeast of Palmdale along Southern Pacific Railroad (lat. 34°32'20" N, long. 118°06'20" W; at S line sec. 2, T 5 N, R 12 W); the place is 0.5 mile south-southeast of Harold. Named on Palmdale (1937) 6' quadrangle. United States Board on Geographic Names (1960b, p. 8) rejected the name "Alpine" for nearby Harold. Los Angeles County (1935) map has the name "Alpine Spgs. Cany." for a feature located west of the site of Alpine (1) (sec. 10, 11, T 5 N, R 12 W).

(2) *locality,* 7 miles east of Solemint along Southern Pacific Railroad (lat. 34°26'15" N, long. 118°20'15" W; near S line sec. 10, T 4 N, R 14 W). Named on Lang (1933) 6' quadrangle. Los Angeles County (1935) map shows a feature called Alpine Canyon that opens into Soledad Canyon near Alpine (2) (at N line sec. 15, T 4 N, R 14 W).

Alpine: see **Harold** [LOS ANGELES].

Alpine Butte [LOS ANGELES]: *mountain,* 9.5 miles north-northeast of Littlerock (lat. 34°37'50" N, long. 117°53'50" W; at SW cor. sec. 1, T 6 N, R 10 W). Altitude 3259 feet. Named on Alpine Butte (1957) and Littlerock (1957) 7.5' quadrangles.

Alpine Canyon [LOS ANGELES]: *canyon,* nearly 2 miles long, 2.25 miles southeast of Crystal Lake (lat. 34°17'40" N, long. 117°49'10" W). Named on Crystal Lake (1958) 7.5' quadrangle.

Alpine Canyon: see **Agua Dulce Canyon** [LOS ANGELES]; **Alpine** [LOS ANGELES] (2).

Alpine Springs Canyon: see **Alpine** [LOS ANGELES] (1).

Alpine Springs Colony: see **Littlerock** [LOS ANGELES].

Alsace [LOS ANGELES]: *locality,* 6.25 miles north of Manhattan Beach city hall along Pacific Electric Railroad (lat. 33°58'45" N, long. 118°25' W). Named on Venice (1950) 7.5' quadrangle.

Altacanyada [LOS ANGELES]: *district,* 6.5 miles north-northwest of present Pasadena city hall (lat. 34°13'20" N, long. 118°12'25" W; near N line sec. 35, T 2 N, R 13 W). Named on La Crescenta (1939) 6' quadrangle. Los Angeles County (1935) map has the form "Alta Canyada" for the name.

Altadena [LOS ANGELES]: *city,* 3 miles north-northeast of Pasadena city hall (lat. 34°11'30" N, long. 118°07'30" W). Named on Mount Wilson (1953) and Pasadena (1953) 7.5' quadrangles. Postal authorities established Altadena post office in 1894 (Frickstad, p. 70). The name, applied in 1887, is from the position of the community above Pasadena (Gudde, 1949, p. 9). California Mining Bureau's (1917) map shows a place called La Vina located about 3 miles north of Altadena. Postal authorities established La Vina post office in 1915 (Salley, p. 119).

Altamira Canyon [LOS ANGELES]: *canyon,* drained by a stream that flows 1.25 miles to the sea 7.25 miles south of Redondo Beach city hall (lat. 33°44'25" N, long. 118°22'35" W). Named on San Pedro (1964) and Torrance (1964) 7.5' quadrangles.

Alvarado Hot Springs [LOS ANGELES]: *locality,* 4.5 miles northeast of La Habra [ORANGE] (lat. 33°58'35" N, long. 117°53'10" W). Named on La Habra (1952) 7.5' quadrangle. On La Habra (1964) 7.5' quadrangle, the name applies to a water feature. According to Berkstresser (p. A-7), water at a temperature of 112° Fahrenheit is pumped from a large-diameter oil test well drilled to about 5,000 feet in 1910—natural gas produced with the water heats a bath house

Amargo: see **Malibu Junction** [LOS ANGELES].

Amargosa Creek [LOS ANGELES]: *stream* and *dry wash,* extends for 30 miles in an interrupted watercourse to Lancaster (lat. 34°41'20" N, long, 118°09'30" W; at N line sec. 21, T 7 N, R 12 W). Named on Del Sur (1958), Lancaster West (1958), Ritter Ridge (1958), and Sleepy Valley (1958) 7.5' quadrangles

Amargosa Creek [VENTURA]: *stream,* flows 7 miles to Lockwood Creek 13 miles northeast of Reyes Peak (lat. 34°44'05" N, long. 119°04'40" W). Named on Cuddy Valley (1943), Lockwood Valley (1943), and Sawmill Mountain (1943) 7.5' quadrangles. Called Bitter Creek on Mount Pinos (1903) 30' quadrangle, but United States Board on Geographic Names (1939, p. 4) rejected this name for the stream.

Amarillo Beach [LOS ANGELES]: *beach,* 1.25 miles west of Malibu Point along the coast (lat. 34°01'50" N, long. 118°42'20" W). Named on Malibu Beach (1951) 7.5' quadrangle. Called Amarilla Beach on Solstice Canyon (1932) 6' quadrangle.

Amarillo Canyon: see **Winter Canyon** [LOS ANGELES].

Amarus Lake: see **Santa Ana River** [ORANGE].

Anacapa Island [VENTURA]: *islands,* three,

20 miles south-southwest of Ventura (lat. 34°00'55" N, long. 119°21'25" W at east end; lat. 34°00'50" N, long. 119°26'35" W at west end). Named on Anacapa Island (1973) quadrangle. Anacapa Island is one of the group called Santa Barbara Islands, which in turn is part of the larger group called Channel Islands (United States Coast and Geodetic Survey, p. 106). Early Spanish explorers gave the cluster of islands that forms present Anacapa Island the name "Tres Isleos," and in 1770 Costanso referred to one island as Falsa Vela because it looked like a ship; he called the other two islands Las Mesitas (Wagner, p. 372). Juan Perez called the cluster Islotes de Santo Tomas in 1774 (Wagner, p. 514). Yates (p. 171-173) referred to the three islands as the Anacapas, and to the individual islands as Eastern Anacapa, Middle Anacapa, and Western Anacapa. The name "Anacapa" is of Indian origin (Kroeber, p. 34).

Anacapa Passage [VENTURA]: *water feature,* between Anacapa Island and Santa Cruz Island, which is west of Anacapa Island in Santa Barbara County—the water passage is as narrow as 4.5 miles. Named on Los Angeles (1975) 1°x 2° quadrangle.

Anaheim [ORANGE]: *city,* 7 miles north-north-west of Santa Ana city hall (lat. 33°50'10" N, long. 117°54'40" W). Named on Anaheim (1965), Los Alamitos (1964), Orange (1964), and Yorba Linda (1964, photorevised 1981) 7.5' quadrangles. Postal authorities established Anaheim post office in 1861 (Frickstad, p. 115), and the city incorporated in 1878. A group of Germans, mainly from San Francisco, started a colony at the place in 1857—for years the community was known as Campo Aleman to its Spanish-speaking neighbors (Hoover, Rensch, and Rensch, p. 263). The name "Anaheim" is from Santa Ana River and *heim,* which means "home" in German (Bancroft, 1888, p. 522).

Anaheim: see **South Anaheim** [ORANGE]; **West Anaheim** [ORANGE].

Anaheim Bay [ORANGE]: *bay,* opens to the sea 7.5 miles northwest of Huntington Beach civic center (lat. 33°44'05" N, long. 118°05'40" W); the feature is along the lower part of former Anaheim Creek. Named on Seal Beach (1965) 7.5' quadrangle.

Anaheim Bay: see **Huntington Harbor** [ORANGE] (1).

Anaheim Creek [ORANGE]: *stream,* flows 8 miles to the sea 7.5 miles northwest of present Huntington Beach civic center (lat. 33° 44' N, long. 118°06' W). Named on Downey (1902) and Las Bolsas (1896) 15' quadrangles. The feature is an overflow channel of Santa Ana River (Meadows, p. 21).

Anaheim Junction: see **West Anaheim Junction** [ORANGE].

Anaheim Landing [ORANGE]: *locality,* 7.5 miles northwest of present Huntington Beach civic center along the coast (lat. 33°44' 05" N, long. 118°06' W); the site is at the mouth of Anaheim Creek. Named on Las Bolsas (1896) 15' quadrangle. The place was called El Piojo in the early days (Meadows, p. 21). Later it was a shipping point for residents of Anaheim; lighters carried produce to schooners anchored offshore and brought back supplies; the navy took over the site during World War II as part of an ammunition and net depot (Gleason, p. 101).

Anaheim Tower [ORANGE]: *locality,* 7 miles southeast of present Buena Park civic center where Atchison, Topeka and Santa Fe Railroad crossed Southern Pacific Railroad (lat. 33°48'30" N, long. 117°53'35" W; sec. 23, T 4 S, R 10 W). Named on Anaheim (1950) 7.5' quadrangle. Called Miraflores on Corona (1902) 30' quadrangle.

Anaheim Union Reservoir [ORANGE]: *lake,* 1300 feet long, 3 miles west-northwest of Yorba Linda (lat. 33°54'15" N, long. 117°51'55" W; on S line sec. 18, T 3 S, R 9 W). Named on Yorba Linda (1964) 7.5' quadrangle.

Anaverde Creek [LOS ANGELES]: *stream,* flows 7.25 miles to lowlands 1.5 miles southwest of downtown Palmdale (lat. 34°34'10" N, long. 118°08' W; sec. 34, T 6 N, R 12 W); the stream goes through Anaverde Valley. Named on Ritter Ridge (1958) 7.5' quadrangle.

Anaverde Valley [LOS ANGELES]: *valley,* 3.25 miles west-southwest of Palmdale (lat. 34°34'15" N, long. 118°10'15" W). Named on Ritter Ridge (1958) 7.5' quadrangle.

Andrade Corner [LOS ANGELES]: *locality,* 4 miles east-southeast of the village of Lake Hughes (lat. 34°38'55" N, long. 118°22'35" W; on E line sec. 32, T 7 N, R 14 W). Named on Lake Hughes (1957) 7.5' quadrangle. Called Talamantes on Lake (1937) 6' quadrangle, but United States Board of Geographic Names (1960a, p. 11) rejected this designation for the place. The name "Andrade" recalls Andrada stage station that Pedro Andrada built in the 1880's (Hoover, Rensch, and Rensch, p. 168).

Andrews' Station: see **Lyon's Station**, under **San Fernando Pass** [LOS ANGELES].

Angles Pass [VENTURA]: *pass,* 3.5 miles west-northwest of Piru (lat. 34°26'15" N, long. 118°50'45" W; near SW cor. sec. 11, T 4 N, R 19 W). Named on Piru (1952) 7.5' quadrangle.

Anlauf Canyon [VENTURA]: *canyon,* drained by a stream that flows 2 miles to Santa Paula Creek 4.25 miles west-southwest of Santa Paula Peak (lat. 34°25'20" N, long. 119°04'55" W; near S line sec. 16, T 4 N, R 21 W). Named on Santa Paula Peak (1951) 7.5' quadrangle. Called Onlauf Canyon on Santa Paula (1903) 15' quadrangle. The name is for the Anlauf family of Santa Paula, landowners in the neighborhood (Gudde, 1949, p. 243).

Ant Canyon [LOS ANGELES]: *canyon,* drained by a stream that flows 0.5 mile to Pacoima Canyon 6.5 miles north-northwest of Sunland (lat. 34°20'45" N, long. 118°21'55" W; sec. 17, T 3 N, R 14 W). Named on Sunland (1953) 7.5' quadrangle.

Antelope Acres [LOS ANGELES]: *settlement,* 4.5 miles north of Del Sur (lat. 34°45'15" N, long. 118°17'15" W; sec. 29, 30, 31, T 8 N, R 13 W); the place is in Antelope Valley. Named on Del Sur (1958) and Little Buttes (1965) 7.5' quadrangles.

Antelope Buttes [LOS ANGELES]: *ridge,* west-southwest-trending, 2.5 miles long, 5.5 miles north-northeast of the village of Lake Hughes (lat. 34°44'15" N, long. 118°23'15" W). Named on Del Sur (1958), Fairmont Butte (1965), Lake Hughes (1957), and Little Buttes (1965) 7.5' quadrangles.

Antelope Center [LOS ANGELES]: *locality,* 4 miles north of Littlerock (lat. 34°34'45" N, long. 117°58'05" W; on W line sec. 29, T 6 N, R 10 W). Named on Littlerock (1957) 7.5' quadrangle.

Antelope Valley [LOS ANGELES]: *valley,* part of Mojave Desert north of San Gabriel Mountains on Los Angeles-Kern county line. Named on Los Angeles (1975) and San Bernardino (1957) 1°x 2° quadrangles. Called Palma Plain on Williamson's (1853a) map. The name "Antelope" is from antelope herds in the valley in the early days (Hoover, Rensch, and Rensch, p. 148).

Antelope Valley: see **El Mirage Valley** [LOS ANGELES].

Antimony Canyon [LOS ANGELES]: *canyon,* drained by a stream that flows less than 1 mile to Kings Canyon 4 miles northeast of Burnt Peak (lat. 34°43' N, long. 118°31'05" W; near SW cor. sec. 6, T 7 N, R 15 W). Named on Burnt Peak (1958) 7.5' quadrangle.

Apache Canyon [VENTURA]: *canyon,* drained by a stream that flows 16 miles to Cuyama River 11 miles northwest of Reyes Peak (lat. 34°44'45" N, long. 119°24'40" W). Named on Apache Canyon (1943), Cuyama Peak (1943), Rancho Nuevo Creek (1943), and Sawmill Mountain (1943) 7.5' quadrangles.

Apache Potrero [VENTURA]: *area,* 16 miles north of Reyes Peak (lat. 34°52' N, long. 119°19'30" W; sec. 15, T 9 N, R 23 W); the place is 5 miles north of Apache Canyon. Named on Apache Canyon (1943) 7.5' quadrangle.

Apple Canyon [LOS ANGELES]: *canyon,* drained by a stream that flows nearly 4 miles to Cañada de Los Alamos 8.5 miles southeast of Gorman (lat. 34°41'10" N, long. 118°47'10" W; near E line sec. 21, T 7 N, R 18 W). Named on Black Mountain (1958) 7.5' quadrangle.

Apple Tree Flat [LOS ANGELES]: *area,* 1.5 miles west-northwest of Big Pines (lat. 34°23'15" N, long. 117°42'40" W). Named on Mescal Creek (1956) 7.5' quadrangle.

Aqueduct Spring [LOS ANGELES]: *spring,* 5 miles south of the village of Lake Hughes (lat. 34°36' N, long. 118°26'45" W); the spring is less than 0.5 mile east of the aqueduct that brings Owens Valley water to Los Angeles. Named on Green Valley (1958) 7.5' quadrangle.

Arbolada [VENTURA]: *locality,* less than 1 mile west of downtown Ojai (lat. 34°27' N, long. 119°15'25" W). Named on Matilija (1952) 7.5' quadrangle.

Arcadia [LOS ANGELES]: *city,* 6 miles south-southeast of Mount Wilson (1) (lat. 34°08'30" N, long. 118°01'45" W). Named on Baldwin Park (1966), El Monte (1953), and Mount Wilson (1953) 7.5' quadrangles. Postal authorities established Arcadia post office in 1888 and named it for Dona Arcadia de Baker (Salley, p. 9). The city incorporated in 1903. Herman A. Unruh of San Gabriel Valley Railroad platted the place about 1888 (Gudde, 1949, p. 13).

Arcadia: see **West Arcadia** [LOS ANGELES].

Arch Beach [ORANGE]: *beach,* 2 miles south-southeast of Laguna Beach city hall along the coast (lat. 33°31'15" N, long. 117°45'50" W; sec. 36, T 7 S, R 9 W). Named on Laguna Beach (1965) 7.5' quadrangle. On Santa Ana (1901) 15' quadrangle, the name applies to an inhabited place at the site. Postal authorities established Arch Beach post office in 1889 and discontinued it in 1894 (Frickstad, p. 116). Hubbard Goff built a hotel at the site about 1886; in 1887 Goff and his brother Henry laid out a subdivision around the hotel and called it Arch Beach from an arched rock on the shore—the subdivision was unsuccessful (Meadows, p. 22). Fairview Development Company and Santa Ana Immigration Association laid out a town called Catalina-on-the-Main southeast of Arch Beach in 1888, but this venture also failed (Meadows, p. 51).

Arch Rock [ORANGE]: *relief feature,* nearly 6 miles west-northwest of Laguna Beach city hall along the coast at Corona del Mar (lat. 33°35'15" N, long. 117°52' W). Named on Laguna Beach (1965) 7.5' quadrangle. Called Hollow Rock on Corona (1902) 30' quadrangle.

Arch Rock [VENTURA]: *rock,* off the east end of Anacapa Island (lat. 34°01' N, long. 119°21'20" W). Named on Anacapa Island (1973) quadrangle. About 1936 a storm destroyed the arch that gave the rock its name; the feature also was called Grand Arch (Doran, 1980, p. 130).

Arena [LOS ANGELES]: *locality,* less than 1 mile northeast of present Manhattan Beach city hall along a railroad (lat. 33°53'45" N, long, 118°24' W). Named on Redondo (1896) 15' quadrangle.

Army Camp Beach: see **San Nicolas Island** [VENTURA].

Arnold: see **Port Hueneme** [VENTURA].

Arrastre Canyon [LOS ANGELES]: *canyon,* drained by a stream that flows 4.5 miles to Soledad Canyon 2 miles south-southwest of Acton (lat. 34°26'40" N, long. 118°12'30" W; sec. 11, T 4 N, R 13 W). Named on Acton (1959) 7.5' quadrangle.

Arrastra Flat [VENTURA]: *valley,* 2 miles east-southeast of Frazier Mountain (lat. 34°45'40" N, long. 118°56'30" W; around SE cor. sec. 24, T 8 N, R 20 W). Named on Frazier Mountain (1958) 7.5' quadrangle.

Arrow Point [LOS ANGELES]: *promontory,* 2.25 miles northeast of Silver Peak on the north side of Santa Catalina Island (lat. 33°28'40" N, long. 118°32'15" W). Named on Santa Catalina West (1943) 7.5' quadrangle. Doran (1980, p. 66) gave the alternate names "Ram Point" and "Stony Point" for the feature.

Arroyo Calabasas [LOS ANGELES]: *stream,* flows 7 miles to join Bell Creek and form Los Angeles River 0.5 mile southwest of the center of Canoga Park (lat. 34°11'40" N, long. 118°36'05" W); the stream goes through Calabasas. United States Board on Geographic Names (1933, p. 183) rejected the forms "Arroyo Calabaces" and "Arroyo Calabazas" for the name.

Arroyo Colorado [VENTURA]: *gully,* extends for 2.25 miles to Honda Barranca 6 miles south of Santa Paula (lat. 34°16' N, long. 119°03'15" W). Named on Santa Paula (1951) 7.5' quadrangle.

Arroyo Conejo: see **Conejo Creek** [VENTURA].

Arroyo de la Quema: see **San Juan Creek** [ORANGE].

Arroyo del Mupu: see **Santa Paula Creek** [VENTURA].

Arroyo Hondo: see **San Rafael** [LOS ANGELES].

Arroyo Jalisco [LOS ANGELES]: *stream,* flows 1.25 miles to Tacobi Creek 3.5 miles west-northwest of La Habra [ORANGE] (lat. 33°57'10" N, long. 117°59'55" W; sec. 35, T 2 S, R 11 W). Named on La Habra (1952) 7.5' quadrangle.

Arroyo las Posas [VENTURA]: *stream,* flows 10 miles to Calleguas Creek 2.25 miles northeast of downtown Camarillo (lat. 34°14'20" N, long. 119°00'20" W). Named on Camarillo (1950), Moorpark (1951), and Newbury Park (1951) 7.5' quadrangles.

Arroyo Pescadero [LOS ANGELES]: *stream,* flows 2.25 miles to La Canada Verde Creek 1.5 miles east-southeast of present Whittier city hall (lat. 33°57'40" N, long. 118°00'35" W; near SW cor. sec. 26, T 2 S, R 11 W). Named on La Habra (1952) and Whittier (1949) 7.5' quadrangles.

Arroyo Salada [ORANGE]: *stream,* flows 1 mile to Salt Creek 3 miles west of San Juan Capistrano (lat. 33°29'35" N, long. 117° 43'

7

W; sec. 9, T 8 S, R 8 W). Named on Dana Point (1968) and San Juan Capistrano (1968) 7.5' quadrangles. On Dana Point (1949) 7.5' quadrangle, the name applies to the canyon of the stream.

Arroyo Salada: see **Salt Creek** [ORANGE]; **Sulphur Creek** [ORANGE].

Arroyo Salinas [LOS ANGELES]: *stream,* flows 1.25 miles to Arroyo Jalisco 3.25 miles west-northwest of La Habra [ORANGE] (lat. 33°57'20" N, long. 117°59'35" W; sec. 36, T 2 S, R 11 W). Named on La Habra (1952) 7.5' quadrangle.

Arroyo San Miguel [LOS ANGELES]: *stream,* flows nearly 2 miles to Tacobi Creek 3.5 miles northwest of La Habra [ORANGE] (lat. 33°57'25" N, long. 117°59'50" W; sec. 35, T 2 S, R 11 W). Named on La Habra (1952) 7.5' quadrangle.

Arroyo San Nicolas: see **Nicholas Canyon** [LOS ANGELES].

Arroyo Santa Rosa [VENTURA]: *stream,* flows 3 miles to Santa Rosa Valley nearly 4 miles north of Newbury Park (lat. 34°14'20" N, long. 118°54'25" W). Named on Moorpark (1951), Newbury Park (1951), and Simi (1951) 7.5' quadrangles.

Arroyo Seco [LOS ANGELES]: *stream,* flows 23 miles to Los Angeles River 2 miles northnortheast of Los Angeles city hall (lat. 34°04'45" N, long. 118°13'30" W). Named on Chilao Flat (1959), Condor Peak (1959), Los Angeles (1953), and Pasadena (1953) 7.5' quadrangles. On Tujunga (1900) 15' quadrangle, the name "Long Canyon" applies to the upper part of the canyon of present Arroyo Seco.

Arroyo Sequit [LOS ANGELES-VENTURA]: *stream,* formed by the confluence of East Fork and West Fork, flows 3 miles to the sea 8 miles west-northwest of Point Dume (lat. 34°02'40" N, long. 118° 55'55" W); the mouth of the stream is just east of Sequit Point. Named on Triunfo Pass (1950) 7.5' quadrangle. United States Board on Geographic Names (1933, p. 682) rejected the forms "Arroyo Siquis" and "Arroyo Siquit" for the name. East Fork and West Fork (which heads in Ventura County) each are 2.5 miles long and are named on Triunfo Pass (1950) 7.5' quadrangle.

Arroyo Simi [VENTURA]: *stream,* flows 19 miles to Arroyo Las Posas 2.25 miles westsouthwest of Moorpark (lat. 34°16'10" N, long. 118°54'30" W; sec. 7, T 2 N, R 19 W); the stream goes through Simi Valley. Named on Moorpark (1951), Santa Susana (1951), and Simi (1951) 7.5' quadrangles.

Arroyo Susal: see **Los Sauces Creek** [VENTURA].

Arroyo Trabuco [ORANGE]: *stream,* flows 15 miles from the mouth of Trabuco Canyon to San Juan Creek less than 1 mile south of the center of San Juan Capistrano (lat. 33°29'25" N, long. 117°39'55" W; sec. 12, T 8 S, R 8

W). Named on Cañada Gobernadora (1968), San Juan Capistrano (1968), and Santiago Peak (1954) 7.5' quadrangles. Called Trabuco Creek on Dana Point (1968) 7.5' quadrangle. On Corona (1902) 30' quadrangle, the name applies to the canyon of the stream.

Artesia [LOS ANGELES]: *town,* 9 miles northeast of Long Beach city hall (lat. 33°51'55" N, long. 118°04'55" W). Named on Los Alamitos (1964) 7.5' quadrangle. Postal authorities established Artesia post office in 1882, discontinued it in 1902, and reestablished it in 1906 (Frickstad, p. 70). The town incorporated in 1959. Officials of Artesia Company founded and named the town in the 1870's—the company drilled artesian-water wells (Gudde, 1949, p. 16).

Artesian Spring Campgrounds [LOS ANGELES]: *locality,* 5.5 miles southwest of the village of Leona Valley (lat. 34°34'10" N, long. 118°21'51" W; sec. 33, T 6 N, R 14 W). Named on Sleepy Valley (1958) 7.5' quadrangle. Bouquet Reservoir (1937) 6' quadrangle shows an artesian spring at the site.

Arundell Barranca [VENTURA]: *gully,* extends for 4 miles from the mouth of Sexton Canyon to the sea 2.25 miles south-southeast of downtown Ventura (lat. 34°15'10" N, long. 119°16'10" W). Named on Saticoy (1951) and Ventura (1951) 7.5' quadrangles.

Arundell Peak [VENTURA]: *peak,* 3.5 miles north of Piru (lat. 34° 28' N, long. 118°47'55" W; near NE cor. sec. 6, T 4 N, R 18 W). Altitude 3216 feet. Named on Piru (1952) 7.5' quadrangle

Arundell Spring [VENTURA]: *spring,* 3.5 miles north of Piru (lat. 34°27'55" N, long. 118°47'20" W; near N line sec. 5, T 4 N, R 18 W); the spring is 0.5 mile east of Arundell Peak. Named on Piru (1952) 7.5' quadrangle.

Ascot Reservoir [LOS ANGELES]: *intermittent lake,* 1000 feet long, 3.5 miles east-northeast of Los Angeles city hall (lat. 34°04'40" N, long. 118°11'20" W; near SE cor. sec. 13, T 1 S, R 13 W). Named on Los Angeles (1953) 7.5' quadrangle.

Athens [LOS ANGELES]: *district,* 5.25 miles southeast of Inglewood city hall (lat. 33°55'20" N, long. 118°16'45" W). Named on Inglewood (1952) 7.5' quadrangle.

Atherton Canyon: see **Bouquet Canyon** [LOS ANGELES].

Atmore Meadows [LOS ANGELES]: *area,* 1.5 miles west-northwest of Burnt Peak (lat. 34°41'30" N, long. 118°36'15" W). Named on Burnt Peak (1958) 7.5' quadrangle.

Atwater [LOS ANGELES]: *district,* 4.25 miles north of Los Angeles city hall (lat. 34°06'55" N, long. 118°15'25" W). Named on Hollywood (1953) 7.5' quadrangle.

Atwood [ORANGE]: *village,* 5.5 miles northnortheast of Orange city hall (lat. 33°52'05" N, long. 117°49'50" W). Named on Orange (1964) 7.5' quadrangle. Called Richfields on

Corona (1902) 30' quadrangle. Postal authorities established Atwood post office in 1924 (Frickstad, p. 116). Promoters laid out a new townsite called Richfield, but when postal authorities refused to allow the name "Richfield" for a post office, the community took the name "Atwood" from W.J. Atwood, purchasing agent of Chanselor-Canfield Midway Oil Company (Meadows, p. 23). The residents of Atwood voted in 1970 to join Placenta (Carpenter, p. 242).

Aurant [LOS ANGELES]: *locality,* 5 miles eastnortheast of Los Angeles city hall along Southern Pacific Railroad (lat. 34°04'40" N, long. 118°09'50" W). Named on Los Angeles (1966) 7.5' quadrangle.

Avalon [LOS ANGELES]: *town,* near the southeast end of Santa Catalina Island (lat. 33°20'35" N, long. 118°19'40" W). Named on Santa Catalina East (1950) 7.5' quadrangle. Postal authorities established Avalon post office in 1889 (Frickstad, p. 70), and the town incorporated in 1913. The community is at the site of Timm's Landing, where A.W. Timm raised sheep and goats in the early days (Gleason, p. 20). The town first was known as Shatto, for George R. Shatto, who bought the island in 1887 (Hanna, p. 20). Shatto's sister, Mrs. E.J. Whitney, renamed the place Avalon, a name from Tennyson's *Idylls of the King* (Gleason, p. 20).

Avalon Bay [LOS ANGELES]: *embayment,* at Avalon on Santa Catalina Island (lat. 33°20'45" N, long. 118°19'20" W). Named on Santa Catalina East (1950) 7.5' quadrangle. Preston (1890b, map following p. 278) called the feature Dakin's Cove; United States Board on Geographic Names (1936a, p. 8) rejected the name "Dakin Bay" for it. The embayment also was called "Timms Bay" and "Timms Cove" from A.W. Timm of Timm's Landing (Hanna, p. 20)

Avalon Village [LOS ANGELES]: *locality,* 4.5 miles east-southeast of Torrance city hall (lat. 33°48'50" N, long. 118°15'50" W). Named on Torrance (1964) 7.5' quadrangle.

Aventura: see **Camp Aventura** [LOS ANGELES].

Averill Canyon [LOS ANGELES]: *canyon,* less than 1 mile long, nearly 3 miles northwest of Point Fermin (lat. 33°44'10" N, long. 118°19'20" W). Named on San Pedro (1964) 7.5' quadrangle.

Avocado Creek [LOS ANGELES]: *stream,* flows nearly 2 miles to San Gabriel River 2 miles southeast of El Monte city hall (lat. 34°02'45" N, long. 118°00'35" W). Named on Baldwin Park (1953) and El Monte (1966) 7.5' quadrangles.

Ayars Canyon [LOS ANGELES]: *canyon,* less than 1 mile long, 6.5 miles west-northwest of Pasadena city hall (lat. 34°11'40" N, long. 118°14'30" W). Named on Pasadena (1953) 7.5' quadrangle.

Ayers Creek [VENTURA]: *stream,* flows 1.5 miles to Lake Casitas 7.5 miles north-northwest of Ventura (lat. 34°22'25" N, long. 119° 21'20" W). Named on Ventura (1951, photorevised 1967) 7.5' quadrangle. The name is for Robert Ayers, who came to the vicinity in 1868 (Ricard).

Azusa [LOS ANGELES]:
(1) *land grant,* at Duarte. Named on Azusa (1953), Baldwin Park (1953), El Monte (1953), and Mount Wilson (1953) 7.5' quadrangles. Andres Duarte received the land in 1841 and claimed 6596 acres patented in 1878 (Cowan, p. 18). The name is from an Indian village (Kroeber, p. 35).
(2) *land grant,* at Azusa. Named on Azusa (1953) and Baldwin Park (1953) 7.5' quadrangles. Luis Arenas received the land in 1841 and Harry Dalton claimed 4331 acres patented in 1876 (Cowan, p. 17-18). According to Perez (p. 54), Henry Dalton was the grantee in 1846.
(3) *city,* 20 miles east-northeast of Los Angeles city hall (lat. 34°08'05" N, long. 117°54'15" W); the place is on Azusa (2) grant. Named on Baldwin Park (1953) 7.5' quadrangle. Postal authorities established Azusa post office in 1874 and moved it 0.5 mile northeast in 1887 (Salley, p. 13). The city incorporated in 1898. Jonathan Slauson organized Azusa Land and Water Company in 1886, platted a town, and was ready to sell lots in 1887; Henry Dalton had platted a town called Benton at the same place 32 years earlier (Jackson, p. 244-245).

Azusa Avenue [LOS ANGELES]: *locality,* 3.25 miles east of Baldwin Park city hall along Pacific Electric Railroad (lat. 34°05'30" N, long, 117°54'15" W; near W line sec. 14, T 1 S, R 10 W). Named on Baldwin Park (1953) 7.5' quadrangle.

Azusa Canon: see **San Gabriel Canyon** [LOS ANGELES].

– B –

Backus Summit: see **Castro Peak** [LOS ANGELES].

Bacon Creek [LOS ANGELES]: *stream,* flows less than 1 mile to end 1 mile east-southeast of present Whittier city hall (lat. 33°58'10" N, long. 118°01' W). Named on Whittier (1949) 7.5' quadrangle.

Bad Canyon [LOS ANGELES]: *canyon,* drained by a stream that flows 2 miles to Pacoima Canyon 7.25 miles north of Sunland (lat. 34°21'50" N, long. 118°17'35" W; near NE cor. sec. 12, T 3 N, R 14 W). Named on Agua Dulce (1960) and Sunland (1953) 7.5' quadrangles.

Baden-Powell: see **Mount Baden-Powell** [LOS ANGELES].

Bahia de los Fumos: see **San Pedro Bay** [LOS ANGELES].

Bahia de San Juan Capistrano: see **Dana Cove** [ORANGE].
Bahia de San Pedro: see **San Pedro Bay** [LOS ANGELES].
Bailey Canyon [LOS ANGELES]: *canyon,* 1.25 miles long, 3 miles south of Mount Wilson (1) (lat. 34°11' N, long. 118°03'35" W; sec. 8, 17, T 1 N, R 11 W). Named on Mount Wilson (1953) 7.5' quadrangle. Called Baile Canyon on Pasadena (1900) 15' quadrangle.
Baird Canyon [LOS ANGELES]: *canyon,* drained by a stream that flows 1 mile to San Francisquito Canyon nearly 8 miles southsouthwest of the village of Lake Hughes (lat. 34°34' N, long. 118° 28'05" W). Named on Green Valley (1958) 7.5' quadrangle.
Baird Park [LOS ANGELES]: *locality,* 4 miles northeast of Los Angeles city hall (lat. 34°05'10" N, long. 118°11' W). Named on Alhambra (1926) 6' quadrangle. Postal authorities established Bairdstown post office 5 miles east of Los Angeles post office in 1904 and discontinued it in 1917; the name was for Llewelin Baird, founder of the place (Salley, p. 13).
Bairdstown: see **Baird Park** [LOS ANGELES].
Baker Cabin [VENTURA]: *locality,* 3.5 miles northeast of McDonald Peak along Snowy Creek (lat. 34°40'20" N, long. 118°53'40" W; sec. 28, T 7 N, R 19 W). Named on McDonald Peak (1958) 7.5' quadrangle.
Baker Canyon [LOS ANGELES]: *canyon,* 2 miles long, opens into Mint Canyon (1) 3.5 miles northeast of Solemint (lat. 34°27'15" N, long. 118°25' W; near SE cor. sec. 2, T 4 N, R 15 W). Named on Mint Canyon (1960) 7.5' quadrangle.
Baker Canyon [ORANGE]: *canyon,* drained by a stream that flows 5 miles to the canyon of Santiago Creek 6.25 miles south of Sierra Peak (lat. 33°45'35" N, long. 117°40'25" W). Named on Black Star Canyon (1967) 7.5' quadrangle. The feature was called Cañada de la Vieja—*Cañada de la Vieja* means "Canyon of the Old Woman" in Spanish—before W.H. Hall took up a homestead there; for years it was called Hall's Canyon, but after Charles Baker moved there it became Baker's Canyon (Meadows, p. 49; Stephenson, p. 24-25).
Baker Wash [LOS ANGELES]: *stream,* heads in San Jose Hills and flows 2.5 miles to end in lowlands 3.25 miles southeast of Baldwin Park city hall (lat. 34°03'20" N, long. 117°54'55" W). Named on Baldwin Park (1953) 7.5' quadrangle.
Balanced Rock: see **Pyramid Head** [LOS ANGELES].
Balboa [ORANGE]: *district,* 7 miles southeast of Huntington Beach civic center in Newport Beach (lat. 33°36'10" N, long. 117°53'55" W). Named on Newport Beach (1965) 7.5' quadrangle. Postal authorities established Balboa post office in 1907 (Salley, p. 13). Officials of Newport Bay Investment Company had the

community laid out in 1905; E.J. Louis, Peruvian consul in Los Angeles, suggested naming the place for the discoverer of the Pacific Ocean (Gudde, 1949, p. 20). Edward J. Abbot had bought swamp and overflow land there from the state in 1892 and built a house and a small pier known as Abbott's Landing (Gleason, p. 94-95).
Balboa Beach [ORANGE]: *beach,* 7 miles southeast of Huntington Beach civic center along the coast (lat. 33°36' N, long. 117°54' W); the beach is at Balboa. Named on Newport Beach (1965) 7.5' quadrangle.
Balboa Island [ORANGE]: *island,* 4400 feet long, 7 miles east-southeast of Huntington Beach civic center in Newport Bay (lat. 33°36'25" N, long. 117°53'30" W). Named on Newport Beach (1965) 7.5' quadrangle. Postal authorities established Balisle post office in 1927 and changed the name to Balboa Island in 1928 (Frickstad, p. 116). W.S. Collins had the island made in 1906 by dredging bay mud onto a sand flat in Newport Bay; Newport Beach annexed the island in 1916 (Meadows, p. 23). The eastern tip of the island is separated from the main part by a waterway, and this cutoff section of land is called Little Island (Gleason, p. 98).
Balboa Palisades: see **Corona del Mar** [ORANGE].
Balboa Reach: see **Newport Bay** [ORANGE].
Balcom Canyon [VENTURA]: *canyon,* drained by a stream that flows 2.5 miles to the valley of Santa Clara River 5.25 miles southwest of Fillmore (lat. 34°21' N, long. 118°58'55" W; at W line sec. 9, T 3 N, R 20 W). Named on Moorpark (1951) 7.5' quadrangle. Called Sulphur Canyon on Piru (1921) 15' quadrangle.
Bald Mountain [LOS ANGELES]: *ridge,* northwest-trending, 1.25 miles long, 7.5 miles east-southeast of Gorman (lat. 34°44'45" N, long. 118°43'50" W; around NW cor. sec. 31, T 8 N, R 17 W). Named on La Liebre Ranch (1965) and Liebre Mountain (1958) 7.5' quadrangles.
Bald Peak [ORANGE]: *peak,* 5 miles southeast of Pleasants Peak on Orange-Riverside county line (lat. 33°45'20" N, long. 117°32'05" W). Altitude 3947 feet. Named on Corona South (1967) 7.5' quadrangle.
Baldwin Canyon: see **Baldwin Grade Canyon** [LOS ANGELES].
Baldwin Grade Canyon [LOS ANGELES]: *canyon,* drained by a stream that flows 1.5 miles to lowlands 5.25 miles north-northeast of Burnt Peak (lat. 34°45'10" N, long. 118°32'05" W; sec. 25, T 8 N, R 16 W). Named on Burnt Peak (1958) 7.5' quadrangle. Called Baldwin Canyon on Los Angeles County (1935) map.
Baldwin Hills [LOS ANGELES]: *range,* 3 miles north-northwest of Inglewood city hall (lat. 34°00' N, long. 118°22'30" W). Named on

Beverly Hills (1950), Hollywood (1953), Inglewood (1952), and Venice (1964) 7.5' quadrangles.

Baldwin Hills Reservoir [LOS ANGELES]: *lake,* 1250 feet long, 7.5 miles west-southwest of Los Angeles city hall (lat. 34°00'30" N, long. 118°21'45" W); the feature is in Baldwin Hills. Named on Hollwood (1953) 7.5' quadrangle.

Baldwin Park [LOS ANGELES]: *city,* 4.25 miles southwest of Azusa city hall (lat. 34°05'10" N, long, 117°57'30" W); the city is on Santa Anita grant. Named on Baldwin Park (1953) 7.5' quadrangle. Pomona (1904) 15' quadrangle shows a place called Vineland at present Baldwin Park (lat. 34°05'25" N, long. 117°57'45" W). Postal authorities established Vineland post office in 1887 and changed the name to Baldwin Park in 1907 (Frickstad, p. 83). The city incorporated in 1956. The name "Baldwin" commemorates Elias Jackson "Lucky" Baldwin, who bought Santa Anita grant in 1875 (Hanna, p. 23).

Baldy [VENTURA]: *peak,* 2.5 miles north of Piru (lat. 34°27'15" N, long. 118°47'55" W; near SE cor. sec. 6, T 4 N, R 18 W). Altitude 3416 feet. Named on Piru (1952) 7.5' quadrangle.

Baldy: see **Mount Baldy** [LOS ANGELES]; **North Baldy**, under **Mount Baden-Powell** [LOS ANGELES]; **Mount San Antonio** [LOS ANGELES].

Baldy Peak: see **North Baldy Peak**, under **Throop Peak** [LOS ANGELES].

Balisle: see **Balboa Island** [ORANGE].

Ballast Point [LOS ANGELES]: *promontory,* 4 miles east-southeast of Silver Peak on Santa Catalina Island (lat. 33°25'50" N, long. 118°30'15" W). Named on Santa Catalina West (1943) 7.5' quadrangle.

Ball Flat [LOS ANGELES]: *area,* 2.5 miles northwest of Big Pines (lat. 34°24'15" N, long. 117°43'30" W). Named on Mescal Creek (1956) 7.5' quadrangle.

Ballinger Canyon [VENTURA]: *canyon,* drained by a stream that heads in Kern County and flows 4.25 miles in Ventura County to enter Santa Barbara County nearly 20 miles north-northwest of Reyes Peak (lat. 34°53'10" N, long. 119°26'30" W; near N line sec. 9, T 9 N, R 24 W). Named on Ballinger Canyon (1943) and Cuyama Peak (1943) 7.5' quadrangles.

Ballona [LOS ANGELES]: *land grant,* at Venice, Playa del Rey, and Culver City. Named on Beverly Hills (1950), Hollywood (1953), Inglewood (1964), and Venice (1950) 7.5' quadrangles. Called La Ballona on Inglewood (1952) 7.5' quadrangle. Agustin Machado, Ignacio Machado, Felipe Talamantes, and Tomas Talamantes received the land in 1839 and claimed 13,920 acres patented in 1873 (Cowan, p. 18; Cowan gave the alternate name "Paso de las Carretas" for the grant). Accord-

ing to tradition in the Talamantes family, the name "Ballona" is from Bayona, a city in Spain that was the home of a family ancestor (Gudde, 1949, p. 22).

Ballona: see **Port Ballona**, under **Playa del Rey** [LOS ANGELES].

Ballona Creek [LOS ANGELES]: *stream,* flows 8.5 miles to the sea nearly 6 miles north-northwest of Manhattan Beach city hall (lat. 33°57'40" N, long. 118°27'20" W); the stream crosses Ballona grant. Named on Beverly Hills (1950), Hollywood (1953), and Venice (1950) 7.5' quadrangles. Called Sanjon de Agua con Alisos on a diseño of Rincon de Los Bueyes grant (Becker, 1969).

Ballona Harbor: see **Ballona Lagoon** [LOS ANGELES].

Ballona Junction: see **Redondo Junction** [LOS ANGELES].

Ballona Lagoon [LOS ANGELES] *water feature,* extends north-northwest parallel to the coast from a point on Ballona Creek 6 miles north-northwest of Manhattan Beach city hall (lat. 33°58' N, long. 118°27'15" W). Named on Venice (1950) 7.5' quadrangle. On Redondo (1896) 15' quadrangle, the name applies to a larger water feature and adjacent marsh. Venice (1964) 7.5' quadrangle has the name "Marina del Rey" at the place, and Lankershim Ranch Land and Water Company's (1888) map shows Ballona Harbor there.

Bandini [LOS ANGELES]:
(1) *district,* 5.5 miles southeast of Los Angeles city hall (lat. 34°00'25" N, long. 118°10' W). Named on Los Angeles (1953) 7.5' quadrangle.
(2) *locality,* 5 miles west of present Whittier city hall along Atchison, Topeka and Santa Fe Railroad (lat. 33°58'55" N, long. 118°07'05" W). Named on Whittier (1951) 7.5' quadrangle. On Bell (1936) 6' quadrangle, the name applies to a place located about 1 mile farther west-northwest along the railroad.

Bangle [LOS ANGELES]: *locality,* 4.25 miles north-northwest of Long Beach city hall along a railroad (lat. 33°49'30" N, long. 118° 13'40" W). Named on Long Beach (1949) 7.5' quadrangle.

Banning: see **Mount Banning** [LOS ANGELES]; **Mount Banning**, under **Black Jack Mountain** [LOS ANGELES].

Banning Beach [LOS ANGELES]: *beach,* 2.5 miles northwest of Avalon on the northeast side of Santa Catalina Island (lat. 33°22'30" N, long. 118°21'10" W). Named on Santa Catalina East (1943) 7.5' quadrangle.

Barber City [ORANGE]: *district,* 7.5 miles south-southwest of Buena Park civic center in Westminister (lat. 33°45'25" N, long. 118°01'45" W; sec. 9, T 5 S, R 11 W). Named on Los Alamitos (1950) 7.5' quadrangle. Henry Barber laid out the place in 1924 (Meadows, p. 24).

Bardsdale [VENTURA]: *town,* 2 miles south-southwest of Fillmore (lat. 34°22'30" N, long. 118°55'50" W). Named on Fillmore (1951) and Moorpark (1951) 7.5' quadrangles. Postal authorities established Bardsdale post office in 1887 and discontinued it in 1906 (Frickstad, p. 217). R.G. Surdam founded the town in 1887 on land purchased from Thomas R. Bard, the first president of Union Oil Company, and named the town for Bard (Hanna, p. 25) An earlier community at the site commonly was called Stringtown because it was strung out along a water ditch (Ricard).

Bare Mountain [LOS ANGELES]: *peak,* 8.5 miles west-southwest of Valyermo (lat. 34°23'55" N, long. 117°59'30" W). Altitude 6388 feet. Named on Juniper Hills (1959) 7.5' quadrangle.

Bare Mountain Canyon [LOS ANGELES]: *canyon,* drained by a stream that flows 5.5 miles to Little Rock Creek 8.5 miles west of Valyermo (lat. 34°26'15" N, long. 117°59'50" W). Named on Juniper Hills (1959) and Pacifico Mountain (1959) 7.5' quadrangles. West Fork branches southwest 3.25 miles north-northeast of Pacifico Mountain; it is 2 miles long and is named on Pacifico Mountain (1959) 7.5' quadrangle.

Barley Flats [LOS ANGELES]: *area,* 7.5 miles south-southwest of Pacifico Mountain (lat. 34°16'45" N, long. 118°04'30" W; sec. 7, T 2 N, R 11 W). Named on Chilao Flat (1959) 7.5' quadrangle. Wild rye growing at the place gives it the appearance of a barley field (Robinson, J.W., 1977, p. 190).

Barlow Canyon [VENTURA]: *canyon,* drained by a stream that flows 2.25 miles to the valley of Santa Clara River 5.25 miles west of Saticoy (lat. 34°17' N, long. 119°14'25" W). Named on Saticoy (1951) 7.5' quadrangle.

Barney Knob [LOS ANGELES]: *peak,* 6.5 miles northwest of Point Dume (lat. 34°04'40" N, long. 118°52'40" W; near S line sec. 16, T 1 S, R 19 W). Altitude 1729 feet. Named on Triunfo Pass (1950) 7.5' quadrangle.

Barrel Spring [LOS ANGELES]: *spring,* 5.5 miles north-northwest of Sunland (lat. 34°05'05" N, long. 118°20'30" W; near NW cor. sec. 22, T 3 N, R 14 W). Named on Sunland (1966) 7.5' quadrangle.

Barrel Springs [LOS ANGELES]: *springs,* 4 miles southeast of Palmdale (lat. 34°32' N, long. 118°04'05" W; sec. 7, T 5 N, R 11 E). Named on Palmdale (1958) 7.5' quadrangle.

Barrett: see **Sawtelle**, under **West Los Angeles** [LOS ANGELES].

Barrett Canyon [LOS ANGELES]: *canyon,* drained by a stream that heads in San Bernardino County and flows 1.25 miles to San Antonio Canyon 12.5 miles north-northeast of Pomona city hall just inside Los Angeles County (lat. 34°13'05" N, long. 117°39'50" W; sec. 36, T 2 N, R 8 W). Named on Mount Baldy (1954) 7.5' quadrangle. Called

Kerkhoff Canyon on Camp Baldy (1940) 6' quadrangle, where present Cascade Canyon is called Barrett Canyon.

Bartholomaus Canyon [LOS ANGELES]: *canyon,* drained by a stream that flows 1.5 miles to lowlands 3.5 miles east of downtown San Fernando (lat. 34°17' N, long. 118°22'35" W; at E line sec. 6, T 2 N, R 14 W). Named on San Fernando (1953) 7.5' quadrangle. Called Batholem Canyon on Los Angeles County (1935) map.

Bartlett: see **Camp Bartlett** [VENTURA].

Bartolo [LOS ANGELES]: *locality,* 3.5 miles south of El Monte city hall along Union Pacific Railroad (lat. 34°01'10" N, long. 118°02'35" W); the place is on Paso de Bartolo grant. Named on El Monte (1953) 7.5' quadrangle.

Bartolo: see **Saint Helens Spur** [LOS ANGELES].

Barton Mound: see **East Irvine** [ORANGE].

Bassett [LOS ANGELES]: *town,* 2.25 miles southeast of El Monte city hall (lat. 34°03' N, long. 118°00' W). Named on Baldwin Park (1953) and El Monte (1953) 7.5' quadrangles. Postal authorities established Bassett post office in 1957; after O.T. Bassett purchased the site in 1895, the place was known as Bassett ranch and was developed in the 1930's as Bassett Village (Salley, p. 15).

Bassett Village: see **Bassett** [LOS ANGELES].

Bass Rock [VENTURA]: *relief feature,* 5.5 miles southwest of Triunfo Pass along the coast (lat. 34°03'55" N, long. 118°59'40" W; sec. 20, T 1 S., R 20 W). Named on Triunfo Pass (1950) 7.5' quadrangle.

Bastanchury: see **Sunny Hills** [ORANGE].

Batholem Canyon: see **Bartholomaus Canyon** [LOS ANGELES].

Baughman Spring [LOS ANGELES]: *spring,* 4.5 miles west-southwest of Pacifico Mountain along Mill Creek (lat. 34°21'20" N, long. 118°06'35" W). Named on Chilao Flat (1959) 7.5' quadrangle.

Bay City: see **Seal Beach** [ORANGE].

Bay Island [ORANGE]: *island,* 450 feet long, 6.5 miles east-southeast of Huntington Beach civic center in Newport Bay (lat. 33° 36'25" N, long. 117°54'15" W). Named on Newport Beach (1965) 7.5' quadrangle. The feature was a low-lying mud flat before the level was raised by material from dredging operations; the place was called Modjeska Island after Polish actress Helene Modjeska bought a home there in 1907 (Gleason, p. 96-97).

Bay of San Pedro: see **San Pedro Bay** [LOS ANGELES-ORANGE].

Beacon Bay [ORANGE]: *embayment,* 7 miles east-southeast of Huntington Beach civic center in Newport Bay (lat. 33°36'35" N, long. 117°53'40" W). Named on Newport Beach (1965) 7.5' quadrangle.

Beale's Cut: see **San Fernando Pass** [LOS ANGELES].

Bear Canyon [LOS ANGELES]:
(1) *canyon,* drained by a stream that flows 5 miles to Cienaga Canyon 12 miles southeast of Gorman (lat. 34°39'35" N, long. 118°40'10" W; near N line sec. 34, T 7 N, R 17 W). Named on Liebre Mountain (1958) 7.5' quadrangle.
(2) *canyon,* nearly 2 miles long, 14 miles north-northeast of Pomona city hall on Los Angeles-San Bernardino county line (lat. 34°14'45" N, long. 117°39'20" W). Named on Mount Baldy (1954) 7.5' quadrangle. West Fork branches north less than 1 mile above the mouth of the main canyon; it is 1.25 miles long and is named on Mount Baldy (1954) and Mount San Antonio (1955) 7.5' quadrangles.
(3) *canyon,* drained by a stream that flows nearly 5 miles to Santa Clara River 6.25 miles east of Solemint (lat. 34°25'35" N, long. 118°20'50" W; sec. 16, T 4 N, R 14 W). Named on Agua Dulce (1960) 7.5' quadrangle. Called Little Bear Canyon on Los Angeles County (1935) map.
(4) *canyon,* drained by a stream that flows about 2 miles to Sand Canyon (2) 4 miles southeast of Solemint (lat. 34°22'45" N, long. 118°24'10" W; sec. 1, T 3 N, R 15 W). Named on Mint Canyon (1960) and San Fernando (1953) 7.5' quadrangles.
(5) *canyon,* drained by a stream that flows 3.5 miles to Arroyo Seco 6.5 miles southeast of Condor Peak (lat. 34°15'05" N, long. 118°08'55" W). Named on Condor Peak (1959), Mount Wilson (1953), and Pasadena (1953) 7.5' quadrangles.
(6) *canyon,* 1.5 miles long, 1.5 miles north of Gorman on Los Angeles-Kern county line (lat. 34°49'05" N, long. 118°51'10" W; at NW cor. sec. 1, T 8 N, R 19 W). Named on Lebec (1958) 7.5' quadrangle.
Bear Canyon [VENTURA]:
(1) *canyon,* drained by a stream that flows 3.25 miles to Cuyama River 5.5 miles northwest of Reyes Peak (lat. 34°41'05" N, long. 119°21'25" W; sec. 19, T 7 N, R 23 W). Named on Rancho Nuevo Creek (1943) and Reyes Peak (1943) 7.5' quadrangles.
(2) *canyon,* drained by a stream that flows 3.5 miles to Sespe Creek 11 miles east-northeast of Wheeler Springs (lat. 34°33'30" N, long. 119°06'10" W; near N line sec. 5, T 5 N, R 21 W). Named on Topatopa Mountains (1943) 7.5' quadrangle.
(3) *canyon,* drained by a stream that flows 3 miles to Sisar Creek 6.5 miles west of Santa Paula Peak (lat. 34°25'55" N, long. 119°07'20" W). Named on Santa Paula Peak (1951) 7.5' quadrangle.
Bear Canyon: see **Little Bear Canyon** [LOS ANGELES]; **O'Hara Canyon** [VENTURA]; **South Portal Canyon** [LOS ANGELES].
Bear Creek [LOS ANGELES]: *stream,* flows 10.5 miles to West Fork San Gabriel River 7.5

miles north of Azusa city hall (lat. 34°14'25" N, long. 117°53'W). Named on Azusa (1953), Crystal Lake (1958), and Waterman Mountain (1959) 7.5' quadrangles. West Fork enters from the west 5.25 miles south-southeast of Waterman Mountain; it is 4.5 miles long and is named on Waterman Mountain (1959) 7.5' quadrangle.
Bear Creek [VENTURA]: *stream,* flows nearly 1 mile to Maple Creek 5.5 miles north of Fillmore (lat. 34°28'55" N, long. 118°53'20" W; near N line sec. 32, T 5 N, R 19 W). Named on Fillmore (1951) 7.5' quadrangle.
Bear Creek: see **Maple Creek** [VENTURA]; **Rancho Nuevo Creek** [VENTURA].
Bear Divide [LOS ANGELES]: *pass,* 6 miles north-northeast of downtown San Fernando (lat. 34°21'35" N, long. 118°23'30" W; sec. 7, T 3 N, R 14 W); the feature is near the head of Bear Canyon (4). Named on San Fernando (1966) 7.5' quadrangle.
Beardsley Wash [VENTURA]: *stream,* flows 3.5 miles to lowlands 4 miles west-northwest of Camarillo (lat. 34°14'10" N, long. 119°06'15" W). Named on Camarillo (1950) and Santa Paula (1951) 7.5' quadrangles.
Bear Flat [ORANGE]: *area,* 3.5 miles west-northwest of Santiago Peak at the head of Halfway Canyon (lat. 33°44'10" N, long. 117°35'15" W). Named on Santiago Peak (1943) 7.5' quadrangle. On Santiago Peak (1943) 15' quadrangle, the name applies to a place located 1.25 miles north-northwest of Santiago Peak (lat. 33°43'35" N, long. 117°32'40" W). The name is from the bear that Jonathan Watson killed at the site (Sleeper, 1976, p. 79).
Bear Gulch [LOS ANGELES]: *canyon,* drained by a stream that flows 1.25 miles to Prairie Fork 5.5 miles northwest of Mount San Antonio (lat. 34°20'55" N, long. 117°42'35" W; at W line sec. 15, T 3 N, R 8 W). Named on Mount San Antonio (1955) 7.5' quadrangle.
Bear Gulch [VENTURA]: *canyon,* nearly 2 miles long, opens into the canyon of Piru Creek 6 miles northeast of McDonald Peak (lat. 34° 42'05" N, long. 118°52'15" W; near W line sec. 14, T 7 N, R 19 W); the canyon heads northeast of Bear Mountain. Named on Black Mountain (1958) and McDonald Peak (1958) 7.5' quadrangles.
Bear Gulch: see **Halfway Canyon** [ORANGE].
Bear Gulch Camp [LOS ANGELES]: *locality,* 13 miles east-southeast of Gorman on Liebre Mountain (lat. 34°42'45" N, long. 118° 37'50" W; sec. 12, T 7 N, R 17 W); the place is near the head of Bear Canyon (1). Named on Liebre Mountain (1958) 7.5' quadrangle.
Bear Heaven [VENTURA]: *area,* 7.5 miles northwest of Fillmore (lat. 34°29' N, long. 118°59' W). Named on Fillmore (1951) and Santa Paula Peak (1951) 7.5' quadrangles.
Bear Mountain [VENTURA]: *peak,* 5.5 miles north-northeast of McDonald Peak (lat. 34°42'20" N, long. 118°53'30" W; near NE

cor. sec. 16, T 7 N, R 19 W). Altitude 4777 feet. Named on McDonald Peak (1958) 7.5' quadrangle.

Bear Spring [LOS ANGELES]: *spring,* 3.5 miles south-southwest of the village of Leona Valley (lat. 34°34'10" N, long. 118°18'55" W; sec. 36, T 6 N, R 14 W). Named on Sleepy Valley (1958) 7.5' quadrangle. Los Angeles County (1935) map shows Bear Spring located a little farther north (sec. 25, T 6 N, R 14 W), and shows a feature called Pidgeon Spg. situated about 1 mile west-southwest of Bear Spring (sec. 35, T 6 N, R 14 W).

Bear Spring: see **Los Pinos Spring** [ORANGE].

Bear Trap Canyon [ORANGE]: *canyon,* drained by a stream that flows 1.25 miles to Santiago Canyon 2.5 miles west-southwest of Santiago Peak (lat. 33°41'30" N, long. 117°34'20" W; at W line sec. 36, T 5 S, R 7 W). Named on Santiago Peak (1954) 7.5' quadrangle.

Beartrap Canyon [LOS ANGELES]:
(1) *canyon,* drained by a stream that flows 2.25 miles to Piru Creek 10.5 miles south-southeast of Gorman (lat. 34°39'20" N, long. 118° 46'50" W; sec. 34, T 7 N, R 18 W). Named on Black Mountain (1958) 7.5' quadrangle. Los Angeles County (1935) map shows a place called Horse Thief Flat located about 1 mile west of the mouth of Beartrap Canyon along a southern tributary of Piru Creek.
(2) *canyon,* 3.25 miles long, opens into Aliso Canyon (1) 4.25 miles east-southeast of Acton (lat. 34°26'15" N, long. 118°07'50" W; at NW cor. sec. 15, T 4 N, R 12 W). Named on Acton (1959) and Pacifico Mountain (1959) 7.5' quadrangles. A grizzly bear trapped in the canyon in 1889 was sent to the zoo in San Francisco, where it lived until 1911 (Robinson, J.W., 1977, p. 190, 195).

Beartrap Creek [VENTURA]: *stream,* flows 7.25 miles to join Alamo Creek (2) and form Cuyama River 4 miles north of Reyes Peak (lat. 34°41'25" N, long. 119°17'30" W; sec. 23, T 7 N, R 23 W). Named on Reyes Peak (1943) and San Guillermo (1943) 7.5' quadrangles.

Beartrap Spring [LOS ANGELES]: *spring,* 11 miles south-southeast of Gorman in Beartrap Canyon (1) (lat. 34°38'35" N, long. 118°47'25" W). Named on Black Mountain (1958) 7.5' quadrangle.

Beatty Canyon [LOS ANGELES]: *canyon,* 1 mile long, 1.25 miles north-northeast of Azusa city hall (lat. 34°09'05" N, long. 117°53'45" W; sec. 23, 26, T 1 N, R 10 W). Named on Azusa (1953) 7.5' quadrangle.

Beckley: see **Hall Beckley Canyon** [LOS ANGELES].

Bedford Peak [ORANGE]: *peak,* 2.5 miles southeast of Pleasants Peak on Orange-Riverside county line (lat. 33°46' N, long. 117°34'35" W). Named on Corona South

(1967) 7.5' quadrangle. The name is from a pioneer of Riverside County (Meadows, p. 26).

Bee Canyon [LOS ANGELES]:
(1) *canyon,* drained by a stream that flows 3 miles to San Francisquito Canyon 7.5 miles south of the village of Lake Hughes (lat. 34°34'05" N, long. 118°27'45" W). Named on Green Valley (1958) 7.5' quadrangle.
(2) *canyon,* drained by a stream that flows 2.5 miles to Santa Clara River 5.25 miles east-northeast of Solemint (lat. 34°26'15" N, long. 118°21'55" W; near N line sec. 17, T 4 N, R 14 W). Named on Agua Dulce (1960) 7.5' quadrangle.
(3) *canyon,* drained by a stream that flows 0.5 mile to Pacoima Canyon 7 miles north-north-west of Sunland (lat. 34°21'05" N, long. 118°21'25" W; near SW cor. sec. 9, T 3 N, R 14 W). Named on Sunland (1953) 7.5' quadrangle.
(4) *canyon,* drained by a stream that flows 2.5 miles to lowlands 5 miles south of Newhall (lat. 34°18'25" N, long. 118°30'35" W). Named on Oat Mountain (1952) 7.5' quadrangle.

Bee Canyon [ORANGE]:
(1) *canyon,* 0.5 mile long, opens into Santa Ana Canyon 2.5 miles south-southeast of San Juan Hill (lat. 33°52'40" N, long. 117°43'15" W). Named on Prado Dam (1967) 7.5' quadrangle.
(2) *canyon,* drained by a stream that flows 2 miles to lowlands 5.5 miles north-northwest of El Toro (lat. 33°42'05" N, long. 117°42'45" W). Named on El Toro (1968) 7.5' quadrangle.

Bee Canyon: see **Round Canyon** [ORANGE].

Bee Canyon Wash [ORANGE]: *stream,* flows 4.5 miles from the mouth of Bee Canyon (2) to San Diego Creek 9 miles southeast of Santa Ana city hall (lat. 33°39'15" N, long. 117°45'30" W). Named on El Toro (1968) and Tustin (1965) 7.5' quadrangles.

Bee Rock [LOS ANGELES]: *relief feature,* 3.5 miles south-southeast of Burbank city hall (lat. 34°08'05" N, long. 118°17'35" W). Named on Burbank (1953) 7.5' quadrangle.

Bel Air [LOS ANGELES]: *district,* 3.25 miles west-northwest of Beverly Hills city hall in Los Angeles (lat. 34°05'10" N, long. 118° 27' W). Named on Beverly Hills (1950) 7.5' quadrangle.

Bell [LOS ANGELES]: *city,* 2 miles north-north-east of South Gate city hall (lat. 33°58'45" N, long. 118°11'15" W). Named on South Gate (1952) 7.5' quadrangle. The city incorporated in 1923. Downey (1902) 15' quadrangle has the names "Obed" and "Bell Sta." for a place situated along Los Angeles Terminal Railroad about 1 mile west of present Bell city hall (lat. 33°58'40" N, long. 118°12'20" W). Postal authorities established Obed post office—named for Obed, Kentucky—in 1892 and changed the name to Bell in 1898; James G. Bell, who owned the land there, was the first postmaster of both post offices (Hanna, p. 28; Salley, p. 17, 159).

Bell Canyon [LOS ANGELES]: *canyon,* 2 miles long, joins Volfe Canyon to form Big Dalton Canyon 5 miles northeast of Glendora city hall (lat. 34°10'55" N, long. 117°47'45" W; sec. 11, T 1 N, R 9 W). Named on Glendora (1953) 7.5' quadrangle.

Bell Canyon [LOS ANGELES-VENTURA]: *canyon,* 6 miles long, on Los Angeles-Ventura county line along Bell Creek above a point 5 miles south-southwest of Chatsworth (lat. 34°11'50" N, long. 118° 39'15" W). Named on Calabasas (1952) 7.5' quadrangle.

Bell Canyon [ORANGE]: *canyon,* drained by a stream that flows 13 miles to San Juan Creek nearly 7 miles east-northeast of San Juan Capistrano (lat. 33°32'05" N, long. 117°33'15" W; near NW cor. sec. 30, T 7 S, R 6 W). Named on Alberhill (1954), Cañada Gobernadora (1968), and Santiago Peak (1954) 7.5' quadrangles. The name is the anglicized form of the Spanish name *Cañada de la Campaña,* given to the canyon in Spanish days because of a boulder there that gave off a clear tone when struck (Meadows, p. 26).

Bell Canyon: see **Hot Spring Canyon** [ORANGE].

Bell Creek [LOS ANGELES-VENTURA]: *stream,* heads just inside Ventura County and flows 3 miles to join Arroyo Calabasas and form Los Angeles River 0.5 mile southwest of the center of Canoga Park (lat. 34°11'40" N, long. 118°36'05" W). Named on Calabasas (1952) and Canoga Park (1952) 7.5' quadrangles. South Branch enters from the southwest 1.5 miles above the mouth of the main stream; it is 0.5 mile long and is named on Calabasas (1952) 7.5' quadrangle.

Bellflower [LOS ANGELES]: *city,* 8 miles southwest of Whittier city hall (lat. 33°52'55" N, long. 118°07'15" W). Named on Long Beach (1949), Los Alamitos (1950), South Gate (1952), and Whittier (1965) 7.5' quadrangles. Postal authorities established Bellflower post office in 1910 (Frickstad, p. 70), and the city incorporated in 1957. F.E. Woodruff founded the community in 1906 and called it Somerset, but postal authorities rejected this designation; an orchard of bellflower apples suggested the present name (Gudde, 1949, p. 27).

Bell Gardens [LOS ANGELES]: *city,* 2 miles east-southeast of South Gate city hall (lat. 33°58' N, long. 118°09'30" W). Named on South Gate (1964) 7.5' quadrangle. Postal authorities established Gardens post office in 1930 and changed the name to Bell Gardens in 1943 (Salley, p. 82). The city incorporated in 1961. The community began in 1930 when promoters subdivided vegetable tracts developed there by Japanese gardeners (Gudde, 1969, p. 25).

Bell Station: see **Bell** [LOS ANGELES].

Belmont Shore [LOS ANGELES]: *district,* 3.25 miles east-southeast of Long Beach city hall (lat. 33°45'30" N, long. 118°08'05" W). Named on Long Beach (1964) 7.5' quadrangle. Postal authorities established Belmont Shore post office in 1930 and discontinued it in 1962; the place, now part of Long Beach, was settled in the early 1900's as a seashore vacation spot (Salley, p. 18).

Belvedere [LOS ANGELES]:
(1) *district,* 4.5 miles east-southeast of Los Angeles city hall (lat. 34°02'10" N, long. 118°09'45" W). Named on Los Angeles (1953) 7.5' quadrangle.
(2) *locality,* 2.5 miles northeast of Redondo (present Redondo Beach) along a rail line (lat. 33°51'50" N, long. 118°21'25" W). Named on Redondo (1896) 15' quadrangle.

Belvedere Gardens [LOS ANGELES]: *district,* 5 miles east-southeast of Los Angeles city hall (lat. 34°01'40" N, long. 118°10' W). Named on Alhambra (1926) 6' quadrangle.

Benedict: see **Stanton** [ORANGE].

Benedict Canyon [LOS ANGELES]: *canyon,* 3.25 miles long, 3 miles northwest of Beverly Hills city hall (lat. 34°06'15" N, long. 118°26'10" W). Named on Beverly Hills (1950) and Van Nuys (1953) 7.5' quadrangles. The name commemorates Edson A. Benedict, a storekeeper in Los Angeles who claimed the canyon in 1868 (Gudde, 1949, p. 28).

Bennington [LOS ANGELES]: *locality,* 3 miles north of Los Angeles city hall along Los Angeles Terminal Railroad (lat. 34°05'45" N, long. 118°14' W). Named on Pasadena (1900) 15' quadrangle.

Benton: see **Azusa** [LOS ANGELES] (3).

Bent Spring Canyon [LOS ANGELES]: *canyon,* 2.25 miles long, 4 miles south of Torrance city hall (lat. 33°46'40" N, long. 118°40'15" W). Named on Torrance (1964) 7.5' quadrangle.

Ben Weston Beach [LOS ANGELES]: *beach,* 3 miles west-southwest of Mount Banning on the west side of Santa Catalina Island (lat. 33°21'45" N, long. 118°29' W); the beach is less than 0.5 mile north-northeast of Ben Weston Point. Named on Santa Catalina South (1943) 7.5' quadrangle.

Ben Weston Point [LOS ANGELES]: *promontory,* 3.25 miles west-southwest of Mount Banning on the west side of Santa Catalina Island (lat. 33°21'25" N, long. 118°29'15" W). Named on Santa Catalina South (1943) 7.5' quadrangle. The name recalls Ben Weston, an early squatter on the island (Doran, 1980, p. 76).**Berry Canyon** [LOS ANGELES]: *canyon,* 1.25 miles long, 5 miles southeast of Van Nuys (lat. 34°07'55" N, long. 118°23'10" W). Named on Van Nuys (1953) 7.5' quadrangle.

Berryfield: see **Garden Grove** [ORANGE].

Berry Flat [LOS ANGELES]: *area,* 4.25 miles north of Glendora city hall (lat. 34°11'55" N, long. 117°51'10" W; near W line sec. 5, T 1

N, R 9 W). Named on Glendora (1953) 7.5'
quadrangle.
Beverly: see **Beverly Hills** [LOS ANGELES].
Beverly Glen [LOS ANGELES]: *locality,* 3.5
miles northwest of Beverly Hills city hall in
Brown Canyon (2) (lat. 34°06'30" N, long.
118°26'45" W). Named on Beverly Hills
(1950) 7.5' quadrangle. Postal authorities established Beverly Glen post office in 1913 and
discontinued it in 1916 (Frickstad, p. 71).
Beverly Hills [LOS ANGELES]: *city,* 9 miles
west of Los Angeles city hall (lat. 34°04'20"
N, long. 118°24' W). Named on Beverly Hills
(1950) and Hollywood (1953) 7.5' quadrangles. Postal authorities established Beverly
post office in 1907 and changed the name to
Beverly Hills in 1911 (Salley, p. 20). The city
incorporated in 1914. De Las Aguas Association of San Francisco bought Rodeo de los
Aguas grant in 1869 and subdivided it to form
a German colony called Santa Maria—the
association reserved land for a town of Santa
Maria at a site in the heart of present Beverly
Hills (Robinson, W.W., p. 23-24). Another
early-day community called Morocco also
occupied part of present Beverly Hills (Hanna,
p. 31). The name "Beverly Hills" is from Beverly Farms, Massachusetts, former home of
Burton E. Green, an official of Rodeo Land
and Water Company, which promoted the city
(Gudde, 1949, p. 30).
Bichota Canyon [LOS ANGELES]: *canyon,*
drained by a stream that flows nearly 4 miles
to North Fork San Gabriel River 4 miles south
of Crystal Lake (lat. 34°15'40" N, long.
117°50'35" W). Named on Crystal lake (1958)
7.5' quadrangle.
Bichota Mesa [LOS ANGELES]: *area,* 4 miles
south of Crystal Lake (lat. 34°15'45" N, long.
117°50'45" W); the place is opposite the
mouth of Bichota Canyon. Named on Crystal Lake (1958) 7.5' quadrangle.
Big Canyon [ORANGE]: *canyon,* drained by a
stream that flows nearly 3 miles to lowlands
along Upper Newport Bay 7 miles east-southeast of Huntington Beach city hall (lat.
33°37'50" N, long. 117°52'55" W). Named
on Laguna Beach (1965), Newport Beach
(1965), and Tustin (1965) 7.5' quadrangles.
Big Canyon [VENTURA]: *canyon,* drained by
a stream that flows 1.5 miles to Upper Ojai
Valley nearly 4 miles east-southeast of the
town of Ojai (lat. 34°25'50" N, long.
119°09'40" W). Named on Ojai (1952) 7.5'
quadrangle. The feature first was called Cataract Canyon for natural asphalt cataracts or
tar seeps in it, and then it was called Pinkerton Canyon for a family of early landowners
in the vicinity (Ricard).
Big Canyon Reservoir [ORANGE]: *lake,* 1350
feet long, 6.25 miles northwest of Laguna
Beach city hall (lat. 33°36'40" N, long. 117°
51'20" W); the lake is at the head of a branch
of Big Canyon. Named on Laguna Beach

(1965) 7.5' quadrangle.
Big Cedar Creek [VENTURA]: *stream,* flows
1.5 miles to Snowy Creek 2.5 miles northeast
of McDonald Peak (lat. 34°39'25" N, long.
118°54'25" W; near W line sec. 33, T 7 N, R
19 W). Named on McDonald Peak (1958) 7.5'
quadrangle.
Big Cienega [LOS ANGELES]:
(1) *canyon,* drained by a stream that flows less
than 1 mile to Trail Canyon nearly 1 mile
northwest of Condor Peak (lat. 34°20' N, long.
118°13'45" W). Named on Condor Peak
(1959) 7.5' quadrangle.
(2) *spring,* 1.5 miles north-northeast of Crystal Lake (lat. 34°20'15" N, long. 117°49'50"
W). Named on Crystal Lake (1958) 7.5' quadrangle. On Crystal Lake (1941) 6' quadrangle,
the name "Big Cienega" applies to a relief
feature at the place.
Big Cienega Spring [LOS ANGELES]: *spring,*
3.25 miles east-northeast of Glendora city hall
(lat. 34°09'30" N, long. 117°48'45" W; sec.
22, T 1 N, R 9 W). Named on Glendora (1953)
7.5' quadrangle.
Big Cone Camp [VENTURA]: *locality,* 2.5
miles west of Santa Paula Peak at the mouth
of East Fork Santa Paula Canyon (lat.
34°26'55" N, long. 119°03'20" W). Named
on Santa Paula Peak (1951) 7.5' quadrangle.
Big Cone Spring [ORANGE]: *spring,* 2 miles
north-northwest of Santiago Peak (lat.
33°44'20" N, long. 117°32'45" W). Named
on Santiago Peak (1954) 7.5' quadrangle. The
name is from some bigcone-spruce trees that
grow near the spring (Meadows, p. 27).
Big Dalton Canyon [LOS ANGELES]: *canyon,*
3.5 miles long, opens into lowlands 2 miles
northeast of Glendora city hall (lat. 34°09'10"
N, long. 117°50'10" W; at W line sec. 21, T 1
N, R 9 W). Named on Glendora (1953) 7.5'
quadrangle. The canyon divides at the head
to form Volfe Canyon and Bell Canyon. The
name "Dalton" commemorates Henry Dalton,
who claimed Azusa grant and Santa Anita
grant (Gudde, 1949, p. 87). Spaniards called
the feature El Cañon de la Boca Negra, supposedly for dark foliage that marked the entrance to the canyon—*El Cañon de la Boca
Negra* means "the canyon with the Black
Mouth" in Spanish (Robinson, J.W., 1983, p.
13).
Big Dalton Reservoir [LOS ANGELES]: *lake,*
behind a dam 4 miles northeast of Glendora
city hall (lat. 34°10'10" N, long. 117°48'30"
W; sec. 15, T 1 N, R 9 W); the lake is in Big
Dalton Canyon. Named on Glendora (1966)
7.5' quadrangle.
Big Dalton Wash [LOS ANGELES]: *stream* and
dry wash, extends for nearly 11 miles from
the mouth of Big Dalton Canyon to Walnut
Creek 1.5 miles south-southwest of Baldwin
Park city hall (lat. 34°04' N, long. 117°58'15"
W). Named on Baldwin Park (1953), Glendora (1953), and San Dimas (1954) 7.5' quad-

rangles. East Branch extends for 1.25 miles from the mouth of Shuler Canyon to Big Dalton Wash 1.25 miles east-southeast of Glendora city hall. East Branch is named on Glendora (1966) 7.5' quadrangle; the upper part of present East Branch is called Shuler Creek on Glendora (1953) 7.5' quadrangle.

Bighorn: see **Valyermo** [LOS ANGELES].

Big Horn Ridge [LOS ANGELES]: *ridge,* southwest-trending, 3 miles long, center 2.25 southwest of Mount San Antonio (lat. 34° 16'15" N, long. 117°40'40" W). Named on Mount San Antonio (1955) 7.5' quadrangle.

Big John Flat [LOS ANGELES]: *area,* 4 miles northwest of Big Pines (lat. 34°25'05" N, long. 117°44'30" W; sec. 19, 20, T 4 N, R 8 W). Named on Mescal Creek (1956) and Valyermo (1958) 7.5' quadrangles. Called Big John Flats on Los Angeles County (1935) map.

Big Mermaids Canyon [LOS ANGELES]: *canyon,* drained by a stream that flows 2.5 miles to West Fork San Gabriel River 7.5 miles north of Azusa city hall (lat. 34°14'45" N, long. 117°54' W); the mouth of the canyon is 1650 feet east of the mouth of Little Mermaids Canyon. Named on Azusa (1953) and Waterman Mountain (1959) 7.5' quadrangles.

Big Moore Canyon: see **Wickham Canyon** [LOS ANGELES].

Big Mountain [VENTURA]: *ridge,* west-trending, 8 miles long, center 6 miles northeast of Moorpark (lat. 34°20'15" N, long. 118° 47'45" W). Named on Santa Susana (1951) and Simi (1951) 7.5' quadrangles.

Big Narrows [VENTURA]: *narrows,* 3.25 miles south-southeast of Cobblestone Mountain along Agua Blanca Creek (lat. 34°34' N, long. 118°50'25" W; near E line sec. 36, T 6 N, R 19 W). Named on Cobblestone Mountain (1958) 7.5' quadrangle.

Big Oak Flat [LOS ANGELES]: *area,* 2.5 miles east of Whitaker Peak (lat. 34°34'35" N, long. 118°41'30" W; sec. 28, 33, T 6 N, R 17 W). Named on Whitaker Peak (1958) 7.5' quadrangle.

Big Oak Spring [LOS ANGELES]: *spring,* 4 miles southwest of the village of Leona Valley (lat. 34°34'25" N, long. 118°20'20" W; near SW cor. sec. 26, T 6 N, R 14 E). Named on Sleepy Valley (1958) 7.5' quadrangle.

Big Pines [LOS ANGELES]: *village,* nearly 7 miles north-northwest of Mount San Antonio (lat. 34°22'45" N, long. 117°41'20" W; near W line sec. 2, T 3 N, R 8 W). Named on Mescal Creek (1956) 7.5' quadrangle. Swarthout (1941) 6' quadrangle shows a place called Swarthout located 0.5 mile west-northwest of the west end of Swarthout Valley at present Big Pines. Postal authorities established Swartout post office (with the misspelled name) in 1926 and discontinued it in 1942 (Frickstad, p. 82).

Big Rock [LOS ANGELES]: *rock,* 7 miles west-northwest of present Santa Monica city hall,

and 100 feet offshore (lat. 34°02'10" N, long. 118°36'30" W). Named on Las Flores (1932) 6' quadrangle.

Big Rock Beach [LOS ANGELES]: *beach,* 7.25 miles west-northwest of Santa Monica city hall (lat. 34°02'15" N, long. 118°37' W; sec. 36, T 1 S, R 17 W); Big Rock is near the east end of the beach, which is at the mouth of Piedra Gorda Canyon. Named on Topanga (1952) 7.5' quadrangle.

Big Rock Campground [LOS ANGELES]: *locality,* 5.5 miles southeast of Valyermo (lat. 34°23'15" N, long. 117°46'45" W; sec. 36, T 4 N, R 9 W). Named on Valyermo (1958) 7.5' quadrangle.

Big Rock Creek [LOS ANGELES]: *stream,* flows 11 miles to lowlands 1.5 miles north-northwest of Valyermo (lat. 34°28'30" N, long. 117°51'15" W; sec. 31, T 5 N, R 9 W). Named on Valyermo (1958) 7.5' quadrangle. Thompson (1929, p. 291) noted that the stream was called both Rock Creek and Rio del Llano, but United States Board on Geographic Names (1960d, p. 15) rejected these names for the feature. South Fork enters from the south 3 miles southeast of Valyermo; it is 5.5 miles long and is named on Crystal Lake (1958) and Valyermo (1958) 7.5' quadrangles.

Big Rock Springs [LOS ANGELES]: *locality,* 1 mile southeast of Valyermo (lat. 34°26'05" N, long. 117°50'05" W; at E line sec. 17, T 4 N, R 9 W); the place is along Big Rock Creek. Named on Valyermo (1958) 7.5' quadrangle. Rock Creek (1903) 15' quadrangle has the name "Big Rock Villa" near the site.

Big Rock Villa: see **Big Rock Springs** [LOS ANGELES].

Big Rock Wash [LOS ANGELES]: *stream* and *dry wash,* extends for 15 miles from the mouth of the canyon of Big Rock Creek to end 12 miles north-northeast of Littlerock (lat. 34°40' N, long. 117°52'15" W; sec. 30, T 7 N, R 9 W). Named on Hi Vista (1957), Littlerock (1957), Lovejoy Buttes (1957), and Valyermo (1958) 7.5' quadrangles. United States Board on Geographic Names (1961b, p. 8) rejected the names "Rio del Llano," "Rock Creek Wash," and "Rock Wash" for the feature.

Big Springs Canyon [LOS ANGELES]: *canyon,* drained by a stream that flows nearly 3 miles to the sea 2.5 miles west-northwest of Mount Banning on Santa Catalina Island (lat. 33°23'10" N, long. 118°28'25" W); the feature is east of Little Springs Canyon. Named on Santa Catalina North (1950) 7.5' quadrangle.

Big Springs Reservoir [LOS ANGELES]: *lake,* 200 feet long, 4.5 miles north-northwest of Mount Banning on Santa Catalina Island (lat. 33°26' N, long. 118°27'40" W). Named on Santa Catalina North (1950) 7.5' quadrangle.

Big Sycamore Canyon [VENTURA]: *canyon,* drained by a stream that flows 10 miles to the sea 5 miles east-southeast of Point Mugu (lat.

34°04'15" N, long. 119°00'50" W). Named on Newbury Park (1951), Point Mugu (1949), and Triunfo Pass (1950) 7.5' quadrangles. Called Sycamore Canyon on Camulos (1903) 30' quadrangle, but United States Board on Geographic Names (1961b, p. 8) rejected this name for the feature.

Big Tujunga Canyon [LOS ANGELES]: *canyon,* 19 miles long, opens into Tujunga Valley 1 mile north-northwest of Sunland (lat. 34°16'30" N, long. 118°18'50" W). Named on Chilao Flat (1959), Condor Peak (1959), and Sunland (1953) 7.5' quadrangles. Called Tujunga Canyon on San Fernando (1900) 15' quadrangle, which shows Tujunga River in it. Marcou (p. 160) referred to "the large cañon of the Big Tujunja or Tujunga." United States Board on Geographic Names (1968b, p. 4) rejected the names "Tahunga Canyon," "Tajunga Canyon," "Tujunga Canyon," "Tujunga Creek," and "Tuyanga Canyon." The name, which is from Tujunga grant (Robinson, J.W., 1977, p. 145), evidently is of Indian origin (Kroeber, p. 62). The canyon divides at the head to form Upper Big Tujunga Canyon and the canyon of Alder Creek (2). Present Upper Big Tujunga Canyon is called Big Tujunga Canyon on Mount Wilson (1939) 6' quadrangle, but United States Board on Geographic Names (1968b, p. 7) rejected the names "Big Tujunga Canyon," "Tahunga Canyon," "Tajunga Canyon," "Tujunga Canyon," "Tujunga Creek," and "Tuyanga Canyon" for present Upper Big Tujunga Canyon. The Board (1976a, p. 5) approved the name "Big Tujunga Creek" for the stream that flows through Upper Big Tujunga Canyon and Big Tujunga Canyon, and gave the names "Tujunga Creek" and "Tujunga River" as variants.

Big Tujunga Creek: see **Big Tujunga Canyon** [LOS ANGELES]:

Big Tujunga Station [LOS ANGELES]: *locality,* nearly 3 miles south of Condor Peak (lat. 34°17'10" N, long. 118°13'30" W; sec. 3, T 2 N, R 13 W); the place is in Big Tujunga Canyon. Named on Condor Peak (1959) 7.5' quadrangle.

Bill Lane Camp: see **Camp Bill Lane** [LOS ANGELES].

Bingham [ORANGE]: *locality,* 3.5 miles west-southwest of present Buena Park civic center along Pacific Electric Railroad at Los Angeles-Orange county line (lat. 33°50'45" N, long. 118°03'30" W). Named on Los Alamitos (1935) 7.5' quadrangle.

Binnacle Rock [LOS ANGELES]: *rock,* about 3 miles south of Avalon near the southeast end of Santa Catalina Island, and 225 feet offshore (lat. 33°18'05" N, long, 118°20' W). Named on Santa Catalina East (1950) 7.5' quadrangle.

Bird: see **John Bird Canyon** [LOS ANGELES].

Bird Rock [LOS ANGELES]: *rock,* 6.25 miles north-northwest of Mount Banning on the north side of Santa Catalina Island, and 1800 feet offshore (lat. 33°27'05" N, long. 118°29'10" W). Named on Santa Catalina North (1950) 7.5' quadrangle. Preston (1890b, map following p. 278) called the feature White Rock, but United States Board on Geographic Names (1936a, p. 9 rejected this name for it.

Bird Rock: see **Ship Rock** [LOS ANGELES].

Bisket [LOS ANGELES]: *relief feature,* 4.5 miles northeast of downtown San Fernando (lat. 34°19'50" N, long. 118°23'20" W; sec. 19, T 3 N, R 14 W). Named on San Fernando (1966) 7.5' quadrangle.

Bit Rock [LOS ANGELES]: *rock,* 3.25 miles south-southwest of Redondo Beach city hall, and 700 feet offshore at Flat Rock Point (lat. 33°47'45" N, long. 118°24'35" W). Named on Redondo Beach (1963) 7.5' quadrangle.

Bitter Canyon [LOS ANGELES]: *canyon,* drained by a stream that flows 3 miles to Charlie Canyon 6.5 miles south of Warm Springs Mountain (lat. 34°30'10" N, long. 118°34'45" W; sec. 20, T 5 N, R 16 W). Named on Warm Springs Mountain (1958) 7.5' quadrangle. Tejon (1903) 30' quadrangle has the name "Bitter Creek" for the stream in the canyon. Los Angeles County (1935) map shows a feature called Shaw Canyon that opens into Charlie Canyon from the north less than 1 mile east of the mouth of Bitter Canyon (near W line sec. 21, T 5 N, R 16 W), and a feature called McRay Canyon that opens into Charlie Canyon about 2 miles east-northeast of the mouth of Bitter Canyon (near W line sec. 15, T 5 N, R 16 W).

Bitter Creek: see **Amargosa Creek** [VENTURA]; **Bitter Canyon** [LOS ANGELES].

Bitter Point: see **Santa Ana River** [ORANGE].

Bitterwater Lake: see **Amarus Lake**, under **Santa Ana River** [ORANGE].

Bixby [LOS ANGELES]: *locality,* 4.25 miles north-northeast of present Long Beach city hall along Union Pacific Railroad (lat. 33°49'40" N, long. 118°09'50" W). Named on Clearwater (1925) 6' quadrangle.

Bixby: see **Bixby Knolls** [LOS ANGELES].

Bixby Knolls [LOS ANGELES]: *district,* 4.5 miles north of Long Beach city hall (lat. 33°50'05" N, long. 118°10'40" W). Named on Long Beach (1949) 7.5' quadrangle. Postal authorities established Bixby post office 4 miles north of Long Beach post office in 1946; the name commemorates Jotham Bixby, pioneer of Long Beach (Salley, p. 22).

Bixby Slough: see **Harbor Lake** [LOS ANGELES].

Black Butte [LOS ANGELES]: *hill,* 15 miles east-northeast of Littlerock (lat. 34°33'25" N, long. 117°43'20" W; on N line sec. 4, T 5 N, R 8 W). Altitude 3581 feet. Named on El Mirage (1956) 7.5' quadrangle.

Black Canyon [VENTURA]: *canyon,* drained by a stream that flows less than 1 mile to Simi Valley (1) 2.25 miles west-southwest of Santa

Susana Pass (lat. 34°15'45" N, long. 118°40'15" W; near NE cor. sec. 16, T 2 N, R 17 W). Named on Santa Susana (1951) 7.5' quadrangle.

Black Jack Camp [LOS ANGELES]: *locality,* 2 miles east-northeast of Mount Banning on Santa Catalina Island (lat. 33°23'05" N, long. 118°24'20" W); the place is 0.25 mile west-southwest of Black Jack Mountain. Named on Santa Catalina North (1950) 7.5' quadrangle.

Black Jack Mountain [LOS ANGELES]: *peak,* 2.25 miles east-northeast of Mount Banning on Santa Catalina Island (lat. 33°23'15" N, long. 118°24' W). Altitude 2010 feet. Named on Santa Catalina North (1950) 7.5' quadrangle. The name is from zinc blende, also called black jack, found in some veins on spurs of the peak (Preston, 1890b, p. 278). The feature is called Mount Banning on some older maps (Doran, 1980, p. 77).

Black Mountain [VENTURA]:
(1) *peak,* 4.5 miles east-northeast of McDonald Peak (lat. 34°39'15" N, long. 118°51'40" W; sec. 35, T 7 N, R 19 W). Altitude 6216 feet. Named on Black Mountain (1958) 7.5' quadrangle.
(2) *ridge,* west-trending, 2 miles long, 1.5 miles southeast of the town of Ojai (lat. 34°25'55" N, long. 119°13'15" W). Named on Ojai (1952) 7.5' quadrangle.

Black Point [LOS ANGELES]: *promontory,* 1.25 miles north-northwest of Silver Peak on the north side of Santa Catalina Island (lat. 33°28'30" N, long. 118°34'40" W). Named on Santa Catalina West (1943) 7.5' quadrangle.

Black Star Canyon [ORANGE]: *canyon,* drained by Black Star Creek, which flows 5 miles to Santiago Creek 5.5 miles south-southwest of Sierra Peak (lat. 33°46'20" N, long. 117°40'50" W). Named on Black Star Canyon (1967) 7.5' quadrangle, which shows Black Star coal mine near the mouth of the canyon. The feature first was called Cañada de los Indios (Meadows, p. 27). After August Witte discovered coal there in 1879, the canyon took the name of his mine (Hoover, Rensch, and Rensch, p. 264).

Black Star Creek [ORANGE]: *stream,* flows 5 miles to Santiago Creek 5.5 miles south-southwest of Sierra Peak (lat. 33°46'20" N, long. 117°40'50" W); the stream drains Black Star Canyon. Named on Black Star Canyon (1967) 7'5' quadrangle.

Blanchard Canyon [LOS ANGELES]: *canyon,* 1 mile long, 3 miles east of Sunland (lat. 34°15'35" N, long. 118°15'45" W; sec. 17, T 2 N, R 13 W). Named on Sunland (1953) 7.5' quadrangle.

Blanchard Canyon [VENTURA]: *canyon,* drained by a stream that flows 2.25 miles to Piru Canyon nearly 3 miles northeast of Piru (lat. 34°26'35" N, long. 118°45'30" W).

Named on Piru (1952) 7.5' quadrangle. The name commemorates Hooper Crews Blanchard (Ricard).

Blanchards: see **Santa Paula** [VENTURA].

Bleich Canyon [LOS ANGELES]: *canyon,* drained by a stream that flows 2.5 miles to lowlands 4 miles north-northeast of the village of Lake Hughes (lat. 34°43'45" N, long. 118°28'30" W; near N line sec. 4, T 7 N, R 15 W). Named on Lake Hughes (1957) 7.5' quadrangle. Called Bly Canyon on Fairmont (1937) 6' quadrangle, but United States Board on Geographic Names (1960a, p. 12) rejected this name for the feature.

Bleich Flat [LOS ANGELES]: *area,* nearly 5 miles northeast of Burnt Peak (lat. 34°43'35" N, long. 118°30'35" W; sec. 6, T 7 N, R 15 W). Named on Burnt Peak (1958) 7.5' quadrangle.

Blind Canyon [LOS ANGELES]: *canyon,* drained by a stream that flows less than 1 mile to Coldwater Canyon (2) 4.5 miles west-southwest of Mount San Antonio (lat. 34°15'15" N, long. 117°42'45" W). Named on Mount San Antonio (1955) 7.5' quadrangle.

Blind Canyon [LOS ANGELES-VENTURA]: *canyon,* drained by a stream that heads just inside Ventura County and flows 2 miles to Devil Canyon 2.5 miles north-northwest of Chatsworth in Los Angeles County (lat. 34°17'45" N, long. 118°37'05" W; sec. 36, T 3 N, R 17 W). Named on Oat Mountain (1952) and Santa Susana (1951) 7.5' quadrangles. Los Angeles County (1935) map has the name "Caradas Creek" for the stream in present Blind Canyon, and in Devil Canyon below the junction of Blind Canyon and Devil Canyon.

Blind Canyon [ORANGE]:
(1) *canyon,* drained by a stream that flows 2.5 miles to Santiago Creek 6 miles southwest of Sierra Peak (lat. 33°47'40" N, long. 117°43'50" W). Named on Black Star Canyon (1967) 7.5' quadrangle. Corona (1942) 15' quadrangle has the name "Fremont Creek" for the stream in this canyon, and has the name "Sierra Canyon" for present Fremont Canyon.
(2) *canyon,* drained by a stream that flows 2.5 miles to Christianitos Canyon about 4 miles northeast of San Clemente civic center (lat. 33°28' N, long. 117°33'45" W; near N line sec. 24, T 8 S, R 7 W). Named on San Clemente (1968) 7.5' quadrangle.

Bliss: see **Mount Bliss** [LOS ANGELES].

Bliss Canyon [LOS ANGELES]: *canyon,* 1.25 miles long, 4 miles west-northwest of Azusa city hall (lat. 34°09'50" N, long. 117° 58' W; sec. 17, 18, 19, T 1 N, R 10 W). Named on Azusa (1953) 7.5' quadrangle.

Bluebird Canyon [ORANGE]: *canyon,* 1.5 miles long, opens to the sea about 1 mile south-southeast of Laguna Beach city hall (lat. 33° 31'45" N, long. 117°46'20" W; sec. 25, T 7 S, R 9 W). Named on Laguna Beach (1965) 7.5' quadrangle. The feature first was called

19

Rim Rock Canyon, but now that name is restricted to an upper branch (Meadows, p. 119).

Blue Cavern Point [LOS ANGELES]: *promontory,* 5.5 miles north-northwest of Mount Banning on the north side of Santa Catalina Island (lat. 33°26'55" N, long. 118°28'35" W). Named on Santa Catalina North (1950) 7.5' quadrangle.

Bluegum Canyon [LOS ANGELES]: *canyon,* nearly 1 mile long, 2.5 miles east of Sunland (lat. 34°15'35" N, long. 118°16'10" W; sec. 17, 18, T 2 N, R 13 W). Named on Sunland (1953) 7.5' quadrangle. Los Angeles County (1935) map has the form "Blue Gum Canyon" for the name.

Blue Mud Canyon [ORANGE]: *canyon,* drained by a stream that flows 3 miles to Santa Ana Canyon 2.25 miles east of Yorba Linda (lat. 33°52'50" N, long. 117°45'20" W). Named on Prado Dam (1967) and Yorba Linda (1964, photorevised 1981) 7.5' quadrangles.

Blue Point [VENTURA]: *promontory,* 8 miles southeast of Cobblestone Mountain on the west side of Piru Creek (lat. 34°31'35" N, long. 118°45'40" W; near SW cor. sec. 10, T 5 N, R 18 W). Named on Cobblestone Mountain (1958) 7.5' quadrangle.

Blue Point Campground [VENTURA]: *locality,* 8 miles southeast of Cobblestone Mountain along Piru Creek (lat. 34°31'50" N, long. 118°45'25" W; sec. 10, T 5 N, R 18 W); the place is just north of Blue Point. Named on Cobblestone Mountain (1958) 7.5' quadrangle.

Blue Ridge [LOS ANGELES]: *ridge,* northwest- to west-trending 9 miles long, center 6 miles north-northwest of Mount San Antonio (lat. 34°22' N, long. 117°41'30" W). Named on Mescal Creek (1956), Mount San Antonio (1955), and Valyermo (1958) 7.5' quadrangles. The southeasternmost end of the ridge is in San Bernardino County.

Blue Ridge Camp [LOS ANGELES]: *locality,* 5.5 miles north-northwest of Mount San Antonio (lat. 34°21'35" N, long. 117°41'10" W; sec. 11, T 3 N, R 8 W); the place is on Blue Ridge. Named on Mount San Antonio (1955) 7.5' quadrangle.

Blue Rock Spring [VENTURA]: *spring,* 15 miles north-northwest of Reyes Peak (lat. 34°50'40" N, long. 119°20'55" W; at SE cor. sec. 20, T 9 N, R 23 W). Named on Apache Canyon (1943) 7.5' quadrangle.

Bluff Camp [VENTURA]: *locality,* 1.5 miles north of Santa Paula Peak (lat. 34°27'40" N, long. 119°00'30" W; near E line sec. 6, T 4 N, R 20 W). Named on Santa Paula Peak (1951) 7.5' quadrangle.

Bluff Cove [LOS ANGELES]: *embayment,* 3.5 miles south of Redondo Beach city hall along the coast (lat. 33°47'30" N, long. 118°24'25" W). Named on Redondo Beach (1951) 7.5' quadrangle.

Bly Canyon: see **Bleich Canyon** [LOS ANGELES].

Boat Canyon [ORANGE]: *canyon,* drained by a stream that flows nearly 2 miles to the sea less than 1 mile west of Laguna Beach city hall (lat. 33°32'40" N, long. 117°47'40" W). Named on Laguna Beach (1965) 7.5' quadrangle. Commercial fishermen landed their rowboats on the beach at the mouth of the canyon in the early days (Meadows, p. 28).

Bobcat Canyon [LOS ANGELES]:
(1) *canyon,* drained by a stream that flows 2 miles to Santa Clara River 10 miles east of Solemint (lat. 34°26'25" N, long. 118°17' W; sec. 7, T 4 N, R 13 W). Named on Agua Dulce (1960) 7.5' quadrangle.
(2) *canyon,* drained by a stream that flows 3.5 mile to West Fork San Gabriel River 3.5 miles east-northeast of Mount Wilson (1) (lat. 34°14'25" N, long. 118°00' W; sec. 23, T 2 N, R 11 W). Named on Chilao Flat (1959), Mount Wilson (1953), and Waterman Mountain (1959) 7.5' quadrangles.

Bobs Canyon: see **Bobs Gap** [LOS ANGELES].

Bobs Gap [LOS ANGELES]: *pass,* 2.25 miles east-northeast of Valyermo (lat. 34°27'15" N, long. 117°48'45" W; on S line sec. 3, T 4 N, R 9 W). Named on Valyermo (1958) 7.5' quadrangle. Los Angeles County (1935) map shows a feature called Bobs Canyon located about 3 miles southeast of Bobs Gap.

Boca de la Playa [ORANGE]: *land grant,* between Capistrano Beach and San Clemente. Named on Dana Point (1949) and San Clemente (1968) 7.5' quadrangles. Emigdio Vejar received 1.5 leagues in 1846 and claimed 6607 acres patented in 1879 (Cowan, p. 61).

Boca de Santa Monica [LOS ANGELES]: *land grant,* extends from Santa Monica Canyon to Topanga Canyon. Named on Beverly Hills (1950) and Topanga (1952) 7.5' quadrangles. Isidro Reyes and others received 1.5 leagues in 1839 and claimed 6657 acres patented in 1882 (Cowan, p. 94). Perez (p. 55) gave 1881 as the year of the patent.

Bodie Peak: see **Lobo Canyon** [LOS ANGELES] (1).

Boiler Canyon: see **Bouquet Canyon** [LOS ANGELES].

Boiling Point [LOS ANGELES]: *locality,* nearly 7 miles south-southeast of the village of Leona Valley at the head of Agua Dulce Canyon (lat. 34°31'20" N, long. 118°15'45" W; near N line sec. 17, T 5 N, R 13 W). Named on Sleepy Valley (1958) 7.5' quadrangle.

Bolsa [ORANGE]: *locality,* 6.25 miles north-northeast of present Huntington Beach civic center (lat. 33°44'40" N, long. 117°57'15" W; at NW cor. sec. 17, T 5 S, R 10 W); the place is on Las Bolsas grant. Named on Newport Beach (1951) 7.5' quadrangle. Postal authorities established Bolsa post office in 1886, discontinued it in 1891, reestablished it in 1895, discontinued it in 1904, and reestablished it 1971 (Salley, p. 24).

Bolsa Bay [ORANGE]: *water feature,* 4.25 miles

northwest of Huntington Beach civic center (lat. 33°42'10" N, long. 118°03'10" W); the feature is on La Bolsa Chica grant. Named on Seal Beach (1965) 7.5' quadrangle. In the early days, a feature called Freeman River headed at some large springs located just south of Westminister and reached the sea through Bolsa Bay; the stream was named was for J.G. Freeman, who owned land along it (Meadows, p. 64).

Bolsa de Quigara: see **Newport Bay** [OR-ANGE].

Bolsa de San Joaquin: see **Newport Bay** [OR-ANGE].

Bolsas Creek [ORANGE]: *stream*, flows through marsh to the sea 4 miles northwest of present Huntington Beach civic center (lat. 33° 42'20" N, long. 118°03'35" W); Bolsa Bay now occupies part of the old stream course. Named on Las Bolsas (1896) 15' quadrangle.

Bommer Canyon [ORANGE]: *canyon*, drained by a stream that flows 2.25 miles to Bonita Creek 8 miles south of Santa Ana city hall (lat. 33°37'50" N, long. 117°50'35" W). Named on Laguna Beach (1965) and Tustin (1965) 7.5' quadrangles.

Bonebreak Canyon: see **Meier Canyon** [VEN-TURA].

Boneyard Canyon [LOS ANGELES]: *canyon*, on Los Angeles-San Bernardino county line, drained by a stream that flows 1.25 miles to lowlands 3.5 miles north-northeast of Big Pines (lat. 34°25'30" N, long. 117°39'25" W; near SW cor. sec. 18, T 4 N, R 7 W). Named on Mescal Creek (1956) 7.5' quadrangle.

Boney Mountain:[VENTURA]: *ridge*, mainly southwest-trending, 4 miles long, 2 miles west-northwest of Triunfo Pass (lat. 34°07'15" N, long. 118°57' W). Named on Newbury Park (1951) and Triunfo Pass (1950) 7.5' quadrangles. The feature has a series of sharp crags and was known in the early days as Old Boney (Ricard).

Bonita: see **Camp Bonita** [LOS ANGELES].

Bonita Creek [ORANGE]: *stream*, flows 3.5 miles to San Diego Creek 6.5 miles south of Santa Ana city hall (lat. 33°39'05" N, long. 117°51'35" W). Named on Tustin (1965) 7.5' quadrangle. Tustin (1935) 7.5' quadrangle has the name "Coyote Creek" for the lower part of the stream.

Bonita Reservoir [ORANGE]: *lake*, 1600 feet long, behind a dam 8 miles south of Santa Ana city hall (lat. 33°37'55" N, long. 117°50'50" W); the lake is along Bonita Creek. Named on Tustin (1965) 7.5' quadrangle.

Boone Canyon [VENTURA]: *canyon*, drained by a stream that flows 1.5 miles to Fox Canyon 4 miles south-southeast of Santa Paula (lat. 34°18'15" N, long. 119°01'15" W). Named on Santa Paula (1951) 7.5' quadrangle.

Bootleggers Canyon [LOS ANGELES]: *can-yon*, drained by a stream that flows 1.5 miles to Soledad Canyon 2.5 miles south-southwest of Acton (lat. 34°26'10" N, long. 118°13'05" W; at W line sec. 14, T 4 N, R 13 W). Named on Acton (1959) 7.5' quadrangle.

Border City: see **Valyermo** [LOS ANGELES].

Borrego Canyon [ORANGE]: *canyon*, drained by a stream that flows 4.5 miles to lowlands 3 miles north of El Toro (lat. 33°40'05" N, long. 117°42' W). Named on El Toro (1968) 7.5' quadrangle.

Borrego Canyon Wash [ORANGE]: *stream*, flows 2.5 miles to Agua Chinon Wash 3.25 miles northwest of El Toro (lat. 33°39'15" N, long. 117°44'15" W). Named on El Toro (1968) 7.5' quadrangle.

Boston Heights [LOS ANGELES]: *district*, 2.5 miles east of present Los Angeles city hall (lat. 34°03'35" N, long. 118°11'45" W). Named on Alhambra (1926) 6' quadrangle.

Boulder Canyon [LOS ANGELES]:
(1) *canyon*, drained by a stream that flows 3 miles to lowlands 5.25 miles northwest of Big Pines (lat. 34°26'15" N, long. 117°45' W; sec. 18, T 4 N, R 8 W). Named on Mescal Creek (1956) 7.5' quadrangle.
(2) *canyon*, drained by a stream that flows 1.5 miles to Gold Creek 4 miles north of Sunland (lat. 34°19'10" N, long. 118°19'05" W; sec. 26, T 3 N, R 14 W). Named on Sunland (1953) 7.5' quadrangle. Los Angeles County (1935) map shows Boulder Creek in the canyon.

Boulder Canyon [VENTURA]: *canyon*, drained by a stream that flows 3.5 miles to the canyon of Cuyama River 5.25 miles northwest of Reyes Peak (lat. 34°41'05" N, long. 119°20'50" W; at W line sec. 20, T 7 N, R 23 W). Named on Reyes Peak (1943) 7.5' quadrangle.

Boulder Creek [VENTURA]: *stream*, flows 5.5 miles to Santa Clara River 2.5 miles west-southwest of Fillmore (lat. 34°23' N, long. 118°57'10" W; near W line sec. 35, T 4 N, R 20 W). Named on Fillmore (1951) 7.5' quadrangle.

Boulder Creek: see **Boulder Canyon** [LOS ANGELES] (2).

Boulevard Gardens [ORANGE]: *locality*, 4.5 miles north of present Huntington Beach civic center (lat. 33°43'40" N, long. 117°59'20" W; at E line sec. 23, T 5 S, R 11 W). Named on Newport Beach (1951) 7.5' quadrangle.

Bouquet Campground Number 4 [LOS AN-GELES]: *locality*, 8 miles south-southeast of the village of Lake Hughes (lat. 34°33'40" N, long. 118°24'05" W; near S line sec. 31, T 6 N, R 14 W); the place is in Bouquet Canyon. Named on Green Valley (1958) 7.5' quadrangle.

Bouquet Campground Number 3 [LOS AN-GELES]: *locality*, 8.5 miles south-southeast of the village of Lake Hughes (lat. 34°33'15" N, long. 118°24'35" W; near W line sec. 1, T 5 N, R 15 W); the place is in Bouquet Canyon. Named on Green Valley (1958) 7.5' quadrangle.

Bouquet Canyon [LOS ANGELES]: *canyon,* drained by a stream that flows 20 miles to Santa Clara River nearly 3 miles north-northwest of Newhall (lat. 34°25'30" N, long. 118°32'30" W). Named on Green Valley (1958), Mint Canyon (1960), Newhall (1952), and Sleepy Valley (1958) 7.5' quadrangles. Called Deadman Canyon on Camulos (1903) 30' quadrangle, and on Fernando (1900) 15' quadrangle. Storms (p. 248) mentioned the name "La Cañon de Los Murtes," presumably for present Bouquet Canyon. Francisco Chari, a French sailor known to the Spaniards by the nickname "El Buque"—*El Buque* means means "The Ship" in Spanish— took up land in the canyon; surveyors later misspelled his nickname when they named the canyon for him (Gudde, 1949, p. 38). Los Angeles County (1935) map names several branches of Bouquet Canyon: Boiler Canyon, which opens into Bouquet Canyon from the north about 3.5 miles north-northwest of Solemint (near W line sec. 5, T 4 N, R 15 W); Era Canyon, which opens into Bouquet Canyon from the north 0.5 mile below the mouth of Boiler Canyon (sec. 6, T 4 N, R 15 W); Kane Canyon, which opens into Bouquet Canyon from the east nearly 4 miles north of Solemint (near SE cor. sec. 32, T 5 N, R 15 W); and Atherton Canyon, which opens into Bouquet Canyon just below the mouth of Kane Canyon (at N line sec. 5, T 4 N, R 15 W).

Bouquet Canyon Reservoir: see **Bouquet Reservoir** [LOS ANGELES].

Bouquet Juntion [LOS ANGELES]: *locality,* 2.5 miles north of Newhall (lat. 34°25'20" N, long. 118°32'25" W); the road to Bouquet Canyon branches from the road to Soledad Canyon at the place. Named on Newhall (1952) 7.5' quadrangle.

Bouquet Reservoir [LOS ANGELES]: *lake,* behind a dam 7.5 miles south-southeast of the village of Lake Hughes (lat. 34°34'35" N, long. 118°23'05" W; sec. 29, T 6 N, R 14 W); the lake is in Bouquet Canyon. Named on Green Valley (1958) and Sleepy Valley (1958) 7.5' quadrangles. Called Bouquet Canyon Reservoir on Los Angeles County (1935) map.

Bouton Lake [LOS ANGELES]: *lake,* 2000 feet long, 5 miles north-northeast of Long Beach city hall (lat. 33°50'05" N, long. 118°08'50" W). Named on Long Beach (1949) 7.5' quadrangle.

Box Canyon [LOS ANGELES-VENTURA]: *canyon,* drained by a stream that heads in Ventura County and flows nearly 3 miles to Chatsworth Reservoir 2.5 miles southwest of Chatsworth in Los Angeles County (lat. 34°14' N, long. 118°38'25" W). Named on Calabasas (1952) and Santa Susana (1951) 7.5' quadrangles.

Box Canyon [ORANGE]: *canyon,* drained by a stream that flows 1.25 miles to Santa Ana Canyon 2 miles south of San Juan Hill (lat. 33°52'55" N, long. 117°44' W). Named on Prado Dam (1967) 7.5' quadrangle.

Boyle: see **Boyle Heights** [LOS ANGELES].

Boyle Heights [LOS ANGELES]: *district,* 1.5 miles southeast of Los Angeles city hall (lat. 34°02' N, long. 118°12'15" W). Named on Los Angeles (1953) 7.5' quadrangle. Postal authorities established Boyle post office in the district in 1952 (Salley, p. 25). The place was known to the Spaniards as El Paredon Blanco—*El Paredon Blanco* means "The White Bluffs" in Spanish; the name "Boyle Heights" is from Boyle Workman, who subdivided the district in 1874 (Latta, p. 11).

Brace Canyon [LOS ANGELES]: *canyon,* 1 mile long, 2.25 miles north-northwest of Burbank city hall (lat. 34°12'50" N, long. 118° 19'20" W; sec. 35, T 2 N, R 14 W). Named on Burbank (1966) 7.5' quadrangle.

Bradbury [LOS ANGELES]: *town,* 3.5 miles west of Azusa city hall (lat. 34°08'40" N, long. 117°58'05" W); the place is at the mouth of Bradbury Canyon. Named on Azusa (1966) 7.5' quadrangle. Postal authorities established Bradbury post office in 1957 (Salley, p. 25), and the town incorporated the same year. The name commemorates L.L. Bradbury, who owned land at the site about 1900 (Gudde, 1969, p. 36).

Bradbury Canyon [LOS ANGELES]: *canyon,* nearly 1 mile long, 3.5 miles west-northwest of Azusa city hall (lat. 34°09'35" N, long. 117°57'40" W; mainly in sec. 19, 20, T 1 N, R 10 W). Named on Azusa (1953) 7.5' quadrangle. Los Angeles County (1935) map has the form "Bradberry Canyon" for the name.

Brainard Canyon [LOS ANGELES]: *canyon,* 3.5 miles long, opens into lowlands 8.5 miles west-northwest of Valyermo (lat. 34°29' N, long. 117°58'15" W; near NW cor. sec. 31, T 5 N, R 10 W). Named on Juniper Hills (1959) 7.5' quadrangle.

Branagan: see **Newport Beach** [ORANGE] (2).

Brand Canyon [LOS ANGELES]: *canyon,* 1.25 miles long, 1.25 miles east-northeast of Burbank city hall (lat. 34°11'30" N, long. 118°16'10" W). Named on Burbank (1953) 7.5' quadrangle.

Branscomb Camp: see **Follows Camp** [LOS ANGELES].

Brea [ORANGE]: *city,* 12 miles north of Santa Ana (lat. 33°55' N, long. 117°54' W). Named on La Habra (1964) 7.5' quadrangle. Postal authorities established Brea post office in 1912 (Frickstad, p. 116), and the city incorporated in 1917. The school building of Randolph school district was built in Brea Canyon about 1.5 miles north of the center of present Brea in 1902; Officials of Ontario Investment Company had a townsite called Randolph laid out below the school in 1908, but the community that developed there took the name "Brea" in 1911 (Meadows, p. 118). Meadows (p. 111, 131) noted two flag stops along Pacific Electric Railroad near Brea: Pillsbury, located 0.5 mile west-northwest of the center of town, and Stewart, situated 1 mile west of the center of town—the name "Stewart" was for W.L. Stewart, vice president and general manager of Union Oil Company.

Brea Canyon [LOS ANGELES-ORANGE]: *canyon,* 12.5 miles long, along Brea Creek on Los Angeles-Orange county line above a point 4 miles south-southeast of La Habra (lat. 33°52'45" N, long. 117°55'20" W); the feature is partly on Rincon de la Brea grant. Named on La Habra (1964) and Yorba Linda (1964) 7.5' quadrangles. Called La Brea Canyon on Coyote Hills (1935) 7.5' quadrangle, called Rodeo Canyon on Anaheim (1942) 15' quadrangle—where present Tonner Canyon is called La Brea Canyon, and called Canada del Rodeo on Watts' (1898-1899) map. Watts (p. 33) noted that the feature was known locally as Rincon de la Brea.

Brea Canyon [VENTURA]: *canyon,* drained by a stream that flows 3.25 miles to Arroyo Simi 4.5 miles east of Moorpark (lat. 34° 16'45" N, long. 118°48'10" W; at S line sec. 6, T 2 N, R 18 W). Named on Simi (1951) 7.5' quadrangle.

Brea Canyon: see **Tonner Canyon** [LOS ANGELES-ORANGE].

Brea Chem [ORANGE]: *locality,* 3.5 miles west-northwest of Yorba Linda along Pacific Electric Railroad (lat. 33°55' N, long. 117°52'10" W; near NW cor. sec. 18, T 3 S, R 9 W). Named on Yorba Linda (1964) 7.5' quadrangle.

Brea Creek [ORANGE]: *stream,* flows nearly 6 miles from the mouth of Brea Canyon [LOS ANGELES-ORANGE] to Coyote Creek 1.25 miles northwest of Buena Park civic center (lat. 33°52'40" N, long. 118°00'30" W; near W line sec. 26, T 3 S, R 11 W). Named on Anaheim (1965), La Habra (1964), and Whittier (1965) 7.5' quadrangles. The stream is called Coyote Creek on Whittier (1949) 7.5' quadrangle.

Breakneck Canyon [LOS ANGELES]: *canyon,* drained by a stream that flows nearly 1 mile to Big Tujunga Canyon 3 miles south-southeast of Condor Peak (lat. 34°17' N, long. 118°11'45" W; sec. 1, T 2 N, R 13 W). Named on Condor Peak (1959) 7.5' quadrangle. On Tujunga (1900) 15' quadrangle, the stream in the canyon is called Breakneck Creek.

Breakneck Creek: see **Breakneck Canyon** [LOS ANGELES].

Brents: see **Brents Mountain** [LOS ANGELES].

Brents Junction [LOS ANGELES]: *locality,* 2.25 miles east of Agoura (lat. 34°08'50" N, long. 118°41'50" W; on N line sec. 30, T 1 N,

R 17 W). Named on Calabasas (1952) 7.5' quadrangle.

Brents Mountain [LOS ANGELES]: *peak,* 4.5 miles north-northwest of Malibu Point (lat. 34°05'10" N, long. 118°43'20" W; sec. 13, T 1 S, R 18 W). Altitude 1713 feet. Named on Malibu Beach (1951) 7.5' quadrangle. Solstice Canyon (1932) 6' quadrangle shows a place called Brents Mountain Crag Camp located 0.5 mile east of Brents Mountain; Malibu Beach (1951) 7.5' quadrangle has the name "Salvation Army Camp" at the same place, and Los Angeles County (1935) map has the name "Brents" there.

Brents Mountain Crag Camp: see **Brents Mountain** [LOS ANGELES].

Brentwood [LOS ANGELES]: *district,* 4.5 miles west-southwest of Beverly Hills city hall in Los Angeles (lat. 34°03'10" N, long. 118° 28'45" W). Named on Beverly Hills (1966) 7.5' quadrangle. The place includes former Brentwood Park and Westgate.

Brentwood Heights [LOS ANGELES]: *district,* 4.5 miles west of Beverly Hills city hall in Los Angeles (lat. 34°03'40" N, long. 118° 28'35" W). Named on Beverly Hills (1950) 7.5' quadrangle. Called Westgate Heights on Sawtelle (1934) 6' quadrangle. Postal authorities established Brentwood Heights Hot Springs post office in 1926, changed the name to Brentwood Heights in 1927, and discontinued it in 1935 (Salley, p. 26).

Brentwood Heights Hot Springs: see **Brentwood Heights** [LOS ANGELES].

Brentwood Park [LOS ANGELES]: *district,* 5 miles west-southwest of Beverly Hills city hall in Los Angeles (lat. 34°03'15" N, long. 118°29' W). Named on Beverly Hills (1950) 7.5' quadrangle. On Beverly Hills (1966) 7.5' quadrangle, this district is shown as part of present Brentwood. Postal authorities established Brentwood Park post office in 1908 and discontinued it in 1909 (Salley, p. 26).

Briggs Terrace [LOS ANGELES]: *locality,* 8 miles northwest of Pasadena city hall in Pickens Canyon (lat. 34°14'25" N, long. 118° 13'30" W; near SE cor. sec. 22, T 2 N, R 13 W). Named on Pasadena (1953) 7.5' quadrangle.

Broadacres Gardens: see **Compton** [LOS ANGELES].

Broad Canyon [LOS ANGELES]:
(1) *canyon,* drained by a stream that flows 3 miles to lowlands 3.5 miles north-northwest of the village of Lake Hughes (lat. 34°43'30" N, long. 118°27'30" W; sec. 3, T 7 N, R 15 W). Named on Lake Hughes (1957) 7.5' quadrangle.
(2) *canyon,* drained by a stream that flows 3.5 miles to lowlands 7.5 miles north-northeast of the village of Lake Hughes (lat. 34°46'20" N, long. 118°22'35" W; near NW cor. sec. 21, T 8 N, R 14 W). Named on Fairmont Butte (1965) 7.5' quadrangle.

Brookhurst [ORANGE]: *locality,* 2.5 miles east-southeast of present Buena Park civic center along Southern Pacific Railroad (lat. 33° 50'40" N, long. 117°57'30" W). Named on Garden Grove (1935) 7.5' quadrangle. A loading platform for Brookhurst Ranch Company was at the site (Meadows, p. 30).

Brooklyn Heights [LOS ANGELES]: *district,* 1.5 miles east of present Los Angeles city hall (lat. 34°02'55" N, long. 118°13' W). Named on Pasadena (1900) 15' quadrangle.

Brookmann Canyon [LOS ANGELES]: *canyon,* 0.5 mile long, 3 miles east of Burbank city hall (lat. 34°10'25" N, long. 118°15'25" W). Named on Burbank (1953) 7.5' quadrangle.

Brookside Canyon [LOS ANGELES]: *canyon,* drained by a stream that flows 1.25 miles to Topanga Canyon 5.5 miles west-northwest of Santa Monica city hall (lat. 34°02'55" N, long. 118°34'50" W). Named on Topanga (1952) 7.5' quadrangle.

Brown: see **John Brown Peak**, under **Mount Lowe** [LOS ANGELES] (1).

Brown Barranca [VENTURA]: *gully,* extends from the mouth of Long Canyon (2) to Santa Clara River 0.5 mile south-southeast of Saticoy (lat. 34°16'30" N, long. 119°08'40" W). Named on Saticoy (1951) 7.5' quadrangle.

Brown Canyon [LOS ANGELES]:
(1) *canyon,* drained by a stream that flows nearly 1 mile to Arroyo Seco 7 miles north-northwest of Pasadena city hall (lat. 34°14'25" N, long. 118°11' W). Named on Pasadena (1953) 7.5' quadrangle.
(2) *canyon,* 3 miles long, 2 miles northwest of Beverly Hills city hall (lat. 34°06'15" N, long. 118°25'20" W). Named on Beverly Hills (1950) 7.5' quadrangle.

Browning [ORANGE]: *locality,* 4 miles east-southeast of Santa Ana city hall along Atchison, Topeka and Santa Fe Railroad (lat. 33° 44' N, long. 117°48' W). Named on Tustin (1965) 7.5' quadrangle. The name commemorates Frank Browning, who leased land near the site (Meadows, p. 30-31).

Brown Mountain [LOS ANGELES]: *peak,* 6 miles north of Pasadena city hall (lat. 34°06'40" N, long. 118°08'45" W). Altitude 4454 feet. Named on Pasadena (1953) 7.5' quadrangle. Jason Brown and Owen Brown named the feature for their father, abolitionist John Brown (Robinson, J.W., 1977, p. 103, 105).

Browns Canyon [LOS ANGELES]: *canyon,* 4 miles long, opens into lowlands 1.25 miles northeast of Chatsworth (lat. 34°16'20" N, long. 118°35'25" W). Named on Oat Mountain (1952) 7.5' quadrangle.

Browns Canyon Wash [LOS ANGELES]: *stream,* flows nearly 6 miles from the mouth of Browns Canyon to Los Angeles River 1 mile east-southeast of the center of Canoga Park (lat. 34°11'40" N, long. 116°34'50" W). Named on Canoga Park (1952) and Oat Mountain (1952) 7.5' quadrangles

Browns Flat [LOS ANGELES]: *area,* 9.5 miles north of Pomona city hall (lat. 34°11'15" N, long. 117°43'15" W; sec. 9, T 1 N, R 8 W). Named on Mount Baldy (1954) 7.5' quadrangle.

Browns Gulch [LOS ANGELES]: *canyon,* drained by a stream that flows 2.5 miles to San Gabriel Canyon 4.5 miles north of Glendora city hall (lat. 34°12'15" N, long. 117°51'45" W; sec. 6, T 1 N, R 9 W). Named on Azusa (1953) and Glendora (1966) 7.5' quadrangles.

Brownstone [VENTURA]: *locality,* 1.5 miles west-northwest of Fillmore along Southern Pacific Railroad (lat. 34°24'25" N, long. 118° 56'15" W). Named on Piru (1921) 15' quadrangle. Stone from Sespe Cañon brownstone quarry, located 5 miles to the north, was shipped from the spot (Huguenin, p. 769).

Brownstone Reservoir [VENTURA]: *lake,* 225 feet long, 2 miles west-northwest of Fillmore (lat. 34°24'55" N, long. 118°56'35" W; sec. 23, T 4 N, R 20 W). Named on Fillmore (1951) 7.5' quadrangle.

Brubaker Canyon [VENTURA]: *canyon,* drained by a stream that heads in Santa Barbara County and flows 1.5 miles in Ventura County to Cuyama River 12 miles northwest of Reyes Peak (lat. 34°45'25" N, long. 119°25'20" W; sec. 28, T 8 N, R 24 W). Named on Cuyama Peak (1943) and Rancho Nuevo Creek (1943) 7.5' quadrangles.

Brush Canyon [LOS ANGELES]: *canyon,* 2 miles long, 6.25 miles northwest of Los Angeles city hall (lat. 34°07'10" N, long. 118°18'55" W'; on S line sec. 35, T 1 N, R 14 W). Named on Burbank (1953) and Hollywood (1953) 7.5' quadrangles.

Bryant Canyon [LOS ANGELES]: *canyon,* drained by a stream that flows nearly 2 miles to Big Tujunga Canyon 3.5 miles northeast of Sunland (lat. 34°18' N, long. 118°16'25" W; near E line sec. 31, T 3 N, R 13 W). Named on Sunland (1953) 7.5' quadrangle.

Buaro: see **Santa Ana** [ORANGE].

Buck Canyon [LOS ANGELES]:
(1) *canyon,* drained by a stream that flows 2.5 miles to Little Tujunga Canyon 5 miles north-northwest of Sunland (lat. 34°19'35" N, long. 118°20'15" W; sec. 22, T 3 N, R 14 W). Named on Sunland (1953) 7.5' quadrangle.
(2) *canyon,* drained by a stream that flows less than 1 mile to Pacoima Canyon 2.5 miles north-northwest of Condor Peak (lat. 34°21'35" N, long. 118°14'15" W). Named on Condor Peak (1959) 7.5' quadrangle.

Buck Creek [VENTURA]: *stream,* flows 5.25 miles to Piru Creek 7 miles east-northeast of McDonald Peak (lat. 34°39'55" N, long. 118°49'25" W). Named on Black Mountain (1958) and McDonald Peak (1958) 7.5' quadrangles. Los Angeles County (1935) map shows a feature called Mine Canyon that opens into the canyon of Piru Creek less than 1 mile northwest of the mouth of Buck Creek.

Buck Creek Campground [VENTURA]: *locality,* 4 miles east of McDonald Peak (lat. 34°38'15" N, long. 118°52'05" W; near SW cor. sec. 2, T 6 N, R 19 W); the place is along Buck Creek. Named on Black Mountain (1958) 7.5' quadrangle.

Buck Creek Spring [VENTURA]: *spring,* 4 miles east of McDonald Peak (lat. 34°38'15" N, long. 118°52'10" W; near SW cor. sec. 2, T 6 N, R 19 W); the spring is along Buck Creek. Named on Black Mountain (1958) 7.5' quadrangle.

Buck Gully [ORANGE]: *canyon,* drained by a stream that flows 3.5 miles to the sea 6 miles west-northwest of Laguna Beach city hall (lat. 33°35'15" N, long. 117°51'55" W). Named on Laguna Beach (1965) 7.5' quadrangle.

Buckhorn [VENTURA]: *locality,* 1.5 miles southwest of Piru (lat. 34° 24'05" N, long. 118°48'55" W; sec. 25, T 4 N, R 19 W). Named on Piru (1952) 7.5' quadrangle. Postal authorities established Buckhorn post office in 1900 and discontinued it in 1906; deer antlers that decorated the post office building suggested the name (Salley, p. 28).

Buckhorn Canyon: see **Buckhorn Flat** [LOS ANGELES].

Buckhorn Flat [LOS ANGELES]: *area,* 1.5 miles east-northeast of Waterman Mountain (lat. 34°20'45" N, long. 117°54'45" W; sec. 15, T 3 N, R 10 W). Named on Waterman Mountain (1959) 7.5' quadrangle. Los Angeles County (1935) map has the form "Buckhorn Flats" for the name, and shows a feature called Buckhorn Canyon that extends for 2.5 miles from Waterman Mountain through Buckhorn Flats to Cooper Canyon.

Buckhorn Spring [LOS ANGELES]: *spring,* 1.5 miles east-northeast of Waterman Mountain (lat. 34°20'30" N, long. 117°24'30" W; sec. 15, T 3 N, R 10 W); the spring is near Buckhorn Flat. Named on Waterman Mountain (1959) 7.5' quadrangle.

Bucksnort Spring [VENTURA]: *spring,* 4.5 miles east of Devils Heart Peak (lat. 34°33'10" N, long. 118°53'35" W). Named on Devils Heart Peak (1943) 7.5' quadrangle.

Buena Park [ORANGE]: *city,* 11 miles northwest of Santa Ana (lat. 33°51'50" N, long 117°59'50" W). Named on Anaheim (1965), La Habra (1964), Los Alamitos (1964), and Whittier (1965) 7.5' quadrangles. Postal authorities established Buena Park post office in 1887 (Frickstad, p. 116), and the city incorporated in 1953. James A. Whitaker founded the community in 1887 on 960 acres of land that he bought the year before (Meadows, p. 31).

Buffalo Corral Reservoir: see **Lower Buffalo Corral Reservoir** [LOS ANGELES]; **Upper**

Buffalo Corral Reservoir [LOS ANGELES].

Buffalo Springs Reservoirs [LOS ANGELES]: *lakes,* two, largest 150 feet long, 2.5 miles north-northeast of Mount Banning on Santa Catalina Island (lat. 33°24'25" N, long. 118°25' W). Named on Santa Catalina North (1950) 7.5' quadrangle.

Buford Canyon [LOS ANGELES]: *canyon,* drained by a stream that flows 1 mile to Swarthout Valley 5.5 miles north of Mount San Antonio (lat. 34°21'55" N, long. 117°39'40" W; near NE cor. sec. 12, T 3 N, R 8 W). Named on Mount San Antonio (1955) 7.5' quadrangle.

Bull Canyon [LOS ANGELES]: *canyon,* drained by a stream that flows 12 miles to Los Angeles River 2 miles southwest of Van Nuys (lat. 34°10'10" N, long. 118°28'25" W). Named on Oat Mountain (1952), San Fernando (1953), and Van Nuys (1953) 7.5' quadrangles. The stream in Bull Canyon below a point about 3 miles west of downtown San Fernando is called Bull Creek on San Fernando (1966) 7.5' quadrangle, which shows the confluence of the stream with Los Angeles River about 1.5 miles west-northwest of the location of the mouth of Bull Canyon shown on Van Nuys (1953) 7.5' quadrangle.

Bull Creek: see **Bull Canyon** [LOS ANGELES].

Burbank [LOS ANGELES]: *city,* 9.5 miles north-northwest of Los Angeles city hall (lat. 34°10'55" N, long. 118°18'25" W). Named on Burbank (1953) 7.5' quadrangle. Postal authorities established Burbank post office in 1887 (Frickstad, p. 71), and the city incorporated in 1911. The name is from Dr. David Burbank, a dentist in Los Angeles who was one of the subdividers of the property (Gudde, 1949, p. 45). California Mining Bureau's (1917) map shows a place called Roberts located about 4 miles northwest of Burbank along the railroad. Postal authorities established Roberts post office 4.5 miles northwest of Burbank post office in 1912 and discontinued it in 1916; the name was from the given name of Robert B. Reed, first postmaster, who developed the site (Salley, p. 187).

Burbank Canyon [LOS ANGELES]: *canyon,* less than 1 mile long, 6.5 miles north-northeast of Pomona city hall (lat. 34°08'40" N, long. 117°43'05" W; sec. 27, 28, T 1 N, R 8 W). Named on Mount Baldy (1954) 7.5' quadrangle.

Burbank Junction [LOS ANGELES]: *locality,* less than 1 mile west-northwest of Burbank city hall along Southern Pacific Railroad (lat. 34°11'10" N, long. 118°19'15" W). Named on Burbank (1953) 7.5' quadrangle.

Burges Canyon [VENTURA]: *canyon,* drained by a stream that flows 6.5 miles to Santa Barbara County 14 miles northwest of Reyes Peak (lat. 34°47'25" N, long. 119°26'30" W; sec. 17, T 8 N, R 24 W). Named on Apache Canyon (1943) and Cuyama Peak (1943) 7.5' quadrangles. Hess (p. 28) mentioned "a hill known as French Point" situated south of the lower part of Burges Canyon (sec. 16, T 8 N, R 24 W).

Burke Canyon: see **Agua Dulce Canyon** [LOS ANGELES].

Burkhart Saddle [LOS ANGELES]: *pass,* 4.5 miles south-southwest of Valyermo (lat. 34°23'10" N, long. 117°53'35" W; sec. 35, T 4 N, R 10 W). Named on Juniper Hills (1959) 7.5' quadrangle.

Burnett: see **Long Beach** [LOS ANGELES].

Burnham: see **Mount Burnham** [LOS ANGELES].

Burns Canyon [LOS ANGELES]: *canyon,* drained by a stream that flows nearly 1.5 miles to lowlands 3.5 miles east-southeast of the village of Lake Hughes (lat. 34°39'05" N, long. 118°23'15" W; sec. 32, T 7 N, R 14 W). Named on Lake Hughes (1957) 7.5' quadrangle.

Burnside Canyon [LOS ANGELES]: *canyon,* 2 miles long, opens into lowlands 17 miles east-southeast of Gorman (lat. 34°45'30" N, long. 118°33'50" W; near N line sec. 27, T 8 N, R 16 W). Named on Burnt Peak (1958) and Neenach School (1965) 7.5' quadrangles.

Burnt Peak [LOS ANGELES]: *peak,* 17 miles east-southeast of Gorman (lat. 34°41' N, long. 118°34'30" W). Altitude 5788 feet. Named on Burnt Peak (1958) 7.5' quadrangle.

Burnt Peak: see **Little Burnt Peak** [LOS ANGELES].

Burnt Peak Canyon [LOS ANGELES]: *canyon,* drained by a stream that flows 4.5 miles to Fish Canyon (1) 2.5 miles south-southwest of Burnt Peak (lat. 34°39' N, long. 118°35'45" W); the canyon heads east of Burnt Peak. Named on Burnt Peak (1958) 7.5' quadrangle.

Burro Canyon [LOS ANGELES]:
(1) *canyon,* drained by a stream that flows 2.25 miles to Fish Canyon (1) 4.25 miles southwest of Burnt Peak (lat. 34°38'15" N, long. 118°37'35" W). Named on Burnt Peak (1958) 7.5' quadrangle.
(2) *canyon,* drained by a stream that flows 2 miles to San Gabriel Reservoir 7 miles north of Glendora city hall (lat. 34°14'10" N, long. 117°50'20" W). Named on Crystal Lake (1958) and Glendora (1953) 7.5' quadrangles. Called Burrow Canyon on Rock Creek (1903) 15' quadrangle.

Burro Creek [VENTURA]: *stream,* flows 3.5 miles to Sespe Creek 6 miles north-northwest of Wheeler Springs (lat. 34°35'35" N, long. 119°18'45" W). Named on Reyes Peak (1943) and Wheeler Springs (1943) 7.5' quadrangles.

Burro Flats [VENTURA]: *area,* 8 miles northeast of Thousand Oaks (lat. 34°13'45" N, long. 118°42'40" W). Named on Calabasas (1952) 7.5' quadrangle.

Burro Peak [LOS ANGELES]: *peak,* 4.25 miles south of Crystal Lake (lat. 34°15'20" N, long. 117°50'40" W). Altitude 3200 feet. Named on

Crystal Lake (1958) 7.5' quadrangle.

Burrow Canyon: see **Burro Canyon** [LOS ANGELES] (2).

Burruel Point [ORANGE]: *promontory,* 4 miles north-northeast of Orange city hall (lat. 33°50'15" N, long. 117°49'30" W). Named on Orange (1964) 7.5' quadrangle. The name recalls Desiderio Burruel, son-in-law of Teodocio Yorba (Meadows, p. 31).

Burruel Ridge: see **Peralta Hills** [ORANGE] (1).

Bus Canyon [VENTURA]: *canyon,* 2.5 miles long, opens into Simi Valley (1) 6 miles north-northeast of Thousand Oaks (lat. 34°14'30" N, long. 118°46'40" W). Named on Thousand Oaks (1952) 7.5' quadrangle.

Bushard: see **Huntington Beach** [ORANGE].

Bushnell Summit [LOS ANGELES]: *pass,* 3 miles east-northeast of Burnt Peak (lat. 34°42'10" N, long. 118°31'40" W; near S line sec. 12, T 7 N, R 16 W). Named on Burnt Peak (1958) 7.5' quadrangle.

Butler [LOS ANGELES]: *locality,* 3.5 miles west of Azusa city hall along Atchison, Topeka and Santa Fe Railroad (lat. 34°07'55" N, long. 117°57'50" W; sec. 31, T 1 N, R 10 W). Named on Azusa (1953) 7.5' quadrangle.

Butterfield Canyon [LOS ANGELES]: *canyon,* drained by a stream that flows 2 miles to West Fork San Gabriel River nearly 8 miles north-northwest of Azusa city hall (lat. 34°14'35" N, long. 117°56'50" W). Named on Azusa (1953) 7.5' quadrangle.

Butte Street Junction [LOS ANGELES]: *locality,* 2.5 miles south-southeast of Los Angeles city hall along Union Pacific Railroad (lat. 34°01'05" N, long. 118°13'50" W). Named on Los Angeles (1966) 7.5' quadrangle.

Button Shell Beach [LOS ANGELES]: *beach,* 5 miles north-northwest of Avalon on the northeast side of Santa Catalina Island (lat. 33°24'15" N, long. 118°22'05" W). Named on Santa Catalina East (1950) 7.5' quadrangle. United States Board on Geographic Names (1976b, p. 3) gave the form "Buttonshell Beach" as a variant.

Buzzard Peak [LOS ANGELES]: *peak,* 5.5 miles west of Pomona city hall in San Jose Hills (lat. 34°03'20" N, long. 117°51' W). Altitude 1375 feet. Named on San Dimas (1954) 7.5' quadrangle.

– C –

Caballero Creek [LOS ANGELES]: *stream,* flows nearly 4.5 miles to Los Angeles River 4 miles east-southeast of the center of Canoga Park (lat. 34°11'10" N, long. 118°31'40" W). Named on Canoga Park (1952) 7.5' quadrangle.

Cabin Canyon [LOS ANGELES]: *canyon,* drained by a stream that flows 1.25 miles to Aliso Canyon (1) 4.25 miles northwest of

Pacifico Mountain (lat. 34°25'05" N, long. 118°05'35" W; sec. 24, T 4 N, R 12 W). Named on Pacifico Mountain 1959) 7.5' quadrangle.

Cabin Flat [LOS ANGELES]: *area,* 4.5 miles northwest of Mount San Antonio along Prairie Fork (lat. 34°20'35" N, long. 117°41'50" W; sec. 15, T 3 N, R 8 W). Named on Mount San Antonio (1955) 7.5' quadrangle.

Cabrillo Harbor [LOS ANGELES]: *embayment,* nearly 4 miles north-northeast of Mount Banning on the north side of Santa Catalina Island (lat. 33°25'15" N, long. 118°24'15" W). Named on Santa Catalina North (1950) 7.5' quadrangle.

Cabrini Canyon [LOS ANGELES]: *canyon,* 1 mile long, nearly 3 miles north-northwest of Burbank city hall (lat. 34°12'55" N, long. 118°20' W; in and near sec. 34, T 2 N, R 14 W). Named on Burbank (1953) 7.5' quadrangle.

Cactus Bay [LOS ANGELES]: *embayment,* 1.5 miles west-northwest of Silver Peak on the south side of Santa Catalina Island (lat. 33° 28' N, long. 118°35'35" W). Named on Santa Catalina West (1943) 7.5' quadrangle.

Cactus Peak [LOS ANGELES]: *peak,* 2.25 miles south-southwest of Mount Banning on Santa Catalina Island (lat. 33°20'15" N, long. 118°26'40" W). Altitude 1560 feet. Named on Santa Catalina South (1943) 7.5' quadrangle. The feature also was called Mount Vizcaino (Doran, 1980, p. 77).

Cactus Point [ORANGE]: *promontory,* nearly 1.5 miles south-southeast of Laguna Beach city hall along the coast (lat. 33°31'35" N, long. 117°46'15" W; at N line sec. 35, T 7 S, R 9 W). Named on Laguna Beach (1965) 7.5' quadrangle.

Cagney Island: see **Collins Island** [ORANGE].

Cahuenga [LOS ANGELES]: *land grant,* 2 miles south-southwest of Burbank city hall. Named on Burbank (1966) 7.5' quadrangle. Jose M. Triunfo was the grantee in 1843, and David W. Alexander was the patentee for 388.34 acres in 1872 (Perez, p. 57).

Cahuenga: see **Hollywood** [LOS ANGELES]; **Universal City** [LOS ANGELES].

Cahuenga Pass [LOS ANGELES]: *pass,* 7.5 miles northwest of Los Angeles city hall (lat. 34°07'30" N, long. 118°20'35" W). Named on Burbank (1953) and Hollywood (1953) 7.5' quadrangles. Marcou (p. 158) referred to Cahunga Pass, and Preston (1890a, p. 189) mentioned Cahuengo Pass. The name undoubtedly is of Indian origin (Kroeber, p. 36).

Cahuenga Peak [LOS ANGELES]: *peak,* 3.25 miles south-southwest of Burbank city hall (lat. 34°08'15" N, long. 118°19'30" W); the peak is 1.25 miles northeast of Cahuenga Pass. Altitude 1821 feet. Named on Burbank (1953) 7.5' quadrangle.

Calabasas [LOS ANGELES]: *village,* 6 miles east of Agoura (lat. 34° 09'25" N, long.

118°38'15" W; sec. 23, T 1 N, R 17 W). Named on Calabasas (1952) 7.5' quadrangle, which shows Calabasas P.O. located 1.25 miles west-southwest of Calabasas (on W line sec. 22, T 1 N, R 17 W). Calabasas (1903) 15' quadrangle has the name "Calabasas" at both places, and Dry Canyon (1932) 6' quadrangle shows Calabasas school at the site of present Calabasas post office. Postal authorities established Calabasas post office in 1888, moved it 1 mile west in 1889, discontinued it in 1897, and reestablished it in 1898 (Salley, p. 32). The name is the Spanish version of an Indian word for "place of wild gourds," and means "pumpkin," "squash," or "wild gourd" in Spanish (Hanna, p. 49). United States Board on Geographic Names (1933, p. 183) rejected the forms "Calabaces" and "Calabazas" for the name. Postal authorities established Daices post office—named for Wencil Daic, first postmaster—6 miles west of Calabasas in 1891, changed the name to Liberty in 1899, and discontinued it in 1900 (Salley, p. 54, 122).

Calabasas Highlands [LOS ANGELES]: *locality,* 2 miles south of Calabasas (lat. 34°07'50" N, long. 118°38'40" W; near NE cor. sec. 34, T 1 N, R 17 W). Named on Calabasas (1952) 7.5' quadrangle.

Calabasas Peak [LOS ANGELES]: *peak,* 6 miles north-northeast of Malibu Point (lat. 34°06'45" N, long. 118°39' W; sec. 3, T 1 S, R 17 W); the peak is 3.25 miles south-southwest of Calabasas. Altitude 2163 feet. Named on Malibu Beach (1951) 7.5' quadrangle.

Cal-Baden Mineral Spring: see **Sycamore Canyon** [LOS ANGELES] (5).

Caldwell Lake [LOS ANGELES]: *lake,* 650 feet long, 4.5 miles east-southeast of Valyermo (lat. 34°24'50" N, long. 117°46'40" W; sec. 24, T 4 N, R 9 W). Named on Valyermo (1958) 7.5' quadrangle.

California Heights [LOS ANGELES]: *district,* 4 miles north of Long Beach city hall (lat. 33°49'30" N, long. 118°10'45" W). Named on Long Beach (1949) 7.5' quadrangle.

California Street [LOS ANGELES]: *locality,* 1 mile south-southwest of present Pasadena city hall along Los Angeles Terminal Railroad (lat. 34°08'05" N, long. 118°09'10" W). Named on Pasadena (1900) 15' quadrangle.

Calleguas [VENTURA]: *land grant,* east of Camarillo. Named on Camarillo (1950) and Newbury Park (1951) 7.5' quadrangles. Jose Pedro Ruiz received the land in 1837; Gabriel Ruiz claimed 9998 acres patented in 1866 (Cowan, p. 22). The name is from the designation of an Indian rancheria (Kroeber, p. 37).

Calleguas Creek [VENTURA]: *stream,* flows 13 miles to Mugu Lagoon 2.25 miles northwest of Point Mugu (lat. 34°06'20" N, long. 119°05'30" W); the stream is partly on Calleguas grant. Named on Camarillo (1950) and Point Mugu (1949) 7.5' quadrangles.

Called Rio Simi on Parke's (1854-1855) map. Antisell (p. 75) used the name "Semee creek." **Calumet Canyon** [VENTURA]: *canyon,* drained by a stream that flows nearly 2 miles to the valley of Santa Clara River 5 miles west-southwest of Piru (lat. 34°22'55" N, long. 118°52'10" W; sec. 33, T 4 N, R 19 W). Named on Piru (1952) and Simi (1951) 7.5' quadrangles.

Camarillo [VENTURA]: *city,* 8.5 miles east of Oxnard (lat. 34°13' N, long. 119°02'10" W). Named on Camarillo (1950) 7.5' quadrangle. Postal authorities established Camarillo post office in 1899 (Frickstad, p. 217), and the city incorporated in 1964. The name commemorates Juan Camarillo, who purchased Callequas grant (Hoover, Rensch, and Rensch, p. 581).

Camarillo Hills [VENTURA]: *ridge,* west-southwest-trending, 6 miles long, center 2.5 miles north-northwest of downtown Camarillo (lat. 34°15' N, long. 119°03'30" W). Named on Camarillo (1950) and Santa Paula (1951) 7.5' quadrangles.

Camerons Canyon: see **Cañada de Aliso** [VENTURA].

Camp Ah-DA-HI [LOS ANGELES]: *locality,* nearly 2 miles north of Mount Wilson (lat. 34°14'55" N, long. 118°03'55" W; near NE cor. sec. 19, T 2 N, R 11 W). Named on Mount Wilson (1953) 7.5' quadrangle

Camp Aventura [LOS ANGELES]: *locality,* 1 mile north-northwest of Glendora city hall (lat. 34°09'05" N, long. 117°52'15" W; at SW cor. sec. 19, T 1 N, R 9 W). Named on Glendora (1966) 7.5' quadrangle.

Camp Bartlett [VENTURA]: *locality,* 5.5 miles west of Santa Paula Peak along Sisar Creek (lat. 34°25'40" N, long. 119°06'25" W). Named on Santa Paula Peak (1951) 7.5' quadrangle.

Camp Bill Lane [LOS ANGELES]: *locality,* 1 mile north of Sunland (lat. 34°16'30" N, long. 118°18'20" W). Named on Sunland (1953) 7.5' quadrangle. Called Bill Lane Camp on Sunland (1966) 7.5' quadrangle.

Camp Bonita [LOS ANGELES]: *locality,* 8.5 miles northeast of Glendora city hall near the mouth of Cattle Canyon (lat. 34°13'45" N, long. 117°46'05" W). Named on Camp Bonita (1940) 6' quadrangle. Jay Gardner Scott founded a resort called Scott's Camp at the site in 1909 and soon changed the name to Camp Bonita; a flood destroyed the place in 1938 (Robinson, J.W., 1983, p. 96).

Camp Caula [LOS ANGELES]: *locality,* 2 miles north-northeast of Whitaker Peak (lat. 34°35'55" N, long. 118°43'20" W; sec. 19, T 6 N, R 18 W). Named on Whitaker Peak (1958) 7.5' quadrangle.

Camp Chiquita [LOS ANGELES]: *locality,* 4.25 miles north of Pasadena city hall (lat. 34°12'40" N, long. 118°08'20" W); the place is near Chiquita Canyon. Named on Pasadena

(1953) 7.5' quadrangle.

Camp Christian [LOS ANGELES]: *locality,* 5.5 miles west-northwest of Waterman Mountain (lat. 34°20'55" N, long. 117°59'55" W; sec. 14, T 3 N, R 11 W). Named on Waterman Mountain (1959) 7.5' quadrangle.

Camp Comfort [VENTURA]: *locality,* 1.5 miles south-southwest of downtown Ojai along San Antonio Creek (lat. 34°25'35" N, long. 119°15'30" W). Named on Matilija (1952) 7.5' quadrangle.

Camp Cumorah Crest [LOS ANGELES]: *locality,* 3 miles west-northwest of Waterman Mountain (lat. 34°20'55" N, long. 117°59'05" W; sec. 13, T 3 N, R 11 W). Named on Waterman Mountain (1959) 7.5' quadrangle. Waterman Mountain (1941) 6' minute quadrangle has the name "Cumorah Crest" for a relief feature located near the place.

Camp Drum: see **Wilmington** [LOS ANGELES].

Camp Glenwood [LOS ANGELES]: *locality,* 1.5 miles northwest of Waterman Mountain (lat. 34°21'10" N, long. 117°57'25" W; near NW cor. sec. 17, T 3 N, R 10 W). Named on Waterman Mountain (1959) 7.5' quadrangle.

Camp Hawthorne [LOS ANGELES]: *locality,* 2 miles west-northwest of Big Pines (lat. 34°23'35" N, long. 117°43'15" W). Named on Mescal Creek (1956) 7.5' quadrangle.

Camp Hemohme [LOS ANGELES]: *locality,* 2 miles west-northwest of Big Pines (lat. 34°23'20" N, long. 117°43'15" W). Named on Mescal Creek (1956) 7.5' quadrangle.

Camp Hidden Valley [LOS ANGELES]: *locality,* 3 miles southeast of Pacifico Mountain (lat. 34°21' N, long. 118°00'10" W; sec. 14, T 3 N, R 11 W). Named on Chilao Flat (1959) 7.5' quadrangle.

Camp Hi-Hill [LOS ANGELES]: *locality,* 9.5 miles south-southwest of Pacifico Mountain near the head of West Fork San Gabriel River (lat. 34°15'15" N, long. 118°05'40" W). Named on Chilao Flat (1959) 7.5' quadrangle. Called Opids Camp on Mount Wilson (1939) 6' quadrangle. John T. Opid took out a resort lease in 1913 at what then was called Stony Gulch and began construction of a popular hostelry called Opid's Camp; the place now is known as Camp Hi-Hill (Robinson, J.W., 1977, p. 159, 161). Ernest DeVore, Chorie DeVore, and J.P. Nevins built a place called Camp West Fork in 1913 about 5 miles downstream from Opid's Camp; it lasted until the mid-1920's (Robinson, J.W., 1977, p. 162).

Camp Huntington [LOS ANGELES]: *locality,* 4 miles west-southwest of Mount Wilson (1) in Rubio Canyon (lat. 34°12' N, long. 118°07'15" W; sec. 3, T 1 N, R 12 W). Named on Mount Wilson (1953) 7.5' quadrangle.

Camp Idle Hour: see **Idlehour Camp** [LOS ANGELES].

Camp Ivy [LOS ANGELES]: *locality,* 2 miles southeast of Mount Wilson (1) in Winter Canyon (lat. 34°12'30" N, long. 118°02' W; on S line sec. 33, T 2 N, R 11 W). Named on Mount Wilson (1953) 7.5' quadrangle. The place first was called Hoegee's Camp; Arie Hoegee and his family founded the resort in 1908 (Robinson, J.W., 1977, p. 134). It was called Camp LeRoy before LeRoy Haynes sold it to Ivy Holzer in 1947; Holzer changed the name to Camp Ivy (Owens, p. 88). A fire destroyed the place in 1953 (Robinson, J.W., 1977, p. 134).

Camp Josepho [LOS ANGELES]: *locality*, 5 miles north-northwest of Santa Monica city hall in Rustic Canyon (lat. 34°04'50" N, long. 118°31'10" W). Named on Topanga (1952) 7.5' quadrangle.

Camp Jubilee [LOS ANGELES]: *locality*, 2.5 miles north-northeast of Big Pines (lat. 34°24'40" N, long. 117°40'10" W; near N line sec. 25, T 4 N, R 8 W). Named on Mescal Creek (1956) 7.5' quadrangle.

Camp Junipero Serra [LOS ANGELES]: *locality*, 2.5 miles west-northwest of Big Pines (lat. 34°23'35" N, long. 117°43'45" W). Named on Mescal Creek (1956) 7.5' quadrangle.

Camp Kole [LOS ANGELES]: *locality*, 9 miles south-southwest of Pacifico Mountain (lat. 34°15'10" N, long. 118°04'25" W; near S line sec. 18, T 2 N, R 11 W); the place is at the mouth of Valley Forge Canyon. Named on Chilao Flat (1959) 7.5' quadrangle. Mount Wilson (1939) 6' quadrangle shows Valley Forge Lodge at the site. Ernest DeVore and Cherie DeVore took a Forest Service lease in 1922 and started a resort that they called Valley Forge Lodge (Robinson, J.W., 1977, p. 162).

Camp LeRoy: see **Camp Ivy** [LOS ANGELES].

Camp Losadena: see **Switzer Camp** [LOS ANGELES].

Camp Lupin [LOS ANGELES]: *locality*, 3 miles north-northwest of Mount San Antonio (lat. 34°19'40" N, long. 117°40' W; sec. 24, T 3 N, R 8 W). Named on Mount San Antonio (1955) 7.5' quadrangle.

Camp Manzanita [LOS ANGELES]: *locality*, 2.5 miles west-northwest of Big Pines (lat. 34°23'40" N, long. 117°43'35" W). Named on Mescal Creek (1956) 7.5' quadrangle.

Camp Marion [LOS ANGELES]: *locality*, 0.5 mile east-northeast of Mescal Creek (lat. 34°22'35" N, long. 117°40'50" W; sec. 2, T 3 N, R 8 W). Named on Mescal Creek (1956) 7.5' quadrangle.

Camp McClellan [LOS ANGELES]: *locality*, 0.25 mile north of Big Pines (lat. 34°23' N, long. 117°41'20" W; near NW cor. sec. 2, T 3 N, R 8 W). Named on Mescal Creek (1956) 7.5' quadrangle.

Camp McKiwanis [LOS ANGELES]: *locality*, 1.5 miles west-northwest of Big Pines (lat. 34°23'20" N, long. 117°43' W). Named on Mescal Creek (1956) 7.5' quadrangle.

Camp Merriam: see **Camp Sierra** [LOS ANGELES].

Camp Metaka [LOS ANGELES]: *locality*, 1.25 miles west-northwest of Big Pines (lat. 34°23'20" N, long. 117°42'35" W). Named on Mescal Creek (1956) 7.5' quadrangle.

Camp Oak Grove [LOS ANGELES]: *locality*, 7.5 miles north-northeast of Glendora city hall (lat. 34°14'15" N, long. 117°49'15" W). Named on Glendora (1966) 7.5' quadrangle.

Camp Oak Wilde: see **Oakwilde** [LOS ANGELES].

Campo Aleman: see **Anaheim** [ORANGE].

Campo de Cahunga: see **Universal City** [LOS ANGELES].

Camp Pajarito [LOS ANGELES]: *locality*, 1 mile north-northwest of Waterman Mountain (lat. 34°21' N, long. 117°56'30" W; near E line sec. 17, T 3 N, R 10 W). Named on Waterman Mountain (1959) 7.5' quadrangle.

Camp Rathke: see **Santiago Reservoir** [ORANGE].

Camp Rosenita [LOS ANGELES]: *locality*, 2.25 miles southeast of Pacifico Mountain (lat. 34°21'20" N, long. 118°00'40" W; near SE cor. sec. 10, T 3 N, R 11 W). Named on Chilao Flat (1959) 7.5' quadrangle.

Camp San Pedro: see **Drum Barracks**, under **Wilmington** [LOS ANGELES].

Camp Sierra [LOS ANGELES]: *locality*, nearly 5 miles north of Pasadena city hall (lat. 34°13' N, long. 118°07'55" W; near W line sec. 34, T 2 N, R 12 W). Named on Pasadena (1953) 7.5' quadrangle. Judge J.H. Merriam founded a place called Camp Merriam high on Sunset Ridge above Millard Canyon in 1904; C.W. Siefert took over the place and changed the name to Camp Sierra (Robinson, J.W., 1977, p. 137-138).

Camp Singing Pines [LOS ANGELES]: *locality*, 3.5 miles west-northwest of Waterman Mountain (lat. 34°21'05" N, long. 117°59'30" W; near NW cor. sec. 13, T 3 N, R 11 W). Named on Waterman Mountain (1959) 7.5' quadrangle. Called Squaw Camp on Waterman Mountain (1941) 6' quadrangle.

Camp Slauson [LOS ANGELES]: *locality*, 5.5 miles north-northeast of Malibu Point in Red Rock Canyon (3) (lat. 34°06'15" N, long. 118°38'30" W; at SE cor. sec. 3, T 1 S, R 17 W). Named on Malibu Beach (1951) 7.5' quadrangle.

Camp Sterling [LOS ANGELES]: *locality*, 2.5 miles north-northeast of Sunland in Big Tujunga Canyon (lat. 34°17'35" N, long. 118°17'05" W; near NW cor. sec. 6, T 2 N, R 13 W). Named on La Crescenta (1939) 6' quadrangle.

Camp Sturtevant: see **Sturtevant Camp** [LOS ANGELES].

Camp Teresita Pines [LOS ANGELES]: *locality*, 1.5 miles west-northwest of Big Pines (lat. 34°23'30" N, long. 117°42'55" W). Named on Mescal Creek (1956) 7.5' quadrangle.

Camp Toyon [LOS ANGELES]: *locality*, 2.5 miles northwest of Avalon on Santa Catalina Island (lat. 33°22'25" N, long. 118°21'15" W); the place is at Toyon Bay. Named on Santa Catalina East (1950) 7.5' quadrangle.

Camp 2 [LOS ANGELES]: *locality*, 8.5 miles south of the present village of Lake Hughes in Bouquet Canyon (lat. 34°33'15" N, long. 118°25'15" W; sec. 2, T 5 N, R 15 W). Named on San Francisquito (1937) 6' quadrangle.

Camp Valcrest [LOS ANGELES]: *locality*, 2.5 miles west-northwest of Waterman Mountain (lat. 34°20'40" N, long. 117°58'40" W; near E line sec. 13, T 3 N, R 11 W). Named on Waterman Mountain (1959) 7.5' quadrangle. Waterman Mountain (1941) 6' quadrangle has the name "Valcrest" at the place.

Camp Verdugo Pines [LOS ANGELES]: *locality*, 2.25 miles west-northwest of Big Pines (lat. 34°23'20" N, long. 117°43'35" W). Named on Mescal Creek (1956) 7.5' quadrangle.

Camp West Fork: see Camp Hi-Hill [LOS ANGELES].

Camp Wilson: see Martins Camp [LOS ANGELES].

Camulas: see Camulos [VENTURA].

Camulos [VENTURA]: *locality*, 2.25 miles east-southeast of Piru (lat. 34°24'20" N, long. 118°45'20" W). Named on Piru (1952) 7.5' quadrangle. Postal authorities established Camulas post office in 1885, changed the name to Camulos in 1886, and discontinued it in 1914 (Frickstad, p. 218). The name is of Indian origin (Kroeber, p. 37).

Cañada Chiquita [ORANGE]: *canyon*, drained by a stream that flows 6.5 miles to San Juan Creek 3.5 miles east-northeast of San Juan Capistrano (lat. 33°31'35" N, long. 117°36'35" W; near NE cor. sec. 33, T 7 S, R 7 W). Named on Cañada Gobernadora (1968) 7.5' quadrangle.

Cañada de Agua Chinon: see Limestone Canyon [ORANGE].

Cañada de Aliso [VENTURA]: *canyon*, drained by a stream that flows 3.25 miles to Cañada Larga 5 miles north-northeast of Ventura (lat. 34°21' N, long. 119°15'30" W). Named on Ventura (1951) 7.5' quadrangle. Called Cañada del Aliso on Matilija (1952) 7.5' quadrangle. The feature also was called Camerons Canyon for Alexander M. Cameron, who owned land there (Ricard).

Cañada de la Brea: see Rincon de la Brea [LOS ANGELES-ORANGE].

Cañada de la Campaña: see Bell Canyon [ORANGE].

Cañada de la Habra: see La Habra [LOS ANGELES-ORANGE].

Cañada de la Madera: see Silverado Canyon [ORANGE]; Walnut Canyon [ORANGE].

Canada de la Madra: see Shady Canyon [ORANGE].

Cañada de la Oasis: see Oso Canyon [LOS ANGELES].

Cañada de las Encinas [VENTURA]: *canyon*, drained by a stream that flows 0.5 mile to the canyon of Ventura River 3.25 miles north of Ventura (lat. 34°19'35" N, long. 119°17'05" W). Named on Ventura (1951) 7.5' quadrangle.

Canada de las Lagunas: see Laguna Canyon [ORANGE].

Canada de las Ranas: see Peters Canyon [ORANGE].

Cañada de la Vieja: see Baker Canyon [ORANGE].

Cañada del Diablo [VENTURA]: *canyon*, drained by a stream that flows 4.5 miles to Ventura River 2 miles north-northwest of downtown Ventura (lat. 34°18'15" N, long. 119°18'10" W). Named on Ventura (1951) 7.5' quadrangle.

Canada de Leon: see Lion Canyon [VENTURA] (2).

Canada del Incendio: see San Juan Creek [ORANGE].

Cañada de Los Alamos [LOS ANGELES]: *canyon*, nearly 7 miles long, opens into the canyon of Piru Creek 9 miles south-southeast of Gorman (lat. 34°39'15" N, long. 118°46'30" W; sec. 34, T 7 N, R 18 W). Named on Black Mountain (1958) 7.5' quadrangle, where the upper part of the feature is called Lower Hungry Valley. Beartrap Canyon (1938) and Gorman (1938) 6' quadrangles have the form "Cañada de los Alamos" (with the lower-case "l" in "los") for the name.

Cañada de los Alisos [ORANGE]: *land grant*, at and north of El Toro. Named on El Toro (1950), San Juan Capistrano (1949), and Santiago Peak (1954) 7.5' quadrangles. Jose Serrano received 2 leagues in 1842 and more land in 1846; he claimed 10,669 acres patented in 1871 (Cowan, p. 15).

Cañada de los Indios: see Black Star Canyon [ORANGE].

Cañada de los Nogales [LOS ANGELES]: *land grant*, 4 miles north of Los Angeles city hall. Named on Los Angeles (1953) 7.5' quadrangle. Jose M. Aguila received 0.5 league in 1844 and claimed 1200 acres patented in 1882 (Cowan, p. 53).

Canada del Rodeo: see Brea Canyon [LOS ANGELES-ORANGE].

Canada del Toro: see Serrano Creek [ORANGE].

Cañada de Palos Verdes: see Harbor Lake [LOS ANGELES].

Cañada de Rodriguez [VENTURA]: *canyon*, drained by a stream that flows 2.25 miles to Ventura River 3.5 miles north of Ventura (lat. 34°20' N, long. 119°17'55" W); the canyon is on Cañada de San Miguelito grant, which Ramon Rodriquez received in 1846. Named on Ventura (1951) 7.5' quadrangle.

Cañada de San Joaquin [VENTURA]: *canyon*, drained by a stream that flows 1.5 miles to the canyon of Ventura River 2 miles north of downtown Ventura (lat. 34°18'30" N, long. 119°17'30" W). Named on Ventura (1951) 7.5' quadrangle.

Cañada de San Miguelito [VENTURA]: *land grant,* northwest of Ventura. Named on Ventura (1951) 7.5' quadrangle. Ramon Rodriguez received 2 leagues in 1846 and his heirs claimed 8877 acres patented in 1871 (Cowan, p. 86).

Cañada de Santa Ana: see **Cañon de Santa Ana** [ORANGE].

Cañada de Santa Clara: see **Santa Clara River** [VENTURA].

Cañada Gobernadora [ORANGE]: *canyon,* drained by a stream that flows 8.5 miles to San Juan Creek 4 miles east-northeast of San Juan Capistrano (lat. 33°31'25" N, long. 117°35'50" W; sec. 34, T 7 S, R 7 W). Named on Cañada Gobernadora (1968) and Santiago Peak (1954) 7.5' quadrangles. Called Canada Gubernadora on Corona (1902) 30' quadrangle. *Gobernadora* means "greasewood" in Spanish (Meadows, p. 66).

Cañada Larga [VENTURA]: *canyon,* drained by a stream that flows 7.5 miles to Ventura River 4 miles north of Ventura (lat. 34°20'15" N, long. 119°17'45" W); the feature is on Cañada Larga o Verde grant. Named on Saticoy (1951) and Ventura (1951) 7.5' quadrangles. Postal authorities established Verdi post office at the mouth of the canyon in 1894 and discontinued it in 1898 (Ricard; Salley, p. 230).

Cañada Larga o Verde [VENTURA]: *land grant,* north of Ventura. Named on Matilija (1952), Ojai (1952), Saticoy (1951), and Ventura (1951) 7.5' quadrangles. Joaquina Alvarado received 0.5 league in 1841 and claimed 6659 acres patented in 1873 (Cowan, p. 44; Cowan listed the grant under the name "Cañada Larga y Verde").

Cañada Niguel: see **Salt Creek** [ORANGE].

Canada of Alamos: see **San Francisquito Canyon** [LOS ANGELES].

Canada Salada: see **Sulphur Creek** [ORANGE].

Cañada San Nicolas: see **Nicholas Canyon** [LOS ANGELES].

Cañada Seca [VENTURA]: *canyon,* drained by a stream that flows 2 miles to Cañada Larga 4.5 miles north-northeast of Ventura (lat. 34°20'40" N, long. 119°15'35" W). Named on Saticoy (1951) and Ventura (1951) 7.5' quadrangles.

Cañada Seco: see **Williams Canyon** [ORANGE].

Canal de Santa Barbara: see **Santa Barbara Channel** [VENTURA].

Canal Street Station [LOS ANGELES]: *locality,* 6 miles southeast of present Torrance city hall along Pacific Electric Railroad (lat. 33°46'25" N, long. 118°15'40" W). Named on Wilmington (1925) 6' quadrangle.

Canet: see **Weldons** [VENTURA].

Canoga: see **Canoga Park** [LOS ANGELES].

Canoga Park [LOS ANGELES]: *district,* 23 miles west-northwest of Los Angeles city hall (lat. 34°12'05" N, long. 118°35'45" W). Named on Canoga Park (1952) 7.5' quadrangle. Camulos (1903) 30' quadrangle shows a place called Canoga along the railroad at the site. Called Owensmouth on Chatsworth (1927) 6' quadrangle. Postal authorities established Owensmouth post office in 1912 and changed the name to Canoga Park in 1931 (Frickstad, p. 78). Harrison Gray Otis, publisher of *Los Angeles Times,* gave the name "Owensmouth" to the place because it used water brought by aqueduct from Owens River in Inyo County (Hanna, p. 54). The west part of Canoga Park withdrew from the district to form an incorporated community called West Hills.

Cañon de la Horca: see **Fremont Canyon** [ORANGE].

Cañon de Santa Ana [ORANGE]: *land grant,* extends from Yorba Linda to Santa Ana Canyon. Named on Black Star Canyon (1950), Orange (1950), Prado Dam (1950), and Yorba Linda (1950) 7.5' quadrangles. Bernardo Yorba received 3 leagues in 1834 and claimed 13,329 acres patented in 1866 (Cowan, p. 90; Cowan used the form "Cañada de Santa Ana" for the name).

Canterbury Lake: see **Lake Sherwood** [VENTURA].

Canton Canyon [LOS ANGELES-VENTURA]: *canyon,* drained by a stream that heads in Los Angeles County and flows 8.5 miles to Lake Piru 9 miles southeast of Cobblestone Mountain in Ventura County (lat. 34°30'45" N, long. 118°45'15" W; near S line sec. 15, T 5 N, R 18 W). Named on Cobblestone Mountain (1958) and Whitaker Peak (1958) 7.5' quadrangles. The lower part of the feature is called Stockton Canyon on Whitaker Peak (1935) 6' quadrangle, but United States Board on Geographic Names (1960b, p. 6) rejected the names "Stockton Canyon" and "Stocton Canyon" for it.

Canyon Acres [ORANGE]: *locality,* less than 1 mile northeast of Laguna Beach city hall in a branch of Laguna Canyon (lat. 33°33'10" N, long. 117°46'15" W; sec. 24, T 7 S, R 9 W). Named on Laguna Beach (1965) 7.5' quadrangle.

Cape Canyon [LOS ANGELES]: *canyon,* drained by a stream that flows 3.25 miles to Middle Canyon 1.25 miles south of Mount Banning on Santa Catalina Island (lat. 33°21'15" N, long. 118° 26' W). Named on Santa Catalina North (1950) and Santa Catalina South (1943) 7.5' quadrangles.

Cape Canyon Reservoir [LOS ANGELES]: *lake,* 300 feet long, 2.5 miles east of Mount Banning on Santa Catalina Island (lat. 33°22'40" N, long. 118°23'30" W); the feature is at the head of Cape Canyon. Named on Santa Catalina North (1950) 7.5' quadrangle.

Cape Cortes [LOS ANGELES]: *promontory,* 3 miles southeast of Silver Peak on the south side of Santa Catalina Island (lat. 33°25'45" N, long. 118°31'55" W). Named on Santa Catalina West (1943) 7.5' quadrangle.

Cape Horn Canyon [LOS ANGELES]: *canyon,* drained by a stream that flows 1.5 miles to San Gabriel River 7.5 miles north-northeast of Glendora city hall (lat. 34°13'50" N, long. 117°47'55" W). Named on Glendora (1953) 7.5' quadrangle.

Capistrano: see **San Juan Capistrano** [ORANGE].

Capistrano Beach [ORANGE]: *town,* 2.5 miles south-southwest of San Juan Capistrano (lat. 33°27'55" N, long. 117°40'40" W); the place is at the mouth of San Juan Creek. Named on Dana Point (1968) 7.5' quadrangle, which shows a railroad station called Serra at the town. Capistrano (1902) 30' quadrangle has the name "San Juan" at or near the site. Postal authorities established Capistrano Beach post office in 1925, changed the name to Doheny Park in 1931, and changed it back to Capistrano Beach in 1948 (Frickstad, p. 116). United States Board Geographic Names (1963, p. 13) rejected the names "Doheny Park," "San Juan by the Sea," and "Serra" for the town. Promoters laid out a subdivision called San Juan-by-the-Sea at the site in 1887, but the development failed; it was revived in 1925 under the name "Capistrano Beach," and eventually the E.L. Doheny interests took over the enterprise (Meadows, p. 50).

Capistrano Bight [ORANGE]: *water feature,* extends southeast along the coast from Dana Point to San Mateo Point [ORANGE]. Named on Dana Point (1968) and San Clemente (1968) 7.5' quadrangles.

Caradas Creek: see **Blind Canyon** [LOS ANGELES-VENTURA].

Carbon Beach [LOS ANGELES]: *beach,* 1.5 miles east-northeast of Malibu Point (lat. 34°02'20" N, long. 118°39'30" W); the beach is west of the mouth of Carbon Canyon. Named on Malibu Beach (1951) 7.5' quadrangle.

Carbon Canyon [LOS ANGELES]: *canyon,* drained by a stream that flows nearly 3 miles to the sea 2 miles southeast of Malibu Point (lat. 34°02'15" N, long. 118°38'50" W). Named on Malibu Beach (1951) 7.5' quadrangle. Called Coal Canyon on Camulos (1903) 30' quadrangle.

Carbon Canyon [ORANGE]: *canyon,* 7 miles long, heads in San Bernardino County and opens into lowlands 2.5 miles northwest of Yorba Linda (lat. 33°55' N, long. 117°50'20" W). Named on Yorba Linda (1964) 7.5' quadrangle.

Carbon Canyon Creek: see **Carbon Creek** [ORANGE].

Carbon Canyon Wash: see **Carbon Creek** [ORANGE].

Carbon Creek [ORANGE]: *stream,* flows 17 miles to Coyote Creek [LOS ANGELES-ORANGE] 5.5 miles southwest of Buena Park civic center (lat. 33°48'55" N, long. 118°04'10" W; near N line sec. 19, T 4 S, R 11 W). Named on Anaheim (1965), Los Alamitos (1964), and Orange (1964) 7.5' quadrangles. Called Carbon Canyon Creek on Anaheim (1950), Orange (1950), and Yorba Linda (1950) 7.5' quadrangles. Anaheim (1950) 7.5' quadrangle also has the name "Carbon Canyon Wash" for part of the feature (sec. 9, T 4 S, R 10 W).

Carbondale: see **Silverado Canyon** [ORANGE].

Carey: see **Saugus** [LOS ANGELES].

Carlos Canyon [LOS ANGELES]: *canyon,* drained by a stream that flows 2 miles to Piru Creek 10 miles south-southeast of Gorman (lat. 34°39'30" N, long. 118°46'55" W; sec. 34, T 7 N, R 18 W). Named on Black Mountain (1958) 7.5' quadrangle.

Carlton [ORANGE]: *locality,* 1.5 miles west-northwest of Yorba Linda along Pacific Electric Railroad (lat. 33°54'05" N, long. 117°50'10" W; near NW cor. sec. 21, T 3 S, R 9 W). Named on Yorba Linda (1950) 7.5' quadrangle. The place preserves the name of a community called Carlton that started in 1887; by the middle of 1889 the residents were leaving, and eventually the buildings were hauled away (Carpenter, p. 94).

Carmenita [LOS ANGELES]: *locality,* 5.5 miles south of present Whittier city hall (lat. 33°53'25" N, long. 118°02'40" W; near SW cor. sec. 21, T 3 S, R 11 W). Named on Whittier (1949) 7.5' quadrangle. Postal authorities established Carmenita post office in 1887 and discontinued it in 1892 (Frickstad, p. 71).

Carmicle: see **Kevet** [VENTURA].

Carr Canyon [LOS ANGELES]: *canyon,* drained by a stream that flows 3 miles to Little Rock Wash 7 miles southeast of Palmdale (lat. 34°30'35" N, long. 118°01'20" W; sec. 22, T 5 N, R 11 W). Named on Juniper Hills (1959), Pacifico Mountain (1959), and Palmdale (1958) 7.5' quadrangles.

Carson [LOS ANGELES]: *city,* 3.5 miles east of Torrance city hall (lat. 33°49'45" N, long. 118°17' W). Named on Torrance (1964) 7.5' quadrangle. Postal authorities established North Wilmington post office in 1953 and changed the name to Carson in 1955 (Salley, p. 157). The city incorporated in 1968.

Carter's Camp: see **Little Santa Anita Canyon** [LOS ANGELES].

Casa Desierto: see **Redman** [LOS ANGELES].

Casa Loma: see **Yorba Linda** [ORANGE].

Casa Verdugo: see **Tropico** [LOS ANGELES].

Cascade Canyon [LOS ANGELES]: *canyon,* drained by a stream that heads in San Bernardino County and flows 1.25 miles to San Antonio Canyon 12 miles north-northeast of Pomona city hall in Los Angeles County (lat. 34°12'55" N, long. 117°40'05" W; sec. 36, T 2 N, R 8 W). Named on Mount Baldy (1954) 7.5' quadrangle. Called Barrett Can. on Camp Baldy (1940) 6' quadrangle, where present Barrett Canyon is called Kerkhoff Canyon.

Cascade Picnic Area: see **Cascade Public Camp** [LOS ANGELES].

Cascade Public Camp [LOS ANGELES]: *locality,* 2.25 miles east of Mount Wilson (1) in Santa Anita Canyon (lat. 34°13'05" N, long. 118°01'20" W; sec. 34, T 2 N, R 11 W). Named on Mount Wilson (1953) 7.5' quadrangle. Called Cascade Picnic Area on Mount Wilson (1966) 7.5' quadrangle.

Casells: see **Caswell** [LOS ANGELES].

Casino Point [LOS ANGELES]: *promontory,* 0.25 mile north of Avalon on the northeast side of Santa Catalina Island (lat. 33°20'55" N, long. 118°19'30" W). Named on Santa Catalina East (1950) 7.5' quadrangle. United States Board on Geographic Names (1936a, p. 10) rejected the name "Sugarloaf Point" for the feature.

Casitas [VENTURA]: *locality,* 5.5 miles north of Ventura along Southern Pacific Railroad (lat. 34°21'30" N, long. 119°18'35" W). Named on Ventura (1904) 7.5' quadrangle.

Casitas: see **Lake Casitas** [VENTURA].

Casitas Creek [VENTURA]: *stream,* flows 2.5 miles to Rincon Creek 6 miles south-southwest of White Ledge Peak (lat. 34°23'45" N, long. 119°27'10" W); the stream heads at West Casitas Pass. Named on White Ledge Peak (1952) 7.5' quadrangle.

Casitas Pass: see **East Casitas Pass** [VENTURA]; **West Casitas Pass** [VENTURA].

Casitas Reservoir: see **Lake Casitas** [VENTURA].

Casitas Springs [VENTURA]: *town,* 6 miles north of Ventura along Ventura River (lat. 34°22' N, long. 119°18'20" W). Named on Ventura (1951) 7.5' quadrangle. Postal authorities established Casitas Springs post office in 1928 and discontinued it in 1969 (Salley, p. 39).

Casitas Valley [VENTURA]: *valley,* 6 miles south of White Ledge Peak (lat. 34°22'55" N, long. 119°24' W; sec. 33, T 4 N, R 24 W); the feature is between East Casitas Pass and West Casitas Pass. Named on White Ledge Peak (1952) 7.5' quadrangle. The name is from little willow-thatched houses used by Indians in the neighborhood—*casitas* means "little houses" in Spanish (Hoover, Rensch, and Rensch, p. 578).

Cassara Canyon [LOS ANGELES]: *canyon,* drained by a stream that flows less than 1 mile to Tujunga Valley 3 miles west-northwest of Sunland (lat. 34°16'45" N, long. 118°21'20" W; at S line sec. 4, T 2 N, R 14 W). Named on Sunland (1966) 7.5' quadrangle.

Castac: see **Castaic** [LOS ANGELES].

Castac Creek: see **Castaic Creek** [LOS ANGELES].

Castac Valley [LOS ANGELES]: *valley,* mainly in Kern County, but extends southwest into Los Angeles County 2.5 miles northwest of Gorman (lat. 34°49'05" N, long. 118°53' W; at N line sec. 3, T 8 N, R 19 W). Named on Frazier Mountain (1958) 7.5' quadrangle. Called Castaic Valley on Frazier Mountain (1944) 7.5' quadrangle, but United States Board on Geographic Names (1960d, p. 16) rejected this designation for the feature. Antisell (p. 91) used the form "Cestek" for the name.

Castac Valley: see **Castaic Valley** [LOS ANGELES].

Castaic [LOS ANGELES]: *town,* 9 miles northwest of Newhall (lat. 34°29'20" N, long. 118°36'55" W; sec. 25, T 5 N, R 17 W); the place is along Castaic Creek in Castaic Valley. Named on Newhall (1952) 7.5' quadrangle. Postal authorities established Castaic post office in 1894, discontinued it in 1895, and reestablished it in 1917 (Frickstad, p. 71). The name is from Castac grant in Kern County (Hanna, p. 58), but United States Board on Geographic Names (1960d, p. 16) rejected the name "Castac" for the town. California Mining Bureau's (1917) map shows a place called Kemp situated about 4 miles west-southwest of Castaic along the railroad. Los Angeles County (1935) map shows a feature called Nicholson Canyon located west of Castaic (sec. 25, 26, T 5 N, R 17 W).

Castaic: see **Castaic Junction** [LOS ANGELES].

Castaic Afterbay: see **Elderberry Forebay** [LOS ANGELES].

Castaic Canyon: see **Castaic Valley** [LOS ANGELES].

Castaic Creek [LOS ANGELES]: *stream,* flows 23 miles to Santa Clara River 6.5 miles west-northwest of Newhall (lat. 34°25'10" N, long. 118°37'45" W). Named on Liebre Mountain (1958), Newhall (1952), Val Verde (1952), Warm Springs Mountain (1958), and Whitaker Peak (1958) 7.5' quadrangles. Preston (1890a, p. 201) used the form "Castaca Cañon" for the name. United States Board on Geographic Names (1960d, p. 17) rejected the names "Castac Creek" and "Castiac Creek" for the feature. The name is from an Indian village located near the mouth of the stream (Kroeber, p. 37).

Castaic Forebay: see **Elderberry Forebay** [LOS ANGELES].

Castaic Junction [LOS ANGELES]: *locality,* nearly 6 miles northeast of Newhall (lat. 34°26'25" N, long. 118°36'20" W); the place is 3.5 miles south of Castaic, where the road to Castaic joins the road that lies along Santa Clara River. Named on Newhall (1952) 7.5' quadrangle. Santa Susana (1903) 15' quadrangle shows a place called Castaic located along the railroad at the site, and Castaic (1940) 6' quadrangle shows Castaic Sta. there. Newhall (1952, photorevised 1988) 7.5' quadrangle has the name "Valencia" near the place; Valencia is a new town founded after Newhall (1952) 7.5' quadrangle was made. Postal authorities established Valencia post office in 1965 (Salley, p. 229). Los Angeles County (1935) map has the name "San Jose Canyon" for a feature, about 1.5 miles long, that opens into the valley of Santa Clara River from the south near Castaic Junction, and has the name "Potrero Canyon" for a feature, about 2.5 miles long, that is parallel to San Jose Canyon and situated 0.5 mile farther east

Castaic Lagoon [LOS ANGELES]: *lake,* 6.5 miles south-southwest of Warm Springs Mountain along Castaic Creek below the dam that forms Castaic Lake (lat. 34°30'15" N, long. 118°36'30" W; on and near E line sec. 24, T 5 N, R 17 W). Named on Warm Springs Mountain (1958, photorevised 1988) 7.5' quadrangle.

Castaic Lake [LOS ANGELES]: *lake,* behind a dam on Castaic Creek 5.5 miles south-south-west of Warm Springs Mountain (lat. 34°31'10" N, long. 118°36'20" W; on W line sec. 18, T 5 N, R 16 W). Named on Warm Springs Mountain (1958, photorevised 1988) and Whitaker Peak (1958, photorevised 1974) 7.5' quadrangles.

Castaic Pumping Forebay: see **Elderberry Forebay** [LOS ANGELES].

Castaic Pumping Plant Afterbay: see **Elderberry Forebay** [LOS ANGELES].

Castaic Reservoir: see **Elderberry Forebay** [LOS ANGELES].

Castaic Station: see **Castaic Junction** [LOS ANGELES].

Castaic Valley [LOS ANGELES]: *valley,* along Castaic Creek above the entrance of the creek into the valley of Santa Clara River. Named on Newhall (1952) and Warm Springs Mountain (1958) 7.5' quadrangles. Called Castac Valley on Camulos (1903) 30' quadrangle, and Storms (p. 248) mentioned Casteca Cañon. United States Board on Geographic Names (1960d, p. 17) rejected the names "Castac Valley" and "Castaic Canyon" for the feature.

Castaic Valley: see **Castac Valley** [LOS ANGELES].

Casteca Cañon: see **Castaic Valley** [LOS ANGELES].

Castellammare: see **Castellammare Mesa** [LOS ANGELES].

Castellammare Mesa [LOS ANGELES]: *area,* 4.5 miles west-northwest of Santa Monica city hall (lat. 34°02'35" N, long. 118°33'40" W). Named on Topanga (1952) 7.5' quadrangle. Topanga Canyon (1928) 6' quadrangle has the name "Castellammare" for a locality at the place.

Castiac Creek: see **Castaic Creek** [LOS ANGELES].

Castle Canyon [LOS ANGELES]: *canyon,* drained by a stream that flows about 0.5 mile to Rubio Canyon 3.25 miles west of Mount Wilson (1) (lat. 34°12'55" N, long. 118°07' W). Named on Mount Wilson (1966) 7.5' quadrangle.

Castle Canyon [VENTURA]: *canyon,* drained by a stream that flows nearly 4 miles to Cuyama River 7.5 miles northwest of Reyes Peak (lat. 34°42'35" N, long. 119°22'40" W). Named on Reyes Peak (1943) 7.5' quadrangle.

Castle Rock [LOS ANGELES]:
(1) *relief feature,* 4.5 miles west-northwest of present Santa Monica city hall along the coast (lat. 34°02'30" N, long. 118°33'55" W). Named on Topanga Canyon (1928) 6' quadrangle.
(2) *rock,* 1.5 miles west of Northwest Harbor on San Clemente Island, and 2000 feet offshore (lat. 33°02'05" N, long. 118°36'50" W). Named on San Clemente Island North (1943) 7.5' quadrangle.

Castro Peak [LOS ANGELES]: *peak,* 6 miles north of Point Dume (lat. 34°05'10" N, long. 118°47'05" W; sec. 17, T 1 S, R 18 W). Altitude 2824 feet. Named on Point Dume (1951) 7.5' quadrangle. Los Angeles County (1935) map shows a place called Backus Summit situated 1.25 miles west of Castro Peak.

Caswell [LOS ANGELES]: *locality,* 5.5 miles south-southeast of Gorman in Peace Valley (lat. 34°43'20" N, long. 118°47'50" W; at S line sec. 4, T 7 N, R 18 W). Named on Black Mountain (1958) 7.5' quadrangle. Called Casells on Black Mountain (1943) 7.5' quadrangle.

Catalina Channel: see **San Pedro Channel** [LOS ANGELES].

Catalina Harbor [LOS ANGELES]: *embayment,* 4 miles east-southeast of Silver Peak on the south side of Santa Catalina Island (lat. 33°25'45" N, long. 118°30'25" W). Named on Santa Catalina West (1943) 7.5' quadrangle.

Catalina Head [LOS ANGELES]: *peak,* 4 miles southeast of Silver Peak on Santa Catalina Island (lat. 33°25'25" N, long. 118°30'50" W); the feature is just west of the entrance to Catalina Harbor. Named on Santa Catalina West (1943) 7.5' quadrangle.

Catalina-on-the-Main: see **Arch Beach** [ORANGE].

Cataract Canyon: see **Big Canyon** [VENTURA].

Cat Canyon [LOS ANGELES]: *canyon,* drained by a stream that flows nearly 1 mile to San Antonio Canyon 11 miles north-northeast of Pomona city hall (lat. 34°11'50" N, long. 117°40'35" W; sec. 1, T 1 N, R 8 W). Named on Mount Baldy (1954) 7.5' quadrangle.

Catharina Creek [VENTURA]: *stream,* flows 1.5 miles to Rincon Creek 4 miles southwest of White Ledge Peak (lat. 34°25'45" N, long. 119°26'35" W; near E line sec. 13, T 4 N, R 25 W). Named on White Ledge Peak (1952) 7.5' quadrangle. Called East Fork [of Rincon

Creek] on Ventura (1904) 15' quadrangle.
Cat Rock [VENTURA]: *island,* 425 feet long, off the south side of the western Anacapa Island (lat. 34°00'15" N, long. 119°25'15" W). Named on Anacapa Island (1973) quadrangle.
Cattle Canyon [LOS ANGELES]: *canyon,* 8.5 miles long, opens into the canyon of San Gabriel River 8.5 miles northeast of Glendora city hall (lat. 34°13'45" N, long. 117°46'05" W). Named on Glendora (1953), Mount Baldy (1954), and Mount San Antonio (1955) 7.5' quadrangles.
Caula: see **Camp Caula** [LOS ANGELES].
Cavin [VENTURA]: *locality,* 3.5 miles westsouthwest of Piru along Southern Pacific Railroad (lat. 34°23'40" N, long. 118°51' W; near SE cor. sec. 27, T 4 N, R 19 W). Named on Piru (1952) 7.5' quadrangle. California Division of Highways' (1934) map shows a place called Wilshire located 1.5 miles west of Cavin along the railroad.
CCC Ridge [LOS ANGELES]: *ridge,* southeast-trending, 1 mile long, 5 miles south-south-east of Condor Peak (lat. 34°15'25" N, long. 118°11'30" W; mainly in sec. 13, T 2 N, R 13 W). Named on Condor Peak (1959) 7.5' quadrangle.
Cedar Camp: see **Fish Fork** [LOS ANGELES].
Cedar Canyon [LOS ANGELES]:
(1) *canyon,* drained by a stream that flows less than 1 mile to Arroyo Seco 9 miles south-southwest of Pacifico Mountain (lat. 34°15'15" N, long. 118°05' W). Named on Chilao Flat (1959) and Mount Wilson (1953) 7.5' quadrangles.
(2) *canyon,* drained by a stream that flows 1.5 miles to Mescal Creek 2 miles northwest of Big Pines (lat. 34°23'45" N, long. 117° 43' W). Named on Mescal Creek (1956) 7.5' quadrangle.
(3) *canyon,* drained by a stream that flows 1 mile to Cogswell Reservoir 8.5 miles north-northwest of Azusa city hall (lat. 34° 14'10" N, long. 117°59'10" W; near N line sec. 25, T 2 N, R 11 W). Named on Azusa (1953) 7.5' quadrangle.
Cedar Creek [LOS ANGELES]: *stream,* flows 2.25 miles to Soldier Creek 1 mile east-south-east of Crystal Lake (lat. 34°18'40" N, long. 117°50' W). Named on Crystal Lake (1958) 7.5' quadrangle.
Cedar Creek [VENTURA]: *stream,* flows nearly 2 miles to South Fork Piru Creek 8.5 miles east of Reyes Peak (lat. 34°38'15" N, long. 119°07'35" W; sec. 5, T 6 N, R 21 W). Named on San Guillermo (1943) 7.5' quadrangle. United States Board on Geographic Names (1990, p. 6) rejected the name "South Fork Piru Creek" for the stream.
Cedar Creek: see **Big Cedar Creek** [VENTURA].
Cedars Campground: see **Little Cedars Campground** [LOS ANGELES].
Cedar Springs [LOS ANGELES]: *locality,* 3

miles east-northeast of Waterman Mountain (lat. 34°21'05" N, long. 117°53'05" W; near NW cor. sec. 13, T 3 N, R 10 W). Named on Waterman Mountain (1959) 7.5' quadrangle. Crystal Lake (1941) 6' quadrangle shows a spring called Cedar Spring at the site.
Celery [ORANGE]: *locality,* 2.5 miles south-east of present Huntington Beach civic center along Southern Pacific Railroad (lat. 33° 38' N, long. 117°58' W). Named on Santa Ana (1901) 15' quadrangle.
Cemetery Barranca: see **Sanjon Barranca** [VENTURA].
Cemetery Ravine: see **Chavez Ravine** [LOS ANGELES].
Centennial Creek [VENTURA]: *stream,* flows 1.5 miles to Little Sespe Creek 4 miles north of Fillmore (lat. 34°27'40" N, long. 118° 54'35" W; sec. 6, T 4 N, R 19 W). Named on Fillmore (1951) 7.5' quadrangle.
Center Creek [LOS ANGELES]: *stream,* flows 1 mile to Gold Creek 4.25 miles north of Sunland (lat. 34°19'20" N, long. 118°18'40" W; at N line sec. 26, T 3 N, R 14 W). Named on Sunland (1953) 7.5' quadrangle.
Centinela [LOS ANGELES]: *locality,* less than 1 mile northeast of present Inglewood city hall along Atchison, Topeka and Santa Fe Railroad (lat. 33°58'15" N, long. 118°20'30" W); the place is on Aguaje de la Centinela grant. Named on Redondo (1896) 15' quadrangle. Postal authorities established Centinela post office in 1889 and discontinued it in 1895 (Salley, p. 41).
Centinela Creek [LOS ANGELES]: *stream,* flows 7.5 miles to Ballona Lagoon about 5.5 miles north-northwest of present Manhattan Beach city hall (lat. 33°57'45" N, long. 118°27' W); the stream heads near Centinela. Named on Redondo (1896) 15' quadrangle. Venice (1964) 7.5' quadrangle shows a feature called Centinela Creek Channel that joins Ballona Creek 2.25 miles above the mouth of that creek.
Centinela Valley Camp [LOS ANGELES]: *locality,* 0.5 mile northwest of Big Pines (lat. 34°23'05" N, long. 117°41'50" W). Named on Mescal Creek (1956) 7.5' quadrangle.
Central Avenue [LOS ANGELES]: *locality,* 5.5 miles east-northeast of present Inglewood city hall along Atchison, Topeka and Santa Fe Railroad (lat. 33°59'10" N, long. 118°15'20" W). Named on Redondo (1896) 15' quadrangle.
Centro: see **Covina** [LOS ANGELES].
Cerrito de las Ranas: see **Red Hill** [ORANGE].
Cerritos [LOS ANGELES]: *city,* 10 miles north-east of Long Beach city hall (lat. 33°51'30" N, long. 118°03'30" W). Named on Los Alamitos (1964, photorevised 1981) and Whittier, (1965, photorevised 1981) 7.5' quadrangles. Called Dairy Valley on Los Alamitos (1964) and Whittier (1965) 7.5' quadrangles. Postal authorities established Dairy Valley post office in 1962 and changed the name to

Cerritos in 1967 (Salley, p. 54). The city incorporated with the name "Dairy Valley" in 1956, and changed the name to Cerritos in 1967. The place was incorporated to preserve the land for dairy farms, but by the late 1960's most of the dairy activity was gone (Van Kampen, p. 39, 41, 43).

Cerritos: see **Elftman** [LOS ANGELES].

Cerritos Channel [LOS ANGELES]: *water feature,* 3 miles west of Long Beach city hall between Terminal Island and the mainland (lat. 33°45'55" N, long. 118°14'30" W). Named on Long Beach (1964) and Torrance (1964) 7.5' quadrangles.

Cerro Colorado: see **Red Hill** [ORANGE].

Cerro Villa Heights [ORANGE]: *locality,* 4 miles northeast of Orange city hall (lat. 33°49'35" N, long. 117°48'05" W). Named on Orange (1964) 7.5' quadrangle.

Chaffee Island: see **Island Chaffee** [LOS ANGELES].

Chalk Hills [LOS ANGELES]: *ridge,* north-northwest-trending, 2 miles long, 2.5 miles south-southeast of Canoga Park (lat. 34°10'10" N, long. 118°34'40" W). Named on Canoga Park (1952) 7.5' quadrangle.

Chandler Canyon [LOS ANGELES]: *canyon,* 1 mile long, 3.5 miles northwest of Burbank city hall (lat. 34°13'30" N, long. 118°20'35" W; sec. 27, 28, T 2 N, R 14 W). Named on Burbank (1953) 7.5' quadrangle.

Chandlers [LOS ANGELES]: *locality,* 2 miles west-northwest of Gorman (lat. 34°48'40" N, long. 118°53' W). Named on Frazier Mountain (1944) 7.5' quadrangle. Called Chandler on Gorman (1938) 6' quadrangle.

Chaneys Point [ORANGE]: *promontory,* 0.5 mile south of Laguna Beach city hall along the coast (lat. 33°32'15" N, long. 117°46'45" W; at W line sec. 25, T 7 S, R 9 W). Named on Laguna Beach (1965) 7.5' quadrangle.

Channel Islands: see **Santa Barbara Channel** [VENTURA].

Channel Islands Harbor: see **Port Hueneme** [VENTURA].

Chantry Flat [LOS ANGELES]: *area,* 3 miles southeast of Mount Wilson (1) (lat. 34°11'40" N, long. 118°01'20" W; on S line sec. 3, T 1 N, R 11 W). Named on Mount Wilson (1953) 7.5' quadrangle. Called Chantry Flats on Los Angeles County (1935) map. Charles E. Chantry received use of 20 acres at the place in 1907 (Owens, p. 17-18).

Chaparral Campground [LOS ANGELES]: *locality,* 8.5 miles south-southeast of the village of Lake Hughes (lat. 34°33'30" N, long. 118°24'20" W; near N line sec. 1, T 5 N, R 15 W). Named on Green Valley (1958) 7.5' quadrangle.

Chapman [LOS ANGELES]: *locality,* 6.5 miles south of Mount Wilson (1) along Southern Pacific Railroad (lat. 34°07'35" N, long. 118°04'30" W). Named on Pasadena (1900) 15' quadrangle.

Chapman: see **Chapman Siding** [LOS ANGELES].

Chapman Siding [LOS ANGELES]: *locality,* 5.25 miles south-southwest of Mount Wilson (1) along Atchison, Topeka and Santa Fe Railroad (lat. 34°08'55" N, long. 118°04'55" W). Named on Mount Wilson (1953) 7.5' quadrangle. Mount Wilson (1966) 7.5' quadrangle has the name "Chapman" at the place.

Charles Cañon: see **Charlie Canyon** [LOS ANGELES].

Charlie Canyon [LOS ANGELES]: *canyon,* drained by a stream that flows 9 miles to Castaic Valley 8 miles north-northwest of Newhall (lat. 34°29' N, long. 118°36'30" W; near SE cor. sec. 25, T 5 N, R 17 W). Named on Newhall (1952) and Warm Springs Mountain (1958) 7.5' quadrangles. Preston (1890a, p. 202) called the feature Charles Cañon.

Charlton Flats [LOS ANGELES]: *area,* 5.5 miles south of Pacifico Mountain along East Fork Alder Creek (lat. 34°18'15" N, long. 118°01' W). Named on Alder Creek (1941) 6' quadrangle. The place first was called Pine Flat, but in 1925 the name was changed to honor Rush H. Charlton, who was retiring as forest supervisor (Robinson, J.W., 1977, p. 193).

Charlton Flats Picnic Ground [LOS ANGELES]: *locality,* 6 miles south of Pacifico Mountain (lat. 34°17'40" N, long. 118°01'05" W; at N line sec. 3, T 2 N, R 11 W); the place is at the south end of Charlton Flats. Named on Chilao Flat (1959) 7.5' quadrangle.

Charlton Station [LOS ANGELES]: *locality,* 6 miles south-southeast of Pacifico Mountain (lat. 34°17'55" N, long. 118°00'20" W; near S line sec. 35, T 3 N, R 11 W). Named on Chilao Flat (1959) 7.5' quadrangle.

Charter Oak [LOS ANGELES]: *district,* 6.5 miles west-northwest of Pomona city hall (lat. 34°06' N, long. 117°51' W). Named on San Dimas (1966) 7.5' quadrangle. Postal authorities established Charter Oak post office in 1899, discontinued it in 1954, and reestablished it in 1956 (Salley, p. 42).

Charter Oak Creek [LOS ANGELES]: *stream,* flows 3 miles to Walnut Creek 3.25 miles east-southeast of Baldwin Park city hall (lat. 34°04'10" N, long. 117°53'10" W); the stream heads at Charter Oak district. Named on Baldwin Park (1966) and San Dimas (1966) 7.5' quadrangles.

Chatsworth [LOS ANGELES]: *district,* 9 miles west-southwest of San Fernando in Los Angeles (lat. 34°15'25" N, long. 118°36'20" W). Named on Oat Mountain (1952) 7.5' quadrangle. Called Chatworth on California Mining Bureau's (1909b) map. Postal authorities established Chatsworth post office in 1890 and moved it 0.75 mile south in 1898 (Salley, p. 42). The name is from Chatsworth, England (Gudde, 1949, p. 64). California Mining Bureau's (1917) map shows a place called

Hasson located along the railroad northwest of Chatsworth near present Santa Susana Pass. The same map shows a place called Pisgah Grande situated about 11 miles north-north-west of Chatsworth, and north-northwest of Hasson. Postal authorities established Pisgah Grande post office 10 miles northwest of Chatsworth post office (sec. 15, T 3 N, R 17 W) in 1915 and discontinued it in 1920 (Salley, p. 173)—Finis E. Yoakum founded a religious utopian colony at the place (Hoover, Rensch, and Rensch, p. 169).

Chatsworth Creek [LOS ANGELES]: *stream,* flows 2 miles to Bell Creek 1.25 miles west of the center of Canoga Park (lat. 34°11'55" N, long. 118°37' W); the stream heads at Chatsworth Reservoir. Named on Calabasas (1952) and Canoga Park (1952) 7.5' quadrangles.

Chatsworth Lake Manor [LOS ANGELES-VENTURA]: *locality,* 2 miles south of Santa Susana Pass on Los Angeles-Ventura county line (lat. 34°14'25" N, long. 118°38'05" W); the place is at the north side of Chatsworth Reservoir. Named on Calabasas (1952) 7.5' quadrangle.

Chatsworth Peak [VENTURA]: *peak,* 1 mile south-southwest of Santa Susana Pass (lat. 34°15'25" N, long. 118°38'25" W). Altitude 2314 feet. Named on Santa Susana (1951) 7.5' quadrangle. The name is from the nearby town of Chatsworth [LOS ANGELES] (Ricard).

Chatsworth Reservoir [LOS ANGELES]: *lake,* behind a dam on Chatsworth Creek 2.5 miles south-southwest of Chatsworth (lat. 34°13'35" N, long. 118°37'45" W). Named on Calabasas (1952) and Canoga Park (1952) 7.5' quadrangles.

Chavez Ravine [LOS ANGELES]: *canyon,* 1.5 miles long, 1.25 miles north of Los Angeles city hall (lat. 34°04'30" N, long. 118°14'50" W). Named on Los Angeles (1953) 7.5' quadrangle. Stevenson's (1884) map shows four south-trending canyons east of Chavez Ravine between the ravine and Los Angeles River: Sulphur Ravine, just east of Chavez Ravine; Cemetery Ravine, the second canyon to the east; Solano Ravine, the third canyon to the east; and Reservoir Ravine, the canyon farthest to the east. Hanson's (1868) map has the name "Stone Quarry Hills" for the range that contains Chavez Ravine and the four canyons.

Cheeseboro Canyon [LOS ANGELES-VENTURA]: *canyon,* drained by a stream that heads in Ventura County and flows 5 miles to Palo Comado Canyon 0.5 mile north-northeast of Agoura in Los Angeles County (lat. 34°09'05" N, long. 118°44' W). Named on Calabasas (1952) 7.5' quadrangle.

Cherry Canyon [LOS ANGELES]:
(1) *canyon,* drained by a stream that flows 2.5 miles to Piru Creek 3.5 miles north of Whitaker Peak (lat. 34°37'20" N, long. 118°44'40" W; near W line sec. 12, T 6 N, R

18 W). Named on Liebre Mountain (1958) and Whitaker Peak (1958) 7.5' quadrangles.
(2) *canyon,* drained by a stream that flows 3.5 miles to San Francisquito Canyon nearly 6 miles south of the village of Lake Hughes (lat. 34°35'25" N, long. 118°26'50" W). Named on Green Valley (1958) 7.5' quadrangle.

Cherry Cove [LOS ANGELES]: *embayment,* 4 miles east of Silver Peak on the north side of Santa Catalina Island (lat. 33°27'05" N, long. 118°30'05" W); the feature is at the mouth of Cherry Valley. Named on Santa Catalina West (1943) 7.5' quadrangle. Preston (1890b, p. 280) called the embayment Cherry Valley Harbor.

Cherry Creek [VENTURA]: *stream,* flows 2.5 miles to Sespe Creek 7.5 miles north-north-west of Wheeler Springs (lat. 34°36'15" N, long. 119°21'20" W; near S line sec. 18, T 6 N, R 23 W). Named on Wheeler Springs (1943) 7.5' quadrangle.

Cherry Creek Campground [VENTURA]: *locality,* 7 miles north-northwest of Wheeler Springs (lat. 34°35'50" N, long. 119°21'10" W; sec. 19, T 6 N, R 23 W); the place is along Cherry Creek. Named on Wheeler Springs (1943) 7.5' quadrangle.

Cherry Valley [LOS ANGELES]: *canyon,* drained by a stream that flows 1 mile to the sea nearly 4 miles east of Silver Peak on the north side of Santa Catalina Island (lat. 33°27' N, long. 118°30'05" W). Named on Santa Catalina West (1943) 7.5' quadrangle.

Cherry Valley Harbor: see **Cherry Cove** [LOS ANGELES].

Chicken Canyon [LOS ANGELES]: *canyon,* 0.5 mile long, 8 miles north-northeast of Pomona city hall (lat. 34°09'30" N, long. 117°41'35" W; sec. 23, T 1 N, R 8 W). Named on Mount Baldy (1954) 7.5' quadrangle.

Chilao Campground [LOS ANGELES]: *locality,* 4 miles south of Pacifico Mountain (lat. 34°19'25" N, long. 118°01'05" W; near N line sec. 27, T 3 N, R 11 W); the place is at Chilao Flat. Named on Chilao Flat (1959) 7.5' quadrangle.

Chilao Creek [LOS ANGELES]: *stream,* flows 3.5 miles to East Fork Alder Creek (2) 4 miles south of Pacifico Mountain (lat. 34°19'20" N, long. 118°01'35" W; near NW cor. sec. 27, T 3 N, R 11 W). Named on Chilao Flat (1959) and Waterman Mountain (1959) 7.5' quadrangles.

Chilao Flat [LOS ANGELES]: *area,* 3.5 miles south of Pacifico Mountain (lat. 34°19'50" N, long. 118°01'20" W; mainly in sec. 21, 22, T 3 N, R 11 W). Named on Chilao Flat (1959) 7.5' quadrangle. Called Pine Flats on Tujunga (1900) 15' quadrangle. The name is for Chileo Silvas, who reportedly herded cattle and lassoed bears at the place for 40 years (Robinson, J.W., 1983, p. 217).

Chilao Station [LOS ANGELES]: *locality,* nearly 4 miles south-southeast of Pacifico

Mountain (lat. 34°19'40" N, long. 118°00'30" W; sec. 22, T 3 N, R 11 W); the place is at Chilao Flat. Named on Chilao Flat (1959) 7.5' quadrangle.

Childs Canyon [LOS ANGELES]: *canyon,* 1 mile long, 1.5 miles northeast of Burbank city hall (lat. 34°11'30" N, long. 118°16'35" W). Named on Burbank (1953) 7.5' quadrangle.

Chileno Canyon [LOS ANGELES]: *canyon,* drained by a stream that flows 2.25 miles to West Fork San Gabriel River 8 miles north-northwest of Azusa city hall (lat. 34°14'30" N, long. 117°56'55" W). Named on Azusa (1953) and Waterman Mountain (1959) 7.5' quadrangles.

Chimney Canyon [LOS ANGELES]: *canyon,* drained by a stream that flows nearly 1.5 miles to Pacoima Canyon 2.5 miles north of Condor Peak (lat. 34°21'40" N, long. 118°12'35" W). Named on Acton (1959) and Condor Peak (1959) 7.5' quadrangles.

China Flat [VENTURA]: *area,* 4.25 miles northeast of Thousand Oaks (lat. 34°12'30" N, long. 118°46'05" W; near S line sec. 33, T 2 N, R 18 W). Named on Thousand Oaks (1952) 7.5' quadrangle.

China Point [LOS ANGELES]:
(1) *promontory,* 3.5 miles south-southwest of Mount Banning on the south side of Santa Catalina Island (lat. 33°19'45" N, long. 118° 28' W). Named on Santa Catalina South (1943) 7.5' quadrangle.
(2) *promontory,* 4.5 miles west-northwest of Pyramid Point at the south end of San Clemente Island (lat. 32°48'05" N, long. 118°25'30" W). Named on San Clemente Island South (1943) 7.5' quadrangle.

Chino Creek [LOS ANGELES]: *stream,* flows 2 miles to San Bernardino County 2.5 miles south-southeast of Pomona city hall (lat. 34° 01'05" N, long. 117°44'05" W). Named on Ontario (1954) and San Dimas (1954) 7.5' quadrangles.

Chino Flat [VENTURA]: *area,* 2.5 miles north of Piru (lat. 34°27'05" N, long. 118°47'05" W; near N line sec. 8, T 4 N, R 18 W). Named on Piru (1952) 7.5' quadrangle.

Chino Hills [LOS ANGELES-ORANGE]: *range,* extends east in Los Angeles, Orange, and San Bernardino Counties from Brea Canyon to Santa Ana River; the range is south of Chino, which is in San Bernardino County. Named on Prado Dam (1967) and Yorba Linda (1950) 7.5' quadrangles.

Chiquita: see Camp Chiquita [LOS ANGELES].

Chiquita Canyon [LOS ANGELES]: *canyon,* 1.5 miles long, 4.25 miles north of Pasadena city hall (lat. 34°12'30" N, long. 118°08'30" W). Named on Pasadena (1953) 7.5' quadrangle. Called Chiquita Ravine on Los Angeles County (1935) map.

Chiquita Ravine: see Chiquita Canyon [LOS ANGELES].

Chiquito Spring [ORANGE]: *spring,* 4.5 miles south of Trabuco Peak (lat. 33°38'20" N, long. 117°28'10" W). Named on Alberhill (1954) 7.5' quadrangle. Kenneth Munhall, a forest ranger, named the spring in 1927 for his horse (Meadows, p. 52).

Chismahoo Creek [VENTURA]: *stream,* flows less than 1 mile to Lake Casitas 8 miles southwest of the town of Ojai (lat. 34°23' N, long. 119°22'10" W). Named on Matilija (1952, photorevised 1967) and White Ledge Peak (1952) 7.5' quadrangles.

Chismahoo Mountain [VENTURA]: *peak,* 2.25 miles southwest of White Ledge Peak (lat. 34°26'40" N, long. 119°25'10" W; sec. 8, T 4 N, R 24 W). Altitude 2923 feet. Named on White Ledge Peak (1952) 7.5' quadrangle.

Chitwood Canyon: see Acton Camp [LOS ANGELES].

Chivo Canyon [LOS ANGELES-VENTURA]: *canyon,* drained by a stream that heads in Los Angeles County and flows 5 miles to Simi Valley (1) 4 miles west-northwest of Santa Susana Pass in Ventura County (lat. 34°18' N, long. 118°41'30" W; near E line sec. 31, T 3 N, R 17 W). Named on Santa Susana (1951) 7.5' quadrangle.

Chorro Grande Canyon [VENTURA]: *canyon,* drained by a stream that flows 3.5 miles to Sespe Creek 6.25 miles north-northwest of Wheeler Springs (lat. 34°35'35" N, long. 119°19'35" W; sec. 21, T 6 N, R 23 W). Named on Reyes Peak (1943) and Wheeler Springs (1943) 7.5' quadrangles.

Chrisman [VENTURA]: *locality,* 1.5 miles north-northwest of downtown Ventura along Southern Pacific Railroad (lat. 34°17'50" N, long. 119°18'05" W). Named on Ventura (1951) 7.5' quadrangle.

Christian: see Camp Christian [LOS ANGELES].

Chuchupate Campground [VENTURA]: *locality,* 2 miles west-northwest of Frazier Mountain (lat. 34°47'15" N, long. 118°59'55" W; sec. 16, T 8 N, R 20 W). Named on Frazier Mountain (1958) 7.5' quadrangle. The name is of Indian origin (Ricard).

Church Rock [LOS ANGELES]: *rock,* 3 miles south of Avalon at the southeast end of Santa Catalina Island, and 750 feet offshore (lat. 33°17'50" N, long. 118°19'35" W). Named on Santa Catalina East (1950) 7.5' quadrangle.

Cienaga Campground [LOS ANGELES]: *locality,* 6.25 miles east-northeast of Whitaker Peak in Fish Canyon (1) (lat. 34°37'10" N, long. 118°38'10" W; near SW cor. sec. 12, T 6 N, R 17 W); the place is near Cienaga Spring. Named on Whitaker Peak (1958) 7.5' quadrangle. Called Cienaga Camp on Redrock Mountain (1936) 6' quadrangle.

Cienaga Canyon [LOS ANGELES]: *canyon,* 5 miles long, along Castaic Creek above a point 15 miles southeast of Gorman (lat. 34° 38'15" N, long. 118°40'10" W; sec. 3, T 6 N, R 17

W). Named on Liebre Mountain (1958) 7.5' quadrangle.

Cienaga Spring [LOS ANGELES]: *spring,* 6.25 miles east-northeast of Whitaker Peak (lat. 34°37'05" N, long. 118°38'15" W; sec. 12, T 6 N, R 17 W). Named on Whitaker Peak (1958) 7.5' quadrangle.

Cienega [LOS ANGELES]: *locality,* 5.25 miles west-southwest of Los Angeles city hall along Southern Pacific Railroad (lat. 34°01'15" N, long. 118°19'35" W); the place is at the boundary of Las Cienegas grant. Named on Hollywood (1966) 7.5' quadrangle.

Cienega Camp [VENTURA]: *locality,* 0.5 mile northwest of Santa Paula Peak (lat. 34°26'55" N, long. 119°00'55" W; sec. 7, T 4 N, R 20 W). Named on Santa Paula Peak (1951) 7.5' quadrangle.

Cienega de la San Joaquin: see **Newport Bay** [ORANGE].

Cienega de las Ranas: see **Upper Newport Bay** [ORANGE].

Cienega de San Joaquin: see **Cienega de las Ranas**, under **Upper Newport Bay** [ORANGE].

Cienega o Paso de la Tijera [LOS ANGELES]: *land grant,* at Baldwin Hills. Named on Hollywood (1953) and Inglewood (1952) 7.5' quadrangles. Vicente Sanchez received the land in 1843; Tomas Sanchez and others claimed 4481 acres patented in 1873 (Cowan, p. 28). The term "Cienega" in the name is from natural springs and marsh; the term "Paso de la Tijera" in the name is from the fancied resemblance of two narrow valleys to an open pair of scissors (Hoover, Rensch, and Rensch, p. 162)—*tijera* means "scissors" in Spanish. Postal authorities established La Tijera post office, named for the grant, in 1938 (Salley, p. 119).

Cima Mesa [LOS ANGELES]: *area,* 6 miles west-northwest of Valyermo (lat. 34°27'45" N, long. 117°57'15" W; at W line sec. 5, T 4 N, R 10 W). Named on Juniper Hills (1959) 7.5' quadrangle.

Circle Camp: see **Coldwater Canyon** [LOS ANGELES] (1).

Citrus: see **Covina** [LOS ANGELES].

City Lands of Los Angeles [LOS ANGELES]: *land grant,* at downtown Los Angeles. Named on Hollywood (1953) and Los Angeles (1953) 7.5' quadrangles.

City of Commerce: see **Commerce** [LOS ANGELES].

City of Industry: see **Industry** [LOS ANGELES].

City of Orangethorpe: see **Placentia** [ORANGE].

City Terrace [LOS ANGELES]:
(1) *district,* 3.5 miles east of Los Angeles city hall (lat. 34°03'05" N, long. 118°10'55" W). Named on Los Angeles (1953) 7.5' quadrangle.
(2) *locality,* nearly 4 miles east of Los Angeles city hall along Pacific Electric Railroad (lat.

34°03'35" N, long. 118°10'40" W); the place is northeast of City Terrace (1). Named on Alhambra (1926) 6' quadrangle.

Clair [ORANGE]: *locality,* 4.25 miles south of Buena Park along Southern Pacific Railroad (lat. 33°48'20" N, long. 117°59'05" W). Named on Corona (1902) 30' quadrangle. Postal authorities established Clair post office in 1895 and discontinued it in 1900 (Frickstad, p. 116).

Clamshell Canyon [LOS ANGELES]: *canyon,* drained by a stream that flows 1.5 miles to Santa Anita Wash 4 miles southeast of Mount Wilson (1). lat. 34°10'30" N, long. 118°01'05" W; sec. 15, T 1 N, R 11 W). Named on Mount Wilson (1953) 7.5' quadrangle.

Clamshell Peak [LOS ANGELES]: *peak,* 7 miles northwest of Azusa city hall (lat. 34°12'05" N, long. 117°59'50" W; near E line sec. 2, T 1 N, R 11 W). Named on Azusa (1953) 7.5' quadrangle.

Clapp Canon: see **Soquel Canyon** [ORANGE].

Claremont [LOS ANGELES]: *city,* 3.5 miles northeast of Pomona city hall (lat. 34°05'45" N, long. 117°43' W). Named on Mount Baldy (1967) and Ontario (1967) 7.5' quadrangles. Postal authorities established Claremont post office in 1887 (Frickstad, p. 72), and the city incorporated in 1907. Officials of Pacific Land and Improvement Company had the town platted in 1887 and named it for Claremont, New Hampshire, former home of a director of the company (Gudde, 1949, p. 69). Lankershim Ranch Land and Water Company's (1888) map shows a place called Palomares located along the railroad west of Claremont, between Claremont and Lordsburg.

Clark Gulch [LOS ANGELES]: *canyon,* drained by a stream that flows 1.5 miles to San Gabriel River 5.25 miles west of Mount San Antonio (lat. 34°18' N, long. 117°44'10" W). Named on Mount San Antonio (1955) 7.5' quadrangle. Called Clarks Gulch on Los Angeles County (1935) map.

Clarks Peak [VENTURA]: *peak,* 3.25 miles southwest of Triunfo Pass (lat. 34°05' N, long. 118°57'45" W; sec. 15, T 1 N, R 20 W). Altitude 1965 feet. Named on Triunfo Pass (1950) 7.5' quadrangle. The name commemorates a pioneer family in the neighborhood (Ricard).

Clayton [LOS ANGELES]: *locality,* 2.5 miles south of El Monte city hall along Union Pacific Railroad (lat. 34°01'35" N, long. 118°01'55" W). Named on El Monte (1953) 7.5' quadrangle.

Clear Creek [LOS ANGELES]: *stream,* flows 3.5 miles to Big Tujunga Canyon 3.25 miles south-southeast of Condor Peak (lat. 34°16'55" N, long. 118°11'50" W; near S line sec. 1, T 2 N, R 13 W). Named on Condor Peak (1959) 7.5' quadrangle.

Clear Creek Station [LOS ANGELES]: *locality,* 5.25 miles southeast of Condor Peak (lat.

DURHAM'S PLACE-NAMES

34°16'15" N, long. 118°09'10" W); the place is near the head of Clear Creek. Named on Condor Peak (1959) 7.5' quadrangle.
Clear Spring [LOS ANGELES]: *spring,* 2 miles southeast of the village of Lake Hughes (lat. 34°39'10" N, long. 118°25'20" W; sec. 36, T 7 N, R 15 W). Named on Lake Hughes (1957) 7.5' quadrangle.
Clearwater: see **Clearwater Canyon** [LOS ANGELES]; **Clearwater Station** [LOS ANGELES]; **South Clearwater**, under **Paramount** [LOS ANGELES].
Clearwater Canyon [LOS ANGELES]: *canyon,* drained by a stream that flows 2.25 miles to San Francisquito Canyon 6 miles south of the village of Lake Hughes (lat. 34°35' N, long. 118°27'10" W). Named on Green Valley (1958) 7.5' quadrangle. Thompson's (1921) map shows a place called Clearwater situated near the mouth of Clearwarer Canyon.
Clearwater Station [LOS ANGELES]: *locality,* 4.5 miles southeast of South Gate city hall along Pacific Electric Railroad (lat. 33°54'10" N, long. 118°09'30" W). Named on South Gate (1952) 7.5' quadrangle. Downey (1902) 15' quadrangle shows a community called Clearwater located less than 1 mile southwest of present Clearwater Station (lat. 33°53'35" N, long. 118°09'45" W). Postal authorities established Clearwater post office in 1888 and discontinued it in 1953; the name was from a small lake created by water from artesian wells (Salley, p. 45).
Clef: see **Mount Clef** [VENTURA].
Clement Junction [LOS ANGELES]: *locality,* nearly 3 miles south of Los Angeles city hall along Southern Pacific Railroad (lat. 34°00'50" N, long. 118°14'20" W). Named on Los Angeles (1966) 7.5' quadrangle.
Clifton [LOS ANGELES]: *district,* 1.25 miles south-southeast of Redondo Beach city hall (lat. 33°40'35" N, long. 118°22'45" W). Named on Redondo Beach (1951) and Torrance (1964) 7.5' quadrangles. Called Clifton Heights on Los Angeles County (1935) map.
Clifton Heights: see **Clifton** [LOS ANGELES].
Cloudburst Canyon [LOS ANGELES]:
(1) *canyon,* drained by a stream that flows less than 1 mile to Arroyo Seco 9.5 miles south-southwest of Pacifico Mountain (lat. 34°15'40" N, long. 118°07' W). Named on Chilao Flat (1959) 7.5' quadrangle.
(2) *canyon,* drained by a stream that flows 1.5 miles to Squaw Canyon 2 miles north-north-west of Waterman Mountain (lat. 34° 21'45" N, long. 117°57'15" W; sec. 8, T 3 N, R 10 W). Named on Waterman Mountain (1959) 7.5' quadrangle.
(3) *canyon,* 1.5 miles long, nearly 2 miles southeast of Crystal Lake (lat. 34°18'05" N, long. 117°49'25" W). Named on Crystal Lake (1958) 7.5' quadrangle.
Cloudburst Summit [LOS ANGELES]: *pass,* 1 mile north of Waterman Mountain (lat.

34°21'05" N, long. 117°56' W; near N line sec. 16, T 3 N, R 10 W); the pass is at the head of Cloudburst Canyon (2). Named on Waterman Mountain (1959) 7.5' quadrangle.
Coal Canyon [ORANGE]: *canyon,* drained by a stream that flows 2.25 miles to Santa Ana Canyon 2.5 miles northwest of Sierra Peak (lat. 33°52'20" N, long. 117°41'15" W). Named on Black Star Canyon (1967) 7.5' quadrangle. Corona (1942) 15' quadrangle has the name "Coal Cr." for the stream in the canyon.
Coal Canyon: see **Carbon Canyon** [LOS ANGELES].
Coal Creek: see **Coal Canyon** [ORANGE].
Coarse Gold Canyon [LOS ANGELES]: *canyon,* drained by a stream that flows nearly 1.5 miles to Bouquet Canyon 4.5 miles north of Solemint (lat. 34°25' N, long. 118°27'15" W; sec. 21, T 4 N, R 15 W). Named on Mint Canyon (1960) 7.5' quadrangle.
Coast Guard Beach: see **San Nicolas Island** [VENTURA].
Cobal Canyon [LOS ANGELES]: *canyon,* drained by a stream that flows 1.25 miles to lowlands 6.5 miles north-northeast of Pomona city hall (lat. 34°08'35" N, long. 117°42'30" W; sec. 27, T 1 N, R 8 W). Named on Mount Baldy (1954) 7.5' quadrangle.
Cobblestone Mountain [VENTURA]: *peak,* 14 miles north of Fillmore (lat. 34°36'30" N, long. 118°52' W; sec. 14, T 6 N, R 19 W). Altitude 6730 feet. Named on Cobblestone Mountain (1958) 7.5' quadrangle.
Cobblestone Spring [VENTURA]: *spring,* 0.5 mile east of Cobblestone Mountain (lat. 34°36'25" N, long. 118°51'20" W; at E line sec. 14, T 6 N, R 19 E). Named on Cobblestone Mountain (1958) 7.5' quadrangle.
Coche Canyon [VENTURA]: *canyon,* drained by a stream that flows 3.5 miles to Cañada Larga nearly 8 miles northwest of Saticoy (lat. 34°21'45" N, long. 119°14'50" W). Named on Matilija (1952), Ojai (1952), and Saticoy (1951) 7.5' quadrangles.
Cogswell Reservoir [LOS ANGELES]: *lake,* behind a dam on West Fork San Gabriel River 8 miles north-northwest of Azusa city hall (lat. 34°14'40" N, long. 117°57'50" W). Named on Azusa (1953) 7.5' quadrangle.
Colby Canyon [LOS ANGELES]: *canyon,* drained by a stream that flows nearly 2 miles to Arroyo Seco 6 miles southeast of Condor Peak (lat. 34°15'55" N, long. 118°08'35" W). Named on Chilao Flat (1959) and Condor Peak (1959) 7.5' quadrangles.
Cold Brook: see **Coldbrook Camp** [LOS ANGELES].
Coldbrook Camp [LOS ANGELES]: *locality,* 2 miles south of Crystal Lake (lat. 34°17'40" N, long. 117°50'20" W); the place is at the mouth of Coldbrook Creek. Named on Camp Rincon (1940) 6' quadrangle. Postal authorities established Cold Brook post office in

1911 and discontinued it in 1916; the name was from Cold Brook Camp (Salley, p. 47). R.W. Dawson took over management of a resort at the place in 1904 and named it Coldbrook Camp; the site had the early name "Sycamore Flats" (Robinson, J.W., 1983, p. 57, 92).

Coldbrook Creek [LOS ANGELES]: *stream,* flows less than 2 miles to join Soldier Creek and form North Fork San Gabriel River 2 miles south of Crystal Lake (lat. 34°17'25" N, long. 117°50'20" W). Named on Crystal Lake (1958) 7.5' quadrangle.

Cold Canyon [LOS ANGELES]: *canyon,* drained by a stream that flows 2.5 miles to Salt Creek 9 miles southeast of Gorman (lat. 34° 41'55" N, long. 118°42'20" W; sec. 17, T 7 S, R 17 W). Named on Liebre Mountain (1958) 7.5' quadrangle.

Cold Creek [LOS ANGELES]: *stream,* flows 4.5 miles to Malibu Creek 3.5 miles north-northwest of Malibu Point (lat. 34°04'40" N, long. 118°42'05" W; sec. 18, T 1 S, R 17 W). Named on Malibu Beach (1951) 7.5' quadrangle.

Cold Spring Canyon [ORANGE]: *canyon,* drained by a stream that flows 4.5 miles to San Juan Creek 10 miles northeast of San Juan Capistrano (lat. 33°35'10" N, long. 117°31'10" W; near W line sec. 4, T 7 S, R 6 W). Named on Cañada Gobernadora (1968) and Santiago Peak (1954) 7.5' quadrangles.

Cold Springs Canyon [LOS ANGELES]: *canyon,* drained by a stream that flows 1.5 miles to Fish Canyon (2) 5 miles north-northwest of Azusa city hall (lat. 34°12' N, long. 117°56'30" W; near W line sec. 4, T 1 N, R 10 W). Named on Azusa (1953) 7.5' quadrangle.

Coldwater Canyon [LOS ANGELES]:
(1) *canyon,* drained by a stream that flows 1.25 miles to Big Tujunga Canyon 7 miles southwest of Pacifico Mountain (lat. 34° 18'35" N, long. 118°06'55" W). Named on Chilao Flat (1959) 7.5' quadrangle. Los Angeles County (1935) map shows a place called Circle Camp located about 0.25 mile north of the mouth of Coldwater Canyon (1) in Big Tujunga Canyon.
(2) *canyon,* drained by a stream that flows nearly 7 miles to Cattle Canyon 12.5 miles north of Pomona city hall (lat. 34°14'05" N, long. 117°43'40" W). Named on Mount Baldy (1954) and Mount San Antonio (1955) 7.5' quadrangles.
(3) *canyon,* 2 miles long, 2.5 miles north of Beverly Hills city hall (lat. 34°06'30" N, long. 118°24'15" W). Named on Beverly Hills (1950) 7.5' quadrangle.

Coldwater Canyon [VENTURA]: *canyon,* drained by a stream that flows 2 miles to Sespe Creek 5 miles north-northwest of Fillmore (lat. 34°27'55" N, long. 118°56'35" W; near N line sec. 2, T 4 N, R 20 W). Named on Fillmore (1951) 7.5' quadrangle.

Coldwater Fork [VENTURA]: *stream,* flows 3.5 miles to Hot Springs Canyon 2.5 miles north-northwest of Devils Heart Peak (lat. 34°34'55" N, long. 118°59'25" W; sec. 27, T 6 N, R 20 W). Named on Devils Heart Peak (1943) 7.5' quadrangle.

Colegrove [LOS ANGELES]: *district,* 5.5 miles west-northwest of present Los Angeles city hall (lat. 34°05'30" N, long. 118°19'45" W). Named on Santa Monica (1902) 15' quadrangle. Postal authorities established Colegrove post office in 1888 and discontinued it in 1917; the name was for Seward Cole, first postmaster and promoter of the community (Salley, p. 47). A spa called Radium Sulphur Spring was situated near Colegrove (Merrill, 1919, p. 508); the place, which also was called Hollywood Spa, obtained water from an old oil test well, probably drilled in 1905 (Berkstresser, p. A-7).

Colima [LOS ANGELES]: *locality,* 2.25 miles south-southeast of Whittier city hall along Southern Pacific Railroad (lat. 33°56'40" N, long. 118°00'55" W). Named on Whittier (1965) 7.5' quadrangle.

College Settlement: see **Downey** [LOS ANGELES].

Collins Island [ORANGE]: *island,* 325 feet long, nearly 7 miles east-southeast of Huntington Beach civic center in Newport Bay at the northwest tip of Balboa Island (lat. 33°36'30" N, long. 117°53'55" W). Named on Newport Beach (1965) 7.5' quadrangle. The name commemorates W.S. Collins, who created this feature and nearby Balboa Island; Collins Island also was called Cagney Island for the movie star who later owned it (Gleason, p. 97).

Colonia Independencia [ORANGE]: *locality,* 4.25 miles south-southeast of present Buena Park civic center (lat. 33°48'20" N, long. 117°58'05" W; near S line sec. 19, T 4 S, R 10 W). Named on Anaheim (1950) 7.5' quadrangle.

Colonia Juarez [ORANGE]: *locality,* 4.5 miles northeast of present Huntington Beach civic center (lat. 33°42'50" N, long. 117°56'45" W; sec. 29, T 5 S, R 10 W). Named on Newport Beach (1951) 7.5' quadrangle.

Colonia Manzanillo [ORANGE]: *locality,* 8 miles south-southeast of present Buena Park civic center (lat. 33°45'30" N, long. 117°56'05" W; near NW cor. sec. 9, T 5 S, R 10 W). Named on Anaheim (1950) 7.5' quadrangle.

Colorado Lagoon [LOS ANGELES]: *lake,* 1750 feet long, 3.25 miles east of Long Beach city hall (lat. 33°46'15" N, long. 118°08' W). Named on Long Beach (1964) 7.5' quadrangle.

Coltrell Flat [VENTURA]: *area,* 2.5 miles north-northwest of Devils Heart Peak along Sespe Creek (lat. 34°34'40" N, long. 118°59'45" W; at SW cor. sec. 27, T 6 N, R

20 W). Named on Devils Heart Peak (1943) 7.5' quadrangle. United States Board on Geographic Names (1990, p. 7) approved the name "Cottriel Flat" for the feature, and pointed out that the name is for George W. Cottriel, who patented land at the place in 1891.

Columbine Spring [LOS ANGELES]: *spring,* 2.5 miles north-northwest of Mount San Antonio (lat. 34°19'20" N, long. 117°40' W; near N line sec. 25, T 3 N, R 8 W). Named on Mount San Antonio (1955) 7.5' quadrangle.

Comfort: see **Camp Comfort** [VENTURA]; **Old Point Comfort** [LOS ANGELES].

Commerce [LOS ANGELES]: *town,* 6 miles southeast of Los Angeles city hall (lat. 34°00'05" N, long. 118°09'15" W). Named on Los Angeles (1966) and South Gate (1964) 7.5' quadrangles. Postal authorities established City of Commerce post office there in 1963 (Salley, p. 44). The place is an industrial enclave that incorporated in 1960.

Community Center: see **Simi Valley** [VENTURA] (2).

Como [ORANGE]: *locality,* 5.25 miles southeast of Santa Ana city hall along Atchison Topeka and Santa Fe Railroad (lat. 33°41'55" N, long. 117°47'30" W). Named on Tustin (1965) 7.5' quadrangle.

Compton [LOS ANGELES]: *city,* 4.25 miles south-southwest of South Gate (lat. 33°53'40" N, long. 118°13'25" W). Named on Inglewood (1952) and South Gate (1952) 7.5' quadrangles. Postal authorities established Compton post office in 1869 (Frickstad, p. 72), and the city incorporated in 1888. The Reverend G.D. Compton started the community, first called Comptonville, in 1869 under the sponsorship of the Methodist Church (Hanna, p. 70). Lankershim Ranch Land and Water Company's (1888) map shows a place called Broadacres Gardens located just southeast of Compton.

Compton Creek [LOS ANGELES]: *stream,* flows 8.5 miles to Los Angeles River 5 miles north of Long Beach city hall (lat. 33°50'30" N, long. 118°12'10" W). Named on Inglewood (1952) and South Gate (1952) 7.5' quadrangles. Before 1938, when part of the watercourse was paved and joined to Los Angeles River, the creek flowed to San Pedro Bay through Wilmington Lagoon (Poland, Garrett, and Sinnott, p. 21).

Comptonville: see **Compton** [LOS ANGELES].

Condor Canyon [LOS ANGELES]: *canyon,* drained by a stream that flows 1.25 miles to Trail Canyon 5.5 miles northeast of Sunland (lat. 34°19'30" N, long. 118°15'15" W); the canyon heads near Condor Peak. Named on Condor Peak (1959) and Sunland (1953) 7.5' quadrangles.

Condor Peak [LOS ANGELES]: *peak,* 19 miles north of Los Angeles city hall (lat. 34°19'30" N, long. 118°13'10" W). Named on Condor Peak (1959) 7.5' quadrangle.

Conejo Creek [VENTURA]: *stream,* flows 19 miles to Calleguas Creek 2 miles south-south-east of Camarillo (lat. 34°11'20" N, long. 119°01'20" W). Named on Camarillo (1950) and Newbury Park (1951) 7.5' quadrangles. The feature is called Arroyo Conejo above Santa Rosa Valley on Newbury Park (1951) and Thousand Oaks (1952) 7.5' quadrangles. North Fork Arroyo Conejo enters 2 miles north-northwest of Newbury Park; it is 6.25 miles long and is named on Newbury Park (1951) 7.5' quadrangle. South Branch Arroyo Conejo enters from the south 0.5 mile northeast of Newbury Park; it is 6.25 miles long—including an interruption of the stream course through Conejo Valley—and is named on Newbury Park (1951) 7.5' quadrangle.

Conejo Mountain [VENTURA]: *peak,* 4.25 miles west of Newbury Park (lat. 34°11'15" N, long. 118°59' W); the peak is 1.5 miles west of Conejo Valley. Altitude 1814 feet. Named on Newbury Park (1951) 7.5' quadrangle.

Conejo Valley [VENTURA]: *valley,* west of Newbury Park (lat. 34° 11' N, long. 118°56' W); the feature is on El Conejo grant. Named on Newbury Park (1951) 7.5' quadrangle.

Coney Island [ORANGE]: *hill,* nearly 7 miles east-southeast of Huntington Beach civic center along Newport Bay (lat. 33°37'10" N, long. 117°53'30" W). Named on Newport Beach (1965) 7.5' quadrangle. Newport Beach (1951) 7.5' quadrangle shows the feature surrounded by marsh and water.

Conservation Camp 37 [LOS ANGELES]: *locality,* 6.25 miles south-southwest of Valyermo (lat. 34°21'15" N, long. 117°52'40" W; near S line sec. 12, T 3 N, R 10 W). Named on Waterman Mountain (1959) 7.5' quadrangle.

Contract Point [LOS ANGELES]: *relief feature,* 4.5 miles north-northeast of downtown San Fernando (lat. 34°20'30" N, long. 118° 24'25" W; sec. 13, T 3 N, R 15 W). Named on San Fernando (1966, photorevised 1972) 7.5' quadrangle.

Cooks Canyon [LOS ANGELES]: *canyon,* 1 mile long, 3.5 miles east of Sunland (lat. 34°15'25" N, long. 118°15'05" W; mainly in sec. 16, T 2 N, R 13 W). Named on Condor Peak (1959) and Sunland (1953) 7.5' quadrangles. Called Cook Cany. on Los Angeles County (1935) map.

Coon Canyon: see **Fern Canyon** [LOS ANGELES] (1).

Cooper Canyon [LOS ANGELES]: *canyon,* drained by a stream that flows 2.5 miles to Little Rock Creek 2.5 miles northeast of Waterman Mountain (lat. 34°21'45" N, long. 117°54' W; sec. 11, T 3 N, R 10 W). Named on Waterman Mountain (1959) 7.5' quadrangle. The name commemorates brothers Ike Cooper and Tom Cooper, hunters who favored the canyon (Robinson, J.W., 1977, p. 189).

Cooper Canyon [VENTURA]: *canyon,* 1 mile

long, opens into Santa Ana Valley 5 miles west of the town of Ojai (lat. 34°26'15" N, long. 119°19'50" W). Named on Matilija (1952) 7.5' quadrangle. Joseph Harrison Cooper once owned the canyon (Ricard).

Copter Ridge [LOS ANGELES]: *ridge,* south-southeast-trending, 3 miles long, 3.25 miles east of Crystal Lake (lat. 34°19'30" N, long. 117°47'30" W) Named on Crystal Lake (1958) 7.5' quadrangle.

Cordero: see **Huntington Beach** [ORANGE].

Cordorniz: see **Garden Grove** [ORANGE].

Cordova Canyon: see **Elderberry Canyon** [LOS ANGELES].

Cornell [LOS ANGELES]: *village,* 8 miles north of Point Dume in Triunfo Canyon (lat. 34°06'50" N, long. 118°46'35" W; sec. 4, T 1 S, R 18 W). Named on Point Dume (1951) 7.5' quadrangle.

Cornell: see **Seminole Hot Springs** [LOS ANGELES].

Corona del Mar [ORANGE]: *district,* 6.25 miles west-northwest of Laguna Beach city hall in Newport Beach (lat. 33°35'30" N, long. 117°52'15" W). Named on Laguna Beach (1965) and Newport Beach (1965) 7.5' quadrangles. Postal authorities established Corona Del Mar (with a capital "D") post office in 1926, moved it about 0.25 mile northwest in 1940, moved it 0.5 mile southeast in 1941, and changed the name to Corona del Mar (with a lower-case "d") in 1950 (Salley, p. 50). George E. Hart developed and named the place in 1904; F.D. Cornell Company acquired it in 1915 and named it Balboa Palisades, but the old name was restored (Gudde, 1949, p. 79). The place was called Pacific Palisades for a short time after a hotel called Palisades Inn was built there (Meadows, p. 109).

Corral Beach [LOS ANGELES]: *beach,* 3 miles west of Malibu Point along the coast (lat. 34°02' N, long. 118°44' W); the beach is at the mouth of Corral Canyon. Named on Malibu Beach (1951) 7.5' quadrangle.

Corral Canyon [LOS ANGELES]: *canyon,* drained by a stream that flows to the sea 3 miles west of Malibu Point (lat. 34°02' N, long. 118°44' W). Named on Malibu Beach (1951) 7.5' quadrangle.

Corral Canyon [VENTURA]: *canyon,* drained by a stream that flows 5.5 miles to Cuyama River 9 miles northwest of Reyes Peak (lat. 34°43'30" N, long. 119°23'15" W). Named on Apache Canyon (1943), Rancho Nuevo Creek (1943), and Reyes Peak (1943) 7.5' quadrangles.

Corral Harbor: see **San Nicolas Island** [VENTURA].

Corriganville [VENTURA]: *locality,* 1.25 miles west-southwest of Santa Susana Pass (lat. 34°15'50" N, long. 118°39'10" W). Named on Santa Susana (1951) 7.5' quadrangle. Ray "Crash" Corrigan made western movies at the place (Ricard).

Cortelyou Spring [LOS ANGELES]: *spring,* 2.5 miles north of Crystal Lake (lat. 34°21'20" N; long. 117°50'35" W; sec. 8, T 3 N, R 9 W). Named on Crystal Lake (1958) 7.5' quadrangle.

Cortes: see **Cape Cortes** [LOS ANGELES].

Corvallis: see **Norwalk** [LOS ANGELES].

Costa Mesa [ORANGE]: *city,* 4.5 miles east-southeast of Huntington Beach civic center (lat. 33°38'35" N, long. 117°55'35" W). Named on Newport Beach (1965) and Tustin (1965) 7.5' quadrangles. Postal authorities established Harper post office 3 miles northeast of Newport Beach post office in 1909 and changed the name to Costa Mesa in 1920 (Salley, p. 93). The name "Harper" was for a local rancher; Alice Plummer's entry "Costa Mesa" won a contest held in 1915 to choose a new name for the community (Hanna, p. 75).

Cota [LOS ANGELES]: *locality,* 5 miles north of Long Beach city hall along a railroad (lat. 33°50'20" N, long. 118°12'20" W). Named on Long Beach (1949) 7.5' quadrangle.

Cottonwood Campground [LOS ANGELES]: *locality,* 5 miles southeast of Burnt Peak in Elizabeth Lake Canyon (lat. 34°38'25" N, long. 118°30'15" W). Named on Burnt Peak (1958) 7.5' quadrangle.

Cottonwood Canyon [LOS ANGELES]:
(1) *canyon,* drained by a stream that flows 1 mile to Little Tujunga Canyon 3.5 miles north-northwest of Sunland (lat. 34°18'10" N, long. 118°20'45" W; sec. 33, T 3 N, R 14 W). Named on Sunland (1966) 7.5' quadrangle.
(2) *canyon,* drained by a stream that flows 5.25 miles to the sea 2.5 miles west of Mount Banning on Santa Catalina Island (lat. 33°22'35" N, long. 118°28'40" W). Named on Santa Catalina North (1950) 7.5' quadrangle.

Cottonwood Creek: see **Little Cottonwood Creek**, under **Oso Canyon** [LOS ANGELES].

Cottonwood Glen [LOS ANGELES]: *locality,* 3.5 miles north-northwest of Sunland in Little Tujunga Canyon (lat. 34°18'05" N, long. 118°20'50" W; sec. 33, T 3 N, R 14 W); the place is at the mouth of Cottonwood Canyon (1). Named on Sunland (1953) 7.5' quadrangle.

Cottriel Flat: see **Coltrell Flat** [VENTURA].

Couger Canyon [LOS ANGELES]: *canyon,* nearly 1 mile long, opens into Pacoima Canyon 5 miles north-northeast of downtown San Fernando (lat. 34°20'35" N, long. 118°23'35" W; sec. 18, T 3 N, R 14 W). Named on San Fernando (1953) 7.5' quadrangle.

County Farm: see **Poor Farm Station** [LOS ANGELES].

Cove Campground [VENTURA]: *locality,* 4.5 miles south-southeast of Cobblestone Mountain along Agua Blanca Creek (lat. 34°33'10" N, long. 118°49'35" W). Named on Cobblestone Mountain (1958) 7.5' quadrangle.

Covina [LOS ANGELES]: *city,* 4 miles east of Baldwin Park city hall (lat. 34°05'15" N, long. 117°53'20" W). Named on Baldwin Park (1966) and San Dimas (1966) 7.5' quadrangles. Postal authorities established Covina post office in 1887 (Frickstad, p. 72), and the city incorporated in 1901. J.S. Phillips, landowner in the neighborhood, and Fred Eaton, engineer and surveyor, named the community in 1882 for its covelike setting and the large number of abandoned grape vines there (Hanna, p. 75-76). Postal authorities established Citrus post office at the site of present Covina in 1878 and discontinued in 1887 (Salley, p. 44). They established Centro post office 1.25 miles north of Citrus post office in 1885, changed the name to Gladstone in 1888, and discontinued it in 1892—an admirer of the British Prime Minister was responsible for the name "Gladstone" (Salley, p. 41, 85).

Covina: see **West Covina** [LOS ANGELES].

Cowan Heights [ORANGE]: *locality,* 4.5 miles east-southeast of Orange city hall (lat. 33°46'30" N, long. 117°46'15" W). Named on Orange (1964) 7.5' quadrangle.

Cow Canyon [LOS ANGELES]: *canyon,* drained by a stream that flows 4.25 miles to Cattle Canyon 12.5 miles north of Pomona city hall (lat. 34°13'45" N, long. 117°43'15" W). Named on Mount Baldy (1954) 7.5' quadrangle.

Cow Canyon Saddle [LOS ANGELES]: *pass,* 12 miles north-northeast of Pomona city hall (lat. 34°13'40" N, long. 117°40'10" W; sec. 25, T 2 N, R 8 W); the pass is at the head of Cow Canyon. Named on Mount Baldy (1954) 7.5' quadrangle.

Cowhead Potrero [VENTURA]: *area,* 16 miles north of Reyes Peak (lat. 34°52'15" N, long. 119°17'10" W; at N line sec. 12, T 9 N, R 23 W). Named on Apache Canyon (1943) 7.5' quadrangle.

Cow Spring [VENTURA]: *spring,* 4 miles east-northeast of Devils Heart Peak (lat. 34°33'35" N, long. 119°54'25" W). Named on Devils Heart Peak (1943) 7.5' quadrangle.

Cow Spring Canyon [LOS ANGELES]: *canyon,* drained by a stream that flows 5 miles to lowlands 12 miles east of Gorman (lat. 34°46'45" N, long. 118°38'10" W; sec. 13, T 8 N, R 17 W). Named on La Liebre Ranch (1965) and Liebre Mountain (1958) 7.5' quadrangles. Called Cow Springs Canyon on Liebre (1938) 6' quadrangle, but United States Board on Geographic Names (1959, p. 6) rejected this form of the name.

Coyote Bluff [ORANGE]: *relief feature,* nearly 3 miles south-southeast of San Juan Capistrano along Prima Deshecha Canyon (lat. 33°27'50" N, long. 117°38'30" W; on E line sec. 19, T 8 S, R 7 W). Named on Dana Point (1968) 7.5' quadrangle.

Coyote Canyon [LOS ANGELES]:
(1) *canyon,* drained by a stream that flows 2.25 miles to Cañada de Los Alamos 7.25 miles south-southeast of Gorman (lat. 34°41'40" N, long. 118°47'30" W); near S line sec. 16, T 7 N, R 18 W). Named on Black Mountain (1958) 7.5' quadrangle.
(2) *canyon,* drained by a stream that flows nearly 2 miles to Sand Canyon (2) 3.5 miles southeast of Solemint (lat. 34°22'45" N, long. 118°24'30" W; near NW cor. sec. 1, T 3 N, R 15 W). Named on Mint Canyon (1960) and San Fernando (1953) 7.5' quadrangles.

Coyote Canyon [ORANGE]: *canyon,* 2.5 miles long, opens into the canyon of Bonita Creek 8 miles south of Santa Ana city hall (lat. 33°37'50" N, long. 117°50'30" W). Named on Laguna Beach (1965) and Tustin (1965) 7.5' quadrangles. On Tustin (1935) 7.5' quadrangle, the name "Coyote Creek" applies to present Bonita Creek below the mouth of present Coyote Canyon.

Coyote Canyon [VENTURA]: *canyon,* drained by a stream that flows 6.25 miles to Arroyo Las Posas 6.5 miles west-southwest of Moorpark (lat. 34°15'30" N, long. 118°59'15" W). Named on Moorpark (1951) and Santa Paula (1951) 7.5' quadrangles.

Coyote Creek [LOS ANGELES-ORANGE]: *stream,* heads in Orange County and flows 13 miles in and out of Orange County across Los Angeles-Orange county line to San Gabriel River 6.5 miles east-northeast of Long Beach city hall in Los Angeles County (lat. 33° 47'40" N, long. 118°05'20" W; sec. 25, T 4 S, R 12 W). Named on La Habra (1952), Los Alamitos (1964), and Whittier (1965) 7.5' quadrangles. Los Alamitos (1950) 7.5' quadrangle shows the creek formed by the confluence of East Fork and Middle Fork 7 miles above the mouth of the stream—on this map the present main stream is called East Fork, and present La Cañada Verde Creek is called West Fork. On Whittier (1949) 7.5' quadrangle, the name "Coyote Creek" applies to present Brea Creek.

Coyote Creek [VENTURA]: *stream,* flows nearly 15 miles to Ventura River 5.25 miles north-northwest of Ventura (lat. 34°21'15" N, long. 119°18'35" W). Named on Matilija (1952), Ventura (1951), and White Ledge Peak (1952) 7.5' quadrangles. East Fork enters 3.5 miles south-southeast of White Ledge Peak; it is 2.5 miles long and is named on Matilija (1952) and White Ledge Peak (1952) 7.5' quadrangles. West Fork enters from the southwest 3.25 miles south of White Ledge Peak; it is nearly 3 miles long and is named on White Ledge Peak (1952) 7.5' quadrangle.

Coyote Creek: see **Bonita Creek** [ORANGE].

Coyote Flat [LOS ANGELES]: *area,* nearly 9 miles northeast of Glendora city hall along San Gabriel River (lat. 34°14'05" N, long. 117°46' W). Named on Glendora (1966) 7.5' quadrangle.

Coyote Hills: see **East Coyote Hills** [ORANGE]; **West Coyote Hills** [ORANGE].

Coyote Pass [LOS ANGELES]: *canyons,* two, that provide a passage through highlands in Monterey Park 5.25 miles east of Los Angeles city hall (lat. 34°03'15" N, long. 118°08'50" W). Named on Los Angeles (1953) 7.5' quadrangle. The feature also is called Monterey Pass (Gudde, 1949, p. 223).

Cozy Dell Canyon [VENTURA]: *canyon,* drained by a stream that flows 3.25 miles to Ojai Valley nearly 3 miles west-northwest of the town of Ojai (lat. 34°28'05" N, long. 119°17'05" W; near SE cor. sec. 33, T 5 N, R 23 W). Named on Matilija (1952) 7.5' quadrangle.

Crab Hollow Diggings: see **San Gabriel River** [LOS ANGELES].

Craig Beach: see **Mills Landing** [LOS ANGELES].

Craig Canyon [LOS ANGELES]: *canyon,* 0.5 mile long, nearly 2 miles north-northwest of Burbank city hall (lat. 34°12'25" N, long. 118°19' W). Named on Burbank (1953) 7.5' quadrangle.

Craig Spring [LOS ANGELES]: *spring,* 4 miles southwest of the village of Lake Hughes in San Francisquito Canyon (lat. 34°37'40" N, long. 118°23'50" W; near NE cor. sec. 7, T 6 N, R 14 W). Named on Lake Hughes (1957) 7.5' quadrangle.

Crane Canyon [LOS ANGELES]: *canyon,* 2 miles long, 2 miles north-northeast of Gorman on Los Angeles-Kern county line (lat. 34°49'05" N, long. 118°50'10" W; near NW cor. sec. 6, T 8 N, R 18 W). Named on Lebec (1958) 7.5' quadrangle.

Crane Lake: see **Quail Lake** [LOS ANGELES].

Crater Camp [LOS ANGELES]: *locality,* 3.5 miles north-northwest of Malibu Point (lat. 34°04'45" N, long. 118°41'55" W; sec. 18, T 1 S, R 17 W). Named on Malibu Beach (1951) 7.5' quadrangle.

Crater Lake: see **Echo Lake** [LOS ANGELES].

Crawfish George's: see **San Pedro** [LOS ANGELES] (2).

Crawfish Rock [ORANGE]: *rock,* 3.5 miles south-southwest of San Juan Capistrano, and 0.5 mile offshore (lat. 33°27'15" N, long. 117°41'15" W). Named on Dana Point (1968) 7.5' quadrangle.

Crawford Canyon [ORANGE]: *canyon,* less than 1 mile long, 3.25 miles east of Orange city hall (lat. 33°47' N, long. 117°47'40" W). Named on Orange (1964) 7.5' quadrangle.

Crescent [LOS ANGELES]: *district,* 8 miles west-northwest of present Los Angeles city hall (lat. 34°05'25" N, long. 118°22'25" W). Named on Hollywood (1926) 6' quadrangle.

Crescent Bay [ORANGE]: *embayment,* 1.25 miles west of Laguna Beach city hall along the coast (lat. 33°32'45" N, long. 117°48'05" W). Named on Laguna Beach (1965) 7.5' quadrangle.

Cristianitos Canyon [ORANGE]: *canyon,* 4.25 miles long, along Cristianitos Creek above a

point 3 miles northeast of San Clemente civic center (lat. 33°27'15" N, long. 117°34'05" W). Named on Cañada Gobernadora (1968) and San Clemente (1968) 7.5' quadrangles.

Cristianitos Creek [ORANGE]: *stream,* heads in Orange County and flows 6.5 miles to San Mateo Creek 2.25 miles east-southeast of San Clemente civic center in San Diego County (lat. 33°25'10" N, long. 117°34'10" W; sec. 1, T 9 S, R 7 W). Named on San Clemente (1968) 7.5' quadrangle. The name recalls two little Indian girls who were ill and who became Christians when the padres with Portola baptized them at the place in 1769—*Cristianitos* means "little Christians" in Spanish (Hoover, Rensch, and Rensch, p. 259).

Croswell Springs: see **Lovejoy Springs** [LOS ANGELES].

Crow Canyon [ORANGE]: *canyon,* drained by a stream that flows 4.25 miles to Bell Canyon 8 miles northeast of San Juan Capistrano (lat. 33°35' N, long. 117°34'05" W; near N line sec. 12, T 7 S, R 7 W). Named on Cañada Gobernadora (1968) and Santiago Peak (1954) 7.5' quadrangles.

Crow Spring [ORANGE]: *spring,* 11 miles northeast of San Juan Capistrano (lat. 33°37'05" N, long. 117°32' W; sec. 29, T 6 S, R 6 W); the spring is in Crow Canyon. Named on Cañada Gobernadora (1968) 7.5' quadrangle.

Crushton [LOS ANGELES]: *locality,* less than 1 mile northeast of Baldwin Park city hall along Pacific Electric Railroad (lat. 34°05'30" N, long. 117°57' W; on N line sec. 17, T 1 S, R 10 W). Named on Baldwin Park (1953) 7.5' quadrangle.

Cruthers Creek [LOS ANGELES]: *stream,* flows 4.5 miles to Holmes Creek 2.25 west of Valyermo (lat. 34°26'40" W; long. 117°53'20" W; near SE cor. sec. 11, T 4 N, R 10 W). Named on Juniper Hills (1959) 7.5' quadrangle. On Los Angeles County (1935) map, present Holmes Creek is called East Fork Cruthers Creek. The same map shows a feature called Moss Spring located hear the head of Cruthers Creek (sec. 35, T 4 N, R 10 W).

Cruzan Canyon: see **Cruzan Mesa** [LOS ANGELES].

Cruzan Mesa [LOS ANGELES]: *area,* 3.25 miles north-northeast of Solemint (lat. 34°27'45" N, long. 118°26'25" W; mainly in sec. 3, T 4 N, R 15 W). Named on Mint Canyon (1960) 7.5' quadrangle. Los Angeles County (1935) map has the name "Cruzan Canyon" for a feature, 1.25 miles long, that opens into Mint Canyon (1) 1 mile east-southeast of present Cruzan Mesa.

Crystal Cove [ORANGE]: *locality,* 4 miles west-northwest of Laguna Beach city hall along the coast (lat. 33°34'30" N, long. 117°50'25" W). Named on Laguna Beach (1965) 7.5' quadrangle.

Crystal Lake [LOS ANGELES]: *lake,* 650 feet long, 5 miles east-southeast of Waterman Mountain (lat. 34°19'10" W; long. 117°50'45" W). Named on Crystal Lake (1958) 7.5' quadrangle. R.W. Dawson visited the lake in 1876 and laid claim to it; Dawson was a pioneer settler at Sycamore Flat (2), and apparently he gave the name "Sycamore Lake" to the feature (Robinson, J.W., 1983, p. 105).

Crystal Spring [LOS ANGELES]: *spring,* nearly 3 miles west of Mount Wilson (1) (lat. 34°13'30" N, long. 118°06'35" W). Named on Pasadena (1900) 15' quadrangle. Water from the spring was bottled for table use (Waring, p. 367).

Cuati: see Prospero Tract [LOS ANGELES].

Cudahy [LOS ANGELES]: *town,* 1.25 miles east-southeast of South Gate city hall (lat. 33°57'45" N, long. 118°10'45" W). Named on South Gate (1964) 7.5' quadrangle. Postal authorities established Cudahy post office in 1930; the name was for Peter Cudahy, who settled at the place and founded Cudahy Meat Packing Company (Salley, p. 53). The town incorporated in 1960. Bell (1936) 6' quadrangle shows Cudahy Sta. located along the railroad in the town (lat. 33°57'20" N, long. 118°11' W).

Cudahy Station: see Cudahy [LOS ANGELES].

Cuddy Peak: see Frazier Mountain [VENTURA].

Culver: see Culver City [LOS ANGELES].

Culver City [LOS ANGELES]: *city,* 3.5 miles south of Beverly Hills city hall (lat. 34°01'15" N, long. 118°23'45" W). Named on Beverly Hills (1950), Hollywood (1953), and Venice (1950) 7.5' quadrangles. Called Culver on Sawtelle (1925) 6' quadrangle. Postal authorities established Culver City post office in 1915 (Frickstad, p. 72), and the city incorporated in 1917. T. McCarey named the place for Harry H. Culver when Culver Investment Company announced plans for the community in 1913 (Hanna, p. 79).

Culver Garden [LOS ANGELES]: *district,* 7.5 miles north of present Manhattan Beach city hall (lat. 33°59'45" N, long. 118°25'20" W). Named on Venice (1924) 6' quadrangle.

Culver Junction [LOS ANGELES]: *locality,* 3 miles south of Beverly Hills city hall along Southern Pacific Railroad (lat. 34°01'40" N, long. 118°23'20" W); a branch rail line to Culver City joins the main rail line at the place. Named on Beverly Hills (1966) 7.5' quadrangle.

Cumorah Crest: see Camp Cumorah Crest [LOS ANGELES].

Cunnane Barranca: see Prince Barranca [VENTURA].

Cunningham Canyon [LOS ANGELES]. *canyon,* drained by a stream that flows less than 1 mile to Verdugo Wash 4 miles northeast of Burbank city hall (lat. 34°13'25" N, long.

118°15'25" W). Named on Burbank (1966) 7.5' quadrangle.

Cuyama River [VENTURA]: *stream,* formed by the confluence of Beartrap Creek and Alamo Creek (2), flows 12.5 miles to Santa Barbara County 14 miles northwest of Reyes Peak (lat. 34°47' N, long. 119°26'30" W; sec. 17, T 8 N, R 24 W). Named on Cuyama Peak (1943), Rancho Nuevo Creek (1943), and Reyes Peak (1943) 7.5' quadrangles. Called Guyamas River on Goddard's (1857) map, Rio S. Maria on Parke's (1854-1855) map, and Santa Maria River on California Mining Bureau's (1909a) map.

Cypave [LOS ANGELES]. *locality,* 3.5 miles south-southeast of present Inglewood city hall along Pacific Electric Railroad (lat. 33° 55'10" N, long. 118°19'35" W). Named on Inglewood (1924) 6' quadrangle.

Cypress [ORANGE]: *city,* 3.5 miles southwest of Buena Park civic center (lat. 33°49'15" N, long. 118°02'10" W). Named on Los Alamitos (1964) 7.5' quadrangle. Postal authorities established Cypress post office in 1927 (Frickstad, p. 116), and the city incorporated in 1956. The name recalls Cypress school district, organized in 1895 (Meadows, p. 56). The community began in 1899 and first was called Waterville because it was practically surrounded by the uncontrolled flow of water from artesian wells; the residents disliked the name "Waterville" and chose the new name "Cypress" about 1905 (Hanna, p. 80).

Cypress Grove [LOS ANGELES]. *locality,* 7.25 miles north of present Manhattan Beach city hall along Pacific Electric Railroad (lat. 34°59'30" N, long, 118°25'15" W). Named on Venice (1924) 6' quadrangle.

– D –

Dagger Flat [LOS ANGELES]. *area,* 7 miles north-northwest of Sunland in Pacoima Canyon (lat. 34°21'35" N, long. 118°20'30" W; at W line sec. 10, T 3 N, R 14 W). Named on Sunland (1953) 7.5' quadrangle.

Dagger Flat Canyon [LOS ANGELES]: *canyon,* drained by a stream that flows 2 miles to Pacoima Canyon 7 miles north-northwest of Sunland (lat. 34°21'35" N, long. 118°20'30" W; at W line sec. 10, T 3 N, R 14 W); the mouth of the canyon is at Dagger Flat. Named on Agua Dulce (1960) and Sunland (1953) 7.5' quadrangles.

Daices: see Calabasas [LOS ANGELES].

Dairyland: see La Palma [ORANGE].

Dairy Valley: see Cerritos [LOS ANGELES].

Daisy Canyon [LOS ANGELES]: *canyon,* drained by a stream that flows 1.25 miles to Colby Canyon 6 miles southeast of Condor Peak (lat. 34°16'15" N, long. 118°08'05" W). Named on Chilao Flat (1959) and Condor Peak (1959) 7.5' quadrangles.

Dakin Bay: see **Avalon Bay** [LOS ANGELES].
Dakin's Cove: see **Avalon Bay** [LOS ANGELES].
Dalewood [ORANGE]: *locality,* 6 miles south of present Buena Park civic center (lat. 33°46'40" N, long. 117°58'50" W; sec. 36, T 4 S, R 11 W). Named on Anaheim (1950) 7.5' quadrangle.
Dalton Campground: see **Little Dalton Campground** [LOS ANGELES].
Dalton Canyon: see **Big Dalton Canyon** [LOS ANGELES]; **Little Dalton Canyon** [LOS ANGELES].
Dalton Reservoir: see **Big Dalton Reservoir** [LOS ANGELES].
Dalton Wash: see **Big Dalton Wash** [LOS ANGELES]; **Little Dalton Wash** [LOS ANGELES].
Dana Cove [ORANGE]: *embayment,* 3.5 miles southwest of San Juan Capistrano (lat. 33°27'45" N, long. 117°42'15" W). Named on Dana Point (1968) 7.5' quadrangle. The feature was called Bahia de San Juan Capistrano when it was used as an anchorage for San Juan Capistrano mission (Gudde, 1949, p. 88). The name "Dana" recalls Richard Henry Dana, who described the embayment in his book *Two Years before the Mast* (Hoover, Rensch, and Rensch, p. 261).
Dana Point [ORANGE]:
(1) *promontory,* 4 miles southwest of San Juan Capistrano along the coast (lat. 33°27'40" N, long. 117°42'55" W); the feature is west of Dana Cove. Named on Dana Point (1968) 7.5' quadrangle. Called San Juan Capistrano Point on San Juan Capistrano (1941) 15' quadrangle, but United States Board on Geographic Names (1938, p. 17) rejected the names "San Juan Capistrano Point" and "San Juan Point" for the feature. Wagner (p. 410) noted that the promontory was called Punta de Arbolada on a Spanish chart. Richard Egan is credited with applying the name "Dana" to the promontory in the 1870's after he visited the spot with Richard Henry Dana's son (Hanna, p. 82).
(2) *town,* 3 miles southwest of San Juan Capistrano (lat. 33°28'05" N, long. 117°41'50" W); the center of the town is 1 mile northeast of Dana Point (1). Named on Dana Point (1968) 7.5' quadrangle. Postal authorities established Dana Point post office in 1929 (Frickstad, p. 116). S.H. Woodruff laid out the town in 1924 (Meadows, p. 57).
Dana Point Harbor [ORANGE]: *water feature,* 3.5 miles southwest of San Juan Capistrano along the coast at Dana Cove (lat. 33°27'35" N, long. 117°41'50" W). Named on Dana Point (1968) 7.5' quadrangle.
Dark Canyon [LOS ANGELES]:
(1) *canyon,* drained by a stream that flows 1.5 miles to Arroyo Seco 7 miles north-northwest of Pasadena city hall (lat. 34°14'45" N, long. 118°11' W). Named on Condor Peak (1959)

and Pasadena (1953) 7.5' quadrangles.
(2) *canyon,* drained by a stream that flows 2 miles to Cold Canyon 4.5 miles north of Malibu Point (lat. 34°04'55" N, long. 118°41'25" W; near W line sec. 17, T 1 S, R 17 W). Named on Malibu Beach (1951) 7.5' quadrangle.
(3) *canyon,* 0.5 mile long, 3.5 miles southsouthwest of Burbank city hall (lat. 34°08'20" N, long. 118°20'25" W). Named on Burbank (1953) 7.5' quadrangle.
Dark Canyon: see **Sycamore Canyon** [LOS ANGELES] (5).
Daum [ORANGE]: *locality,* 1.5 miles westnorthwest of Yorba Linda along Atchison, Topeka and Santa Fe Railroad (lat. 33°53'50" N, long. 117°50'15" W). Named on Olinda (1935) 7.5' quadrangle.
Davidson City: see **Dominguez** [LOS ANGELES] (2).
Dawson Saddle [LOS ANGELES]: *pass,* 4 miles north-northeast of Crystal Lake (lat. 34°22'05" N, long. 117°48'10" W; near SE cor. sec. 3, T 3 N, R 9 W). Named on Crystal Lake (1958) 7.5' quadrangle.
Dayton Avenue [LOS ANGELES]: *locality,* 2.25 miles north-northeast of Los Angeles city hall along Southern Pacific Railroad (lat. 34°05' N, long. 118°13'30" W). Named on Los Angeles (1966) 7.5' quadrangle.
Dayton Canyon [LOS ANGELES]: *canyon,* 1.25 miles long, drained by Dayton Creek above a point 3.5 miles southwest of Chatsworth (lat. 34°13'10" N, long. 118°38'45" W). Named on Calabasas (1952) 7.5' quadrangle.
Dayton Creek [LOS ANGELES]: *stream,* flows 2.25 miles to Chatsworth Creek 3 miles southsouthwest of Chatsworth (lat. 34°12'55" N, long. 118°37'30" W); the stream drains Dayton Canyon. Named on Calabasas (1952) 7.5' quadrangle.
Dead Horse Canyon [LOS ANGELES]: *canyon,* 2 miles long, 6 miles west-northwest of Pasadena city hall (lat. 34°10'20" N, long. 118° 14'45" W). Named on Burbank (1953) and Pasadena (1953) 7.5' quadrangles.
Deadhorse Canyon [LOS ANGELES]: *canyon,* drained by a stream that flows less than 1 mile to South Long Canyon 4.5 miles northeast of Burnt Peak (lat. 34°43'30" N, long. 118°31'05" W; near W line sec. 6, T 7 N, R 15 W). Named on Burnt Peak (1958) 7.5' quadrangle.
Deadhorse Canyon: see **Dead Horse Creek** [VENTURA].
Dead Horse Creek [VENTURA]: *stream,* flows 2 miles to Snowy Creek 4.5 miles northeast of McDonald Peak (lat. 34°40'30" N, long. 118°52'30" W; sec. 27, T 7 N, R 19 W). Named on Black Mountain (1958) and McDonald Peak (1958) 7.5' quadrangles. Called Deadhorse Cr. on Tejon (1903) 30' quadrangle. The canyon of the stream is called

Deadhorse Canyon on Los Angeles County (1935) map.

Deadman Canyon: see **Bouquet Canyon** [LOS ANGELES].

Deadman Island: see **Reservation Point** [LOS ANGELES].

Deal Canyon [VENTURA]: *canyon,* drained by a stream that flows 4.5 miles to Rancho Nuevo Creek 8.5 miles west-northwest of Reyes Peak (lat. 34°41'20" N, long. 119°24'50" W). Named on Rancho Nuevo Creek (1943) 7.5' quadrangle.

Deals Flat [VENTURA]: *area,* 3.5 miles west-southwest of Triunfo Pass (lat. 34°05'15" N, long. 118°58'15" W; at NE cor. sec. 16, T 1 S, R 20 W). Named on Triunfo Pass (1950) 7.5' quadrangle.

Decker Canyon: see **Agua Dulce Canyon** [LOS ANGELES].

Deep Canyon [ORANGE]: *canyon,* 1 mile long, 2.25 miles south-southeast of San Juan Capistrano (lat. 33°28'15" N, long. 117°38'55" W). Named on Dana Point (1968) 7.5' quadrangle.

Deep Tank Reservoir [LOS ANGELES]: *lake,* 300 feet long, nearly 4 miles north of Mount Banning on Santa Catalina Island (lat. 33°25'30" N, long. 118°27' W). Named on Santa Catalina North (1950) 7.5' quadrangle.

Deer Canyon [LOS ANGELES]:

(1) *canyon,* drained by a stream that flows nearly 2 miles to Elizabeth Lake Canyon 3.25 miles southwest of the village of Lake Hughes (lat. 34°38'50" N, long. 118°29'10" W; near SE cor. sec. 32, T 7 N, R 15 W). Named on Lake Hughes (1957) 7.5' quadrangle. On Los Angeles County (1935) map, the name "Aliso Canyon" applies to the lower part of present Deer Canyon (1) and to a western branch of that canyon.

(2) *canyon,* drained by a stream that flows nearly 1 mile to Sunset Canyon 2 miles northeast of Burbank (lat. 34°12'05" W; long. 118°17'10" W). Named on Burbank (1953) 7.5' quadrangle.

Deer Canyon [VENTURA]: *canyon,* drained by a stream that flows 2.25 miles to the sea 5.25 miles southwest of Triunfo Pass (lat. 34°03'40" N, long. 118°59'05" W; sec. 21, T 1 S, R 20 W). Named on Triunfo Pass (1950) 7.5' quadrangle.

Deer Creek [LOS ANGELES]: *stream,* flows 1.5 miles to Verdugo Canyon 6 miles west-northwest of Pasadena city hall (lat. 34°11'35" N, long. 118°14'05" W). Named on Burbank (1953) and Pasadena (1953) 7.5' quadrangles.

Deer Flat Campground [LOS ANGELES]: *locality,* 1 mile north-northeast of Crystal Lake (lat. 34°20' N, long. 117°50'15" W). Named on Crystal Lake (1958) 7.5' quadrangle.

Deer Lake Highlands [LOS ANGELES]: *locality,* 2 miles north-northeast of Chatsworth (lat. 34°17' N, long. 118°35'45" W; sec. 6, T 2 N, R 16 W). Named on Oat Mountain (1952) 7.5' quadrangle. Called Twin Lakes on Chatsworth

(1940) and Zelzah (1941) 6' quadrangles, and called Twin Lakes Park on Santa Susana (1943) 15' quadrangle.

Deer Lodge [LOS ANGELES]: *locality,* 3 miles north of Burnt Peak (lat. 34°43'35" N, long. 118°34'25" W; near E line sec. 4, T 7 N, R 16 W). Named on Burnt Peak (1958) 7.5' quadrangle.

Deer Park [LOS ANGELES]: *locality,* 5.5 miles northwest of Azusa city hall (lat. 34°11'40" N, long. 117°57'50" W; on S line sec. 6, T 1 N, R 10 W). Named on Azusa (1953) 7.5' quadrangle. The name is from the abundance of deer at the place in the 1880's (Robinson, J.W., 1983, p. 74).

Deer Park Branch [LOS ANGELES]: *stream,* flows 1 mile to Eaton Canyon 1.5 miles west-southwest of Mount Wilson (1) (lat. 34°13'05" N, long. 118°05'05" W). Named on Mount Wilson (1953) 7.5' quadrangle.

Deer Park Canyon [VENTURA]: *canyon,* drained by a stream that flows 2.25 miles to Santa Barbara County 18 miles north-northwest of Reyes Peak (lat. 34°51'10" N, long. 119°26'30" W; sec. 21, T 9 N, R 24 W). Named on Cuyama Peak (1943) 7.5' quadrangle.

Deer Ridge Camp [LOS ANGELES]: *locality,* 0.5 mile east-southeast of Big Pines (lat. 34°22'35" N, long. 117°40'55" W; sec. 2, T 3 N, R 8 W). Named on Mescal Creek (1956) 7.5' quadrangle.

Deer Spring [LOS ANGELES]: *spring,* 6.5 miles south of Acton (lat. 34°22'35" N, long. 118°10'50" W). Named on Acton (1959) 7.5' quadrangle. Los Angeles County (1935) map has the plural form "Deer Springs" for the name.

Deer Spring Campground [LOS ANGELES]: *locality,* 4 miles north-northeast of Condor Peak (lat. 34°22'30" N, long. 118°10'55" W); the campground is near Deer Spring. Named on Condor Peak (1959) 7.5' quadrangle.

Del Amo [LOS ANGELES]: *locality,* 5.5 miles north of Long Beach city hall along Pacific Electric Railroad (lat. 33°50'50" N, long. 118°12'35" W). Named on Long Beach (1949) 7.5' quadrangle.

Delhi [ORANGE]: *locality,* 2.5 miles south-southeast of Santa Ana along Southern Pacific Railroad (lat. 33°42'50" N, long. 117°51'15" W). Named on Tustin (1935) 7.5' quadrangle, which shows Gloryetta post office at the place. Postal authorities established Harbor post office in 1914, changed the name to Gloryetta in 1915, and discontinued it in 1936 (Frickstad, p. 117). The name "Delhi" is from Delhi, New York, former home of the McFaldden brothers, who developed several hundred acres of land in Orange County (Meadows, p. 57).

Del Rey [LOS ANGELES]: *locality,* 7 miles north of present Manhattan Beach city hall along Pacific Electric Railroad (lat. 33°59'10"

N, long. 118°25'30" W). Named on Venice (1924) 6' quadrangle.

Del Sur [LOS ANGELES]: *locality,* 8.5 miles east of the village of Lake Hughes (lat. 34°41'20" N, long. 118°17'20" W; at NE cor. sec. 19, T 7 N, R 13 W). Named on Del Sur (1958) 7.5' quadrangle. Postal authorities established Maynard post office in 1884, moved it 0.5 mile east in 1890, changed the name to Del Sur the same year, moved it 0.5 mile west in 1891, and discontinued it in 1925; the name "Maynard" was for Levi C. Maynard, first postmaster (Salley, p. 57, 135).

Del Sur Ridge [LOS ANGELES]: *ridge,* 7.5 miles long, center about 11 miles south of the village of Lake Hughes (lat. 34°31' N, long. 118°28'15" W). Named on Green Valley (1958) and Mint Canyon (1960) 7.5' quadrangles.

Delta [LOS ANGELES]: *locality,* 3.5 miles south-southeast of Inglewood city hall (lat. 33°55'10" N, long. 118°19'15" W; sec. 11, T 3 S, R 14 W). Named on Inglewood (1964) 7.5' quadrangle.

Delta Canyon [LOS ANGELES]: *canyon,* 1.5 miles long, opens into Big Tujunga Canyon 4 miles northeast of Sunland (lat. 34°18'05" N, long. 118°15'35" W). Named on Condor Peak (1959) and Sunland (1953) 7.5' quadrangles.

Del Valle [LOS ANGELES]: *locality,* 8 miles west-northwest of Newhall along Southern Pacific Railroad (lat. 34°25'05" N, long. 118°39'25" W); the place is on San Francisco grant, which Antonio del Valle received. Named on Val Verde (1952) 7.5' quadrangle. Camulos (1903) 30' quadrangle had the form "Delvalle" for the name.

Denis [LOS ANGELES]: *locality,* 6 miles south of Lancaster along Southern Pacific Railroad (lat. 34°38' N, long. 118°07'30" W; sec. 2, 11, T 6 N, R 12 W). Named on Lancaster East (1958), Lancaster West (1958), and Palmdale (1958) 7.5' quadrangles.

Dennis Park: see **Mission Hills** [LOS ANGELES].

Derrydale Creek [VENTURA]: *stream,* flows 3.5 miles to Sespe Creek 5.5 miles northnortheast of Wheeler Springs (lat. 34°35' N, long. 119°15'40" W; near E line sec. 25, T 6 N, R 23 E). Named on Lion Canyon (1943) and Wheeler Springs (1943) 7.5' quadrangles.

Descanso Bay [LOS ANGELES]: *embayment,* 0.5 mile north of Avalon on the northeast side of Santa Catalina Island (lat. 33°21'05" N, long. 118°19'35" W). Named on Santa Catalina East (1950) 7.5' quadrangle.

Des Moines [ORANGE]: *locality,* 1.5 miles west of downtown La Habra along Pacific Electric Railroad (lat. 33°55'40" N, long. 117° 58' W). Named on La Habra (1964) 7.5' quadrangle. The site also had the name "Laon Junction" (Meadows, p. 77).

De Soto Heights: see **Soto Street Junction** [LOS ANGELES].

Devil Canyon [LOS ANGELES]: *canyon,* drained by a stream that flows 4.5 miles to Browns Canyon 1.5 miles north-northwest of Chatsworth (lat. 34°16'40" N, long. 118°35'30" W). Named on Oat Mountain (1952) and Santa Susana (1951) 7.5' quadrangles. Camulos (1903) 30' quadrangle has the name "Aliso Canyon" for the upper part of present Devil Canyon, and shows Devil Creek in the lower part. Santa Susana (1903) 15' quadrangle has the name "Ybarra Canyon" for the upper part of present Devil Canyon, and leaves present Ybarra Canyon unnamed. Los Angeles County (1935) map shows Devils Canyon Creek in present Devil Canyon.

Devil Canyon [LOS ANGELES-VENTURA]: *canyon,* drained by a stream that heads in Los Angels County and flows 6 miles to Lake Piru 6 miles north-northeast of Piru in Ventura County (lat. 34°29'15" N, long. 118°44'25" W). Named on Val Verde (1952, photorevised 1969) and Whitaker Peak (1958) 7.5' quadrangles. Los Angeles County (1935) map has the form "Devils Canyon" for the name.

Devil Creek: see **Devil Canyon** [LOS ANGELES].

Devil Gulch [LOS ANGELES]: *canyon,* drained by a stream that flows 2.5 miles to San Gabriel River 6 miles east-southeast of Crystal Lake (lat. 34°16'50" N, long. 117°45'10" W). Named on Crystal Lake (1958) 7.5' quadrangle. Called Devils Canyon on Rock Creek (1903) 15' quadrangle, but United States Board on Geographic Names (1939, p. 13) rejected this form for the name.

Devil Gulch: see **Devils Gulch** [VENTURA].

Devils Canyon [LOS ANGELES]: *canyon,* nearly 10 miles long, opens into the canyon of West Fork San Gabriel River 8.5 miles north-northwest of Azusa city hall (lat. 34°14'30" N, long. 117°58'15" W). Named on Azusa (1953) and Waterman Mountain (1959) 7.5' quadrangles.

Devils Canyon: see **Devil Canyon** [LOS ANGELES-VENTURA]; **Devil Gulch** [LOS ANGELES].

Devils Canyon Creek: see **Devil Canyon** [LOS ANGELES].

Devils Chair [LOS ANGELES]: *relief feature,* 3 miles south of Valyermo (lat. 34°24'05" N, long. 117°50'50" W; sec. 29, T 4 N, R 9 W). Named on Valyermo (1958) 7.5' quadrangle.

Devils Gate [LOS ANGELES]:

(1) *narrows,* 3 miles north-northwest of present Pasadena city hall along Arroyo Seco (lat. 34°11'05" N, long. 118°10'30" W). Named on Pasadena (1900) 15' quadrangle.

(2) *locality,* 2.5 miles north-northwest of present Pasadena city hall along Los Angeles Terminal Railroad (lat. 34°10'50" N, long. 118° 10'05" W); the place is 0.5 mile eastsoutheast of Devils Gate (1). Named on Pasadena (1900) 15' quadrangle.

Devils Gate [VENTURA]: *narrows,* 4.5 miles

north-northwest of Fillmore along Sespe Creek (lat. 34°27'50" N, long. 118°56'35" W; sec. 2, T 4 N, R 20 W). Named on Fillmore (1951) 7.5' quadrangle.

Devils Gate Reservoir [LOS ANGELES]: *intermittent lake,* behind a dam three miles north-northwest of Pasadena along Arroyo Seco (lat. 34°11'05" N, long. 118°10'30" W); the dam is at Devils Gate (1). Named on Pasadena (1966) 7.5' quadrangle.

Devils Gateway [VENTURA]: *narrows,* 5.5 miles southeast of Cobblestone Mountain along Agua Blanca Creek (lat. 34°33' N, long. 118°48'05" W; sec. 6, T 5 N, R 18 W). Named on Cobblestone Mountain (1958) 7.5' quadrangle.

Devils Gulch [LOS ANGELES]: *canyon,* 1 mile long, 2 miles north-northeast of Burnt Peak (lat. 34°42'20" N, long. 118°33'25" W; on S line sec. 10, T 7 N, R 16 W). Named on Burnt Peak (1958) 7.5' quadrangle.

Devils Gulch [VENTURA]: *relief feature,* 5 miles southwest of the town of Ojai near Ventura River (lat. 34°24'25" N, long. 119°17'50" W). Named on Matilija (1952) 7.5' quadrangle. Called Devil Gulch on Ventura (1904) 15' quadrangle.

Devils Heart Peak [VENTURA]: *peak,* 10.5 miles north-northwest of Fillmore (lat. 34°32'45" N, long. 118°58'30" W). Altitude 5203 feet. Named on Devils Heart Peak (1943) 7.5' quadrangle.

Devils Potrero [VENTURA]: *area,* 6 miles southeast of Cobblestone Mountain (lat. 34°32'10" N, long. 118°48'25" W; sec. 7, T 5 N, R 18 W). Named on Cobblestone Mountain (1958) 7.5' quadrangle.

Devils Punchbowl [LOS ANGELES]: *relief feature,* 1.5 miles south of Valyermo (lat. 34°25'15" N, long. 117°51'10" W; sec. 18, 19, 20, T 4 N, R 9 W). Named on Valyermo (1958) 7.5' quadrangle.

Devore Campground [LOS ANGELES]: *locality,* 2 miles northeast of Mount Wilson (1) along West Fork San Gabriel River (lat. 34°14'35" N, long. 118°02'05" W; sec. 21, T 2 N, R 11 W). Named on Mount Wilson (1966) 7.5' quadrangle.

Dewitt Canyon [LOS ANGELES]: *canyon,* drained by a stream that flows nearly 2 miles to Pico Canyon 3.25 miles west of Newhall (lat. 34°22'35" N, long. 118°35'15" W; near NW cor. sec. 5, T 3 N, R 16 W). Named on Oat Mountain (1952) 7.5' quadrangle.

Diamond Bar [LOS ANGELES]: *town,* 4 miles west-southwest of Pomona city hall (lat. 34°01'30" N, long. 117°48'45" W). Named on San Dimas (1966, photorevised 1981) and Yorba Linda (1964, photorevised 1981) 7.5' quadrangles.

Diamond Bar Creek [LOS ANGELES]: *stream,* flows nearly 3 miles to San Jose Creek 7.25 miles west-southwest of Pomona city hall (lat. 34°00'15" N, long. 117°51'45" W). Named on San Dimas (1966) 7.5' quadrangle.

Diamond Campground [LOS ANGELES]: *locality,* about 8 miles north-northeast of Sunland in Pacoima Canyon (lat. 34°22'10" N, long. 118°15'55" W). Named on Sunland (1966) 7.5' quadrangle.

Dillon Divide [LOS ANGELES]: *pass,* 6.25 miles north-northwest of Sunland (lat. 34°20'40" N, long. 118°20'55" W; sec. 16, T 3 N, R 14 W). Named on Sunland (1966) 7.5' quadrangle, which shows Dillon ranch located 0.5 mile west-northwest of the pass.

Dime Canyon [LOS ANGELES]: *canyon,* drained by a stream that flows less than 1 mile to Cattle Canyon 8.5 miles northeast of Glendora city hall (lat. 34°13'40" N, long. 117°45'50" W). Named on Glendora (1966) 7.5' quadrangle.

Disappointment: see **Mount Disappointment** [LOS ANGELES].

Divide Forest Camp [VENTURA]: *locality,* 2.5 miles east-northeast of McDonald Peak at the head of Big Cedar Creek (lat. 34°38'35" N, long. 118°53'40" W; sec. 4, T 6 N, R 19 W). Named on McDonald Peak (1958) 7.5' quadrangle.

Dix Canyon [LOS ANGELES]: *canyon,* drained by a stream that flows 1.5 miles to Topanga Canyon 7.5 miles northwest of Santa Monica city hall (lat. 34°04'55" N, long. 118°35'45" W; sec. 18, T 1 S, R 16 W). Named on Topanga (1952) 7.5' quadrangle.

Doane Canyon [LOS ANGELES]: *canyon,* drained by a stream that flows 2 miles to Big Tujunga Canyon 1 mile north of Sunland (lat. 34°16'35" N, long. 118°18'40" W). Named on Sunland (1953) 7.5' quadrangle.

Doe Flat [LOS ANGELES]: *area,* 8.5 miles north-northeast of Glendora city hall (lat. 34°14'50" N, long. 117°48' W). Named on Crystal Lake (1958) and Glendora (1966) 7.5' quadrangles.

Doe Spring [LOS ANGELES]: *spring,* 4.5 miles southwest of Waterman Mountain (lat. 34°18' N, long. 118°00' W). Named on Waterman Mountain (1959) 7.5' quadrangle.

Doheny Cattle Camp Number 2 [LOS ANGELES]: *locality,* 13 miles west-northwest of Newhall at the mouth of Oak Canyon (1) (lat. 34°28'35" N, long. 118°43'05" W). Named on Santa Felicia Canyon (1935) 6' quadrangle.

Doheny Park: see **Capistrano Beach** [ORANGE].

Delanco Junction [LOS ANGELES]: *locality,* 2.25 miles east of Torrance city hall (lat. 33°50'45" N, long. 118°17'55" W). Named on Torrance (1964) 7.5' quadrangle. Called Dolanco on Compton (1930) 6' quadrangle.

Dolgeville: see **Shorb** [LOS ANGELES].

Dolley [LOS ANGELES]: *locality,* 9 miles northeast of present Long Beach city hall along Pacific Electric Railroad (lat. 33°51'55" N, long. 118°05'25" W). Named on Artesia (1925) 6' quadrangle.

Dolores [LOS ANGELES]: *locality,* nearly 5

miles north-northwest of Long Beach city hall along Southern Pacific Railroad (lat. 33° 50' N, long. 118°13'30" W). Named on Long Beach (1964) 7.5' quadrangle.

Dome Mountain [LOS ANGELES-VENTURA]: *peak,* 4 miles east-northeast of Cobblestone Mountain on Los Angeles-Ventura county line (lat. 34°37'45" N, long. 118°48'05" W). Named on Black Mountain (1958) 7.5' quadrangle.

Dominguez [LOS ANGELES]:
(1) *district,* nearly 5 miles north-northwest of Long Beach city hall (lat. 33°50'10" N, long. 118°13'10" W). Named on Long Beach (1949) 7.5' quadrangle.
(2) *locality,* 7 miles north of present Long Beach city hall along Southern Pacific Railroad (lat. 33°52' N, long. 118°13' W). Named on Downey (1902) 15' quadrangle. Compton (1930) 6' quadrangle shows a place called Davidson City at the site. Davidson City was named for Davidson Investment Company (Gudde, 1949, p. 97).

Dominguez Campground [VENTURA]: *locality,* 4.5 miles north of Piru (lat. 34°28'50" N, long. 118°47'50" W; near NW cor. sec. 32, T 5 N, R 18 W); the place is in Dominguez Canyon. Named on Piru (1952) 7.5' quadrangle.

Dominguez Canyon [VENTURA]: *canyon,* drained by a stream that flows 3 miles to Reasoner Canyon 4.5 miles north-northeast of Piru (lat. 34°28'45" N, long. 118°46'15" W; sec. 33, T 5 N, R 18 W). Named on Piru (1952) 7.5' quadrangle. Called Reasoner Canyon on Camulos (1903) 30' quadrangle.

Dominguez Channel [LOS ANGELES]: *water feature,* extends for 16 miles to Los Angeles Harbor 3.25 miles west of Long Beach city hall (lat. 33°46'05" N, long. 118°15' W). Named on Inglewood (1964), Long Beach (1964), and Torrance (1964) 7.5' quadrangles. Inglewood (1952) 7.5' quadrangle has the name "Laguna Dominguez" for marsh situated mainly at the upper part of present Dominguez Channel; Los Angeles Board of Supervisors adopted the name "Laguna Dominguez" in 1938 for the swampy lake formerly called Nigger Slough (Gudde, 1949, p. 97).

Dominguez Hills [LOS ANGELES]: *ridge,* east-northeast-trending, about 3 miles long, 2 miles north-northeast of Dominguez (lat. 33° 51'45" N, long. 118°14'15" W). Named on Inglewood (1964), Long Beach (1964), South Gate (1964), and Torrance (1964) 7.5' quadrangles. On Downey (1902) 15' quadrangle, the name "Dominguez Hill" applies to the high point on present Dominguez Hills.

Dominguez Junction [LOS ANGELES]: *locality,* 6.5 miles north of Long Beach city hall along the railroad (lat. 33°51'45" N, long. 118°12'55" W); the place is near the east end of Dominguez Hills. Named on Long Beach (1949) 7.5' quadrangle.

Dominguez Reservoir [LOS ANGELES]: *lake,* 450 feet long, 0.5 mile north-northwest of present Torrance city hall (lat. 33°50'45" N, long. 118°20'30" W). Named on Torrance (1924) 6' quadrangle.

Dorothy Canyon [LOS ANGELES]: *canyon,* drained by a stream that flows 1.5 miles to Pacoima Canyon 7 miles north of Sunland (lat. 34°21'45" N, long. 118°19'35" W; near NE cor. sec. 10, T 3 N, R 14 W). Named on Sunland (1953) 7.5' quadrangle.

Dorr Canyon [LOS ANGELES]: *canyon,* drained by a stream that flows 3 miles to Big Rock Creek nearly 5 miles southeast of Valyermo (lat. 34°23'35" N, long. 117°47'45" W; near NW cor. sec. 35, T 4 N, R 9 W). Named on Crystal Lake (1958) and Valyermo (1958) 7.5' quadrangles.

Dougherty Peak: see **Throop Peak** [LOS ANGELES].

Dough Flat [VENTURA]: *area,* 5 miles east-southeast of Devils Heart Peak (lat. 34°31'20" N, long. 118°53'35" W; sec. 17, T 5 N, R 19 W). Named on Devils Heart Peak (1943) 7.5' quadrangle.

Douglas Junction [LOS ANGELES]: *locality,* 6 miles north-northeast of Long Beach city hall along Union Pacific Railroad (lat. 33°51'20" N, long. 118°09'50" W). Named on Long Beach (1949) 7.5' quadrangle.

Dove Canyon [ORANGE]: *canyon,* drained by a stream that flows 3 miles to Bell Canyon 10 miles northeast of San Juan Capistrano (lat. 33°37'10" N, long. 117°33'45" W; sec. 25, T 6 S, R 7 W). Named on Cañada Gobernadora (1968) and Santiago Peak (1954) 7.5' quadrangles. The name is from the abundance of mourning doves in the canyon (Meadows, p. 58).

Dove Canyon: see **Peters Canyon** [ORANGE].

Dowd Canyon [LOS ANGELES]: *canyon,* drained by a stream that flows 3 miles to San Francisquito Canyon 4.25 miles south-southeast of the village of Lake Hughes (lat. 34°37' N, long. 118°25' W; at S line sec. 12, T 6 N, R 15 W). Named on Green Valley (1958) and Sleepy Valley (1958) 7.5' quadrangles.

Downey [LOS ANGELES]: *city,* 4.5 miles east-southeast of South Gate city hall (lat. 33°56'25" N, long. 118°07'45" W). Named on South Gate (1964) and Whittier (1949) 7.5' quadrangles. Called Downey City on Stevenson's (1884) map. Postal authorities established Downey post office in 1876 (Salley, p. 61), and the city incorporated in 1956. The name commemorates John G. Downey, governor California from 1860 until 1862, who subdivided Santa Gertrudis grant where the city lies (Gudde, 1949, p. 98). Bancroft (1888, p. 522) referred to Downey City, "which absorbed Gallatin and College Settlement." The community called Gallatin was started in 1868, and a church and a college opened in 1869 at a place called College

51

DURHAM'S PLACE-NAMES

Settlement—both Gallatin and College Settlement were moved to Downey when Downey was founded (Thompson and West, p. 150). Postal authorities established Vultee Field post office 1.75 miles south of Downey post office in 1940 and discontinued it in 1947; the name was for Vultee Aircraft, Incorporated, military aircraft manufacturers in World War II (Salley, p. 233).

Downey: see **Mount Downey**, under **Santiago Peak** [ORANGE].

Downey Road [LOS ANGELES]: *locality*, 3.5 miles southeast of Los Angeles city hall (lat. 34°00'50" N, long. 118°12'15" W). Named on Los Angeles (1966) 7.5' quadrangle.

Drinkwater Canyon [LOS ANGELES]: *canyon*, drained by a stream that flows 1.5 miles to San Francisquito Canyon 5.5 miles south-southeast of Warm Springs Mountain (lat. 34°31'40" N, long. 118°31'40" W; near S line sec. 11, T 5 N, R 16 W). Named on Warm Springs Mountain (1958) 7.5' quadrangle. Los Angeles County (1935) map shows several canyons related to San Francisquito Canyon: LeBrun Canyon, which opens into San Francisquito Canyon from the north about 2 miles north-northeast of the mouth of Drinkwater Canyon; Peters Canyon, which opens into LeBrun Canyon from the north near the mouth of LeBrun Canyon; and Hunter Canyon, which opens into San Francisquito Canyon about 1.5 miles northeast of the mouth of LeBrun Canyon. According to Outland (1963, p. 27), Raggio ranch and stage station was located about 0.5 mile below the mouth Drinkwater Canyon.

Drinkwater Flat [LOS ANGELES]: *area*, 9.5 miles south-southwest of the village of Lake Hughes in Dry Canyon (1) (lat. 34°32'30" N, long. 118°30' W). Named on Green Valley (1958) and Warm Springs Mountain (1958) 7.5' quadrangles. Red Mountain (1936) 6' quadrangle has the name "Drinkwater Flat" for a place located about 0.5 mile farther west at the head of Drinkwater Canyon.

Drinkwater Reservoir [LOS ANGELES]: *lake*, 600 feet long, 4.5 miles southeast of Warm Springs Mountain (lat. 34°31'50" N, long. 118°31'15" W; near E line sec. 11, T 5 N, R 16 W); the feature is near Drinkwater Canyon. Named on Warm Springs Mountain (1958) 7.5' quadrangle.

Dripping Springs [VENTURA]: *spring*, 3.5 miles northeast of Devils Heart Peak (lat. 34°34'30" N, long. 118°55'20" W; near N line sec. 32, T 6 N, R 19 W). Named on Devils Heart Peak (1943) 7.5' quadrangle.

Drum Barracks: see **Wilmington** [LOS ANGELES].

Dry Canyon [LOS ANGELES]:
(1) *canyon*, drained by a stream that flows 18 miles to Bouquet Canyon 3 miles north of Newhall (lat. 34°25'50" N, long. 118°32' W). Named on Green Valley (1958), Newhall

(1952), and Warm Springs Mountain (1958) 7.5' quadrangles.
(2) *canyon*, drained by a stream that flows 2.5 miles to lowlands less than 1 mile southeast of Calabasas (lat. 34°08'50" N, long. 118°37'45" W; at N line sec. 26, T 1 N, R 17 W). Named on Calabasas (1952) 7.5' quadrangle.
(3) *canyon*, 2.5 miles long, 4 miles west-northwest of Beverly Hills city hall (lat. 34°05'45" N, long. 118°27'45" W). Named on Beverly Hills (1950) 7.5' quadrangle.
(4) *canyon*, drained by a stream that flows nearly 2 miles to Solstice Canyon 3.5 miles west of Malibu Point (lat. 34°02'15" N, long. 118°44'45" W). Named on Malibu Beach (1951) 7.5' quadrangle.

Dry Canyon [VENTURA]:
(1) *canyon*, drained by a stream that flows about 2 miles to Simi Valley (1) 6.5 miles west-northwest of Santa Susana Pass (lat. 34° 17'25" N, long. 118°44'45" W; sec. 3, T 2 N, R 18 W). Named on Santa Susana (1951) 7.5' quadrangle. Called Oak Canyon on Santa Susana (1943) 15' quadrangle.
(2) *canyon*, drained by a stream that flows 10 miles to Cuyama River 4 miles north of Reyes Peak (lat. 34°41'25" N, long. 119°17'30" W; sec. 23, T 7 N, R 23 W). Named on Reyes Peak (1943), San Guillermo (1943), and Sawmill Mountain (1943) 7.5' quadrangles. West Fork branches north-northwest nearly 4 miles above the mouth of the main canyon; it is 3 miles long and is named on Apache Canyon (1943) and Reyes Peak (1943) 7.5' quadrangles.

Dry Canyon: see **Gillibrand Canyon** [VENTURA].

Dry Canyon Reservoir [LOS ANGELES]: *lake*, 3700 feet long, behind a dam 6.5 miles north of Newhall (lat. 34°28'55" N, long. 118°31'30" W; on S line sec. 26, T 5 N, R 16 W); the lake is in Dry Canyon (1). Named on Newhall (1952) 7.5' quadrangle.

Dry Creek [VENTURA]: *stream*, flows about 5.5 miles to end 6.5 miles north-northeast of McDonald Peak (lat. 34°43'40" N, long. 118°54'35" W; sec. 5, T 7 N, R 19 W). Named on McDonald Peak (1958) 7.5' quadrangle.

Dry Gulch [LOS ANGELES]:
(1) *canyon*, drained by a stream that flows 2.5 miles to Elizabeth Lake Canyon 3 miles south of Warm Springs Mountain (lat. 34°33'10" N, long. 118°34'35" W; sec. 5, T 5 N, R 16 W). Named on Warm Springs Mountain (1958) 7.5' quadrangle.
(2) *canyon*, drained by a stream that flows 1.5 miles to Coldwater Canyon (2) nearly 4 miles west-southwest of Mount San Antonio (lat. 34°15'55" N, long. 117°42'20" W). Named on Mount San Antonio (1955) 7.5' quadrangle.

Dry Lake Canyon [LOS ANGELES]: *canyon*, drained by a stream that flows 1 mile to San

Antonio Canyon 11 miles north-northeast of Pomona city hall (lat. 34°12'10" N, long. 117°40'30" W; sec. 1, T 1 N, R 8 W). Named on Mount Baldy (1954) 7.5' quadrangle.

Duarte [LOS ANGELES]: *town*, 3.5 miles west of Azusa city hall (lat. 34°08'25" N, long. 117°58'10" W); the place is on Andres Duarte's Azusa (1) grant. Named on Azusa (1966) and Baldwin Park (1966) 7.5' quadrangles. Postal authorities established Duarte post office in 1882 (Frickstad, p. 72), and the town incorporated in 1957. The community began with subdivision of Azusa (1) grant in 1864 and 1865 (Gudde, 1949, p. 100).

Dudmore [LOS ANGELES]: *locality*, 1.5 miles north-northwest of Torrance city hall along Atchison, Topeka and Santa Fe Railroad (lat. 33°51'25" N, long. 118°21' W). Named on Torrance (1964) 7.5' quadrangle.

Duena: see **Santa Ana** [ORANGE].

Dulah [VENTURA]: *settlement*, 4.5 miles westnorthwest of Ventura along the coast (lat. 34°18'45" N, long. 119°21'30" W). Named on Ventura (1951) 7.5' quadrangle.

Dume: see **Point Dume** [LOS ANGELES].

Dume Canyon: see **Zuma Canyon** [LOS ANGELES].

Dume Cove [LOS ANGELES]: *embayment*, just northeast of Point Dume along the coast (lat. 34°00'15" N, long. 118°48' W). Named on Point Dume (1951) 7.5' quadrangle. United States Board on Geographic Names (1961b, p. 13) rejected the name "Dume Cove" for present Paradise Cove.

Dume Point: see **Point Dume** [LOS ANGELES].

Dumetz: see **Point Dumetz**, under **Point Dume** [LOS ANGELES].

Dundee [LOS ANGELES]: *locality*, 3.5 miles northwest of present Burbank city hall along Southern Pacific Railroad (lat. 34°12'30" N, long. 118°21'20" W). Named on Santa Monica (1902) 15' quadrangle. Postal authorities established Dundee post office in 1887 and discontinued it in 1909; the name was from Dundee, Scotland (Salley, p. 62).

Dunsmore Canyon [LOS ANGELES]: *canyon*, 1.5 miles long, 5 miles south-southwest of Condor Peak (lat. 34°15'30" N, long. 118°14'20" W; mainly in sec. 15, 16, T 2 N, R 13 W). Named on Condor Peak (1959) 7.5' quadrangle.

Dutch Harbor [VENTURA]: *embayment*, on the south side of San Nicolas Island (lat. 33°13'05" N, long. 119°29'10" W). Named on San Nicolas Island (1943) quadrangle.

Dutch Louie Camp [LOS ANGELES]: *locality*, 7 miles north-northwest of Sunland in Pacoima Canyon (lat. 34°21'30" N, long. 118° 21'10" W; sec. 9, T 3 N, R 14 W). Named on Sunland (1953) 7.5' quadrangle. Called Dutch Louie Campground on Sunland (1966) 7.5' quadrangle.

Dutchmans Camp [VENTURA]: *locality*, 2.5

miles northwest of McDonald Peak (lat. 34°39'50" N, long. 119°58'05" W; near S line sec. 26, T 7 N, R 20 W). Named on McDonald Peak (1958) 7.5' quadrangle.

Dyer [ORANGE]: *locality*, 2.5 miles southsoutheast of Santa Ana city hall along Southern Pacific Railroad (lat. 33°42'35" N, long. 117°51'15" W). Named on Tustin (1965) 7.5' quadrangle.

— E —

Eagle Canyon [LOS ANGELES]: *canyon*, 1.5 miles long, 8.5 miles northwest of Pasadena city hall (lat. 34°14'40" N, long. 118°14'10" W; sec. 22, T 2 N, R 13 W). Named on Condor Peak (1959) and Pasadena (1953) 7.5' quadrangles.

Eagle Canyon Channel [LOS ANGELES]: *stream*, extends for 1.5 miles to Verdugo Wash nearly 8 miles northwest of Pasadena city hall (lat. 34°13'05" N, long. 118°14'55" W); the feature heads at the mouth of Eagle Canyon. Named on Pasadena (1966) 7.5' quadrangle.

Eagle Reef: see **Isthmus Cove** [LOS ANGELES].

Eagle Rock [LOS ANGELES]:
(1) *relief feature*, 2.25 miles west of Pasadena city hall (lat. 34°08'35" N, long. 118°10'55" W). Named on Pasadena (1953) 7.5' quadrangle. The name is from the figure of an eagle in flight caused by shadows cast on the face of the feature by an overhanging rock outcrop (Diller and others, p. 98).
(2) *rock*, 2.25 miles west-northwest of Silver Peak near the west end of Santa Catalina Island, and 750 feet offshore (lat. 33°28'20" N, long. 118°36'15" W). Named on Santa Catalina West (1943) 7.5' quadrangle.
(3) *district*, 3.5 miles west-southwest of Pasadena city hall in Los Angeles (lat. 34°08' N, long. 118°12' W); the place is southwest of Eagle Rock (1). Named on Pasadena (1953) 7.5' quadrangle.

Eagle Rock Reservoir [LOS ANGELES]: *lake*, 1100 feet long, 2.5 miles west of Pasadena city hall (lat. 34°08'50" N, long. 118°11'20" W); the feature is northeast of Eagle Rock district. Named on Pasadena (1953) 7.5' quadrangle.

Eagle Rock Valley [LOS ANGELES]: *valley*, 3.5 miles west-southwest of present Pasadena city hall (lat. 34°08'20" N, long. 118°12'30" W); the place is at and around present Eagle Rock district. Named on Pasadena (1900) 15' quadrangle.

Eagles Nest [LOS ANGELES]: *ridge*, generally west-trending, about 1 mile long, 1 mile southwest of Mount Banning on Santa Catalina Island (lat. 33°21'45" N, long. 118°26'45" W). Named on Santa Catalina South (1943) 7.5' quadrangle.

Eagle Spring [LOS ANGELES]: *spring*, 8 miles

DURHAM'S PLACE-NAMES

northwest of Santa Monica city hall (lat. 34°06'25" N, long. 118°34' W). Named on Topanga (1952) 7.5' quadrangle.

Earlham: see **El Modeno** [ORANGE].

Earthquake Bay: see **Gulf of Santa Catalina** [ORANGE].

East Canyon [LOS ANGELES]: *canyon,* drained by a stream that flows 1.25 miles to Gavin Canyon 2 miles south-southwest of Newhall (lat. 34°20'45" N, long. 118°32'30" W; sec. 15, T 3 N, R 16 W). Named on Oat Mountain (1952) 7.5' quadrangle.

East Canyon Channel [LOS ANGELES]: *water feature,* extends for 2.5 miles to Pacoima Wash 1.25 miles south of downtown San Fernando (lat. 34°15'45" N, long. 118°26'30" W). Named on San Fernando (1966) 7.5' quadrangle.

East Casitas Pass [VENTURA]: *pass,* nearly 6 miles south of White Ledge Peak (lat. 34°23'10" N, long. 119°22'50" W; sec. 34, T 4 N, R 24 W); the feature is 2 miles east of West Casitas Pass. Named on White Ledge Peak (1952) 7.5' quadrangle.

East Coyote Hills [ORANGE]: *range,* 4 miles southeast of downtown La Habra (lat. 33°53'30" N, long. 117°54' W); the feature is east of West Coyote Hills. Named on La Habra (1964) 7.5' quadrangle.

Eastern Anacapa: see **Anacapa Island** [VENTURA].

East Fish Camp [VENTURA]: *locality,* on the south side of the middle Anacapa Island (lat. 34°00'25" N, long. 119°23'05" W). Named on Anacapa Island (1973) quadrangle.

East Irvine [ORANGE]: *village,* 8 miles southeast of Santa Ana city hall (lat. 33°40'35" N, long. 117°45'35" W); the place is about 3.5 miles east of the center of present Irvine. Named on Tustin (1965, photorevised 1981) 7.5' quadrangle. Tustin (1965) 7.5' quadrangle has the designation "Irvine (Valencia Siding)" at the site, but United States Board on Geographic Names (1965c, p. 8) rejected the name "Irvine" for the village. Corona (1902) 30' quadrangle has both the names "Irvine" and "Myford" along Atchison, Topeka and Santa Fe Railroad at the place. Postal authorities established Myford post office in 1899, changed the name to Irvine in 1914, and to East Irvine in 1965; the name "Myford" was for Myford Irvine, first postmaster (Salley, p. 64, 149). Atchison, Topeka and Santa Fe Railroad established a shipping center at the site in 1888 and named it Irvine for Irvine ranch, owned by James Irvine; because a post office named Irvine already existed in California, the post office at the site was called Myford for Irvine's son; the village and post office became East Irvine when the new city of Irvine was started nearby (Meadows, p. 73). A feature called Barton Mound lies 1.5 miles south of East Irvine; the name recalls Sheriff James Barton, whom outlaws killed there in

1857 (Hoover, Rensch, and Rensch, p. 265; Meadows, p. 24).

East Las Virgenes Canyon [VENTURA]: *canyon,* drained by a stream that flows 2 miles to Las Virgenes Canyon 7.5 miles east of Thousand Oaks (lat. 34°10'15" N, long. 118°42'05" W). Named on Calabasas (1952) 7.5' quadrangle. Called East Fork on Camulos (1903) 30' quadrangle.

East Los Angeles [LOS ANGELES]:
(1) *district,* 2 miles northeast of present Los Angeles city hall (lat. 34°04'35" N, long. 118°12'45" W). Named on Pasadena (1900) 15' quadrangle.
(2) *district,* 4.5 miles southeast of Los Angeles city hall (lat. 34°00'55" N, long. 118°10'45" W). Named on Los Angeles (1953) 7.5' quadrangle.

Eastmont [LOS ANGELES]: *district,* 5.5 miles east-southeast of Los Angeles city hall (lat. 34°01'25" N, long. 118°09' W). Named on Alhambra (1926) 6' quadrangle.

East Pasadena [LOS ANGELES]: *district,* east of the main part of Pasadena (lat. 34°09' N, long. 118°05'30" W). Named on Mount Wilson (1953) 7.5' quadrangle. Pasadena (1900) 15' quadrangle has the name "Lamanda" along the railroad at the place, and Mount Wilson (1966) 7.5' quadrangle has the name "Lamanda Park" for the railroad station at East Pasadena. Postal authorities established Lamanda Park post office in 1886, changed the name to Lamanda in 1894, to La Manda in 1905, to Lamanda Park in 1920, and to East Pasadena in 1930 (Salley, p. 116). They first established East Pasadena post office in 1887, discontinued it in 1896, reestablished it in 1904, discontinued it in 1907, and reestablished it in 1930 (Salley, p. 64). The name "Lamanda" is from Amanda Rose—her husband, Lenard J. Rose, owned the land at the place (Gudde, 1949, p. 102).

East San Gabriel [LOS ANGELES]: *locality,* 3.25 miles west-northwest of El Monte city hall along Southern Pacific Railroad (lat. 34°05'35" N, long. 118°04'50" W); the place is 1.5 miles east of downtown San Gabriel. Named on El Monte (1953) 7.5' quadrangle.

East San Pedro [LOS ANGELES]: *locality,* 3 miles northeast of Point Fermin on Terminal Island (lat. 33°44'15' N, long. 118°15'45" W). Named on San Pedro (1964) 7.5' quadrangle. Postal authorities established East San Pedro post office 1 mile east of San Pedro post office in 1906 and discontinued in 1924 (Salley, p. 64).

East Whittier [LOS ANGELES]: *district,* 1.25 miles southeast of present Whittier city hall (lat. 33°57'50" N, long. 118°01' W). Named on Whittier (1949) 7.5' quadrangle.

East Whittier Siding [LOS ANGELES]: *locality,* nearly 3 miles south-southeast of present Whittier city hall along Atchison, Topeka and Santa Fe Railroad (lat. 33°56'10" N, long.

118°00'50" W). Named on Whittier (1949) 7.5' quadrangle.

East Wilmington: see **Wilmington** [LOS ANGELES].

Eaton Canyon [LOS ANGELES]: *canyon,* drained by a stream that flows 5 miles to leave San Gabriel Mountains 3.25 miles southwest of Mount Wilson (lat. 34°11'30" N, long. 118°06'10" W; at S line sec. 2, T 1 N, R 12 W). Named on Mount Wilson (1953) 7.5' quadrangle. The name commemorates Judge Benjamin S. Eaton, who had property 3 miles below the mouth of the canyon; the feature had the early name "Precipicio Canyon" (Robinson, J.W., 1977, p. 102).

Eaton Canyon Wash: see **Eaton Wash** [LOS ANGELES].

Eaton Wash [LOS ANGELES]: *stream,* extends for 9.5 miles from the mouth of Eaton Canyon to Rio Hondo 1.5 miles west of El Monte city hall (lat. 34°04'10" N, long. 118°03'20" W). Named on El Monte (1966) and Mount Wilson (1953) 7.5' quadrangles. El Monte (1926) 6' quadrangle has the name "Eaton Canyon Wash" for the stream.

Ebey Canyon [LOS ANGELES]: *canyon,* drained by a stream that flows nearly 1.5 miles to Tujunga Valley 1 mile north-northwest of Sunland (lat. 34°16'25" N, long. 118°19'05" W). Named on Sunland (1953) 7.5' quadrangle. Called Ebe Cany. on Los Angeles County (1935) map.

Echo Falls Canyon [VENTURA]: *canyon,* drained by a stream that flows 2.5 miles to Santa Paula Canyon 4 miles west of Santa Paula Peak (lat. 34°26'30" N, long. 119°04'45" W). Named on Santa Paula Peak (1951) 7.5' quadrangle.

Echo Lake [LOS ANGELES]: *lake,* 400 feet long, 3.25 miles northeast of Mount Banning on Santa Catalina Island (lat. 33°24' N, long. 118°23'25" W). Named on Santa Catalina North (1950) 7.5' quadrangle. Doran (1980, p. 77) gave the alternate name "Crater Lake" for the feature.

Echo Mountain [LOS ANGELES]: *locality,* 3.5 miles west-southwest of Mount Wilson (lat. 34°12'45" N, long. 118°07'15" W; sec. 34, T 2 N, R 12 W). Site named on Mount Wilson (1953) 7.5' quadrangle. Pasadena (1900) 15' quadrangle has both the names "Echo Mountain" and "Mount Lowe Hotel" at the spot. Mount Lowe (1939) 6' quadrangle has the name "Echo Mountain" for a place along the Pacific Electric incline cable, and Mount Wilson (1966) 7.5' quadrangle has the name "Echo Mountain" for a peak at the place. Postal authorities established Echo Mountain post office in 1893, moved it 3.5 miles northeast in 1904, and changed the name to Mount Lowe in 1910 (Salley, p. 65).

Echo Rock [LOS ANGELES]: *peak,* 0.25 mile northeast of Mount Wilson (1) (lat. 34°13'30" N, long. 118°03'20" W). Named on Pasadena (1900) 15' quadrangle.

Edendale [LOS ANGELES]: *locality,* 2.5 miles north-northwest of Los Angeles city hall (lat. 34°05'25" N, long. 118°15'25" W). Named on Hollywood (1953) 7.5' quadrangle. Postal authorities established Edendale post office in 1952 (Salley, p. 65).

Edfu: see **Lemon** [VENTURA].

Edgemont [LOS ANGELES]: *locality,* 4.5 miles northwest of present Los Angeles city hall (lat. 34°06'35" N, long. 118°17'35" W). Named on Santa Monica (1902) 15' quadrangle.

Edwards Air Force Base: see **Rosamond Lake** [LOS ANGELES].

Edwards Canyon [VENTURA]: *canyon,* drained by a stream that flows 1 mile to the valley of Santa Clara River 1 mile west of Piru (lat. 34°24'45" N, long. 118°48'35" W; sec. 19, T 4 N, R 18 W). Named on Piru (1952) 7.5' quadrangle.

Eel Point [LOS ANGELES]: *promontory,* 8 miles south-southeast of Northwest Harbor on the west side of San Clemente Island (lat. 32°55'05" N, long. 118°32'45" W). Named on San Clemente Island Central (1943) 7.5' quadrangle.

Elayon [LOS ANGELES]: *locality,* less than 1 mile south-southeast of Newhall along Southern Pacific Railroad (lat. 34°22'15" N, long. 118°31'20" W). Named on Santa Susana (1903) 15' quadrangle.

El Cañon de la Boca Negra: see **Big Dalton Canyon** [LOS ANGELES].

El Conejo [LOS ANGELES-VENTURA]: *land grant,* around Newbury Park and Thousands Oaks; mainly in Ventura County, but extends south into Los Angeles County. Named on Newbury Park (1951), Point Dume (1951), Thousand Oaks (1952), and Triunfo Pass (1950) 7.5' quadrangles. Jose Polanco and Ignacio Rodriguez received 11 leagues in 1803; Jose de la Guerra y Noriega received the grant in 1822 and claimed 48,672 acres patented in 1873 (Cowan, p. 29; Cowan gave the name "Señora de Altagracia" as an alternate). Font first used the name "Conejo" in the neighborhood in 1776—*conejo* means "rabbit" in Spanish (Ricard).

Elderberry Canyon [LOS ANGELES]: *canyon,* drained by a stream that flows 3.5 miles to Castaic Creek nearly 6 miles east of Whitaker Peak (lat. 34°34'05" N, long. 118°37'50" W; sec. 36, T 6 N, R 17 W). Named on Warm Springs Mountain (1958) and Whitaker Peak (1958) 7.5' quadrangles. Los Angeles County (1935) map names several other branches of the canyon of Castaic Creek: Simon Canyon, which opens into the canyon of Castaic Creek from the east about 0.5 mile downstream from the mouth of Elderberry Canyon; Cordova Canyon, which opens into the canyon of Castaic Creek from the northeast about 0.25 mile upstream from the mouth of Elderberry Canyon; Funks Canyon, which opens into the canyon of Castaic Creek from the north about

1 mile upstream from the mouth of Elderberry Canyon; Haynes Canyon, which opens into the canyon of Castaic Creek from the northeast about 1 mile upstream from the mouth of Funks Canyon; Sycamore Canyon, which opens into the canyon of Castaic Creek from the southwest about 0.25 mile upstream from the mouth of Haynes Canyon; and Randolph Canyon, which opens into the canyon of Castaic Creek from the southwest about 0.5 mile upstream from the mouth of Sycamore Canyon.

Elderberry Forebay [LOS ANGELES]: *water feature,* behind a dam on Castaic Creek 6 miles east of Whitaker Peak (lat. 34°33'40" N, long. 118°37'45" W; near S line sec. 36, T 6 N, R 17 W); the feature is at and above the mouth of Elderberry Canyon. Named on Whitaker Peak (1958, photorevised 1974) 7.5' quadrangle. United States Board on Geographic Names (1973, p. 3) gave the variant names "Castaic Afterbay," "Castaic Forebay," "Castaic Pumping Forebay," "Castaic Pumping Plant Afterbay," and "Castaic Reservoir" for the feature.

Eldon: see **Lancaster** [LOS ANGELES].

Eldoradoville: see **Eldoradoville Campground** [LOS ANGELES].

Eldoradoville Campground [LOS ANGELES]: *locality,* 8.5 miles northeast of Glendora city hall along San Gabriel River (lat. 34° 13'45" N, long. 117°46'10" W). Named on Glendora (1966) 7.5' quadrangle. The name recalls the mining camp of Eldoradoville, which was situated near the intersection of East Fork San Gabriel River and Cattle Canyon; the first settlement at the site, called Prospect Bar, was destroyed by a flood in 1859, and Eldoradoville was wiped out by a flood in 1862—a shanty settlement of unemployed men and their families at the site in the depression years of the early 1930's had the informal name "Hooverville" (Robinson, J.W., 1983, p. 18-20, 40).

Eleanor: see **Lake Eleanor** [VENTURA].

Electric: see **Pico Heights** [LOS ANGELES].

El Encanto [LOS ANGELES]: *locality,* 2 miles north-northeast of Azusa city hall (lat. 34°09'40" N, long. 117°53'30" W; near E line sec. 23, T 1 N, R 10 W). Named on Azusa (1953) 7.5' quadrangle.

El Encino[LOS ANGELES]: *land grant,* at and north of Encino. Named on Canoga Park (1952) and Van Nuys (1966) 7.5' quadrangles. Ramon, Francisco, and Roque (presumably Indians) received 1 league in 1845; Vicente de la Ossa claimed 4461 acres patented in 1873 (Cowan, p. 34).

Elephant Hill [LOS ANGELES]: *peak,* 2.5 miles west of Pomona city hall (lat. 34°03'05" N, long. 117°47'45" W). Altitude 1160 feet. Named on San Dimas (1954) 7.5' quadrangle.

El Escorpion [LOS ANGELES]: *land grant,* north of Calabasas. Named on Calabasas

(1952) 7.5' quadrangle. Odon, Urbano, and Manuel (who were Indians) received the land in 1845 and claimed 1110 acres patented in 1876 (Cowan, p. 34).

Elftman [LOS ANGELES]: *locality,* 5 miles north-northwest of Long Beach city hall along Southern Pacific Railroad (lat. 33°50'25" N, long. 118°13'20" W). Named on Long Beach (1964) 7.5' quadrangle. Downey (1902) 15' quadrangle has the name "Cerritos" at the site. Postal authorities established Cerritos post office in 1888, discontinued it in 1890, reestablished it in 1902, and discontinued it in 1903 (Salley, p. 41).

Elisio: see **Santa Paula** [VENTURA].

Elizabeth Lake [LOS ANGELES]:
(1) *intermittent lake,* 1.25 miles long, 2.25 miles east-southeast of the village of Lake Hughes (lat. 34°40' N, long. 118°24'10" W; mainly in sec. 30, T 7 N, R 14 W). Named on Lake Hughes (1957) 7.5' quadrangle. Baker's (1911) map shows two lakes at the place, and has the name "Elizabeth Lakes" for them. Elizabeth Lake (1917) 30' quadrangle shows one permanent lake there. Hughes Lake (1937) 6' quadrangles shows two lakes at the place, and has the name "Elizabeth Lake" for the pair. The feature long was known as La Laguna de Chico Lopez for its owner; the present name came after Elizabeth Wingfield fell into the lake (Latta, p. 29, 81). It also was called Laguna del Diablo (Bell, p. 202) and Rabbit Lake (Barras, p. 17). Blake (p. 57) used the form "Lake Elizabeth" for the name.
(2) *locality,* 3.25 miles east-southeast of the present village of Lake Hughes (lat. 34°39'45" N, long. 118°22'50" W; near S line sec. 29, T 7 N, R 14 W); the place is less than 0.5 mile east-southeast of the east end of Elizabeth Lake (1). Named on Elizabeth Lake (1917) 30' quadrangle. Postal authorities established Elizabeth Lake post office in 1878, discontinued it in 1892, reestablished it in 1893, discontinued it in 1918, reestablished it in 1923, and discontinued it finally in 1925 (Frickstad, p. 73). California Mining Bureau's (1917) map shows a place called Pinchot located 6 miles southwest of Elizabeth Lake (2). Postal authorities established Pinchot post office in 1908 and discontinued it in 1911; the name was for Gifford Pinchot, head of the Forest Service (Salley, p. 171).

Elizabeth Lake Campground [LOS ANGELES]: *locality,* 2.25 miles northeast of Warm Springs Mountain (lat. 34°37'15" N, long. 118° 33'25" W); the place is in Elizabeth Lake Canyon. Named on Warm Springs Mountain (1958) 7.5' quadrangle.

Elizabeth Lake Canyon [LOS ANGELES]: *canyon,* drained by a stream that flows 16 miles to Castaic Creek 5.5 miles south-southwest of Warm Springs Mountain (lat. 34°31' N, long. 118°36'15" W; near W line sec. 18, T 5 N, R 16 W); the feature heads 3 miles west of Elizabeth Lake (1). Named on Burnt Peak (1958), Lake Hughes (1957), and Warm Springs Mountain (1958) 7.5' quadrangles.

Elkhorn Camp [LOS ANGELES]: *locality,* 6.25 miles northwest of present Santa Monica city hall in Topanga Canyon (lat. 34°03'35" N, long. 118°35' W). Named on Topanga Canyon (1928) 6' quadrangle.

Elkhorn Lodge [LOS ANGELES]: *locality,* 10 miles northeast of Solemint (lat. 34°29'40" N, long. 118°18'30" W; near NE cor. sec. 26, T 5 N, R 14 W). Named on Lang (1933) 6' quadrangle.

Eller Slough [LOS ANGELES]: *stream,* flows 4 miles to end 5.25 miles north-northwest of Black Butte (lat. 34°37'40" N, long. 117° 44'40" W; sec. 8, T 6 N, R 8 W)). Named on Adobe Mountain (1955) and El Mirage (1956) 7.5' quadrangles.

Ellis Apiary Campground [VENTURA]: *locality,* 6 miles east-southeast of Cobblestone Mountain (lat. 34°34' N, long. 118°46'40" W). Named on Cobblestone Mountain (1958) 7.5' quadrangle. A small commercial beehive operation was at the site (Gagnon, p. 79).

Ellsworth Barranca [VENTURA]: *gully,* extends for 2 miles from the mouth of Aliso Canyon to Santa Clara River 1 mile east-northeast of Saticoy (lat. 34°17'30" N, long. 119°07'50" W). Named on Saticoy (1951) 7.5' quadrangle. The name commemorates Daniel Ellsworth and Charles Ellsworth, farmers near Saticoy in the 1870's (Ricard).

Elm Creek [VENTURA]: *stream,* flows 1.5 miles to Tar Creek 6.5 miles north of Fillmore (lat. 34°29'35" N, long. 118°53'05" W; near E line sec. 29, T 5 N, R 19 W). Named on Cobblestone Mountain (1958) and Fillmore (1951) 7.5' quadrangles.

El Merrie Dell [LOS ANGELES]: *locality,* 4.5 miles northwest of Sunland in Kagel Canyon (lat. 34°17'45" N, long. 118°22'35" W; on E line sec. 31, T 3 N, R 14 W). Named on Sunland (1942) 6' quadrangle.

El Mirage Valley [LOS ANGELES]: *valley,* mainly in San Bernardino County, but extends northwest into Los Angeles County 12 miles north-northeast of Black Butte (lat. 34°44' N, long. 117°40' W). Named on Adobe Mountain (1955) and Jackrabbit Hill (1973) 7.5' quadrangles. Called Mirage Valley on Kramer (1942) 15' quadrangle, and called Antelope Valley on Adobe (1934) 6' quadrangle.

El Modena: see **El Modeno** [ORANGE].

El Modena Station [ORANGE]: *locality,* 2.25 miles east-southeast of present Orange city hall (lat. 33°46'50" N, long. 117°48'40" W). Named on Orange (1963) 7.5' quadrangle.

El Modeno [ORANGE]: *district,* 2 miles east of Orange city hall (lat. 33°47'15" N, long. 117°48'45" W). Named on Orange (1964) 7.5' quadrangle. Called El Modena on Corona (1902) 30' quadrangle. Lankershim Ranch Land and Water Company's (1888) map has

the form "Elmodena" for the name. Postal authorities established Earlham post office in 1887 and changed the name to El Modena in 1888, to El Modino in 1910, and back to El Modena in 1970; a group from Earlham, Indiana, planned to found a university at the spot and gave the site the name "Earlham" (Salley, p. 63, 68). United States Board on Geographic Names (1965b, p. 11) rejected the names "El Modena" and "Modena" for the place, but later (1970a, p. 2) approved the name "El Modena" and listed the names "El Modeno" and "Modena" as variants. Earlham began in 1886 as a Quaker settlement; the name was changed to Modena for the city in Italy, but postal authorities added the Spanish article "El" to the name to distinguish the post office from another one in California— later the terminal letter "a" was changed to "o" apparently in the mistaken belief that the gender of the word should agree with the Spanish article "El" (Hanna, p. 196).

El Molino [LOS ANGELES]: *district,* 6 miles west-northwest of El Monte city hall in San Marino (lat. 34°06'40" N, long. 118°07'15" W). Named on El Monte (1953) 7.5' quadrangle.

El Monte [LOS ANGELES]: *city,* 12 miles east of Los Angeles city hall (lat. 34°04'15" N, long. 118°01'45" W). Named on El Monte (1953) 7.5' quadrangle. A.W. Whipple (p. 135) referred to "the town of Monte," and Trask (p. 19) used the name "the Monte" for the place. Postal authorities established Monte post office in 1853, changed the name to Elmonte in 1875, and changed it to El Monte in 1905 (Salley, p. 68, 145). The city incorporated in 1912. Squatters came to the site in 1852, and a dense stand of willows there gave the name "El Monte" to the place—*el monte* means "the thicket" in Spanish (Gudde, 1949, p. 106). Henry Dalton laid out the town, which by 1852 had a dozen frame buildings and was called Lexington, Lickskillit, and El Monte; it was the first town of English-speaking people in Southern California (Jackson, p. 150). Postal authorities established Four Corners post office 6 miles northeast of El Monte post office (NE quarter sec. 17, T 1 S, R 10 W) in 1876 and discontinued it in 1878 (Salley, p. 79).

El Monte: see **South El Monte** [LOS ANGELES].

Elmwood Canyon [LOS ANGELES]: *canyon,* 1 mile long, 1.5 miles east-northeast of Burbank city hall (lat. 34°11'40" N, long. 118°16'55" W). Named on Burbank (1953) 7.5' quadrangle.

El Nido [LOS ANGELES]:

(1) *locality,* 3.5 miles west-northwest of Malibu Point (lat. 34°02'35" N, long. 118°44'20" W; sec. 35, T 1 S, R 18 W). Named on Malibu Beach (1951) 7.5' quadrangle.

(2) *district,* 2.25 miles north-northwest of Torrance city hall (lat. 33°51'55" N, long.

118°21'25" W). Named on Torrance (1964) 7.5' quadrangle.

El Paredon Blanco: see **Boyle Heights** [LOS ANGELES].

El Piojo: see **Anaheim Landing** [ORANGE].

El Prieto [LOS ANGELES]: *canyon*, drained by a stream that flows 1.5 miles to Arroyo Seco 4.5 miles north-northwest of Pasadena city hall (lat. 34°12'30" N, long. 118°10'10" W; at SE cor. sec. 31, T 2 N, R 12 W). Named on Pasadena (1953) 7.5' quadrangle. Called El Prieto Cany. on Los Angeles County (1935) map. For many years the feature was called Negro Canyon, for Robert Owen, a freed slave who lived there in the 1850's (Robinson, J.W., 1977, p. 103).

El Prieto Canyon: see **El Prieto** [LOS ANGELES].

El Pueblo de Nuestra Señora la Reina de los Angeles de la Porciuncula: see **Los Angeles** [LOS ANGELES].

El Rincon [VENTURA]: *land grant*, at Rincon Point on Ventura-Santa Barbara county line. Named on White Ledge Peak (1952) 7.5' quadrangle. Teodoro Arellanes received 1 league in 1835 and claimed 4460 acres patented in 1872 (Cowan, p. 68).

El Rio [VENTURA]: *town*, 2.5 miles north of Oxnard (lat. 34°14'05" N, long. 119°10'15" W); the place is near Santa Clara River. Named on Oxnard (1949) 7.5' quadrangle. Called Elrio on Hueneme (1904) 15' quadrangle. Postal authorities established New Jerusalem post office in 1882, changed the name to Jerusalem in 1895, changed it to El Rio the same year, discontinued it in 1911, reestablished it in 1953, and discontinued it in 1966 (Salley, p. 68, 107). The name "Jerusalem" was from Jewish merchants at the place (Ricard).

El Rio de los Temblores: see **San Gabriel River** [LOS ANGELES-ORANGE].

El Segundo [LOS ANGELES]: *town*, 2.25 miles north of Manhattan Beach city hall (lat. 33°55'05" N, long. 118°25' W). Named on Venice (1950) 7.5' quadrangle. Postal authorities established El Segundo post office in 1911 (Frickstad, p. 73), and the town incorporated in 1917. Colonel Rheem of Standard Oil Company applied the name "El Segundo" to the refinery that the company had at the place, the second refinery of the company in California—*el segundo* means "the second" in Spanish (Gudde, 1949, p. 107).

El Segundo Station [LOS ANGELES]:
(1) *locality*, 2 miles northeast of Manhattan Beach city hall along Atchison, Topeka and Santa Fe Railroad (lat. 33°54'30" N, long. 118°23' W). Named on Venice (1950) 7.5' quadrangle.
(2) *locality*, 1.25 miles north-northwest of present Manhattan Beach city hall along Pacific Electric Railroad (lat. 33°55' N, long. 118° 25'40" W). Named on Venice (1924) 6' quadrangle.

El Sereno [LOS ANGELES]: *district*, 4.25 miles east-northeast of Los Angeles city hall (lat. 34°04'55" N, long. 118°10'30" W; sec. 18, T 1 S, R 12 W). Named on Los Angeles (1953) 7.5' quadrangle. Postal authorities established El Sereno post office in 1949 (Salley, p. 68).

Elsmere Canyon [LOS ANGELES]: *canyon*, nearly 3 miles long, opens into the canyon of Newhall Creek 2 miles southeast of Newhall (lat. 34°21'40" N, long. 118°30'15" W). Named on San Fernando (1953) 7.5' quadrangle. On San Fernando (1945) 15' quadrangle, the name follows a southeasterly branch of the canyon rather than the present main canyon above the mouth of the branch.

El Toro [ORANGE]: *city*, 18 miles southeast of Santa Ana (lat. 33° 37'35" N, long. 117°41'35" W); the city is on Cañada de los Alisos grant. Named on El Toro (1968) and San Juan Capistrano (1968) 7.5' quadrangles. Postal authorities established Eltoro post office in 1888 and changed the name to El Toro in 1905 (Salley, p. 69). A townsite called Aliso City laid out at the place in 1887 failed to develop as planned (Meadows, p. 19). When railroad officials asked Mrs. Dwight Whiting to name their station at the site, she selected the designation "El Toro" from a bull that had fallen into a well there and drowned—*el toro* means "the bull" in Spanish (Hanna, p. 332).

El Toro Air Station: see **El Toro Marine Corps Air Station** [ORANGE].

El Toro Canyon [LOS ANGELES]: *canyon*, drained by a stream that flows nearly 2 miles to Las Llajas Canyon [LOS ANGELES-VENTURA] 7.5 miles west-southwest of Newhall (lat. 34°19'35" N, long. 118°38'45" W). Named on Santa Susana (1951) 7.5' quadrangle.

El Toro Marine Corps Air Station [ORANGE]: *military installation*, 4 miles north-northwest of El Toro (lat. 33°40'45" N, long. 117°43'30" W). Named on El Toro (1968) 7.5' quadrangle. Called El Toro Air Station on El Toro (1950) 7.5' quadrangle.

El Toro Reservoir [ORANGE]: *lake*, 0.25 mile long, 1.5 miles east of El Toro (lat. 33°37'25" N, long. 118°39'55" W; at N line sec. 25, T 6 S, R 8 W). Named on El Toro (1968) and San Juan Capistrano (1968) 7.5' quadrangles.

El Valle de Santa Catalina de Bononia de los Encinos: see **San Fernando Valley** [LOS ANGELES].

El Venado: see **Point Dume** [LOS ANGELES].

Elysian Garden [LOS ANGELES]: *locality*, 3.5 miles north-northwest of Los Angeles city hall (lat. 34°06'20" N, long. 118°15'30" W); the place is north of present Elysian Heights. Named on Glendale (1928) 6' quadrangle.

Elysian Heights [LOS ANGELES]: *district*, 2.5 miles north of Los Angeles city hall (lat. 34°05'15" N, long. 118°15' W). Named on

Hollywood (1953) and Los Angeles (1953) 7.5' quadrangles.

Emerald Bay [LOS ANGELES]: *embayment,* 2.5 miles east of Silver Peak on the north side of Santa Catalina Island (lat. 33°27'55" N, long. 118°31'25" W). Named on Santa Catalina West (1943) 7.5' quadrangle. The feature also was called Wilson's Cove, for Spencer H. Wilson (Doran, 1980, p. 68). During the mining boom of the 1860's, streets were laid out on the shore of Emerald Bay for a town to be called Queen City (Doran, 1963, p. 100; Gleason, p. 15-16).

Emerald Bay [ORANGE]: *village,* 1.5 miles west of Laguna Beach city hall along the coast (lat. 33°33'05" N, long. 117°48'20" W). Named on Laguna Beach (1965) 7.5' quadrangle. Los Angeles Title Insurance Company developed the exclusive residential community in 1929 (Meadows, p. 60).

Emerald Canyon [ORANGE]: *canyon,* drained by a stream that flows 3.25 miles to the sea 1.5 miles west-northwest of Laguna Beach city hall (lat. 33°33'05" N, long. 117°48'25" W); the mouth of the canyon is at Emerald Bay. Named on Laguna Beach (1965, photorevised 1981) 7.5' quadrangle. Called Niger Canyon on Santa Ana (1942) 15' quadrangle, and called Nigger Canyon on Laguna Beach (1949) 7.5' quadrangle. United States Board on Geographic Names (1969a, p. 3) rejected the names "Niger Canyon" and "Mayate Canyon" for the feature. The word "Nigger" was a corruption of the name "Niguel" (Meadows, p. 105).

Emerson Flats [LOS ANGELES]: *area,* 5.5 miles west-northwest of Azusa city hall (lat. 34°10'35" N, long. 117°59'15" W; sec. 13, T 1 N, R 11 W). Named on Azusa (1953) 7.5' quadrangle. The name commemorates L.H. Emerson, who filed for land just below the junction of Monrovia Canyon and Sawpit Canyon, and built a log cabin there in the 1880's (Robinson, J.W., 1983, p. 73-74).

Emma: see **Mount Emma** [LOS ANGELES].

Empire Landing [LOS ANGELES]: *locality,* 4 miles north of Mount Banning on the north side of Santa Catalina Island (lat. 33°25'35" N, long. 118°26' W). Named on Santa Catalina North (1950) 7.5' quadrangle. The place also was known as Pot Hole Harbor (Doran, 1980, p. 72).

Enchanto: see **Lake Enchanto** [LOS ANGELES].

Encinal Canyon [LOS ANGELES]: *canyon,* drained by a stream that flows 2.5 miles to the sea 4.5 miles northwest of Point Dume (lat. 34°02'10" N, long. 118°52'10" W). Named on Point Dume (1951) 7.5' quadrangle.

Encino [LOS ANGELES]: *district,* 6.25 miles east-southeast of the center of Canoga Park in Los Angeles (lat. 34°09'35" N, long. 118° 30' W); the place is on El Encino grant. Named

on Canoga Park (1952) and Van Nuys (1953) 7.5' quadrangles. Called Encino Park on Reseda (1928) 6' quadrangle. Postal authorities established En Cino post office in 1873, discontinued in it 1877, and reestablished it 1 mile farther north with the name "Encino" in 1938 (Salley, p. 70).

Encino Creek [LOS ANGELES]: *stream,* flows 2 miles to Los Angeles River 2 miles southsouthwest of Van Nuys (lat. 34°10'05" N, long. 118°28'25" W); the stream is in Encino. Named on Van Nuys (1966) 7.5' quadrangle.

Encino Park: see **Encino** [LOS ANGELES].

Encino Reservoir [LOS ANGELES]: *lake,* 0.5 mile long, 6 miles southeast of the center of Canoga Park (lat. 34°08'45" N, long. 118°30'45" W); the feature is 1.25 miles southwest of Encino. Named on Canoga Park (1952) 7.5' quadrangle.

Encino Siding [LOS ANGELES]: *locality,* 5.5 miles east of the center of Canoga Park along Southern Pacific Railroad (lat. 34°11'10" N, long. 118°30'15" W); the place is 2 miles north of Encino. Named on Canoga Park (1952) 7.5' quadrangle. Reseda (1928) 6' quadrangle shows a place called "Encino" located along the railroad 0.25 mile farther south before the rails were realigned.

Engleheard Canyon [LOS ANGELES]: *canyon,* drained by a stream that flows 1.5 miles to Verdugo Wash 7 miles northwest of Pasadena city hall (lat. 34°12'25" N, long. 118°14'25" W). Named on Burbank (1953) and Pasadena (1966) 7.5' quadrangles.

Englewild Canyon [LOS ANGELES]: *canyon,* 1 mile long, 2 miles north-northeast of Glendora city hall (lat. 34°09'40" N, long. 117° 51'05" W; mainly in sec. 20, T 1 N, R 9 W). Named on Glendora (1953) 7.5' quadrangle.

English Canyon [ORANGE]: *canyon,* drained by a stream that flows 3.5 miles to Aliso Creek less than 1 mile east of El Toro (lat. 33° 37'45" N, long. 117°40'50" W). Named on El Toro (1968) 7.5' quadrangle. The name is from settlers who came to the place from England in 1890 (Meadows, p. 61).

Ensenada de San Andres: see **San Pedro Bay** [LOS ANGELES-ORANGE].

Epworth [VENTURA]: *locality,* 2 miles northnorthwest of Moorpark (lat. 34°18'55" N, long. 118°53'25" W; sec. 29, T 3 N, R 19 W). Named on Moorpark (1951) 7.5' quadrangle.

Era Canyon: see **Bouquet Canyon** [LOS ANGELES].

Escondido Beach [LOS ANGELES]: *beach,* 2.5 miles northeast of Point Dume along the coast (lat. 34°01'30" N, long. 118°46' W); the beach is at the mouth of Escondido Canyon (2). Named on Point Dume (1951) 7.5' quadrangle.

Escondido Canyon [LOS ANGELES]:
  (1) *canyon,* drained by a stream that flows 6 miles to Agua Dulce Canyon 8 miles east-

northeast of Solemint (lat. 34°27'50" N, long. 118°19'45" W; near NE cor. sec. 3, T 4 N, R 14 W). Named on Agua Dulce (1960) 7.5' quadrangle. Los Angeles County (1935) map shows North Fork opening into the main canyon from the northeast about 1.5 miles above the mouth of the main canyon.
(2) *canyon,* drained by a stream that flows 4.5 miles to the sea 3 miles northeast of Point Dume (lat. 34°01'30" N, long. 118°45'50" W). Named on Point Dume (1951) 7.5' quadrangle.

Esperanza [ORANGE]: *locality,* 3.5 miles east-southeast of Yorba Linda along Atchison, Topeka and Santa Fe Railroad (lat. 33°52'35" N, long. 117°45'15" W). Named on Orange (1964), Prado Dam (1967), and Yorba Linda (1950) 7.5' quadrangles. The name is for Esperanza Yorba, daughter of Prudencio Yorba (Meadows, p. 61).

Esperanza: see **Lancaster** [LOS ANGELES].

Eureka Canyon [VENTURA]: *canyon,* drained by a stream that flows 4 miles to the valley of Santa Clara River 1.5 miles south-southeast of Piru (lat. 34°23'35" N, long. 118°46'55" W). Named on Piru (1952), Santa Susana (1951), and Val Verde (1952) 7.5' quadrangles.

Evergreen [LOS ANGELES]: *locality,* nearly 1 mile west-southwest of present Whittier city hall along Southern Pacific Railroad (lat. 33°58' N, long. 118°02'55" W). Named on Downey (1902) 15' quadrangle.

Evey Canyon [LOS ANGELES]: *canyon,* drained by a stream that flows 2 miles to San Antonio Canyon 8.5 miles north-northeast of Pomona city hall (lat. 34°09'45" N, long. 117°40'50" W; near NE cor. sec. 23, T 1 N, R 8 W). Named on Mount Baldy (1954) 7.5' quadrangle. The name commemorates Judge Evey, who settled in San Antonio Canyon in the late 1870's (Robinson, J.W., 1983, p. 136).

Ex Mission de San Fernando [LOS ANGELES]: *land grant,* in San Fernando Valley at and around San Fernando mission. Named on Calabasas (1952), Canoga Park (1952), Oat Mountain (1952), San Fernando (1953), Sunland (1953), and Van Nuys (1953) 7.5' quadrangles. Eulogio de Célis bought 13 leagues in 1846 and claimed 116,858 acres patented in 1873 (Cowan, p. 76).

Eyrie: see **The Eyrie**, under **Mount Harvard** [LOS ANGELES].

— F —

Fagan Canyon [VENTURA]: *canyon,* drained by a stream that flows 3 miles to the valley of Santa Clara River 1 mile west of downtown Santa Paula (lat. 34°21'20" N, long. 119°04'40" W). Named on Santa Paula (1951) and Santa Paula Peak (1951) 7.5' quadrangles. The name commemorates Michael Fagan, who settled in Ventura County in 1869 and

raised sheep in the canyon (Ricard).

Fairmont [LOS ANGELES]: *locality,* 4 miles north-northeast of the village of Lake Hughes (lat. 34°44'05" N, long. 118°25'25" W; sec. 36, T 8 N, R 15 W). Named on Lake Hughes (1957) 7.5' quadrangle. Postal authorities established Fairmont post office in 1888 and discontinued it in 1939; the name was transferred from a place in Illinois (Salley, p. 72).

Fairmont Butte [LOS ANGELES]: *ridge,* generally north-northeast-trending, nearly 2 miles long, 6 miles north-northeast of the village of Lake Hughes (lat. 34°45'30" N, long. 118°24' W). Named on Fairmont Butte (1965) and Lake Hughes (1957) 7.5' quadrangles.

Fairmont Reservoir [LOS ANGELES]: *lake,* 4300 feet long, 2 miles north of the village of Lake Hughes (lat. 34°42'25" N, long. 118° 25'55" W; sec. 11, 12, T 7 N, R 15 W); the feature is 2 miles south-southwest of Fairmont. Named on Lake Hughes (1957) 7.5' quadrangle. Johnson's (1911) map shows an inhabited place called North Portal located at present Fairmont Reservoir at the north end of a tunnel for the aqueduct that brings Owens Valley water from Inyo County to Los Angeles—the place was a temporary headquarters for operations at the north end of the tunnel (Johnson, p. 9).

Fair Oaks [LOS ANGELES]: *locality,* 6.5 miles northeast of present Los Angeles city hall along a rail line (lat. 34°07'05" N, long. 118° 09'15" W). Named on Pasadena (1900) 15' quadrangle.

Fairview [ORANGE]: *locality,* 6 miles southsouthwest of Santa Ana (lat. 33°40'15" N, long. 117°55' W). Named on Corona (1902) 30' quadrangle. Postal authorities established Fairview post office in 1888 and discontinued it in 1903 (Frickstad, p. 116). Promoters bought land in 1887 and laid out a town of Fairview, but the enterprise failed and the land reverted to farming; Santa Ana Army Air Base was established at the site in 1943 (Meadows, p. 62, 123-124). Waring (p. 37) described a place called Fairview Hot Spring that was located south of Santa Ana; water for the establishment originally came from a spring, but later from an artesian well 700 feet deep—in 1908 a hotel and cottages accommodated about 50 people.

Fairview [VENTURA]: *locality,* 3 miles northwest of Moorpark (lat. 34°18'55" N, long. 118°54'50" W; sec. 30, T 3 N, R 19 W). Named on Moorpark (1951) 7.5' quadrangle.

Fairview Canyon [VENTURA]: *canyon,* drained by a stream that flows 1.25 miles to the valley of Santa Clara River 4 miles westsouthwest of Piru (lat. 34°23'55" N, long. 118°51'40" W; sec. 27, T 4 N, R 19 W). Named on Piru (1952) 7.5' quadrangle.

Fairview Hot Spring: see **Fairview** [ORANGE].

Fall Canyon [LOS ANGELES]: *canyon,* drained by a stream that flows nearly 3 miles to Texas

Canyon 11 miles south of the village of Lake Hughes (lat. 34°30'55" N, long. 118°24'20" W; sec. 13, T 5 N, R 15 W). Named on Green Valley (1958) 7.5' quadrangle. On Los Angeles County (1935) map, the stream in the canyon is called Fall Creek.

Fall Creek [LOS ANGELES]: *stream,* flows 1.5 miles to Big Tujunga Canyon 3.5 miles east-southeast of Condor Peak (lat. 34°18'20" N, long. 118°09'45" W). Named on Condor Peak (1959) 7.5' quadrangle, which shows waterfalls near the mouth of the creek.

Fall Creek: see **Fall Canyon** [LOS ANGELES].

Fallen Leaf Spring [LOS ANGELES]: *spring,* 11.5 miles north-northeast of Pomona city hall (lat. 34°13'05" N, long. 117°41'50" W). Named on Mount Baldy (1954) 7.5' quadrangle.

Falling Springs [LOS ANGELES]: *locality,* 1.25 miles south-southeast of Crystal Lake (lat. 34°18'10" N, long. 117°50'15" W). Named on Crystal Lake (1958) 7.5' quadrangle. Called La Cienega on Crystal Lake (1941) 6' quadrangle, but United States Board on Geographic Names (1962, p. 11) rejected this name. The site first was known as Little Cienega; Frank Headlee built a small resort there in 1931 that he called La Cienega, then Headlee's, and finally Falling Springs Resort (Robinson, J.W., 1983, p. 94).

Fallon: see **Rowland** [LOS ANGELES].

Falls Canyon [LOS ANGELES]:
(1) *canyon,* drained by a stream that flows nearly 1.5 miles to West Fork San Gabriel River 9 miles south-southwest of Pacifico Mountain (lat. 34°15'10" N, long. 118°04'20" W; near S line sec. 18, T 2 N, R 11 W). Named on Chilao Flat (1959) and Mount Wilson (1953) 7.5' quadrangles.
(2) *canyon,* drained by a stream that flows nearly 1 mile to Arroyo Seco 6.25 miles north-northwest of Pasadena city hall (lat. 34° 14' N, long. 118°10'40" W). Named on Pasadena (1953) 7.5' quadrangle.

Falls Canyon [ORANGE]: *canyon,* drained by a stream that flows 1.5 miles to Trabuco Canyon 2.5 miles south of Santiago Peak (lat. 33° 40'25" N, long. 117°32'10" W; near W line sec. 5, T 6 S, R 6 W). Named on Santiago Peak (1954) 7.5' quadrangle. A place called Surprise City was situated at the mouth of Falls Canyon; it provided housing for workers associated with the tin mine in Trabuco Canyon from about 1902 until 1908 (Meadows, p. 132). A flood in 1916 swept away the abandoned houses there (Sleeper, 1968, p. 166).

Falls Creek [LOS ANGELES]: *stream,* flows 2.5 miles to Devil Canyon 1.5 miles north of Chatsworth (lat. 34°16'55" N, long. 118° 36'20" W; at E line sec. 1, T 2 N, R 17 W). Named on Oat Mountain (1952) 7.5' quadrangle. The canyon of the stream has the name "Twin Lakes Canyon" on Los Angeles County (1935) map.

Falls Gulch [LOS ANGELES]: *canyon,* drained by a stream that flows 1.25 miles to San Gabriel River 5 miles west of Mount San Antonio (lat. 34°18'10" N, long. 117°44' W; sec. 32, T 3 N, R 8 W). Named on Mount San Antonio (1955) 7.5' quadrangle.

Falsa Vela: see **Anacapa Island** [VENTURA].

Farnsworth Bank: see **Lands End** [LOS ANGELES].

Fascination Spring [LOS ANGELES]: *spring,* 2.25 miles north-northwest of Sunland (lat. 34°17'30" N, long. 118°19'20" W; near NW cor. sec. 2, T 2 N, R 14 W). Named on Sunland (1953) 7.5' quadrangle.

Fellowship Farm [LOS ANGELES]: *locality,* 3 miles south-southeast of Baldwin Park (lat. 34°02'45" N, long. 117°56'15" W). Named on Puente (1927) 6' quadrangle.

Fenner Canyon [LOS ANGELES]: *canyon,* drained by a stream that flows 1.5 miles to Big Rock Creek 5.5 miles southeast of Valyermo (lat. 34°23'25" N, long. 117°46'40" W). Named on Valyermo (1958) 7.5' quadrangle.

Fermin: see **Point Fermin** [LOS ANGELES].

Fernandez: see **Juan Fernandez Spring** [VENTURA].

Fernando: see **San Fernando** [LOS ANGELES].

Fernando Pass: see **San Fernando Pass** [LOS ANGELES].

Fern Ann Falls [LOS ANGELES]: *locality,* 2 miles north-northwest of Chatsworth (lat. 34°17'05" N, long. 118°36'55" W; sec. 1, T 2 N, R 17 W); the place is along Falls Creek. Named on Oat Mountain (1952) 7.5' quadrangle.

Fern Canyon [LOS ANGELES]:
(1) *canyon,* drained by a stream that flows 2 miles to Arroyo Seco (lat. 34°12'50" N, long. 118°10'20" W; sec. 31, T 2 N, R 12 W). Named on Pasadena (1953) 7.5' quadrangle. Los Angeles County (1935) map shows a feature called Coon Canyon situated between Fern Canyon (1) and El Prieto.
(2) *canyon,* drained by a stream that flows less than 1 mile to Fish Canyon (2) 2.5 miles north-northwest of Azusa city hall (lat. 34° 10'10" N, long. 117°55'30" W; near E line sec. 16, T 1 N, R 10 W). Named on Azusa (1953) 7.5' quadrangle.
(3) *canyon,* drained by a stream that flows 3.5 miles to East Fork San Dimas Canyon nearly 10 miles north of Pomona city hall (lat. 34°11'45" N, long. 117°44'20" W; near S line sec. 5, T 1 N, R 8 W). Named on Mount Baldy (1954) 7.5' quadrangle.
(4) *canyon,* 0.5 mile long, nearly 4 miles south-southeast of Burbank city hall (lat. 34°07'45" N, long. 118°17'05" W). Named on Burbank (1953) 7.5' quadrangle.

Fern Lodge [LOS ANGELES]: *locality,* 2.5 miles east-southeast of Mount Wilson (1) in Santa Anita Canyon (lat. 34°12'30" N, long. 118°01' W; on N line sec. 3, T 1 N, R 11 W).

Named

DURHAM'S PLACE-NAMES

Named on Mount Wilson (1953) 7.5' quadrangle. Earl Topping built Fern Lodge in 1916 (Robinson, J.W., 1977, p. 134).

Fern Springs [LOS ANGELES]: *spring,* 6.25 miles north of Glendora city hall (lat. 34°13'40" W, long. 117°52'10" W; sec. 30, T 2 N, R 9 W). Named on Glendora (1953) 7.5' quadrangle.

Fernwood [LOS ANGELES]: *settlement,* 8 miles northwest of Santa Monica city hall (lat. 34°04'45" N, long. 118°36' W; sec. 18, T 1 S, R 16 W). Named on Topanga (1952) 7.5' quadrangle. Called Wildwood on Topanga Canyon (1928) 6' quadrangle.

Fillmore [VENTURA]: *town,* 9 miles east-northeast of Santa Paula (lat. 34°24'05" N, long. 118°54'40" W; sec. 30, T 4 N, R 19 W). Named on Fillmore (1951) 7.5' quadrangle. Postal authorities established Fillmore post office in 1887 (Frickstad, p. 218), and the town incorporated in 1914. The name is for J.A. Fillmore of Southern Pacific Railroad (Hanna, p. 105). Postal authorities established Scenega post office 12 miles east of Santa Paula in 1875, discontinued it for a time in 1876, and discontinued it finally in 1888—the name was a corruption of the Spanish word *cienega* (Salley, p. 199).

Fillmore: see **North Fillmore** [VENTURA].

Fine Gold Canyon: see **Santa Felicia Canyon** [LOS ANGELES-VENTURA].

Firestone Park [LOS ANGELES]: *locality,* 1.5 miles west-northwest of South Gate city hall along Southern Pacific Railroad (lat. 33°57'50" N, long. 118°13'55" W). Named on South Gate (1964) 7.5' quadrangle. Called Firestone Park Sta. on South Gate (1952) 7.5' quadrangle.

Firestone Park Station: see **Firestone Park** [LOS ANGELES].

Firmin: see **Point Fermin** [LOS ANGELES].

Firth: see **Paramount** [LOS ANGELES].

Fish Camp: see **East Fish Camp** [VENTURA].

Fish Canyon [LOS ANGELES].

(1) *canyon,* drained by a stream that flows 12 miles to Castaic Creek 4.5 miles east-northeast of Whitaker Peak (lat. 34°36'05" N, long. 118°39'50" W; near N line sec. 22, T 6 N, R 17 W). Named on Burnt Peak (1958), Liebre Mountain (1958), and Whitaker Peak (1958) 7.5' quadrangles. East Fork branches east 6.5 miles east-northeast of Whitaker Peak; it is 3.5 miles long and is named on Burnt Peak (1958), Warm Springs Mountain (1958), and Whitaker Peak (1958) 7.5' quadrangles. North Fork branches north 1 mile west-northwest of Burnt Peak; it is 1.5 miles long and is named on Burnt Peak (1958) 7.5' quadrangle.

(2) *canyon,* drained by a stream that flows 6.25 miles to lowlands 2 miles north-northwest of Azusa city hall (lat. 34°09'30" N, long. 117°55'25" W; at W line sec. 22, T 1 N, R 10 W). Named on Azusa (1953) 7.5' quadrangle.

Fish Creek [LOS ANGELES]: *stream,* flows 4 miles to Elizabeth Lake Canyon 4.25 miles southeast of Burnt Peak (lat. 34°38'30" N, long. 118°31'15" W). Named on Burnt Peak (1958) 7.5' quadrangle.

Fish Creek [VENTURA]: *stream,* flows 5 miles to Piru Creek 4 miles east of Cobblestone Mountain (lat. 34°36'30" N, long. 118°47'45" W). Named on Cobblestone Mountain (1958) 7.5' quadrangle. North Fork enters from the north 1.25 miles above the mouth of the main stream; it is 3 miles long and is named on Black Mountain (1958) and Cobblestone Mountain (1958) 7.5' quadrangles.

Fisher Canyon [LOS ANGELES]: *canyon,* 1 mile long, 3.25 miles northwest of Burbank city hall (lat. 34°12'50" N, long. 118°20'15" W; in and near sec. 34, T 2 N, R 14 W). Named on Burbank (1953) 7.5' quadrangle.

Fishermans Cove [LOS ANGELES]: *embayment,* nearly 6 miles north-northwest of Mount Banning on the north side of Santa Catalina Island (lat. 33°26'40" N, long. 118°29'05" W). Named on Santa Catalina North (1950) 7.5' quadrangle. United States Coast and Geodetic Survey (p. 108) used the form "Fisherman Cove" for the name.

Fisher Spring [LOS ANGELES]: *spring,* 1.5 miles northeast of Whitaker Peak (lat. 34°35'25" N, long. 118°42'55" W; near SE cor. sec. 19, T 6 N, R 17 W). Named on Whitaker Peak (1958) 7.5' quadrangle.

Fish Fork [LOS ANGELES]: *stream,* flows 4 miles to San Gabriel River 5 miles west of Mount San Antonio (lat. 34°18'20" N, long. 117°43'55" W; sec. 32, T 3 N, R 8 W). Named on Mount San Antonio (1955) 7.5' quadrangle. Los Angeles County (1935) map shows a place called Cedar Camp located 2 miles northwest of San Antonio Peak (present Mount San Antonio) along a tributary to Fish Fork (sec. 36, T 3 N, R 8 W).

Fish Fork Camp [LOS ANGELES]: *locality,* 5 miles west of Mount San Antonio along San Gabriel River (lat. 34°18'20" N, long. 117° 43'55" W; sec. 32, T 3 N, R 8 W); the place is opposite the mouth of Fish Fork. Named on Mount San Antonio (1955) 7.5' quadrangle.

Fish Harbor [LOS ANGELES]: *water feature,* 2.5 miles northeast of Point Fermin at the southwest end of Terminal Island (lat. 33°44'10" N, long. 118°16' W). Named on San Pedro (1964) 7.5' quadrangle.

Five Points [LOS ANGELES]: *locality,* less than 1 mile southeast of El Monte city hall (lat. 34°03'45" N, long. 118°01'05" W). Named on El Monte (1953) 7.5' quadrangle.

Flat Rock [LOS ANGELES]: *rock,* 3.25 miles south-southwest of Redondo Beach city hall, and 500 feet offshore (lat. 33°47'45" N, long. 118°24'35" W). Named on Redondo Beach (1963) 7.5' quadrangle.

Flat Rock Point [LOS ANGELES]: *promontory,* 3.25 miles south-southwest of Redondo Beach city hall along the coast (lat. 33°47'50" N, long. 118°24'30" W); Flat Rock is off the promontory. Named on Redondo Beach (1963) 7.5' quadrangle. Redondo Beach (1951) 7.5' quadrangle has the form "Flatrock Point" for the name.

Flint Peak [LOS ANGELES]: *peak,* 3.25 miles west-northwest of Pasadena city hall (lat. 34°09'50" N, long. 118°11'45" W). Altitude 1888 feet. Named on Pasadena (1953) 7.5' quadrangle.

Flintridge [LOS ANGELES]: *district,* 4 miles northwest of Pasadena city hall (lat. 34°11' N, long. 118°11'45" W). Named on Pasadena (1953) 7.5' quadrangle. The place was subdivided in 1920 and Frank P. Flint, senator from California from 1905 until 1911, named it (Gudde, 1949, p. 116). Flintridge and La Cañada (2) incorporated in 1976 with the name "La Cañada Flintridge."

Florence [LOS ANGELES]: *district,* 3 miles west-northwest of South Gate city hall (lat. 33°58'30" N, long. 118°14'55" W). Named on Inglewood (1964) and South Gate (1964) 7.5' quadrangles. Postal authorities established Florence post office in 1878, discontinued it in 1918, and reestablished it in 1926 (Salley, p. 76). Downey (1902) 15' quadrangle has the name "Florence" for a place located along Southern Pacific Railroad in present Florence (lat. 33°58'25" N, long. 118°14'05" W), and has the name "Florence Sta." for a place situated along the railroad less than 1 mile farther south (lat. 33°57'45" N, long. 118°14' W).

Florence Station: see **Florence** [LOS ANGELES].

Flume Canyon [LOS ANGELES]: *canyon,* drained by a stream that heads in Los Angeles County and flows 1.5 miles to Swarthout Valley 5.25 miles north of Mount San Antonio in San Bernandino County (lat. 34°21'50" N, long. 117°39'05" W; sec. 7, T 3 N, R 7 W). Named on Mount San Antonio (1955) 7.5' quadrangle. On Los Angeles County (1935) map, the stream in the canyon is called Flume Creek.

Flume Creek: see **Flume Canyon** [LOS ANGELES].

Follows Camp [LOS ANGELES]: *locality,* 7.5 miles north-northeast of Glendora city hall along San Gabriel River (lat. 34°14' N, long. 117°48'10" W; near NE cor. sec. 27, T 2 N, R 9 W). Named on Glendora (1966) 7.5' quadrangle. Ralph Follows came to live along San Gabriel River to restore his health in 1891 and soon started the camp that bears his name (Robinson, J.W., 1983, p. 86-87). A place called Branscomb Camp started just east of Follows Camp in 1913 and washed away the next year (Robinson, J.W., 1983, p. 97).

Follows Camp West: see **Shady Oaks Camp** [LOS ANGELES].

Folsom Ridge [ORANGE]: *ridge,* generally west-trending, less than 1 mile long, 2.25 miles south-southeast of San Juan Capistrano

(lat. 33°28'05" N, long. 117°39'15" W). Named on Dana Point (1968) 7.5' quadrangle.

Foothill Station: see **Sulphur Springs** [LOS ANGELES].

Forbes Siding [LOS ANGELES]: *locality,* 5.5 miles northwest of present Pomona city hall along Atchison, Topeka and Santa Fe Railroad (lat. 34°07'05" N, long. 117°49'45" W). Named on Glendora (1927) 6' quadrangle.

Forest Park [LOS ANGELES]: *settlement,* 2.5 miles north-northeast of Solemint (lat. 34°26'45" N, long. 118°25'40" W; sec. 11, T 4 N, R 15 W). Named on Mint Canyon (1960) 7.5' quadrangle.

Forster Lake [ORANGE]: *lake,* behind a dam 3.5 miles south-southeast of San Juan Capistrano in Prima Deshecha Canyon (lat. 33°26'55" N, long. 117°38'45" W). Named on Dana Point (1949) 7.5' quadrangle.

Forsythe Canyon [LOS ANGELES]: *canyon,* drained by a stream that flows 1 mile to Pine Canyon (3) 2 miles west-northwest of the village of Lake Hughes (lat. 34°41'20" N, long. 118°28'45" W; sec. 21, T 7 N, R 15 W). Named on Lake Hughes (1957) 7.5' quadrangle.

Fort Hill: see **Los Angeles** [LOS ANGELES].

Fort Latham: see **Playa del Rey** [LOS ANGELES].

Fort MacArthur [LOS ANGELES]: *military installation,* near Point Fermin. Fort MacArthur Upper Reservation is 0.5 mile north of Point Fermin (lat. 33°42'45" N, long. 118°17'40" W), and Fort MacArthur Lower Reservation is 1 mile north-northeast of Point Fermin (lat. 33°43' N, long. 118°17'10" W). Named on San Pedro (1964) 7.5' quadrangle, which also shows Fort MacArthur Military Reservation situated 1.5 miles northwest of Point Fermin (lat. 33° 43'05" N, long. 118°18'50" W). Land for the lower reservation was reserved in 1888, and land for the upper reservation was purchased in 1910; when construction of the facility began in 1914, the army named the installation to honor Lieutenant General Arthur MacArthur (Gudde, 1949, p. 198; Whiting and Whiting, p. 43).

Fort Moore: see **Los Angeles** [LOS ANGELES].

Fort Tejon Pass: see **Tejon Pass** [LOS ANGELES].

Fossil Canyon [LOS ANGELES]: *canyon,* drained by a stream that flows 1 mile to Coldwater Canyon (2) 4.5 miles southwest of Mount San Antonio (lat. 34°15'20" N, long. 117°42'40" W). Named on Mount San Antonio (1955) 7.5' quadrangle.

Foster Park [VENTURA]: *town,* 5 miles north of Ventura along Ventura River (lat. 34°21'10" N, long. 119°18'15" W). Named on Los Angeles (1975) 1°x 2° quadrangle. Postal authorities established Foster Park post office in 1952 and discontinued it in 1966 (Salley, p. 79). The name is from Foster Memorial

Park, located nearby and given to the county by Mr. and Mrs. Eugene P. Foster in memory of their son; freeway construction destroyed the community in 1969 (Ricard).

Fountainhead Spring [LOS ANGELES]: *spring,* 0.5 mile east-southeast of Pacifico Mountain (lat. 34°22'45" N, long. 118°01'40" W; near NW cor. sec. 3, T 3 N, R 11 W). Named on Pacifico Mountain (1959) 7.5' quadrangle.

Fountain Valley [ORANGE]: *city,* 4.25 miles northeast of Huntington Beach civic center (lat. 33°42'30" N, long. 117°57' W). Named on Newport Beach (1965) 7.5' quadrangle. Postal authorities established Fountain Valley post office in 1958 (Salley, p. 79); the city had incorporated in 1957. Santa Ana River changed its course in 1828 and left about 30,000 acres of marsh land between the old and new courses; this area was called Squatters Country because of illegal residents there, it was called Fountain Valley for the abundance of artesian water in the neighborhood, and it was called Gospel Swamp for the devout residents who held camp meetings there; the city of Fountain Valley now covers most of the area (Meadows, p. 63, 67).

Four Corners: see **El Monte** [LOS ANGELES].

Fourfork Creek [VENTURA]: *stream,* flows 1.5 miles to Little Sespe Creek 4 miles north of Fillmore (lat. 34°27'40" N, long. 118°54'35" W; sec. 6, T 4 N, R 19 W); Fourfork Creek and Centennial Creek join Little Sespe Creek at the same point, so that stream courses radiate in four directions from the place. Named on Fillmore (1951) 7.5' quadrangle.

Four Points [LOS ANGELES]: *locality,* 5.5 miles east-southeast of Palmdale (lat. 34°32'35" N, long. 118°01'45" W; near NE cor. sec. 9, T 5 N, R 11 W). Named on Palmdale (1958) 7.5' quadrangle.

Fourth of July Cove [LOS ANGELES]: *embayment,* 4 miles east-southeast of Silver Peak on the north side of Santa Catalina Island (lat. 33°26'50" N, long. 118°30' W). Named on Santa Catalina North (1950) and Santa Catalina West (1943) 7.5' quadrangles. Preston (1890b, p. 280) referred to July Harbor.

Fox Barranca [VENTURA]: *gully,* extends for 3.25 miles from the mouth of Fox Canyon to Arroyo Las Posas 6.5 miles west-southwest of Moorpark (lat. 34°15'30" N, long. 118°59'15" W). Named on Santa Paula (1951) 7.5' quadrangle.

Fox Canyon [ORANGE]: *canyon,* drained by a stream that flows 1.25 miles to Bell Canyon 10.5 miles northeast of San Juan Capistrano (lat. 33°37'25" N, long. 117°33'25" W). Named on Cañada Gobernadora (1968) 7.5' quadrangle. The name commemorates Samuel Fox, who homesteaded on the ridge between Fox Canyon and Crow Canyon in 1879 (Meadows, p. 64).

Fox Canyon [VENTURA]: *canyon,* drained by a stream that flows 3.25 miles to lowlands 5 miles south-southeast of Santa Paula (lat. 34°17'10" N, long. 119°01'25" W). Named on Santa Paula (1951) 7.5' quadrangle.

Fox Creek [LOS ANGELES]: *stream,* flows 7 miles to Big Tujunga Canyon 3 miles east-southeast of Condor Peak (lat. 34°18'10" N, long. 118°10'35" W). Named on Condor Peak (1959) 7.5' quadrangle. West Fork enters from the northwest 2.5 miles upstream from the mouth of the main creek; it is 3 miles long and is named on Condor Peak (1959) 7.5' quadrangle. A place called Wagon Wheels Camp was situated near the mouth of Fox Creek; the name was from a pair of wagon wheels abandoned at the site (Robinson, J.W., 1977, p. 145).

Frances [ORANGE]: *locality,* 6.25 miles east-southeast of Santa Ana city hall along Atchison, Topeka and Santa Fe Railroad (lat. 33°42'40" N, long. 117°45'45" W). Named on Tustin (1965) 7.5' quadrangle. The name commemorates Frances Anita Plum, first wife of James Irvine, Jr. (Meadows, p. 64).

Franklin Canyon [LOS ANGELES]: *canyon,* 2.5 miles long, 2.5 miles north-northwest of Beverly Hills city hall (lat. 34°06'30" N, long. 118°24'50" W). Named on Beverly Hills (1950) 7.5' quadrangle.

Franklin Canyon Reservoir [LOS ANGELES]: *lake,* 3300 feet long, behind a dam 1.5 miles north-northwest of Beverly Hills city hall (lat. 34°05'40" N, long. 118°24'35" W); the lake is in Franklin Canyon. Named on Beverly Hills (1950) 7.5' quadrangle.

Franklin Canyon Reservoir: see **Upper Franklin Canyon Reservoir** [LOS ANGELES].

Frazier Creek [VENTURA]: *stream,* flows 3.5 miles to Piru Creek 4 miles north-northeast of McDonald Peak (lat. 34°41'20" N, long. 118°54'40" W; sec. 20, T 7 N, R 19 W). Named on McDonald Peak (1958) 7.5' quadrangle.

Frazier Mountain [VENTURA]: *peak,* 26 miles north of Fillmore (lat. 34°46'30" N, long. 118°58'05" W; at S line sec. 14, T 8 N, R 20 W). Named on Frazier Mountain (1958) 7.5' quadrangle. United States Board on Geographic Names (1933, p. 311) rejected the name "Cuddy Peak" for the feature. The name "Frazier" is for a pioneer family of the neighborhood (Ricard).

Frazier's Station: see **Carlsbad.**

Freeman Canyon [LOS ANGELES]: *canyon,* drained by a stream that flows 6 miles to Cañada de Los Alamos 6.5 miles south-southeast of Gorman (lat. 34°42'30" N, long. 118°49' W; near SW cor. sec. 8, T 7 N, R 18 W). Named on Black Mountain (1958) and Lebec (1958) 7.5' quadrangles.

Freeman Island: see **Island Freeman** [LOS ANGELES].

Freeman River: see **Bolsa Bay** [ORANGE].

Freeway Park [ORANGE]: *locality,* 2.25 miles southeast of present Buena Park civic center (lat. 33°50'40" N, long. 117°57'45" W; near NE cor. sec. 7, T 4 S, R 10 W). Named on Anaheim (1950) 7.5' quadrangle.

Fremont Canyon [ORANGE]: *canyon,* drained by a stream that flows nearly 7 miles to Santiago Creek 7 miles southwest of Sierra Peak (lat. 33°47'30" N, long. 117°43'35" W). Named on Black Star Canyon (1967) 7.5' quadrangle. Called Sierra Canyon on Corona (1902) 30' quadrangle. In the early days the feature was called Cañon de la Horca because it narrows down to a gorge—*Cañon de la Horca* means "Canyon that was Choked" in Spanish; later it was called Sierra Canyon because it heads at Sierra Peak, and finally it took the nickname of a shepherd called "Fremont" Smith because he had campaigned with John C. Fremont (Meadows, p. 64-65). A large depression in the cliff on the east side of Fremont Canyon 1.4 miles above its mouth is called Robbers Cave (Meadows, p. 120).

Fremont Creek: see **Blind Canyon** [ORANGE] (1).

Fremont Pass: see **San Fernando Pass** [LOS ANGELES].

Fremontville [VENTURA]: *locality,* 2 miles west of Moorpark (lat. 34°16'40" N, long. 118°54'30" W). Named on Camulos (1903) 30' quadrangle. Postal authorities established Fremontville post office in 1894 and discontinued it in 1905 (Frickstad, p. 218).

French Flat: see **Frenchmans Flat** [LOS ANGELES].

French Hill [ORANGE]: *peak,* 7.5 miles south-southeast of Santa Ana city hall (lat. 33°39' N, long. 117°48'30" W). Altitude 426 feet. Named on Tustin (1965) 7.5' quadrangle. The name commemorates C.E. French, first superintendent of Irvine ranch (Meadows, p. 65).

Frenchmans Flat [LOS ANGELES]: *area,* 3 miles north-northwest of Whitaker Peak along Piru Creek (lat. 34°36'55" N, long. 118°44'45" W; near NW cor. sec. 13, T 6 N, R 18 W). Named on Whitaker Peak (1958) 7.5' quadrangle. Called French Flat on Beartrap Canyon (1938) 6' quadrangle, but United States Board on Geographic Names (1960b, p. 8) rejected this name for the place. The name "Frenchmans Flat" recalls Harry Latour and Pete Augustura, who had a cabin at the site (Suter, p. 20).

Frenchmans Flat Campground [LOS ANGELES]: *locality,* 3 miles north of Whitaker Peak (lat. 34°37' N, long. 118°44'35" W; near NW cor. sec. 13, T 6 N, R 18 W); the place is at Frenchman Flat. Named on Whitaker Peak (1958) 7.5' quadrangle.

French Point: see **Burges Canyon** [VENTURA].

Frenchys Cove [VENTURA]: *embayment,* on the north side of the gap between middle

Anacapa Island and western Anacapa Island (lat. 34°00'25" N, long. 119°24'25" W). Named on Anacapa Island (1973) quadrangle.

Fresno Canyon [VENTURA]: *canyon,* drained by a stream that flows 2.5 miles to Ventura River 6 miles north of Ventura (lat. 34°21'50" N, long. 119°18'30" W). Named on Matilija (1952) and Ventura (1951) 7.5' quadrangles.

Frey Canyon [VENTURA]: *canyon,* drained by a stream that flows 2 miles to the valley of Santa Clara River 4.25 miles southwest of Piru (lat. 34°22'50" N, long. 118°51'20" W; sec. 34, T 4 N, R 19 W). Named on Piru (1952) and Simi (1951) 7.5' quadrangles. Called Guiberson Canyon on Piru (1921) 15' quadrangle, and called Garberson Canyon on Eldridge and Arnold's (1907) map.

Friendly Hills [LOS ANGELES]: *district,* 2.25 miles east-southeast of Whittier city hall (lat. 33°59' N, long. 118°00' W). Named on La Habra (1964) and Whittier (1965) 7.5' quadrangles.

Frog Rock [LOS ANGELES]: *rock,* 1.25 miles north-northwest of Avalon, and 75 feet offshore on the northeast side of Santa Catalina Island (lat. 33°21'40" N, long. 118°20'05" W). Named on Santa Catalina East (1950) 7.5' quadrangle.

Fruitland [LOS ANGELES]: *locality,* 10 miles west of Whittier along Los Angeles Terminal Railroad (lat. 33°59'50" N, long. 118°12'25" W). Named on Downey (1902) 15' quadrangle.

Fryer Canyon [LOS ANGELES]: *canyon,* drained by a stream that flows 1 mile to Soledad Canyon (lat. 34°26'15" N, long. 118°16' W; at N line sec. 17, T 4 N, R 13 W). Named on Agua Dulce (1960) 7.5' quadrangle.

Fryingpan Springs [LOS ANGELES]: *springs,* 4 miles south of the village of Leona Valley (lat. 34°33'35" N, long. 118°17'25" W; near SE cor. sec. 31, T 6 N, R 13 W). Named on Sleepy Valley (1958) 7.5' quadrangle.

Fryman Canyon [LOS ANGELES]: *canyon,* drained by a stream that flows 1 mile to Berry Canyon 5 miles southeast of Van Nuys (lat. 34°08' N, long. 118°23'25" W). Named on Beverly Hills (1950) and Van Nuys (1953) 7.5' quadrangles.

Fuller Park [ORANGE]: *locality,* 1 mile east-northeast of present Buena Park civic center (lat. 33°52'05" N, long. 117°58'35" W; near E line sec. 36, T 3 S, R 11 W). Named on Anaheim (1950) 7.5' quadrangle.

Fullerton [ORANGE]: *city,* 4 miles east of Buena Park civic center (lat. 33°52'15" N, long. 117°55'45" W). Named on Anaheim (1965), La Habra (1964), and Yorba Linda (1964) 7.5' quadrangles. Postal authorities established Fullerton post office in 1888 (Frickstad, p. 116), and the city incorporated in 1904. George H. Amerige and Edward R. Amerige purchased land at the place and laid out a townsite; Fullerton Land and Trust Company, a subsidiary of Atchison, Topeka and Santa Fe Railroad, acquired an interest in the project and the community was named to honor George H. Fullerton, president of the company; after Fullerton lost his position with the company, officials of the railroad called their station at the site La Habra, but the residents of the community insisted on retaining the old name (Meadows, p. 65).

Fullerton Creek [ORANGE]: *stream,* flows 12.5 miles to Coyote Creek 2.25 miles west of Buena Park civic center (lat. 33°51'50" N, long. 118°02'05" W; sec. 33, T 3 S, R 11 W). Named on Anaheim (1965), La Habra (1964), and Los Alamitos (1964) 7.5' quadrangles.

Fulton Wells: see **Santa Fe Springs** [LOS ANGELES].

Funks Canyon: see **Elderberry Canyon** [LOS ANGELES].

Fusier Canyon [LOS ANGELES]: *canyon,* drained by a stream that flows 2.5 miles to Big Tujunga Canyon 3.25 miles south of Condor Peak (lat. 34°16'45" N, long. 118°12'30" W). Named on Condor Peak (1959) 7.5' quadrangle.

Fustero Point [VENTURA]: *promontory,* 9 miles southeast of Cobblestone Mountain on the east side of Lake Piru (lat. 34°30'40" N, long. 118°45'10" W; near N line sec. 22, T 5 N, R 18 W). Named on Cobblestone Mountain (1958) 7.5' quadrangle. The name commemorates Juan Fustero, an Indian who lived at the place (Ricard).

– G –

Gabino Canyon [ORANGE]: *canyon,* drained by a stream that flows nearly 7 miles to Christianitos Canyon about 4 miles northeast of San Clemente civic center (lat. 33°28' N, long. 117°33'45" W; near N line sec. 24, T 8 S, R 7 W). Named on Cañada Gobernadora (1968) and San Clemente (1968) 7.5' quadrangles.

Gable Promontory: see **South Gable Promontory**, under **Mount Harvard** [LOS ANGELES].

Gage [LOS ANGELES]: *locality,* 4.5 miles east-northeast of present South Gate city hall along Pacific Electric Railroad (lat. 33°58'30" N, long. 118°07'30" W). Named on Bell (1936) 6' quadrangle.

Gail Canyon [LOS ANGELES]: *canyon,* 0.5 mile long, 6 miles north-northeast of Pomona city hall (lat. 34°08'20" N, long. 117°43'15" W; sec. 28, T 1 N, R 8 W). Named on Mount Baldy (1954) 7.5' quadrangle.

Gallagher Beach [LOS ANGELES]: *beach,* 2.25 miles north-northwest of Avalon on the northeast side of Santa Catalina Island (lat. 33°22'15" N, long. 118°20'55" W; the beach is at the mouth of Gallagher Canyon. Named

on Santa Catalina East (1950) 7.5' quadrangle. The name commemorates Tom Gallagher, who lived at the place as a squatter for many years (Gudde, 1949, p. 123-124).

Gallagher Canyon [LOS ANGELES]: *canyon,* drained by a stream that flows 1.25 miles to the sea 2.25 miles north-northwest of Avalon on the northeast side of Santa Catalina Island (lat. 33°22'10" N, long. 118°20'50" W). Named on Santa Catalina East (1950) 7.5' quadrangle.

Gallatin: see **Downey** [LOS ANGELES].

Gamewell: see **Huntington Beach** [ORANGE].

Ganesha Junction [LOS ANGELES]: *locality,* nearly 2 miles north-northwest of present Pomona city hall (lat. 34°04'50" N, long. 117° 45'35" W). Named on Claremont (1928) 6' quadrangle.

Ganesha Park [LOS ANGELES]: *district,* 1.5 miles north-northwest of present Pomona city hall (lat. 34°04'30" N, long. 117°45'40" W). Named on Claremont (1928) 6' quadrangle.

Garapito Creek [LOS ANGELES]: *stream,* flows 2.5 miles to Topanga Canyon 9 miles northwest of Santa Monica city hall (lat. 34°06'45" N, long. 118°35'25" W; sec. 6, T 1 S, R 16 W). Named on Topanga (1952) 7.5' quadrangle. Calabasas (1903) 15' quadrangle shows Garapito Creek in present Topanga Canyon above the mouth of present Old Topanga Canyon.

Garberson Canyon: see **Frey Canyon** [VENTURA].

Garcia Canyon [LOS ANGELES]: *canyon,* drained by a stream that flows 1 mile to Morris Reservoir nearly 4 miles north of San Dimas city hall (lat. 34°11'25" N, long. 117°51'30" W; near NE cor. sec. 7, T 1 N, R 9 W). Named on Glendora (1953) 7.5' quadrangle.

Gardena [LOS ANGELES]: *city,* 6 miles south-southeast of Inglewood city hall (lat. 33°52'55" N, long. 118°18'20" W). Named on Inglewood (1964) and Torrance (1964) 7.5' quadrangles. Postal authorities established Gardena post office in 1890 and moved it 1.5 miles southeast in 1892; the name recalls truck gardens at the site (Salley, p. 82). The city incorporated in 1930.

Garden Acres [ORANGE]: *locality,* 6 miles south of present Buena Park civic center (lat. 33°46'35" N, long. 117°58'25" W; near SW cor. sec. 31, T 4 S, R 10 W). Named on Anaheim (1950) 7.5' quadrangle.

Garden Grove [ORANGE]: *city,* 7 miles south-southeast of Buena Park civic center (lat. 33°46'35" N, long. 117°56' W). Named on Anaheim (1965) and Los Alamitos (1964, photorevised 1981) 7.5' quadrangles. California Mining Bureau's (1909b) map has the form "Gardengrove" for the name. Postal authorities established Garden Grove post office in 1877 (Frickstad, p. 117), and the city incorporated in 1956. Dr. A.G. Cook and

Converse Howe founded the community in 1877 (Guinn, p. 195). A loading platform situated along Pacific Electric Railroad about 2 miles west-northwest of present Garden Grove city hall was called Berryfield, and later it was known as Harperville (Meadows, p. 26-27). A flag stop located along Pacific Electric Railroad 2.5 miles northwest of present Garden Grove city hall was called Cordorniz, and a flag stop located along the same railroad 1.25 miles northwest of present Garden Grove city hall was called Mesto (Meadows, p. 54, 99).

Garden Gulch [LOS ANGELES]: *canyon,* drained by a stream that flows 1.25 miles to an unnamed canyon 4 miles north-northwest of Burnt Peak (lat. 34°43'40" N, long. 118°36'50" W; sec. 6, T 7 N, R 16 W). Named on Burnt Peak (1958) 7.5' quadrangle.

Garden of the Gods [LOS ANGELES]: *area,* 1 mile north-northwest of Chatsworth (lat. 34°16'25" N, long. 118°36'35" W; sec. 12, T 2 N, R 17 W). Named on Oat Mountain (1952) 7.5' quadrangle.

Gardens: see **Bell Gardens** [LOS ANGELES].

Garnsey [LOS ANGELES]: *locality,* 3 miles east-southeast of Van Nuys along Southern Pacific Railroad (lat. 34°10'10" N, long. 118°24'15" W). Named on Van Nuys (1926) 6' quadrangle.

Garvalia: see **San Gabriel** [LOS ANGELES].

Garvanza [LOS ANGELES]: *district,* 3.5 miles northeast of Los Angeles city hall in Los Angeles (lat. 34°07' N, long. 118°10'30" W). Named on Los Angeles (1953) 7.5' quadrangle. Postal authorities established Garvanza post office in 1887 and discontinued it in 1921; the name is from chickpeas planted at the place—*garbanzo* means "chickpeas" in Spanish (Salley, p. 83). United States Board on Geographic Names (1933, p. 319) rejected the form "Garvanzo" for the name.

Garvanza Station [LOS ANGELES]: *locality,* nearly 5 miles northeast of present Los Angeles city hall along Atchison, Topeka and Santa Fe Railroad (lat. 34°06'35" N, long. 118°11'35" W); the place is 0.5 mile west-southwest of Garvanza. Named on Pasadena (1900) 15' quadrangle.

Garvey: see **South San Gabriel** [LOS ANGELES].

Garvey Avenue: see **South San Gabriel** [LOS ANGELES].

Garvey Reservoir [LOS ANGELES]: *lake,* 5 miles west-southwest of El Monte city hall (lat. 34°03' N, long. 118°07' W); the feature is southwest of South San Gabriel, which also was called Garvey. Named on El Monte (1966) 7.5' quadrangle.

Gaspur [LOS ANGELES]: *locality,* 1.5 miles west-northwest of Long Beach city hall along Pacific Electric Railroad (lat. 33°46'55" N, long. 118°13'05" W). Named on Long Beach (1949) 7.5' quadrangle.

Gaston [LOS ANGELES]: *locality,* 4 miles north of present Los Angeles city hall along Los Angeles Terminal Railroad (lat. 34°06'30" N, long. 118°14'40" W). Named on Pasadena (1900) 15' quadrangle.

Gates Canyon [LOS ANGELES-VENTURA]: *canyon,* drained by a stream that heads just inside Ventura County and flows 1.5 miles to Las Virgenes Creek 2.5 miles east-northeast of Agoura (lat. 34°09'10" N, long. 118°41'45" W; sec. 19, T 1 N, R 17 W). Named on Calabasas (1952) 7.5' quadrangle.

Gavilan [ORANGE]: *locality,* 4.5 miles north of San Juan Capistrano along Atchison, Topeka and Santa Fe Railroad (lat. 33°34'10" N, long. 117°40'25" W). Named on San Juan Capistrano (1968) 7.5' quadrangle. Construction of the railroad in 1887 destroyed springs called Aguaje del Cuate that were situated 0.6 mile north of Gavilan; travelers had always found fresh water at the springs (Meadows, p. 18).

Gavin Canyon [LOS ANGELES]: *canyon,* drained by a stream that flows 3 miles to lowlands nearly 2 miles west-southwest of downtown Newhall (lat. 34°22'30" N, long. 118°33' W). Named on Oat Mountain (1952) 7.5' quadrangle.

Gemco [LOS ANGELES]: *locality,* 2 miles north-northeast of Van Nuys along Southern Pacific Railroad (lat. 34°12'35" N, long. 118°26'05" W). Named on Van Nuys (1966) 7.5' quadrangle.

George Canyon [LOS ANGELES]: *canyon,* 2 miles long, 5 miles south of Torrance city hall (lat. 33°45'45" N, long. 118°20'10" W). Named on Torrance (1964) 7.5' quadrangle.

Georges Gap [LOS ANGELES]: *pass,* 5 miles southeast of Condor Peak (lat. 34°16'10" N, long. 118°10' W). Named on Condor Peak (1959) 7.5' quadrangle.

German [LOS ANGELES]: *locality,* 2.25 miles east-southeast of Gorman (lat. 34°47' N, long. 118°49' W; near NW cor. sec. 17, T 8 N, R 18 W). Named on Tejon (1903) 30' quadrangle.

German Canyon: see **Gorman Canyon** [LOS ANGELES].

Gibraltar: see **Little Gibraltar** [LOS ANGELES].

Gibson: see **Point Fermin** [LOS ANGELES].

Gillibrand Canyon [VENTURA]: *canyon,* drained by a stream that flows 4 miles to Tapo Canyon (1) 6 miles west-northwest of Santa Susana Pass (lat. 34°19' N, long. 118°43' W; sec. 25, T 3 N, R 18 E). Named on Santa Susana (1951) 7.5' quadrangle. Called Dry Canyon on Santa Susana (1903) 15' quadrangle. The name "Gillibrand Canyon" is for Edward Clayton Gillibrand, who settled in the neighborhood about 1889 (Ricard).

Gilman Peak [ORANGE]: *peak,* 3 miles northeast of Yorba Linda (lat. 33°55'25" N, long. 117°46'30" W; sec. 12, T 3 S, R 9 W). Altitude 1678 feet. Named on Yorba Linda (1950)

7.5' quadrangle. The name commemorates Richard Hall Gilman, an early settler (Meadows, p. 66).

Girard: see **Woodland Hills** [LOS ANGELES].

Girard Reservoir [LOS ANGELES]: *lake*, 400 feet long, 3.5 miles south of Canoga Park (lat. 34°09'05" N, long. 118°36'35" W); the feature is just south of Woodland Hills, which once was called Girard. Named on Canoga Park (1952) 7.5' quadrangle.

Gladstone: see **Covina** [LOS ANGELES].

Glassell Park [LOS ANGELES]: *district*, 4 miles north of Los Angeles city hall (lat. 34°06'40" N, long. 118°14'20" W). Named on Los Angeles (1953) 7.5' quadrangle.

Gleason Canyon [LOS ANGELES]: *canyon*, drained by a stream that flows 5.5 miles to Aliso Canyon (1) 3 miles east-southeast of Acton (lat. 34°26'40" N, long. 118°08'55" W; at E line sec. 8, T 4 N, R 12 W); the canyon heads near Mount Gleason. Named on Acton (1959) 7.5' quadrangle.

Gleason Mountain: see **Mount Gleason** [LOS ANGELES].

Glen Campground [LOS ANGELES]: *locality*, nearly 8 miles west-northwest of Azusa city hall along West Fork San Gabriel River (lat. 34°14'25" N, long. 117°57'05" W). Named on Azusa (1966) 7.5' quadrangle.

Glen Canyon [LOS ANGELES]: *canyon*, drained by a stream that flows 2 miles to West Fork San Gabriel River nearly 8 miles north-northwest of Azusa city hall (lat. 34°14'25" N, long. 117°57'05" W). Named on Azusa (1953) 7.5' quadrangle.

Glendale [LOS ANGELES]: *city*, 6 miles west of Pasadena city hall (lat. 34°08'50" N, long. 118°14'50" W). Named on Burbank (1953), Hollywood (1953), Pasadena (1966), and Sunland (1953) 7.5' quadrangles. Called Riverdale on Stevenson's (1884) map. Postal authorities established Mason post office in 1886 and changed the name Glendale in 1891 (Salley, p. 134). The city incorporated in 1906. The community began soon after the railroad was built from Los Angeles to San Fernando in 1873 and 1874; it first was called Riverdale, but postal authorities rejected this name and called the post office there Mason (Gudde, 1949, p. 128). The place also was called Verdugo before 1883, when an artist from Chicago proposed the name "Glendale," which was adopted by popular acclaim (Hanna, p. 121).

Glendale: see **North Glendale** [LOS ANGELES]; **West Glendale** [LOS ANGELES].

Glendale Junction [LOS ANGELES]: *locality*, 2 miles north-northeast of Los Angeles city hall along a rail line (lat. 34°04'30" N, long. 118°13'25" W). Named on Los Angeles (1966) 7.5' quadrangle.

Glendora [LOS ANGELES]: *city*, 2.5 miles east of Azusa city hall (lat. 34°08'10" N, long. 117°51'50" W). Named on Azusa (1953),

Glendora (1953), and San Dimas (1966) 7.5' quadrangles. Postal authorities established Alosta post office in 1883 and moved it 0.5 mile west in 1887, when they changed the name to Glendora; they reestablished Alosta post office in 1888 and discontinued it in 1899—when it was discontinued finally, Alosta post office was situated 1 mile south of Glendora post office (Salley, p. 5, 86). Glendora incorporated in 1911. George Whitcomb coined the name "Glendora" in 1887 from the word "glen" and his wife's name "Ledora" (Gudde, 1949, p. 128).

Glendora Mountain [LOS ANGELES]: *peak*, 4 miles north-northeast of Glendora city hall (lat. 34°11'30" N, long. 117°50'15" W; near NE cor. sec. 8, T 1 N, R 9 W). Altitude 3322 feet. Named on Glendora (1966) 7.5' quadrangle.

Glenview [LOS ANGELES]: *locality*, 10 miles northwest of Santa Monica city hall near the head of Topanga Canyon (lat. 34°07'30" N, long. 118°36' W). Named on Canoga Park (1952) and Topanga (1952) 7.5' quadrangles. Called Mohn Springs on Dry Canyon (1932) 6' quadrangle. Los Angeles County (1935) map shows a place called Veteran Springs located in Topanga Canyon at or near present Glenview. Sampson (p. 206) mentioned Mohn Mineral Springs and noted that the water was bottled for sale.

Glenwood: see **Camp Glenwood** [LOS ANGELES].

Gloryetta: see **Delhi** [ORANGE].

Goat Buttes [LOS ANGELES]: *relief feature*, 5.5 miles northwest of Malibu Point (lat. 34°05'50" N, long. 118°44'25" W; mainly in sec. 11, T 1 S, R 18 W). Named on Malibu Beach (1951) 7.5' quadrangle.

Goat Canyon: see **Tick Canyon** [LOS ANGELES].

Goat Harbor [LOS ANGELES]: *embayment*, 4 miles northeast of Mount Banning on the north side of Santa Catalina Island (lat. 33°25' N, long. 118°23'40" W). Named on Santa Catalina North (1950) 7.5' quadrangle.

Godde Pass [LOS ANGELES]: *pass*, 8.5 miles southwest of Lancaster (lat. 34°36'30" N, long. 118°14'35" W; sec. 15, T 6 N, R 13 W). Named on Ritter Ridge (1958) 7.5' quadrangle.

Godwin Canyon [VENTURA]: *canyon*, drained by a stream that flows nearly 4 miles to Sespe Creek 7 miles north-northwest of Wheeler Springs (lat. 34°36' N, long. 119°20'50" W; near W line sec. 20, T 6 N, R 23 W). Named on Reyes Peak (1943) and Wheeler Springs (1943) 7.5' quadrangles.

Goff Island [ORANGE]: *peninsula*, 2.5 miles southeast of Laguna Beach city hall along the coast (lat. 33°30'50" N, long, 117°45'35" W; near S line sec. 31, T 7 S, R 8 W). Named on Laguna Beach (1965) 7.5' quadrangle. On Santa Ana (1901) 15' quadrangle, the name applies to a small island at the site. The name commemorates four Goff brothers who settled along the coast near the feature in the early 1870's (Meadows, p. 66-67).

Gold Canyon [LOS ANGELES]: *canyon,* drained by a stream that flows 2.25 miles to Big Tujunga Canyon 3.5 miles northeast of Sunland (lat. 34°18'05" N, long. 118°16'15" W; near W line sec. 32, T 3 N, R 13 W). Named on Sunland (1953) 7.5' quadrangle.

Gold Canyon Saddle [LOS ANGELES]: *pass,* 4 miles north of Sunland (lat. 34°19' N, long. 118°17'35" W; sec. 25, T 3 N, R 14 W); the feature is at the head of Gold Canyon. Named on Sunland (1966) 7.5' quadrangle.

Gold Creek [LOS ANGELES]: *stream,* flows nearly 6 miles to Little Tujunga Canyon 4 miles north-northwest of Sunland (lat. 34°18'35" N, long. 118°20'40" W; near SE cor. sec. 28, T 3 N, R 14 W). Named on Sunland (1953) 7.5' quadrangle. Gold-mining operations along Gold Creek around the turn of the century constituted what was called Little Nugget Placers (Robinson, J.W., 1973, p. 36).

Gold Creek Saddle [LOS ANGELES]: *pass,* 5.25 miles north-northeast of Sunland (lat. 34°19'50" N, long. 118°16'35" W). Named on Sunland (1966) 7.5' quadrangle.

Goldenrod Spring [LOS ANGELES]: *spring,* 2 miles north-northwest of Sunland (lat. 34°17'25" N, long. 118°19'10" W; sec. 2, T 2 N, R 14 W). Named on Sunland (1966) 7.5' quadrangle.

Gold Hill [VENTURA]: *peak,* 5 miles north-northeast of McDonald Peak (lat. 34°42'15" N, long 118°55' W; sec. 17, T 7 N, R 19 W). Altitude 4838 feet. Named on McDonald Peak (1958) 7.5' quadrangle.

Gold Hill Campground [VENTURA]: *locality,* 5 miles north of McDonald Peak (lat. 34°42'15" N, long. 118°56'05" W; sec. 18, T 7 N, R 19 W); the place is 1 mile west of Gold Hill. Named on McDonald Peak (1958) 7.5' quadrangle.

Gookin Gulch: see **Pine Canyon** [LOS ANGELES] (1).

Gookins Dry Lake [LOS ANGELES]: *dry lake,* 500 feet long, 11 miles east-southeast of Gorman (lat. 34°44'35" N, long. 118°37'45" W; on N line sec. 36, T 8 N, R 17 W). Named on Liebre Mountain (1958) 7.5' quadrangle.

Gooseberry Canyon [LOS ANGELES]: *canyon,* drained by a stream that flows 1 mile to Pacoima Canyon 7 miles north of Sunland (lat. 34°21'45" N, long. 118°18'45" W; sec. 11, T 3 N, R 14 W). Named on Sunland (1953) 7.5' quadrangle.

Gooseberry Spring: see **Little Jimmy Spring** [LOS ANGELES].

Gordon Canyon [LOS ANGELES]:
(1) *canyon,* drained by a stream that flows less than 1 mile to Pacoima Canyon 7 miles north of Sunland (lat. 34°21'45" N, long. 118°19'15"

W; sec. 11, T 3 N, R 14 W). Named on Sunland (1966) 7.5' quadrangle.
(2) *canyon,* 1 mile long, 2.25 miles east-northeast of Glendora city hall (lat. 34°08'45" N, long. 117°49'30" W; sec. 21, 28, T 1 N, R 9 W). Named on Glendora (1953) 7.5' quadrangle.

Gorman [LOS ANGELES]: *village,* 42 miles northwest of San Fernando (lat. 34°47'45" N, long. 118°51'10" W; at W line sec. 12, T 8 N, R 19 W). Named on Lebec (1958) 7.5' quadrangle. Postal authorities established Gorman's Station post office in 1877, discontinued it 1878, reestablished it the same year, changed the name to Gorman Station in 1894, discontinued it in 1896, reestablished it with name "Gorman" in 1896, discontinued it in 1898, reestablished it in 1904, discontinued it in 1908, and reestablished it in 1915; the name was for Henry Gorman, first postmaster (Salley, p. 87). Gorman was a soldier at Fort Tejon in Kern County who settled in the neighborhood after his discharge in 1864 (Hanna, p. 124).

Gorman Canyon [LOS ANGELES]: *canyon,* drained by a stream that flows 1.5 miles to Sand Canyon (2) 3.5 miles southeast of Solemint (lat. 34°22'45" N, long. 118°24'40" W; near NW cor. sec. 1, T 3 N, R 15 W). Named on Mint Canyon (1960) and San Fernando (1953) 7.5' quadrangles. Called German Canyon on San Fernando (1900) 15' quadrangle.

Gorman Creek [LOS ANGELES]: *stream,* flows 10.5 miles to Cañada de Los Alamos 7 miles south-southeast of Gorman (lat. 34°42'10" N, long. 118°47'40" W; sec. 16, T 7 N, R 18 W); Gorman is along upper reaches of the creek. Named on Black Mountain (1958) and Lebec (1958) 7.5' quadrangles.

Gorman's Station: see **Gorman** [LOS ANGELES].

Gosnell Hill [VENTURA]: *relief feature,* 2 miles north of downtown Ventura (lat. 34°18'40" N, long. 119°17'25" W). Named on Ventura (1951) 7.5' quadrangle. The name commemorates Truman Barrick Gosnell, who farmed at the place in the 1890's (Ricard).

Gospel Swamp: see **Fountain Valley** [ORANGE].

Goss Canyon [LOS ANGELES]: *canyon,* nearly 1 mile long, 8 miles northwest of Pasadena city hall (lat. 34°14'20" N, long. 118°13'55" W; heads in sec. 22, T 2 N, R 13 W). Named on Pasadena (1953) 7.5' quadrangle.

Gould Canyon [LOS ANGELES]: *canyon,* 1.5 miles long, 6 miles north-northwest of Pasadena city hall (lat. 34°13'15" N, long. 118°11'40" W; sec. 25, 36, T 2 N, R 13 W). Named on Pasadena (1953) 7.5' quadrangle.

Government Canyon [LOS ANGELES]: *canyon,* drained by a stream that flows 1 mile to Swarthout Valley 5.5 miles north-northwest of Mount San Antonio (lat. 34°22'05" N, long.

117°40'05" W; at N line sec. 12, T 3 N, R 8 W). Named on Mount San Antonio (1955) 7.5' quadrangle.

Grabino Canyon [ORANGE]: *canyon,* drained by a stream that flows 7 miles to Cristianitos Canyon about 4 miles northeast of San Clemente civic center (lat. 33°28' N, long. 117°33'45" W; near N line sec. 24, T 8 S, R 7 W). Named on Cañada Gobernadora (1968) and San Clemente (1968) 7.5' quadrangles.

Grace Hill [LOS ANGELES]: *hill,* 1.5 miles south-southwest of Pasadena city hall (lat. 34°07'35" N, long. 118°09'05" W). Named on Pasadena (1953) 7.5' quadrangle.

Graham [LOS ANGELES]: *district,* 2.25 miles west-southwest of present South Gate city hall (lat. 33°56'40" N, long. 118°14'35" W). Named on Watts (1937) 6' quadrangle. Postal authorities established Seal Garden post office 1 mile north of Watts post office in 1908, changed the name to Graham Station in 1911, and discontinued it in 1918; the name "Seal Garden" was for a farm project that failed, and the name "Graham Station" was for a place along Pacific Electric Railroad (Salley, p. 87, 200).

Graham Canyon [LOS ANGELES]: *canyon,* drained by a stream that flows 2.25 miles to lowlands 5.5 miles north-northwest of Big Pines (lat. 34°27'15" N, long. 117°43'50" W; near NE cor. sec. 8, T 4 N, R 8 W). Named on Mescal Creek (1956) 7.5' quadrangle.

Graham Station: see **Graham** [LOS ANGELES].

Granada: see **Granada Hills** [LOS ANGELES].

Granada Hills [LOS ANGELES]: *district,* 5 miles east of Chatsworth in Los Angeles (lat. 34°16' N, long. 118°31' W). Named on Oat Mountain (1952) and San Fernando (1966) 7.5' quadrangles. Called Granada on Zelzah (1941) 6' quadrangle. Postal authorities established Granada Hills post office in 1942 (Salley, p. 88).

Grand Arch: see **Arch Rock** [VENTURA].

Grand Canyon [LOS ANGELES]:
(1) *canyon,* drained by a stream that flows 1 mile to Millard Canyon 5.5 miles north of Pasadena city hall (lat. 34°13'45" N, long. 118° 07'40" W). Named on Mount Wilson (1953) and Pasadena (1953) 7.5' quadrangles.
(2) *canyon,* drained by a stream that flows 2.25 miles to Silver Canyon 3 miles west of Avalon on Santa Catalina Island (lat. 33° 20'05" N, long. 118°22'30" W). Named on Santa Catalina East (1950) 7.5' quadrangle.

Grandview Canyon [LOS ANGELES]: *canyon,* drained by a stream that flows 4.5 miles to lowlands nearly 5 miles east of Valyermo (lat. 34°26'15" N, long. 117°46' W; near NE cor. sec. 13, T 4 N, R 9 W). Named on Mescal Creek (1956) and Valyermo (1958) 7.5' quadrangles.

Granite Mountain [LOS ANGELES]: *peak,*

2.25 miles west-southwest of Pacifico Mountain (lat. 34°22'15" N, long. 118°04'10" W; sec. 6, T 3 N, R 11 W). Named on Chilao Flat (1959) 7.5' quadrangle.

Grape Arbor [LOS ANGELES]: *locality,* 1 mile east-southeast of present Agoura in Liberty Canyon (lat. 34°08'15" N, long. 118°43'30" W). Named on Camulos (1903) 30' quadrangle.

Grapevine Canyon [LOS ANGELES]: *canyon,* 1.5 miles long, opens into lowlands 3.5 miles northwest of downtown San Fernando (lat. 34°18'55" N, long. 118°29'10" W). Named on San Fernando (1953) 7.5' quadrangle.

Grasshopper Canyon [LOS ANGELES]: *canyon,* drained by a stream that flows 5.25 miles to Castaic Creek 6.25 miles south-southwest of Warm Springs Mountain (lat. 34°30'30" N, long. 118°36'45" W; near N line sec. 24, T 5 N, R 17 W). Named on Warm Springs Mountain (1958) 7.5' quadrangle.

Grass Mountain [LOS ANGELES]: *peak,* nearly 3 miles south-southeast of the village of Lake Hughes (lat. 34°38'30" N, long. 118°24'45" W). Altitude 4605 feet. Named on Lake Hughes (1957) 7.5' quadrangle.

Grassy Hollow [LOS ANGELES]: *area,* 2 miles west of Big Pines (lat. 34°22'35" N, long. 117°43'25" W; sec. 4, T 3 N, R 8 W). Named on Mescal Creek (1956) 7.5' quadrangle.

Graveyard Barranca: see **Sanjon Barranca** [VENTURA].

Graveyard Canyon [LOS ANGELES]: *canyon,* drained by a stream that flows nearly 4 miles to San Gabriel River 7.5 miles north-north-east of Glendora city hall (lat. 34°14'10" N, long. 117°48'35" W). Named on Crystal Lake (1958) and Glendora (1953) 7.5' quadrangles. The name is from Indian burial grounds (Gudde, 1969, p. 127).

Greenleaf Canyon [LOS ANGELES]: *canyon,* drained by a stream that flows 2.5 miles to Topanga Canyon 8.5 miles northwest of Santa Monica city hall (lat. 34°05'25" N, long. 118°36'15" W). Named on Topanga (1952) 7.5' quadrangle.

Green Meadows [LOS ANGELES]: *locality,* 5 miles east of Inglewood (lat. 33°57'30" N, long. 118°16' W). Named on Redondo (1896) 15' quadrangle. Postal authorities established Green Meadows post office at a farming community in 1894 and discontinued it in 1902 (Salley, p. 89).

Green Valley [LOS ANGELES]: *settlement,* 4.25 miles south-southeast of the village of Lake Hughes (lat. 34°37'15" N, long. 118°24'45" W). Named on Lake Hughes (1957) 7.5' quadrangle. Hughes Lake (1937) 6' quadrangle has the name "La Joya" at the site.

Green Verdugo Reservoir [LOS ANGELES]: *intermittent lake,* 500 feet long, 1.25 miles west of downtown Sunland (lat. 34°15'25" N, long. 118°20'05" W). Named on Sunland (1966) 7.5' quadrangle.

Greenville [ORANGE]: *locality,* 6 miles east-northeast of Huntington Beach civic center (lat. 33°42'10" N, long. 117°54'25" W). Named on Newport Beach (1965) 7.5' quadrangle. Newport school was built at the site in 1874, and after the community of Newport Beach was started, the village around the school was referred to as Old Newport (Meadows, p. 106-107). A flag stop located along Pacific Electric Railroad 0.5 mile west of Greenville was called Von Schritz (Meadows, p. 137).

Greenwich Village [VENTURA]: *locality,* about 1.5 miles west-northwest of downtown Thousand Oaks (lat. 34°10'50" N, long. 118°51'45" W; sec. 10, T 1 N, R 19 W). Named on Thousand Oaks (1952) 7.5' quadrangle.

Gridley Canyon [VENTURA]: *canyon,* drained by a stream that flows 3.5 miles to Ojai Valley 2.5 miles east-northeast of the town of Ojai (lat. 34°28' N, long. 119°12'10" W; sec. 32, T 5 N, R 22 E). Named on Ojai (1952) 7.5' quadrangle.

Griffin [VENTURA]: *locality,* 15 miles east-northeast of Reyes Peak at the east end of Lockwood Valley (lat. 34°44' N, long. 119°02'45" W; near SW cor. sec. 31, T 8 N, R 20 W). Named on Mount Pinos (1903) 30' quadrangle. Postal authorities established Griffin post office in 1896 and discontinued it in 1905 (Frickstad, p. 218).

Grimes Canyon [VENTURA]: *canyon,* drained by a stream that flows 3.25 miles to the valley of Santa Clara River 2.25 miles south of Fillmore (lat. 34°22' N, long. 118°55'10" W; near SE cor. sec. 1, T 3 N, R 20 W). Named on Moorpark (1951) 7.5' quadrangle. The name commemorates Brice Grimes of Bardsdale (Ricard).

Grissom Island: see **Island Grissom** [LOS ANGELES].

Grizzly Flat [LOS ANGELES]: *area,* 4 miles south of Condor Peak (lat. 34°16'10" N, long. 118°12'25" W; sec. 11, T 2 N, R 13 W). Named on Condor Peak (1959) 7.5' quadrangle. Called Grizzly Flats on Los Angeles County (1935) map.

Grotto Creek [LOS ANGELES]: *stream,* flows 1.5 miles to Big Tujunga Canyon 7 miles southwest of Pacifico Mountain (lat. 34° 18'35" N, long. 118°07'05" W). Named on Chilao Flat (1959) 7.5' quadrangle.

Grotto Spring [ORANGE]: *spring,* 1.25 miles west-northwest of Santiago Peak (lat. 33°43'15" N, long. 117°33'05" W; sec. 19, T 5 S, R 6 W). Named on Santiago Peak (1954) 7.5' quadrangle.

Guadalasca [VENTURA]: *land grant,* at Point Mugu and inland to Conejo Mountain. Named on Camarillo (1950), Newbury Park (1951), Point Mugu (1949), and Triunfo Pass (1950) 7.5' quadrangles. Isabel Yorba received 6 leagues in 1836 and claimed 30,594 acres patented in 1873 (Cowan, p. 37-38; Cowan gave

the alternate name "La Laguna" for the grant).

Guard Canyon: see **Morgan Canyon** [LOS ANGELES].

Guffy Camp [LOS ANGELES]: *locality,* 3.5 miles north of Mount San Antonio (lat. 34°20'30" N, long. 117°39'15" W; at S line sec. 18, T 3 N, R 7 W). Named on Mount San Antonio (1955) 7.5' quadrangle. Called Guffys Camp on Swarthout (1941) 6' quadrangle.

Guiberson Canyon: see **Frey Canyon** [VENTURA].

Gulf of Santa Catalina [LOS ANGELES-ORANGE]: *water feature,* separates the mainland from Santa Catalina and San Clemente Islands. Named on Long Beach (1957) and Santa Ana (1959) 1°x 2° quadrangles. On Blake's (1857) map, the name "Earthquake Bay" applies to the sea along the coast from San Pedro to San Diego.

Guyamas River: see **Cuyama River** [VENTURA].

Gypsum [ORANGE]: *locality,* 3.25 miles southeast of San Juan Hill along Atchison, Topeka and Santa Fe Railroad (lat. 33°52'40" N, long. 117°42' W); the place is north of the mouth of Gypsum Canyon. Named on Prado Dam (1950) 7.5' quadrangle.

Gypsum Canyon [ORANGE]: *canyon,* drained by a stream that flows 3.5 miles to Santa Ana Canyon 3.5 miles west-northwest of Sierra Peak (lat. 33°52' N, long. 117°42'35" W). Named on Black Star Canyon (1967) 7.5' quadrangle. Corona (1942) 15' quadrangle has the name "Gypsum Creek" for the stream in the canyon. A deposit of gypsum occurs in the canyon (Tucker, 1925, p. 67).

Gypsum Creek: see **Gypsum Canyon** [ORANGE].

— H —

Hacienda Heights [LOS ANGELES]: *city,* 5.5 miles south of Baldwin Park city hall (lat. 34°00'20" N, long. 117°57'50" W). Named on Baldwin Park (1966) and La Habra (1964) 7.5' quadrangles.

Hahaonuput: see **San Rafael** [LOS ANGELES].

Haines [VENTURA]: *locality,* 3 miles southwest of Santa Paula along Southern Pacific Railroad (lat. 34°19'30" N, long. 119°06'05" W); the place is near Haines Barranca. Named on Santa Paula (1951) 7.5' quadrangle. The name commemorates Abner Haines, who came to the neighborhood in 1867 (Ricard).

Haines Barranca [VENTURA]: *gully,* extends for 2 miles from the mouth of O'Hara Canyon to Santa Clara River nearly 3 miles southwest of Santa Paula (lat. 34°19'15" N, long. 119°05'20" W). Named on Santa Paula (1951) 7.5' quadrangle.

Haines Canyon [LOS ANGELES]: *canyon,*

drained by a stream that flows 2.5 miles to lowlands 2 miles east of Sunland, where it enters Haines Canyon Channel (lat. 34°15'30" N, long. 118°16'35" W; sec. 18, T 2 N, R 13 W). Named on Condor Peak (1959) and Sunland (1953) 7.5' quadrangles.

Haines Canyon [VENTURA]: *canyon,* 1 mile long, opens into the valley of Santa Clara River 2.25 miles east of Fillmore (lat. 34°23'50" N, long. 118°52'20" W; near S line sec. 28, T 4 N, R 19 W). Named on Camulos (1903) 30' quadrangle. The name commemorates Herman Haines, who was killed by gunfire on the main street of Santa Paula in 1886 (Ricard).

Haines Canyon Channel [LOS ANGELES]: *stream,* flows 3.5 miles from the mouth of Haines Canyon to Tujunga Valley 0.5 mile northwest of the center of Sunland (lat. 34°16' N, long. 118°19'05" W). Named on Burbank (1953) and Sunland (1953) 7.5' quadrangles.

Halcon [ORANGE]: *locality,* 3 miles southwest of present Buena Park civic center along Pacific Electric Railroad (lat. 33°49'40" N, long. 118°01'40" W). Named on Los Alamitos (1935) 7.5' quadrangle.

Halfway Canyon [ORANGE]: *canyon,* drained by a stream that flows 1 mile to Silverado Canyon nearly 4 miles northwest of Santiago Peak (lat. 33°44'45" N, long. 117°35'05" W; near S line sec. 11, T 5 S, R 7 W); Bear Flat (1) is at the head of the canyon. Named on Santiago Peak (1954) 7.5' quadrangle. The feature also was called Bear Gulch ·(Sleeper, 1976, p. 79).

Halfway House: see **Martins Camp** [LOS ANGELES].

Halfway Inn [LOS ANGELES]: *locality,* 10 miles southeast of Gorman (lat. 34°41'05" N, long. 118°43'45" W; at W line sec. 19, T 7 N, R 17 W). Named on Liebre Mountain (1958) 7.5' quadrangle.

Halfway Rock [ORANGE]: *rock,* 1 mile south of Laguna Beach city hall, and 400 feet offshore (lat. 33°31'50" N, long. 117°46'30" W). Named on Laguna Beach (1965) 7.5' quadrangle. The feature is half way between Laguna Beach and Arch Beach (Meadows, p. 68).

Halfway Spring Campground [VENTURA]: *locality,* 3.5 miles east-southeast of Cobblestone Mountain (lat. 34°35' N, long. 118°48'55" W; sec. 29, T 6 N, R 18 W). Named on Cobblestone Mountain (1958) 7.5' quadrangle.

Hall Beckley Canyon [LOS ANGELES]: *canyon,* 1.5 miles long, 7 miles north-northwest of Pasadena city hall (lat. 34°14' N, long. 118°12'30" W; sec. 23, 26, T 2 N, R 13 W). Named on Pasadena (1953) 7.5' quadrangle. Called Hall Canyon on Los Angeles County (1935) map.

Hall Canyon [VENTURA]: *canyon,* drained by a stream that flows 4 miles to lowlands 2 miles east of downtown Ventura (lat. 34°16'55" N, long. 119°15'25" W). Named on Ventura (1951) 7.5' quadrangle. The name commemorates brothers Dick Hall and Bill Hall, who raised sheep in the canyon in the 1870's (Ricard). East Fork branches northeast nearly 2 miles above the mouth of the main canyon; it is 3.5 miles long and is named on Saticoy (1951) and Ventura (1951) 7.5' quadrangles.

Hall Canyon [ORANGE]: *canyon,* drained by a stream that flows nearly 2 miles to Baker Canyon 6.25 miles south of Sierra Peak (lat. 33°45'35" N, long. 117°39'40" W; sec. 1, T 5 S, R 8 W). Named on Black Star Canyon (1967) 7.5' quadrangle. Meadows (p. 68) associated the name with W.H. Hall, who kept bees in present Baker Canyon.

Hall Canyon: see **Hall Beckley Canyon** [LOS ANGELES].

Hall's Canyon: see **Baker Canyon** [ORANGE].

Halls Canyon Channel [LOS ANGELES]: *stream,* extends for 2 miles from the mouth of Hall Beckley Canyon to Verdugo Wash 6.5 miles northwest of Pasadena city hall (lat. 34°12'15" N, long. 118°14'15" W). Named on Pasadena (1966) 7.5' quadrangle.

Halsey Canyon [LOS ANGELES]: *canyon,* drained by a stream that flows 5 miles to Castaic Creek 6.25 miles northwest of Newhall (lat. 34°26'25" N, long. 118°37'10" W). Named on Newhall (1952) and Val Verde (1952) 7.5' quadrangles. Called Hasley Canyon on Santa Susana (1903) 15' quadrangle. Los Angeles County (1935) map shows a feature called Stevens Canyon that opens into Halsey Canyon from the west near the mouth of Halsey Canyon.

Ham Canyon [LOS ANGELES]: *canyon,* 1.5 miles long, 4.5 miles east of Glendora city hall (lat. 34°08'45" N, long. 117°47'15" W; mainly in sec. 26, T 1 N, R 9 W). Named on Glendora (1953) 7.5' quadrangle.

Hamilton Beach [LOS ANGELES]: *beach,* less than 1 mile north of Avalon on the northeast side of Santa Catalina Island (lat. 33°21'15" N, long. 118°19'45" W). Named on Santa Catalina East (1950) 7.5' quadrangle.

Hammell: see **Ventura** [VENTURA].

Hammond Canyon [VENTURA]: *canyon,* drained by a stream that flows 4.5 miles to Sulphur Canyon 8 miles northwest of Saticoy (lat. 34°22'20" N, long. 119°14'05" W). Named on Ojai (1952) and Saticoy (1951) 7.5' quadrangles. The name is for Elisha George Hammond and his wife, who owned land in the canyon in 1875 (Ricard).

Hampton Canyon [VENTURA]: *canyon,* drained by a stream that flows 2.5 miles to Wheeler Canyon 4.25 miles north of Saticoy (lat. 34°20'50" N, long. 119°08'45" W). Named on Saticoy (1951) 7.5' quadrangle. The name commemorates Wade Hampton, who reportedly was in the region as early as 1867 (Ricard).

Handy Creek [ORANGE]: *stream,* flows 2.5 miles to the canyon of Santiago Creek 4 miles east-northeast of Orange city hall (lat. 33° 48'45" N, long. 117°47'15" W). Named on Orange (1964) 7.5' quadrangle.

Hansen [ORANGE]: *locality,* 3.25 miles south-southwest of Buena Park civic center along Southern Pacific Railroad (lat. 33°49' N, long. 118°00'35" W). Named on Los Alamitos (1964) 7.5' quadrangle. The name recalls Charles Hansen and Peter Hansen, who raised wheat in the neighborhood in the 1880's (Meadows, p. 69). A flag stop called Lobo was situated along Pacific Electric Railroad less than 1 mile southeast of Hansen (Meadows, p. 79).

Hansen Canyon [LOS ANGELES]: *canyon,* drained by a stream that flows nearly 1 mile to Big Tujunga Canyon 3 miles south-southeast of Condor Peak (lat. 34°17'20" N, long. 118°11'40" W; sec. 1, T 2 N, R 13 W). Named on Condor Peak (1959) 7.5' quadrangle.

Hansen Flood Control Basin: see **Hansen Lake** [LOS ANGELES].

Hansen Lake [LOS ANGELES]: *lake,* 3 miles east-southeast of downtown San Fernando along Tujunga Wash (lat. 34°16' N, long. 118°23'15" W). Named on San Fernando (1966) 7.5' quadrangle. San Fernando (1953) 7.5' quadrangle shows Hansen Flood Control Basin at the place.

Happy Camp [VENTURA]: *locality,* 35 miles north of Moorpark (lat. 34°20'15" N, long. 118°51'55" W; near SE cor. sec. 16, T 3 N, R 19 W). Named on Simi (1951) 7.5' quadrangle.

Happy Camp Canyon [VENTURA]: *canyon,* drained by a stream that flows 10 miles to Arroyo Simi 1 mile east of Moorpark (lat. 34°17'10" N, long. 118°51'40" W; sec. 3, T 2 N, R 19 W); Happy Camp is in the canyon. Named on Simi (1951) 7.5' quadrangle.

Happy Valley [LOS ANGELES]:
(1) *canyon,* 1 mile long, opens into Pine Canyon (1) 14 miles east of Gorman (lat. 34°45'20" N, long. 118°36' W). Named on Burnt Peak (1958) and Neenach School (1965) 7.5' quadrangles.
(2) *district,* 3.5 miles northeast of Los Angels city hall (lat. 34°05'10" N, long. 118°11'50" W). Named on Los Angeles (1953) 7.5' quadrangle.

Harbor: see **Delhi** [ORANGE].

Harbor City [LOS ANGELES]: *district,* 4 miles southeast of Torrance city hall in Los Angeles (lat. 33°47'30" N, long. 118°17'45" W). Named on Torrance (1964) 7.5' quadrangle. Postal authorities established Harbor City post office in 1916; the full name of the place is Harbor Industrial City (Salley, p. 93).

Harbor Hills [LOS ANGELES]: *district,* 4.25 miles south-southeast of Torrance city hall (lat. 33°46'50" N, long. 118°18'40" W). Named on Torrance (1964) 7.5' quadrangle.

Harbor Industrial City: see **Harbor City** [LOS ANGELES].

Harbor Island [ORANGE]: *island,* 1200 feet long, 6.5 miles east-southeast of Huntington Beach civic center in Newport Bay (lat. 33°36'40" N, long. 117°54'10" W). Named on Newport Beach (1965) 7.5' quadrangle. Joseph A. Beck created the island in 1926 by adding fill to a sandbar (Meadows, p. 69).

Harbor Island Reach: see **Newport Bay** [ORANGE].

Harbor Lake [LOS ANGELES]: *lake,* crescent shaped, 1.5 miles long, 4.5 miles southeast of Torrance city hall (lat. 33°47'05" N, long. 118°37'35" W). Named on Torrance (1964) 7.5' quadrangle. Called Bixby Slough on Redondo (1896) 15' quadrangle. The old name "Bixby Slough" was for Jotham Bixby, a pioneer landowner; the feature was called Cañada de Palos Verdes in Spanish days (Gudde, 1949, p. 32). It also was called Machado Lake or Lake Machado (Fink, p. 22).

Harding Canyon [ORANGE]: *canyon,* drained by a stream that flows 5.5 miles to Santiago Creek nearly 7 miles northeast of El Toro (lat. 33°42'30" N, long. 117°37'40" W; sec. 29, T 5 S, R 7 W). Named on El Toro (1950) and Santiago Peak (1954) 7.5' quadrangles. The name commemorates Isaac Harding, who homesteaded at the place; Harding sold out to Madame Modjeska in 1898 (Meadows, p. 69). The feature first was called Shrewsbury Canyon for Lewis Shrewsbury, who had an apiary there (Sleeper, 1976. p. 87, 89).

Hardluck Campground [VENTURA]: *locality,* 6.5 miles northeast of McDonald Peak along Piru Creek (lat. 34°41'30" N, long. 118° 51' W; at N line sec. 24, T 7 N, R 19 W). Named on Black Mountain (1958) 7.5' quadrangle.

Hargraves: see **Orange** [ORANGE].

Harmon Barranca [VENTURA]: *gully,* extends for 3 miles from the mouth of Harmon Canyon to Santa Clara River 3.5 miles north of Oxnard (lat. 34°14'45" N, long. 119°11'30" W). Named on Saticoy (1951) 7.5' quadrangle.

Harmon Canyon [VENTURA]: *canyon,* drained by a stream that flows 4.25 miles to the valley of Santa Clara River 2.5 miles west of Saticoy (lat. 34°17'20" N, long. 119°11'50" W). Named on Saticoy (1951) 7.5' quadrangle. The name commemorates Silas Solon Harmon, a Presbyterian minister who farmed at the place in the late 1860's (Ricard).

Harold [LOS ANGELES]: *locality,* 2.5 miles south of Palmdale along Southern Pacific Railroad (lat. 34°32'40" N, long. 118°06'30" W; sec. 2, T 5 N, R 12 W). Named on Palmdale (1958) 7.5' quadrangle. Postal authorities established Trego post office in 1884, changed the name to Harold in 1890, discontinued it in 1894, reestablished it in 1895, and discontinued it finally in 1901 (Salley, p. 93, 224). United States Board on Geographic Names

(1960b, p. 8) rejected the name "Alpine" for the place. Los Angeles County (1935) map shows a feature called Harold Canyon located southwest of Harold (mainly in sec. 10, T 5 N, R 12 W). Postal authorities established Myrtle post office 10 miles east of Harold in 1891, moved it 4 miles east in 1894, discontinued it for a time in 1895, moved it 1.5 miles west in 1899, and discontinued it in 1902 (Salley, p. 149).

Harold Canyon: see **Harold** [LOS ANGELES].

Harold Lake: see **Lake Palmdale** [LOS ANGELES].

Harold Reservoir: see **Lake Palmdale** [LOS ANGELES].

Harper: see **Costa Mesa** [ORANGE].

Harperville: see **Garden Grove** [ORANGE].

Harrisburg: see **Carbondale**, under **Silverado Canyon** [ORANGE].

Harrow Canyon [LOS ANGELES]: *canyon,* 1 mile long, 1.5 miles north of Glendora city hall (lat. 34°09'25" N, long. 117°51'40" W; sec. 19, T 1 N, R 9 W). Named on Glendora (1953) 7.5' quadrangle.

Hartford [LOS ANGELES]: *locality,* 7 miles west-southwest of present Pomona city hall (lat. 34°00'20" N, long. 117°51'20" W). Named on Pomona (1904) 15' quadrangle. Postal authorities established Hartford post office in 1893 and discontinued it in 1895 (Frickstad, p. 74).

Hart's Ranch: see **San Fernando Pass** [LOS ANGELES].

Harvard: see **Mount Harvard** [LOS ANGELES].

Harvard Branch [LOS ANGELES]: *stream,* flows nearly 1 mile to Eaton Canyon 1.5 miles southwest of Mount Wilson (1) (lat. 34° 12'25" N, long. 118°05' W). Named on Mount Wilson (1953) 7.5' quadrangle.

Harvard Observatory Point: see **Mount Wilson** [LOS ANGELES] (1).

Haskell Canyon [LOS ANGELES]: *canyon,* drained by a stream that flows 8.5 miles to Bouquet Canyon 4.25 miles north of Newhall (lat. 34°26'45" N, long. 118°30'40" W; sec. 12, T 4 N, R 16 E). Named on Green Valley (1958), Mint Canyon (1960), and Newhall (1952) 7.5' quadrangles. The name commemorates John Haskell, who bought a ranch in the canyon in 1890 and mined gold there (Robinson, J.W., 1973, p. 19).

Hasley Canyon: see **Halsey Canyon** [LOS ANGELES].

Hasson: see **Chatsworth** [LOS ANGELES].

Hastings Canyon [LOS ANGELES]: *canyon,* 1 mile long, 3 miles south of Mount Wilson (1) (lat. 34°10'50" N, long. 118°04'05" W; sec. 7, 18, T 1 N, R 11 W). Named on Mount Wilson (1953) 7.5' quadrangle.

Hauser Canyon [LOS ANGELES]: *canyon,* drained by a stream that flows 2.25 miles to Sierra Pelona Valley 6 miles south of the village of Leona Valley (lat. 34°31'45" N, long.

118°16'35" W; sec. 7, T 5 N, R 13 W). Named on Sleepy Valley (1958) 7.5' quadrangle. Red Rover (1937) 6' quadrangle shows Hauser ranch in the canyon.

Hawaiian Gardens [LOS ANGELES]: *town,* 8.5 miles east-northeast of Long Beach city hall (lat. 33°49'45" N, long. 118°04'15" W). Named on Los Alamitos (1964) 7.5' quadrangle. Postal authorities established Hawaiian Gardens post office in 1951 (Salley, p. 94), and the town incorporated in 1964.

Hawkins: see **Mount Hawkins** [LOS ANGELES]; **South Mount Hawkins** [LOS ANGELES].

Hawthorne [LOS ANGELES]: *city,* 3 miles south of Inglewood city hall (lat. 33°55'05" N, long. 118°21'15" W). Named on Inglewood (1952) and Venice (1964) 7.5' quadrangles. Postal authorities established Hawthorne post office in 1908 (Frickstad, p. 74), and the city incorporated in 1922. Mrs. Laurine H. Woolwine, whose father was a founder of the city, named the place about 1906 for Nathaniel Hawthorne (Gudde, 1949, p. 144).

Hawthorne: see **Camp Hawthorne** [LOS ANGELES].

Hay Canyon [LOS ANGELES]: *canyon,* less than 1 mile long, 6.5 miles north-northwest of Pasadena city hall (lat. 34°13'35" N, long. 118°12'05" W; mainly in sec. 25, T 2 N, R 13 W). Named on Pasadena (1953) 7.5' quadrangle. Los Angeles County (1935) map shows a feature called Sargent Canyon located east of Hay Canyon, between Hay Canyon and Gould Canyon.

Hayes [LOS ANGELES]: *locality,* less than 1 mile east of El Monte along Pacific Electric Railroad (lat. 34°04'30" N, long. 118°01'05" W). Named on El Monte (1926) 6' quadrangle.

Haynes Canyon: see **Elderberry Canyon** [LOS ANGELES].

Haypress Reservoir [LOS ANGELES]: *lake,* 950 feet long, 2 miles west-northwest of Avalon on Santa Catalina Island (lat. 33°21'10" N, long. 118°21'40" W). Named on Santa Catalina East (1950) 7.5' quadrangle.

Headlee's: see **Falling Springs** [LOS ANGELES].

Heaton Flat [LOS ANGELES]: *area,* 9 miles northeast of Glendora city hall along San Gabriel River (lat. 34°14'25" N, long. 117°45'35" W). Named on Glendora (1953) 7.5' quadrangle. William Tecumseh Heaton came to the neighborhood in 1891 and settled at Peachtree Flat, which now is called Heaton Flat (Robinson, J.W., 1983, p. 35).

Hemohme: see **Camp Hemohme** [LOS ANGELES].

Henderson Canyon [LOS ANGELES]: *canyon,* drained by a stream that flows 1.5 miles to Verdugo Wash 7.5 miles northwest of Pasadena city hall (lat. 34°12'55" N, long. 118°14'50" W). Named on Burbank (1966) 7.5' quadrangle.

Henninger Flats [LOS ANGELES]: *area,* 2.5 miles south-southwest of Mount Wilson (1) (lat. 34°11'35" N, long. 118°05'10" W; at N line sec. 12, T 1 N, R 12 W). Named on Mount Wilson (1953) 7.5' quadrangle. The name recalls William K. Henninger, who built a house at the place in 1884 (Robinson, J.W., 1977, p. 67).

Hen Rock [LOS ANGELES]: *rock,* 4.5 miles north-northwest of Avalon off Santa Catalina Island (lat. 33°24' N, long. 118°22' W). Named on Santa Catalina East (1950) 7.5' quadrangle.

Henry Ridge [LOS ANGELES]: *ridge,* south-trending, 2.25 miles long, 9.5 miles northwest of Santa Monica city hall (lat. 34°06'30" N, long. 118°36'40" W). Named on Topanga (1952) 7.5' quadrangle.

Hermon: see **Highland Park** [LOS ANGELES].

Hermosa: see **Hermosa Beach** [LOS ANGELES]; **South Pasadena** [LOS ANGELES].

Hermosa Beach [LOS ANGELES]: *town,* 1.5 miles north-northwest of Redondo Beach city hall (lat. 33°51'45" N, long. 118°23'55" W). Named on Redondo Beach (1951) and Venice (1950) 7.5' quadrangles. Postal authorities established Hermosa Beach post office in 1903 (Frickstad, p. 75), and the town incorporated in 1907. Called Hermosa on California Mining Bureau's (1917) map.

Hermosillo: see **Hermosillo Station** [LOS ANGELES].

Hermosillo Station [LOS ANGELES]: *locality,* 6.5 miles south-southeast of Inglewood city hall (lat. 33°52'45" N, long. 118°17'50" W). Named on Inglewood (1952) 7.5' quadrangle. Called Hermosillo on Compton (1930) 6' quadrangle.

Herrick Canyon: see **Marek Canyon** [LOS ANGELES].

Heryford Canyon [LOS ANGELES]: *canyon,* 1.25 miles long, 2 miles northeast of Burnt Peak (lat. 34°42' N, long. 118°33' W; sec. 11, 14, T 7 N, R 16 W). Named on Burnt Peak (1958) 7.5' quadrangle.

Hewes Park [ORANGE]: *locality,* 2.25 miles east of present Orange city hall (lat. 33°46'50" N, long. 117°48'35" W). Named on Orange (1964) 7.5' quadrangle. David Hewes planned to build a home at the site as early as 1886, but when the house was not built, the property was open to the public as a park—the place was subdivided in 1928 (Meadows, p. 70).

Hewitt [LOS ANGELES]: *locality,* 3.5 miles east-northeast of Van Nuys along Southern Pacific Railroad (lat. 34°12' N, long. 118°23'25" W). Named on Van Nuys (1953) 7.5' quadrangle.

Hialeah Springs [LOS ANGELES]: *spring,* 9 miles southwest of Newhall (lat. 34°16'40" N, long. 118°37'45" W). Named on Santa Susana (1951) 7.5' quadrangle. Los Angeles County (1935) map has the name "Hi-Lea Canyon"

for the canyon that contains Hialeah Springs.

Hiatt Canyon [LOS ANGELES]: *canyon,* drained by a stream that flows 2 miles to Elizabeth Lake Canyon 1.25 miles southwest of the village of Lake Hughes (lat. 34°39'45" N, long. 118°27'20" W; sec. 27, T 7 N, R 15 W). Named on Lake Hughes (1957) 7.5' quadrangle.

Hickey Canyon [ORANGE]: *canyon,* drained by a stream that flows 2.5 miles to Arroyo Trabuco 5 miles southwest of Santiago Peak (lat. 33°39'20" N, long. 117°40' W; near NE cor. sec. 15, T 6 S, R 7 W). Named on Santiago Peak (1954) 7.5' quadrangle. The name commemorates Jim Hickey, who came to the canyon in 1877 and kept bees there (Meadows, p. 70). The feature first was called Weakly Canyon for Labon Weakly, who was a pioneer beekeeper in the mid-1870's; later it was called Rowell Canyon for Edward Rowell, a resident of the place (Sleeper, 1976, p. 165-166).

Hicks Canyon [ORANGE]: *canyon,* drained by a stream that flows 2 miles to lowlands about 7 miles north-northwest of El Toro (lat. 33°43'10" N, long. 117°44' W). Named on El Toro (1968) 7.5' quadrangle. The name is from Jim Hickey, who moved his bees to the canyon in the 1880's (Meadows, p. 70).

Hick's Canyon: see **Rose Canyon** [ORANGE].

Hicks Canyon Wash [ORANGE]: *stream,* flows 2.5 miles from the mouth of Hicks Canyon to Rattlesnake Canyon Wash 5.5 miles east-southeast of Santa Ana city hall (lat. 33°43'35" N, long. 117° 46'15" W). Named on El Toro (1968) and Tustin (1965) 7.5' quadrangles.

Hickson [LOS ANGELES]: *locality,* 2.5 miles southwest of downtown San Fernando along Pacific Electric Railroad (lat. 34°15'25" N, long. 118°28' W). Named on Pacoima (1927) 6' quadrangle.

Hidden Hills [LOS ANGELES]: *town,* northwest of Calabasas (lat. 34°09'45" N, long. 118°39' W). Named on Calabasas (1952, photorevised 1967) 7.5' quadrangle. The town incorporated in 1961.

Hidden Lake [LOS ANGELES]: *lake,* 300 feet long, 2.5 miles northeast of Burnt Peak (lat. 34°42'30" N, long. 118°32'45" W; sec. 11, T 7 N, R 16 W). Named on Burnt Peak (1958) 7.5' quadrangle. Manzana (1938) 6' quadrangle shows an intermittent lake.

Hidden Springs [LOS ANGELES]: *locality,* 5 miles east of Condor Peak along Mill Creek (lat. 34°19'05" N, long. 118°07'50" W). Named on Condor Peak (1959) 7.5' quadrangle. Los Angeles County (1935) map has the singular form "Hidden Spring" for the name.

Hidden Valley [VENTURA]: *valley,* 2.5 miles south of Newbury Park (lat. 34°08'50" N, long. 118°54'20" W). Named on Newbury Park (1951) 7.5' quadrangle. Called Potrero on Camulos (1903) 30' quadrangle.

DURHAM'S PLACE-NAMES

Hidden Valley: see **Camp Hidden Valley** [LOS ANGELES].
Hideaway Canyon [LOS ANGELES]: *canyon,* about 1 mile long, 2.5 miles northeast of Burnt Peak (lat. 34°42'15" N, long. 118°32'30" W; sec. 11, 14, T 7 N, R 16 W). Named on Burnt Peak (1958) 7.5' quadrangle.
Higgins Canyon [LOS ANGELES]: *canyon,* 2.5 miles long, 2.5 miles north-northwest of Beverly Hills city hall (lat. 34°06'20" N, long. 118°25' W). Named on Beverly Hills (1950) 7.5' quadrangle.
Highland Park [LOS ANGELES]: *district,* 5 miles north-northeast of Los Angeles city hall (lat. 34°06'45" N, long. 118°12' W). Named on Los Angeles (1953) 7.5' quadrangle. Postal authorities established Highland Park post office in 1892 (Salley, p. 97). They established Hermon post office in 1904 and discontinued it in 1916; the name was for the developer of a community that now is in Highland Park (Salley, p. 96).
Highland Park: see **North Highland Park** [LOS ANGELES].
Highline Saddle [LOS ANGELES]: *pass,* 6.25 miles north of downtown Sunland on Mendenhall Ridge (lat. 34°21'05" N, long. 118°19'30" W; at NE cor. sec. 15, T 3 N, R 14 W). Named on Sunland (1966) 7.5' quadrangle.
Highway Highlands [LOS ANGELES]: *locality,* 4.5 miles northeast of Burbank city hall (lat. 34°14'15" N, long. 118°15'55" W). Named on Burbank (1953) 7.5' quadrangle. Postal authorities established Highway Highlands post office in 1925 and discontinued it in 1954 (Salley, p. 97). Mark S. Collins, one of the promoters of the place, named it in 1923 for its position along a state highway (Gudde, 1949, p. 148).
Hi-Hill: see **Camp Hi-Hill** [LOS ANGELES].
Hi-Lea Canyon: see **Hialeah Springs** [LOS ANGELES].
Hillcrest Canyon [LOS ANGELES]: *canyon,* less than 1 mile long, 2.5 miles east of Burbank city hall (lat. 34°10'40" N, long. 118°15'40" W). Named on Burbank (1953) 7.5' quadrangle.
Hillgrove [LOS ANGELES]: *district,* nearly 5 miles south-southwest of Baldwin Park city hall (lat. 34°01'05" N, long. 117°58'45" W). Named on Baldwin Park (1966) 7.5' quadrangle. On Puente (1927) 6' quadrangle, the name "Hill Grove" applies to a place along a rail line.
Hillyer: see **Mount Hillyer** [LOS ANGELES].
Hines Peak [VENTURA]: *peak,* 12 miles east of Wheeler Springs at the west end of Topatopa Mountains (lat. 34°30'40" N, long. 119° 04'30" W; near SW cor. sec. 15, T 5 N, R 21 W). Altitude 6704 feet. Named on Topatopa Mountains (1943) 7.5' quadrangle. The name is for Colonel J.D. Hines, first superior court judge in Ventura County (Outland, 1969, p. 7).

Hi Vista [LOS ANGELES]: *locality,* 19 miles northeast of Littlerock (lat. 34°44'05" N, long. 117°46'35" W; on S line sec. 36, T 8 N, R 9 W). Named on Hi Vista (1957) 7.5' quadrangle. Mrs. M.R. Card, wife of the developer of the site, named the place in 1930 for the view from there (Gudde, 1949, p. 148).
Hoagland Canyon: see **Stokes Canyon** [LOS ANGELES].
Hoar: see **Mount Hoar**, under **Rincon Mountain** [VENTURA].
Hobart [LOS ANGELES]: *locality,* 3.5 miles southeast of Los Angeles city hall along Atchison, Topeka and Santa Fe Railroad (lat. 34°00'40" N, long. 118°12'10" W). Named on Los Angeles (1953) 7.5' quadrangle. Called Manhattan on Pasadena (1900) 15' quadrangle.
Hobo Canyon [ORANGE]: *canyon,* 1 mile long, opens to the sea 2.25 miles south-southeast of Laguna Beach city hall (lat. 33°31' N, long. 117°45'35" W; sec. 31, T 7 S, R 8 W). Named on Laguna Beach (1965) 7.5' quadrangle.
Hoegee Campground [LOS ANGELES]: *locality,* 2 miles southeast of Mount Wilson (1) along Winter Creek (lat. 34°12'25" N, long. 118°01'55" W; near NE cor. sec. 4, T 1 N, R 11 W). Named on Mount Wilson (1966) 7.5' quadrangle. The name recalls Arie Hoegee and his family, founders of Hoegee's Camp, later called Camp Ivy (Robinson, J.W., 1977, p. 134).
Hoegee's Camp: see **Camp Ivy** [LOS ANGELES].
Hog Back [LOS ANGELES]: *relief feature,* 12.5 miles north-northeast of Pomona city hall (lat. 34°13'10" N, long. 117°40' W; sec. 36, T 2 N, R 8 W). Named on Mount Baldy (1954) 7.5' quadrangle. Camp Baldy (1940) 6' quadrangle has the form "Hogback" for the name.
Hogback: see **The Hogback**, under **Mount Harvard** [LOS ANGELES].
Hog Canyon [LOS ANGELES]: *canyon,* 1.25 miles long, opens into lowlands 3.5 miles north-northwest of downtown San Fernando (lat. 34°19'45" N, long. 118°27'50" W; near W line sec. 21, T 3 N, R 15 W). Named on San Fernando (1953) 7.5' quadrangle.
Hog Canyon: see **Tapo Canyon** [VENTURA] (1).
Hog Island [ORANGE]: *island,* 6.5 miles northwest of Huntington Beach civic center in marsh along Anaheim Bay (lat. 33°43'55" N, long. 118°04'20" W). Named on Seal Beach (1965) 7.5' quadrangle.
Holcomb Canyon [LOS ANGELES]: *canyon,* drained by a stream that flows 3.5 miles to Big Rock Creek 2 miles south-southeast of Valyermo (lat. 34°25' N, long. 117°50'15" W; sec. 20, T 4 N, R 9 W). Named on Valyermo (1958) 7.5' quadrangle. Los Angeles County (1935) map has the name "Holcomb Creek" for the stream in the canyon.
Holcomb Creek: see **Holcomb Canyon** [LOS ANGELES].

76

Holcomb Ridge [LOS ANGELES]: *ridge,* west-to west-northwest-trending, 3 miles long, center 1 mile northeast of Valyermo (lat. 34°27'30" N, long. 117°50'30" W). Named on Valyermo (1958) 7.5' quadrangle.

Holdansville: see **San Francisquito Canyon** [LOS ANGELES].

Hole-in-the-Wall [VENTURA]: *relief feature,* 7 miles south-southeast of Cobblestone Mountain along Hopper Canyon (lat. 34°30'40" N, long. 118°50'10" W). Named on Cobblestone Mountain (1958) 7.5' quadrangle.

Holiday Lake [LOS ANGELES]: *lake,* 15 miles east of Gorman (lat. 34°47'55" N, long. 118°34'25" W; sec. 9, T 8 N, R 16 W). Named on Neenach School (1965) 7.5' quadrangle.

Holland Summit: see **Tejon Pass** [LOS ANGELES].

Hollister Campground [VENTURA]: *locality,* 5 miles southeast of Cobblestone Mountain along Agua Blanca Creek (lat. 34°32'55" N, long. 118°49' W). Named on Cobblestone Mountain (1958) 7.5' quadrangle.

Hollow Rock: see **Arch Rock** [ORANGE].

Hollydale [LOS ANGELES]: *district,* 4 miles southeast of South Gate city hall (lat. 33°54'55" N, long. 118°09'35" W). Named on South Gate (1952) 7.5' quadrangle. Postal authorities established Hollydale post office in 1926 (Salley, p. 99).

Hollywood [LOS ANGELES]: *district,* 5 miles west-northwest of Los Angeles city hall in Los Angeles (lat. 34°05'30" N, long. 118° 19' W). Named on Hollywood (1953) 7.5' quadrangle. Postal authorities established Hollywood post office in 1897 (Salley, p. 99). Horace H. Wilcox laid out the community in 1886; his wife suggested the name (Gudde, 1969, p. 143). Promoters projected an elaborate townsite called Cahuenga at present Hollywood in 1888, but the older community of Hollywood soon eclipsed it (Hanna, p. 48).

Hollywood: see **Mount Hollywood** [LOS ANGELES]; **North Hollywood** [LOS ANGELES]; **West Hollywood** [LOS ANGELES].

Hollywood Beach [VENTURA]: *settlement,* 3.5 miles southwest of Oxnard along the coast (lat. 34°10'05" N, long. 119°13'50" W). Named on Oxnard (1949) 7.5' quadrangle. The name, given after a movie called *The Sheik* was filmed at the place, was supposed to attract residents (Ricard).

Hollywood by the Sea [VENTURA]: *town,* 3.5 miles southwest of Oxnard along the coast (lat. 34°09'35" N, long. 119°13'25" W). Named on Oxnard (1949) 7.5' quadrangle. The name has the same origin as the name of neighboring Hollywood Beach (Ricard).

Hollywood Lake: see **Hollywood Reservoir** [LOS ANGELES].

Hollywood Reservoir [LOS ANGELES]: *lake,* 0.5 mile long, 7 miles northwest of Los Angeles city hall (lat. 34°07'15" N, long.

118°19'55" W; on S line sec. 34, T 1 N, R 14 W). Named on Burbank (1953) and Hollywood (1953) 7.5' quadrangles. Called Hollywood Lake on Burbank (1926) 6' quadrangle.

Hollywood Riviera [LOS ANGELES]: *district,* 2 miles south-southeast of Redondo Beach city hall (lat. 33°48'45" N, long. 118°22'50" W). Named on Redondo Beach (1951) 7.5' quadrangle.

Hollywood Spa: see **Colegrove** [LOS ANGELES].

Holmes Creek [LOS ANGELES]: *stream,* flows 4 miles to Pallett Creek 2 miles west-northwest of Valyermo (lat. 34°27'10" N, long. 117°53'45" W; sec. 11, T 4 N, R 10 W). Named on Juniper Hills (1959) 7.5' quadrangle. On Los Angeles County (1935) map, present Holmes Creek above its confluence with Cruthers Creek is called East Fork Cruthers Creek.

Holser Canyon [LOS ANGELES-VENTURA]: *canyon,* drained by a stream that heads in Los Angeles County and flows 3.5 miles to Piru Canyon 3 miles northeast of Piru in Ventura County (lat. 34° 26'25" N, long. 118°45'10" W). Named on Piru (1952) and Val Verde (1952) 7.5' quadrangles. The name commemorates a family of landowners in the canyon (Ricard).

Holt Canyon: see **Humphreys** [LOS ANGELES].

Holton [LOS ANGELES]: *locality,* 3.5 miles north-northwest of present Manhattan Beach city hall along Pacific Electric Railroad (lat. 33°56'50" N, long. 118°26'35" W). Named on Venice (1924) 6' quadrangle.

Holton: see **Karl Holton Camp** [LOS ANGELES].

Holy Jim Canyon [ORANGE]: *canyon,* drained by a stream that flows nearly 3 miles to Trabuco Canyon 2.5 miles south-southeast of Santiago Peak (lat. 33°40'35" N, long. 117°31' W; at W line sec. 4, T 6 S, R 6 W). On Santiago Peak (1943) 15' quadrangle, the name applies to the lower part of the canyon and to a northeast branch. The feature was named in jest for James "Cussin' Jim" Smith, who had an apiary in the canyon (Gudde, 1949, p. 151).

Home Junction [LOS ANGELES]: *locality,* 3.25 miles southwest of Beverly Hills city hall along Southern Pacific Railroad (lat. 34°02'05" N, long. 118°26' W). Named on Beverly Hills (1966) 7.5' quadrangle. Beverly Hills (1950) 7.5' quadrangle shows the place along Pacific Electric Railroad. On Santa Monica (1902) 15' quadrangle, a branch rail line to Soldiers Home joins the main line at the site.

Honby [LOS ANGELES]: *locality,* 2.25 miles west of Solemint along Southern Pacific Railroad (lat. 34°25'15" N, long. 118°29'40" W; near N line sec. 19, T 4 N, R 15 W). Named on Mint Canyon (1960) 7.5' quadrangle. Los

Angeles County (1935) map shows a feature called McCoy Canyon that opens into Solemint Canyon from the northeast 0.5 mile northwest of Honby.

Honda Barranca [VENTURA]: *gully,* extends for 3.5 miles to Beardsley Wash 7 miles south of Santa Paula (lat. 34°15'15" N, long. 119°04'05" W). Named on Santa Paula (1951) 7.5' quadrangle.

Hondo: see **Poor Farm Station** [LOS ANGELES].

Hondo Canyon [LOS ANGELES]: *canyon,* drained by a stream that flows 1.5 miles to Old Topanga Canyon 9 miles northwest of Santa Monica city hall (lat. 34°05'50" N, long. 118°36'55" W; sec. 12, T 1 S, R 17 W). Named on Topanga (1952) 7.5' quadrangle.

Honeybee Campground [LOS ANGELES]: *locality,* 7 miles north-northwest of Sunland in Pacoima Canyon (lat. 34°21'15" N, long. 118°21'10" W; near S line sec. 9, T 3 N, R 14 W). Named on Sunland (1966) 7.5' quadrangle. The place is at the mouth of a feature called Honey Bee Canyon on Los Angels County (1935) map.

Honey Bee Canyon: see **Honeybee Campground** [LOS ANGELES].

Hooverville: see **Eldoradoville Campground** [LOS ANGELES].

Hopper Canyon [VENTURA]: *canyon,* drained by a stream that flows 11 miles to the valley of Santa Clara River 2 miles west of Piru (lat. 34°24'30" N, long. 118°49'40" W; near SW cor. sec. 24, T 4 N, R 19 W); the canyon is east of Hopper Mountain. Named on Cobblestone Mountain (1958) and Piru (1952) 7.5' quadrangles. The name commemorates Ari Hopper, a mountaineer who homesteaded above the canyon (Outland, 1969, p. 27).

Hopper Mountain [VENTURA]: *peak,* 6 miles northwest of Piru (lat. 34°28'40" N, long. 118°51'50" W; near W line sec. 34, T 5 N, R 19 W). Altitude 4524 feet. Named on Piru (1952) 7.5' quadrangle.

Horn Canyon [VENTURA]: *canyon,* 2.5 miles long, along Thatcher Creek above a point 4 miles east-northeast of the town of Ojai (lat. 34°27'50" N, long. 119°10'40" W; near SW cor. sec. 34, T 5 N, R 22 W). Named on Ojai (1952) 7.5' quadrangle.

Horno Creek [ORANGE]: *stream,* flows 5.5 miles to San Juan Creek 0.5 mile east-southeast of San Juan Capistrano (lat. 33°29'55" N, long. 117°39'15" W; at S line sec. 6, T 8 S, R 7 W). Named on San Juan Capistrano (1968) 7.5' quadrangle. The name is from kilns situated along the stream that were used to make roof tiles and floor tiles for San Juan Capistrano mission—*horno* means "kiln" in Spanish (Meadows, p. 71).

Horse Camp [LOS ANGELES]: *locality,* 9.5 miles east-southeast of Gorman (lat. 34°43'40" N, long. 118°39'40" W). Named on Liebre (1938) 6' quadrangle.

Horse Camp Canyon [LOS ANGELES]: *canyon,* 4 miles long (the course of the canyon is interrupted by San Andreas rift zone), opens into lowlands 11 miles east of Gorman (lat. 34°46'50" N, long. 118°39'20" W; sec. 14, T 8 N, R 17 W); Horse Camp is in the canyon. Named on La Liebre Ranch (1965) and Liebre Mountain (1958) 7.5' quadrangles.

Horse Canyon [LOS ANGELES]: *canyon,* drained by a stream that flows 2.25 miles to San Gabriel River nearly 8 miles north-northeast of Glendora city hall (lat. 34°13'55" N, long. 117°47'30" W). Named on Glendora (1953) 7.5' quadrangle. East Fork branches southeast 0.5 mile above the mouth of the main canyon; it is nearly 1.5 miles long and is named on Glendora (1953) 7.5' quadrangle.

Horse Canyon Saddle [LOS ANGELES]: *pass,* 5.5 miles north-northeast of Glendora city hall (lat. 34°12'15" N, long. 117°48'30" W; sec. 3, T 1 N, R 9 W). Named on Glendora (1953) 7.5' quadrangle.

Horse Flats [LOS ANGELES]:
(1) *area,* 4 miles northeast of Chatsworth (lat. 34°17'45" N, long. 118°33' W; around SW cor. sec. 34, T 3 N, R 16 W). Named on Oat Mountain (1952) 7.5' quadrangle.
(2) *area,* 3 miles south-southeast of Pacifico Mountain (lat. 34°20'45" N, long. 118°00'30" W). Named on Alder Creek (1941) 6' quadrangle.

Horse Flats Campground [LOS ANGELES]: *locality,* 3 miles south-southeast of Pacifico Mountain (lat. 34°20'35" N, long. 118°00'30" W; near W line sec. 14, T 3 N, R 11 W); the place is at Horse Flats (2). Named on Chilao Flat (1959) 7.5' quadrangle.

Horseshoe Bend [ORANGE]:
(1) *bend,* 2 miles south of San Juan Hill along Santa Ana River (lat. 33°52'50" N, long. 117°44'15" W). Named on Prado Dam (1967) 7.5' quadrangle.
(2) *locality,* 2.5 miles south-southwest of San Juan Hill along Atchison, Topeka and Santa Fe Railroad (lat. 33°52'50" N, long. 117°44'40" W); the place is near Horseshoe Bend (1). Named on Prado (1941) 7.5' quadrangle.

Horse Thief Flat: see **Beartrap Canyon** [LOS ANGELES] (1).

Horse Trail Campground [LOS ANGELES]: *locality,* 11.5 miles east-southeast of Gorman (lat. 34°34'15" N, long. 118°39'15" W; sec. 35, T 8 N, R 17 W). Named on Liebre Mountain (1958) 7.5' quadrangle.

Horsetrough Spring [ORANGE]: *spring,* 2.25 miles south of Sierra Peak (lat. 33°49'05" N, long. 117°38'55" W; sec. 18, T 4 S, R 7 W). Named on Black Star Canyon (1967) 7.5' quadrangle.

Hot Spring Canyon [ORANGE]: *canyon,* drained by a stream that flows 7.25 miles to San Juan Creek 10 miles northeast of San Juan Capistrano (lat. 33°35'15" N, long.

117°30'55" W; sec. 4, T 7 S, R 6 W). Named on Alberhill (1954), Cañada Gobernadora (1968), and Santiago Peak (1954) 7.5' quadrangles. Cañada Gobernadora (1968) 7.5' quadrangle shows a hot spring near the mouth of the canyon. Called Bell Canyon on Lake Elsinore (1942) 15' quadrangle, where present Bell Canyon is unnamed.

Hot Springs Canyon [VENTURA]: *canyon,* drained by a stream that flows 5.25 miles to Sespe Creek 2.25 miles north-northwest of Devils Heart Peak (lat. 34°34'35" N, long. 118°59'05" W; at S line sec. 27, T 6 N, R 20 W); the feature called Sespe Hot Springs is in the canyon. Named on Devils Heart Peak (1943) and Topatopa Mountains (1943) 7.5' quadrangles. Called Hot Spring Canyon on Mount Pinos (1903) 30' quadrangle. Tejon (1903) 30' quadrangle has the name "Hot Springs Cr." for the stream in the canyon.

Hot Springs Creek: see **Hot Springs Canyon** [VENTURA].

Howard Creek [VENTURA]: *stream,* flows 3.5 miles to Sespe Creek 6 miles northeast of Wheeler Springs (lat. 34°33'20" N, long. 119° 12'20" W; near N line sec. 5, T 5 N, R 22 W). Named on Lion Canyon (1943) 7.5' quadrangle. The name commemorates Jeff Howard, a homesteader in the neighborhood in the 1870's (Ricard).

Howard Summit [LOS ANGELES]: *locality,* 4.5 miles southeast of Inglewood along a rail line (lat. 33°55'15" N, long. 118°17'35" W). Named on Redondo (1896) 15' quadrangle. Postal authorities established Howard Summit post office on a small hill (NE quarter sec. 12, T 3 S, R 13 W) in 1892, changed the name to Loma Vista in 1902, and discontinued it in 1904; the name "Howard Summit" was for William W. Howard, first postmaster (Salley, p. 101, 125).

Hudsons Bay Camp [LOS ANGELES]: *locality,* 8 miles north-northeast of Glendora city hall along San Gabriel River (lat. 34°13'55" N, long. 117°47'30" W). Named on Glendora (1966) 7.5' quadrangle.

Hueneme: see **Port Hueneme** [VENTURA].

Hueneme Point: see **Point Hueneme** [VENTURA].

Huerta de Cuati [LOS ANGELES]: *land grant,* at San Marino. Named on El Monte (1953) and Mount Wilson (1953) 7.5' quadrangles. Victoria Reid received the land in 1830 or 1838, and claimed 128 acres patented in 1859 (Cowan, p. 31; Cowan used the form "Huerta de Coati" for the name).

Hughes: see **Lake Hughes** [LOS ANGELES].

Hughes Canyon [LOS ANGELES]: *canyon,* drained by a stream that flows nearly 3 miles to Santa Clara River 12 miles east of Solemint (lat. 34°26'25" N, long. 118°15'15" W; near SE cor. sec. 8, T 4 N, R 13 W). Named on Acton (1959) and Agua Dulce (1960) 7.5' quadrangles.

Hughes Canyon: see **Price Canyon** [LOS ANGELES].

Hughes Lake [LOS ANGELES]: *lake,* 2000 feet long, at the village of Lake Hughes (lat. 34°40'35" N, long. 118°26'40" W; near SW cor. sec. 23, T 7 N, R 15 W). Named on Lake Hughes (1957) 7.5' quadrangle. G.O. Hughes owned land along the lake (Gudde, 1949, p. 156). The lake is in what was known as Tweedy Canyon as late as 1875; Bill Tweedy and his family lived there for years (Latta, p. 211). Los Angeles County (1935) map shows a place called Judahy Flats located 1.5 miles northwest of Hughes Lake (SW cor. sec. 15, T 7 N, R 15 W).

Hughes Lake: see **Lake Hughes** [LOS ANGELES].

Humingbird Creek [LOS ANGELES]: *stream,* flows less than 1 mile to San Dimas Canyon nearly 8 miles northeast of Glendora city hall (lat. 34°12'20" N, long. 117°45'15" W; sec. 6, T 1 N, R 8 W). Named on Glendora (1966) 7.5' quadrangle.

Humphreys [LOS ANGELES]: *locality,* 1 mile east-southeast of Solemint along Southern Pacific Railroad (lat. 34°24'35" N, long. 118°26'25" W; near S line sec. 22, T 4 N, R 15 W). Named on Mint Canyon (1960) 7.5' quadrangle. Los Angeles County (1935) map shows a feature called Holt Canyon that opens into Solemint Canyon from the south at present Humphreys. Lankershim Ranch Land and Water Company's (1888) map shows a place called Kent Sta. located along the railroad between Saugus and Lang, at or near the site of present Humphreys.

Hungry Valley [VENTURA]: *valley,* 8.5 miles north-northeast of McDonald Peak (lat. 34°44'40" N, long. 118°52'30" W). Named on Black Mountain (1958), Frazier Mountain (1958), Lebec (1958), and McDonald Peak (1958) 7.5' quadrangles.

Hungry Valley: see **Lower Hungry Valley**, under **Cañada de Los Alamos** [LOS ANGELES].

Hunt Canyon [LOS ANGELES]: *canyon,* 3.25 miles long, 7.5 miles north-northwest of Pacifico Mountain (lat. 34°29'20" N, long. 118° 03'50" W). Named on Pacifico Mountain (1959) 7.5' quadrangle. Los Angeles County (1935) map has the form "Hunts Cany." for the name.

Hunter Canyon: see **Drinkwater Canyon** [LOS ANGELES].

Huntington: see **Camp Huntington** [LOS ANGELES].

Huntington Beach [ORANGE]: *city,* 10 miles southwest of Santa Ana (lat. 33°39'40" N, long. 117°59'55" W). Named on Los Alamitos (1964), Newport Beach (1965), and Seal Beach (1965) 7.5' quadrangles. Postal authorities established Huntington Beach post office in 1903 (Frickstad, p. 117), and the city incorporated in 1909. Philip Stanton and others laid out a community called Pacific City in 1901 at what was known as Shell Beach; after Henry E. Huntington bought controlling interest in the project in 1902, the town was renamed Huntington Beach (Meadows, p. 72). Meadows listed several stops situated along Pacific Electric Railroad in and near Huntington Beach: Bushard, named for John B. Bushard, a farmer, located 2.25 miles east-northeast of Huntington Beach civic center (p. 31); Cordero, located 3 miles northeast of the civic center (p. 54); Gamewell, located 1.5 miles southeast of the civic center (p. 65); Lambs, located 2.5 miles northeast of the civic center (p. 77); Nimock, located 3.25 miles north-northeast of the civic center (p. 106); Thompsonville, located a little more than 0.5 mile north-northeast of the civic center (p. 134); and Xalisco, located 1.5 miles east of the civic center (p. 140).

Huntington Harbour [ORANGE]:
(1) *water feature,* 5.5 miles northwest of Huntington Beach civic center (lat. 33°43'15" N, long. 118°03'45" W); the feature is inland from Sunset Beach. Named on Seal Beach (1965) 7.5' quadrangle. Seal Beach (1950) 7.5' quadrangle has the name "Sunset Bay" at the place. United States Board on Geographic Names (1978b, p. 4) rejected the names "Anaheim Bay" and "Huntington Harbor" for the feature.
(2) *district,* 5 miles northwest of Huntington Beach civic center (lat. 33°43' N, long. 118°03'15" W); the place is at Huntington Harbour (1). Named on Seal Beach (1965, photorevised 1981) 7.5' quadrangle.

Huntington Park [LOS ANGELES]: *city,* less than 2 miles north-northwest of South Gate city hall (lat. 33°58'45" N, long. 118°13'05" W). Named on South Gate (1952) 7.5' quadrangle. Postal authorities established La Park post office in 1904 and changed the name to Huntington Park in 1906 (Salley, p. 117). The city incorporated in 1906. E.V. Baker laid out the community in 1903 and named it for Henry E. Huntington (Gudde, 1949, p. 157).

Hunts Canyon: see **Hunt Canyon** [LOS ANGELES].

Hutak Canyon [LOS ANGELES]: *canyon,* 1 mile long, 6 miles west of Valyermo (lat. 34°26'15" N, long. 117°57' W; sec. 8, 17, T 4 N, R 10 W). Named on Juniper Hills (1959) 7.5' quadrangle.

Hutton Peak [VENTURA]: *peak,* 3.25 miles west-northwest of Piru (lat. 34°26' N, long. 118°50'40" W; sec. 14, T 4 N, R 19 W). Altitude 2239 feet. Named on Piru (1952) 7.5' quadrangle.

Hyde Park [LOS ANGELES]: *district,* 2 miles east of Inglewood city hall (lat. 33°57'55" N, long. 118°19'15" W). Named on Inglewood (1952) 7.5' quadrangle. On Inglewood (1964) 7.5' quadrangle, the name applies to a place

located 1 mile farther north-northwest. Postal authorities established Hyde Park post office in 1888, changed the name to Hydepark in 1895, changed it back to Hyde Park in 1924, and discontinued the post office in 1969 (Salley, p. 102). Moses L. Wicks laid out a community at the place in 1887 and named it for the owner of a lumber yard there (Gudde, 1949, p. 158).

Hynes: see **Paramount** [LOS ANGELES].

Hyperion [LOS ANGELES]: *locality,* 3 miles north-northwest of present Manhattan Beach city hall along Pacific Electric Railroad (lat. 33°55'35" N, long. 118°25'55" W). Named on Venice (1924) 6' quadrangle.

– I –

Icy Springs [LOS ANGELES]: *spring,* 6.25 miles southeast of Valyermo along Big Rock Creek (lat. 34°22'55" N, long. 117°46'15" W; near N line sec. 1, T 3 N, R 9 W). Named on Valyermo (1958) 7.5' quadrangle.

Idlehour Camp [LOS ANGELES]: *locality,* 1.5 miles southwest of Mount Wilson (1) (lat. 34°12'35" N, long. 118°05' W). Named on Mount Wilson (1953) 7.5' quadrangle. The name recalls Camp Idle Hour, which Emile Gunther started in 1915 in Eaton Canyon (Robinson, J.W., 1977, p. 134). Mount Wilson (1966) 7.5' quadrangle shows a place called Idlehour Campground located about 400 feet farther south.

Idlewood Canyon [LOS ANGELES]: *canyon,* less than 0.5 mile long, 2 miles east of Burbank city hall (lat. 34°10'50" N, long. 118°16'10" W). Named on Burbank (1953) 7.5' quadrangle.

Ikanhoffer Canyon: see **Maple Canyon** [LOS ANGELES] (1).

Imperial Crest [LOS ANGELES]: *locality,* 4 miles southwest of present Whittier city hall (lat. 33°55'35" N, long. 118°04'25" W). Named on Whittier (1949) 7.5' quadrangle. The place includes a crescent-shaped street, and is located off of Imperial Highway.

Inceville [LOS ANGELES]: *locality,* 4 miles west-northwest of present Santa Monica city hall along the coast (lat. 34°02'20" N, long. 118°33'20" W). Named on Topanga Canyon (1928) 6' quadrangle.

Indiana Colony: see **Pasadena** [LOS ANGELES].

Indian Ben Saddle [LOS ANGELES]: *pass,* 2 miles north of Condor Peak (lat. 34°21'10" N, long. 118°12'50" W). Named on Condor Peak (1959) 7.5' quadrangle.

Indian Bill Canyon [LOS ANGELES]: *canyon,* nearly 2 miles long, 6 miles west of Valyermo (lat. 34°26'20" N, long. 117°57'25" W). Named on Juniper Hills (1959) 7.5' quadrangle.

Indian Canyon [LOS ANGELES]:

(1) *canyon,* drained by a stream that flows 3.25 miles to Santa Clara River 10 miles east of Solemint (lat. 34°26'20" N, long. 118°16'40" W; near S line sec. 7, T 4 N, R 13 W). Named on Agua Dulce (1960) 7.5' quadrangle. On Ravenna (1934) 6' quadrangle, the stream in the canyon is called Indian Creek.

(2) *canyon,* drained by a stream that flows 1.25 miles to Lopez Canyon 2.5 miles east-northeast of downtown San Fernando (lat. 34°17'45" N, long. 118°23'55" W; near SE cor. sec. 36, T 3 N, R 15 W). Named on San Fernando (1953) 7.5' quadrangle.

Indian Canyon Campground [LOS ANGELES]: *locality,* 11 miles east of Solemint (lat. 34°25'10" N, long. 118°16' W); the place is in present Indian Canyon (1). Named on Ravena (1934, reprinted 1949) 6' quadrangle.

Indian Creek: see **Indian Canyon** [LOS ANGELES] (1).

Indian Hill [LOS ANGELES]: *relief feature,* 4.5 miles north-northeast of Pomona city hall (lat. 34°06'55" N, long. 117°42'50" W; on W line sec. 3, T 1 S, R 8 W). Named on Ontario (1954) 7.5' quadrangle. The name recalls an Indian rancheria that was the last of its kind in the vicinity; smallpox decimated the Indians in 1892 and 1893 (Anonymous, 1976, p. 2).

Indian Rock [LOS ANGELES]: *rock,* 2.5 miles east-northeast of Silver Peak, and 600 feet offshore on the north side of Catalina Island (lat. 33°28'05" N, long. 118°31'35" W). Named on Santa Catalina West (1943) 7.5' quadrangle.

Indian Spring [LOS ANGELES]: *spring,* nearly 3 miles east-northeast of the village of Lake Hughes (lat. 34°41'40" N, long. 118°23'40" W; near E line sec. 18, T 7 N, R 14 W). Named on Lake Hughes (1957) 7.5' quadrangle.

Indian Springs [LOS ANGELES]:

(1) *spring,* 5.5 miles north-northwest of Sunland (lat. 34°20'10" N, long. 118°20'05" W; near N line sec. 22, T 3 N, R 14 W). Named on Sunland (1966) 7.5' quadrangle.

(2) *locality,* 5 miles north-northwest of Sunland (lat. 34°19'55" N, long. 118°20' W; sec. 22, T 3 N, R 14 W); the place is 0.5 mile south of Indian Springs (1). Named on Sunland (1953) 7.5' quadrangle. Los Angeles County (1935) map has the form "Indian Spring" for the name.

Industry [LOS ANGELES]: *town,* the city hall is 4.5 miles south of Baldwin Park city hall (lat. 34°01'15" N, long. 117°57'20" W). Named on Baldwin Park (1966), El Monte (1966), La Habra (1964), San Dimas (1966), and Yorba Linda (1964) 7.5' quadrangles. Postal authorities established City of Industry post office at the place in 1957 (Salley, p. 44). The town incorporated in 1957 to promote and protect industrial development.

Inglewood [LOS ANGELES]: *city,* 16 miles northwest of Long Beach city hall (lat.

33°57'50" N, long. 118°21'10" W). Named on Inglewood (1952) 7.5' quadrangle. Postal authorities established Inglewood post office in 1895 (Salley, p. 104), and the city incorporated in 1908.

Inglewood Rancho: see **Lennox** [LOS ANGELES].

Inspiration Point [LOS ANGELES]:

(1) *peak,* nearly 3 miles west of Mount Wilson (1) (lat. 34°13'20" N, long. 118°06'35" W; at S line sec. 26, T 2 N, R 12 W). Altitude 4715 feet. Named on Mount Wilson (1953) 7.5' quadrangle.

(2) *promontory,* nearly 5 miles west-northwest of Point Fermin along the coast (lat. 33°44'10" N, long. 118°22'05" W). Named on San Pedro (1964) 7.5' quadrangle.

Iredell Canyon [LOS ANGELES]: *canyon,* drained by a stream that flows less than 1 mile to Fryman Canyon 5 miles southeast of Van Nuys (lat. 34°07'55" N, long. 118°23'25" W). Named on Van Nuys (1953) 7.5' quadrangle.

Iron Bound Bay [LOS ANGELES]: *embayment,* 1 mile south-southwest of Silver Peak on the south side of Santa Catalina Island (lat. 33°26'50" N, long. 118°34'25" W). Named on Santa Catalina West (1943) 7.5' quadrangle.

Iron Canyon [LOS ANGELES]:

(1) *canyon,* drained by a stream that flows 4.5 miles to Sand Canyon (2) 2.5 miles east-southeast of Solemint (lat. 34°23'50" N, long. 118°25' W; near SE cor. sec. 26, T 4 N, R 15 W). Name on Agua Dulce (1960) and Mint Canyon (1960) 7.5' quadrangles.

(2) *canyon,* drained by a stream that flows 2 miles to Pacoima Canyon 3 miles north-northwest of Condor Peak (lat. 34°21'45" N, long. 118°14'40" W). Named on Acton (1959) and Condor Peak (1959) 7.5' quadrangles.

Iron Fork [LOS ANGELES]: *stream,* flows 6 miles to San Gabriel River 5.5 miles west of Mount San Antonio (lat. 34°17'45" N, long. 117°44'25" W). Named on Crystal Lake (1958) and Mount San Antonio (1955) 7.5' quadrangles. South Fork enters 5 miles east of Crystal Lake; it is 4.25 miles long and is named on Crystal Lake (1958) 7.5' quadrangle.

Iron Mountain: see **Magic Mountain** [LOS ANGELES].

Iron Mountain Saddle [LOS ANGELES]: *pass,* 7 miles north-northeast of Sunland (lat. 34°21' N, long. 118°15'30" W). Named on Sunland (1966) 7.5' quadrangle.

Iron Peak [LOS ANGELES]:

(1) *peak,* 1.5 miles north-northwest of Condor Peak (lat. 34°20'55" N, long. 118°13'40" W). Altitude 5635 feet. Named on Condor Peak (1959) 7.5' quadrangle.

(2) *peak,* 4.5 miles southwest of Pacifico Mountain (lat. 34°20'20" N, long. 118°05'25" W). Named on Chilao Flat (1959) 7.5' quadrangle.

(3) *peak,* nearly 4 miles west of Mount San

81

Antonio (lat. 34°17'20" N, long. 117°42'45" W). Altitude 8002 feet. Named on Mount San Antonio (1955) 7.5' quadrangle.

Ironsides [LOS ANGELES]: *locality,* nearly 3 miles southeast of Torrance city hall along Atchison, Topeka and Santa Fe Railroad (lat. 33°48'35" N, long. 118°18'10" W). Named on Torrance (1964) 7.5' quadrangle.

Iron Trough Canyon [VENTURA]: *canyon,* drained by a stream that flows 1.25 miles to Tripas Canyon nearly 7 miles northwest of Santa Susana Pass (lat. 34°19'55" N, long. 118°43'20" W; sec. 24, T 3 N, R 18 W). Named on Santa Susana (1951) 7.5' quadrangle.

Irvine: [ORANGE]: *city,* 5 miles southeast of Santa Ana city hall (lat. 33°41' N, long. 117°49' W). Named on Tustin (1965, photorevised 1981) 7.5' quadrangle. Postal authorities transferred Irvine post office to the place from present East Irvine in 1965 (Salley, p. 105), and the city incorporated in 1971.

Irvine: see **East Irvine** [ORANGE].

Irvine Lake: see **Santiago Reservoir** [ORANGE].

Irvine Mesa [ORANGE]: *area,* 8 miles north-northeast of El Toro on the ridge between Silverado Canyon and Santiago Creek (lat. 33° 44'30" N, long. 117°39'30" W). Named on El Toro (1968) 7.5' quadrangle.

Irvine Siding [ORANGE]: *locality,* 3.5 miles southeast of Santa Ana city hall along Atchison, Topeka and Santa Fe Railroad (lat. 33° 43' N, long. 117°49' W). Named on Tustin (1965) 7.5' quadrangle. Called Venta on Tustin (1950) 7.5' quadrangle.

Irwin Canyon: see **Solemint** [LOS ANGELES].

Irwindale [LOS ANGELES]:
(1) *town,* 2 miles northeast of Baldwin Park city hall (lat. 34°06'15" N, long. 117°56' W). Named on Azusa (1966), Baldwin Park (1966), and El Monte (1966) 7.5' quadrangles. Postal authorities established Irwindale post office in 1899 (Frickstad, p. 75), and the town incorporated in 1957. The name commemorates a citrus grower (Gudde, 1969, p. 153).
(2) *locality,* 1.5 miles east-northeast of Baldwin Park city hall along Pacific Electric Railroad (lat. 34°05'30" N, long. 117°56' W; sec. 16, T 1 S, R 10 W). Named on Baldwin Park (1953) 7.5' quadrangle.

Irwindale Siding [LOS ANGELES]: *locality,* 1.5 miles northeast of Baldwin Park city hall along Southern Pacific Railroad (lat. 34°05'50" N, long. 117°56'20" W; sec. 9, T 1 S, R 10 W). Named on Baldwin Park (1966) 7.5' quadrangle.

Isla Hermosa Camp Ground [LOS ANGELES]: *locality,* 2.5 miles south-southeast of Valyermo along Big Rock Creek (lat. 34°24'50" N, long. 117°49'45" W; sec. 21, T 4 N, R 9 W). Named on Valyermo (1940) 6' quadrangle.

Island Chaffee [LOS ANGELES]: *island,* 850 feet long, 3.5 miles southeast of Long Beach city hall, and 4600 feet offshore (lat. 33°44'25" N, long. 118°08'20" W). Named on Long Beach (1964) 7.5' quadrangle. Called Chaffee Island on Long Beach (1964, photorevised 1972) 7.5' quadrangle, but United States Board on Geographic Names (1979, p. 5) rejected this form of the name; the Board noted that officials of Long Beach named the feature to honor American astronaut Roger B. Chaffee. The island is artificial and is used for oil wells.

Island Freeman [LOS ANGELES]: *island,* 1100 feet long, 2.5 miles southeast of Long Beach city hall, and 1.25 miles offshore (lat. 33° 44'30" N, long. 118°09'40" W). Named on Long Beach (1964) 7.5' quadrangle. Called Freeman Island on Long Beach (1964, photorevised 1972) 7.5' quadrangle, but United States Board on Geographic Names (1979, p. 6) rejected this form of the name; the Board noted that officials of Long Beach named the feature to honor American astronaut Theodore C. Freeman. The island is artificial and is used for oil wells.

Island Grissom [LOS ANGELES]: *island,* 950 feet long, 1 mile southeast of Long Beach city hall, and 1100 feet offshore (lat. 33° 45'35" N, long. 118°10'50" W). Named on Long Beach (1964) 7.5' quadrangle. Called Grissom Island on Long Beach (1964, photorevised 1972) 7.5' quadrangle, but United States Board on Geographic Names (1979, p. 6) rejected this form of the name; the Board noted that officials of Long Beach named the feature to honor American Astronaut Virgil I. Grissom. The island is artificial and is used for oil wells.

Island White [LOS ANGELES]: *island,* 950 feet long, 2.25 miles east-southeast of Long Beach city hall, and 0.5 mile offshore (lat. 33°45'10" N, long. 118°09'30" W). Named on Long Beach (1964) 7.5' quadrangle. Called White Island on Long Beach (1964, photorevised 1972) 7.5' quadrangle, but United States Board on Geographic Names (1979, p. 9) rejected this form of the name; the Board noted that officials of the city of Long Beach named the feature to honor American astronaut Edward H. White. The island is artificial and is used for oil wells.

Islip: see **Mount Islip** [LOS ANGELES].

Islip Canyon [LOS ANGELES]: *canyon,* drained by a stream that flows 1.5 miles to Morris Reservoir 4 miles north of Glendora city hall (lat. 34°11'35" N, long. 117°51'50" W; near N line sec. 7, T 1 N, R 9 W). Named on Azusa (1953) and Glendora (1953) 7.5' quadrangles.

Islip Saddle [LOS ANGELES]: *pass,* 2.5 miles north of Crystal Lake (lat. 34°21'25" N, long. 117°51' W; sec. 8, T 3 N, R 9 W); the pass is 1 mile northwest of Mount Islip. Named on Crystal Lake (1958) 7.5' quadrangle.

Islotes de Santo Tomas: see **Anacapa Island** [VENTURA].

Isthmus: see **The Isthmus** [LOS ANGELES].

Isthmus Cove [LOS ANGELES]: *embayment,* 6 miles northwest of Mount Banning on the north side of Santa Catalina Island (lat. 33°26'35" N, long. 118°29'40" W). Named on Santa Catalina North (1950) 7.5' quadrangle. Isthmus Cove, Fourth of July Cove, and Fishermans Cove together were called Union Bay in Civil War times; Union Bay was used by the vessel that transported troops and supplies to the island (Gleason, p. 17). A feature called Eagle Reef is west of the entrance to Isthmus Cove (United States Coast and Geodetic Survey, p. 108).

Italian Gardens [LOS ANGELES]: *locality,* 4 miles northeast of Mount Banning on the north side of Santa Catalina Island (lat. 33°24'40" N, long. 118°22'55" W). Named on Santa Catalina North (1950) 7.5' quadrangle.

Iva [LOS ANGELES]: *locality,* 18 miles east of Gorman (lat. 34°46' N, long. 118°31'40" W). Named on Tejon (1903) 30' quadrangle.

Ivanhoe [LOS ANGELES]:
(1) *locality,* 4 miles north-northwest of present Los Angeles city hall (lat. 34°0630" N, long. 118°16'30" W). Named on Santa Monica (1902) 15' quadrangle. Postal authorities established Ivanhoe post office in 1904, changed the name to Sunset Hills in 1908, and discontinued it in 1911 (Salley, p. 105, 216).
(2) *locality,* 4.5 miles north-northwest of present Los Angeles city hall along Pacific Electric Railroad (lat. 34°06'35" N, long. 118°15'45" W). Named on Glendale (1928) 6' quadrangle.

Ivy:[LOS ANGELES]: *locality,* 3 miles south of present Beverly Hills city hall (lat. 34°01'35" N, long. 118°23'15" W). Named on Santa Monica (1902) 15' quadrangle.

Ivy: see **Camp Ivy** [LOS ANGELES].

— J —

Jackson Camp [VENTURA]: *locality,* 3 miles west-northwest of Santa Paula Peak in Santa Paula Canyon (lat. 34°27'45" N, long. 119°03'20" W). Named on Santa Paula Peak (1951) 7.5' quadrangle

Jackson Flat [LOS ANGELES]: *area,* 2.5 miles west of Big Pines (lat. 34°22'50" N, long. 117°44' W; at N line sec. 5, T 3 N, R 8 W). Named on Mescal Creek (1956) 7.5' quadrangle.

Jackson Hill: see **San Nicolas Island** [VENTURA].

Jackson Lake [LOS ANGELES]: *lake,* 0.25 mile long, 2.25 miles west-northwest of Big Pines (lat. 34°23'30" N, long. 117°43'30" W). Named on Mescal Creek (1956) 7.5' quadrangle.

James Canyon: see **Mint Canyon** [LOS ANGELES] (1).

Jamison Spring [ORANGE]: *spring,* 0.5 mile west of Santiago Peak (lat. 33°42'35" N, long. 117°32'45" W; near N line sec. 30, T 5 S, R 6 W). Named on Santiago Peak (1954) 7.5' quadrangle. The name commemorates a miner and hunter who settled near the spring in the 1880's (Meadows, p. 74).

Javon Canyon [VENTURA]: *canyon,* drained by a stream that flows nearly 3 miles to the sea 1.25 miles northwest of Pitas Point (lat. 34°19'55" N, long. 119°24'05" W; sec. 21, T 3 N, R 24 W). Named on Pitas Point (1950) 7.5' quadrangle. The name is from *jabón,* which means "soap" in Spanish—an abrasive material called rock-soap was produced in the canyon in the 1870's (Gudde, 1949, p. 165).

Jefferson [LOS ANGELES]: *locality,* 2.25 miles southwest of Los Angeles city hall along Southern Pacific Railroad (lat. 34°01'05" N, long. 118°16'25" W). Named on Hollywood (1966) 7.5' quadrangle.

Jefferson: see **Lennox** [LOS ANGELES].

Jeffrey [LOS ANGELES]: *locality,* 2.5 miles north-northeast of present Los Angeles city hall along Los Angeles Terminal Railroad (lat. 34°05'20" N, long. 118°13'30" W). Named on Pasadena (1900) 15' quadrangle.

Jeffries Canyon [LOS ANGELES]: *canyon,* less than 1 mile long, 3.25 miles northwest of Burbank city hall (lat. 34°13'05" N, long. 118°20'35" W; sec. 27, 33, 34, T 2 N, R 14 W). Named on Burbank (1953) 7.5' quadrangle.

Jehemy Beach: see **San Nicolas Island** [VENTURA].

Jerusalem: see **El Rio** [VENTURA].

Jesus Canyon [LOS ANGELES]: *canyon,* drained by a stream that flows 4 miles to lowlands 4.5 miles north of Big Pines (lat. 34°26'45" N, long. 117°41'35" W; at E line sec. 10, T 4 N, R 8 W). Named on Mescal Creek (1956) 7.5' quadrangle.

Jewfish Point [LOS ANGELES]: *promontory,* 2 miles southeast of Avalon near the southeast end of Santa Catalina Island (lat. 33°19'10" N, long. 118°18'10" W). Named on Santa Catalina East (1950) 7.5' quadrangle.

Jimmy Campground: see **Little Jimmy Campground** [LOS ANGELES].

Jimmy Spring: see **Little Jimmy Spring** [LOS ANGELES].

Joaquin Valley: see **Little Joaquin Valley** [ORANGE].

John Bird Canyon [LOS ANGELES]: *canyon,* 1 mile long, 4.25 miles west-southwest of Valyermo (lat. 34°25'20" N, long. 117°55'20" W; sec. 21, 22, T 4 N, R 10 W). Named on Juniper Hills (1959) 7.5' quadrangle.

John Brown Peak: see **Mount Lowe** [LOS ANGELES] (1).

John Muirs Peak: see **Muir Peak**, under **Mount Wilson** [LOS ANGELES] (1)

83

DURHAM'S PLACE-NAMES

Johns Canyon: see Agua Dulce Canyon [LOS ANGELES].
Johnson Ridge: see Johnston Ridge, under Mutau Flat [VENTURA].
Johnsons Landing [LOS ANGELES]: locality, 2.25 miles east-northeast of Silver Peak on the north side of Santa Catalina Island (lat. 33°28'05" N, long. 118°31'50" W). Named on Santa Catalina West (1943) 7.5' quadrangle.
Johnson Summit [LOS ANGELES]: pass, 4.25 miles west-southwest of Del Sur on Portal Ridge (lat. 34°39'30" N, long. 118°21'15" W; near NW cor. sec. 34, T 7 N, R 14 W). Named on Del Sur (1958) 7.5' quadrangle.
Johnstone Peak [LOS ANGELES]: peak, 4.25 miles east-northeast of Glendora city hall (lat. 34°09'40" N, long. 117°47'45" W; sec. 23, T 1 N, R 9 W). Altitude 3201 feet. Named on Glendora (1953) 7.5' quadrangle. The name commemorates W.A. Johnstone, a conservation leader in California (United States Board on Geographic Names, 1940, p. 23). The feature first was called San Dimas Peak (Robinson, J.W., 1983, p. 125).
Johnston Ridge: see Mutau Flat [VENTURA].
Jones Canyon [LOS ANGELES]: canyon, drained by a stream that flows nearly 2 miles to lowlands 1.25 miles northwest of Acton (lat. 34°28'55" N, long. 118°12'40" W; near S line sec. 26, T 5 N, R 13 W). Named on Acton (1959) 7.5' quadrangle.
Josephine Creek [LOS ANGELES]: stream, flows 1.5 miles to Big Tujunga Canyon 3 miles east-southeast of Condor Peak (lat. 34°18'05" N, long. 118°10'20" W); the stream heads near Josephine Peak. Named on Condor Peak (1959) 7.5' quadrangle.
Josephine Mountain: see Josephine Peak [LOS ANGELES].
Josephine Peak [LOS ANGELES]: peak, 4.5 miles southeast of Condor Peak (lat. 34°17'10" N, long. 118°09'10" W). Altitude 5558 feet. Named on Condor Peak (1959) 7.5' quadrangle. Called Josephine Mt. on Tujunga (1900) 15' quadrangle. Joseph Barlow Lippencott used the peak as a triangulation point and named it for his wife when he was mapping Tujunga quadrangle for United States Geological Survey in 1894 (Robinson, J.W., 1977, p. 154).
Josephine Saddle [LOS ANGELES]: pass, nearly 6 miles east-southeast of Condor Peak (lat. 34°16'55" N, long. 118°08' W); the pass is 1 mile east of Josephine Peak. Named on Condor Peak (1959) 7.5' quadrangle.
Josepho: see Camp Josepho [LOS ANGELES].
Juan Fernandez Spring [VENTURA]: spring, nearly 6 miles north-northeast of Piru (lat. 34°29'40" N, long. 118°45'35" W; sec. 27, T 5 N, R 18 W). Named on Piru (1952) 7.5' quadrangle. The name is for Juan Bautista Fernandez and his son (Ricard).
Jubilee: see Camp Jubilee [LOS ANGELES].

Judahy Flats: see Hughes Lake [LOS ANGELES].
July Harbor: see Fourth of July Harbor [LOS ANGELES].
Juniper Hills [LOS ANGELES]: locality, 4.5 miles west of Valyermo (lat. 34°26'40" N, long. 117°56' W; sec. 9, T 4 N, R 10 W). Named on Juniper Hills (1959) 7.5' quadrangle.
Junipero Serra: see Camp Junipero Serra [LOS ANGELES].
Jupiter Mountain [LOS ANGELES]: ridge, generally west-trending, 3 miles long, 5.25 miles south-southeast of Lake Hughes (lat. 34°36'20" N, long. 118°24'40" W). Named on Green Valley (1958) 7.5' quadrangle.

– K –

Kagel Canyon [LOS ANGELES]: canyon, nearly 4 miles long, opens into Little Tujunga Canyon 4 miles west-northwest of Sunland (lat. 34°16'55" N, long. 118°22'20" W). Named on San Fernando (1953) and Sunland (1953) 7.5' quadrangles. The name commemorates Henry Kagel, who claimed land at the mouth of the canyon (Gudde, 1949, p. 170).
Kagel Divide [LOS ANGELES]: pass, 5.25 miles northwest of Sunland (lat. 34°19'20" N, long. 118°21'50" W; on N line sec. 29, T 3 N, R 14 W); the pass is at the head of a branch of Kagel Canyon. Named on Sunland (1966) 7.5' quadrangle.
Kagel Mountain [LOS ANGELES]: peak, nearly 5 miles northeast of downtown San Fernando (lat. 34°20' N, long. 118°23' W; sec. 19, T 3 N, R 14 W). Named on San Fernando (1966) 7.5' quadrangle.
Kane Canyon: see Bouquet Canyon [LOS ANGELES].
Kanoshaz Spur [LOS ANGELES]: locality, 6 miles southwest of El Monte city hall along Union Pacific Railroad (lat. 34°00'20" N, long. 118°05'50" W). Named on El Monte (1966) 7.5' quadrangle.
Kanter Canyon [LOS ANGELES]: canyon, 2 miles long, 5.25 miles west of Beverly Hills city hall (lat. 34°05' N, long. 118°29'30" W). Named on Beverly Hills (1950) 7.5' quadrangle.
Karl Holton Camp [LOS ANGELES]: locality, 4 miles northwest of Sunland in Marek Canyon (lat. 34°18'05" N, long. 118°21'35" W; on W line sec. 33, T 3 N, R 14 W). Named on Sunland (1966) 7.5' quadrangle.
Kashmere Canyon [LOS ANGELES]: canyon, drained by a stream that flows nearly 2 miles to lowlands at Acton (lat. 34°28'25" N, long. 118°04'35" W; at E line sec. 35, T 5 N, R 13 W). Named on Acton (1959) 7.5' quadrangle.
Kathryn [ORANGE]: locality, 7.25 miles east-southeast of Santa Ana city hall along

84

Atchison, Topeka and Santa Fe Railroad (lat. 33°42'15" N, long., 117°45'10" W). Named on Tustin (1965) 7.5' quadrangle. The name is for Kathryn Helene Irvine, daughter of James Irvine, Jr. (Meadows, p. 75).

Katrina: see **Lake Katrina**, under **Tweedy Lake** [LOS ANGELES].

Keeler Flats [LOS ANGELES]: *area*, 4.5 miles east-northeast of Burnt Peak (lat. 34°42'50" N, long. 118°30' W; sec. 7, 8, T 7 N, R 15 W). Named on Burnt Peak (1958) and Lake Hughes (1957) 7.5' quadrangles.

Keith [VENTURA]: *locality*, 3 miles west of Fillmore along Southern Pacific Railroad (lat. 34°23'40" N, long. 118°57'30" W; at S line sec. 27, T 4 N, R 20 W). Named on Fillmore (1951) 7.5' quadrangle. The name is from Keith Spalding, owner of Sespe grant (Ricard).

Kellers Shelter [LOS ANGELES]: *embayment*, just east of Malibu Point along the coast (lat. 34°02'10" N, long. 118°40'30" W). Named on Malibu Beach (1951) 7.5' quadrangle. The name commemorates Mathew Keller, first American owner of the feature (Femling, p. 65).

Kelp Point [LOS ANGELES]: *promontory*, 2.25 miles southeast of Silver Peak on the south side of Santa Catalina Island (lat. 33° 26' N, long. 118°32'30" W). Named on Santa Catalina West (1943) 7.5' quadrangle.

Kemp: see **Castaic** [LOS ANGELES].

Kennedy Canyon [VENTURA]: *canyon*, drained by a stream that flows 2 miles to Ventura River 3.25 miles west-northwest of Ojai (lat. 34°28'25" N, long. 119°17'25" W; sec. 33, T 5 N, R 23 W). Named on Matilija (1952) 7.5' quadrangle. The name commemorates John Logan Kennedy, who came to Ventura in 1872 (Ricard).

Kent Station: see **Humphreys** [LOS ANGELES].

Kentucky Springs [LOS ANGELES]: *springs*, 6 miles northwest of Pacifico Mountain (lat. 34°26'45" N, long. 118°06'30" W; sec. 11, T 4 N, R 12 W). Named on Pacifico Mountain (1959) 7.5' quadrangle. On Tujunga (1900) 15' quadrangle, the name applies to a locality near the site of the springs.

Kentucky Springs Canyon [LOS ANGELES]: *canyon*, drained by a stream that flows 7 miles to Soledad Canyon 3.25 miles east-northeast of Acton (lat. 34°28'50" N, long. 118°08'30" W; near S line sec. 28, T 5 N, R 12 W); Kentucky Springs are in the canyon. Named on Acton (1959) and Pacifico Mountain (1959) 7.5' quadrangles.

Keril Canyon [LOS ANGELES]: *canyon*, drained by a stream that flows less than 1 mile to Big Dalton Canyon 4 miles northeast of Glendora city hall (lat. 34°10'10" N, long. 117°48'30" W; sec. 15, T 1 N, R 9 W). Named on Glendora (1953) 7.5' quadrangle.

Kerkhoff Canyon [LOS ANGELES]: *canyon*, drained by a stream that heads in San Bernardino County and flows 2 miles to San Antonio Canyon 13 miles north-northeast of Pomona city hall in Los Angeles County (lat. 34°13'35" N, long. 117°39'55" W; sec. 25, T 2 N, R 8 W). Named on Mount Baldy (1954) 7.5' quadrangle. Present Barrett Canyon is called Kerkhoff Canyon on Camp Baldy (1940) 6' quadrangle.

Kester [LOS ANGELES]: *locality*, 1.5 miles east-southeast of Van Nuys along Southern Pacific Railroad (lat. 34°10'25" N, long. 118° 25'20" W). Named on Van Nuys (1926) 6' quadrangle.

Kester Canyon: see **Sharps Canyon** [LOS ANGELES-VENTURA].

Kesters Camp [VENTURA]: *locality*, 7.5 miles southeast of Cobblestone Mountain near the mouth of Agua Blanca Creek (lat. 34°32'30" N, long. 118°45'50" W; near SE cor. sec. 4, T 5 N, R 18 W). Named on Cobblestone Mountain (1958) 7.5' quadrangle.

Kevet [VENTURA]: *locality*, 1.25 miles east-northeast of downtown Santa Paula along Southern Pacific Railroad (lat. 34°21'45" N, long. 119°02'15" W; at N line sec. 12, T 3 N, R 21 W). Named on Santa Paula (1951) 7.5' quadrangle. California Mining Bureau's (1917) map shows a place called Carmicle located about 1.5 miles north-northeast of Kevet along the railroad.

Kewen Lake [LOS ANGELES]: *lake*, 1100 feet long, 6.25 miles west-northwest of present El Monte city hall (lat. 34°07' N, long. 118°07'30" W). Named on Pasadena (1900) 15' quadrangle.

Keystone [LOS ANGELES]: *district*, 3.5 miles east of Torrance city hall (lat. 33°49'40" N, long. 118°16'35" W). Named on Torrance (1964) 7.5' quadrangle.

Kimball [VENTURA]: *locality*, 3 miles southwest of Saticoy along Southern Pacific Railroad (lat. 34°15'20" N, long. 119°11'15" W). Named on Saticoy (1951) 7.5' quadrangle.

Kimbrough Canyon [LOS ANGELES]: *canyon*, drained by a stream that flows 1 mile to Oakdale Canyon (1) 4.25 miles north-northwest of Burnt Peak (lat. 34°44'10" N, long. 118°37' W; sec. 31, T 8 N, R 16 W). Named on Burnt Peak (1958) and Liebre Mountain (1958) 7.5' quadrangles.

Kincaid [LOS ANGELES]: *locality*, 1.5 miles west-southwest of Azusa city hall along Atchison, Topeka and Santa Fe Railroad (lat. 34°07'45" N, long. 117°55'45" W; at E line sec. 33, T 1 N, R 10 W). Named on Azusa (1953) 7.5' quadrangle.

Kincaid Cabin [VENTURA]: *locality*, 14 miles east-northeast of Reyes Peak along Piru Creek (lat. 34°40'25" N, long. 119°02'10" W; sec. 30, T 7 N, R 20 W). Named on Lockwood Valley (1943) 7.5' quadrangle.

Kincloa Canyon: see **Pasadena Glen** [LOS ANGELES].

King Harbor [LOS ANGELES]: *water feature,* 0.5 mile west of Redondo Beach city hall along the coast (lat. 33°50'45" N, long. 118°23'45" W). Named on Redondo Beach (1963) 7.5' quadrangle.

Kings Campground [VENTURA]: *locality,* 5.5 miles north of McDonald Peak (lat. 34°43' N, long. 118°55'40" W; sec. 7, T 7 N, R 19 W). Named on McDonald Peak (1958) 7.5' quadrangle.

Kings Canyon [LOS ANGELES]: *canyon,* drained by a stream that flows 4.25 miles to lowlands 4.5 miles northwest of the village of Lake Hughes (lat. 34°43'50" N, long. 118°29'15" W; near N line sec. 5, T 7 N, R 15 W). Named on Burnt Peak (1958) and Lake Hughes (1957) 7.5' quadrangles.

Kingsley Canyon: see Necktie Canyon [LOS ANGELES].

Kinneyloa: see Mount Kinneyloa, under Mount Wilson [LOS ANGELES] (1).

Kirby Canyon [LOS ANGELES]: *canyon,* 0.5 miles long, 4.5 miles west-northwest of Pasadena city hall (lat. 34°10'20" N, long. 118°13'10" W). Named on Pasadena (1953) 7.5' quadrangle.

Kitter Canyon [LOS ANGELES]: *canyon,* drained by a stream that flows 2.5 miles to Little Rock Creek 4.5 miles north-northeast of Pacifico Mountain (lat. 34°26'40" N, long. 118°00'35" W). Named on Pacifico Mountain (1959) 7.5' quadrangle.

Kleine Canyon [LOS ANGELES]: *canyon,* drained by a stream that flows nearly 2 miles to Elizabeth Lake Canyon 2 miles north-northeast of Warm Springs Mountain (lat. 34°37'20" N, long. 118° 33'20" W). Named on Burnt Peak (1958) and Warm Springs Mountain (1958) 7.5' quadrangles.

Klondike Canyon [LOS ANGELES]: *canyon,* 1 mile long, 4.5 miles northwest of Point Fermin (lat. 33°44'40" N, long. 118°21'10" W). Named on San Pedro (1964) 7.5' quadrangle.

Kole: see Camp Kole [LOS ANGELES].

Kratka Ridge [LOS ANGELES]: *ridge,* generally southwest- to west-trending, 2.5 miles long, 3 miles east-northeast of Waterman Mountain (lat. 34°21' N, long. 117°53' W). Named on Waterman Mountain (1959) 7.5' quadrangle.

Krotona Hill [VENTURA]: *ridge,* west-northwest-trending, 1.25 miles long, 2 miles west-southwest of downtown Ojai (lat. 34°26'15" N, long. 119°16'25" W). Named on Matilija (1952) 7.5' quadrangle. The name is from a Theosophical colony called Krotona that Albert P. Warrington founded in 1911 and moved to the place in 1924 (Hine, p. 57).

Krum Reservoir [ORANGE]: *water feature,* 1.5 miles southeast of San Juan Capistrano (lat. 33°29'05" N, long. 117°38'40" W; near SE cor. sec. 7, T 8 S, R 7 W). Named on Dana Point (1968) 7.5' quadrangle.

– L –

La Ballona: see Ballona [LOS ANGELES].

La Bolsa [ORANGE]: *locality,* less than 2 miles north of present Huntington Beach civic center along Southern Pacific Railroad (lat. 33°41'10" N, long. 117°59'50" W; at N line sec. 2, T 6 S, R 11 W); the place is on Las Bolsas grant. Named on Newport Beach (1951) 7.5' quadrangle.

La Bolsa Chica [ORANGE]: *land grant,* inland from Sunset Beach. Named on Los Alamitos (1950), Newport Beach (1951), and Seal Beach (1950) 7.5' quadrangles. Joaquin Ruiz received 2 leagues in 1841 and claimed 8107 acres patented in 1874 (Cowan, p. 19).

La Brea [LOS ANGELES]: *land grant,* southwest of Hollywood. Named on Beverly Hills (1950) and Hollywood (1953) 7.5' quadrangles. Jose Antonio Bocha received 1 league in 1828 and claimed 4439 acres patented in 1873 (Cowan, p. 20).

La Brea Canyon: see Brea Canyon [LOS ANGELES-ORANGE]; Tonner Canyon [LOS ANGELES-ORANGE].

La Broche Canyon [VENTURA]: *canyon,* drained by a stream that flows 1.5 miles to Santa Paula Canyon 4.25 miles west of Santa Paula Peak (lat. 34°26'40" N, long. 119°05' W). Named on Santa Paula Peak (1951) 7.5' quadrangle.

La Brun [LOS ANGELES]: *locality,* 8.5 miles south-southwest of the present village of Lake Hughes in San Francisquito Canyon (lat. 34°33'30" N, long. 118°29'15" W; near N line sec. 6, T 5 N, R 15 W). Named on Elizabeth Lake (1917) 30' quadrangle.

La Cañada [LOS ANGELES]:

(1) *land grant,* north of Verdugo Mountains and San Rafael Hills at La Cañada and La Crescenta. Named on Burbank (1953), Pasadena (1953), and Sunland (1953) 7.5' quadrangles. Ignacio Coronel received 2 leagues in 1843; J.R. Scott and others claimed 5832 acres patented in 1866 (Cowan, p. 23).

(2) *town,* 5 miles northwest of Pasadena city hall (lat. 34°12'15" N, long. 118°12' W); the town is on La Cañada grant. Named on Pasadena (1953) 7.5' quadrangle. Postal authorities established La Canada post office in 1884 and discontinued it for a time in 1888 (Frickstad, p. 75). La Cañada and nearby Flintridge incorporated in 1976 with the name "La Cañada Flintridge." United States Board on Geographic Names (1979, p. 7) rejected both the names "La Canada" and "Flintridge" for the newly incorporated community.

La Cañada del Violin: see Violin Canyon [LOS ANGELES].

La Cañada Flintridge: see La Cañada [LOS ANGELES] (2).

La Cañada Verde Creek [LOS ANGELES-ORANGE]: *stream,* heads in Los Angeles

County and flows 9.5 miles to Coyote Creek 12 miles northeast of Long Beach city hall just inside Orange County.(lat. 33°52'05" N, long. 118°01'55" W; sec. 33, T 3 S, R 11 W). Named on La Habra (1952) and Los Alamitos (1964) 7.5' quadrangles. The stream is called West Fork [of Coyote Creek] on Los Alamitos (1950) 7.5' quadrangle.

La Cañon de Los Murtes: see **Bouquet Canyon** [LOS ANGELES].

Lachusa Canyon [LOS ANGELES]: *canyon,* drained by a stream that flows nearly 3 miles to the sea 5.5 miles west-northwest of Point Dume (lat. 34°02'20" N, long. 118°53'40" W). Named on Triunfo Pass (1950) 7.5' quadrangle. Called Lechuza Canyon on Camulos (1903) 30' quadrangle

Lachusa Point: see **Lechuza Point** [LOS ANGELES].

La Cienega: see **Falling Springs** [LOS ANGELES].

Lacosca Creek [VENTURA]: *stream,* flows nearly 3 miles to Agua Blanca Creek 5 miles southeast of Cobblestone Mountain (lat. 34° 32'50" N, long. 118°48'55" W). Named on Cobblestone Mountain (1958) 7.5' quadrangle.

La Costa Beach [LOS ANGELES]: *beach,* 2.25 miles east-northeast of Malibu Point (lat. 34°02'15" N, long. 118°38'30" W). Named on Malibu Beach (1951) 7.5' quadrangle.

La Crescenta [LOS ANGELES]: *town,* 7.5 miles northwest of Pasadena city hall (lat. 34°05'55" N, long. 118°14'20" W). Named on Pasadena (1953) 7.5' quadrangle. Postal authorities established La Crescenta post office in 1888 (Frickstad, p. 75). Dr. Benjamin Briggs is said to have named the community for the crescent shape of the alluvial fans that he could see from his home at the place (Hanna, p. 76).

La Cross: see **Lacrosse** [VENTURA].

Lacrosse [VENTURA]: *locality,* 7 miles north of Ventura along Southern Pacific Railroad (lat. 34°22'35" N, long. 119°18'25" W). Named on Ventura (1904) 15' quadrangle. California Division of Highways' (1934) map has the form "La Cross" for the name.

Ladd Canyon [ORANGE]: *canyon,* drained by a stream that flows 5 miles to Silverado Canyon 9 miles north-northeast of El Toro (lat. 33°44'55" N, long. 117°38'20" W); Mustang Spring in on the side of the canyon. Named on Black Star Canyon (1967), Corona South (1967), and El Toro (1968) 7.5' quadrangles. Present Ladd Canyon was called Mustang Spring Canyon before H.C. Ladd settled there in 1872 (Meadows, p. 76, 103). East Fork branches northeast 2 miles south of Pleasants Peak; it heads in Riverside County, is 2 miles long, and is named on Corona South (1967) 7.5' quadrangle. West Fork branches north 2.5 miles south-southwest of Pleasants Peak; it is 2.5 miles long and is named on Corona South (1967) 7.5' quadrangle. On Corona (1942) 15'

quadrangle, Ladd Canyon divides at the head to form East Fork and West Fork.

Ladybug Canyon [LOS ANGELES]: *canyon,* drained by a stream that flows 1.25 miles to Arroyo Seco 9.5 miles south-southwest of Pacifico Mountain (lat. 34°15'40" N, long. 118°07' W). Named on Chilao Flat (1959) 7.5' quadrangle.

Ladybug Creek [VENTURA]: *stream,* flows 2.25 miles to Sespe Creek 6.25 miles north-northwest of Wheeler Springs (lat. 34°35'45" N, long. 119°19'45" W; sec. 21, T 6 N, R 23 W). Named on Wheeler Springs (1943) 7.5' quadrangle.

Ladyface [LOS ANGELES]: *peak,* 2 miles west-southwest of Agoura (lat. 34°08'05" N, long. 118°46'20" W). Altitude 2036 feet. Named on Thousand Oaks (1952) 7.5' quadrangle.

Lady Waterman Mountain: see **Waterman Mountain** [LOS ANGELES].

La Fetra [LOS ANGELES]: *locality,* 1.25 miles east-northeast of Azusa city hall along Pacific Electric Railroad (lat. 34°08'20" N, long. 117°52'50" W). Named on Azusa (1953) 7.5' quadrangle.

La Fresa [LOS ANGELES]: *district,* 2.5 miles north of Torrance city hall (lat. 33°52'25" N, long. 118°20' W). Named on Torrance (1964) 7.5' quadrangle.

Lagol [VENTURA]: *locality,* 4.25 miles west-southwest of Moorpark along Southern Pacific Railroad (lat. 34°16'10" N, long. 118° 57' W). Named on Moorpark (1951) 7.5' quadrangle. Called Lagol Siding on Camulos (1903) 30' quadrangle.

Lagona: see **Laguna Beach** [ORANGE].

Lagona Beach: see **Laguna Beach** [ORANGE].

La Granada Mountain [VENTURA]: *peak,* 4 miles south-southwest of White Ledge Peak (lat. 34°25'05" N, long. 119°25'20" W; at W line sec. 20, T 4 N, R 24 W). Altitude 2291 feet. Named on White Ledge Peak (1952) 7.5' quadrangle.

Laguna [LOS ANGELES]:

(1) *lake,* 6.5 miles west of Whittier (lat. 33°59'15" N, long. 118° 09' W). Named on Downey (1902) 15' quadrangle.

(2) *locality,* 6 miles west of Whittier along Atchison, Topeka and Santa Fe Railroad (lat. 33°59'15" N, long. 118°08'10" W); the place is just east of Laguna (1). Named on Downey (1902) 15' quadrangle.

(3) *locality,* 4 miles east-northeast of South Gate city hall along Southern Pacific Railroad (lat. 33°58'40" N, long. 118°08'25" W). Named on South Gate (1964, photorevised 1981) 7.5' quadrangle.

Laguna: see **Laguna Beach** [ORANGE]; **Lagunas** [ORANGE]; **South Laguna** [ORANGE].

Laguna Beach [ORANGE]: *town,* 17 miles south-southeast of Santa Ana along the coast (lat. 33°32'45" N, long. 117°46'50" W); the town is at the mouth of Laguna Canyon.

Named on Laguna Beach (1965) and San Juan Capistrano (1968) 7.5' quadrangles. Called Laguna on Santa Ana (1896) 15' quadrangle. Postal authorities established Lagona Beach post office in 1891 and discontinued it in 1893; they established Lagona post office in 1894 and changed the name to Laguna Beach in 1904 (Salley, p. 114). The town incorporated in 1927. George Rogers purchased land at the mouth of Laguna Canyon in 1887 and laid out the town (Meadows, p. 76).

Laguna Canyon [ORANGE]: *canyon,* 6.25 miles long, opens to the sea 0.25 mile southwest of Laguna Beach city hall (lat. 33°32'35" N, long. 117°47'05" W). Named on Laguna Beach (1965) 7.5' quadrangle. The feature was called Canada de las Lagunas in the early days for fresh-water lagoons situated near its head (Meadows, p. 32).

Laguna Creek [VENTURA]: *stream,* flows 1.25 miles to Rincon Creek 5.25 miles south-southwest of White Ledge Peak (lat. 34°24'25" N, long. 119°26'40" W; near NE cor. sec. 25, T 4 N, R 25 W). Named on White Ledge Peak (1952) 7.5' quadrangle.

Laguna del Diablo: see **Elizabeth Lake** [LOS ANGELES] (1).

Laguna Dominguez: see **Dominguez Channel** [LOS ANGELES].

Laguna Hills [ORANGE]: *city,* 1.5 miles southwest of El Toro (lat. 33°36'45" N, long. 117°43' W). Named on San Juan Capistrano (1968) 7.5' quadrangle. Postal authorities established Laguna Hills post office in 1964; the post office name is from a retirement community called Leisure World Laguna Beach Hills (Salley, p. 114).

Laguna Lake [ORANGE]: *lake,* 1500 feet long, nearly 2 miles south-southeast of downtown La Habra (lat. 33°54'30" N, long. 117°56'10" W). Named on La Habra (1964) 7.5' quadrangle.

Laguna Niguel [ORANGE]: *town,* 3.5 miles west-northwest of San Juan Capistrano (lat. 33°31'15" N, long. 117°42'45" W); the town is on Niguel grant. Named on San Juan Capistrano (1968) 7.5' quadrangle. Postal authorities established Laguna Niguel post office in 1968 (Salley, p. 114).

Laguna Peak [VENTURA]: *peak,* 1.5 miles north of Point Mugu (lat. 34°06'30" N, long. 119°03'50" W). Named on Point Mugu (1949) 7.5' quadrangle.

Laguna Point [VENTURA]: *promontory,* 3 miles west-northwest of Point Mugu along the coast (lat. 34°05'40" N, long. 119°06'30" W). Named on Point Mugu (1949) 7.5' quadrangle. Point Mugu (1950) 7.5' quadrangle gives the alternate name "Sandy Point" for the feature.

Laguna Reservoir [ORANGE]: *lake,* 1600 feet long, 9.5 miles southeast of Santa Ana city hall (lat. 33°38'30" N, long. 117°45'30" W). Named on Tustin (1965) 7.5' quadrangle. The

feature is at the head of a stream called Agua del Palo Verde in the early days (Meadows, p. 17).

Laguna Ridge [VENTURA]: *ridge,* west-trending, 3.5 miles long, 4.5 miles south of White Ledge Peak (lat. 34°24'10" N, long. 119°23'10" W). Named on Matilija (1952) and White Ledge Peak (1952) 7.5' quadrangles.

Lagunas [ORANGE]: *intermittent lakes,* largest 1000 feet long, 4.5 miles north-northeast of Laguna Beach city hall (lat. 33°36'35" N, long. 117°45'25" W); the features are in Laguna Canyon. Named on Laguna Beach (1965) 7.5' quadrangle. Santa Ana (1901) 15' quadrangle shows a single lake called Laguna at the place.

Laguna Seca: see **Nigger Slough** [LOS ANGELES].

La Habra [LOS ANGELES-ORANGE]: *land grant,* at and near the city of La Habra [ORANGE]. Named on La Habra (1964) 7.5' quadrangle. Maríano Roldan received 1.5 leagues in 1839; Andres Pico and others claimed 6699 acres patented in 1872 (Cowan, p. 39; Cowan used the name "Cañada de la Habra" for the grant).

La Habra [ORANGE]: *city,* 13 miles northnorthwest of Santa Ana (lat. 33°55'55" N, long. 117°56'45" W); the city is on La Habra [LOS ANGELES-ORANGE] grant. Named on La Habra (1964) 7.5' quadrangle. Postal authorities established La Habra post office in 1895, discontinued it in 1903, and reestablished it in 1912 (Frickstad, p. 117). The city incorporated in 1925.

La Habra: see **Fullerton** [ORANGE].

La Habra Heights [LOS ANGELES]: *town,* 2 miles north of La Habra [ORANGE] (lat. 33°57'30" N, long. 117°57' W). Named on La Habra (1952) 7.5' quadrangle. The town incorporated in 1978.

Lairport [LOS ANGELES]: *locality,* 3 miles north-northeast of Manhattan Beach city hall along Atchison, Topeka and Santa Fe Railroad (lat. 33°55'25" N, long. 118°22'40" W). Named on Venice (1964) 7.5' quadrangle. Called Wiseburn on Redondo (1896) 15' quadrangle. Postal authorities established Wiseburn post office in 1891, discontinued it the same year, reestablished it in 1896, moved it 2 miles southeast in 1898, and discontinued it in 1906 (Salley, p. 242).

La Isla de la Culebra de Cascabel: see **Terminal Island** [LOS ANGELES] (1).

La Isla del Muerto: see **Reservation Point** [LOS ANGELES].

La Jolla [ORANGE]: *locality,* 5 miles northnorthwest of Orange city hall (lat. 33°51'30" N, long. 117°52'25" W). Named on Anaheim (1950) and Orange (1964) 7.5' quadrangles.

La Jolla Canyon [VENTURA]: *canyon,* 1.5 miles long, opens to the sea 1.5 miles east of Point Mugu (lat. 34°05' N, long. 119°02'05"

W); the feature heads at La Jolla Valley. Named on Point Mugu (1949) 7.5' quadrangle.

La Jolla Peak [VENTURA]: *peak,* 2 miles north-northeast of Point Mugu (lat. 34°06'55" N, long. 119°02'55" W). Altitude 1567 feet. Named on Point Mugu (1949) 7.5' quadrangle. Called La Joya Pk. on Hueneme (1904) 15' quadrangle, but United States Board on Geographic Names (1961b, p. 10) rejected this name for the feature.

La Jolla Valley [VENTURA]: *valley,* 1.25 miles north-northeast of Point Mugu (lat. 34°06'15" N, long. 119°03'05" W); the feature is less than 1 mile south of La Jolla Peak. Named on Point Mugu (1949) 7.5' quadrangle.

La Joya: see **Green Valley** [LOS ANGELES].

La Joya Peak: see **La Jolla Peak** [VENTURA].

Lake Campground [LOS ANGELES]: *locality,* 2 miles west-northwest of Big Pines (lat. 34°23'25" N, long. 117°43'20" W); the place is near Jackson Lake. Named on Mescal Creek (1956) 7.5' quadrangle.

Lake Canyon [VENTURA]: *canyon,* drained by a stream that flows 2.5 miles to Sexton Canyon 4 miles west-northwest of Saticoy (lat. 34°18' N, long. 119°13'05" W). Named on Saticoy (1951) 7.5' quadrangle.

Lake Casitas [VENTURA]: *lake,* behind a dam on Coyote Creek 7 miles north-northwest of Ventura (lat. 34°22'15" N, long. 119° 20' W). Named on Matilija (1952, photorevised 1967) and Ventura (1951, photorevised 1967) 7.5' quadrangles. United States Board on Geographic Names (1960a, p. 13) first approved and then (1962a, p. 9) rejected the name "Casitas Reservoir" for the lake.

Lake Eleanor [VENTURA]: *intermittent lake,* behind a dam on Lake Eleanor Creek 2.5 miles south-southwest of Thousand Oaks (lat. 34°08'05" N, long. 119°51' W; at E line sec. 27, T 1 N, R 19 W). Named on Thousand Oaks (1952) 7.5' quadrangle.

Lake Eleanor Creek [LOS ANGELES-VENTURA]: *stream,* heads in Los Angeles County and flows nearly 3 miles to Potrero Valley about 2 miles south-southwest of Thousand Oaks in Ventura County (lat. 34°08'45" N, long. 118°50'55" W; near NW cor. sec. 26, T 1 N, R 19 W). Named on Thousand Oaks (1952) 7.5' quadrangle.

Lake Elizabeth: see **Elizabeth Lake** [LOS ANGELES]; **West Lake Elizabeth,** under **Lake Hughes** [LOS ANGELES].

Lake Enchanto [LOS ANGELES]: *lake,* 1450 feet long, 8 miles north of Point Dume in Triunfo Canyon (lat. 34°06'50" N, long. 118°46'40" W; near W line sec. 4, T 1 S, R 18 W). Named on Point Dume (1951) 7.5' quadrangle.

Lake Hughes [LOS ANGELES]: *village,* 26 miles north of San Fernando (lat. 34°40'35" N, long. 118°26'25" W; in and near sec. 23, T 7 N, R 15 W); the village is near Hughes Lake.

Named on Lake Hughes (1957) 7.5' quadrangle. Hughes Lake (1937) 6' quadrangle has the name "Hughes Lake" for the village, and shows Lake Hughes P.O. at the place. Postal authorities established Lake Hughes post office in 1925; the name was for G.O. Hughes, owner of the land—the community first was known as West Lake Elizabeth (Salley, p. 115).

Lake Katarina: see **Tweedy Lake** [LOS ANGELES].

Lake Machado: see **Harbor Lake** [LOS ANGELES].

Lake Mathiessen: see **Lake Sherwood** [VENTURA].

Lake Palmdale [LOS ANGELES]: *lake,* 1 mile long, 2 miles south of Palmdale (lat. 34°33'05" N, mainly in sec. 3, T 5 N, R 12 W). Named on Palmdale (1958) and Ritter Ridge (1958) 7.5' quadrangles. Called Harold Reservoir on Elizabeth Lake (1917) 30' quadrangle, and called Palmdale Reservoir on Palmdale (1937) 6' quadrangle, but United States Board on Geographic Names (1960a, p. 16) rejected the names "Harold Lake," "Harold Reservoir," "Palmdale Lake," "Palmdale Reservoir," and "Shoulder Lake" for the feature.

Lake Piru [VENTURA]: *lake,* behind a dam 4 miles northeast of Piru (lat. 34°27'40" N, long. 118°45'05" W); the lake is along Piru Creek. Named on Cobblestone Mountain (1958), Piru (1952, photorevised 1969), and Val Verde (1952, photorevised 1969) 7.5' quadrangles. United Water Conservation District built the dam that formed the lake in 1956 (Ricard).

Lake Salinas: see **Salt Pond** [LOS ANGELES].

Lake Shangri La [LOS ANGELES]: *dry lake,* nearly 2 miles west of Baldwin Park city hall in a gravel pit (lat. 34°05'25" N, long. 117° 59'30" W; sec. 13, T 1 S, R 11 W). Named on Baldwin Park (1953) 7.5' quadrangle.

Lake Sherwood [VENTURA]: *lake,* behind a dam on Potrero Valley Creek 2.25 miles south-southwest of Thousand Oaks (lat. 34°08'20" N, long. 118°51'25" W). Named on Newbury Park (1951) and Thousand Oaks (1952) 7.5' quadrangles. Called Sherwood Lake on Los Angeles County (1935) map. The name is from the filming of the movie *Robin Hood* at the place in 1922; a reservoir built at the site in 1889 was called Canterbury Lake until about 1898, when F.W. Mathiessen, Jr., purchased the land—the early lake then was known as Lake Mathiessen (Ricard).

Lakeside Park [LOS ANGELES]: *locality,* 3.25 miles southwest of Chatsworth (lat. 34°13'40" N, long. 118°38'50" W); the place is west of Chatsworth Reservoir. Named on Calabasas (1952) 7.5' quadrangle.

Lakewood [LOS ANGELES]: *city,* 6.5 miles north-northeast of Long Beach city hall (lat. 33°51' N, long. 118°07'55" W). Named on Los Alamitos (1964) 7.5' quadrangle. Postal authorities established Lakewood post office in 1949 (Salley, p. 116), and the city incorporated in 1954.

Lakewood Village [LOS ANGELES]: *district,* 6 miles northeast of Long Beach city hall (lat. 33°50' N, long. 118°07'30" W). Named on Long Beach (1949) and Los Alamitos (1950) 7.5' quadrangles. Clark J. Bonner and Charles B. Hopper had the community laid out in 1934; the name is from nearby Bouton Lake (Gudde, 1949, p. 180-181).

La Laguna: see **Guadalasca** [VENTURA].

La Laguna de Chico Lopez: see **Elizabeth Lake** [LOS ANGELES] (1).

La Laguna Seca: see **Quail Lake** [LOS ANGELES].

La Liebra [LOS ANGELES]: *land grant,* west of Antelope Valley on Los Angeles-Kern county line. Named on La Liebre Ranch (1965), Lebec (1958), Liebre Mountain (1958), and Neenach School (1965) 7.5' quadrangles. Jose M. Flores received 11 leagues in 1846 and claimed 48,800 acres patented in 1875 (Cowan, p. 45). Johnson's (1911) map shows a feature called Liebre Creek on La Liebra grant; the stream heads east of Quail Lake and flows about 3.5 miles easterly to a spot in the lowlands (sec. 15, T 8 N, R 17 W).

Lamanda: see **East Pasadena** [LOS ANGELES].

Lamanda Park: see **East Pasadena** [LOS ANGELES].

Lambert Reservoir [ORANGE]: *lake,* 1000 feet long, 4.5 miles north-northwest of El Toro (lat. 33°41'35" N, long. 117°42'35" W). Named on El Toro (1968) 7.5' quadrangle. The name is for Ray Lambert, who had a citrus grove at the mouth of Bee Canyon (Meadows, p. 77).

Lambs: see **Huntington Beach** [ORANGE].

Lamel Spring [LOS ANGELES]: *spring,* 6 miles northeast of Crystal Lake (lat. 34°22'05" N, long. 117°45'20" W). Named on Crystal Lake (1958) 7.5' quadrangle.

La Merced [LOS ANGELES]: *land grant,* north of Montebello. Named on El Monte (1953) and Los Angeles (1953) 7.5' quadrangles. Casilda Soto received 1 league in 1844; Francis Pliny F. Temple and others claimed 2364 acres patented in 1872 (Cowan, p. 47).

La Mirada [LOS ANGELES]: *city,* 4 miles south-southeast of Whittier city hall (lat. 33°55'35" N, long. 118°00'40" W); La Mirada Creek goes through the city. Named on La Habra (1964) and Whittier (1965) 7.5' quadrangles. Postal authorities established La Mirada post office in 1895 (Frickstad, p. 76), and the city incorporated in 1960. Whittier (1949) 7.5' quadrangle has the name for a place along Atchison, Topeka and Santa Fe Railroad in the present city of La Mirada (lat. 33°53'40" N, long. 118°01'25" W; sec. 22, T 3 S, R 11 W).

La Mirada Creek [LOS ANGELES-OR-ANGE]: *stream,* heads in Los Angeles County and flows 8.5 miles, partly in Orange County,

to La Cañada Verde Creek nearly 6 miles south of Whittier city hall (lat. 33°53'25" N, long. 118°01'55" W; sec. 21, T 3 S, R 11 W). Named on La Habra (1952) and Whittier (1965) 7.5' quadrangles.

Lancaster [LOS ANGELES]: *city,* 32 miles north-northeast of San Fernando (lat. 34°41'50" N, long. 118°08'15" W). Named on Lancaster East (1958) and Lancaster West (1958) 7.5' quadrangles. Postal authorities established Lancaster post office in 1884 (Frickstad, p. 76), and the city incorporated in 1977. M.L. Wicks laid out the townsite in 1884 and named it for his home town of Lancaster, Pennsylvania (Settle, p. 29). Postal authorities established Eldon post office 13 miles east of Lancaster in 1892 and discontinued it the same year (Salley, p. 66). Johnson's (1911) map shows a place called Esperanza located 5.5 miles west-northwest of Lancaster.

Landing Hill [ORANGE]: *relief feature,* 8 miles northwest of Huntington Beach civic center (lat. 33°44'55" N, long. 118°05'35" W; sec. 11, 12, T 5 S, R 12 W). Named on Los Alamitos (1964) and Seal Beach (1965) 7.5' quadrangles. The name is from Anaheim Landing, which was located about 1 mile south of Landing Hill (Meadows, p. 77).

Lands End [LOS ANGELES]: *promontory,* 2.5 miles west-northwest of Silver Peak at the extreme west end of Santa Catalina Island (lat. 33°28'45" N, long. 118°36'20" W). Named on Santa Catalina West (1943) 7.5' quadrangle, which shows Catalina Island West End light near the place. United States Board on Geographic Names (1978c, p. 5) approved the name "West End" for the promontory. The Board (1936b, p. 22) approved the name "Farnsworth Bank" for a feature situated about 1 mile southwest of Santa Catalina Island (lat. 33°20'36" N, long. 118°31' W)—they noted that name commemorates Samuel Stephen Farnsworth, who built a road on the Island and died there. According to United States Coast and Geodetic Survey (p. 107), Farnsworth Bank is located 9.2 miles southeast of West End.

Lane: see **Camp Bill Lane** [LOS ANGELES].

Lang [LOS ANGELES]: *locality,* 5 miles east of Solemint along Southern Pacific Railroad (lat. 34°26'05" N, long. 118°22'10" W; sec. 17, T 4 N, R 14 W). Named on Agua Dulce (1960) and Mint Canyon (1960) 7.5' quadrangles. Postal authorities established Lang post office in 1881, discontinued it in 1882, reestablished it in 1883, and discontinued it in 1933; the name was for John Lang, first postmaster (Salley, p. 117). The golden spike that marked completion of Southern Pacific Railroad's line connecting Los Angeles and San Francisco was driven at Lang in 1876 (Hanna, p. 167). Los Angeles County (1935) map shows a feature called Lang Canyon that opens into Soledad Canyon from the north about 0.5 mile west of Lang.

Lang Canyon: see **Lang** [LOS ANGELES].

Lankershim: see **North Hollywood** [LOS ANGELES].

Laon Junction: see **Des Moins** [ORANGE].

La Paco [LOS ANGELES]: *locality,* 3 miles west-southwest of present Burbank city hall along Southern Pacific Railroad (lat. 34° 10'05" N, long. 118°21'25" W). Named on Burbank (1926) 6' quadrangle.

La Palma [ORANGE]: *town,* 3 miles west-southwest of Buena Park civic center (lat. 33°50'45" N, long. 118°02'35" W; on S line sec. 4, T 4 S, R 11 W). Named on Los Alamitos (1964) 7.5' quadrangle. Postal authorities established La Palma post office in 1966; the name was from La Palma Avenue (Salley, p. 117). The town incorporated with the name "Dairyland" in 1955; residents changed the name to La Palma in 1957.

La Paloma [ORANGE]: *locality,* 2.25 miles east-southeast of Orange city hall (lat. 33°46'50" N, long. 117°48'10" W). Named on Orange (1964) 7.5' quadrangle. Lawrence Phillips laid out a Latin-American colony at the place in 1923 (Meadows, p. 75).

La Palonia Flat [LOS ANGELES]: *area,* 3 miles south of Condor Peak in Big Tujunga Canyon (lat. 34°17' N, long. 118°13'20" W; sec. 3, T 2 N, R 13 W). Named on Condor Peak (1959) 7.5' quadrangle.

La Park: see **Huntington Park** [LOS ANGELES].

La Paz: see **Mission Viejo or La Paz** [ORANGE].

La Paz Canyon [ORANGE]: *canyon,* drained by a stream that heads in Riverside County and flows 3 miles in Orange County to Gabino Canyon 5.5 miles northeast of San Clemente (lat. 33°28'55" N, long. 117°32'10" W; near W line sec. 8, T 8 S, R 6 W); the feature is on Mission Viejo or La Paz grant. Named on Cañada Gobernadora (1968) and San Clemente (1968) 7.5' quadrangles.

La Placerita Canyon: see **Placerita Canyon** [LOS ANGELES].

La Puente [LOS ANGELES]:
(1) *land grant,* north of Puente Hills between San Gabriel River and San Jose Creek. Named on Baldwin Park (1953), El Monte (1953), La Habra (1952), San Dimas (1954), Whittier (1951), and Yorba Linda (1950) 7.5' quadrangles. John Rowland and William Workman received the land in 1845; they claimed 48,791 acres patented in 1867 (Cowan, p. 64; Cowan listed the grant under the wrong name).
(2) *city,* 4.5 miles south of Baldwin Park city hall (lat. 34°02'10" N, long. 117°57' W); the city is on La Puente (1) grant. Named on Baldwin Park (1966) 7.5' quadrangle. Called Puente on Baldwin Park (1953) 7.5' quadrangle. Postal authorities established Puente post office in 1884 and changed the name to

La Puente in 1956 (Salley, p. 118).

La Quinta [LOS ANGELES]: *locality,* 7.5 miles west-southwest of Newhall in Las Llajas Canyon [LOS ANGELES-VENTURA] (lat. 34°19'40" N, long. 118°38'25" W). Named on Pico (1940) 6' quadrangle.

Largo Vista [LOS ANGELES]: *locality,* 5 miles east-southeast of Valyermo in Grandview Canyon (lat. 34°25'40" N, long. 117°45'55" W; near SE cor. sec. 13, T 4 N, R 9 W). Named on Valyermo (1958) 7.5' quadrangle.

Larres Canyon: see **Potrero Canyon** [LOS ANGELES].

Las Barras Canyon [LOS ANGELES]: *canyon,* less than 1 mile long, 4 miles north-northeast of Burbank city hall (lat. 34°14' N, long. 118°16'35" W). Named on Burbank (1953) 7.5' quadrangle.

Las Bolsas [ORANGE]: *land grant,* at and west of present Fountain Valley. Named on Anaheim (1950), Los Alamitos (1950), Newport Beach (1951), and Seal Beach (1950) 7.5' quadrangles. Catarina Ruis, widow of Manuel Nieto, received confirmation of 7 leagues of this part of the original Los Nietos grant in 1834; Maria C. Nieto claimed half of 33,460 acres patented in 1877, and Ramon Yorba and others claimed the other half, patented in 1874 (Cowan, p. 19).

Las Casetas [LOS ANGELES]: *locality,* 4.5 miles north-northwest of present Pasadena city hall (lat. 34°12'30" N, long. 118°10' W). Named on Pasadena (1900) 15' quadrangle. United States Board on Geographic Names (1933, p. 449) rejected the forms "Las Casitas" and "Los Casitos" for the name. Jason Brown and Owen Brown, sons of John Brown of Civil War fame, laid out a farm at the place in the 1880's and called it Las Casitas—*las casitas* means "the little houses" in Spanish (Robinson, J.W., 1977, p. 103).

Las Casetas Station [LOS ANGELES]: *locality,* 3.25 miles north-northwest of present Pasadena city hall along Los Angeles Terminal Railroad (lat. 34°11'30" N, long. 118°09'30" W); the place is 1.25 miles southeast of Las Casetas. Named on Pasadena (1900) 15' quadrangle.

Las Casitas: see **Las Casetas** [LOS ANGELES].

Las Cienegas [LOS ANGELES]: *land grant,* 5.5 miles west of Los Angeles city hall. Named on Hollywood (1953) 7.5' quadrangle. Januario Avila received 1 league in 1823 and claimed 4439 acres patented in 1871 (Cowan, p. 28). According to Perez (p. 62), Francisco Abila was grantee in 1843, and Januario Abila was patentee in 1871.

Las Flores [LOS ANGELES]: *locality,* nearly 3 miles east of Malibu Point along the coast (lat. 34°02'15" N, long, 118°38' W); the place is on Topanga Malibu Sequit grant at the mouth of Las Flores Canyon. Named on Malibu Beach (1951) 7.5' quadrangle, which shows

Malibu post office at the place. Postal authorities established Malibu post office 1947; the name is from the grant (Salley, p. 131).

Las Flores Canyon [LOS ANGELES]:
(1) *canyon,* 1 mile long, 3.5 miles west of Mount Wilson (1) (lat. 34°12'55" N, long. 118°07'25" W; sec. 34, T 2 N, R 12 W). Named on Mount Wilson (1953) and Pasadena (1953) 7.5' quadrangles.
(2) *canyon,* drained by a stream that flows 3.5 miles to the sea 2.5 miles east of Malibu Point (lat. 34°02'10" N, long. 118°38'05" W). Named on Malibu Beach (1951) 7.5' quadrangle.

Las Flores Canyon: see **Little Las Flores Canyon** [LOS ANGELES].

La Sierra Canyon [LOS ANGELES]: *canyon,* drained by a stream that flows 2.5 miles to Triunfo Canyon 8 miles north of Point Dume (lat. 34°07'05" N, long. 118°47' W). Named on Point Dume (1951) 7.5' quadrangle.

La Sierra de San Gabriel: see **San Gabriel Mountains** [LOS ANGELES].

Laskey Mesa [VENTURA]: *area,* 8.5 miles east of Thousand Oaks (lat. 34°10'30" N, long. 118°40'50" W). Named on Calabasas (1952) 7.5' quadrangle.

Las Llajas Canyon [LOS ANGELES-VENTURA]: *canyon,* drained by a stream that heads in Los Angeles County and flows 5.5 miles to Simi Valley (1) 4 miles west-northwest of Santa Susana Pass in Ventura County (lat. 34°18' N, long. 118°41'30" W; near E line sec. 31, T 3 N, R 17 W). Named on Santa Susana (1951) 7.5' quadrangle.

Las Lomas [LOS ANGELES]: *locality,* 2.5 miles west-northwest of Azusa city hall along Pacific Electric Railroad (lat. 34°08'35" N, long. 117°56'45" W). Named on Azusa (1953) 7.5' quadrangle.

Las Mesitas: see **Anacapa Island** [VENTURA].

La Soledad Pass: see **Soledad Pass** [LOS ANGELES].

Las Pitas: see **Point Las Pitas**, under **Pitas Point** [VENTURA].

Las Posas [VENTURA]: *land grant,* at and around Somis. Named on Camarillo (1950), Moorpark (1951), Newbury Park (1951), and Santa Paula (1951) 7.5' quadrangles. Jose Carrillo received 6 leagues in 1834; Jose de la Guerra y Noriega claimed 26,623 acres patented in 1881 (Cowan, p. 63; Cowan used the form "Las Pozas" for the name). Perez (p. 82) gave the date 1871 for the patent.

Las Posas: see **Saticoy** [VENTURA].

Las Posas Hills [VENTURA]: *ridge,* west-trending, 7 miles long, center 4 miles southwest of Moorpark (lat. 34°15'10" N, long. 118° 56' W). Named on Moorpark (1951) and Newbury Park (1951) 7.5' quadrangles.

Las Pozas: see **Las Posas** [VENTURA].

Las Pulgas Canyon: see **Pulga Canyon** [LOS ANGELES].

Las Salinas: see **Salt Pond** [LOS ANGELES].

Last Chance Camp [VENTURA]: *locality,* 4.5 miles north-northwest of Santa Paula Peak (lat. 34°29'50" N, long. 119°03'15" W). Named on Santa Paula Peak (1951) 7.5' quadrangle.

Las Tunas Beach [LOS ANGELES]: *beach,* 6.25 miles west-northwest of Santa Monica city hall along the coast (lat. 34°02'20" N, long. 118°35'45" W; sec. 31, 32, T 1 S, R 16 W); the beach is at the mouth of Tuna Canyon. Named on Topanga (1952) 7.5' quadrangle.

Las Virgenes [LOS ANGELES]: *land grant,* at and near Agoura. Named on Calabasas (1952), Malibu Beach (1951), Point Dume (1951), and Thousand Oaks (1952) 7.5' quadrangles. Jose Maria Dominguez received the land in 1837; M. Antonio Machado claimed 8885 acres patented in 1883 (Cowan, p. 58; Cowan listed the grant under the name "Paraje de las Virgenes"). Perez (p. 104) gave 8878.76 acres as the size of the grant.

Las Virgenes Canyon [LOS ANGELES-VENTURA]: *canyon,* 6.5 miles long, on Los Angeles-Ventura county line along Las Virgenes Creek above a point 2.25 miles east of Agoura (lat. 34°09' N, long. 118°41'45" W; sec. 19, T 1 N, R 17 E). Named on Calabasas (1952) 7.5' quadrangle.

Las Virgenes Canyon: see **East Las Virgenes Canyon** [VENTURA].

Las Virgenes Creek [LOS ANGELES-VENTURA]: *stream,* heads in Ventura County and flows 10.5 miles in Los Angeles and Ventura Counties to Malibu Creek 5 miles northwest of Malibu Point in Los Angeles County (lat. 34°05'50" N, long. 118°43'15" W; sec. 12, T 1 S, R 18 W). Named on Calabasas (1952) and Malibu Beach (1951) 7.5' quadrangles. Whitney (p. 122) called the stream Virgenes Creek.

Lateen [LOS ANGELES]: *locality,* 2 miles east-northeast of Baldwin Park city hall along Pacific Electric Railroad (lat. 34°05'30" N, long. 117°55'25" W; near W line sec. 15, T 1 S, R 10 W). Named on Baldwin Park (1953) 7.5' quadrangle.

Latham: see **Fort Latham**, under **Playa del Rey** [LOS ANGELES].

Latigo Canyon [LOS ANGELES]: *canyon,* 3 miles long, opens to the sea 3.5 miles northeast of Point Dume (lat. 34°01'50" N, long. 118° 45'10" W). Named on Point Dume (1951) 7.5' quadrangle.

La Tijera: see **Cienega o Paso de La Tijera** [LOS ANGELES].

Latrango Canon: see **Telegraph Canyon** [ORANGE].

La Tuna Canyon [LOS ANGELES]: *canyon,* 5.5 miles long, opens into lowlands 4.5 miles northwest of Burbank city hall (lat. 34° 14' N, long. 118°21'30" W; near NW cor. sec. 28, T 2 N, R 14 W). Named on Burbank (1953) 7.5' quadrangle.

Laurel Canyon [LOS ANGELES]: (1) *canyon*, drained by a stream that flows 1.25 miles to Pacoima Canyon 7 miles north of Sunland (lat. 34°21'35" N, long. 118° 20' W; sec. 10, T 3 N, R 14 W). Named on Sunland (1953) 7.5' quadrangle. (2) *canyon*, 1.5 miles long, 8.5 miles west-northwest of Los Angeles city hall (lat. 34°06'50" N, long. 118°22'20" W). Named on Hollywood (1966) 7.5' quadrangle.

Laurel Gulch [LOS ANGELES]: *canyon*, drained by a stream that flows 2.5 miles to San Gabriel River 6 miles west-southwest of Mount San Antonio (lat. 34°15'30" N, long. 117°44'45" W). Named on Mount San Antonio (1955) 7.5' quadrangle.

Laurel Spring [ORANGE]: *spring*, nearly 3 miles west of Santiago Peak (lat. 33°42'50" N, long. 117°34'50" W). Named on Santiago Peak (1954) 7.5' quadrangle.

La Verne [LOS ANGELES]: *town*, 3.25 miles north-northwest of Pomona city hall (lat. 34°06' N, long. 117°46'10" W). Named on Glendora (1966) and San Dimas (1954) 7.5' quadrangles. Pomona (1904) 15' quadrangle has the name "Lordsburg" at present La Verne, and has the name "La Verne" for a place located about 1.25 miles farther northwest. Postal authorities established Lordsburg post office in 1887; they established La Vern post office 2 miles northwest of Lordsburg post office in 1888 and moved it to Lordsburg in 1889; they changed the name of Lordsburg post office to La Verne in 1918 (Salley, p. 119, 126). La Verne incorporated in 1906. Lordsburg, named for its founder, I.W. Lord, originally was a Dunkard colony (Garner, p. 209). The name "La Verne" is from La Verne Heights, a subdivision that had the given name of its promoter (Gudde, 1949, p. 184).

Lavida Hot Springs: see **La Vida Mineral Springs** [ORANGE].

La Vida Mineral Springs [ORANGE]: *locality*, 3 miles north-northeast of Yorba Linda in Carbon Canyon (lat. 33°56' N, long. 117°47'35" W; near S line sec. 2, T 3 S, R 9 W). Named on Yorba Linda (1950) 7.5' quadrangle. Anaheim (1942) 15' quadrangle shows a water feature called Lavida Hot Springs at the site. A resort at the place uses water from an artesian well drilled at or near a former natural spring (Berkstresser, p. A-9).

La Vina: see **Altadena** [LOS ANGELES].

Lawlor: see **Mount Lawlor** [LOS ANGELES].

Lawndale [LOS ANGELES]: *town*, 4.5 miles south of Inglewood city hall (lat. 33°53'10" N, long. 118°21' W). Named on Inglewood (1964) 7.5' quadrangle. Postal authorities established Lawndale post office in 1906 (Frickstad, p. 76), and the town incorporated in 1959. Charles Hopper founded and named the community in 1905 (Gudde, 1949, p. 184).

La Zanja: see **San Rafael** [LOS ANGELES].

Leach Canyon [ORANGE]: *canyon*, drained by a stream that flows 0.5 mile to Riverside County 3.5 miles southeast of Trabuco Peak (lat. 33°40'15" N, long. 117°25'40" W; near N line sec. 8, T 6 S, R 5 W). Named on Alberhill (1954) 7.5' quadrangle.

Leaming Canyon [LOS ANGELES]: *canyon*, drained by a stream that flows 1 mile to Gavin Canyon 2.25 miles south-southwest of Newhall (lat. 34°21'05" N, long. 118°32'50" W; near N line sec. 15, T 3 N, R 16 W). Named on Oat Mountain (1952) 7.5' quadrangle. The name commemorates Christopher Leaming, a pioneer of the 1860's (Reynolds, p. 13).

Le Brun Canyon: see **Drinkwater Canyon** [LOS ANGELES].

Lechler Canyon [LOS ANGELES-VENTURA]: *canyon*, drained by a stream that heads in Los Angeles County and flows nearly 3 miles to Lake Piru 5.5 miles northeast of Piru in Ventura County (lat. 34°28'10" N, long. 118°44' W). Named on Val Verde (1952, photorevised 1969) 7.5' quadrangle, which shows Lechler ranch in nearby in Oak Canyon [LOS ANGELES] (1). Called Lechler Canyon on Santa Susana (1903) 15' quadrangle.

Lechuza Canyon: see **Lachusa Canyon** [LOS ANGELES].

Lechuza Point [LOS ANGELES]: *promontory*, 4 miles northwest of Point Dume (lat. 34°02'05" N, long. 118°51'40" W). Named on Point Dume (1951) 7.5' quadrangle. Called Lachusa Point on Dume Point (1932) 6' quadrangle.

Leckler Canyon: see **Lechler Canyon** [LOS ANGELES-VENTURA].

Lee: see **Mount Lee** [LOS ANGELES].

Leesdale [VENTURA]: *locality*, 4 miles west-southwest of Camarillo along Southern Pacific Railroad (lat. 34°11'50" N, long. 119°05'50" W). Named on Camarillo (1950) 7.5' quadrangle.

Lees Lake [LOS ANGELES]: *lake*, 650 feet long, nearly 3 miles south-southwest of Chatsworth along Chatsworth Creek (lat. 34° 13'20" N, long. 118°37'45" W). Named on Calabasas (1952) 7.5' quadrangle.

Leffingwell [LOS ANGELES]: *locality*, 2.5 miles west of La Habra [ORANGE] along Union Pacific Railroad (lat. 33°56' N, long. 117° 59'30" W). Named on La Habra (1952) 7.5' quadrangle.

Leffingwell Creek [LOS ANGELES-ORANGE]: *stream*, heads in Los Angeles County and flows 3.5 miles, partly in Orange County, to La Cañada Verde Creek 2.5 miles south of present Whittier city hall (lat. 33°56'20" N, long. 118°01'25" W). Named on La Habra (1952) and Whittier (1949) 7.5' quadrangles.

Legg Lake [LOS ANGELES]: *lakes*, two, largest 2000 feet long, 3 miles south-southwest of El Monte city hall in a flood control basin of San Gabriel River and Rio Hondo (lat. 34°02' N, long. 118°03'30" W). Named on El

Monte (1966) 7.5' quadrangle.
Lemon [VENTURA]: *locality,* 2.25 miles east-southeast of downtown Ventura along Southern Pacific Railroad (lat. 34°15'45" N, long. 119°15'20" W). Named on Ventura (1951) 7.5' quadrangle. The name is from a packing house for lemons (Ricard). California Division of Highways' (1934) map shows a place called Edfu located along the railroad 1 mile east-southeast of Lemon.
Lemon: see **Walnut** [LOS ANGELES].
Lemon Creek [LOS ANGELES]: *stream,* flows 3 miles to San Jose Creek 7.25 miles southwest of Pomona city hall (lat. 34°00'20" N, long. 117°51'40" W); the stream goes through Walnut, which formerly was called Lemon. Named on San Dimas (1966) 7.5' quadrangle.
Lemon Heights [ORANGE]: *locality,* 4.5 miles east-southeast of Orange city hall (lat. 33°45'30" N, long. 117°46'45" W). Named on Orange (1964) 7.5' quadrangle.
Le Montaine Creek [LOS ANGELES]: *stream,* flows 3.5 miles to lowlands 3.5 miles northnortheast of Big Pines (lat. 34°25'30" N, long. 117°40' W; near N line sec. 24, T 4 N, R 8 W). Named on Mescal Creek (1956) 7.5' quadrangle.
Lennox [LOS ANGELES]: *town,* 1.5 miles south of Inglewood city hall (lat. 33°56'25" N, long. 118°21' W). Named on Inglewood (1952) 7.5' quadrangle. Postal authorities established Lennox post office in 1930, discontinued it in 1936, and reestablished it in 1940 (Salley, p. 121). The name is from Lennox, Massachusetts, former home of a resident of the place; it also was known as Inglewood Rancho and as Jefferson (Gudde, 1949, p. 186).
Leona Valley [LOS ANGELES]:
(1) *valley,* 11 miles long, center 10 miles west-southwest of Lancaster (lat. 34°37'15" N, long. 118°17'30" W). Named on Del Sur (1958), Ritter Ridge (1958), and Sleepy Valley (1958) 7.5' quadrangles. Called Leonis Valley on Elizabeth Lake (1917) 30' quadrangle, but United States Board on Geographic Names (1959, p. 6-7) rejected this name, which is from Miguel Leonis, a Basque shepherd (Gudde, 1949, p. 186).
(2) *village,* 9.5 miles east-southeast of the village of Lake Hughes (lat. 34°37'05" N, long. 118°17'15" W; near SW cor. sec. 8, T 6 N, R 13 W); the village is in Leona Valley (1). Named on Sleepy Valley (1958) 7.5' quadrangle.
Leon Canyon [VENTURA]: *canyon,* drained by a stream that flows 2.5 miles to Cañada Larga 5.5 miles north-northeast of Ventura (lat. 34°21'25" N, long. 119°15'05" W). Named on Saticoy (1951) 7.5' quadrangle.
Leonis Valley: see **Leona Valley** [LOS ANGELES].
LeRoy: see **Camp LeRoy**, under **Camp Ivy** [LOS ANGELES]
Latteau Canyon [LOS ANGELES]: *canyon,*

drained by a stream that flows 2 miles to Sierra Pelona Valley 6 miles south of the village of Lenna Valley (lat. 34°31'45" N, long. 118°16'40" W; sec. 7, T 5 N, R 13 W). Named on Sleepy Valley (1958) 7.5' quadrangle.
Lewis: see **Mount Lewis** [LOS ANGELES].
Lewis Paul Canyon [LOS ANGELES]: *canyon,* drained by a stream that flows 1.25 miles to Big Dalton Canyon nearly 4 miles northeast of Glendora city hall (lat. 34°10'10" N, long. 117°48'35" W; sec. 15, T 1 N, R 9 W). Named on Glendora (1953) 7.5' quadrangle.
Lexington: see **El Monte** [LOS ANGELES]; **Lockwood Flat** [VENTURA].
Lexington Wash: see **Rio Hondo** [LOS ANGELES] (1).
Liberty: see **Calabasas** [LOS ANGELES].
Liberty Canyon [LOS ANGELES]: *canyon,* drained by a stream that flows nearly 4 miles to Las Virgenes Creek 5.5 miles north-northwest of Malibu Point (lat. 34°06'20" N, long. 118°42'40" W; near SE cor. sec. 1, T 1 S, R 18 W). Named on Calabasas (1952) and Malibu Beach (1951) 7.5' quadrangles.
Liberty Park [ORANGE]: *locality,* 3.25 miles north of present Huntington Beach civic center (lat. 33°42'25" N, long. 117°59'20" W; at E line sec. 26, T 5 S, R 11 W). Named on Newport Beach (1951) 7.5' quadrangle.
Lickskillit: see **El Monte** [LOS ANGELES].
Lido Isle [ORANGE]: *island,* 1 mile long, 6 miles southeast of Huntington Beach civic center in Newport Bay (lat. 33°36'45" N, long. 117°55' W). Named on Newport Beach (1965) 7.5' quadrangle. W.K. Parkinson purchased the property from Pacific Electric Land Company in 1923, had the island built up with dredged material, and opened a subdivision there in 1928—the name is from an island southeast of Venice, Italy (Meadows, p. 78). When Henry E. Huntington owned the place, it was known as Pacific Electric Island (Gleason, p. 98).
Lido Isle Reach: see **Newport Bay** [ORANGE].
Liebre Creek: see **La Liebra** [LOS ANGELES].
Liebre Gulch [LOS ANGELES]: *canyon,* drained by a stream that flows 8 miles to Piru Creek 11 miles south-southeast of Gorman (lat. 34°38'50" N, long. 118°45'45" W; near N line sec. 2, T 6 N, R 18 W); the canyon heads near the west end of Liebre Mountain. Named on Black Mountain (1958) and Liebre Mountain (1958) 7.5' quadrangles. West Fork branches off about 0.5 mile above the mouth of the main canyon; it is 7 miles long and is named on Black Mountain (1958) 7.5' quadrangle. United States Board on Geographic Names (1960c, p. 19) rejected the name "West Liebre Gulch" for West Fork.
Liebre Mountain [LOS ANGELES]: *ridge,* west-northwest-trending, 6 miles long, 12.5 miles east-southeast of Gorman (lat. 34°43' N, long. 118°40' W). Named on Burnt Peak (1958) and Liebre Mountain (1958) 7.5' quad-

rangles. Called Liebre Mountains on Neenach (1943) 15' quadrangle. Fairbanks (p. 493) referred to a range called Sierra Libre, and Marcou (p. 166) mentioned a range that he called both Sierra Liebra and Sierra de Liebre.

Lilly Meadows [VENTURA]: *area,* 12.5 miles northeast of Reyes Peak (lat. 34°46' N, long. 119°08' W; at W line sec. 20, T 8 N, R 21 W). Named on Sawmill Mountain (1943) 7.5' quadrangle.

Lily Spring [LOS ANGELES]: *spring,* nearly 3 miles northeast of Crystal Lake (lat. 34°20'40" N, long. 117°48'30" W). Named on Crystal Lake (1958) 7.5' quadrangle.

Limco: see **Limon** [VENTURA].

Lime Canyon [VENTURA]:
(1) *canyon,* drained by a stream that flows 3 miles to Piru Canyon 3.25 miles north-northeast of Piru (lat. 34°27'15" N, long. 118°45'40" W). Named on Piru (1952) 7.5' quadrangle.
(2) *canyon,* drained by a stream that flows nearly 2 miles to Matilija Creek 4.5 miles west of Wheeler Springs (lat. 34°30'10" N, long. 119°22'10" W; near W line sec. 23, T 5 N, R 24 W). Named on Matilija (1952) and White Ledge Peak (1952) 7.5' quadrangles.

Limekiln Canyon [LOS ANGELES]:
(1) *canyon,* 4 miles long, opens into lowlands 3 miles east-northeast of Chatsworth (lat. 34°16'20" N, long. 118°33'25" W; sec. 9, T 2 N, R 16 W). Named on Oat Mountain (1952) 7.5' quadrangle.
(2) *canyon,* 1.5 miles long, opens into lowlands 3.5 miles northeast of San Fernando (lat. 34°19'10" N, long. 118°23'50" W; sec. 25, T 3 N, R 15 W). Named on San Fernando (1953) 7.5' quadrangle.

Limekiln Canyon Wash [LOS ANGELES]: *stream,* flows nearly 4 miles to Aliso Canyon Wash 3.5 miles northeast of the center of Canoga Park (lat. 34°13'50" N, long. 118°32'40" W); the stream heads at the mouth of Limekiln Canyon (1). Named on Canoga Park (1952) and Oat Mountain (1952) 7.5' quadrangles.

Limerock Canyon [LOS ANGELES]: *canyon,* drained by a stream that flows 1.5 miles to Little Tujunga Canyon 4 miles north-northwest of Sunland (lat. 34°18'45" N, long. 118°20'35" W; near E line sec. 28, T 3 N, R 14 W); the canyon is northeast of Limerock Peak. Named on Sunland (1953) 7.5' quadrangle.

Limerock Peak [LOS ANGELES]: *peak,* nearly 5 miles northwest of Sunland (lat. 34°19'05" N, long. 118°21'25" W; sec. 28, T 3 N, R 14 W). Altitude 2986 feet. Named on Sunland (1966) 7.5' quadrangle.

Limestone Canyon [ORANGE]: *canyon,* drained by a stream that flows 5.5 miles to Santiago Reservoir 6.5 miles south-southwest of Sierra Peak (lat. 33°45'50" N, long. 117°42'35" W). Named on Black Star Can-

yon (1967) and El Toro (1968) 7.5' quadrangles. Called Rabbit Canyon on Corona (1902) 30' quadrangle. The feature also was called Cañada de Agua Chinon for a spring that was named for a curly-headed man who lived by it—*chinon* means "curly" in Spanish (Meadows, p. 32; Stephenson, p. 99). The name "Limestone Canyon" was given in 1862 when Sam Shrewsbury built a limekiln in the canyon (Meadows, p. 78).

Limon [VENTURA]: *locality,* 3.5 miles southwest of Santa Paula along Southern Pacific Railroad (lat. 34°19'15" N, long. 119°06'25" W); a spur rail line to Limoneira leaves the main line at the place. Named on Santa Paula (1951) 7.5' quadrangle. Called Limco on California Mining Bureau's (1917) map.

Limoneira [VENTURA]: *locality,* 4 miles west-southwest of Santa Paula (lat. 34°19'50" N, long. 119°07'25" W). Named on Santa Paula (1951) and Saticoy (1951) 7.5' quadrangles. The name is from a packing house for lemons (Ricard).

Lincoln Crest [LOS ANGELES]: *pass,* 2.25 miles south-southwest of the village of Leona Valley at the head of Bouquet Canyon (lat. 34°35'10" N, long. 118°18'15" W; at NW cor. sec. 30, T 6 N, R 13 W). Named on Sleepy Valley (1958) 7.5' quadrangle.

Lincoln Heights [LOS ANGELES]: *district,* 2.5 miles east-northeast of Los Angeles city hall (lat. 34°04'15" N, long. 118°12'15" W). Named on Los Angeles (1953) 7.5' quadrangle. Alhambra (1926) 6' quadrangle has the name "Lincoln Park" at the place. Postal authorities established Lincoln Heights post office in 1949 (Salley, p. 122).

Lincoln Park [LOS ANGELES]: *locality,* 6 miles west-northwest of present Los Angeles city hall (lat. 34°06'35" N, long. 118°10'30" W). Named on Pasadena (1900) 15' quadrangle.

Lincoln Park: see **Lincoln Heights** [LOS ANGELES].

Lincoln Village [LOS ANGELES]: *district,* 4.5 miles north-northwest of Long Beach city hall (lat. 33°49'45" N, long. 118°13'15" W). Named on Long Beach (1949) 7.5' quadrangle.

Linda Isle [ORANGE]: *island,* 1500 feet long, 6.5 miles east-southeast of Huntington Beach civic center in Newport Bay (lat. 33°36'50" N, long. 117°54'05" W). Named on Newport Beach (1965) 7.5' quadrangle. Called Shark Island on Newport Beach 7.5' (1951) quadrangle, but United States Board on Geographic Names (1967a, p. 3) rejected this designation. Teenagers found the place a romantic playground and named it Shark Island in the 1930's; the name "Linda Isle" is for a granddaughter of James Irvine, Jr. (Meadows, p. 78, 127).

Linda Vista [LOS ANGELES]: *locality,* 3.5 miles northwest of Pasadena city hall (lat. 34°10'15" N, long. 118°10'40" W). Named on Pasadena (1953) 7.5' quadrangle.

Lindero Canyon [LOS ANGELES-VENTURA]: *canyon*, drained by a stream that heads in Ventura County and flows 6.5 miles to Medea Creek 1 mile west of Agoura in Los Angeles County (lat. 34°08'20" N, long. 118°45'30" W). Named on Thousand Oaks (1952) 7.5' quadrangle. The feature is on the boundary between two land grants—*lindero* means "boundary" in Spanish (Ricard).

Lindys: see **Nintynine Oaks** [LOS ANGELES].

Lion Canyon [LOS ANGELES]: *canyon*, drained by a stream that flows 1.25 miles to Burnt Peak Canyon 2.25 miles south of Burnt Peak (lat. 34°38'50" N, long. 118°34'40" W). Named on Burnt Peak (1958) 7.5' quadrangle.

Lion Canyon [ORANGE]: *canyon*, drained by a stream that flows nearly 4 miles to San Juan Canyon 7 miles south of Trabuco Peak (lat. 33°36'05" N, long. 117°27'35" W; sec. 36, T 6 S, R 6 W). Named on Alberhill (1954) and Sitton Peak (1954) 7.5' quadrangles.

Lion Canyon [VENTURA]:
(1) *canyon*, drained by a stream that flows 6.5 miles to Sespe Creek 8 miles east-northeast of Wheeler Springs (lat. 34°33'35" N, long. 119°09'35" W; near NW cor. sec. 2, T 5 N, R 22 W). Named on Lion Canyon (1943) and Topatopa Mountains (1943) 7.5' quadrangles.
(2) *canyon*, 4.5 miles long, along Lion Creek above a point 2 miles south-southwest of the town of Ojai (lat. 34°25'20" N, long. 119° 15'50" W). Named on Matilija (1952) and Ojai (1952) 7.5' quadrangles. Called Cañada de Leon on Peckham's (1866) map.

Lion Creek [VENTURA]: *stream*, flows 8 miles to San Antonio Creek 2 miles south-southwest of the town of Ojai (lat. 34°25'20" N, long. 119°15'50" W); the stream passes through Lion Canyon (2). Named on Ojai (1952) 7.5' quadrangle.

Lion Head: see **Lions Head** [LOS ANGELES].

Lions Canyon [LOS ANGELES-ORANGE]: *canyon*, drained by a stream that heads in Los Angeles County and flows 1.5 miles, partly in San Bernardino County, to Carbon Canyon 4.25 miles north-northeast of Yorba Linda just inside Orange County (lat. 33°56'40" N, long. 117°46'50" W; near NW cor. sec. 1, T 3 S, R 9 W). Named on Yorba Linda (1950) 7.5' quadrangle.

Lions Head [LOS ANGELES]: *promontory*, 4 miles east of Silver Peak on the north side of Santa Catalina Island (lat. 33°27'10" N, long. 118°30' W). Named on Santa Catalina West (1943) 7.5' quadrangle. United States Board on Geographic Names (1976b, p. 4) approved the singular form "Lion Head" for the name, and gave the names "Lions Head" and "Lions Head Point" as variants.

Lions Head Point: see **Lions Head** [LOS ANGELES].

Little Bear Canyon [LOS ANGELES]: *canyon*, drained by a stream that flows 2 miles to Arroyo Seco 6.5 miles southeast of Condor Peak (lat. 34°15'10" N, long. 118°08'55" W); the mouth of the canyon is 500 feet north of the mouth of Bear Canyon (5). Named on Condor Peak (1959) 7.5' quadrangle. Tujunga (1900) 15' quadrangle has the name "Little Bear Creek" for the stream in the canyon.

Little Bear Canyon: see **Bear Canyon** [LOS ANGELES] (3).

Little Bear Creek: see **Little Bear Canyon** [LOS ANGELES].

Little Burnt Peak [LOS ANGELES]: *peak*, 0.5 mile north of Burnt Peak (lat. 34°41'20" N, long. 118°34'35" W). Named on Burnt Peak (1958) 7.5' quadrangle.

Little Buttes [LOS ANGELES]: *hill*, 11.5 miles northeast of the village of Lake Hughes (lat. 34°47'55" N, long. 118°18'10" W; sec. 7, T 8 N, R 13 W). Named on Little Buttes (1965) 7.5' quadrangle.

Little Cedars Campground [LOS ANGELES]: *locality*, 7.5 miles west-southwest of Valyermo along South Fork Little Rock Creek (lat. 34°23'50" N, long. 117°58'10" W; near S line sec. 30, T 4 N, R 10 W). Named on Juniper Hills (1959) 7.5' quadrangle.

Little Cienega: see **Falling Spring** [LOS ANGELES].

Little Cottonwood Creek: see **Oso Canyon** [LOS ANGELES].

Little Dalton Campground [LOS ANGELES]: *locality*, 2.5 miles north-northeast of Glendora city hall (lat. 34°10'05" N, long. 117° 50'15" W; near SE cor. sec. 17, T 1 N, R 9 W); the place is in Little Dalton Canyon. Named on Glendora (1953) 7.5' quadrangle. Glendora (1966) 7.5' quadrangle shows Little Dalton Picnic Area at the site

Little Dalton Canyon [LOS ANGELES]: *canyon*, 4 miles long, opens into lowlands 2 miles northeast of Glendora city hall (lat. 34°09'15" N, long. 117°50'15" W; at E line sec. 20, T 1 N, R 9 W); the mouth of the canyon is just west of the mouth of Big Dalton Canyon. Named on Glendora (1953) 7.5' quadrangle.

Little Dalton Wash [LOS ANGELES]: *stream*, flows nearly 7 miles from the mouth of Little Dalton Canyon to Big Dalton Wash 2.5 miles east-northeast of Baldwin Park city hall (lat. 34°06' N, long. 117°55'25" W; near W line sec. 10, T 1 S, R 10 W). Named on Baldwin Park (1953) 7.5' quadrangle.

Little Gibraltar [LOS ANGELES]: *promontory*, nearly 4 miles north-northeast of Mount Banning on the north side of Santa Catalina Island (lat. 33°25'20" N, long. 118°24'15" W). Named on Santa Catalina North (1950) 7.5' quadrangle.

Little Harbor [LOS ANGELES]: *embayment*, 2.5 miles west-northwest of Mount Banning on the west side of Santa Catalina Island (lat. 33°23' N, long. 118°28'30" W). Named on Santa Catalina North (1950) 7.5' quadrangle.

Little Island: see **Balboa Island** [ORANGE].

Little Jimmy Campground [LOS ANGELES]: *locality,* 2 miles north-northeast of Crystal Lake (lat. 34°20'50" N, long. 117°49'45" W); the place is 750 feet north of Little Jimmy Spring. Named on Crystal Lake (1958) 7.5' quadrangle.

Little Jimmy Spring [LOS ANGELES]: *spring,* 2 miles north-northeast of Crystal Lake (lat. 34°20'45" N, long. 117°49'40" W). Named on Crystal Lake (1958) 7.5' quadrangle. The feature first was called Gooseberry Spring for the gooseberry bushes around it; Jimmy Swinnerton, a well-known newspaper cartoonist, camped at the place in 1909 and painted a likeness of his cartoon character "Little Jimmy" on a tree stump—the spring took the name of the character, and the place was called Swinnerton Camp (Robinson, J.W., 1983, p. 109).

Little Joaquin Valley [ORANGE]: *valley,* 6.5 miles east of Santa Ana city hall (lat. 33°44'50" N, long. 117°45'15" W). Named on Orange (1964) and Tustin (1965) 7'5 quadrangles. The name is from the fancied resemblance of the feature to a miniature version of San Joaquin Valley of central California (Meadows, p. 78).

Little Lake [LOS ANGELES]: *intermittent lake,* 800 feet long, 4 miles southwest of present Whittier city hall (lat. 33°55'50" N, long. 118°04'55" W). Named on Whittier (1925) 6' quadrangle.

Littlelands: see **Tujunga** [LOS ANGELES] (2).

Little Las Flores Canyon [LOS ANGELES]: *canyon,* drained by a stream that flows 1.5 miles to Las Flores Canyon (2) 3 miles northeast of Malibu Point (lat. 34°03'25" N, long. 118°38'10" W; near NW cor. sec. 26, T 1 S, R 17 W). Named on Malibu Beach (1951) and Topanga (1952) 7.5' quadrangles.

Little Mermaids Canyon [LOS ANGELES]: *canyon,* drained by a stream that flows 2.25 miles to West Fork San Gabriel River 7.5 miles north of Azusa city hall (lat. 34°14'45" N, long. 117°54'20" W); the mouth of the canyon is 1650 feet west of the mouth of Big Mermaid Canyon. Named on Azusa (1953) and Waterman Mountain (1959) 7.5' quadrangles.

Little Mutau Creek [VENTURA]: *stream,* flows 5 miles to Mutau Creek 15 miles east of Reyes Peak (lat. 34°39'20" N, long. 119°01'30" W; sec. 32, T 7 N, R 20 W). Named on Lockwood Valley (1943) and McDonald Peak (1958) 7.5' quadrangles.

Little Nicholas Canyon: see **Willow Creek** [LOS ANGELES].

Little Nugget Placers: see **Gold Creek** [LOS ANGELES].

Little Rattlesnake Canyon: see **Shoemaker Canyon** [LOS ANGELES] (2).

Littlerock [LOS ANGELES]: *locality,* 27 miles north of Azusa (lat. 34°31'15" N, long. 117°58'50" W; sec. 13, T 5 N, R 11 W).

Named on Littlerock (1957) 7.5' quadrangle. Called Little Rock on Little Rock (1934) 6' quadrangle, but United States Board on Geographic Names (1983b, p. 5) rejected this form of the name. Postal authorities established Little Rock post office in 1893 and changed the name to Littlerock in 1894; the place also was known as Alpine Springs Colony and as Tierra Bonita (Salley, p. 123).

Little Rock Creek [LOS ANGELES]: *stream,* flows 14 miles to Little Rock Reservoir 6 miles north of Pacifico Mountain (lat. 34°28'10" N, long. 118°01'10" W; near S line sec. 34, T 5 N, R 11 W). Named on Crystal Lake (1958), Juniper Hills (1959), Pacifico Mountain (1959), and Waterman Mountain (1959) 7.5' quadrangles. On Mount Emma (1940) 6' quadrangle, the name "Little Rock Creek" applies both to present Little Rock Creek and to present Little Rock Wash, which is below Little Rock Reservoir. South Fork enters from the south 7.25 miles west-southwest of Valyermo; it is 5.5 miles long and is named on Chilao Flat (1959), Juniper Hills (1959), and Waterman Mountain (1959) 7.5' quadrangles.

Little Rock Reservoir [LOS ANGELES]: *lake,* 1.25 miles long, behind a dam 7 miles north of Pacifico Mountain (lat. 34°29'10" N, long. 118°01'20" W; near S line sec. 27, T 5 N, R 11 W); the dam is on Little Rock Creek. Named on Pacifico Mountain (1959) 7.5' quadrangle.

Little Rock Station [LOS ANGELES]: *locality,* nearly 8 miles north of Pacifico Mountain (lat. 34°29'45" N, long. 118°01'35" W; at W line sec. 27, T 5 N, R 11 W); the place is along Little Rock Wash. Named on Pacifico Mountain (1959) 7.5' quadrangle.

Little Rock Wash [LOS ANGELES]: *stream and dry wash,* extends for 19 miles to end 6.5 miles east of Lancaster (lat. 34°42'15" N, long. 118°01'30" W; at N line sec. 15, T 7 N, R 11 W); the feature heads at Little Rock Reservoir. Named on Lancaster East (1958), Littlerock (1957), Pacifico Mountain (1959), and Palmdale (1958) 7.5' quadrangles. Called Little Rock Cr. on Elizabeth Lake (1917) 30' quadrangle.

Little Santa Anita Canyon [LOS ANGELES]: *canyon,* 3.25 miles long, the mouth is 3.5 miles south-southeast of Mount Wilson (1) (lat. 34°10'30" N, long. 118°02'30" W; sec. 18, T 1 N, R 11 W); the mouth of the canyon is about 1.5 miles west of the mouth of Santa Anita Canyon. Named on Mount Wilson (1953) 7.5' quadrangle. The Carter brothers started a resort in 1906 called Carter's Camp that was located just below the mouth of Little Santa Anita Canyon; the place was sold in 1913, subdivided, and renamed Sierra Madre Canyon Park (Robinson, J.W., 1977, p. 128). A place called both Quarterway House and The Old Trading Post was situated 2 miles up the canyon from Carter's Camp (Robinson, J.W., 1977, p. 130).

Little Sespe Creek [VENTURA]: *stream,* flows 2 miles to Sespe Creek 3.5 miles north-northwest of Fillmore (lat. 34°27'05" N, long. 118°55'25" W; at S line sec. 1, T 4 N, R 20 W). Named on Fillmore (1951) 7.5' quadrangle.

Little Simi Valley [VENTURA]: *valley,* at and near Moorpark (lat. 34°16'30" N, long. 118°53'45" W); the feature is along Arroyo Simi. Named on Moorpark (1951) and Simi (1951) 7.5' quadrangles.

Little Springs Canyon [LOS ANGELES]: *canyon,* drained by a stream that flows nearly 4 miles to the sea 2.5 miles west-northwest of Mount Banning on Santa Catalina Island (lat. 33°23'10" N, long. 118°28'25" W); the feature is west of Big Springs Canyon. Named on Santa Catalina North (1950) 7.5' quadrangle.

Little Sycamore Canyon [VENTURA]: *canyon,* drained by a stream that flows nearly 5 miles to the sea 5 miles south-southwest of the mouth of Big Sycamore Canyon (lat. 34°03'10" N, long. 118°57'45" W; sec. 27, T 1 S, R 20 W). Named on Triumfo Pass (1950) 7.5' quadrangle.

Little Tahunga Canyon: see **Little Tujunga Canyon** [LOS ANGELES].

Little Trough Canyon [LOS ANGELES]: *canyon,* 0.5 mile long, opens into Lobo Canyon (1) 8 miles north of Point Dume (lat. 34°07'05" N, long. 118°48'55" W; near SE cor. sec. 36, T 1 N, R 19 W); the mouth of the canyon is 1700 feet west of the mouth of Trough Canyon (2). Named on Point Dume (1951) 7.5' quadrangle.

Little Tujunga Canyon [LOS ANGELES]: *canyon,* drained by a stream that flows 5.5 miles to lowlands 4 miles west-northwest of downtown Sunland (lat. 34°17' N, long. 118°22'10" W; sec. 5, T 2 N, R 14 W). Named on Sunland (1953) 7.5' quadrangle. United States Board on Geographic Names (1933, p. 467) rejected the form "Little Tahunga Canyon" for the name, and (1975, p. 5) approved the name "Little Tujunga Creek" for the stream in the canyon.

Little Tujunga Creek: see **Little Tujunga Canyon** [LOS ANGELES].

Live Oak Acres [VENTURA]: *settlement,* 4.5 miles southwest of the town of Ojai along Ventura River (lat. 34°24'30" N, long. 119°18'25" W). Named on Matilija (1952) 7.5' quadrangle.

Live Oak Campground [LOS ANGELES]: *locality,* 4 miles southeast of Solemint in Sand Canyon (2) (lat. 34°22'45" N, long. 118°24'10" W; sec. 1, T 3 N, R 15 W). Named on Mint Canyon (1960) 7.5' quadrangle.

Live Oak Canyon [LOS ANGELES]: *canyon,* 3 miles long, opens into lowlands 4.5 miles north of Pomona city hall (lat. 34°07'30" N,

long. 117°44'35" W; sec. 32, T 1 N, R 8 W). Named on Mount Baldy (1954) 7.5' quadrangle. Cucamonga (1903) 15' quadrangle has the name "Liveoak Creek" for the stream in the canyon.

Live Oak Canyon [ORANGE]: *canyon,* drained by a stream that flows nearly 3 miles to lowlands along Arroyo Trabuco 5.5 miles southwest of Santiago Peak (lat. 33°39'10" N, long. 117°35'55" W; sec. 15, T 6 S, R 7 W). Named on Santiago Peak (1954) 7.5' quadrangle.

Liveoak Creek: see **Live Oak Canyon** [LOS ANGELES]; **Live Oak Wash** [LOS ANGELES].

Live Oak Spring Canyon: see **Sand Canyon** [LOS ANGELES] (2).

Live Oak Wash [LOS ANGELES]: *stream,* flows 3.5 miles to Puddingstone Reservoir 3.5 miles northwest of Pomona city hall (lat. 34°05'40" N, long. 117°47'15" W). Named on Ontario (1954) and San Dimas (1954) 7.5' quadrangles. Called Liveoak Creek on Cucamonga (1903) 15' quadrangle.

Llano [LOS ANGELES]: *locality,* 10 miles east of Littlerock (lat. 34° 30'20" N, long. 117°49' W; on E line sec. 21, T 5 N, R 9 W). Named on Lovejoy Buttes (1957) 7.5' quadrangle. Llano (1934) 6' quadrangle shows Llano post office located 1 mile farther west (sec. 21, T 5 N, R 9 W). Postal authorities established Llano post office in 1890, discontinued it in 1900, and reestablished it in 1915 (Frickstad, p. 76). The name recalls a socialistic colony called Llano del Rio that operated at the place from 1914 until 1918 (Hoover, Rensch, and Rensch, p. 168).

Llano del Rio: see **Llano** [LOS ANGELES].

Loara: see **West Anaheim** [ORANGE].

Lobe Canyon: see **Lobo Canyon** [LOS ANGELES] (1).

Lobo: see **Hansen** [ORANGE].

Lobo Canyon [LOS ANGELES]:

(1) *canyon,* drained by a stream that flows 3.25 miles to Triunfo Canyon 8.5 miles north of Point Dume (lat. 34°07'25" N, long. 118°47'35" W; sec. 32, T 1 N, R 18 W). Named on Point Dume (1951) 7.5' quadrangle Called Lobe Canyon on Camulos (1903) 30' quadrangle. Los Angeles County (1935) map shows a feature called Bodie Peak located near the head of the canyon (sec. 2, T 1 S, R 19 W).

(2) *canyon,* drained by a stream that flows 1.5 miles to Cogswell Reservoir 9 miles northnorthwest of Azusa city hall (lat. 34°14'30" N, long. 117°59'15" W; sec. 24, T 2 N, R 11 W). Named on Azusa (1953) and Waterman Mountain (1959) 7.5' quadrangles.

Lobster Bay [LOS ANGELES]: *embayment,* 3.25 miles southeast of Silver Peak on the south side of Santa Catalina Island (lat. 33°25'45" N, long. 118°31'30" W). Named on Santa Catalina West (1943) 7.5' quadrangle.

Lobster Point [LOS ANGELES]: *promontory,* 4 miles southeast of Silver Peak on the south side of Santa Catalina Island (lat. 33°25'20" N, long. 118°30'45" W); the feature is east of Lobster Bay. Named on Santa Catalina West (1943) 7.5' quadrangle.

Lockwood Creek [VENTURA]: *stream,* flows 11 miles to Piru Creek 5.5 miles northwest of McDonald Peak (lat. 34°41'55" N, long. 118°59'50" W; near E line sec. 16, T 7 N, R 20 W); the stream goes through Lockwood Valley. Named on Lockwood Valley (1943), McDonald Peak (1958), and San Guillermo (1943) 7.5' quadrangles. North Fork enters in Lockwood; it is 8.5 miles long and is named on Lockwood Valley (1943) and Sawmill Mountain (1943) 7.5' quadrangles. Middle Fork enters North Fork in Lockwood Valley; it is 7 miles long and is named on Cuddy Valley (1943), Lockwood Valley (1943), and Sawmill Mountain (1943) 7.5' quadrangles.

Lockwood Flat [VENTURA]: *valley,* 5.5 miles northwest of McDonald Peak along Piru Creek (lat. 34°42' N, long. 118°59'45" W; on E line sec. 16, T 7 N, R 20 W); the feature is at the mouth of Lockwood Creek. Named on McDonald Peak (1958) 7.5' quadrangle. A town called Lexington was laid out at the place in 1887 during mining excitement (Outland, 1969, p. 54).

Lockwood Valley [VENTURA]: *valley,* 13 miles northeast of Reyes Peak (lat. 34°44'15" N, long. 119°05'30" W); the feature is along Lockwood Creek. Named on Cuddy Valley (1943), Lockwood Valley (1943), San Guillermo (1943), and Sawmill Mountain (1943) 7.5' quadrangles.

Lodgepole Picnic Area [LOS ANGELES]: *locality,* 4.25 miles northeast of Crystal Lake (lat. 34°21'40" N, long. 117°47'30" W; sec. 11, T 3 N, R 9 W). Named on Crystal Lake (1958) 7.5' quadrangle.

Lodi Canyon [LOS ANGELES]: *canyon,* drained by a stream that flows 2 miles to San Dimas Canyon 5.25 miles east of Glendora city hall (lat. 34°09'05" N, long. 117°46'20" W; near S line sec. 24, T 1 N, R 9 W). Named on Glendora (1953) 7.5' quadrangle.

Loftus [ORANGE]: *locality,* 3.25 miles west-northwest of Yorba Linda along Pacific Electric Railroad (lat. 33°54'50" N, long. 117°51'45" W). Named on Olinda (1935) 7.5' quadrangle. The name commemorates William Loftus, an oil man (Meadows, p. 79).

Loftus Canyon [VENTURA]: *canyon,* drained by a stream that flows 0.5 mile to the valley of Santa Clara River 3.25 miles east of Santa Paula (lat. 34°21'05" N, long. 119°00' W; near S line sec. 8, T 3 N, R 20 W). Named on Santa Paula (1951) 7.5' quadrangle.

Log Cabin Campground [VENTURA]: *locality,* 5.5 miles southeast of Cobblestone Mountain along Agua Blanca Creek (lat. 34°32'55" N, long. 118°48'15" W; sec. 6, T 5 N, R 18

W). Named on Cobblestone Mountain (1958) 7.5' quadrangle.

Lomarias de la Costa: see **San Joaquin Hills** [ORANGE].

Loma Ridge [ORANGE]: *ridge,* generally northwest-trending, 6.5 miles long, center about 8 miles north of El Toro (lat. 33°44'45" N, long. 117°42'30" W); the place is on Lomas de Santiago grant. Named on Black Star Canyon (1967), El Toro (1968), and Orange (1964) 7.5' quadrangles.

Lomas de Santiago [ORANGE]: *land grant,* east of Tustin and north of El Toro. Named on Black Star Canyon (1950), El Toro (1950), Orange (1950), Prado Dam (1950), and Tustin (1950) 7.5' quadrangles. Teodosio Yorba received the land in 1846 and claimed 47,227 acres patented in 1868 (Cowan, p. 96).

Loma Verde [LOS ANGELES]: *peak,* 11.5 miles northwest of Newhall (lat. 34°29'45" N, long. 118°40'05" W; on S line sec. 21, T 5 N, R 17 W). Named on Val Verde (1952) 7.5' quadrangle. Called Loma Verde Pk. on Los Angeles County (1935) map.

Loma Verde Peak: see **Loma Verde** [LOS ANGELES].

Loma Vista: see **Howard Summit** [LOS ANGELES].

Lomita [LOS ANGELES]: *town,* 3.5 miles south-southeast of Torrance city hall (lat. 33°47'30" N, long. 118°19' W). Named on Torrance (1964) 7.5' quadrangle. Postal authorities established Lomita post office in 1910 (Frickstad, p. 76), and the town incorporated in 1964. W.I. Hollingsworth Company of Los Angeles founded and named the community in 1907: the place first was planned as a Dunker colony (Hanna, p. 175).

Lone Hill [LOS ANGELES]: *locality,* 5.5 miles northwest of Pomona city hall along Southern Pacific Railroad (lat. 34°06'10" N, long. 117°49'30" W). Named on San Dimas (1966) 7.5' quadrangle. On Glendora (1939) 6' quadrangle, the name "San Dimas Junction" applies to a place situated along the railroad at or near present Lone Hill.

Lone Oak Canyon [VENTURA]: *canyon,* drained by a stream that flows 1 mile to Bus Canyon 5.25 miles northeast of Thousand Oaks (lat. 34°13'10" N, long. 118°45'50" W; sec. 33, T 2 N, R 18 W). Named on Calabasas (1952) and Thousand Oaks (1952) 7.5' quadrangles.

Lone Point: see **Long Point** [LOS ANGELES] (2).

Lonetree Canyon [LOS ANGELES]: *canyon,* drained by a stream that flows 1.5 miles to Pacoima Canyon 8 miles north-northeast of Sunland (lat. 34°22'20" N, long. 118°16'40" W). Named on Agua Dulce (1960) and Sunland (1953) 7.5' quadrangles. Called Long Tree Canyon on Los Angeles County (1935) map.

Long Beach [LOS ANGELES]: *city,* 19 miles

south of Los Angeles city hall (lat. 33°46'10" N, long. 118°11'35" W). Named on Long Beach (1949), Los Alamitos (1950), Seal Beach (1950), and South Gate (1952) 7.5' quadrangles. Postal authorities established Long Beach post office in 1885, changed the name to Longbeach in 1895, and changed it back to Long Beach in 1914 (Salley, p. 125). The city incorporated in 1897. William E. Willmore founded the community in 1882 and called it Willmore City (Gudde, 1949, p. 193). Postal authorities established Burnett post office 3 miles north of Long Beach post office in 1897 and discontinued it in 1929; the name was for the developer of a farming community at the site (Salley, p. 30). They established Roosevelt post office in 1937 and discontinued it in 1942; it was named for Franklin D. Roosevelt and was in Long Beach at Pier G, Navy Landing Building (Salley, p. 188).

Long Beach: see **North Long Beach** [LOS ANGELES].

Long Beach Channel [LOS ANGELES]: *channel*, leads to Long Beach Middle Harbor 2 miles southwest of Long Beach city hall (lat. 33°44'45" N, long. 118°12'55" W). Named on Long Beach (1964) 7.5' quadrangle.

Long Beach Harbor [LOS ANGELES]: *water feature*, 2 miles southwest of Long Beach city hall (lat. 33°45' N, long. 118°13'15" W). Named on Long Beach (1949) 7.5' quadrangle. Called Long Beach Middle Harbor on Long Beach (1964) 7.5' quadrangle, which shows Long Beach Outer Harbor seaward of this feature, and Long Beach Inner Harbor farther inland.

Long Buttes [LOS ANGELES]: *ridge*, northnortheast-trending, 3 miles long, center 17 miles north-northeast of Little Rock near Hi Vista (lat. 34°43' N, long. 117°48'45" W). Named on Alpine Butte (1945) 15' quadrangle.

Long Canyon [LOS ANGELES]:
(1) *canyon*, drained by a stream that flows 2 miles to Santa Clara River 9 miles east of Solemint (lat. 34°26'25" N, long. 118°17'50" W; sec. 12, T 4 N, R 14 W). Named on Agua Dulce (1960) 7.5' quadrangle.
(2) *canyon*, drained by a stream that flows 1 mile to Arroyo Seco 5.5 miles south-south-east of Condor Peak (lat. 34°15'10" N, long. 118°10'20" W). Named on Condor Peak (1959) 7.5' quadrangle. On Tujunga (1900) 15' quadrangle, the name "Long Canyon" applies to the upper part of the canyon of present Arroyo Seco.

Long Canyon [ORANGE]: *canyon*, drained by a stream that flows nearly 3 miles to Riverside County 5.25 miles south-southeast of Trabuco Peak (lat. 33°38'10" N, long. 117°25'50" W). Named on Alberhill (1954) 7.5' quadrangle.

Long Canyon [VENTURA]:
(1) *canyon*, drained by a stream that flows 4

miles to lowlands 4 miles west of Moorpark (lat. 34°17'40" N, long. 118°57' W). Named on Moorpark (1951) 7.5' quadrangle.
(2) *canyon*, drained by a stream that flows 2.25 miles to the valley of Santa Clara River nearly 2 miles west-northwest of Saticoy (lat. 34°17'50" N, long. 119°10'30" W). Named on Saticoy (1951) 7.5' quadrangle.
(3) *canyon*, drained by a stream that flows 5 miles to Apache Canyon 11 miles north-north-west of Reyes Peak (lat. 34°47' N, long. 119°19'45" W; at W line sec. 16, T 8 N, R 23 W). Named on Apache Canyon (1943) 7.5' quadrangle.
(4) *canyon*, drained by a stream that flows 1.5 miles to Oak Canyon (2) 5.5 miles north-northeast of Thousand Oaks (lat. 34° 14'10" N, long. 118°47' W; at S line sec. 20, T 2 N, R 18 W). Named on Thousand Oaks (1952) 7.5' quadrangle.

Long Canyon: see **Arroyo Seco** [LOS ANGELES]; **North Long Canyon** [LOS ANGELES]; **South Long Canyon** [LOS ANGELES].

Long Dave Canyon [VENTURA]: *canyon*, drained by a stream that flows 2.5 miles to Lockwood Creek 6 miles east-northeast of Reyes Peak (lat. 34°42'50" N, long. 119°00'45" W; near W line sec. 9, T 7 N, R 20 W). Named on Lockwood Valley (1943) and McDonald Peak (1958) 7.5' quadrangles.

Long Dave Valley [VENTURA]: *valley*, 8 miles north-northwest of McDonald Peak (lat. 34°44'30" N, long. 118°59'15" W); the valley extends north-northeast from the upper end of Long Dave Canyon. Named on McDonald Peak (1958) 7.5' quadrangle.

Long Grade Canyon [VENTURA]: *canyon*, drained by a stream that flows 3.25 miles to lowlands 3.5 miles south of Camarillo (lat. 34° 09'55" N, long. 119°02'30" W). Named on Camarillo (1950) and Newbury Park (1951) 7.5' quadrangles.

Long Point [LOS ANGELES]:
(1) *promontory*, 7.25 miles south of Redondo Beach city hall along the coast (lat. 33°44'10" N, long. 118°23'50" W). Named on Redondo Beach (1951) 7.5' quadrangle.
(2) *promontory*, 5 miles north-northwest of Avalon on the northeast side of Santa Catalina Island (lat. 33°24'20" N, long. 118°21'55" W). Named on Santa Catalina East (1950) 7.5' quadrangle. Preston (1890b, map following p. 278) called the feature Lone Pt., but United States Board on Geographic Names (1936b, p. 28) rejected this name for the feature.

Long Tree Canyon: see **Lonetree Canyon** [LOS ANGELES].

Long Valley [VENTURA]: *valley*, 2.5 miles west-southwest of downtown Ojai at present Mira Monte (lat. 34°25'45" N, long. 119°16'55" W). Named on Ventura (1904) 15' quadrangle.

Longview [LOS ANGELES]: *locality*, 4 miles

northwest of Valyermo (lat. 34°29'40" N long. 117°53'30" W; sec. 26, T 5 N, R 10 W). Named on Valyermo (1940) 6' quadrangle.

Lookout Gates [LOS ANGELES]: *locality*, 1.5 miles northeast of Chatsworth (lat. 34°16'20" N, long. 118°35'10" W; sec. 8, T 2 N, R 16 W). Named on Oat Mountain (1952) 7.5' quadrangle.

Lookout Mountain [LOS ANGELES]: *peak*, 14 miles north-northeast of Pomona city hall (lat. 34°14'55" N, long. 117°40'25" W). Altitude 6812 feet. Named on Mount Baldy (1954) 7.5' quadrangle. A fire lookout functioned on the peak from 1915 until 1927 (Robinson, J.W., 1983, p. 172).

Lookout Point [LOS ANGELES]: *relief feature*, 2 miles south-southeast of Mount Wilson (1) (lat. 34°11'50" N, long. 118°02'50" W; near E line sec. 5, T 1 N, R 11 W). Named on Mount Wilson (1953) 7.5' quadrangle.

Loop Canyon [LOS ANGELES]: *canyon*, nearly 2 miles long, opens into lowlands 3.5 miles north-northeast of downtown San Fernando (lat. 34°19'35" N, long. 118°24'40" W; near W line sec. 24, T 3 N, R 15 W). Named on San Fernando (1953) 7.5' quadrangle.

Lopez: see **Palmdale** [LOS ANGELES].

Lopez Canyon [LOS ANGELES]: *canyon*, 3.5 miles long, opens into lowlands 2 miles east of downtown San Fernando (lat. 34°17'10" N, long. 118°24'15" W). Named on San Fernando (1953) 7.5' quadrangle.

Lopez Station: see **San Fernando** [LOS ANGELES].

Lordsburg: see **La Verne** [LOS ANGELES].

Lorenzo Beach [LOS ANGELES]: *beach*, 1 mile north of Silver Peak (lat. 33°28'25" N, long. 118°33'50" W). Named on Santa Catalina West (1943) 7.5' quadrangle.

Losadena: see **Camp Losadena**, under **Switzer Camp** [LOS ANGELES].

Los Alamitos [LOS ANGELES-ORANGE]: *land grant*, extends from Long Beach [LOS ANGELES] to the town of Los Alamitos [OR-ANGE]. Named on Anaheim (1950), Long Beach (1949), Los Alamitos (1950), and Seal Beach (1950) 7.5' quadrangles. Juan Jose Nieto received 6 leagues in 1834 and Abel Stearns claimed 28,027 acres patented in 1874 (Cowan, p. 14).

Los Alamitos [ORANGE]: *town*, 6 miles southwest of Buena Park civic center (lat. 33°48'15" N, long. 118°04'15" W); the town is on Los Alamitos grant. Postal authorities established Los Alamitos post office in 1897 (Frickstad, p. 117), and the town incorporated in 1960. The Clark brothers purchased 8000 acres of Los Alamitos grant in 1896 and built a sugar factory there; the town began as a village that grew around the factory (Meadows, p. 79).

Los Alamitos Armed Forces Reserve Center: see **Los Alamitos Naval Air Station** [OR-ANGE].

Los Alamitos Junction [ORANGE]: *locality*, 4 miles south of Buena Park along Southern Pacific Railroad (lat. 33°48'25" N, long. 117° 59'45" W; near E line sec. 23, T 4 S, R 11 W). Named on Anaheim (1965) 7.5' quadrangle.

Los Alamitos Naval Air Station [ORANGE]: *military installation*, 6 miles south-southwest of Buena Park civic center (lat. 33°47'40" N, long. 118°03'15" W); the place is south of the town of Los Alamitos on Los Alamitos grant. Named on Los Alamitos (1964) 7.5' quadrangle. Called Los Alamitos Armed Forces Reserve Center on Los Alamitos (1964, photorevised 1981) 7.5' quadrangle.

Los Alisos Canyon [LOS ANGELES]: *canyon*, drained by a stream that flows nearly 3 miles to the sea 6 miles west-northwest of Point Dume (lat. 34°02'25" N, long. 118°53'50" W). Named on Triunfo Pass (1950) 7.5' quadrangle. Called Nicolas Canyon on Triunfo Pass (1921) 15' quadrangle, and called Nicholas Canyon on Camulos (1903) 30' quadrangle. United States Board on Geographic Names (1943, p. 9) rejected the name "Nicholas Canyon" for the feature.

Los Altos [LOS ANGELES]: *district*, 2.25 miles east-northeast of Long Beach city hall (lat. 33°47'35" N, long. 118°07'35" W). Named on Long Beach (1964) and Los Alamitos (1964) 7.5' quadrangles. Called Los Altos Terrace on Long Beach (1949) and Los Alamitos (1950) 7.5' quadrangles.

Los Altos Terrace: see **Los Altos** [LOS ANGELES].

Los Amigos: see **Poor Farm Station** [LOS ANGELES].

Los Angeles [LOS ANGELES]: *city*, occupies much of the ground from the west end of San Gabriel Mountains to the sea at San Pedro (city hall near lat. 34°03'15" N, long. 118°14'30" W). Named on Long Beach (1957) and Los Angeles (1975) 1°x 2° quadrangles. Called Pueblo de Los Angeles on Parke's (1854-1855) map. Postal authorities established Los Angeles post office in 1850 (Frickstad, p. 76), and the city incorporated the same year. The pueblo that became the city was established in 1781 with the name "El Pueblo de Nuestra Señora la Reina de los Angeles de la Porciuncula" (Hoover, Rensch, and Rensch, p. 149). An elevation called Fort Hill, located less than 1000 feet north of present Los Angeles city hall (Dumke *in* Evans, p. 190) was used as a base during the first American occupation of Los Angeles in 1846; Lieutenant Davidson built Fort Moore there in 1847 and named it to honor Captain Benjamin D. Moore, who was killed in battle at San Pasqual in 1846 (Frazer, p. 28).

Los Angeles: see **East Los Angeles** [LOS ANGELES]; **North Los Angeles**, under **Northridge** [LOS ANGELES]; **Port Los Angeles** [LOS ANGELES]; **South Los Angeles** [LOS ANGELES]; **West Los Angeles** [LOS ANGELES].

Los Angeles Harbor [LOS ANGELES]: *water feature,* 6 miles southwest of Long Beach city hall at the west end of San Pedro Bay. Named on Long Beach (1957) 1°x 2° quadrangle. San Pedro (1964) 7.5' quadrangle shows Los Angeles Outer Harbor east of Point Fermin. United States Coast and Geodetic Survey (p. 97) described Los Angeles Harbor as including the districts of San Pedro and Wilmington, and a major part of Terminal Island.

Los Angeles Lake [LOS ANGELES]: *lake,* 1350 feet long, 7 miles north-northwest of Manhattan Beach city hall (lat. 33°58'50" N, long. 118°27'20" W). Named on Venice (1950) 7.5' quadrangle.

Los Angeles River [LOS ANGELES]: *stream,* flows 50 miles to the sea less than 1 mile west-southwest of Long Beach city hall (lat. 33°45'50" N, long. 118°12'15" W). Named on Burbank (1953), Canoga Park (1952), Hollywood (1953), Long Beach (1949), Los Angeles (1953), South Gate (1952), and Van Nuys (1953) 7.5' quadrangles. Called R. de los Angeles on Eddy's (1854) map. Marcou (p. 158) called it Rio de los Angeles, or Rio de Porciuncula. Members of the Portola expedition camped along the stream in 1769 and gave it the name "Nuestra Señora de los Angeles de Porciuncula" on the day after the feast day of that saint—the cradle of the Franciscan order is the Porciuncula chapel in the basilica of Our Lady of the Angels near Assisi, Italy (Gudde, 1949, p. 194). Los Angeles River reached the sea just north of present Playa del Rey before the flood of 1825 diverted the water to San Gabriel River, which emptied into San Pedro Bay (Poland and others, p. 35). But before 1825, water of Los Angeles River seldom reached the sea at all, for it spread over lowlands where it formed lakes, ponds, and marshes in part of now highly developed Los Angels (Warner, Hayes, and Widney, p. 17-18). United States Board on Geographic Names (1978a, p. 7) approved the name "Queensway Bay" for the place at the present mouth of Los Angeles River in Long Beach (lat. 33°45'30" N, long. 118°11'45" W) where the former British liner *Queen Mary* is permanently anchored.

Los Bueyos Canyon: see **Weir Canyon** [ORANGE].

Los Casitos: see **Las Casetas** [LOS ANGELES].

Los Cerritos [LOS ANGELES]:
(1) *land grant,* north of Long Beach between Los Angeles River and San Gabriel River. Named on Long Beach (1949), Los Alamitos (1950), South Gate (1952) and Whittier (1951) 7.5' quadrangles. Manuela Nieto received 5 leagues in 1834; John Temple claimed 27,054 acres patented in 1867 (Cowan, p. 26).
(2) *locality,* 4 miles north of present Long Beach city hall along Pacific Electric Railroad (lat. 33°49'40" N, long. 118°12' W); the

place is on Los Cerritos grant. Named on Clearwater (1925) 6' quadrangle.

Los Cerritos: see **San Miguel** [VENTURA]; **Signal Hill** [LOS ANGELES] (1).

Los Coyotes [LOS ANGELES-ORANGE]: *land grant,* at and around Buena Park [ORANGE]. Named on Anaheim (1950), La Habra (1952), Los Alamitos (1950), and Whittier (1949) 7.5' quadrangles. Juan Jose Nieto received 10 leagues in 1834; Andres Pico and others claimed 48,806 acres patented in 1875 (Cowan, p. 30-31).

Los Felis [LOS ANGELES]: *land grant,* northeast of Hollywood at the east end of Santa Monica Mountains. Named on Burbank (1953), Hollywood (1953), and Los Angeles (1953) 7.5' quadrangles. Vincente Felix received 1.5 leagues in 1802 and Juan Diego claimed 6647 acres patented in 1871 (Cowan, p. 36). According to Perez (p. 67), Maria Berdugo was the grantee in 1843 and the patentee in 1871.

Los Nietos [LOS ANGELES]: *town,* 2.25 miles west-southwest of present Whittier city hall (lat. 33°57'40" N, long. 118°04'10" W). Named on Whittier (1949) 7.5' quadrangle. Postal authorities established Los Nietos post office in 1867, discontinued it in 1876, reestablished it in 1891, discontinued it in 1904, and reestablished it in 1924 (Salley, p. 128). The name recalls the five heirs of Manuel Nieto (*los Nietos* in Spanish), who were granted again the lands that the elder Nieto got in 1784 (Gudde, 1949, p. 195).

Los Nietos Junction [LOS ANGELES]: *locality,* 2.25 miles west-southwest of Whittier city hall along Southern Pacific Railroad (lat. 33°57'35" N, long. 118°04'10" W); the place is at the south edge of Los Nietos. Named on Whittier (1965) 7.5' quadrangle.

Los Nietos Station [LOS ANGELES]: *locality,* 2.5 miles west-southwest of Whittier city hall along Southern Pacific Railroad (lat. 33° 57'35" N, long. 118°04'30" W). Named on Whittier (1965) 7.5' quadrangle.

Los Nogales [LOS ANGELES]: *land grant,* west-southwest of downtown Pomona. Named on San Dimas (1954) 7.5' quadrangle. Jose de la Cruz Linares received 1 league in 1840; M. de Jesus Garcia and others claimed 1004 acres patented in 1882 (Cowan, p. 52-53).

Los Osos Valley: see **Oso Creek** [ORANGE].

Los Palos Colorados: see **Los Palos Verdes** [LOS ANGELES].

Los Palos Verdes [LOS ANGELES]: *land grant,* at Palos Verdes Hills. Named on Redondo Beach (1951), San Pedro (1964), and Torrance (1964) 7.5' quadrangles. Jose L. Sepulveda and others received the land in 1827 and 1846; they claimed 31,629 acres patented in 1880 (Cowan, p. 57; Cowan gave the alternate name "Los Palos Colorados" for the grant). The name is from Cañada de los Palos Verdes, the early name for the place later called Bixby

Slough—*Cañada de los Palos Verdes* means "Valley of Green Trees" in Spanish (Gudde, 1949, p. 251). Postal authorities established Palos Verdes post office on the grant 3.5 miles northwest of Wilmington post office in 1880 and discontinued it the same year (Salley, p. 166).

Los Patos [ORANGE]: *locality*, 5 miles northwest of Huntington Beach civic center along Pacific Electric Railroad (lat. 33°42'40" N, long. 118°03'50" W). Named on Seal Beach (1950) 7.5' quadrangle.

Los Pinetos Canyon [LOS ANGELES]: *canyon*, drained by a stream that flows 1.5 miles to Placerita Canyon nearly 3 miles south-southeast of Solemint (lat. 34°22'35" N, long. 118°26'35" W; sec. 3, T 3 N, R 15 W). Named on San Fernando (1953) 7.5' quadrangle.

Los Pinetos Spring [LOS ANGELES]: *spring*, 5.25 miles north of downtown San Fernando (lat. 34°21'30" N, long. 118°26'50" W; near W line sec. 10, T 3 N, R 15 W); the spring is near the head of Los Pinetos Canyon. Named on San Fernando (1966) 7.5' quadrangle.

Los Pinos Peak [ORANGE]: *peak*, 2.5 miles south of Trabuco Peak (lat. 33°39'35" N, long. 117°28'15" W; at N line sec. 11, T 6 S, R 6 W). Altitude 4510 feet. Named on Alberhill (1954) 7.5' quadrangle.

Los Pinos Potrero: see **Los Pinos Spring** [ORANGE].

Los Pinos Spring [ORANGE]: *spring*, 3.25 miles south-southeast of Trabuco Peak (lat. 33°39'35" N, long. 117°27'05" W; near E line sec. 12, T 6 S, R 6 W); the place is 1 mile east-southeast of Los Pinos Peak near the head of Hot Spring Canyon. Named on Alberhill (1954) 7.5' quadrangle. Meadows (p. 25) called the feature Bear Spring, but (p. 80) noted that an open grassy area at the head of Hot Spring Canyon is called Los Pinos Potrero.

Los Pitas: see **Point Los Pitas**, under **Pitas Point** [VENTURA].

Los Sauces Creek [VENTURA]: *stream*, flows 4.5 miles to the sea 3 miles northwest of Pitas Point (lat. 34°20'55" N, long. 119°25'20" W; at S line sec. 8, T 3 N, R 24 W). Named on Pitas Point (1950) and White Ledge Peak (1952) 7.5' quadrangles. Called Arroyo Susal on Peckham's (1866) map.

Lost Canyon [LOS ANGELES]: *canyon*, drained by a stream that flows nearly 2 miles to North Fork San Gabriel River 3 miles south of Crystal Lake (lat. 34°16'20" N, long. 117°50'40" W). Named on Crystal Lake (1958) 7.5' quadrangle.

Lost Canyon: see **Oak Spring Canyon** [LOS ANGELES] (1).

Lost Point [LOS ANGELES]: *promontory*, 13 miles south-southeast of Northwest Harbor on the west side of San Clemente Island (lat. 32°51'10" N, long. 118°30' W). Named on San Clemente Island Central (1943) 7.5' quadrangle.

Los Trancos Canyon [ORANGE]: *canyon*, drained by a stream that flows nearly 3 miles to the sea 4 miles west-northwest of Laguna Beach city hall (lat. 33°34'25" N, long. 117°50'05" W). Named on Laguna Beach (1965) 7.5' quadrangle. On Santa Ana (1942) 15' quadrangle, present Muddy Canyon is called Los Trancos Canyon. The name is from bars that kept trespassers out of the canyon—*los trancos* means "the bars" in Spanish (Meadows, p. 97).

Lost Trough Canyon [ORANGE]: *canyon*, drained by a stream that flows nearly 1.5 miles to Bee Canyon (1) 2.25 miles south-southeast of San Juan Hill (lat. 33°53' N, long. 117°43'20" W). Named on Prado Dam (1967) 7.5' quadrangle.

Lost Valley [LOS ANGELES]: *valley*, 2.25 miles west-southwest of the village of Leona Valley (lat. 34°36'20" N, long. 118°19'20" W; at E line sec. 14, T 6 N, R 14 W). Named on Sleepy Valley (1958) 7.5' quadrangle.

Lost Woman Canyon [ORANGE]: *canyon*, drained by a stream that flows 1.5 miles to Silverado Canyon 4 miles southeast of Pleasants Peak (lat. 33°45'10" N, long. 117°33'30" W; sec. 12, T 5 S, R 7 W). Named on Corona South (1967) and Santiago Peak (1954) 7.5' quadrangles.

Louies Cabin [LOS ANGELES]: *locality*, 3.5 miles west of Waterman Mountain (lat. 34°19'50" N, long. 117°59'40" W; near E line sec. 23, T 3 N, R 11 W). Named on Waterman Mountain (1959) 7.5' quadrangle.

Lovejoy Buttes [LOS ANGELES]: *range*, 10 miles northeast of Littlerock (lat. 34°36'15" N, long. 117°50'30" W). Named on Lovejoy Buttes (1957) 7.5' quadrangle. On Los Angeles County (1935) map, the name "Lovejoy Butte" applies to a high point in the range (sec. 20, T 6 N, R 10 W).

Lovejoy Lake [LOS ANGELES]: *lake*, 100 feet long, 10 miles northeast of Littlerock (lat. 34°36'20" N, long. 117°49'45" W); the lake is at Lovejoy Springs. Named on Alpine Butte (1945) 15' quadrangle.

Lovejoy Springs [LOS ANGELES]: *spring*, 10 miles northeast of Littlerock (lat. 34°40'20" N, long. 117°49'40" W; sec. 16, T 6 N, R 9 W); the feature is at Lovejoy Buttes. Named on Lovejoy Buttes (1957) 7.5' quadrangle. Los Angeles County (1935) map has the singular form "Lovejoy Spring" for the name. Johnson (p. 52) gave the alternate name "Croswell Springs" for the feature.

Lovell Canyon [LOS ANGELES]: *canyon*, drained by a stream that flows 1 mile to Little Tujunga Canyon nearly 4 miles north-north-west of Sunland (lat. 34°18'25" N, long. 118°20'45" W; near NE cor. sec. 33, T 3 N, R 14 W). Named on Sunland (1966) 7.5' quadrangle.

Lowe: see **Mount Lowe** [LOS ANGELES].

Lower Buffalo Corral Reservoir [LOS ANGE-

LES]: *lake,* 650 feet long, 3.5 miles north-
west of Mount Banning on Santa Catalina Is-
land in Little Springs Canyon (lat. 33°24'45"
N, long. 118°28'15" W); the feature is 1 mile
south of Upper Buffalo Corral Reservoir.
Named on Santa Catalina North (1950) 7.5'
quadrangle.
Lower Hungry Valley: see **Cañada de Los
Alamos** [LOS ANGELES].
Lower Pacifico Campground [LOS ANGE-
LES]: *locality,* 0.25 mile west-southwest of
Pacifico Mountain (lat. 34°22'50" N, long.
118° 02'20" W; near N line sec. 4, T 3 N, R
11 W). Named on Pacifico Mountain (1959)
7.5' quadrangle.
Lower Peters Canyon Reservoir [ORANGE]:
lake, 750 feet long, 5 miles east-southeast of
Orange city hall (lat. 33°45'35" N, long.
117°46'10" W); the feature is in Peters Canyon. Named on Orange (1964) 7.5' quadrangle.
Lower San Juan Campground [ORANGE]:
locality, 7 miles south of Trabuco Peak (lat.
33°35'55" N, long. 117°27'35" W; near S line
sec. 36, T 6 S, R 6 W); the place is in San
Juan Canyon near Orange-Riverside county
line. Named on Sitton Peak (1954) 7.5' quadrangle, which shows Upper San Juan Campground farther up the canyon in Riverside
County.
Lower Shake Campground [LOS ANGELES]:
locality, 3 miles east-northeast of Burnt Peak
(lat. 34°41'55" N, long. 118°31'30" W; sec.
13, T 7 N, R 16 W); the place is 0.5 mile north-
northeast of Upper Shake Campground.
Named on Burnt Peak (1958) 7.5' quadrangle.
Lower Switzer Campground [LOS ANGE-
LES]: *locality,* nearly 6 miles southeast of
Condor Peak along Arroyo Seco (lat. 34°16'
N, long. 118°08'45" W); the place is 0.25 mile
west of Upper Switzer Campground. Named
on Condor Peak (1959) 7.5' quadrangle.
Lowler: see **Mount Lowler,** under **Mount
Lawlor** [LOS ANGELES].
Lucas: see **Tom Lucas Campground** [LOS
ANGELES].
Lucas Canyon [ORANGE]: *canyon,* drained by
a stream that heads in Riverside County and
flows 5.5 miles to San Juan Creek 7.5 miles
east-northeast of San Juan Capistrano (lat.
33°33'20" N, long. 117° 33' W; sec. 18, T 7 S,
R 6 W). Named on Cañada Gobernadora
(1968) and Sitton Peak (1954) 7.5' quadrangles. The name is for a Christianized Indian who lived in the canyon (Meadows, p.
97).
Lucas Creek [LOS ANGELES]: *stream,* flows
2.25 miles to Big Tujunga Canyon 4 miles
east-southeast of Condor Peak (lat. 34°18'20"
N, long. 118°09'20" W). Named on Condor
Peak (1959) 7.5' quadrangle.
Lucky Canyon [LOS ANGELES]: *canyon,* less
than 1 mile long, 1 mile southeast of the village of Lake Hughes (lat. 34°39'50" N, long.

118°25'40" W; mainly in sec. 25, T 7 N, R 15
W). Named on Lake Hughes (1957) 7.5' quadrangle.]
Lukens: see **Mount Lukens** [LOS ANGELES].
Lunada Bay [LOS ANGELES]: *embayment,*
5.25 miles south-southwest of Redondo Beach
city hall along the coast (lat. 33°46'10" N,
long. 118°25'20" W). Named on Redondo
Beach (1951) 7.5' quadrangle.
Lupin: see **Camp Lupin** [LOS ANGELES].
Lynwood [LOS ANGELES]: *city,* 2 miles south
of South Gate city hall (lat. 33°55'40" N, long.
118°12'40" W). Named on South Gate (1952)
7.5' quadrangle. Postal authorities established
Lynwood post office in 1922 (Frickstad, p.
77). The city incorporated in 1921. The name
is from Lynwood dairy, which the owner of
the dairy named for his wife, Lynn Wood Ses-
sions (Gudde, 1949, p. 198).
Lynwood Gardens [LOS ANGELES]: *district,*
3 miles south-southeast of South Gate city hall
in Lynwood (lat. 33°54'45" N, long.
118°11'30" W). Named on South Gate (1952)
7.5' quadrangle.
Lynwood Station [LOS ANGELES]: *locality,*
2.5 miles south-southwest of South Gate city
hall along Southern Pacific Railroad (lat.
33°55'30" N, long. 118°13'25" W); the place
is at the west side of Lynwood. Named on
South Gate (1964) 7.5' quadrangle.
Lynx Gulch [LOS ANGELES]: *canyon,* drained
by a stream that flows 3.25 miles to Big
Tujunga Canyon 6 miles south-southwest of
Pacifico Mountain (lat. 34°18'35" N, long.
118°05'20" W; near N line sec. 36, T 3 N, R
12 W). Named on Chilao Flat (1959) 7.5'
quadrangle.
Lyon Canyon [LOS ANGELES]: *canyon,*
drained by a stream that flows 3 miles to Gavin
Canyon nearly 2 miles west-southwest of
downtown Newhall (lat. 34°22'15" N, long.
118°33'40" W; sec. 4, T 3 N, R 16 W). Named
on Oat Mountain (1952) 7.5' quadrangle.
Sanford Lyon of Lyon's Station owned the
feature (Reynolds, p. 13).
Lyons Hot Springs: see **Matilija Hot Springs**
[VENTURA].
Lyon Springs: see **Matilija Hot Springs** [VEN-
TURA].
Lyon's Station: see **San Fernando Pass** [LOS
ANGELES].

– M –

MacArthur: see **Fort MacArthur** [LOS AN-
GELES].
Machado [LOS ANGELES]: *locality,* 7.25 miles
north-northwest of Manhattan Beach city hall
along Pacific Electric Railroad (lat. 33° 59'10"
N, long. 118°27'05" W); the place is on
Ballona grant, received by Agustin Machado
and Ignacio Machado. Named on Venice
(1950) 7.5' quadrangle. Called Machada on

Redondo (1896) 15' quadrangle. On Venice (1924) 6' quadrangle, the name "Machado" applies to a place located nearly 0.5 mile farther east-southeast along the rail line. Postal authorities established Machado post office in 1874, discontinued it in 1875, reestablished it in 1878, and discontinued it in 1887 (Salley, p. 130).

Machado Lake: see **Harbor Lake** [LOS ANGELES].

Maddock Canyon [LOS ANGELES]: *canyon,* less than 1 mile long, 3 miles west-northwest of Azusa city hall (lat. 34°09'30" N, long. 117°57' W; sec. 20, T 1 N, R 10 W). Named on Azusa (1953) 7.5' quadrangle.

Madranio Canyon [VENTURA]: *canyon,* drained by a stream that flows 3.5 miles to the sea 2.5 miles northwest of Pitas Point at Sea Cliff (lat. 34°20'40" N, long. 119°25'05" W; sec. 17, T 3 N, R 24 W). Named on Pitas Point (1950) 7.5' quadrangle.

Magic Mountain [LOS ANGELES]: *peak,* 8 miles east-southeast of Solemint (lat. 34°23'10" N, long. 118°19'40" W; sec. 34, T 4 N, R 14 W). Named on Agua Dulce (1960) 7.5' quadrangle. Called Iron Mountain on San Fernando (1900) 15' quadrangle.

Magnolia Park [LOS ANGELES]: *locality,* 2.5 miles west-southwest of Burbank city hall (lat. 34°10'10" N, long. 118°21'10" W). Named on Burbank (1953) 7.5' quadrangle.

Maher Canyon [LOS ANGELES]: *canyon,* drained by a stream that flows 3 miles to Santa Clara River 10 miles east of Solemint (lat. 34°26'25" N, long. 118°17'15" W; near SW cor. sec. 7, T 4 N, R 13 W). Named on Agua Dulce (1960) 7.5' quadrangle.

Maizeland: see **Rivera**, under **Pico Rivera** [LOS ANGELES].

Malaga Canyon [LOS ANGELES]: *canyon,* drained by a stream that flows less than 3 miles to the sea nearly 3 miles south of Redondo Beach city hall (lat. 33°48'10" N, long. 118°23'45" W). Named on Redondo Beach (1951) 7.5' quadrangle

Malaga Cove [LOS ANGELES]: *embayment,* 2.5 miles south of Redondo Beach city hall along the coast (lat. 33°48'15" N, long. 118°23'45" W); the feature is at the mouth of Malaga Canyon. Named on Redondo Beach (1951) 7.5' quadrangle.

Malaga Creek: see **Malibu Creek** [LOS ANGELES].

Malaga Point: see **Malibu Point** [LOS ANGELES].

Maliba Sequit Creek: see **Malibu Creek** [LOS ANGELES].

Maliba Sequit Point: see **Malibu Point** [LOS ANGELES].

Malibo Creek: see **Malibu Creek** [LOS ANGELES].

Malibo Point: see **Malibu Point** [LOS ANGELES].

Malibu: see **Las Flores** [LOS ANGELES]

Malibu Bowl [LOS ANGELES]: *locality,* 4 miles west-northwest of Malibu Point (lat. 34°03'40" N, long. 118°44'30" W; near SW cor. sec. 23, T 1 S, R 18 W). Named on Malibu Beach (1951) 7.5' quadrangle.

Malibu Beach [LOS ANGELES]: *locality,* at and west of Malibu Point (lat. 34°01'55" N, long. 118°41'15" W). Named on Malibu Beach (1951) 7.5' quadrangle.

Malibu Creek [LOS ANGELES]: *stream,* flows 9.5 miles to the sea at Malibu Point (lat. 34°01'55" N, long. 118°40'45" W). Named on Malibu Beach (1951) 7.5' quadrangle. United States Board on Geographic Names (1933, p. 494) rejected the names "Malaga Creek," "Malibo Creek," "Maliba Sequit Creek," and "Topanga Malibu Sequit Creek" for the stream.

Malibu Hills [LOS ANGELES]: *locality,* 3.5 miles west-northwest of Malibu Point (lat. 34°02'50" N, long. 118°44'35" W; near SW cor. sec. 26, T 1 S, R 18 W). Named on Malibu Beach (1951) 7.5' quadrangle.

Malibu Junction [LOS ANGELES]: *locality,* 1 mile west of Agoura (lat. 34°08'35" N, long. 118°45'20" W). Named on Thousand Oaks (1952) 7.5' quadrangle. Camulos (1903) 30' quadrangle shows a place called Vejor located at or near present Malibu Junction. Postal authorities established Amargo post office in 1880 at a place known as Vejar that was situated 7 miles east of Newbury Park [VENTURA] and discontinued it in 1885; Delores M. Vejar was the first postmaster (Salley, p. 6).

Malibu Lake [LOS ANGELES]: *lake,* less than 1 mile long, behind a dam on Malibu Creek nearly 8 miles north-northeast of Point Dume (lat. 34°06'15" N, long. 118°45' W; near S line sec. 3, T 1 S, R 18 W). Named on Malibu Beach (1951) and Point Dume (1951) 7.5' quadrangles. The feature had the early name "Russell's Lake" (Anonymous, 1950, p. 33).

Malibu Mar Vista [LOS ANGELES]: *locality,* nearly 5 miles north-northeast of Point Dume (lat. 34°03'40" N, long. 118°45'50" W). Named on Solstice Canyon (1932) 6' quadrangle.

Malibu Point [LOS ANGELES]: *promontory,* 25 miles west of Los Angeles city hall along the coast (lat. 34°01'50" N, long. 118°40'55" W); the feature is on Topanga Malibu Sequit grant. Named on Malibu Beach (1951) 7.5' quadrangle. United States Board on Geographic Names (1933, p. 494) rejected the names "Malaga Point," "Malibo Point," "Maliba Sequit Point," and "Topanga Malibu Sequit Point" for the promontory.

Malibu Riviera [LOS ANGELES]: *locality,* at and north of Point Dume (lat. 34°00'55" N, long. 118°48'10" W). Named on Point Dume (1951) 7.5' quadrangle.

Malibu Trading Station: see **Trancas** [LOS ANGELES].

Malibu Vista [LOS ANGELES]: *locality,* nearly

4 miles north-northeast of Point Dume (lat. 34°02'55" N, long. 118°46'20" W; sec. 28, T 1 S, R 18 W). Named on Point Dume (1951) 7.5' quadrangle.

Mandalay Beach [VENTURA]: *beach,* nearly 4 miles west of Oxnard along the coast (lat. 34°11'50" N, long. 119°14'50" W). Named on Oxnard (1949) 7.5' quadrangle.

Mand Canyon [LOS ANGELES]: *canyon,* 0.5 mile long, 3 miles east of Burbank city hall (lat. 34°10'20" N, long. 118°15'15" W). Named on Burbank (1953) 7.5' quadrangle.

Mandeville Canyon [LOS ANGELES]: *canyon,* drained by a stream that flows 5 miles to Santa Monica Canyon 5.5 miles west of Beverly Hills city hall (lat. 34°03'40" N, long. 118°29'35" W). Named on Beverly Hills (1950), Canoga Park (1952), and Topanga (1952) 7.5' quadrangles.

Manhattan: see **Hobart** [LOS ANGELES]; **Manhattan Beach** [LOS ANGELES].

Manhattan Beach [LOS ANGELES]: *city,* 15 miles west-northwest of Long Beach city hall (lat. 33°53'15" N, long. 118°24'35" W). Named on Redondo Beach (1951) and Venice (1950) 7.5' quadrangles. Postal authorities established Manhattan post office in 1903 and changed the name to Manhattan Beach in 1927 (Frickstad, p. 77). The city incorporated in 1912. The place first was called Shore Acres; Stewart Merrill, founder of the community, suggested the name Manhattan Beach from Manhattan Island in New York (Gudde, 1949, p. 203).

Manhattan Beach Station [LOS ANGELES]: *locality,* 1.25 miles north-northwest of Manhattan Beach city hall along Pacific Electric Railroad (lat. 33°54'15" N, long. 118°25'15" W). Named on Venice (1924) 6' quadrangle.

Manuel Canyon [VENTURA]: *canyon,* drained by a stream that flows nearly 2 miles to the canyon of Ventura River 3.5 miles north of Ventura (lat. 34°20' N, long. 119°17'05" W). Named on Ventura (1951) 7.5' quadrangle. The name commemorates John Manuel, a native of Portugal who had a farm at the place (Ricard).

Manzana [LOS ANGELES]: *locality,* 18 miles east of Gorman (lat. 34°46' N, long. 118°31'40" W). Named on Tejon (1903) 30' quadrangle. Postal authorities established Manzana post office in 1892, moved it 1.5 miles northeast in 1899, moved it 4 miles south in 1902, and discontinued it in 1908; the place was in an apple-growing region— *manzana* means "apple" in Spanish (Salley, p. 132).

Manzanita: see **Camp Manzanita** [LOS ANGELES].

Manzanita Canyon: see **Oak Spring Canyon** [LOS ANGELES] (1).

Maple Canyon [LOS ANGELES]:
(1) *canyon,* 1.25 miles long, opens into an unnamed canyon 2 miles south of the village of

Leona Valley (lat. 34°35'15" N, long. 118° 17'15" W; near NE cor. sec. 30, T 6 N, R 13 W). Named on Sleepy Valley (1958) 7.5' quadrangle. Los Angeles County (1935) map has the name "Ikanhoffer Canyon" for a presently unnamed canyon at the mouth of Maple Canyon.
(2) *canyon,* drained by a stream that flows 1.25 miles to North Fork San Gabriel River 2.5 miles south of Crystal Lake (lat. 34°16'50" N, long. 117°50'25" W). Named on Crystal Lake (1958) 7.5' quadrangle.
(3) *canyon,* drained by a stream that flows nearly 1 mile to Pacoima Canyon 5.25 miles north east of downtown San Fernando (lat. 34° 20'40" N, long. 118°23' W; sec. 18, T 3 N, R 14 W). Named on San Fernando (1953) 7.5' quadrangle.
(4) *canyon,* drained by a stream that flows less than 1 mile to Big Tujunga Canyon 3 miles south-southeast of Condor Peak (lat. 34° 17'10" N, long. 118°11'35" W; sec. 1, T 2 N, R 13 W). Named on Condor Peak (1959) 7.5' quadrangle.
(5) *canyon,* drained by a stream that flows 1 mile to Sawtooth Canyon 5.25 miles northwest of Azusa city hall (lat. 34°10'40" N, long. 117°58'50" W; near NE cor. sec. 13, T 1 N, R 11 W). Named on Azusa (1953) 7.5' quadrangle.

Maple Canyon [VENTURA]: *canyon,* drained by a stream that flows nearly 1 mile to Dominguez Canyon 4.5 miles north of Piru (lat. 34°28'50" N, long. 118°47'50" W; near NW cor. sec. 32, T 5 N, R 18 W). Named on Piru (1952) 7.5' quadrangle.

Maple Creek [VENTURA]: *stream,* flows nearly 3 miles to Tar Creek 6.25 miles north of Fillmore (lat. 34°29'30" N, long. 118° 55' W). Named on Fillmore (1951) 7.5' quadrangle. Called Bear Cr. on Camulos (1903) 30' quadrangle—Fillmore (1951) 7.5' quadrangle has the name "Bear Creek" for a tributary of Maple Creek.

Maple Spring [ORANGE]: *spring,* 1.5 miles north-northwest of Santiago Peak (lat. 33°43'55" N, long. 117°32'50" W). Named on Santiago Peak (1954) 7.5' quadrangle. The name is for a cluster of maple trees at the spring (Meadows, p. 99).

Marek Canyon [LOS ANGELES]: *canyon,* drained by a stream that flows nearly 2 miles to Little Tujunga Canyon 4 miles northwest of Sunland (lat. 34°17'35" N, long. 118°21'40" W; at NE cor. sec. 5, T 2 N, R 14 W). Named on Sunland (1953) 7.5' quadrangle. Called Herrick Canyon on San Fernando (1900) 15' quadrangle, and called Merrick Canyon on Los Angeles County (1935) map.

Marengo [LOS ANGELES]: *locality,* 3.5 miles north-northwest of present Pasadena city hall along Los Angeles Terminal Railroad (lat. 34°11'15" N, long. 118°09' W). Named on Pasadena (1900) 15' quadrangle.

Marie Canyon [LOS ANGELES]: *canyon,*

drained by a stream that flows 1.5 miles to the sea 1.5 miles west of Malibu Point (lat. 34° 01'50" N, long. 118°42'35" W). Named on Malibu Beach (1951) 7.5' quadrangle.

Marina Del Rey [LOS ANGELES]: *water feature*, boat harbor 6.5 miles north-northwest of Manhattan Beach city hall near the mouth of Ballona Creek (lat. 33°58'30" N, long. 118°27' W). Named on Venice (1964) 7.5' quadrangle. Redondo (1896) 15' quadrangle shows Ballona Lagoon at the site, and Venice (1950) 7.5' quadrangle shows marsh there.

Marion: see **Camp Marion** [LOS ANGELES]; **Reseda** [LOS ANGELES].

Markham: see **Mount Markham** [LOS ANGELES].

Marlboro [ORANGE]: *locality*, nearly 2 miles north-northwest of Orange city hall along Southern Pacific Railroad (lat. 33°48'45" N, long. 117°51'30" W). Named on Orange (1964) 7.5' quadrangle.

Marle Canyon [LOS ANGELES]: *canyon*, drained by a stream that flows 1.5 miles to the sea 1.5 miles west of Malibu Point (lat. 34°01'50" N, long. 118°42'35" W). Named on Malibu Beach (1951) 7.5' quadrangle.

Marmon Canyon: see **Mormon Canyon** [LOS ANGELES].

Marne [LOS ANGELES]: *locality*, 6.25 miles south-southeast of Baldwin Park city hall along Southern Pacific Railroad (lat. 34°00'20" N, long. 117°54'20" W). Named on Baldwin Park (1953) 7.5' quadrangle.

Marple Canyon [LOS ANGELES]: *canyon*, drained by a stream that flows 6.5 miles to Castaic Valley 9 miles north-northwest of downtown Newhall at Castaic (lat. 34°29'25" N, long. 118° 36'45" W; sec. 25, T 5 N, R 17 W). Named on Whitaker Peak (1958) 7.5' quadrangle.

Marshall Canyon [LOS ANGELES]: *canyon*, nearly 1 mile long, along Marshall Creek above a point 7 miles north of Pomona city hall (lat. 34°09'10" N, long. 117°44'50" W; near SW cor. sec. 20, T 1 N, R 8 W). Named on Mount Baldy (1954) 7.5' quadrangle.

Marshall Creek [LOS ANGELES]: *stream*, flows 4.5 miles to end in lowlands 4.5 miles north-northwest of Pomona city hall (lat. 34° 07' N, long. 117°46'25" W). Named on Glendora (1953), Mount Baldy (1954), and San Dimas (1954) 7.5' quadrangles.

Martindale Canyon [LOS ANGELES]: *canyon*, drained by a stream that flows 3.5 miles to Bouquet Reservoir 5.5 miles west-southwest of the village of Leona Valley (lat. 34°34'40" N, long. 118°22'10" W; sec. 28, T 6 N, R 14 W). Named on Sleepy Valley (1958) 7.5' quadrangle.

Martins [LOS ANGELES]: *locality*, 4.25 miles east of Whitaker Peak (lat. 34°33'55" N, long. 118°39'35" W; near W line sec. 35, T 6 N, R 17 W). Named on Whitaker Peak (1958) 7.5' quadrangle.

Martins Camp [LOS ANGELES]: *locality*, 0.5 mile south of Mount Wilson (1) (lat. 34°13' N, long. 118°04' W; on W line sec. 32, T 2 N, R 11 W). Named on Pasadena (1900) 15' quadrangle. Clarence S. Martin bought a place called Steils Camp in 1891 and renamed it Camp Wilson, but to most visitors it was known as Martin's Camp; George Schneider built his Halfway House in 1894 about 4 miles below Martin's Camp (Robinson, J.W., 1977, p. 30, 38).

Martin's Peak: see **Mount Harvard** [LOS ANGELES].

Mar Vista [LOS ANGELES]: *district*, 5 miles south-southwest of Beverly Hills city hall in Los Angeles (lat. 34°00'10" N, long. 118°25'30" W). Named on Beverly Hills (1950) 7.5' quadrangle. Postal authorities established Mar Vista post office in 1925 (Frickstad, p. 77). The place was called Ocean Park Heights before 1904 (Gudde, 1949, p. 206).

Mason: see **Glendale** [LOS ANGELES].

Matay Canyon [LOS ANGELES]: *canyon*, 1.5 miles long, 5.25 miles west of Valyermo (lat. 34°26'15" N, long. 118°56'40" W; sec. 8, 17, T 4 N, R 10 W). Named on Juniper Hills (1959) 7.5' quadrangle.

Mateo: see **Serra** [ORANGE].

Mathiessen: see **Lake Mathiessen**, under **Lake Sherwood** [VENTURA].

Matiliha Cañon: see **Matilija Creek** [VENTURA].

Matilija [VENTURA]: *locality*, 1.25 miles west-southwest of downtown Ojai along Southern Pacific Railroad (lat. 34°26'20" N, long. 119°15'40" W). Named on Ventura (1904) 15' quadrangle. California Division of Highways' (1934) map shows a place called Tico located 1.5 miles west-southwest of Matilija along the railroad.

Matilija: see **Matilija Hot Springs** [VENTURA].

Matilija Creek [VENTURA]: *stream*, flows 15 miles to join its North Fork and form Ventura River 4 miles northwest of the town of Ojai (lat. 34°29'05" N, long. 119°18' W; near W line sec. 28, T 5 N, R 23 W). Named on Matilija (1952), Old Man Mountain (1943), and Wheeler Springs (1943) 7.5' quadrangles. The canyon of the stream is called Matiliha Cañon on Parke's (1854-1855) map. Antisell (p. 67) used the form "Matilihah" for the name, which is of Indian origin (Kroeber, p. 47). North Fork is 7.5 miles long and is named on Matilija (1952) and Wheeler Springs (1943) 7.5' quadrangles; it is called North Fork Ventura River on Wheeler Springs (1944) 7.5' quadrangle. Upper North Fork enters the main stream 5.5 miles west of Wheeler Springs; it is 6.5 miles long and is named on Old Man Mountain (1943) and Wheeler Springs (1943) 7.5' quadrangles. On Ventura (1904) 15' quadrangle, the stream in present Murietta Can-

yon is called West Fork Matilija Cr.
Matilija Hot Springs [VENTURA]: *locality,* 4.25 miles northwest of the town of Ojai (lat. 34°29' N, long. 119°18'15" W; sec. 29, T 5 N, R 23 W); the place is along Matilija Creek. Named on Matilija (1952) 7.5' quadrangle. Called Matilija on Ventura (1904) 15' quadrangle. Postal authorities established Matilija post office in 1889 and discontinued it in 1916 (Frickstad, p. 218). The place was a resort as early as about 1890; in 1908 it had accommodations for 200 guests (Waring, p. 63). Berkstresser (p. A-19) gave the alternate name "Ojai Hot Sulphur Springs" for the place. Ventura (1941) 15' quadrangle shows Lyons Hot Springs along Matilija Creek above Matilija Hot Springs. Waring (p. 278) noted that Lyons Spring is in Matilija Canyon about 1 mile northwest of Matilija Hot Springs. Postal authorities established Nogales post office in 1906, moved it and changed the name to Lyon Springs in 1907, and discontinued it in 1914; the name "Lyon" was for Gertrude A. Lyon, owner of the place, and the name "Nogales" was for native walnut trees at the site—*nogales* means "walnut trees" in Spanish (Salley, p 129-130, 155).
Mattox Canyon [LOS ANGELES]: *canyon,* drained by a stream that flows 2.5 miles to Soledad Canyon 3.5 miles southwest of Acton (lat. 34°26'10" N, long. 118°14'40" W; near N line sec. 16, T 4 N, R 13 W). Named on Acton (1959) and Agua Dulce (1960) 7.5' quadrangles.
Maxson [LOS ANGELES]: *locality,* nearly 2 miles east of El Monte along Pacific Electric Railroad (lat. 34°04'35" N, long. 118°00'25" W). Named on El Monte (1926) 6' quadrangle.
Maxy Canyon [VENTURA]: *canyon,* drained by a stream that flows 6.5 miles to Hungry Valley 7.5 miles north-northeast of McDonald Peak (lat. 34°44'15" N, long. 118°53'20" W; near E line sec. 34, T 8 N, R 19 W). Named on Frazier Mountain (1958) and McDonald Peak (1958) 7.5' quadrangles.
Mayate Canyon: see **Emerald Canyon** [ORANGE].
May Canyon [LOS ANGELES]: *canyon,* nearly 1.5 miles long, opens into lowlands 3.25 miles north of downtown San Fernando (lat. 34° 19'45" N, long. 118°25'40" W; sec. 23, T 3 N, R 15 W). Named on San Fernando (1953) 7.5 quadrangle.
May Canyon Saddle [LOS ANGELES]: *pass,* 5 miles north of downtown San Fernando (lat. 34°21'20" N, long. 118°25'50" W; at W line sec. 11, T 3 N, R 15 W). Named on San Fernando (1966) 7.5' quadrangle.
Mayfair [LOS ANGELES]: *district,* 7.25 miles north-northeast of Long Beach city hall (lat. 33°51'55" N, long. 118°08'15" W). Named on Long Beach (1949) and Los Alamitos (1950) 7.5' quadrangles. Postal authorities established Mayfair post office in 1958 and

discontinued it in 1963 (Salley, p. 135).
Maynard: see **Del Sur** [LOS ANGELES].
Mayo Spur [LOS ANGELES]: *locality,* 9 miles west-northwest of Newhall along Southern Pacific Railroad (lat. 34°24'35" N, long. 118°40'25" W). Named on Val Verde (1952) 7.5' quadrangle.
Maywood [LOS ANGELES]: *town,* 2.5 miles north-northeast of South Gate city hall (lat. 33°59'25" N, long. 118°11'15" W). Named on South Gate (1964) 7.5' quadrangle. Postal authorities established Maywood post office in 1925; the name is from May Wood, who was an employee of Laguna Land and Water Company—the company founded the community (Salley, p. 136). The city incorporated in 1924.
McCampbell [LOS ANGELES]: *locality,* 4.5 miles west of present Whittier city hall along Pacific Electric Railroad (lat. 33°58'20" N, long. 118°06'50" W). Named on Bell (1936) 6' quadrangle.
McClellan: see **Camp McClellan** [LOS ANGELES].
McClure Canyon [LOS ANGELES]:
(1) *canyon,* 1.25 miles long, 4.5 miles westsouthwest of Valyermo (lat. 34°25'25" N, long. 117°55'30" W; sec. 16, 21, T 14 N, R 10 W). Named on Juniper Hills (1959) 7.5' quadrangle.
(2) *canyon,* 1.5 miles long, 2 miles north-northwest of Burbank city hall (lat. 34°12'40" N, long. 118°19'05" W). Named on Burbank (1953) 7.5' quadrangle.
McCorkle Canyon [LOS ANGELES]: *canyon,* drained by a stream that flows 1 mile to Kings Canyon 4.5 miles northeast of Burnt Peak (lat. 34°43'05" N, long. 118°30'40" W; near S line sec. 6, T 7 N, R 15 W). Named on Burnt Peak (1958) 7.5' quadrangle.
McCoy Canyon [LOS ANGELES]: *canyon,* 4 miles long, along Arroyo Calabasas above a point 0.25 mile south-southwest of Calabasas (lat. 34°09' N, long. 118°38'30" W; at E line sec. 22, T 1 N, R 17 W). Named on Calabasas (1952) 7.5' quadrangle.
McCoy Canyon: see **Honby** [LOS ANGELES].
McCraken Reservoir [ORANGE]: *water feature,* 1.5 miles south of San Juan Capistrano (lat. 33°28'45" N, long. 117°39'50" W). Named on Dana Point (1968) 7.5' quadrangle.
McDill: see **Mount McDill** [LOS ANGELES].
McDonald Cabin [VENTURA]: *locality,* 5.25 miles north of Devils Heart Peak (lat. 34°37'10" N, long. 118°57'20" W; at S line sec. 12, T 6 N, R 20 W); the place is 1.25 miles southwest of McDonald Peak. Named on Devils Heart Peak (1943) 7.5' quadrangle.
McDonald Canyon [VENTURA]: *canyon,* drained by a stream that flows 1.5 miles to Ojai Valley 2 miles west-northwest of the town of Ojai (lat. 34°27'25" N, long. 119°16'30" W; sec. 3, T 4 N, R 23 W). Named on Matilija (1952) 7.5' quadrangle.

McDonald Creek [LOS ANGELES]: *stream,* flows 1.5 miles to La Tuna Canyon 4.5 miles north-northwest of Burbank city hall (lat. 34°14'05" N, long. 118°20'55" W; near S line sec. 21, T 2 N, R 14 W). Named on Burbank (1953) 7.5' quadrangle.

McDonald Peak [VENTURA]: *peak,* 16 miles north of Fillmore (lat. 34°38' N, long. 118°56'20" W; near NW cor. sec. 7, T 6 N, R 19 W). Altitude 6870 feet. Named on McDonald Peak (1958) 7.5' quadrangle.

McFadden's Landing: see **Newport Beach** [ORANGE] (2).

McGill: see **Mount McGill**, under **Mount Pinos** [VENTURA].

McGrath: see **Oxnard** [VENTURA].

McGrath Lake [VENTURA]: *lake,* 3000 feet long, 4.25 miles west-northwest of Oxnard near the coast (lat. 34°12'50" N, long. 119°15'10" W). Named on Oxnard (1949) 7.5' quadrangle. The lake is named for a family that had land in the neighborhood (Ricard).

McKinley [LOS ANGELES]: *district,* 3 miles northeast of present Torrance city hall (lat. 33°51'50" N, long. 118°18'05" W). Named on Torrance (1924) 6' quadrangle.

McKinley: see **Mount McKinley** [LOS ANGELES].

McKinley Canyon [LOS ANGELES]: *canyon,* drained by a stream that flows 1.25 miles to Trail Canyon 5.5 miles northeast of Sunland (lat. 34°19'20" N, long. 118°15'20" W); the canyon heads near Mount McKinley. Named on Sunland (1953) 7.5' quadrangle.

McKiwanis: see **Camp McKiwanis** [LOS ANGELES].

McNeil [LOS ANGELES]: *locality,* 2.5 miles west-southwest of present Burbank city hall along Southern Pacific Railroad (lat. 34°10'15" N, long. 118°21' W). Named on Burbank (1926) 6' quadrangle.

McPherson [ORANGE]: *locality,* 1.5 miles east of Orange city hall along Southern Pacific Railroad (lat. 33°47'20" N, long. 117°49'20" W). Named on Orange (1964) 7.5' quadrangle. Postal authorities established McPherson post office in 1886 and discontinued it in 1900; the name was for Robert McPherson, first postmaster (Salley, p. 136-137).

McRay Canyon: see **Bitter Canyon** [LOS ANGELES].

McVicker Canyon [ORANGE]: *canyon,* drained by a stream that flows 1 mile to Riverside County 2.5 miles southeast of Trabuco Peak (lat. 33°40'40" N, long. 117°26'15" W; sec. 6, T 6 S, R 5 W). Named on Alberhill (1954) 7.5' quadrangle.

Medea Creek [LOS ANGELES-VENTURA]: *stream,* heads in Ventura County and flows 7.25 miles to Malibu Lake 8.5 miles north-northeast of Point Dume in Los Angeles County (lat. 34°06'45" N, long. 118°45'20" W; sec. 3, T 1 S, R 18 W). Named on Malibu

Beach (1951), Point Dume (1951), and Thousand Oaks (1952) 7.5' quadrangles.

Meier Canyon [VENTURA]: *canyon,* 3 miles long, opens into Simi Valley (1) 5 miles west of Santa Susana Pass (lat. 34°15'55" N, long. 118°43'15" W; at S line sec. 12, T 2 N, R 18 W). Named on Calabasas (1952) 7.5' quadrangle. The feature first was called Bonebreak Canyon, probably for George H. Bonebreak, then it was called Sycamore Canyon, and finally it was called Meier Canyon for Eddie Meier, who owned land in the neighborhood (Ricard).

Meiners Oaks [VENTURA]: *town,* 2 miles west of downtown Ojai (lat. 34°27' N, long. 119°16'45" W). Named on Matilija (1952) 7.5' quadrangle.

Mendenhall Peak [LOS ANGELES]: *peak,* 6 miles north of Sunland (lat. 34°20'55" N, long. 118°18'45" W; near N line sec. 14, T 3 N, R 14 W); the peak is on Mendenhall Ridge. Named on Sunland (1953) 7.5' quadrangle. Forest Service officials named the feature for Frank Mendenhall, a hunter (Gudde, 1949, p. 210).

Mendenhall Ridge [LOS ANGELES]: *ridge,* generally west-trending, 6 miles long, 6 miles north of Sunland (lat. 34°20'55" N, long. 118° 18'15" W). Named on Sunland (1966) 7.5' quadrangle.

Mendenhall Saddle [LOS ANGELES]: *pass,* 6 miles north of Sunland (lat. 34°20'55" N, long. 118°18'15" W; near NW cor. sec. 13, T 3 N, R 14 W); the pass is near the center of Mendenhall Ridge. Named on Sunland (1966) 7.5' quadrangle.

Mentryville: see **Pico Canyon** [LOS ANGELES].

Mermaids Canyon: see **Big Mermaids Canyon** [LOS ANGELES]; **Little Mermaids Canyon** [LOS ANGELES].

Merriam: see **Camp Merriam**, under **Camp Sierra** [LOS ANGELES].

Merrick Canyon: see **Marek Canyon** [LOS ANGELES].

Mesa: see **Mount Mesa** [LOS ANGELES].

Mesa Peak [LOS ANGELES]: *peak,* 3 miles northwest of Malibu Point (lat. 34°03'45" N, long. 118°43'05" W; near S line sec. 24, T 1 S, R 18 W). Altitude 1844 feet. Named on Malibu Beach (1951) 7.5' quadrangle.

Mescal Campground [LOS ANGELES]: *locality,* 2 miles west-northwest of Big Pines (lat. 34°23'30" N, long. 117°43'15" W); the place is less than 0.5 mile west of Mescal Creek. Named on Mescal Creek (1956) 7.5' quadrangle.

Mescal Creek [LOS ANGELES]: *stream,* flows 5.5 miles to lowlands 5 miles north of Big Pines (lat. 34°27' N, long. 117°42'15" W; sec. 10, T 4 N, R 8 W). Named on Mescal Creek (1956) 7.5' quadrangle.

Mesmer [LOS ANGELES]: *locality,* 6.5 miles north of present Manhattan Beach city hall along Atchison, Topeka and Santa Fe Railroad (lat. 33°59' N, long. 118°24' W). Named on Redondo (1896) 15' quadrangle..

Messenger Flats [LOS ANGELES]: *area,* 6 miles south of Acton (lat. 34°22'55" N, long. 118°11'35" W; at S line sec. 36, T 4 N, R 13 W). Named on Acton (1959) 7.5' quadrangle.

Mesto: see **Garden Grove** [ORANGE].

Metaka: see **Camp Metaka** [LOS ANGELES].

Michael Canyon: se **Michael Creek** [LOS ANGELES-VENTURA].

Michael Creek [LOS ANGELES-VENTURA]: *stream,* heads in Los Angeles County and flows 2.25 miles to Piru Creek 7 miles southeast of Cobblestone Mountain in Ventura County (lat. 34°32'50" N, long. 118°46'15" W; sec. 4, T 5 N, R 18 W). Named on Cobblestone Mountain (1958) and Whitaker Peak (1958) 7.5' quadrangles. Los Angeles County (1935) map has the name "Michael Cany." for the canyon of the stream.

Middle Anacapa: see **Anacapa Island** [VENTURA].

Middle Canyon [LOS ANGELES]: *canyon,* drained by a stream that flows 7.25 miles to the sea nearly 3 miles west of Mount Banning on Santa Catalina Island (lat. 33°22'05" N, long. 118°28'50" W). Named on Santa Catalina South (1943) 7.5' quadrangle.

Middle Lake [LOS ANGELES]: *lake,* 3.5 miles east-southeast of downtown San Fernando (lat. 34°15'45" N, long. 118°22'45" W). Named on San Fernando (1966) 7.5' quadrangle.

Middle Point [VENTURA]: *promontory,* 4 miles west-northwest of Point Mugu along the coast (lat. 34°05'55" N, long. 119°07'45" W); the feature is situated between Hueneme Point (present Point Hueneme) and Mugu Point (present Point Mugu). Named on Hueneme (1904) 15' quadrangle.

Middle Ranch Cove: see **Mills Landing** [LOS ANGELES].

Midway City [ORANGE]: *town,* 6 miles north of Huntington Beach civic center (lat. 33°45' N, long. 117°59' W). Named on Anaheim (1965) and Newport Beach (1965) 7.5' quadrangles. Postal authorities established Midway City post office in 1929 (Frickstad, p. 117).

Mile High [LOS ANGELES]: *locality,* 5.5 miles east-southeast of Valyermo (lat. 34°24'45" N, long. 117°46'20" W; sec. 24, T 4 N, R 9 W). Named on Valyermo (1958) 7.5' quadrangle.

Millard Canyon [LOS ANGELES]: *canyon,* drained by a stream that flows 3.5 miles to Arroyo Seco 4 miles north-northwest of Pasadena city hall (lat. 34°12'15" N, long. 118°09'50" W; sec. 5, T 1 N, R 12 W). Named on Pasadena (1953) 7.5' quadrangle. The name recalls Henry W. Millard and his family, who took up a homestead in the canyon in 1862 (Robinson, J.W., 1977, p. 101).

Mill Canyon [LOS ANGELES]: *canyon,* drained by a stream that flows 5.5 miles to

Soledad Canyon 3.5 miles southwest of Acton (lat. 34°26'10" N, long. 118°14'35" W; near N line sec. 16, T 4 N, R 13 W). Named on Acton (1959) 7.5' quadrangle.

Mill Creek [LOS ANGELES]: *stream,* flows 8 miles to Big Tujunga Canyon 4.5 miles east-southeast of Condor Peak (lat. 34°18'35" N, long. 118°08'30" W). Named on Chilao Flat (1959), Condor Peak (1959), and Pacifico Mountain (1959) 7.5' quadrangles. Middle Fork enters 2.5 miles upstream from the mouth of the main creek; it is nearly 4 miles long and is named on Chilao Flat (1959) and Condor Peak (1959) 7.5' quadrangles. North Fork enters from the north nearly 1 mile upstream from the mouth of the main stream; it is 5.5 miles long and is named on Condor Peak (1959) 7.5' quadrangle.

Mill Creek Picnic Grounds [LOS ANGELES]: *locality,* 5 miles southwest of Pacifico Mountain along Mill Creek (lat. 34°20'35" N, long. 118°06'30" W). Named on Chilao Flat (1959) 7.5' quadrangle.

Mill Creek Summit [LOS ANGELES]: *pass,* nearly 3 miles west-northwest of Pacifico Mountain (lat. 34°23'30" N, long. 118°04'50" W). Named on Pacifico Mountain (1959) 7.5' quadrangle.

Miller Canyon [LOS ANGELES]: *canyon,* 1.25 miles long, 5 miles west of Valyermo (lat. 34°25'45" N, long. 117°56' W; sec. 16, 21, T 4 N, R 10 W). Named on Juniper Hills (1959) 7.5' quadrangle.

Millhouse Canyon: see **Wheeler Canyon** [VENTURA].

Milligan Barranca [VENTURA]: *gully,* extends for 2.5 miles to Honda Barranca nearly 7 miles south of Santa Paula (lat. 34°15'20" N, long. 119°04' W). Named on Santa Paula (1951) 7.5' quadrangle.

Mills Landing [LOS ANGELES]: *locality,* nearly 3 miles west of Mount Banning on the west side of Santa Catalina Island (lat. 33° 22'05" N, long. 118°28'50" W). Named on Santa Catalina South (1943) 7.5' quadrangle. Smith's (1897) map shows Middle Ranch C. [Cove] at the site. The place was called Craig Beach in 1893 (Doran, 1980, p. 76).

Mine Canyon: see **Buck Creek** [VENTURA].

Mine Gulch [LOS ANGELES]: *canyon,* drained by a stream that flows 2.25 miles to San Gabriel River 6 miles northwest of Mount San Antonio (lat. 34°20'35" N, long. 117°43'35" W; at W line sec. 16, T 3 N, R 8 W). Named on Crystal Lake (1958) and Mount San Antonio (1955) 7.5' quadrangles.

Mine Gulch Camp [LOS ANGELES]: *locality,* 6 miles northwest of Mount San Antonio (lat. 34°20'40" N, long. 117°43'30" W; near W line sec. 16, T 3 N, R 8 W); the place is at the mouth of Mine Gulch. Named on Mount San Antonio (1955) 7.5' quadrangle.

Minero Canyon [LOS ANGELES]: *canyon,* drained by a stream that flows 1 mile to San

Gabriel Reservoir 7.25 miles north-northeast of Glendora city hall (lat. 34°14'10" N, long. 117°49'45" W; at N line sec. 28, T 2 N, R 9 W). Named on Glendora (1953) 7.5' quadrangle.

Mint Canyon [LOS ANGELES]:
(1) *canyon,* drained by a stream that flows 15 miles to Santa Clara River at Solemint (lat. 34°24'50" N, long, 118°27'15" W; sec. 21, T 4 N, R 15 W). Named on Green Valley (1958), Mint Canyon (1960), and Sleepy Valley (1958) 7.5' quadrangles. Los Angeles County (1935) map shows a feature called James Canyon that opens into Mint Canyon about 5.5 miles northeast of Solemint (sec. 31, T 5 N, R 14 W), and a feature called Wright Canyon that opens into Mint Canyon about 6 miles northeast of Solemint (at S line sec. 30, T 5 N, R 14 W).
(2) *settlement,* less than 1 mile north-northeast of Solemint (lat. 34°25'45" N, long. 118°26'30" W; sec. 15, T 4 N, R 15 W); the place is in Mint Canyon (1). Named on Mint Canyon (1960) 7.5' quadrangle. Called St. Johns on Humphreys (1932) 6' quadrangle, and called Thompson on San Fernando (1945) 15' quadrangle, although San Fernando (1900) 15' quadrangle has the name "Thompson" at present Solemint. Postal authorities established Thompson post office in 1888 and discontinued it in 1903 (Frickstad, p. 82).

Mint Canyon Campground [LOS ANGELES]: *locality,* 12.5 miles south-southwest of the village of Lake Hughes (lat. 34°30'05" N, long. 118°22'50" W; near E line sec. 19, T 5 N, R 14 W); the place is in Mint Canyon (1). Named on Green Valley (1958) 7.5' quadrangle.

Mint Canyon Spring [LOS ANGELES]: *locality,* 6.5 miles northeast of Solemint (lat. 34°29'35" N, long. 118°23'05" W; sec. 30, T 5 N, R 14 W); the place is in Mint Canyon (1). Named on Mint Canyon (1960) 7.5' quadrangle.

Miraflores: see **Anaheim Tower** [ORANGE].

Mirage Valley: see **El Mirage Valley** [LOS ANGELES].

Miraleste [LOS ANGELES]: *district,* 6 miles south of Torrance city hall (lat. 33°45'05" N, long. 118°19'25" W). Named on Torrance (1964) 7.5' quadrangle. Officials of a land-development company named the place in 1924 (Gudde, 1949, p. 217).

Miraleste Canyon [LOS ANGELES]: *canyon,* 2.5 miles long, nearly 6 miles south-southeast of Torrance city hall (lat. 33°45'20" N, long. 118°18'45" W); Miraleste is in the canyon. Named on Torrance (1964) 7.5' quadrangle.

Mira Monte [VENTURA]: *settlement,* 2.5 miles west-southwest of the town of Ojai (lat. 34°26' N, long. 119°17' W). Named on Matilija (1952) 7.5' quadrangle. Development of the place began in 1928 (Ricard).

Mirror Lake [VENTURA]: *intermittent lake,* 1900 feet long, 3 miles southwest of the town of Ojai (lat. 34°25'20" N, long. 119°17'25" W). Named on Matilija (1952) 7.5' quadrangle.

Mission Acres: see **Sepulveda** [LOS ANGELES] (1).

Mission Creek [LOS ANGELES]: *stream,* flows 1.25 miles from Legg Lake to Rio Hondo 4 miles southwest of El Monte city hall (lat. 34°01'35" N, long. 118°04'20" W). Named on El Monte (1966) 7.5' quadrangle.

Mission Hills [LOS ANGELES]: *district,* 2.25 miles southwest of downtown San Fernando in Los Angeles (lat. 34°15'30" N, long. 118°27'45" W). Named on San Fernando (1966) 7.5' quadrangle. Postal authorities established Dennis Park post office in 1957 and changed the name was to Mission Hills in 1959 (Salley, p. 58).

Mission Junction [LOS ANGELES]: *locality,* 1 mile east-northeast of Los Angeles city hall along a rail line (lat. 34°03'45" N, long. 118°13'35" W). Named on Los Angeles (1966) 7.5' quadrangle.

Mission Peak: see **Mission Point** [LOS ANGELES].

Mission Point [LOS ANGELES]: *peak,* 4.5 miles south of Newhall (lat. 34°18'40" N, long. 118°32' W). Altitude 2771 feet. Named on Oat Mountain (1952) 7.5' quadrangle. Called Mission Pk. on Los Angeles County (1935) map.

Mission Vieja Valley: see **San Juan Canyon,** under **San Juan Creek** [ORANGE].

Mission Viejo [ORANGE]: *city,* 2 miles southeast of El Toro (lat. 33° 36' N, long. 117°40'15" W); the city is north of the northwest end of Mission Viejo or La Paz grant. Named on San Juan Capistrano (1968) 7.5' quadrangle. Postal authorities established Mission Viejo post office in 1966 (Salley, p. 143).

Mission Viejo or La Paz [ORANGE]: *land grant,* east of San Juan Capistrano. Named on Cañada Gobernadora (1968), San Clemente (1968), San Juan Capistrano (1968), and Santiago Peak (1954) 7.5' quadrangles. Called simply Mission Viejo on Cañada Gobernadora (1949), San Clemente (1949), and San Juan Capistrano (1949) 7.5' quadrangles. Agustin Olvera received the land in 1845, and John Forster claimed 46,433 acres patented in 1866 (Cowan, p. 48).

Mixville [LOS ANGELES]: *locality,* 3.25 miles north-northwest of Los Angeles city hall (lat. 34°05'55" N, long. 118°15'30" W). Named on Hollywood (1953) 7.5' quadrangle.

Modelo Canyon [VENTURA]: *canyon,* drained by a stream that flows 2.5 miles to Piru Canyon 1.5 miles east-northeast of Piru (lat. 34°25'30" N, long. 118°46'10" W). Named on Piru (1952) 7.5' quadrangle.

Modelo Peak [VENTURA]: *peak,* 2.5 miles

north of Piru (lat. 34° 27' N, long. 118°48' W; near N line sec. 7, T 4 N, R 18 W); the peak is at the head of Modelo Canyon. Altitude 3298 feet. Named on Piru (1952) 7.5' quadrangle.

Modena: see **El Modino** [ORANGE].

Modie Canyon: see **Moody Canyon** [LOS ANGELES].

Modjeska [ORANGE]: *village,* 6.5 miles northeast of El Toro along Santiago Creek (lat. 33°42'30" N, long. 117°37'45" W; sec. 28, 29, T 5 S, R 7 W). Named on El Toro (1968) and Santiago Peak (1954) 7.5' quadrangles.

Modjeska Canyon [ORANGE]: *canyon,* less than 1 mile long, 6.5 miles northeast of El Toro along Santiago Creek (lat. 33°42'30" N, long. 117°37'45" W). Named on El Toro (1968) 7.5' quadrangle. The name commemorates actress Helena Modjeska, who with her husband financed a Polish farming project in the canyon (Gudde, 1949, p. 218).

Modjeska Island: see **Bay Island** [ORANGE].

Modjeska Peak [ORANGE]: *peak,* nearly 1 mile northwest of Santiago Peak (lat. 33°43'10" N, long. 117°32'35" W; sec. 19, T 5 S, R 6 W). Altitude 5496 feet. Named on Santiago Peak (1954) 7.5' quadrangle. J.B. Stephenson, a forest ranger, named the peak in memory of actress Helena Modjeska after her death in 1909 (Gudde, 1949, p. 218). Previously the feature was known locally as North Peak (Stephenson, p. 7). United States Board on Geographic Names (1961b, p. 12) rejected the name "Santiago Northwest Peak" for the feature.

Modjeska Reservoir [ORANGE]: *lake,* 400 feet long, 5 miles west of Santiago Peak (lat. 33°42'55" N, long. 117°37'20" W; near NW cor. sec. 28, T 5 S, R 7 W); the feature is less than 0.5 mile north-northeast of Modjeska. Named on Santiago Peak (1954) 7.5' quadrangle. Promoters laid out a place called Santiago City in Harding Canyon during the mining excitement of 1878, but it never materialized; water of Modjeska Reservoir now covers the site (Meadows, p. 125).

Mohave Desert: see "Regional setting."

Mohn Springs: see **Glenview** [LOS ANGELES].

Mojave Desert: see "Regional setting."

Monaco [LOS ANGELES]: *locality,* nearly 3 miles north-northwest of Torrance city hall along Atchison Topeka and Santa Fe Railroad (lat. 33°52'30" N, long. 118°21'30" W). Named on Inglewood (1964) and Torrance (1964) 7.5' quadrangles.

Moneta [LOS ANGELES]: *locality,* 6.25 miles south-southeast of Inglewood city hall along Pacific Electric Railroad (lat. 33°52'45" N, long. 118°18'35" W). Named on Inglewood (1952) 7.5' quadrangle. Postal authorities established Moneta post office in 1890 and discontinued it in 1947 (Salley, p. 144).

Monroe Canyon [LOS ANGELES]: *canyon,* drained by a stream that flows 2.25 miles to

Big Dalton Reservoir 4 miles northeast of Glendora city hall (lat. 34°10'25" N, long. 117°48'30" W; sec. 15, T 1 N, R 9 W). Named on Glendora (1966) 7.5' quadrangle.

Monrovia [LOS ANGELES]: *city,* 5.5 miles west of Azusa city hall (lat. 34°08'50" N, long. 117°55'50" W). Named on Azusa (1953), El Monte (1966), and Mount Wilson (1953) 7.5' quadrangles. Postal authorities established Monrovia post office in 1886 (Frickstad, p. 77), and the city incorporated in 1887. The name recalls William N. Monroe, one of the founders of the community in 1886 (Gudde, 1949, p. 221).

Monrovia Canyon [LOS ANGELES]: *canyon,* drained by a stream that flows 2.5 miles to Sawpit canyon 5.5 miles west-northwest of Azusa city hall (lat. 34°10'25" N, long. 117°59'20" W; sec. 13, T 1 N, R 11 W). Named on Azusa (1953) 7.5' quadrangle.

Monrovia Hill: see **Monrovia Peak** [LOS ANGELES].

Monrovia Peak [LOS ANGELES]: *peak,* 6.5 miles northwest of Azusa city hall (lat. 34°12'45" N, long. 117°58'05" W); the peak is 4.5 miles north-northeast of downtown Monrovia. Altitude 5412 feet. Named on Azusa (1953) 7.5' quadrangle. Called Monrovia Hill on Pomona (1904) 15' quadrangle.

Montalvo [VENTURA]: *town,* 4 miles southwest of Saticoy (lat. 34° 15' N, long. 119°12'15" W). Named on Oxnard (1949) and Saticoy (1951) 7.5' quadrangles. Postal authorities established Montalvo post office in 1888 (Frickstad, p. 218). The name commemorates the early Spanish writer who first used the name "California" (Hoover, Rensch, and Rensch, p. 582).

Monte: see **El Monte** [LOS ANGELES].

Montebello [LOS ANGELES]: *city,* 6 miles southwest of El Monte city hall (lat. 34°00'40" N, long. 118°06'15" W). Named on El Monte (1953), Los Angeles (1953), South Gate (1952), and Whittier (1949) 7.5' quadrangles. Postal authorities established Montebello post office in 1902, discontinued it in 1907, and reestablished it in 1913 (Frickstad, p. 77). The city incorporated in 1920. California Mining Bureau's (1917) map shows a place called Newmark located 2.5 miles east of Montebello along a railroad. Harris Newmark bought land at the place in 1887, and in 1889 he and Kaspare Cohn applied the name "Montebello" to their development there, which included a town called Newmark—residents dropped the name "Newmark" in 1920 (Gudde, 1949, p. 222; Hanna, p. 199).

Montebello Gardens [LOS ANGELES]: *district,* 3.5 miles southwest of El Monte city hall in present Pico Rivera (lat. 34°00'30" N, long. 118°05'30" W); the place is east of Montebello. Named on El Monte (1953) 7.5' quadrangle.

Montebello Hills [LOS ANGELES]: *range,* 4.25 miles southwest of El Monte city hall (lat. 34°01'55" N, long. 118°05'15" W); the range is northeast of downtown Montebello. Named on El Monte (1966) 7.5' quadrangle.

Monte Cristo Creek [LOS ANGELES]: *stream,* flows nearly 3 miles to Mill Creek 5 miles west-southwest of Pacifico Mountain (lat. 34°20'40" N, long. 118°06'30" W). Named on Chilao Flat (1959) 7.5' quadrangle, which shows Monte Cristo mine along the stream.

Monte Nido [LOS ANGELES]: *village,* 3.5 miles north of Malibu Point (lat. 34°04'50" N, long. 118°41'10" W; sec. 17, T 1 S, R 17 W). Named on Malibu Beach (1951) 7.5' quadrangle.

Monterey Acres [LOS ANGELES]: *district,* 8.5 miles northeast of Long Beach city hall (lat. 33°50'25" N, long. 118°04'40" W). Named on Los Alamitos (1950) 7.5' quadrangle.

Monterey Park [LOS ANGELES]: *city,* 6.5 miles east of Los Angeles city hall (lat. 34°03'35" N, long. 118°07'30" W). Named on El Monte (1953) and Los Angeles (1953) 7.5' quadrangles. Postal authorities established Monterey Park post office in 1922 (Salley, p. 145). The city incorporated in 1916. A subdivision developed at the site in 1906 was called Ramona Acres; when Monterey Park incorporated it took its name from nearby Monterey Pass (present Coyote Pass) (Gudde, 1949, p. 223).

Monterey Pass: see **Coyote Pass** [LOS ANGELES].

Monteria Lake [LOS ANGELES]: *lake,* 900 feet long, 2 miles east-northeast of Chatsworth (lat. 34°16'05" N, long. 118°34'10" W; on E line sec. 8, T 2 N, R 16 W). Named on Oat Mountain (1952) 7.5' quadrangle.

Monte Vista: see **Sun Valley** [LOS ANGELES] (2).

Montgomery Canyon [VENTURA]: *canyon,* drained by a stream that flows 1 mile to Oak Canyon (2) 5.5 miles north-northeast of Thousand Oaks (lat. 34°14'05" N, long. 118°47' W; at N line sec. 29, T 2 N, R 18 W). Named on Thousand Oaks (1952) 7.5' quadrangle.

Montrose [LOS ANGELES]: *town,* 6.5 miles northwest of Pasadena city hall (lat. 34°12'35" N, long. 118°13'40" W). Named on Pasadena (1953) 7.5' quadrangle. Postal authorities established Montrose post office in 1923 (Frickstad, p. 77). The name of the town was chosen by means of a contest in 1913 (Gudde, 1949, p. 223).

Moody [ORANGE]: *settlement,* 3.5 miles southwest of Buena Park civic center (lat. 33°50'10" N, long. 118°02'50" W; mainly in sec. 8, T 4 S, R 11 W). Named on Los Alamitos (1950) 7.5' quadrangle.

Moody Canyon [LOS ANGELES]: *canyon,* drained by a stream that flows nearly 4 miles to Arrastre Canyon 2.5 miles south of Acton (lat. 34°25'50" N, long. 118°11'20" W; sec.

13, T 4 N, R 13 W). Named on Acton (1959) 7.5' quadrangle. Called Modie Canyon on Acton (1939) 6' quadrangle.

Moody Creek [LOS ANGELES-ORANGE]: *stream,* heads in Orange County and flows 2 miles to Coyote Creek [LOS ANGELES-ORANGE] 4 miles west-southwest of Buena Park civic center just inside Los Angeles County (lat. 33°50'05" N, long. 118°03'35" W; near SW cor. sec. 8, T 4 S, R 11 W). Named on Los Alamitos (1964) 7.5' quadrangle.

Moody Springs [LOS ANGELES]: *springs,* 4 miles north-northeast of Black Butte along Eller Slough (lat. 34°36'45" N, long. 117°42'30" W; sec. 15, T 6 N, R 8 W). Named on El Mirage (1956) 7.5' quadrangle. Shadow Mountains (1942) 15' quadrangle has the singular form "Moody Spr." for the name

Mooney: see **Mount Mooney** [LOS ANGELES].

Moonstone Beach [LOS ANGELES]: *beach,* 4 miles northwest of Avalon on the northeast side of Santa Catalina Island (lat. 33°23'20" N, long. 118°22' W). Named on Santa Catalina East (1950) 7.5' quadrangle. United States Board on Geographic Names (1975, p. 10) approved the name "Moonstone Cove" for the embayment at the place.

Moonstone Cove: see **Moonstone Beach** [LOS ANGELES].

Moore: see **Fort Moore**, under **Los Angeles** [LOS ANGELES].

Moore Canyon: see **Big Moore Canyon**, under **Wickham Canyon** [LOS ANGELES].

Moorpark [VENTURA]: *town,* 8 miles southeast of Fillmore in Little Simi Valley (lat. 34°17'10" N, long. 118°52'45" W; near W line sec. 4, T 2 N, R 19 W). Named on Moorpark (1951) and Simi (1951) 7.5' quadrangles. Postal authorities established Moorpark post office in 1900 (Frickstad, p. 218). The name is from a variety of apricot (Gudde, 1949, p. 224).

Moorpark Home Acres [VENTURA]: *settlement,* 2.25 miles southwest of Moorpark (lat. 34°16' N, long. 118°54'50" W; near SW cor. sec. 7, T 2 N, R 19 W). Named on Moorpark (1951) 7.5' quadrangle.

Moor's: see **San Francisquito Canyon** [LOS ANGELES].

Morgan [LOS ANGELES]: *locality,* 3 miles north-northeast of present Los Angeles city hall along Los Angeles Terminal Railroad (lat. 34°05'15" N, long. 118°12'45" W). Named on Pasadena (1900) 15' quadrangle

Morgan Canyon [LOS ANGELES]: *canyon,* 1.25 miles long, 3 miles east-northeast of Glendora city hall (lat. 34°08'40" N, long. 117°48'55" W; mainly in sec. 27, T 1 N, R 9 W). Named on Glendora (1953) 7.5' quadrangle. Called Guard Canyon on Los Angeles County (1935) map.

Morgan Canyon [VENTURA]: *canyon,* drained by a stream that flows 1.25 miles to the valley of Santa Clara River 1.25 miles east-southeast of downtown Santa Paula (lat. 34°20'55" N, long. 119° 02'10" W; at N line sec. 13, T 3 N, R 21 W). Named on Santa Paula (1951) 7.5' quadrangle.

Mormon Canyon [LOS ANGELES]: *canyon,* drained by a stream that flows 2.25 miles to Browns Canyon 2.5 miles north-northeast of Chatsworth (lat. 34°17'45" N, long. 118°35'30" W; sec. 31, T 3 N, R 16 W). Named on Oat Mountain (1952) 7.5' quadrangle. Called Marmon Canyon on Los Angeles County (1935) map.

Mormon Island [LOS ANGELES]: *area,* nearly 6 miles southeast of Torrance city hall at Los Angeles Harbor (lat. 33°45'35" N, long. 118°15'45" W). Named on Torrance (1964) 7.5' quadrangle. On Redondo (1896) 15' quadrangle, the feature is shown as marsh in Wilmington Lagoon. Some soldiers from the Mormon Battalion settled at the place after they were mustered out in 1848 (Gleason, p. 116).

Morningside Park [LOS ANGELES]: *district,* 1.5 miles east-southeast of Inglewood city hall (lat. 33°57'25" N, long. 118°19'30" W). Named on Inglewood (1964) 7.5' quadrangle.

Moro Canyon [ORANGE]: *canyon,* drained by a stream that flows 3.25 miles to the sea 2.5 miles west-northwest of Laguna Beach city hall (lat. 33°33'40" N, long. 117°49'15" W). Named on Laguna Beach (1965) 7.5' quadrangle. The name is a misspelling of *morro,* which means "round" in Spanish—the name refers to the dome-shaped feature now called Abalone Point (Meadows, p. 102).

Morocco: see **Beverly Hills** [LOS ANGELES].

Morris Reservoir [LOS ANGELES]: *lake,* behind a dam on San Gabriel River 3 miles north-northeast of Azusa city hall (lat. 34°10'25" N, long. 117°52'45" W; sec. 13, T 1 N, R 10 W). Named on Azusa (1953) and Glendora (1953) 7.5' quadrangles.

Morro Bay: see **Abalone Point** [ORANGE].

Morro Hill [VENTURA]: *peak,* 11 miles northwest of Reyes Peak (lat. 34°44'20" N, long. 119°25'40" W). Altitude 4584 feet. Named on Rancho Nuevo Creek (1943) 7.5' quadrangle.

Mortimer Park: see **Santa Susana Knolls** [VENTURA].

Morton [LOS ANGELES]: *locality,* 3.25 miles south-southeast of South Gate city hall along Pacific Electric Railroad (lat. 33°54'50" N, long. 118°10'50" W). Named on South Gate (1952) 7.5' quadrangle.

Mosquito Cove [LOS ANGELES]: *embayment,* 4 miles northwest of Pyramid Head on the northeast side of San Clemente Island (lat. 32°51'35" N, long. 118°23'55" W). Named on San Clemente Island South (1943) 7.5' quadrangle. Doran (1980, p. 52) called the place Mosquito Harbor, and attributed the name to mosquitos that breed in rock basins at the place.

Mosquito Harbor: see **Mosquito Cove** [LOS ANGELES].

Moss Spring: see **Cruthers Creek** [LOS ANGELES].

Motordrome [LOS ANGELES]: *locality,* nearly 6 miles north-northwest of present Manhattan Beach city hall along Pacific Electric Railroad (lat. 33°55'10" N, long. 118°26'15" W). Named on Venice (1924) 6' quadrangle.

Mountain View: see **Villa Park** [ORANGE].

Mount Baden-Powell [LOS ANGELES]: *peak,* 5.5 miles northeast of Crystal Lake (lat. 34°21'30" N, long. 117°45'50" W). Altitude 9399 feet. Named on Crystal Lake (1958) 7.5' quadrangle. Called North Baldy on Rock Creek (1903) 15' quadrangle, but United States Board on Geographic Names (1933, p. 112) rejected this designation for the feature; the present name honors the founder of the Boy Scout movement.

Mount Baldy [LOS ANGELES]: *village,* 14 miles north-northeast of Pomona city hall in San Antonio Canyon on Los Angeles-San Bernardino county line (lat. 34°14'10" N, long. 117°39'25" W; sec. 19, 30, T 2 N, R 7 W). Named on Mount Baldy (1954) 7.5' quadrangle. Postal authorities established Camp Baldy post office in San Bernardino County in 1913, changed the name to Mt. Baldy in 1951, changed it to Mount Baldy in 1966, and changed it back to Mt. Baldy in 1975; the name is from Mount San Antonio, also known as Old Baldy from the lack of vegetation at the top (Salley, p. 33, 148).

Mount Banning [LOS ANGELES]: *peak,* 6.5 miles west-northwest of Avalon on Santa Catalina Island (lat. 33°22'20" N, long. 118°26'05" W). Altitude 1734 feet. Named on Santa Catalina South (1943) 7.5' quadrangle.

Mount Banning: see **Black Jack Mountain** [LOS ANGELES].

Mount Bliss [LOS ANGELES]: *peak,* 4.25 miles northwest of Azusa city hall (lat. 34°11'05" N, long. 117°57' W; sec. 8, T 1 N, R 10 W). Altitude 3725 feet. Named on Azusa (1953) 7.5' quadrangle.

Mount Burnham [LOS ANGELES]: *peak,* 4.5 miles northeast of Crystal Lake (lat. 34°21'35" N, long. 117°46'50" W; near W line sec. 12, T 3 N, R 9 W). Altitude 8997 feet. Named on Crystal Lake (1958) 7.5' quadrangle. The name honors Major Frederick Russell Burnham, explorer and scout leader (United States Board on Geographic Names, 1954, p. 2).

Mount Clef [VENTURA]: *peak,* 3.5 miles north-northeast of Newbury Park (lat. 34°14' N, long. 118°53'10" W). Altitude 994 feet. Named on Newbury Park (1950, photorevised 1967) 7.5' quadrangle.

Mountclef Ridge [VENTURA]: *ridge,* west-southwest-trending, 3 miles long, 3 miles north-northeast of Newbury Park (lat. 34°13'35" N, long. 118°53'50" W); Mount

Clef is on the ridge. Named on Newbury Park (1950, photorevised 1967) and Thousand Oaks (1950, photorevised 1981) 7.5' quadrangles.

Mountclef Village [VENTURA]: *locality,* 3.25 miles northeast of Newbury Park (lat. 34°13'20" N, long. 118°52'35" W); the place is 1 mile south-southeast of Mount Clef. Named on Newbury Park (1950, photorevised 1967) 7.5' quadrangle.

Mount Disappointment [LOS ANGELES]: *peak,* 3 miles west-northwest of Mount Wilson (1) (lat. 34°14'45" N, long. 118°06'15" W). Altitude 5994 feet. Named on Mount Wilson (1953) 7.5' quadrangle. Three members of the Wheeler Survey climbed the peak in 1875 to use it as a triangulation point, but were disappointed to find that it was lower than nearby San Gabriel Peak (Robinson, J.W., 1977, p. 154).

Mount Downey: see **Santiago Peak** [ORANGE].

Mount Emma [LOS ANGELES]: *peak,* 6 miles north-northwest of Pacifico Mountain (lat. 34°27'35" N, long. 118°04'05" W). Altitude 5273 feet. Named on Pacifico Mountain (1959) 7.5' quadrangle.

Mount Emma Ridge [LOS ANGELES]: *ridge,* generally northeast-trending, 2.25 miles long, 6 miles north-northwest of Pacifico Mountain (lat. 34°27'55" N, long. 118°03'45" W); Mount Emma is on the ridge. Named on Pacifico Mountain (1959) 7.5' quadrangle.

Mount Gleason [LOS ANGELES]: *peak,* 6.5 miles south of Acton (lat. 34°22'35" N, long. 118°10'35" W). Named on Acton (1959) 7.5' quadrangle. Called Gleason Mt. on Tujunga (1900) 15' quadrangle. The name commemorates George Gleason, who with his companions discovered gold ore on the slopes of the feature in 1869 (Robinson, J.W., 1973, p. 26).

Mount Gleason Campground [LOS ANGELES]: *locality,* nearly 4 miles north-northeast of Condor Peak (lat. 34°22'20" N, long. 118°10'55" W); the place is 0.5 mile west-southwest of Mount Gleason. Named on Condor Peak (1959) 7.5' quadrangle.

Mount Harvard [LOS ANGELES]: *peak,* less than 1 mile south of Mount Wilson (1) (lat. 34°12'45" N, long. 118°03'40" W; sec. 32, T 2 N, R 11 W). Altitude 5440 feet. Named on Mount Wilson (1953) 7.5' quadrangle. The feature had the names "The Hogback," "South Gable Promontory," and "Martin's Peak" before Charles W. Eliot, president of Harvard University, visited the place in 1892; the peak was renamed Mount Harvard in the hope that Harvard University would build an observatory there—the university did put up a small observatory building in 1889 at what became known as Harvard Observatory Point (Robinson, J.W., 1977, p. 24, 34, 155). Peter Steil started a tent camp in the saddle between Mount Harvard and Mount Wilson and called

the place The Eyrie, but soon it became known as Steil's Camp (Robinson, J.W., 1977, p. 25).

Mount Hawkins [LOS ANGELES]: *peak,* nearly 3 miles northeast of Crystal Lake (lat. 34°20'30" N, long. 117°48'15" W). Altitude 8850 feet. Named on Crystal Lake (1958) 7.5' quadrangle. The name commemorates Nellie Hawkins, who was a popular waitress at a resort along North Fork San Gabriel River from 1901 until about 1906 (Robinson, J.W., 1983, p. 92).

Mount Hawkins: see **South Mount Hawkins** [LOS ANGELES].

Mount Hillyer [LOS ANGELES]: *peak,* 2.5 miles south-southeast of Pacifico Mountain (lat. 34°21' N, long. 118°00'50" W; sec. 15, T 3 N, R 11 W). Altitude 6162 feet. Named on Chilao Flat (1959) 7.5' quadrangle. Forest Service officials named the peak for Margaret Hillyer, a Forest Service employee (Gudde, 1949, p. 149).

Mount Hoar: see **Rincon Mountain** [VENTURA].

Mount Hollywood [LOS ANGELES]: *peak,* nearly 4 miles south of Burbank (lat. 34°07'40" N, long. 118°18' W); the feature is north of Hollywood. Altitude 1652 feet. Named on Burbank (1953) 7.5' quadrangle.

Mount Islip [LOS ANGELES]: *peak,* nearly 2 miles north of Crystal Lake (lat. 34°20'40" N, long. 117°50'20" W). Altitude 8250 feet. Named on Crystal Lake (1958) 7.5' quadrangle. The name commemorates George Islip, who homesteaded in San Gabriel Canyon in the 1880's (Robinson, J.W., 1983, p. 111).

Mount Kinneyloa: see **Mount Wilson** [LOS ANGELES] (1).

Mount Lawlor [LOS ANGELES]: *peak,* 8.5 miles south-southwest of Pacifico Mountain (lat. 34°16'15" N, long. 118°06'10" W). Altitude 5957 feet. Named on Chilao Flat (1959) 7.5' quadrangle. Called Mt. Lowler on Los Angeles County (1935) map. Forest Service officials named the peak about 1890 for Oscar Lawlor, a Los Angeles attorney.(Gudde, 1969, p. 174).

Mount Lee [LOS ANGELES]: *peak,* 3.25 miles south of Burbank city hall (lat. 34°08'05" N, long. 118°19'10" W). Named on Burbank (1966) 7.5' quadrangle. The peak is unnamed on Burbank (1953) 7.5' quadrangle, which shows Don Lee television tower on it.

Mount Lewis [LOS ANGELES]: *peak,* 4.25 miles north-northeast of Crystal Lake (lat. 34°22'20" N, long. 117°48'15" W; sec. 3, T 3 N, R 9 W). Named on Crystal Lake (1958) 7.5' quadrangle.

Mount Lowe [LOS ANGELES]:
(1) *peak,* 2.5 miles west of Mount Wilson (1) (lat. 34°13'55" N, long. 118°06'20" W; sec. 26, T 2 N, R 12 W). Altitude 5593 feet. Named on Mount Wilson (1953) 7.5' quadrangle. Owen Brown and Jason Brown, sons of abo-

litionist John Brown, named the feature John Brown Peak in 1887, but later they transferred the name to another peak; present Mount Lowe then was known as Oak Mountain until it was renamed to honor Professor Thaddeus Sobieski Coulincourt Lowe, who built the incline and electric railroad to Echo Mountain (Hanna, p. 177).
(2) *locality,* 2.5 miles west of Mount Wilson (1) (lat. 34°13'35" N, long. 118°06'30" W; sec. 26, T 2 N, R 12 W); the place is nearly 0.5 mile south-southwest of Mount Lowe (1). Site named on Mount Wilson (1953) 7.5' quadrangle, which shows it at the end of an abandoned Pacific Electric Railroad line. Mount Lowe (1939) 6' quadrangle shows Mt. Lowe Tavern at the site, and Mount Wilson (1966) 7.5' quadrangle shows Mt. Lowe Campground there. Postal authorities established Mount Lowe post office in 1910 and discontinued it in 1937 (Salley, p. 148).

Mount Lowe Campground: see **Mount Lowe** [LOS ANGELES] (2).

Mount Lowe Hotel: see **Echo Mountain** [LOS ANGELES].

Mount Lowe Tavern: see **Mount Lowe** [LOS ANGELES] (2).

Mount Lowler: see **Mount Lawlor** [LOS ANGELES].

Mount Lukens [LOS ANGELES]: *peak,* 4 miles south-southwest of Condor Peak (lat. 34°16'05" N, long. 118°14'15" W; near SE cor. sec. 9, T 2 N, R 13 W). Altitude 5074 feet. Named on Condor Peak (1959) 7.5' quadrangle. Called Sister Elsie Pk. on Tujunga (1900) 15' quadrangle. Members of the Wheeler Survey called the feature Sister Elsie Peak in 1875 to honor the good deeds of a Roman Catholic nun; the name "Mount Lukens" was given in the 1920's to commemorate Theodore P. Lukens, a Pasadena civic and business leader who was appointed acting supervisor of San Gabriel Forest Reserve in 1906 (Robinson, J.W., 1977, p. 69, 154).

Mount Markham [LOS ANGELES]: *peak,* 2.25 miles west-northwest of Mount Wilson (1) (lat. 34°14'10" N, long. 118°05'55" W; near NE cor. sec. 26, T 2 N, R 12 W). Altitude 5752 feet. Named on Mount Wilson (1953) 7.5' quadrangle. The feature first was called Square Top or Table Mountain for its appearance from Mount Wilson; Forest Service officials renamed it in the 1890's to honor Henry H. Markham, a prominent citizen of Pasadena and governor of California from 1891 until 1895 (Robinson, J.W., 1977, p. 155).

Mount McDill [LOS ANGELES]: *peak,* 3.5 miles south-southeast of the village of Leona Valley (lat. 34°34' N, long. 118°16'30" W; sec. 32, T 6 N, R 13 W). Altitude 5187 feet. Named on Sleepy Valley (1958) 7.5' quadrangle.

Mount McGill: see **Mount Pinos** [VENTURA].

Mount McKinley [LOS ANGELES]: *peak,* 6

miles north-northeast of Sunland (lat. 34°20'20" N, long. 118°15'50" W). Altitude 4926 feet. Named on Sunland (1966) 7.5' quadrangle.

Mount Mesa [LOS ANGELES]: *peak,* 10.5 miles east of Redman (lat. 34°46'25" N, long. 117°47'05" W; sec. 24, T 8 N, R 9 W). Altitude 3175 feet. Named on Rogers Lake South (1973) 7.5' quadrangle.

Mount Mooney [LOS ANGELES]: *peak,* 5.5 miles south-southeast of Pacifico Mountain (lat. 34°18'20" N, long. 118°00'25" W; sec. 35, T 3 N, R 11 W). Named on Chilao Flat (1959) 7.5' quadrangle. The name commemorates John L. Mooney, a Forest Service employee who died in France during World War I (United States Board on Geographic Names, 1933, p. 529).

Mount Oak Campground [LOS ANGELES]: *locality,* 2.25 miles west-northwest of Big Pines (lat. 34°23'40" N, long. 117°43'45" W). Named on Mescal Creek (1956) 7.5' quadrangle.

Mount Orizaba [LOS ANGELES]: *peak,* 1 mile east-northeast of Mount Banning on Santa Catalina Island (lat. 33°22'30" N, long. 118°25'05" W). Altitude 2125 feet. Named on Santa Catalina North (1950) 7.5' quadrangle.

Mount Parkinson: see **Parker Mountain** [LOS ANGELES].

Mount Pinos [VENTURA]: *peak,* 15 miles north-northeast of Reyes Peak at Ventura-Kern county line (lat. 34°48'45" N, long. 119°08'40" W; at N line sec. 6, T 8 N, R 21 W). Altitude 8831 feet. Named on Sawmill Mountain (1943) 7.5' quadrangle. United States Board on Geographic Names (1933, p. 606) rejected the name "Mount McGill" for the peak.

Mount Pinos Camp [VENTURA]: *locality,* 15 miles northeast of Reyes Peak (lat. 34°47'10" N, long. 119°04'50" W; near W line sec. 14, T 8 N, R 21 W); the place is 4 miles east-southeast of Mount Pinos. Named on Cuddy Valley (1943) 7.5' quadrangle. Called Mt. Pinos CCC Camp on Cuddy Valley (1944) 7.5' quadrangle.

Mount Sally [LOS ANGELES]: *peak,* 7.5 miles south of Pacifico Peak (lat. 34°16'20" N, long. 118°00'45" W; near E line sec. 10, T 2 N, R 11 W). Altitude 5408 feet. Named on Chilao Flat (1959) 7.5' quadrangle.

Mount San Antonio [LOS ANGELES]: *peak,* 18 miles northeast of Azusa city hall on Los Angeles-San Bernardino county line (lat. 34°17'20" N, long. 117°38'45" W; sec. 6, T 2 N, R 17 W). Named on Mount San Antonio (1955) 7.5' quadrangle. Called San Antonio Peak on Camp Baldy (1940) 6' quadrangle. United States Board on Geographic Names (1961b, p. 14) rejected the names "Baldy," "North Bald," "Old Bald," "Old Baldy Peak," "San Antonia Peak," and "San Antonio Peak" for the feature.

Mount Smith: see **Smith Mountain** [LOS ANGELES].

Mount Torquemada [LOS ANGELES]: *peak*, 3.25 miles east-southeast of Silver Peak on Santa Catalina Island (lat. 33°26'05" N, long. 118°31'15" W). Altitude 1336 feet. Named on Santa Catalina West (1943) 7.5' quadrangle.

Mount Vizcaino: see **Cactus Peak** [LOS ANGELES].

Mount Washington [LOS ANGELES]: *district*, 3.5 miles north-northeast of Los Angeles city hall (lat. 34°06' N, long. 118°13' W). Named on Los Angeles (1953) 7.5' quadrangle.

Mount Waterman: see **Waterman Mountain** [LOS ANGELES].

Mount Williamson [LOS ANGELES]: *peak*, 3.5 miles north of Crystal Lake (lat. 34°22'15" N, long. 117°51'25" W; sec. 6, T 3 N, R 9 W). Altitude 8214 feet. Named on Crystal Lake (1958) 7.5' quadrangle. The name commemorates Lieutenant Robert Stockton Williamson, who made a reconnaissance along the north side of San Gabriel Mountains in 1855 for the Pacific Railroad Survey (Robinson, J.W., 1983, p. 111).

Mount Wilson [LOS ANGELES]:
(1) *peak*, 15 miles northeast of Los Angeles city hall (lat. 34°13'25" N, long. 118°03'40" W; near S line sec. 29, T 2 N, R 11 W). Altitude 5710 feet. Named on Mount Wilson (1953) 7.5' quadrangle. The feature was known as Wilson's Peak after Benjamin D. Wilson built a trail to the top; government surveyors attempted unsuccessfully in 1887 to change the name to Mount Kinneyloa, from Abbot Kinney's ranch called Kinneyloa that was located in present Altadena—Kinney was head of the Board of Forestry of California (Robinson, J.W., 1977, p. 20, 22). Visitors to Mount Wilson in the early days commonly built a huge bonfire on a south-facing promontory—called Signal Point—at the top to let friends below know that they had arrived safely (Robinson, J.W., 1977, p. 21). A feature called Harvard Observatory Point was located near Signal Point: a small observatory building built there in 1889 gave it the name (Robinson, J.W., 1977, p. 24). United States Board on Geographic Names (1992, p. 4) approved the name "Muir Peak" for a feature situated 2.5 miles southwest of Mount Wilson (lat. 34°12'56" N, long. 118°06'05" W; sec. 35, T 2 N, R 12 W), and rejected the names "John Muirs Peak" and "Muirs Peak" for it; the name commemorates naturalist John Muir.
(2) *locality*, less than 0.5 mile northwest of Mount Wilson (1) (lat. 34°13'35" N, long. 118°03'55" W; on W line sec. 29, T 2 N, R 11 W). Named on Mount Wilson (1966) 7.5' quadrangle. Mount Wilson (1953) 7.5' quadrangle shows Mount Wilson P.O. at the place. Postal authorities established Mount Wilson post office in 1904 (Frickstad, p. 77).

Mount Zion [LOS ANGELES]: *peak*, 2 miles east-southeast of Mount Wilson (1) (lat. 34°12'50" N, long. 118°01'35" W; sec. 34, T 2 N, R 11 W). Altitude 3578 feet. Named on Mount Wilson (1953) 7.5' quadrangle.

Moyle: see **Norwalk** [LOS ANGELES].

Mud Creek Canyon [VENTURA]: *canyon*, drained by a stream that flows 3.5 miles to Santa Paula Creek 5 miles southwest of Santa Paula Peak (lat. 34°23'45" N, long. 119°04'30" W; near SW cor. sec. 27, T 4 N, R 21 W). Named on Santa Paula Peak (1951) 7.5' quadrangle.

Muddy Canyon [ORANGE]: *canyon*, drained by a stream that flows nearly 3.5 miles to the sea 3 miles west-northwest of Laguna Beach city hall (lat. 33°33'40" N, long. 117°49'40" W). Named on Laguna Beach (1965) 7.5' quadrangle. Called Los Trancos Canyon on Santa Ana (1942) 15' quadrangle, where present Los Trancos Canyon is unnamed.

Muddy Springs: see **Mud Spring** [LOS ANGELES].

Mud Spring [LOS ANGELES]: *spring*, 2.5 miles north-northeast of the village of Lake Hughes (lat. 34°42'35" N, long. 118°25' W; sec. 12, T 7 N, R 15 W). Named on Lake Hughes (1957) 7.5' quadrangle. Latta (p. 59) called the feature Aguaje Lodoso, or Muddy Springs.

Mud Springs: see **San Dimas** [LOS ANGELES].

Mud Town: see **Watts** [LOS ANGELES].

Mugu Lagoon [VENTURA]: *water feature*, 2.5 miles west-northwest of Point Mugu along the coast (lat. 34°06'05" N, long. 119°06' W). Named on Point Mugu (1949) 7.5' quadrangle. Called Mugu Laguna on Hueneme (1904) 15' quadrangle.

Mugu Laguna: see **Mugu Lagoon** [VENTURA].

Mugu Peak [VENTURA]: *peak*, 0.5 mile northeast of Point Mugu (lat. 34°05'35" N, long. 119°03'15" W). Altitude 1266 feet. Named on Point Mugu (1949) 7.5' quadrangle.

Mugu Point: see **Point Mugu** [VENTURA].

Muir Peak: see **Mount Wilson** [LOS ANGELES] (1).

Mule Fork [LOS ANGELES]: *stream*, flows 2 miles to Alder Creek (2) 4.5 miles southwest of Pacifico Mountain (lat. 34°19'10" N, long. 118°03' W; sec. 29, T 3 N, R 11 W). Named on Chilao Flat (1959) 7.5' quadrangle.

Mullally Canyon [LOS ANGELES]: *canyon*, drained by a steam that flows 1.25 miles to Pickens Canyon 7.5 miles northwest of Pasadena city hall (lat. 34°14'10" N, long. 118°13'30" W; near N line sec. 27, T 2 N, R 13 W). Named on Pasadena (1953) 7.5' quadrangle.

Mull Canyon [LOS ANGELES]: *canyon*, 1 mile long, 2.5 miles east-northeast of Glendora city hall (lat. 34°08'45" N, long. 117°49'20" W; sec. 22, 27, 28, T 1 N, R 9 W). Named on Glendora (1953) 7.5' quadrangle.

Munger Creek [ORANGE]: *stream,* flows 2.5 miles to Aliso Creek at El Toro (lat. 33°37'25" N, long. 117°41'20" W). Named on El Toro (1950) 7.5' quadrangle. The name commemorates Sam Munger and his family, who settled along the creek in the late 1880's (Meadows, p. 103).

Munson Creek [VENTURA]: *stream,* flows 3.5 miles to Sespe Creek 5.5 miles north of Wheeler Springs (lat. 34°35'20" N, long. 119°17'25" W; near S line sec. 23, T 6 N, R 23 W). Named on Reyes Peak (1943) and Wheeler Springs (1943) 7.5' quadrangles.

Munz Canyon [LOS ANGELES]: *canyon,* drained by a stream that flows 1.5 miles to lowlands about 1.5 miles southeast of the village of Lake Hughes (lat. 34°39'50" N, long. 118°25'15" W; sec. 25, T 7 N, R 15 W). Named on Lake Hughes (1957) 7.5' quadrangle, which shows Munz ranch near the mouth of the canyon. Elizabeth Lake (1917) 30' quadrangle has the name "Roosevelt" for a place located near the mouth of present Munz Canyon. Postal authorities established Roosevelt post office in 1902, moved it 1.5 miles southeast in 1906, and discontinued it in 1925; the name was for Theodore Roosevelt (Salley, p. 188).

Munz Lakes [LOS ANGELES]: *lakes,* 0.5 mile east-southeast of the village of Lake Hughes (lat. 34°40'20" N, long. 118°25'50" W; near NE cor. sec. 26, T 7 N, R 15 W). Named on Lake Hughes (1957) 7.5' quadrangle.

Mupu Cañon: see **Santa Paula Canyon** [VENTURA].

Murietta Canyon [VENTURA]: *canyon,* drained by a stream that flows 3.25 miles to the canyon of Matilija Creek 5 miles west of Wheeler Springs (lat. 34°30'20" N, long. 119°22'40" W; sec. 22, T 5 N, R 24 W). Named on Old Man Mountain (1943) and White Ledge Peak (1952) 7.5' quadrangles. The stream in the canyon is called West Fork Matilija Cr. on Ventura (1904) 15' quadrangle.

Murietta Divide [VENTURA]: *pass,* 3 miles west-northwest of White Ledge Peak (lat. 34°29'25" N, long. 119°26'05" W); the pass is at the head of Murietta Canyon. Named on White Ledge Peak (1952) 7.5' quadrangle.

Muroc Dry Lake Center: see **Edwards Air Force Base**, under **Rosamond Lake** [LOS ANGELES].

Mussel Cove [ORANGE]: *embayment,* 4.25 miles west-southwest of San Juan Capistrano along the coast (lat. 33°29'15" N, long. 117°44'05" W). Named on Dana Point (1968) 7.5' quadrangle.

Mustang Spring [ORANGE]: *spring,* 6.5 miles south of Sierra Peak (lat. 33°45'20" N, long. 117°38'10" W; sec. 8, T 5 S, R 7 W). Named on Black Star Canyon (1967) 7.5' quadrangle.

Mustang Spring Canyon: see **Ladd Canyon** [ORANGE].

Mutau Creek [VENTURA]: *stream,* flows 10 miles to Piru Creek 15 miles east-northeast of Reyes Peak (lat. 34°40'55" N, long. 119°01'10" W; sec. 20, T 7 N, R 20 W); the stream goes through Mutau Flat. Named on Lockwood Valley (1943) and Topatopa Mountains (1943) 7.5' quadrangles.

Mutau Creek: see **Little Mutau Creek** [VENTURA].

Mutau Flat [VENTURA]: *valley,* 13 miles east of Reyes Peak (lat. 34°37'30" N, long. 119°02'45" W). Named on Lockwood Valley (1943) and Topatopa Mountains (1943) 7.5' quadrangles. The name commemorates William Mutau, who came to the region in the 1850's—the name "Mutah" in its various spellings may be an Indian alias given to a wanted man by his native wife (Outland, 1969, p. 100). United States Board on Geographic Names (1990, p. 82) approved the name "Johnston Ridge" for a feature that extends for 3.3 miles southeast from Mutau Flat to Hot Springs Canyon, and rejected name "Johnson Ridge" for it.

Myford: see **East Irvine** [ORANGE].

Myrick Canyon [LOS ANGELES]: *canyon,* drained by a stream that flows 5.25 miles to lowlands 5 miles west-northwest of Del Sur (lat. 34°42'55" N, long. 118°22' W; near N line sec. 9, T 7 N, R 14 W). Named on Del Sur (1958) and Lake Hughes (1957) 7.5' quadrangles. Called Myric Canyon on Los Angeles County (1935) map, which also names North Fork.

Myrtle: see **Harold** [LOS ANGELES].

Mystery Spring [VENTURA]: *spring,* 10.5 miles north of Reyes Peak (lat. 34°47'05" N, long. 119°16'55" W; sec. 14, T 8 N, R 23 W). Named on Apache Canyon (1943) 7.5' quadrangle.

Mystic Canyon [LOS ANGELES]:
(1) *canyon,* drained by a stream that flows 2.25 miles to Texas Canyon 11.5 miles south of the village of Lake Hughes (lat. 34°30'40" N, long. 118°25' W; at S line sec. 14, T 5 N, R 15 W). Named on Green Valley (1958) 7.5' quadrangle.
(2) *canyon,* drained by a stream that flows 1.5 miles to Big Dalton Canyon 2.5 miles northeast of Glendora city hall (lat. 34°09'30" N, long. 117°49'40" W; sec. 21, T 1 N, R 9 W). Named on Glendora (1953) 7.5' quadrangle.

– N –

Nadeau [LOS ANGELES]: *locality,* 2.25 miles west-northwest of South Gate city hall along Southern Pacific Railroad (lat. 33°58' N, long. 118°14'35" W). Named on South Gate (1964) 7.5' quadrangle.

Nadeau Canyon: see **Solemint** [LOS ANGELES].

Nadeau Park [LOS ANGELES]: *locality,* 2 miles northwest of present South Gate city hall along Atchison, Topeka and Santa Fe Railroad (lat. 33°59'15" N, long. 118°14'15" W). Named on Downey (1902) 15' quadrangle. The name is from Gernert and Nadeau Beet Sugarie established at the place in 1881 (Gudde, 1949, p. 230).

Nago [ORANGE]: *locality,* 2.5 miles southeast of present Huntington Beach civic center along Pacific Electric Railroad (lat. 33°38'05" N, long. 117°57'45" W). Named on Newport Beach (1951) 7.5' quadrangle.

Naples [LOS ANGELES]: *district,* 4.25 miles east-southeast of Long Beach city hall (lat. 33°45'20" N, long. 118°07'15" W). Named on Long Beach (1949) and Los Alamitos (1950) 7.5' quadrangles.

Natural Arch [LOS ANGELES]: *relief feature,* 5.25 miles west-northwest of present Santa Monica city hall along the coast (lat. 34°02'25" N, long. 118°34'30" W). Named on Topanga Canyon (1928) 6' quadrangle.

Naud Junction [LOS ANGELES]: *locality,* 0.5 mile northeast of Los Angeles city hall along a railroad (lat. 34°03'35" N, long. 118°14'05" W). Named on Los Angeles (1966) 7.5' quadrangle.

Naumann: see Oxnard [VENTURA].

Necktie Basin [LOS ANGELES]: *area,* 0.5 mile west of Warm Springs Mountain (lat. 34°35'45" N, long. 118°35'15" W); the place is near the head of Necktie Canyon. Named on Warm Springs Mountain (1958) 7.5' quadrangle.

Necktie Canyon [LOS ANGELES]: *canyon,* drained by a stream that flows 4 miles to Castaic Creek 4.25 miles south-southwest of Warm Springs Mountain (lat. 34°32'45" N, long. 118°37'20" W; near W line sec. 1, T 5 N, R 17 W). Named on Warm Springs Mountain (1958) 7.5' quadrangle. Los Angeles County (1935) map names three branches of the canyon of Castaic Creek near Necktie Canyon: Owl Canyon, which opens into canyon of Castaic Creek from the northeast about 0.5 mile below the mouth of Necktie Canyon; Oak Canyon, which opens into the canyon of Castaic Creek from the northeast less than 1 mile downstream from the mouth of Owl Canyon; and Kingsley Canyon, which opens into the canyon of Castaic Creek from the northeast less than 0.25 mile below the mouth of Oak Canyon.

Nedo: see Ozena [VENTURA].

Neenach [LOS ANGELES]: *locality,* 13 miles east of Gorman (lat. 34°47' N, long. 118°36'55" W; sec. 18, T 8 N, R 16 W). Named on Tejon (1903) 30' quadrangle. Neenach School (1965) 7.5' quadrangle shows Neenach school situated about 0.5 mile farther east. Postal authorities established Neenach post office in 1888, moved it 2 miles southeast in 1904, moved it 3.5 miles southwest in 1910, and discontinued it in 1929; the place was a gold-mining camp (Salley, p. 152).

Kroeber (p. 50) suggested an Indian origin for the name.

Neff [ORANGE]: *locality,* 5 miles southeast of present Buena Park civic center along Southern Pacific Railroad (lat. 33°48'35" N, long. 117°55'55" W). Named on Garden Grove (1935) 7.5' quadrangle.

Nehr Canyon [LOS ANGELES]: *canyon,* drained by a stream that flows 1.25 miles to Little Tujunga Canyon 4.5 miles north-northwest of Sunland (lat. 34°19'20" N, long. 118°20'15" W; near N line sec. 27, T 3 N, R 14 W). Named on Sunland (1953) 7.5' quadrangle.

Nellus Canyon [LOS ANGELES]: *canyon,* drained by a stream that flows 1.5 miles to Santa Clara River 9 miles east of Solemint (lat. 34°26'25" N, long. 118°17'45" W; sec. 12, T 4 N, R 14 W). Named on Agua Dulce (1960) 7.5' quadrangle.

Nelson Canyon [LOS ANGELES]: *canyon,* drained by a stream that flows 2 miles to Santa Clara River 9.5 miles east of Solemint (lat. 34°26'25" N, long. 118°17'30" W; near cor. sec. 12, T 4 N, R 14 W). Named on Agua Dulce (1960) 7.5' quadrangle. Los Angeles County (1935) map shows a feature called Portland Canyon that opens into Soledad Canyon from the south about 1 mile west of the mouth of Nelson Canyon, and shows a feature called Redman Canyon that opens into Soledad Canyon from the south less than 1 mile west of the mouth of Nelson Canyon.

Nettle Spring [VENTURA]: *spring,* 11 miles north of Reyes Peak (lat. 34°48'10" N, long. 119°17'30" W; sec. 11, T 8 N, R 23 W). Named on Apache Canyon (1943) 7.5' quadrangle.

Nevin [LOS ANGELES]: *locality,* nearly 3 miles south of Los Angeles city hall along Southern Pacific Railroad (lat. 34°00'50" N, long. 118°14'45" W). Named on Los Angeles (1966) 7.5' quadrangle.

Newbury Park [VENTURA]: *town,* 16 miles east of Oxnard (lat. 34° 11' N, long. 118°54'30" W). Named on Newbury Park (1951) 7.5' quadrangle. Postal authorities established Newbury Park post office in Ventura County in 1875, moved it into Los Angeles County in 1882, moved it 1.25 miles north and back into Ventura County in 1883, moved it 5 miles west in 1891, and moved it 1 mile west in 1908; the name is for Egbert S. Newbury, first postmaster (Salley, p. 153). They established Timberville post office 7 miles west of Newbury Park post office in 1888 and discontinued it in 1893 (Salley, p. 222).

Newcomb Pass [LOS ANGELES]: *pass,* 2 miles east-northeast of Mount Wilson (1) (lat. 34°13'55" N, long. 118°01'05" W; sec. 27, T 2 N, R 11 W). Named on Mount Wilson (1953) 7.5' quadrangle. The name commemorates Louie Newcomb, who laid out a trail over

the pass (Robinson, J.W., 1977, p. 125).
Newhall [LOS ANGELES]: *town,* 7.5 miles
north-northwest of San Fernando (lat.
34°23'05" N, long. 118°31'50" W). Named
on Newhall (1952) and Oat Mountain (1952)
7.5' quadrangles. Postal authorities established
Newhall post office in 1877 (Frickstad, p. 78).
Officials of Southern Pacific Railroad built a
station at present Saugus in 1876 and named
it "Newhall" for Henry M. Newhall, owner
of the land; in 1878 they moved the station
and name to present Newhall (Gudde, 1949,
p. 235). Los Angeles County (1935) map
shows a feature called Railroad Canyon that
extends for 2 miles south from Newhall along
the rail line; the same map has the name
"Wildwood Cany." for the next north-trending canyon west of and parallel to Railroad
Canyon.
Newhall Creek [LOS ANGELES]: *stream,* flows
4.25 miles to South Fork Santa Clara River
0.5 miles north-northeast of downtown
Newhall (lat. 34°23'40" N, long. 118°32'15"
W); the stream goes through Newhall. Named
on Newhall (1952) and Oat Mountain (1952)
7.5' quadrangles.
New Jerusalem: see **El Rio** [VENTURA].
Newman Point [LOS ANGELES]: *relief feature,*
4.5 miles north-northeast of Glendora city hall
(lat. 34°11'55" N, long. 117°50'25" W; sec.
5, T 1 N, R 9 W). Named on Glendora (1953)
7.5' quadrangle.
Newmark: see **Montebello** [LOS ANGELES].
New Pass: see **Soledad Pass** [LOS ANGELES].
Newport [ORANGE]: *locality,* 6 miles north-
northwest of Newport Beach (lat. 33°41'45"
N, long. 117°54'15" W). Named on Corona
(1902) 30' quadrangle.
Newport: see **Newport Beach** [ORANGE] (2);
Old Newport, under **Greenville** [ORANGE].
Newport Bay [ORANGE]: *bay,* the entrance
channel is 3.25 miles east-southeast of Newport Beach city hall (lat. 33°35'35" N, long.
117°52'45" W); the bay is at the city of New-
port Beach. Named on Newport Beach (1965)
7.5' quadrangle. Newport Bay and Upper
Newport Bay together are called San Joaquin
Bay on Lankershim Ranch Land and Water
Company's (1888) map. The combined bays
also were called Cienega de la San Joaquin,
Cienega de las Ranas (Hanna, p. 211), Bolsa
de San Joaquin, and Bolsa de Quigara
(Gleason, p. 88-90). Newport Beach (1965)
7.5' quadrangle names three channels in the
bay: Balboa Reach south of Balboa Island,
Harbor Island Reach south of Harbor Island,
and Lido Isle Reach between Lido Isle and
the mainland. Rocky Point was a conspicu-
ous feature on the east side of the entrance to
Newport Bay before jetties were built there
(Meadows, p. 120).
Newport Bay: see **Upper Newport Bay** [OR-
ANGE].
Newport Beach [ORANGE]:

(1) *beach,* 6 miles southeast of Huntington
Beach civic center along the coast (lat.
33°36'20" N, long. 117°55'05" W). Named
on Newport Beach (1965) 7.5' quadrangle.
The feature first was known as Sand Beach
(Meadows, p. 123).
(2) *city,* 5 miles southeast of Huntington Beach
civic center along the coast (lat. 33°37' N,
long. 117°55'45" W). Named on Laguna
Beach (1965), Newport Beach (1965), and
Tustin (1965) 7.5' quadrangles. Postal authorities established Newport Beach post office in
1891 (Frickstad, p. 117), and the city incorporated in 1906. In 1872 Captain S.S.
Dunnells and Mr. D.M. Dorman set up a small
dock and warehouse called Newport Landing just below the bluff that divides Newport
Bay from Upper Newport Bay 1.25 miles east
of present Newport Beach city hall; the
McFadden brothers purchased the facility in
1873, and it became known as McFadden's
Landing and as Port Orange—after the
McFaddens built a wharf along the ocean, it
was called Old Landing (Hoover, Rensch, and
Rensch, p. 264). Postal authorities established
Newport post office at Newport Landing in
1875, discontinued it in 1876, reestablished
it in 1882, and discontinued it in 1901 (Salley,
p. 154). The present city developed around
the long wharf that the McFadden brothers
built in 1888 along the ocean (Meadows, p.
104-105). Branagan Glass Company built a
factory next to the bluff in the city of Newport Beach in 1913, and Southern Pacific
Railroad built a spur line called Branagan for
the factory; the spur line was abandoned in
1927 (Meadows, p. 30).
Newport Heights [ORANGE]: *district,* 5 miles
east-southeast of Huntington Beach civic center (lat. 33°37'25" N, long. 117°55'15" W).
Named on Newport Beach (1965) 7.5' quadrangle.
Newport Island [ORANGE]: *island,* 1400 feet
long, 4.5 miles southeast of Huntington Beach
civic center in Newport Harbor (lat. 33°
37'10" N, long. 117°56' W). Named on New-
port Beach (1965) 7.5' quadrangle.
Newport Landing: see **Newport Beach** [OR-
ANGE] (2).
New River: see **San Gabriel River** [LOS AN-
GELES].
New San Gabriel River: see **San Gabriel River**
[LOS ANGELES-ORANGE].
New San Pedro: see **Wilmington** [LOS ANGE-
LES].
Newton Canyon [LOS ANGELES]: *canyon,*
drained by a stream that flows 2 miles to Zuma
Canyon 5.25 miles north of Point Dume (lat.
34°04'35" N, long. 118°49'05" W; near SE
cor. sec. 13, T 1 S, R 19 W). Named on Point
Dume (1951) 7.5' quadrangle.
Newton Park [LOS ANGELES]: *district,* 4.5
miles northeast of present Los Angeles city
hall (lat. 34°05'25" N, long. 118°10'35" W).

Named on Alhambra (1926) 6' quadrangle.

Newtown: see **Wilmington** [LOS ANGELES].

Nicholas Canyon [LOS ANGELES]: *canyon,* drained by a stream that flows 2.5 miles to the sea 6.5 miles west-northwest of Point Dume (lat. 34°02'30" N, long. 118°54'50" W). Named on Triunfo Pass (1950) 7.5' quadrangle. On Camulos (1903) 30' quadrangle, the name applies to present Los Alisos Canyon. United States Board on Geographic Names (1943, p. 13) approved the name "San Nicolas Canyon" for the feature, and rejected the names "Arroyo San Nicolas," "Cañada San Nicolas," and "Nicholas Canyon."

Nicholas Canyon: see **Little Nicholas Canyon,** under **Willow Creek** [LOS ANGELES]; **Los Alisos Canyon** [LOS ANGELES].

Nicholas Flat [LOS ANGELES]: *area,* 7.25 miles northwest of Point Dume (lat. 34°04' N, long. 118°54'30" W; sec. 19, T 1 S, R 19 W). Named on Triunfo Pass (1950) 7.5' quadrangle, which shows the place near the head of Nicholas Canyon.

Nichols Canyon [LOS ANGELES]: *canyon,* 1.25 miles long, 8 miles west-northwest of Los Angeles city hall (lat. 34°06'45" N, long. 118°21'35" W; at W line sec. 4, T 1 S, R 14 W). Named on Hollywood (1966) 7.5' quadrangle.

Nicholson Canyon: see **Castaic** [LOS ANGELES].

Nicolas Canyon: see **Los Alsiso Canyon** [LOS ANGELES].

Niger Canyon: see **Emerald Canyon** [ORANGE].

Nigger Canyon: see **Emerald Canyon** [ORANGE]; **Warring Canyon** [VENTURA].

Nigger Creek [VENTURA]: *stream,* flows 3.5 miles to Piru Creek 14 miles east-northeast of Reyes Peak (lat. 34°40' N, long. 119°02'30" W; near S line sec. 30, T 7 N, R 20 W). Named on Lockwood Valley (1943) 7.5' quadrangle.

Niggerhead Mountain [LOS ANGELES]: *peak,* 7.5 miles north of Point Dume (lat. 34°06'35" N, long. 118°48'30" W; sec. 6, T 1 S, R 18 W). Altitude 2039 feet. Named on Point Dume (1951) 7.5' quadrangle. Called Niggerhead on Los Angeles County (1935) map. The name is from the outline of the feature (Gudde, 1949, p. 233).

Nigger Slough [LOS ANGELES]: *lake,* 4 miles long, 7 miles east of Redondo (present Redondo Beach) (lat. 33°50'45" N, long. 118°16' W). Named on Redondo (1896) 15' quadrangle. It is called Laguna Seca on a diseño of Sausal Redondo grant (Becker, 1969). Los Angeles Board of Supervisors adopted the name "Laguna Dominguez" for the swamps and lake formerly known as Nigger Slough (Gudde, 1949, p. 97)—present Dominguez Channel extends through the feature.

Nigger Wash [VENTURA]: *stream,* flows 1.5 miles to Santa Clara River 1.25 miles south of Piru (lat. 34°23'50" N, long. 118°47'50"

W; sec. 30, T 4 N, R 18 W); the stream heads at the mouth of Nigger Canyon (present Warring Canyon). Named on Piru (1952) 7.5' quadrangle.

Niguel [ORANGE]: *land grant,* extends southwest from El Toro to Laguna Beach (2). Named on Dana Point (1949), Laguna Beach (1949), and San Juan Capistrano (1949) 7.5' quadrangles. Juan Avila and others received 3 leagues in 1842, and Avila claimed 13,316 acres patented in 1873 (Cowan, p. 52). Perez (p. 78) gave 1875 as the date of the patent. The name is the Spanish rendition of the designation of an Indian village (Meadows, p. 105).

Niguel Hill [ORANGE]: *peak,* 4 miles westnorthwest of San Juan Capistrano (lat. 33°30'45" N, long. 117°44' W); the feature is on Niguel grant. Altitude 926 feet. Named on San Juan Capistrano (1968) 7.5' quadrangle.

Nimock: see **Huntington Beach** [ORANGE].

Nino Canyon [LOS ANGELES]: *canyon,* drained by a stream that flows less than 0.5 mile to Arroyo Seco nearly 6 miles northnorthwest of Pasadena city hall (lat. 34°13'35" N, long. 118°10'45" W). Named on Pasadena (1953) 7.5' quadrangle.

9th Street Junction [LOS ANGELES]: *locality,* nearly 3 miles south-southeast of Los Angeles city hall along Union Pacific Railroad (lat. 34°01'10" N, long. 118°13'10" W). Named on Los Angeles (1953) 7.5' quadrangle.

Nintynine Oaks [LOS ANGELES]: *locality,* 8 miles northwest of Newhall (lat. 34°31' N, long. 118°36'55" W; sec. 36, T 5 N, R 17 W). Named on Newhall (1952) 7.5' quadrangle. Castaic (1940) 6' quadrangle shows a place called Lindys at the site.

Noel Canyon [LOS ANGELES]: *canyon,* drained by a stream that flows 0.5 mile to Pacoima Canyon 7 miles north of Sunland (lat. 34°21'40" N, long. 118°18'10" W; sec. 12, T 3 N, R 14 W). Named on Sunland (1953) 7.5' quadrangle. Called Pinery Canyon on Los Angeles County (1935) map.

Nogales: see **Matilija Hot Springs** [VENTURA].

Nordhoff: see **Ojai** [VENTURA] (2).

Nordhoff Peak [VENTURA]: *peak,* 3.5 miles north of the town of Ojai, which originally was called Nordhoff (lat. 34°29'50" N, long. 119°14'30" W; sec. 24, T 5 N, R 23 W). Altitude 4485 feet. Named on Ojai (1952) 7.5' quadrangle.

Nordhoff Ridge [VENTURA]: *ridge,* westtrending, 3 miles long, 3.5 miles north-northwest of the town of Ojai (lat. 34°29'45" N, long. 119°15'35" W); Nordhoff Peak is at the east end of the ridge. Named on Matilija (1952) and Ojai (1952) 7.5' quadrangles.

North Alhambra [LOS ANGELES]: *locality,* 5.25 miles west northwest of El Monte along Southern Pacific Railroad (lat. 34°05'55" N, long. 118°07'30" W); the place is north of Alhambra. Named on Pasadena (1900) 15' quadrangle.

Northam [ORANGE]: *locality,* 1.25 miles north of Buena Park along Southern California Railroad (lat. 33°52'50" N, long. 118°00' W). Named on Corona (1902) 30' quadrangle. The name commemorates Robert Northam, a landowner and ranch manager (Meadows, p. 106).

North Bald: see **Mount San Antonio** [LOS ANGELES].

North Baldy: see **Mount Baden-Powell** [LOS ANGELES].

North Baldy Peak: see **Throop Peak** [LOS ANGELES].

North Fillmore [VENTURA]: *town,* less than 1 mile west-northwest of downtown Fillmore (lat. 34°24'25" N, long. 118°55'20" W; at NE cor. sec. 25, T 4 N, R 20 W). Named on Fillmore (1951) 7.5' quadrangle.

North Glendale [LOS ANGELES]: *district,* 2.5 miles southeast of Burbank city hall (lat. 34°09'40" N, long. 118°16' W); the district is 1.5 miles northwest of Glendale civic center. Named on Burbank (1953) 7.5' quadrangle.

North Highland Park [LOS ANGELES]: *district,* 5.25 miles north-northeast of present Los Angeles city hall (lat. 34°07'25" N, long. 118°12'20" W); the district is north of Highland Park. Named on Glendale (1928) 6' quadrangle.

North Hollywood [LOS ANGELES]: *district,* 4.25 miles east-southeast of Van Nuys in Los Angeles (lat. 34°10' N, long. 118°22'30" W). Named on Burbank (1953) and Van Nuys (1953) 7.5' quadrangles. Called Toluca on Santa Monica (1902) 15' quadrangle, and called Lankershim on Burbank (1926) 6' quadrangle. Postal authorities established Toluca post office in 1893, changed the name to Lankershim in 1906, and changed it to North Hollywood in 1926 (Salley, p. 117, 223). The name "Lankershim" recalls Isaac Lankershim, a developer of the place (Hanna, p. 140).

North Long Beach [LOS ANGELES]: *district,* 6 miles north of Long Beach city hall (lat. 33°51'20" N, long. 118°11' W). Named on Long Beach (1949) 7.5' quadrangle. Postal authorities established Virginia City post office in 1923 and changed the name to North Long Beach in 1928 (Salley, p. 232).

North Long Canyon [LOS ANGELES]: *canyon,* drained by a stream that flows 1.5 miles to lowlands 5.25 miles northeast of Burnt Peak (lat. 34°44'30" N, long. 118°30'55" W; sec. 31, T 8 N, R 15 W); the feature is less than 1 mile north of South Long Canyon. Named on Burnt Peak (1958) 7.5' quadrangle.

North Los Angeles: see **Northridge** [LOS ANGELES].

North Peak: see **Modjeska Peak** [ORANGE].

North Pomona [LOS ANGELES]: *district,* 2.25 miles north of Pomona city hall (lat. 34°05'20"

N, long. 117°44'45" W). Named on Ontario (1954) 7.5' quadrangle. Postal authorities established North Pomona post office in 1891 and discontinued it in 1949 (Salley, p. 156).

North Portal: see **Fairmont Reservoir** [LOS ANGELES].

Northridge [LOS ANGELES]: *district,* 4 miles east-northeast of the center of Canoga Park in Los Angeles (lat. 34°13'45" N, long. 118° 32'35" W). Named on Canoga Park (1952) 7.5' quadrangle. Called Zelzah on Zelzah (1941) 6' quadrangle, which shows Northridge P.O. and Sta. at the place. Postal authorities established Zelzah post office in 1911, changed the name to North Los Angeles in 1929, and changed it to Northridge in 1938 (Frickstad, p. 78, 84). The name "Zelzah" was given to the place because it, like the biblical Zelzah, was a watering spot in the desert; Carl S. Dentzel proposed the name "Northridge" from Northridge Stampede, which was at the base of the ridge north of San Fernando Valley (Gudde, 1969, p. 224).

North San Gabriel [LOS ANGELES]: *locality,* 4.5 miles northwest of El Monte along Southern Pacific Railroad (lat. 34°07' N, long. 118°06' W); the place is north of San Gabriel. Named on Pasadena (1900) 15' quadrangle.

North Sherman Way [LOS ANGELES]: *locality,* 1 mile north of Van Nuys along Pacific Electric Railroad (lat. 34°12' N, long. 118°26'55" W). Named on Pacoima (1927) and Van Nuys (1926) 6' quadrangles.

Northwest Harbor [LOS ANGELES]: *embayment,* at the north end of San Clemente Island (lat. 33°01'55" N, long. 118°35' W). Named on San Clemente Island North (1943) 7.5' quadrangle.

North Whittier Heights [LOS ANGELES]: *district,* 5.25 miles south-southwest of Baldwin Park city hall (lat. 34°00'50" N, long. 117° 59'10" W). Named on Baldwin Park (1953) 7.5' quadrangle.

North Wilmington: see **Carson** [LOS ANGELES].

Norwalk [LOS ANGELES]: *city,* 4.5 miles south-southwest of Whittier city hall (lat. 33°54'55" N, long. 118°04'15" W). Named on Whittier (1965) 7.5' quadrangle. Postal authorities established Corvallis post office in 1875, and changed the name to Norwalk in 1877 (Frickstad, p. 72). The city incorporated in 1957. Postal authorities established Moyle post office 4.5 miles south of Norwalk post office in 1900 and discontinued it in 1903; the name was for Thomas Moyle, first postmaster (Salley, p. 148). They established Sunshine post office in present Norwalk 4.5 miles southwest of Whittier post office in 1944 and discontinued it in 1962; the name was for the location of the facility along Sunshine Avenue (Salley, p. 216).

Nuevo Canyon [VENTURA]: *canyon,* drained

by a stream that flows 1.25 miles to Holser Canyon 3.25 miles east-northeast of Piru (lat. 34°26'15" N, long. 118°44'25" W; at N line sec. 14, T 4 N, R 18 W). Named on Val Verde (1952) 7.5' quadrangle.

Nutwood [ORANGE]: *locality,* 4.5 miles southeast of Buena Park along Southern Pacific Railroad (lat. 33°48'20" N, long. 117°57'30" W). Named on Corona (1902) 30' quadrangle.

Nyland [VENTURA]: *town,* 3 miles northeast of Oxnard (lat. 34°13'30" N, long. 119°08'05" W). Named on Oxnard (1949) 7.5' quadrangle.

– O –

Oak Canyon [LOS ANGELES]:
(1) *canyon,* drained by a stream that flows 2.25 miles to Santa Felicia Canyon 13 miles west-northwest of Newhall (lat. 34°28'35" N, long. 118°43'05" W). Named on Val Verde (1952) 7.5' quadrangle.
(2) *canyon,* drained by a stream that flows 1.5 miles to San Gabriel River 8 miles northeast of Glendora city hall (lat. 34°13'45" N, long. 117°46'40" W). Named on Glendora (1953) 7.5' quadrangle.

Oak Canyon [VENTURA]:
(1) *canyon,* drained by a stream that flows less than 1 mile to Dry Canyon (1) 7 miles west-northwest of Santa Susana Pass (lat. 34°18'25" N, long. 118°44'40" W; near NE cor. sec. 34, T 3 N, R 18 W). Named on Santa Susana (1951) 7.5' quadrangle.
(2) *canyon,* drained by a stream that flows 2.5 miles to Simi Valley (1) nearly 6 miles northnortheast of Thousand Oaks (lat. 34°14'30" N, long. 118°47' W; sec. 20, T 2 N, R 18 W). Named on Thousand Oaks (1952) 7.5' quadrangle.

Oak Canyon: see **Dry Canyon** [VENTURA] (1); **Necktie Canyon** [LOS ANGELES].

Oakdale Canyon [LOS ANGELES]:
(1) *canyon,* nearly 2 miles long, opens into Pine Canyon (1) 4 miles north-northwest of Burnt Peak (lat. 34°44'05" N, long. 118°36'10" W; sec. 32, T 8 N, R 16 W). Named on Burnt Peak (1958) and Liebre Mountain (1958) 7.5' quadrangles.
(2) *canyon,* 1.5 miles long, opens into the valley of South Fork Santa Clara River 1 mile north of downtown Newhall (lat. 34°24'05" N, long. 118°32'05" W). Named on Newhall (1952) 7.5' quadrangle.

Oak Creek [VENTURA]: *stream,* flows 1 mile to Cuyama River 9 miles northwest of Reyes Peak (lat. 34°43'40" N, long. 119°23'35" W). Named on Rancho Nuevo Creek (1943) 7.5' quadrangle.

Oak Flat [LOS ANGELES]: *area,* 3 miles north-northeast of Burnt Peak (lat. 34°43'15" N, long. 118°36'10" W; near SW cor. sec. 5, T 7

N, R 16 W). Named on Burnt Peak (1958) 7.5' quadrangle.

Oak Flat [ORANGE]: *area,* 1.5 miles south-southeast of Sierra Peak (lat. 33°49'40" N, long. 117°38'15" W; at NW cor. sec. 17, T 4 S, R 7 W). Named on Black Star Canyon (1967) 7.5' quadrangle.

Oak Flat [VENTURA]:
(1) *area,* 13 miles east-northeast of Wheeler Springs along Sespe Creek (lat. 34°33'35" N, long. 119°03'55" W; near N line sec. 3, T 5 N, R 21 W). Named on Topatopa Mountains (1943) 7.5' quadrangle.
(2) *area,* 5 miles north of Fillmore (lat. 34°28'20" N, long. 118°54'25" W). Named on Fillmore (1951) 7.5' quadrangle.

Oak Flat: see **Big Oak Flat** [LOS ANGELES]; **Oak Flats** [LOS ANGELES].

Oak Flats [LOS ANGELES]: *area,* 2.25 miles north of Whitaker Peak (lat. 34°36'15" N, long. 118°43'45" W; at and near SW cor. sec. 18, T 6 N, R 17 W). Named on Whitaker Peak (1958) 7.5' quadrangle. Los Angeles County (1935) map has the singular form "Oak Flat" for the name.

Oak Flat Spring [LOS ANGELES]: *spring,* 2 miles north-northeast of Whitaker Peak at Camp Caula (lat. 34°35'55" N, long. 118°43'20" W; sec. 19, T 6 N, R 17 W); the spring is near the southeast end of Oak Flats. Named on Whitaker Peak (1958) 7.5' quadrangle.

Oak Grove: see **Camp Oak Grove** [LOS ANGELES].

Oakgrove Canyon [LOS ANGELES]: *canyon,* drained by a stream that flows 2 miles to Pine Canyon (1) nearly 4 miles north-northwest of Burnt Peak (lat. 34°44'05" N, long. 118°35'55" W; sec. 32, T 8 N, R 16 W). Named on Burnt Peak (1958) 7.5' quadrangle.

Oak Hill [LOS ANGELES]: *locality,* 4.5 miles north-northeast of Point Dume (lat. 34°03'45" N, long. 118°47' W; sec. 20, T 1 S, R 18 W). Named on Solstice Canyon (1932) 6' quadrangle.

Oak Knoll [LOS ANGELES]: *district,* 8 miles northeast of Los Angeles city hall in Pasadena (lat. 34°07'25" N, long. 118°08'15" W). Named on Los Angeles (1953) 7.5' quadrangle.

Oak Mountain: see **Mount Lowe** [LOS ANGELES] (1).

Oak Ridge [VENTURA]: *ridge,* generally west-trending, 16 miles long, center 5 miles southeast of Fillmore (lat. 34°21'20" N, long. 118°51' W). Named on Moorpark (1951), Piru (1952), Santa Susana (1951), Simi (1951), and Val Verde (1952) 7.5' quadrangles.

Oaks: see **The Oaks** [LOS ANGELES].

Oak Spring [LOS ANGELES]: *spring,* 3.5 miles north of Sunland (lat. 34°18'30" N, long. 118°19'30" W; at NE cor. sec. 34, T 3 N, R 14 W). Named on Sunland (1953) 7.5' quadrangle. Los Angeles County (1935) map has

the plural form "Oak Springs" for the name.
Oak Spring: see **Big Oak Spring** [LOS AN-GELES]; **Oak Spring Canyon** [LOS ANGE-LES] (2).
Oak Spring Canyon [LOS ANGELES]:
(1) *canyon*, drained by a stream that flows nearly 5 miles to Santa Clara River 1.25 miles east-northeast of Solemint (lat. 34°25'30" N, long. 118°25' W; near SE cor. sec. 14, T 4 N, R 15 W). Named on Agua Dulce (1960) and Mint Canyon (1960) 7.5' quadrangles. Called Oak Springs Can. on Los Angeles County (1935) map, where the name follows a branch of present Oak Spring Canyon to the east (sec. 24, T 4 N, R 15 W, and sec. 19, T 4 N, R 14 W); the upper part of present Oak Spring Canyon has the name "Lost Canyon" on this map. Los Angeles County (1935) map also shows a feature called Rabbitt Canyon that opens into present Oak Spring Canyon from the south about 1.25 miles above the mouth of present Oak Spring Canyon (near SE cor. sec. 24, T 4 N, R 15 W), and a feature called Manzanita Canyon that opens into Solemint Canyon from the north opposite the mouth of present Oak Spring Canyon.
(2) *canyon*, drained by a stream that flows 2.25 miles to Little Tujunga Canyon 3.5 miles north-northwest of Sunland (lat. 34°18'20" N, long. 118°20'40" W; near NE cor. sec. 33, T 3 N, R 14 W). Named on Sunland (1953) 7.5' quadrangle. Los Angeles County (1935) map shows Oak Spring in the canyon.
Oak Springs: see **Oak Spring** [LOS ANGE-LES].
Oak View [VENTURA]: *town*, 4.5 miles south-west of the town of Ojai along Ventura River (lat. 34°23'50" N, long. 119°17'55" W). Named on Matilija (1952) 7.5' quadrangle. On Ventura (1904) 15' quadrangle, the name applies to a place along Southern Pacific Railroad. Postal authorities established Oak View post office in 1947; the name is from a real-estate promotion that was called Oak View Home Gardens (Salley, p. 158).
Oak Village [VENTURA]: *locality*, 3 miles west of Fillmore (lat. 34° 23'30" N, long. 118°57'40" W; near N line sec. 34, T 4 N, R 20 W). Named on Fillmore (1951) 7.5' quad-rangle.
Oakwilde [LOS ANGELES]: *locality*, 7 miles north-northwest of Pasadena city hall along Arroyo Seco (lat. 34°14'40" N, long. 118°10'55" W). Named on Pasadena (1953) 7.5' quadrangle. J.R. Phillips obtained a permit in 1911 to build a resort along Arroyo Seco at the mouth of Dark Canyon, and his resort became known as Camp Oak Wilde; a small tourist camp called Teddy's Outpost was situated 2 miles down Arroyo Seco below Camp Oak Wilde (Robinson, J.W., 1977, p. 113, 116).
Oat Mountain [LOS ANGELES]: *ridge*, west-northwest-trending, 5 miles long, 5 miles

southwest of Newhall (lat. 34°19'40" N, long. 118°35'15" W). Named on Oat Mountain (1952) 7.5' quadrangle.
Oat Mountain [VENTURA]: *peak*, 3.25 miles north of Fillmore (lat. 34°26'55" N, long. 118°54'10" W; at NE cor. sec. 7, T 4 N, R 19 W). Altitude 3124 feet. Named on Fillmore (1951) 7.5' quadrangle.
Oban [LOS ANGELES]: *locality*, 5.5 miles north of Lancaster along Southern Pacific Railroad (lat. 34°46'25" N, long. 118°08'50" W; near W line sec. 22, T 8 N, R 12 W). Named on Rosamond (1973) 7.5' quadrangle. On Oban (1933) 6' quadrangle, the name applies to a place located nearly 0.5 mile far-ther north along the railroad—this place is called Oban Siding on Los Angeles County (1935) map, which shows a place called Waterdale situated about 2 miles east of Oban Siding (sec. 14, T 8 N, R 12 W).
Obed: see **Bell** [LOS ANGELES].
Oberg [LOS ANGELES]: *locality*, 5 miles northwest of Newhall along Southern Pacific Railroad (lat. 34°26' N, long. 118°35'30" W). Named on Saugus (1933) 6' quadrangle.
Observatory Peak: see **San Gabriel Peak** [LOS ANGELES].
Occidental Peak [LOS ANGELES]: *peak*, 1.5 miles west-northwest of Mount Wilson (lat. 34°14'05" N, long. 118°05' W). Altitude 5730 feet. Named on Mount Wilson (1953) 7.5' quadrangle. The feature first was called Precipicio Peak for its location above Precipicio Canyon (present Eaton Canyon); students from Occidental College built a trail to the top about 1915, and Forest Service of-ficials named the peak for their school (Rob-inson, J.W., 1977, p. 155).
Ocean Park [LOS ANGELES]: *district*, 0.5 mile southeast of Santa Monica city hall (lat. 34°00'10" N, long. 118°28'55" W). Named on Beverly Hills (1966) 7.5' quadrangle. Postal authorities established Ocean Park post office in 1899 (Salley, p. 159). Abbot Kinney and F.G. Ryan founded and named the place in 1892 (Gudde, 1949, p. 240).
Ocean Park Heights: see **Mar Vista** [LOS ANGELES].
Ocean View [ORANGE]: *locality*, 4 miles north of Huntington Beach civic center (lat. 33°42'55" N, long. 117°59'15" W; at NW cor. sec. 25, T 5 S, R 11 W). Named on Newport Beach (1965) 7.5' quadrangle.
O'Hara Canyon [VENTURA]: *canyon*, drained by a stream that flows nearly 4 miles to the valley of Santa Clara River 3 miles west of Santa Paula (lat. 34°20'40" N, long. 119°06'25" W). Named on Ojai (1952), Santa Paula (1951), and Saticoy (1951) 15' quad-rangles. Members of the O'Hara family settled in the canyon in the 1860's; the feature first was called Bear Canyon (Ricard).
Ojai [VENTURA]:
(1) *land grant*, in Ojai Valley and Upper Ojai

Valley. Named on Matilija (1952), Ojai (1952), and Santa Paula Peak (1951) 7.5' quadrangles. Fernando Tico received 6 leagues in 1837 and claimed 17,717 acres patented in 1870 (Cowan, p. 54). The name is of Indian origin (Kroeber, p. 51).
(2) *town,* 12 miles north of Ventura (lat. 34°26'55" N, long. 119°14'35" W); the place is in Ojai Valley. Named on Matilija (1952) and Ojai (1952) 7.5' quadrangles. Postal authorities established Nordhoff post office in 1874 and changed the name to Ojai in 1917 (Frickstad, p. 218). The town incorporated in 1921. R.G. Surdam laid out the community in 1874 and named it for Charles Nordhoff, who wrote enthusiastically of Ojai Valley; the town was renamed for the valley in 1916 (Gudde, 1949, p. 241).
(3) *locality,* 3 miles west-southwest of downtown Ojai along Southern Pacific Railroad (lat. 34°25'35" N, long. 119°17'20" W). Named on Ventura (1904) 15' quadrangle.
Ojai Hot Sulphur Springs: see **Matilija Hot Springs** [VENTURA].
Ojai Valley [VENTURA]: *valley,* at and near the town of Ojai. Named on Matilija (1952) and Ojai (1952) 7.5' quadrangles.
Ojai Valley: see **Upper Ojai Valley** [VENTURA].
Ojala [VENTURA]: *locality,* 4 miles northwest of the town of Ojai at the head of Ventura River (lat. 34°29'05" N, long. 119°17'50" W; sec. 28, T 5 N, R 23 W). Named on Matilija (1952) 7.5' quadrangle.
Old Baldy: see **Mount San Antonio** [LOS ANGELES].
Old Baldy Peak: see **Mount San Antonio** [LOS ANGELES].
Old Boney: see **Boney Mountain** [VENTURA].
Old Camp [LOS ANGELES]: *locality,* 4 miles south-southeast of Pacifico Mountain along Chilao Creek (lat. 34°19'35" N, long. 118°00'15" W; near S line sec. 23, T 3 N, R 11 W). Named on Chilao Flat (1959) 7.5' quadrangle.
Old Camp [ORANGE]: *locality,* nearly 1.5 miles southeast of Santiago Peak (lat. 33°41'50" N, long. 117°33' W; near NW cor. sec. 31, T 5 S, R 6 W). Named on Santiago Peak (1954) 7.5' quadrangle.
Old Landing: see **Newport Beach** [ORANGE] (2).
Old Man Canyon [VENTURA]: *canyon,* drained by a stream that flows 3.25 miles to Matilija Creek 6.5 miles west of Wheeler Springs (lat. 34°31'05" N, long. 119°24'15" W; sec. 16, T 5 N, R 24 W); the canyon heads at Old Man Mountain, which is in Santa Barbara County. Named on Old Man Mountain (1943) 7.5' quadrangle.
Old Newport: see **Greenville** [ORANGE].
Old Palmdale: see **Palmdale** [LOS ANGELES].
Old Point Comfort [LOS ANGELES]: *locality,* 2.25 miles south-southeast of Valyermo

along Big Rock Creek (lat. 34°24'55" N, long. 117°50' W; at W line sec. 21, T 4 N, R 9 W). Named on Valyermo (1958) 7.5' quadrangle.
Old Saddleback: see **Santiago Peak** [ORANGE].
Old San Gabriel River: see **Rio Hondo**, under **San Gabriel River** [LOS ANGELES-ORANGE].
Old Santa Ana: see **Olive** [ORANGE].
Old Topanga Canyon [LOS ANGELES]: *canyon,* drained by a stream that flows 3.5 miles to Topanga Canyon 8.5 miles northwest of Santa Monica city hall (lat. 34°05'25" N, long. 118°36'15" W; at SW cor. sec. 7, T 1 S, R 16 W). Named on Malibu Beach (1950, photorevised 1981) 7.5' quadrangle. Called Topanga Canyon on Malibu Beach (1951) 7.5' quadrangle, but United States Board on Geographic Names (1960c, p. 18) rejected this name for the feature.
Old Trading Post: see **The Old Trading Post**, under **Little Santa Anita Canyon** [LOS ANGELES].
Oleo [ORANGE]: *locality,* 1 mile east of downtown Brea along Pacific Electric Railroad (lat. 33°55'15" N, long. 117°52'40" W). Named on Coyote Hills (1935) 7.5' quadrangle.
Olga [LOS ANGELES]: *locality,* 6 miles northeast of Los Angeles city hall along Atchison, Topeka and Santa Fe Railroad (lat. 34°06'45" N, long. 118°09'55" W). Named on Los Angeles (1953) 7.5' quadrangle.
Olinda [ORANGE]: *locality,* 2.5 miles northwest of Yorba Linda near the mouth of Carbon Canyon (lat. 33°55'20" N, long. 117°50'10" W; on E line sec. 8, T 3 S, R 9 W). Named on Yorba Linda (1950) 7.5' quadrangle. Goodyear (1888, p. 70) called the place Petrolia. It was built for oil workers and was a busy community in the 1920's, but it was gone by the 1960's (Carpenter, p. 94).
Olive [ORANGE]: *village,* 3.5 miles north of Orange city hall (lat. 33°50'15" N, long. 117°50'40" W). Named on Orange (1964) 7.5' quadrangle. Postal authorities established Olive post office in 1887 and discontinued it for a time in 1900 (Frickstad, p. 117). The Yorba and Peralta families built adobe homes on Santiago de Santa Ana grant at the place, and this cluster of buildings was called Santa Ana, or Santa Ana Abajo—*abajo* means "lower" in Spanish—to distinguish it from Santa Ana Arriba—*arriba* means "upper" in Spanish—which was located on Bernardo Yorba's Cañon de Santa Ana grant farther up Santa Ana River; after the present city of Santa Ana was laid out in 1868, present Olive became known as Old Santa Ana (Hoover, Rensch, and Rensch, p. 261-262; Meadows, p. 107). The name "Olive" came from olive trees on Burruel Point, and was applied to a school district before it was applied to the village (Meadows, p. 107-108). The community was called Olive Heights when it was laid out

DURHAM'S PLACE-NAMES

in 1880, but the name "Olive" was used for the post office (Gudde, 1949, p. 242).

Olive Heights: see **Olive** [ORANGE].

Olive Hill [LOS ANGELES]: *hill,* 4.25 miles northwest of Los Angeles city hall (lat. 34°06' N, long. 118°17'35" W; sec. 12, T 1 S, R 14 W). Named on Hollywood (1953) 7.5' quadrangle.

Olive Hills: see **Peralta Hills** [ORANGE] (1).

Olive Hills Reservoir [ORANGE]: *lake,* 650 feet long, 3.5 miles north-northeast of Orange city hall (lat. 33°50'05" N, long. 117°49'20" W). Named on Orange (1964) 7.5' quadrangle.

Oliver Canyon [LOS ANGELES]: *canyon,* drained by a stream that flows less than 1 mile to Tujunga Valley 2.5 miles west-northwest of Sunland (lat. 34°16'30" N, long. 118°20'55" W; sec. 9, T 2 N, R 14 W). Named on Sunland (1953) 7.5' quadrangle.

Olive View [LOS ANGELES]: *locality,* 3 miles north of downtown San Fernando (lat. 34°19'30" N, long. 118°26'40" W). Named on San Fernando (1966) 7.5' quadrangle. Postal authorities established Olive View post office in 1923 and discontinued it in 1973; the name was from olive orchards present below the place.(Salley, p. 161).

Olive Wood [LOS ANGELES]: *locality,* less than 0.5 mile east-northeast of present Pasadena city hall along Atchison, Topeka and Santa Fe Railroad (lat. 34°09' N, long. 118°08'10" W). Named on Pasadena (1900) 15' quadrangle.

Omaha Heights [LOS ANGELES]: *district,* 3.5 miles northeast of present Los Angeles city hall (lat. 34°04'50" N, long. 118°11'25" W). Named on Alhambra (1926) 6' quadrangle.

Oneonta Park [LOS ANGELES]: *district,* 6 miles east-northeast of present Los Angeles city hall (lat. 34°06'15" N, long. 118°09'20" W). Named on Altadena (1928) 6' quadrangle. The name is for Oneonta, New York, birthplace of Henry E. Huntington (Gudde, 1949, p. 243).

Onlauf Canyon: see **Anlauf Canyon** [VENTURA].

Opids Camp: see **Camp Hi-Hill** [LOS ANGELES].

Orange [ORANGE]: *city,* 6 miles north-northwest of Santa Ana (lat. 33°47'15" N, long. 117°51' W). Named on Anaheim (1965) and Orange (1964) 7.5' quadrangles. Postal authorities established Orange post office in 1873 (Frickstad, p. 117), and the city incorporated in 1888. Chapman and Glassell laid out the community in 1872 and called it Richland; postal authorities refused this name for a post office, and Glassell substituted the name "Orange" from his native county in Virginia (Gudde, 1949, p. 244; Hanna, p. 219). Anaheim (1898) 15' quadrangle shows a place called Orange Station located along Southern Pacific Railroad 1.5 miles west-southwest

of downtown Orange; Corona (1902) 30' quadrangle has the name "Orange" at the site. A Pacific Electric Railroad station called Hargraves was situated less than 1 mile southwest of present Orange city hall (Meadows, p. 69).

Orange: see **Port Orange**, under **Newport Beach** [ORANGE] (2); **West Orange**, under **Santa Ana** [ORANGE].

Orange Avenue Junction [LOS ANGELES]: *locality,* 1 mile east-northeast of Baldwin Park city hall along Southern Pacific Railroad (lat. 34°05'30" N, long. 117°56'30" W). Named on Baldwin Park (1966) 7.5' quadrangle.

Orange Park Acres [ORANGE]: *settlement,* 4 miles east-northeast of Orange city hall (lat. 33°48'05" N, long. 117°46'50" W). Named on Orange (1964) 7.5' quadrangle. E.F. Mead developed the place in 1928 (Meadows, p. 108).

Orange Station: see **Orange** [ORANGE].

Orangethorpe: see **City of Orangethorpe**, under **Placentia** [ORANGE].

Orchard Camp [LOS ANGELES]: *locality,* nearly 2 miles south-southeast of Mount Wilson (1) in Little Santa Anita Canyon (lat. 34°11'55" N, long. 118°03'05" W; sec. 5, T 1 N, R 11 W). Named on Mount Wilson (1953) 7.5' quadrangle. George Islip planted cherry, apple, pear, and plum trees at the place, which came to be called Orchard Camp (Robinson, J.W., 1977, p. 21).

Orcutt Canyon [VENTURA]: *canyon,* drained by a stream that flows 4.25 miles to the valley of Santa Clara River 2 miles northeast of Santa Paula (lat. 34°22'35" N, long. 119°02'15" W; sec. 1, T 3 N, R 21 W). Named on Santa Paula Peak (1951) 7.5' quadrangle. The name commemorates John Hall Orcutt, a pioneer of Santa Paula (Ricard).

Orizaba: see **Mount Orizaba** [LOS ANGELES].

Ormond Beach [VENTURA]: *beach,* 4 miles south of Oxnard along the coast (lat. 34°08'15" N, long. 119°11' W). Named on Oxnard (1949) 7.5' quadrangle.

Oro Fino Canyon [LOS ANGELES]: *canyon,* 1.5 miles long, 2 miles east-northeast of Newhall (lat. 34°23'55" N, long. 118°30' W). Named on Mint Canyon (1960) and Newhall (1952) 7.5' quadrangles.

Orr Spring Canyon [LOS ANGELES]: *canyon,* drained by a stream that flows 0.5 mile to Pine Canyon (3) 2 miles west-northwest of the village of Lake Hughes (lat. 34°41'05" N, long. 118°28'20" W; sec. 21, T 7 N, R 15 W). Named on Lake Hughes (1957) 7.5' quadrangle.

Ortega Hill [VENTURA]: *peak,* nearly 6 miles northwest of Wheeler Springs (lat. 34°34'25" N, long. 119°21'15" W; at N line sec. 31, T 6 N, R 23 W). Named on Wheeler Springs (1943) 7.5' quadrangle.

126

Ortonville [VENTURA]: *village,* 3 miles north of Ventura along Ventura River (lat. 34°19'15" N, long. 119°17'25" W). Named on Ventura (1951) 7.5' quadrangle. The name recalls Robert Orton, a miller at Ventura flour mill; a railroad siding at the place served the mill (Ricard).

Osito Canyon [LOS ANGELES]: *canyon,* drained by a stream that flows 3.5 miles to Piru Creek 3 miles north-northwest of Whitaker Peak at Frenchman Flat (lat. 34°36'55" N, long. 118°44'40" W; near NW cor. sec. 13, T 6 N, R 18 W). Named on Liebre Mountain (1958) and Whitaker Peak (1958) 7.5' quadrangles.

Oso Canyon [LOS ANGELES]: *canyon,* drained by a stream that heads just inside Kern County and flows 8 miles, mainly in Los Angeles County, to Los Angeles-Kern county line 8 miles east of Gorman (lat. 34°49'05" N, long. 118°42'40" W; near NE cor. sec. 6, T 8 N, R 17 W). Named on La Liebra Ranch (1965) and Lebec (1958) 7.5' quadrangles. The stream in the canyon is called Little Cottonwood Creek on Johnson's (1911) map. United States Board on Geographic Names (1967a, p. 4) rejected the name "Canada de la Oasis" for the canyon.

Oso Creek [ORANGE]: *stream,* flows 12.5 miles to Arroyo Trabuco 1.5 miles north-northwest of San Juan Capistrano (lat. 33°31'10" N, long. 117°40'15" W; sec. 36, T 7 S, R 8 W). Named on El Toro (1968), San Juan Capistrano (1968), and Santiago Peak (1954) 7.5' quadrangles. The name "Los Osos Valley" applies to the valley of the upper part of Oso Creek on some early maps (Meadows, p. 80).

Otterbein [LOS ANGELES]: *locality,* 5.5 miles northeast of La Habra [ORANGE] (lat. 33°59'45" N, long. 117°53' W). Named on La Habra (1952) 7.5' quadrangle. Bishop William M. Bell gave the name in 1911 to a settlement for retired ministers of the Church of the United Brethern in Christ; Philip W. Otterbein founded the church (Gudde, 1949, p. 247).

Owensmouth: see **Canoga Park** [LOS ANGELES].

Owl Canyon: see **Necktie Canyon** [LOS ANGELES].

Oxnard [VENTURA]: *city,* 8 miles southeast of Ventura (lat. 34°11'50" N, long. 119°10'45" W). Named on Oxnard (1949) 7.5' quadrangle. Postal authorities established Oxnard post office in 1898 (Frickstad, p. 218), and the city incorporated in 1903. The name is for Henry T. Oxnard, who started a sugar-beet refinery at the place in 1897 (Gudde, 1949, p. 247). California Division of Highways' (1934) map shows a place called McGrath located 4 miles west-northwest of Oxnard at the end of a railroad spur, a place called Todd located 3 miles east of Oxnard along the rail-

road, and a place called Naumann located 4.5 miles east-southeast of Oxnard along the railroad.

Ozena [VENTURA]: *locality,* 5.5 miles northwest of Reyes Peak along Cuyama River at the mouth of Boulder Canyon (lat. 34°41'55" N, long. 119°21' W; at E line sec. 19, T 7 N, R 23 W). Named on Mount Pinos (1903) 30' quadrangle. Postal authorities established Ozena post office in 1890, moved it 3 miles south in 1901, moved it 1 mile east in 1904, moved it 3 miles east in 1909, and discontinued it in 1921 (Salley, p. 164). California Mining Bureau's (1917) map shows a place called Nedo located about 7 miles northwest of Ozena on the southwest side of Cuyama River near Ventura-Santa Barbara county line. Postal authorities established Nedo post office in 1915 and discontinued it in 1918 (Frickstad, p. 218).

– P –

Pacific City: see **Huntington Beach** [ORANGE].

Pacifico Campground: see **Lower Pacifico Campground** [LOS ANGELES]; **Upper Pacifico Campground** [LOS ANGELES].

Pacific Electric Island: see **Lido Isle** [ORANGE].

Pacific Palisades: see **Corona del Mar** [ORANGE].

Pacoima Canyon [LOS ANGELES]: *canyon,* drained by a stream that flows 20 miles to lowlands 3.5 miles north-northeast of downtown San Fernando (lat. 34°19'40" N, long. 118°24'10" W; near S line sec. 24, T 3 N, R 15 W). Named on Acton (1959), Agua Dulce (1960), Condor Peak (1959), San Fernando (1953), and Sunland (1953) 7.5' quadrangles. San Fernando (1900) 15' quadrangle shows Pacoima Creek in the canyon. Marcou (p. 160) gave the name "Pacoña Cañon" as an alternate. North Fork branches northeast 8 miles north-northeast of Sunland; it is 2 miles long and is named on Acton (1959) and Agua Dulce (1960) 7.5' quadrangles. South Fork branches southeast 7.25 miles north of Sunland; it is 2.5 miles long and in named on Sunland (1953) 7.5' quadrangle.

Pacoima Creek: see **Pacoima Canyon** [LOS ANGELES].

Pacoima Reservoir [LOS ANGELES]: *lake,* behind a dam 4.25 miles north-northeast of downtown San Fernando (lat. 34°20'05" N, long. 118°23'45" W; near NW cor. sec. 19, T 3 N, R 14 W); the lake is in Pacoima Canyon. Named on San Fernando (1966) 7.5' quadrangle.

Pacoima Wash [LOS ANGELES]: *stream* and *dry wash,* extends for 9.5 miles from the mouth of Pacoima Canyon to end in central Van Nuys (lat. 34°11'50" N, long. 118°26'45"

DURHAM'S PLACE-NAMES

W). Named on San Fernando (1953) and Van Nuys (1966) 7.5' quadrangles.
Pacoña Cañon: see **Pacoima Canyon** [LOS ANGELES].
Padre Juan Canyon [VENTURA]: *canyon,* drained by a stream that flows 3.5 miles to the sea at Pitas Point (lat. 34°19'10" N, long. 119°23'25" W; near SW cor. sec. 22, T 3 N, R 24 W). Named on Pitas Point (1950) and Ventura (1951) 7.5' quadrangles. The name commemorates Juan Comapla, priest at San Buenavenura mission from 1861 until 1877, who had a small ranch in the canyon (Ricard).
Painter Lagoon [LOS ANGELES]: *lake,* nearly 1 mile long, 2 miles south-southwest of present Whittier city hall (lat. 33°56'40" N, long. 118°02'30" W). Named on Whittier (1949) 7.5' quadrangle. Whittier (1965) 7.5' quadrangle shows a drain through the place.
Painters [LOS ANGELES]: *locality,* 2 miles north-northwest of present Pasadena city hall along Los Angeles Terminal Railroad (lat. 34°10'25" N, long. 118°09'40" W). Named on Pasadena (1900) 15' quadrangle.
Pajarito: see **Camp Pajarito** [LOS ANGELES].
Palisades [LOS ANGELES]: *escarpment,* west-northwest-trending, 3.25 miles long, center 2.5 miles south-southwest of Avalon on the south side of Santa Catalina Island (lat. 33°18'55" N, long. 118°21'15" W). Named on Santa Catalina East (1950) 7.5' quadrangle.
Palisades Beach [LOS ANGELES]: *beach,* 1.25 miles west-northwest of present Santa Monica city hall along the coast (lat. 34°01'20" N, long. 118°30'35" W). Named on Topanga Canyon (1928) 6' quadrangle.
Palisades del Rey: see **Playa del Rey** [LOS ANGELES].
Palisades Reservoir [ORANGE]: *lake,* 650 feet long, 2.5 miles south-southeast of San Juan Capistrano (lat. 33°27'55" N, long. 117°39' W; sec. 19, T 8 S, R 7 W). Named on Dana Point (1968) 7.5' quadrangle.
Pallett [LOS ANGELES]: *locality,* 2.5 miles west-northwest of present Valyermo (lat. 34°27'05" N, long. 117°53'50" W; near N line sec. 11, T 4 N, R 10 W); the place is along Pallett Creek. Named on Rock Creek (1903) 15' quadrangle.
Pallett Creek [LOS ANGELES]: *stream,* flows nearly 7 miles to Big Rock Creek 1.25 miles north-northwest of Valyermo (lat. 34°27'40" N, long. 117°51'50" W; sec. 6, T 4 N, R 9 W). Named on Juniper Hills (1959) and Valyermo (1958) 7.5' quadrangles.
Pallett Mountain [LOS ANGELES]: *peak,* 4.5 miles south-southwest of Valyermo (lat. 34°23'10" N, long. 117°53'05" W; near SW cor. sec. 36, T 4 N, R 10 W); the peak is near the head of Pallett Creek. Named on Juniper Hills (1959) 7.5' quadrangle.
Palma: see **Palms** [LOS ANGELES].
Palma Plain: see **Antelope Valley** [LOS ANGELES].

Palmas: see **Palms** [LOS ANGELES].
Palmdale [LOS ANGELES]: *town,* 8 miles south of Lancaster (lat. 34°34'45" N, long. 118°07' W; in and near sec. 25, 26, T 6 N, R 12 W). Named on Palmdale (1958) and Ritter Ridge (1958) 7.5' quadrangles. Baker's (1911) map shows a place called West Palmdale located about 2 miles west-northwest of Palmdale near the railroad; the place called Palmdale on Baker's (1911) map is called Old Palmdale on Johnson's (1911) map. Postal authorities established Palmenthal post office in 1888, changed the name to Palmdale in 1890, and discontinued it in 1899 when service moved to West Palmdale post office; they changed the name of West Palmdale post office to Palmdale the same year (Frickstad, p. 78, 79). German Lutherans founded the community in 1886 and named it for Joshua trees found there—Joshua trees sometimes were called yucca palms (Gudde, 1949, p. 250). The community began about 2 miles farther east, but eventually it was moved to the railroad (Hanna, p. 227). The site originally was known as Agua Dulce for a spring of sweet water there (Latta, p. 170). Postal authorities established Lopez post office in 1894 and discontinued it in 1896, when service moved to West Palmdale post office (Salley, p. 126).
Palmdale Lake: see **Lake Palmdale** [LOS ANGELES].
Palmdale Reservoir: see **Lake Palmdale** [LOS ANGELES].
Palmenthal: see **Palmdale** [LOS ANGELES].
Palmer Canyon [LOS ANGELES]: *canyon,* drained by a stream that flows 2.5 miles to lowlands 6.5 miles north-northeast of Pomona city hall (lat. 34°08'35" N, long. 117°42'25" W; sec. 27, T 1 N, R 8 W) Named on Mount Baldy (1954) 7.5' quadrangle. West Fork branches northwest 1.25 miles above the mouth of the main canyon; it is less than 1 mile long and is named on Mount Baldy (1954) 7.5' quadrangle.
Palms [LOS ANGELES]: *district,* 3.5 miles south of Beverly Hills city hall in Los Angeles (lat. 34°01'20" N, long. 118°24'15" W). Named on Beverly Hills (1950) 7.5' quadrangle. Called Palmas on California Mining Bureau's (1909b) map, and called Palma on Diller and others' (1915) map. Postal authorities established Palms post office in 1887 (Frickstad, p. 79).
Palo Comado Canyon [LOS ANGELES-VENTURA]: *canyon,* drained by a stream that heads in Ventura County and flows nearly 5 miles to lowlands at Agura in Los Angeles County (lat. 34°09'05" N, long. 118°44' W). Named on Calabasas (1952) 7.5' quadrangle. Called Posita Canyon on Camulos (1903) 30' quadrangle.
Palomares: see **Claremont** [LOS ANGELES].
Palomas Canyon [LOS ANGELES]: *canyon,* drained by a stream that flows 2.25 miles to

Violin Canyon nearly 6 miles southeast of Whitaker Peak (lat. 34°31'10" N, long. 118°39'15" W; sec. 15, T 5 N, R 17 W). Named on Whitaker Peak (1958) 7.5' quadrangle.

Palo Verde [LOS ANGELES]: *locality,* 8 miles south-southwest of present Whittier city hall (lat. 33°52'35" N, long. 118°06'30" W). Named on Whittier (1949) 7.5' quadrangle.

Palos Verdes: see **Los Palos Verdes** [LOS ANGELES].

Palos Verdes Estates [LOS ANGELES]: *town,* 3 miles south of Redondo Beach city hall (lat. 33°48' N, long. 118°23'25" W); the town is in Palos Verdes Hills. Named on Redondo Beach (1963) and Torrance (1964) 7.5' quadrangles. Postal authorities established Palos Verdes Estates post office in 1925 (Frickstad, p. 79).

Palos Verdes Hills [LOS ANGELES]: *range,* 10 miles west of Long Beach city hall (lat. 33°46' N, long. 118°22' W). Named on Redondo Beach (1951), San Pedro (1964), and Torrance (1964) 7.5' quadrangles. Called San Pedro Hills on Redondo (1896) 15' quadrangle.

Palos Verdes Point [LOS ANGELES]: *promontory,* 5.25 miles south-southwest of Redondo Beach city hall along the coast (lat. 33°46'25" N, long. 118°25'40" W); the promontory is at Palos Verdes Hills. Named on Redondo Beach (1951) 7.5' quadrangle. Called Rocky Point on Redondo (1896) 15' quadrangle, but United States Board on Geographic Names (1940, p. 32-33) rejected this name for the feature.

Palos Verdes Reservoir [LOS ANGELES]: *intermittent lake,* 1450 feet long, 4.5 miles south of Torrance city hall (lat. 33°46'20" N, long. 118°19'20" W). Named on Torrance (1964) 7.5' quadrangle.

Pancho Canyon [ORANGE]: *canyon,* drained by a stream that flows less than 1 mile to Santiago Creek 7 miles north-northeast of El Toro (lat. 33°43'30" N, long. 117°38'50" W). Named on El Toro (1968) 7.5' quadrangle.

Panorama City [LOS ANGELES]: *district,* 3 miles north of Van Nuys (lat. 34°13'40" N, long. 118°26'30" W). Named on Van Nuys (1953) 7.5' quadrangle. Postal authorities established Panorama City post office in 1953; the name is from Panorama moving picture studio (Salley, p. 166).

Panorama Heights [ORANGE]: *locality,* 3 miles east-southeast of Orange city hall (lat. 33°46'35" N, long. 117°47'50" W). Named on Orange (1964) 7.5' quadrangle. L.S. Leeson and G.E. Lindley developed the subdivision in 1928 (Meadows, p. 110).

Paradise Canyon [LOS ANGELES]: *canyon,* nearly 1 mile long, 5 miles north-northwest of Pasadena city hall (lat. 34°12'40" N, long. 118°10'50" W; sec. 31, T 2 N, R 12 W). Named on Pasadena (1953) 7.5' quadrangle.

Paradise Cove [LOS ANGELES]: *embayment,* 1.5 miles northeast of Point Dume (lat.

34°01'10" N, long. 118°47'05" W). Named on Point Dume (1951) 7.5' quadrangle. Gleason (p. 121) called the feature Dume Cove, and noted that it has the popular name "Paradise Cove." United States Board on Geographic Names (1961b, p. 13) rejected the name "Dume Cove" for the place.

Paradise Springs [LOS ANGELES]: *locality,* 4.25 miles southeast of Valyermo along Big Rock Creek (lat. 34°23'45" N, long. 117°48'15" W; on S line sec. 27, T 4 N, R 9 W). Named on Valyermo (1958) 7.5' quadrangle.

Paradise Valley [VENTURA]: *locality,* 4.25 miles south of Chatsworth [LOS ANGELES] in Dayton Canyon just inside Ventura County (lat. 34°13'20" N, long. 118°40'05" W). Named on Chatsworth (1940) 6' quadrangle.

Paraje de las Virgenes: see **Las Virgenes** [LOS ANGELES].

Paramount [LOS ANGELES]: *city,* 5.5 miles south-southeast of South Gate city hall (lat. 33°53'05" N, long. 118°09'35" W). Named on South Gate (1964) 7.5' quadrangle. Called South Clearwater on Downey (1902) 15' quadrangle, and called Hynes on Clearwater (1925) 6' quadrangle. Postal authorities established Hynes post office in 1898 and changed the name to Paramount in 1948 (Frickstad, p. 75). The name "Hynes" was for C.B. Hynes, superintendent of Salt Lake Railroad (Gudde, 1949, p. 158). Paramount incorporated in 1957. When the communities of Hynes and Clearwater merged to form a new city, Frank Zamboni proposed the name "Paramount" for the place because Paramount Boulevard was its main street—the boulevard was named for Paramount motion picture company (Gudde, 1969, p. 238). Postal authorities established Firth post office 3 miles east of Hynes post office in 1908 and discontinued it in 1909 (Salley, p. 75).

Pardee [LOS ANGELES]: *locality,* 2 miles north-northwest of Newhall along Southern Pacific Railroad near Saugus (lat. 34°24'55" N, long. 118°32'25" W). Named on Newhall (1952) 7.5' quadrangle.

Paris [LOS ANGELES]: *locality,* 1 mile east of Acton along Southern Pacific Railroad (lat. 34°28'20" N, long. 118°10'50" W; near W line sec. 31, T 5 N, R 12 W). Named on Acton (1959) 7.5' quadrangle.

Park Canyon [VENTURA]: *canyon,* drained by a stream that flows 4 miles to Wagon Road Canyon 7 miles northeast of Reyes Peak (lat. 34°42'35" N, long. 119°12'25" W; at SW cor. sec. 10, T 7 N, R 22 W). Named on San Guillermo (1943) 7.5' quadrangle.

Park Creek [VENTURA]: *stream,* flows 3 miles to Sespe Creek 15 miles east-northeast of Wheeler Springs (lat. 34°34'10" N, long. 119°01'25" W; sec. 32, T 6 N, R 20 W). Named on Devils Heart Peak (1943) and Topatopa Mountains (1943) 7.5' quadrangles.

Parker Canyon [LOS ANGELES]: *canyon,* drained by a stream that flows 1 mile to the sea nearly 5 miles west-northwest of Santa Monica city hall (lat. 34°02'30" N, long. 118°34' W). Named on Topanga (1952) 7.5' quadrangle.

Parker Mesa [LOS ANGELES]: *area,* 5.25 miles west-northwest of Santa Monica city hall (lat. 34°02'40" N, long. 118°34'20" W); the place is west of the lower part of Parker Canyon. Named on Topanga (1952) 7.5' quadrangle.

Parker Mountain [LOS ANGELES]: *peak,* 1.5 miles west-southwest of Acton (lat. 34°27'35" N, long. 118°13'05" W; at W line sec. 2, T 4 N, R 13 W). Altitude 4131 feet. Named on Acton (1959) 7.5' quadrangle. The feature also was called Mount Parkinson (Gudde, 1949, p. 254).

Parkinson: see **Mount Parkinson**, under **Parker Mountain** [LOS ANGELES].

Parsons Landing [LOS ANGELES]: *locality,* 1.5 miles north of Silver Peak on the north side of Santa Catalina Island (lat. 33°28'25" N, long. 118°33' W). Named on Santa Catalina West (1943) 7.5' quadrangle.

Pasadena [LOS ANGELES]: *city,* 8 miles northeast of Los Angeles city hall (lat. 34°08'50" N, long. 118°08'35" W). Named on Los Angeles (1953), Mount Wilson (1953), and Pasadena (1953) 7.5' quadrangles. Postal authorities established Pasadena post office in 1875, discontinued it the same year, and reestablished it in 1876 (Frickstad, p. 79). The city incorporated in 1886. The community first was called Indiana Colony because the original promoters of the place came from Indiana; Dr. T.B. Elliott, president of Indiana Colony, proposed the name "Pasadena," which supposedly is a Chippewa Indian word (Gudde, 1949, p. 254), but Kroeber (p. 54) expressed doubt about an Indian origin for the name.

Pasadena: see **East Pasadena** [LOS ANGELES]; **South Pasadena** [LOS ANGELES].

Pasadena Camp [LOS ANGELES]: *locality,* 3.25 miles west-northwest of Waterman Mountain (lat. 34°21'10" N, long. 117°59'30" W; near NW cor. sec. 13, T 3 N, R 11 W). Named on Waterman Mountain (1959) 7.5' quadrangle.

Pasadena Glen [LOS ANGELES]: *canyon,* 1.5 miles long, 2.5 miles south-southwest of Mount Wilson (1) (lat. 34°11'15" N, long. 118° 04'30" W; mainly in sec. 7, T 1 N, R 11 W). Named on Mount Wilson (1953) 7.5' quadrangle. Los Angeles County (1935) map has the name "Kineloa Canyon" for the canyon just west of Pasadena Glen, where Mount Wilson (1953) 7.5' quadrangle shows Kineloa ranch.

Paso Canyon: see **Agua Dulce Canyon** [LOS ANGELES].

Paso de Bartolo [LOS ANGELES]: *land grant,* at Pico Rivera and Whittier. Named on El Monte (1953) and Whittier (1949) 7.5' quad-

rangles. Juan Crispin Perez received 2 leagues in 1835; Pio Pico and others claimed 8991 acres patented in 1881; Rafael Guirado claimed 876 acres granted in 1836 and patented in 1867; Joaquin Sepulveda claimed 208 acres patented in 1881 (Cowan, p. 18; Cowan listed the grant under the designation "Paso de Bartolo Viejo, (or) San Rafael").

Paso de Bartolo Viejo: see **Paso de Bartolo** [LOS ANGELES].

Paso de las Carretas: see **Ballona** [LOS ANGELES].

Patrick Reservoir [LOS ANGELES]: *lake,* 650 feet long, 2.25 miles west of Avalon on Santa Caltalina Island (lat. 33°21' N, long. 118° 21'50" W). Named on Santa Catalina East (1950) 7.5' quadrangle.

Patricks Shelter [LOS ANGELES]: *locality,* 2.25 miles north-northwest of Avalon on the northeast side of Santa Catalina Island (lat. 33°22'10" N, long. 118°20'45" W). Named on Santa Catalina East (1950) 7.5' quadrangle.

Paul: see **Lewis Paul Canyon** [LOS ANGELES].

Paulerino [ORANGE]: *locality,* 7 miles east of present Huntington Beach civic center along Southern Pacific Railroad (lat. 33°40'55" N, long. 117°52'40" W). Named on Newport Beach (1935) 7.5' quadrangle.

Peace Valley [LOS ANGELES]: *valley,* 9 miles long, along Gorman Creek above the entrance of that creek into Cañada de Los Alamos 7 miles south-southeast of Gorman (lat. 34°42'10" N, long. 118°47'40" W; sec. 16, T 7 N, R 18 W). Named on Black Mountain (1958) and Lebec (1958) 7.5' quadrangles.

Peachtree Flat: see **Heaton Flat** [LOS ANGELES].

Peacock Canyon [LOS ANGELES]: *canyon,* drained by a stream that flows nearly 1 mile to Cattle Canyon 12 miles north of Pomona city hall (lat. 34°13'45" N, long. 117°45' W). Named on Mount Baldy (1954) 7.5' quadrangle.

Peacock Saddle [LOS ANGELES]: *pass,* 8.5 miles northeast of Glendora city hall (lat. 34°13' N, long. 117°45' W); the pass is near the head of Peacock Canyon. Named on Glendora (1953) and Mount Baldy (1954) 7.5' quadrangles.

Pearblossom [LOS ANGELES]: *locality,* 4.25 miles east-southeast of Littlerock (lat. 34°30'20" N, long. 117°54'30" W). Named on Littlerock (1957) 7.5' quadrangle. Called Pearblossom Heights on Alpine Butte (1945) 15' quadrangle. Postal authorities established Pearblossom post office in 1933 (Salley, p. 169). Guy C. Chase named the place in 1924 for the pear orchards that surrounded it (Gudde, 1949, p. 256). Johnson's (1911) map has the name "Almondale" at a spot situated about 0.5 mile west of present Pearblossom.

Pearblossom Heights: see **Pearblossom** [LOS ANGELES].

Pearland [LOS ANGELES]: *village,* 4.25 miles east-southeast of Palmdale (lat. 34°33'40" N, long. 118°02'40" W; near S line sec. 33, T 6 N, R 11 W). Named on Palmdale (1958) 7.5' quadrangle. The name was given to the place in 1919 (Gudde, 1949, p. 256).

Peavine Campground [LOS ANGELES]: *locality,* 1.5 miles west-northwest of Big Pines (lat. 34°23'20" N, long. 117°43' W). Named on Mescal Creek (1956) 7.5' quadrangle.

Peavine Canyon [LOS ANGELES]: *canyon,* nearly 2 miles long, 2.5 miles north-north-west of Beverly Hills city hall (lat. 34°06'15" N, long. 118°25'20" W). Named on Beverly Hills (1950) 7.5' quadrangle.

Pebbly Beach [LOS ANGELES]: *locality,* 1 mile east-southeast of Avalon on the northeast side of Santa Catalina Island (lat. 33°20'05" N, long. 118°18'40" W). Named on Santa Catalina East (1950) 7.5' quadrangle.

Pechner Canyon [LOS ANGELES]: *canyon,* drained by a stream that flows 2 miles to Pallet Creek 3 miles west-southwest of Valyermo (lat. 34°25'30" N, long. 117°53'45" W; near N line sec. 23, T 4 N, R 10 W). Named on Juniper Hills (1959) 7.5' quadrangle.

Pelican Hill [ORANGE]: *peak,* 4.5 miles northwest of Laguna Beach city hall (lat. 33°35'35" N, long. 117°50'15" W); the peak is 1.25 miles northeast of Pelican Point. Named on Laguna Beach (1965) 7.5' quadrangle.

Pelican Point [ORANGE]: *promontory,* nearly 5 miles west-northwest of Laguna Beach city hall along the coast (lat. 33°34'45" N, long. 117°51'10" W). Named on Laguna Beach (1965) 7.5' quadrangle.

Pellissier Spur [LOS ANGELES]: *locality,* 3 miles south of El Monte city hall along Union Pacific Railroad (lat. 34°01'50" N, long. 118°01'30" W). Named on El Monte (1966) 7.5' quadrangle.

Peña Canyon [LOS ANGELES]: *canyon,* drained by a stream that flows nearly 2 miles to the sea 6.25 miles west-northwest of Santa Monica city hall (lat. 34°02'20" N, long. 118°35'45" W). Named on Topanga (1952) 7.5' quadrangle.

Penrose [VENTURA]: *locality,* 3 miles northwest of Moorpark (lat. 34°18'50" N, long. 118°54'35" W). Named on Camulos (1903) 30' quadrangle. Postal authorities established Penrose post office in 1893 and discontinued it in 1905 (Frickstad, p. 219).

Pensinger Canyon: see **Persinger Canyon** [LOS ANGELES].

Peppertree Canyon [VENTURA]: *canyon,* drained by a stream that flows 3.5 miles to the valley of Santa Clara River 1.5 miles north of Saticoy (lat. 34°18'30" N, long. 119°09' W). Named on Saticoy (1951) 7.5' quadrangle.

Peralta: see **Walnut Canyon** [ORANGE].

Peralta Hills [ORANGE]:
(1) *ridge,* west-trending, 3.5 miles long, 4.5 miles northeast of Orange city hall (lat.

33°50'05" N, long. 117°47'45" W). Named on Orange (1964) 7.5' quadrangle. United States Board on Geographic Names (1965c, p. 10) rejected the names "Burruel Ridge" and "Olive Hills" for the feature.
(2) *settlement,* 4.25 miles north-northeast of Orange city hall (lat. 33°50'40" N, long. 117°48'45" W). Named on Orange (1964, photorevised 1981) 7.5' quadrangle.

Perdition Caves [LOS ANGELES]: *caves,* 5.5 miles north-northwest of Mount Banning along the north side of Santa Catalina Island (lat. 33°26'50" N, long. 118°28'35" W). Named on Santa Catalina North (1950) 7.5' quadrangle.

Perry [LOS ANGELES]: *district,* 2 miles north of Torrance city hall (lat. 33°51'55" N, long. 118°20'30" W). Named on Torrance (1964) 7.5' quadrangle. Postal authorities established Perry post office in 1905 and discontinued it in 1916; the name was for the president of Pacific Electric Railroad (Salley, p. 170).

Persinger Canyon [LOS ANGELES]: *canyon,* drained by a stream that flows 2.5 miles to San Gabriel Reservoir 5.5 miles north of Glendora city hall (lat. 34°12'50" N, long. 117°51'05" W; sec. 32, T 2 N, R 9 W). Named on Glendora (1966) 7.5' quadrangle. Called Pensinger Canyon on Glendora (1953) 7.5' quadrangle. The name recalls Bate Persinger and Mary Persinger, who owned a resort at a site now under water of San Gabriel Reservoir (Robinson, J.W., 1983, p. 83-85).

Perspiration Point [LOS ANGELES]: *locality,* 5 miles south of Acton (lat. 34°23'50" N, long. 118°12'05" W; at E line sec. 26, T 4 N, R 13 W). Named on Acton (1959) 7.5' quadrangle.

Peters Canyon [ORANGE]: *canyon,* drained by a stream that flows nearly 2 miles to lowlands 5 miles east-southeast of Orange city hall (lat. 33°45'20" N, long. 117°46'05" W). Named on Orange (1964) 7.5' quadrangle. The name is for James Peters, who farmed land that he leased in the canyon; the feature was known in the early days as Canada de las Ranas from nearby Cienega de las Ranas—hunters called it Rabbit Canyon, Quail Canyon, and Dove Canyon for game there (Stephenson, p. 72, 73, 74).

Peters Canyon: see **Drinkwater Canyon** [LOS ANGELES].

Peters Canyon Reservoir [ORANGE]: *lake,* 2200 feet long, 5 miles east of Orange city hall (lat. 33°46'55" N, long. 117°45'40" W); the feature is at the head of Peters Canyon. Named on Orange (1964) 7.5' quadrangle.

Peters Canyon Reservoir: see **Lower Peters Canyon Reservoir** [ORANGE].

Peters Canyon Wash [ORANGE]: *stream,* flows 8 miles from the mouth of Peters Canyon to San Diego Creek 5.5 miles south-southeast of Santa Ana city hall (lat. 33°40'05" N, long. 117°50'05" W). Named on Orange (1964) and Tustin (1965) 7.5' quadrangles.

Petrolia: see **Olinda** [ORANGE].

Petroliopolis: see **Lyon's Station**, under **San Fernando Pass** [LOS ANGELES].

Pettinger Canyon [LOS ANGELES]: *canyon,* drained by a stream that flows 2.5 miles to Haskell Canyon 7 miles north of Newhall (lat. 34°28'55" N, long. 118°30'30" W; near S line sec. 25, T 5 N, R 16 W). Named on Newhall (1952) and Warm Springs Mountain (1958) 7.5' quadrangles.

Phipps Canyon [LOS ANGELES]: *canyon,* drained by a stream that flows 1 mile to West Fork San Gabriel River 7.25 miles north of Azusa city hall (lat. 34°14'25" N, long. 117°53'35" W). Named on Azusa (1953) 7.5' quadrangle.

Pickens Canyon [LOS ANGELES]: *canyon,* 2.5 miles long, drained by a stream that flows 2.5 miles northwest of Pasadena city hall (lat. 34°14'30" N, long. 118°13'20" W). Named on Condor Peak (1959) and Pasadena (1953) 7.5' quadrangles. On Los Angeles County (1935) map, present Sutton Canyon is called East Fork [Pickens Canyon].

Pickens Canyon Channel [LOS ANGELES]: *stream,* flows 1.25 miles from the mouth of Pickens Canyon to Verdugo Wash 7 miles northwest of Pasadena city Hall (lat. 34°12'25" N, long. 118°14'20" W). Named on Pasadena (1953) 7.5' quadrangle.

Pico [LOS ANGELES]: *locality,* 4.5 miles west of Newhall (lat. 34° 22'40" N, long. 118°36'40" W; at N line sec. 1, T 3 N, R 17 W); the place is in Pico Canyon. Site named on Newhall (1952) 7.5' quadrangle.

Pico: see **Pico Rivera** [LOS ANGELES].

Pico Camp: see **Mentryville**, under **Pico Canyon** [LOS ANGELES].

Pico Canyon [LOS ANGELES]: *canyon,* 4.25 miles long, opens into lowlands 2 miles west of downtown Newhall (lat. 34°23'10" N, long. 118°34' W). Named on Newhall (1952), Oat Mountain (1952), and Santa Susana (1951) 7.5' quadrangles. The name is for Andreas Pico, who in 1855 dipped crude oil from hand-dug pits in the canyon (Franks and Lambert, p. 41). C.A. Mentry, a veteran of Titusville oil fields in Pennsylvania, completed the first commercially productive oil well in California in Pico Canyon in the 1870's; the town that sprang up there was called Mentryville (Harrington, p. 39). The place earlier was called Pico Springs, or Pico Camp (Reynolds, p. 25).

Pico Heights [LOS ANGELES]: *district,* 3.5 miles west of Los Angeles city hall (lat. 34°02'50" N, long. 118°18' W). Named on Santa Monica (1902) 15' quadrangle. Postal authorities established Electric post office in 1887, changed the name to Pico Heights in 1891, discontinued it in 1897, and reestablished it in 1898; the name "Electric" was for Pacific Electric Railroad (Salley, p. 67, 171).

Pico Rivera [LOS ANGELES]: *city,* 3 miles west of Whittier city hall (lat. 33°58'55" N, long. 118°05'15" W). Named on El Monte (1966) and Whittier (1965) 7.5' quadrangles. The communities of Pico and Rivera incorporated under the name "Pico Rivera" in 1958 (Gudde, 1969, p. 245). Pico was 3 miles northwest of present Whittier city hall (lat. 33°59'50" N, long. 118°04'40" W) and is named on El Monte (1953) and Whittier (1949) 7.5' quadrangles. Postal authorities established Pico post office in 1925 and combined it with Rivera post office in 1958 under the name "Pico Rivera" (Salley, p. 171). The place is on the part of Paso de Bartolo grant owned by Pio Pico. Rivera was 4.25 miles west of present Whittier city hall (lat. 33°57'45" N, long. 118°06'30" W) and is named on Whittier (1949) 7.5' quadrangle. Postal authorities established Rivera post office in 1888 and discontinued it in 1958 (Salley, p. 186). The place was called Maizeland in 1866 for corn grown there (Gudde, 1949, p. 288); Senator R.F. del Valle gave the name "Rivera" to the community in 1886 for its position between San Gabriel River and Rio Hondo (Hanna, p. 256).

Pico Springs: see **Mentryville**, under **Pico Canyon** [LOS ANGELES].

Picture City: see **Agoura** [LOS ANGELES].

Pidgeon Spring: see **Bear Spring** [LOS ANGELES].

Piedra Blanca Camp [VENTURA]: *locality,* 8 miles east-northeast of Wheeler Springs along Sespe Creek (lat. 34°33'40" N, long. 119° 09'50" W; at S line sec. 36, T 6 N, R 22 W); the place is less than 1 mile upstream from the mouth of Piedra Blanca Creek. Named on Lion Canyon (1943) 7.5' quadrangle. Called Piedra Blanca CCC Camp on Lion Canyon (1944) 7.5' quadrangle.

Piedra Blanca Creek [VENTURA]: *stream,* flows nearly 9 miles to Sespe Creek 8.5 miles east-northeast of Wheeler Springs (lat. 34° 33'30" N, long. 119°09'05" W; near N line sec. 2, T 5 N, R 22 W). Named on Lion Canyon (1943) and San Guillermo (1943) 7.5' quadrangles. North Fork enters from the northeast 2.5 miles above the mouth of the main stream; it is 3 miles long and is named on Lion Canyon (1943) 7.5' quadrangle.

Piedra Gorda Canyon [LOS ANGELES]: *canyon,* drained by a stream that flows 1.5 miles to the sea 7 miles west-northwest of Santa Monica city hall (lat. 34°02'10" N, long. 118°36'30" W; sec. 36, T 1 S, R 17 W); the mouth of the canyon is at Big Rock Beach. Named on Topanga (1952) 7.5' quadrangle.

Pierpont Bay [VENTURA]:
(1) *embayment,* along the coast at Ventura (lat. 34°16'15" N, long. 119°17'15" W). Named on Ventura (1951) 7.5' quadrangle. The name commemorates Ernest Pierpont, a resident of Ojai Valley in the 1890's (Gudde, 1949, p. 261).
(2) *district,* 1.5 miles southeast of downtown Ventura near the coast (lat. 34°15'45" N, long. 119°16'15" W); the district is east of Pierpont

Bay (1). Named on Ventura (1951) 7.5' quadrangle. The place was laid out in 1925, and Ventura annexed it in 1968 (Ricard).

Pigeon Flat [VENTURA]: *area,* 3 miles east of Devils Heart Peak (lat. 34°32'40" N, long. 118°55'25" W). Named on Devils Heart Peak (1943) 7.5' quadrangle.

Pigeon Ridge [LOS ANGELES]: *ridge,* southwest-trending, 3 miles long, 2.5 miles southeast of Crystal Lake (lat. 34°17'15" N, long. 117°49'05" W). Named on Crystal Lake (1958) 7.5' quadrangle.

Pillsbury: see **Brea** [ORANGE].

Pinchot: see **Elizabeth Lake** [LOS ANGELES] (2).

Pine Canyon [LOS ANGELES]:
(1) *canyon,* 2.25 miles long, opens into lowlands 14 miles east of Neenach (lat. 34°46' N, long. 118°35'45" W; sec. 20, T 8 N, R 16 W). Named on Burnt Peak (1958) and Neenach School (1965) 7.5' quadrangles. Called Gookin Gulch on Johnson's (1911) map. The feature divides at the head to form Oakdale Canyon (1) and Oakgrove Canyon.
(2) *canyon,* drained by a stream that flows 2 miles to Bear Canyon (1) 12 miles southeast of Gorman (lat. 34°40'25" N, long. 118°39'10" W; sec. 26, T 7 N, R 17 W). Named on Burnt Peak (1958) and Liebre Mountain (1958) 7.5' quadrangles.
(3) *canyon,* drained by a stream that flows 4.25 miles to Hughes Lake at the village of Lake Hughes (lat. 34°40'35" N, long. 118° 26'50" W; at E line sec. 22, T 7 N, R 15 W). Named on Burnt Peak (1958) and Lake Hughes (1957) 7.5' quadrangles.
(4) *canyon,* 0.5 mile long, opens into the canyon of Gold Creek 4.5 miles north of Sunland (lat. 34°19'40" N, long. 118°17'55" W; sec. 24, T 3 N, R 14 W). Named on Sunland (1953) 7.5' quadrangle.
(5) *canyon,* drained by a stream that flows 1.25 miles to Arroyo Seco 6.25 miles north-northwest of Pasadena city hall (lat. 34°14'10" N, long. 118°10'35" W). Named on Pasadena (1953) 7.5' quadrangle.
(6) *canyon,* drained by a stream that flows less than 1 mile to Morris Reservoir 3 miles north of Glendora city hall (lat. 34°10'40" N, long. 117°52'05" W; near N line sec. 18, T 1 N, R 9 W). Named on Glendora (1953) 7.5' quadrangle.
(7) *canyon,* drained by a stream that flows less than 1 mile to Big Dalton Canyon nearly 4 miles northeast of Glendora city hall (lat. 34°10'05" N, long. 117°48'35" W; near S line sec. 7, T 1 N, R 9 W). Named on Glendora (1953) 7.5' quadrangle.

Pine Canyon [ORANGE]: *canyon,* drained by a stream that flows 1.5 miles to Silverado Canyon nearly 4 miles northwest of Santiago Peak (lat. 33°44'45" N, long. 117°35' W; sec. 11, T 5 S, R 7 W). Named on Santiago Peak (1954) 7.5' quadrangle.

Pine Canyon [VENTURA]: *canyon,* drained by a stream that flows 3.25 miles to Sespe Creek 4.5 miles north-northwest of Fillmore (lat. 34°27'40" N, long. 118°56'30" W; sec. 2, T 4 N, R 20 W). Named on Fillmore (1951) 7.5' quadrangle.

Pine Creek [LOS ANGELES]: *stream,* flows 2.25 miles to Amargosa Creek 9 miles southwest of Lancaster (lat. 34°36'05" N, long. 118° 14'35" W; at S line sec. 15, T 6 N, R 13 W). Named on Ritter Ridge (1958) and Sleepy Valley (1958) 7.5' quadrangles.

Pine Flat: see **Charlton Flats** [LOS ANGELES]; **Pine Flats** [LOS ANGELES]; **West Pine Flat** [LOS ANGELES].

Pine Flats [LOS ANGELES]: *area,* northeast of Crystal Lake (lat. 34° 19'25" N, long. 117°50'05" W). Named on Crystal Lake (1958) 7.5' quadrangle. Called Pine Flat on Rock Creek (1903) 15' quadrangle, but United States Board on Geographic Names (1962, p. 14) rejected this form of the name.

Pine Flats: see **Chilao Flat** [LOS ANGELES].

Pine Hollow Picnic Area [LOS ANGELES]: *locality,* 2.5 miles north-northeast of Crystal Lake (lat. 34°21'15" N, long. 117°50'05" W; near SW cor. sec. 9, T 3 N, R 9 W). Named on Crystal Lake (1958) 7.5' quadrangle.

Pine Mountain [LOS ANGELES]: *peak,* 6 miles north of Azusa city hall (lat. 34°13'25" N, long. 117°54' W). Altitude 4540 feet. Named on Azusa (1953) 7.5' quadrangle.

Pine Mountain [VENTURA]: *ridge,* generally west-northwest-trending, 10 miles long, center 1 mile east of Reyes Peak (lat. 34°37'55" N, long. 119°15'55" W). Named on Lion Canyon (1943), Reyes Peak (1943), and San Guillermo (1943) 7.5' quadrangles.

Pine Mountain: see **Vetter Mountain** [LOS ANGELES].

Pine Mountain Lodge [VENTURA]: *locality,* 6 miles east of Reyes Peak (lat. 34°37' N, long. 119°10'35" W; near N line sec. 14, T 6 N, R 22 W). Named on Lion Canyon (1943) 7.5' quadrangle.

Pine Mountain Ridge [LOS ANGELES]: *ridge,* west-northwest-trending, 5 miles long, center 3.5 miles northwest of Mount San Antonio on Los Angeles-San Bernardino county line (lat. 34°19'30" N, long. 117°41'05" W); Pine Mountain of San Bernardino County is at the east end of the ridge. Named on Mount San Antonio (1955) 7.5' quadrangle.

Pinery Canyon: see **Noel Canyon** [LOS ANGELES].

Pines Camp Ground: see **The Pines Camp Ground** [VENTURA].

Pine Springs [VENTURA]: *spring,* 9.5 miles east-northeast of Reyes Peak (lat. 34°41'25" N, long. 119°07'55" W; near W line sec. 20, T 7 N, R 21 W). Named on San Guillermo (1943) 7.5' quadrangle.

Pinkerton Canyon: see **Big Canyon** [VENTURA].

Pinnacle: see **The Pinnacle** [LOS ANGELES].
Pinnacle Rocks: see **Twin Rocks** [LOS ANGELES].
Pinos: see **Mount Pinos** [VENTURA].
Pin Rock [LOS ANGELES]: *rock,* near the mouth of Catalina Harbor on the south side of Santa Catalina Island, and 300 feet offshore (lat. 33°25'30" N, long. 118°30'20" W). Named on Santa Catalina West (1943) 7.5' quadrangle.
Pinyon Flats [LOS ANGELES]: *area,* 9 miles west-southwest of Valyermo (lat. 34°22'35" N, long. 117°59'15" W; near NW cor. sec. 1, T 3 N, R 11 W). Named on Juniper Hills (1959) and Waterman Mountain (1959) 7.5' quadrangles.
Pinyon Ridge [LOS ANGELES]: *ridge,* west-northwest-trending, 5.5 miles long, center 4 miles southeast of Valyermo (lat. 34°24'30" N, long., 117°48' W). Named on Valyermo (1958) 7.5' quadrangle.
Pioneer Pass [VENTURA]: *pass,* 1.25 miles southwest of Santa Susana Pass (lat. 34°15'25" N, long. 118°38'55" W). Named on Santa Susana (1951) 7.5' quadrangle.
Pipe Canyon [LOS ANGELES]: *canyon,* drained by a stream that flows 1.5 miles to Big Tujunga Canyon 2.5 miles north-northeast of Sunland (lat. 34°17'35" N, long. 118°17'05" W; sec. 6, T 2 N, R 13 W). Named on Sunland (1953) 7.5' quadrangle.
Piru [VENTURA]: *town,* 7 miles east of Fillmore (lat. 34°24'50" N, long. 118°47'35" W; sec. 20, T 4 N, R 18 W); the place is near the mouth of Piru Creek. Named on Piru (1952) 7.5' quadrangle. Postal authorities established Piru Rancho post office in 1888, changed the name to Piru City the same year, and changed it to Piru in 1903 (Salley, p. 173). David Cook founded the town in 1887 (Hoover, Rensch, and Rensch, p. 580). California Division of Highways' (1934) map shows a place called Rockbank located 0.5 mile east-northeast of Piru along a rail line.
Piru: see **Lake Piru** [VENTURA].
Piru Canyon [VENTURA]: *canyon,* 6.5 miles long, along Piru Creek above Piru (mouth at lat. 34°25'10" N, long. 118°47'15" W). Named on Piru (1952) 7.5' quadrangle.
Piru City: see **Piru** [VENTURA].
Piru Creek [LOS ANGELES-VENTURA]: *stream,* flows 68 miles, partly in Los Angeles County, to Santa Clara River 1 mile south-southeast of Piru in Ventura County (lat. 34°24' N, long. 118° 47' W). Named on Black Mountain (1958), Cobblestone Mountain (1958), Liebre Mountain (1958), Lockwood Valley (1943), McDonald Peak (1958), Piru (1952), San Guillermo (1943), Val Verde (1952), and Whitaker Peak (1958) 7.5' quadrangles. Called Rio Piru on Parke's (1854-1855) map. Antisell (p. 67) referred to Peyrou river, and Marcou (p. 166) used the designation "Rio de Peru." The name is of Indian ori-

gin (Kroeber, p. 54). South Fork enters 10 miles east of Reyes Peak; it is 4.25 miles long and is named on Lockwood Valley (1943) and San Guillermo (1943) 7.5' quadrangles. United States Board on Geographic Names (1990, p. 6) rejected the name "South Fork Piru Creek" for present Cedar Creek [VENTURA].
Piru Gorge [LOS ANGELES]: *narrows,* 11 miles south-southeast of Gorman (lat. 34°38'30" N, long. 118°45'50" W; mainly in sec. 2, T 6 N, R 18 W); the feature is along Piru Creek. Named on Black Mountain (1958) 7.5' quadrangle.
Piru Rancho: see **Piru** [VENTURA].
Pisgah Grande: see **Chatsworth** [LOS ANGELES].
Pitas Point [VENTURA]: *promontory,* 6 miles west-northwest of Ventura along the coast (lat. 34°19'05" N, long. 119°23'15" W; sec. 27, T 3 N, R 24 W). Named on Pitas Point (1950) 7.5' quadrangle. United States Board on Geographic Names (1961b, p. 14) rejected the names "Point las Petes," "Point Las Pitas," and "Point Los Pitas" for the feature, and pointed out that the name is from *los pitos,* which means "the whistles" in Spanish—Portola gave this designation to an Indian village at the place in 1769 after members of his party were kept awake at night by noise that Indians made with pipes or whistles (Hoover, Rensch, and Rensch, p. 577).
Piute Butte [LOS ANGELES]: *hill,* 12.5 miles northeast of Littlerock (lat. 34°39'30" N, long. 117°51' W; mainly in sec. 32, T 7 N, R 9 W). Named on Hi Vista (1957) 7.5' quadrangle.
Piute Ponds [LOS ANGELES]: *lake,* about 1.25 miles long, 6.25 miles north-northeast of Lancaster (lat. 34°47'20" N, long. 118°06'50" W; sec. 13, 14, T 8 N, R 12 W). Named on Rosamond (1973) and Rosamond Lake (1973) 7.5' quadrangles.
Placentia [ORANGE]: *city,* 6 miles north of Orange city hall (lat. 33° 52'15" N, long. 117°52'10" W). Named on Anaheim (1965), La Habra (1964), Orange (1964), and Yorba Linda (1964) 7.5' quadrangles. Postal authorities established Placentia post office in 1893, discontinued it in 1903, and reestablished it in 1911 (Frickstad, p. 117). The city incorporated in 1926. The name is from Placentia school district, which was organized at the place in 1879 (Meadows, p. 111). Residents of an area along Orangethorpe Avenue near Placentia incorporated in 1920 as the City of Orangethorpe to keep neighboring Fullerton from putting a sewer farm in their midst; after the threat from Fullerton passed, the City of Orangethorpe disincorporated (Carpenter, p. 194).
Placerita Canyon [LOS ANGELES]: *canyon,* drained by Placerita Creek, which flows 7 miles to South Fork Santa Clara River at Newhall (lat. 34°23'30" N, long., 118°32'10"

W). Named on Mint Canyon (1960) and Newhall (1952) 7.5' quadrangles. Called La Placerita Canyon on Newhall (1933) 6' quadrangle. Preston (1890a, p. 200) referred to Placerito Cañon. The name recalls placer gold that Francisco Lopez found at the place in 1842 (Bunje and Kean, p. 9).

Placerita Creek [LOS ANGELES]: *stream,* flows 7 miles to South Fork Santa Clara River at Newhall (lat. 34°23'30" N, long. 118°32'10" W). Named on Newhall (1952) 7.5' quadrangle.

Plano Trabuco [ORANGE]: *area,* extends southwest from the mouth of Trabuco Canyon between Arroyo Trabuco and Tiejeras Canyon; center about 6 miles southwest of Santiago Peak (lat. 33°38'15" N, long. 117°36' W). Named on Cañada Gobernadora (1949) and Santiago Peak (1954) 7.5' quadrangles. The feature now is called Trabuco Mesa (Meadows, p. 111).

Playa del Rey [LOS ANGELES]: *district,* 5 miles north-northwest of Manhattan Beach city hall in Los Angeles (lat. 33°57'05" N, long. 118°26'40" W). Named on Venice (1964) 7.5' quadrangle. Postal authorities established Playa del Rey post office in 1904, discontinued it in 1914, reestablished it in 1939, and changed the name to Playa Del Rey (with a capital "D") in 1960 (Salley, p. 174). Redondo (1896) 15' quadrangle shows a place called Port Ballona located at present Playa del Rey near the present mouth of Ballona Creek. Postal authorities established Port Ballona post office in 1887 and discontinued it in 1889 (Salley, p. 176). Moye L. Wicks attempted to develop a port and town called Port Ballona at the mouth of Ballona Creek in 1886, but the promotion failed; the venture was revived in 1902 and renamed Playa del Rey (Gleason, p. 120). A place called Tell's Landing, operated by Captain William Tell, also was situated at present Playa del Rey (Burnham, p. 339). During the Civil War a garrison of California volunteers occupied Fort Latham, which was located just back of present Playa Del Rey; the estuary at the mouth of Ballona Creek was considered a possible shipping and landing place for Southern sympathizers (Bell, p. 75). Venice (1924) 6' quadrangle has the name "Palisades del Rey" at present Playa del Rey.

Playa del Rey Beach [LOS ANGELES]: *beach,* 4 miles north-northwest of Manhattan Beach city hall along the coast (lat. 33°56'30" N, long. 118°26'30" W); the beach is at Playa del Rey. Named on Venice (1950) 7.5' quadrangle.

Pleasant Ranchos [ORANGE]: *locality,* nearly 6 miles south-southeast of present Buena Park civic center (lat. 33°47' N, long. 117°58'05" W; sec. 31, T 4 S, R 10 W). Named on Anaheim (1950) 7.5' quadrangle.

Pleasants Peak [ORANGE]: *peak,* 15 miles east

of Santa Ana on Orange-Riverside county line (lat. 33°47'45" N, long. 117°36'20" W; at E line sec. 28, T 4 S, R 7 W). Altitude 4007 feet. Named on Corona South (1967) 7.5' quadrangle. Called Sugarloaf Peak on Corona (1942) 15' quadrangle, but United States Board on Geographic Names (1934, p. 14) rejected this name for the feature, and noted that Orange County Historical Society suggested the name "Pleasants Peak" to honor J.E. Pleasants, who was associated with the peak since 1860.

Pleasant Valley [VENTURA]: *valley,* at and near Camarillo (lat. 34° 13' N, long. 119°02'15" W). Named on Camarillo (1950) and Newbury Park (1951) 7.5' quadrangles.

Pleasant View Ridge [LOS ANGELES]: *ridge,* generally northwest-trending, 5 miles long, 5 miles southwest of Valyermo (lat. 34°24'45" N, long. 117°55'45" W). Named on Crystal Lake (1958), Juniper Hills (1959), and Valyermo (1958) 7.5' quadrangles.

Plum Canyon [LOS ANGELES]: *canyon,* drained by a stream that flows 4 miles to Bouquet Canyon 3.5 miles northwest of Solemint (lat. 34°27'05" N, long. 118°29'55" W; near NW cor. sec. 7, T 4 N, R 15 W). Named on Mint Canyon (1960) 7.5' quadrangle.

Plum Spring [LOS ANGELES]: *spring,* 6 miles south-southwest of the village of Lake Hughes in Clearwater Canyon (lat. 34°35'35" N, long. 118°28'45" W). Named on Green Valley (1958) 7.5' quadrangle.

Poche [ORANGE]: *locality,* 4.25 miles south-southeast of San Juan Capistrano along Atchison, Topeka and Santa Fe Railroad (lat. 33° 26'30" N, long. 117°38'35" W). Named on Dana Point (1968) 7.5' quadrangle.

Point Comfort: see **Old Point Comfort** [LOS ANGELES].

Point Dume [LOS ANGELES]: *promontory,* 33 miles east of Los Angeles city hall along the coast (lat. 34°00' N, long. 118°48'20" W). Named on Point Dume (1951) 7.5' quadrangle. Called Dume Pt. on Camulos (1903) 30' quadrangle, and called Pt. Duma on Park's (1854-1855) map. Preston (1890a, p. 208) referred to Point Dumas. United States Board on Geographic Names (1933, p. 275) rejected the forms "Point Duma" and "Point Dumetz" for the name. Vancouver (p. 174) named the feature in 1793 to honor Father Francisco Dumetz, but used the misspelled name "Point Dume." California Mining Bureau's (1917) map shows a place called El Venado located about 2.5 miles north of Point Dume. Postal authorities established El Venado post office 27 miles northwest of Santa Monica (SE quarter of SE quarter sec. 20, T 1 S, R 18 W) in 1914 and discontinued it in 1917 (Salley, p. 69).

Point Dumetz: see **Point Dume** [LOS ANGELES].

Point Fermin [LOS ANGELES]: *promontory,*

7.5 miles southwest of Long Beach city hall along the coast (lat. 33°42'15" N, long. 118° 17'35" W). Named on San Pedro (1964) 7.5' quadrangle. Vancouver (p. 63. 176) named the feature in 1793 to honor Fermin Francisco de Lasuen, father president of the Franciscan order. Postal authorities established Firmin post office near Point Fermin in 1911 and moved it in 1912 when they changed the name to Point Fermin; they moved it again in 1918 when they changed the name to Gibson, and discontinued it in 1948 (Salley, p. 75, 84, 174).

Point Gorda: see **Punta Gorda** [VENTURA].

Point Hueneme [VENTURA]: *promontory,* 4 miles south-southwest of Oxnard (lat. 34°08'45" N, long. 119°12'55" W). Named on Oxnard (1949) 7.5' quadrangle. Called Hueneme Point on Hueneme (1904) 15' quadrangle. The name is of Indian origin (Kroeber, p. 43).

Point Las Petes: see **Pitas Point** [VENTURA].

Point Las Pitas: see **Pitas Point** [VENTURA].

Point Los Pitas: see **Pitas Point** [VENTURA].

Point Mugu [VENTURA]: *promontory,* 10 miles southeast of Oxnard along the coast (lat. 34°05'10" N, long. 119°03'35" W). Named on Point Mugu (1949) 7.5' quadrangle. Called Mugu Point on Hueneme (1904) 15' quadrangle. Vizcaino called the feature Punta de Rio Dulce in 1602 because of a stream of fresh water near it; then on the return voyage of the expedition early in 1603 it was called Punta de la Conversion for the conversion of San Pablo, celebrated January 25 (Wagner, p. 399). The name "Mugu" is of Indian origin (Kroeber, p. 49).

Point Mugu Navel Reservation [VENTURA]: *military installation,* at Mugu Lagoon. Named on Point Mugu (1949) 7.5' quadrangle.

Point Vicente [LOS ANGELES]: *promontory,* 7 miles south of Redondo Beach city hall along the coast (lat. 33°44'30" N, long. 118°24'40" W). Named on Redondo Beach (1951) 7.5' quadrangle. Called Point Vincente on San Pedro (1944) 15' quadrangle. United States Board on Geographic Names (1933, p. 789) rejected the forms "Point Vincent" and "Point Vincente" for the feature, although they admitted that Vancouver named it Point Vincente in 1793 for Friar Vincente Santa Maria of Buenaventura mission. It is called Relis del Codo on a diseño of Palos Verdes grant—*Relis del Codo* means "Landslide Corner" in Spanish (Becker, 1964).

Point Vincente: see **Point Vicente** [LOS ANGELES].

Poison Oak Canyon [LOS ANGELES]: *canyon,* 1.25 miles long, 10 miles east-southeast of Gorman (lat. 34°44'15" N, long. 118°41'05" W; mainly in sec. 33, T 8 N, R 17 W). Named on Liebre Mountain (1958) 7.5' quadrangle.

Pole Canyon [LOS ANGELES]: *canyon,* drained by a stream that flows nearly 4 miles to Soledad Canyon 5 miles east-northeast of

Solemint (lat. 34°25'50" N, long. 118°22'20" W; sec. 17, T 4 N, R 14 W). Named on Agua Duce (1960) 7.5' quadrangle.

Pole Canyon: see **Pole Creek** [VENTURA].

Polecat Gulch [LOS ANGELES]: *canyon,* drained by a stream that flows 1.25 miles to San Gabriel Reservoir 5.25 miles north of Glendora city hall (lat. 34°12'40" N, long. 117°51'35" W; sec. 31, T 2 N, R 9 W). Named on Glendora (1953) 7.5' quadrangle.

Pole Creek [VENTURA]: *stream,* flows 6.5 miles to the valley of Santa Clara River at Fillmore (lat. 34°24'35" N, long. 118°54'20" W; near S line sec. 19, T 4 N, R 19 W). Named on Fillmore (1951) 7.5' quadrangle. On Camulos (1903) 30' quadrangle, the canyon of the stream is called Pole Canyon. The name is from some poles found near the stream—poles that were used in the early days for fence posts; the stream also was called Yellow Creek (Ricard).

Pomeroy Canyon [LOS ANGELES]: *canyon,* drained by a stream that flows 1 mile to Brand Canyon 2 miles east of Burbank city hall (lat. 34°11'10" N, long. 118°16'25" W). Named on Burbank (1953) 7.5' quadrangle.

Pomona [LOS ANGELES]: *city,* 28 miles east of Los Angeles city hall (lat. 34°03'20" N, long. 117°45' W). Named on Ontario (1954) and San Dimas (1954) 7.5' quadrangles, which show a siding called Pomona situated 2.5 miles north of Pomona city hall along Atchison, Topeka and Santa Fe Railroad (lat. 34°05'40" N, long. 117°00' W). Postal authorities established Pomona post office in 1875 (Frickstad, p. 79), and the city incorporated in 1888. Solomon Gates submitted the name "Pomona" in a contest to name the new community in 1875; Gates, a nurseryman, was familiar with the Pomona of the Grangers, and with Pomona, goddess of fruit and trees in Roman mythology (Anonymous, 1976, p. 14).

Pomona: see **North Pomona** [LOS ANGELES].

Pomona Junction [LOS ANGELES]: *locality,* nearly 1.5 miles north of present Pomona city hall along Pacific Electric Railroad (lat. 34° 04'30" N, long. 117°45'10" W). Named on Claremont (1928) 6' quadrangle.

Poor Farm Station [LOS ANGELES]: *locality,* 3.25 miles southeast of present South Gate city hall along Los Angeles Terminal Railroad (lat. 33°55'15" N, long. 118°10' W). Named on Downey (1902) 15' quadrangle. Postal authorities established County Farm post office 2.5 miles northeast of Clearwater at the county home for the indigent in 1908, changed the name to Hondo in 1918, and changed it to Los Amigos in 1957 (Salley, p. 51, 99). South Gate (1952) 7.5' quadrangle shows Hondo post office at Rancho Los Amigos, which is by the site of Poor Farm Station.

Poplar Creek [VENTURA]: *stream,* flows 2.25 miles to Hot Springs Canyon 3.5 miles north-

northwest of Devils Heart Peak (lat. 34°35'40"
N, long. 119°00' W; sec. 21,T 6 N, R 20 W).
Named on Devils Heart Peak (1943) 7.5'
quadrangle.
Poplin Creek [VENTURA]: *stream,* flows 2.5
miles to Coyote Creek 7 miles west-southwest
of the town of Ojai (lat. 34°24'45" N, long.
119°21'35" W). Named on Matilija (1952) 7.5'
quadrangle.
Poppy Peak [LOS ANGELES]: *peak,* 2.5 miles
west-southwest of Pasadena city hall (lat.
34°07'50" N, long. 118°10'50" W). Altitude
1038 feet. Named on Pasadena (1953) 7.5'
quadrangle.
Portal Ridge [LOS ANGELES]: *ridge,* west-
northwest-trending, 18 miles long, northeast
of Pine Canyon (1) and Leona Valley (1); center near Elizabeth Lake. Named on Burnt Peak
(1958), Del Sur (1958), Lake Hughes (1957),
Lancaster West (1958), Ritter Ridge (1958),
and Sleepy Valley (1958) 7.5' quadrangles.
Port Ballona: see **Playa del Rey** [LOS ANGE-
LES].
Port Hueneme [VENTURA]: *town,* 3.25 miles
south-southwest of Oxnard near the coast (lat.
34°09' N, long. 119°11'45" W). Named on
Oxnard (1949) 7.5' quadrangle. Called
Hueneme on Hueneme (1904) 15' quadrangle,
but United States Board on Geographic
Names (1950b, p. 6) rejected this name for
the place. Postal authorities established
Wynema post office in 1870, changed the
name to Hueneme in 1874, and to Port
Hueneme in 1940 (Frickstad, p. 219, 220). The
town incorporated in 1948. W.E. Barnard and
a group of squatters started the community
of Wynema in 1870; Thomas R. Bard, owner
of the land, laid out the town of Hueneme in
1872—the name of the place became Port
Hueneme after construction of a harbor there
in 1939 (Ricard). United States Board on
Geographic Names (1965a, p. 13) approved
the name "Channel Islands Harbor" for a place
situated about 1.5 miles northwest of Port
Hueneme (lat. 34°09'45" N, long. 119°13'23"
W), and rejected the name "Ventura County
Small Craft Harbor" for the feature; the name
"Channel Islands Harbor" is from the position of the feature at the gateway to the
northernmost of the Channel Islands. Ricard
listed a place called Arnold located 3 miles
southeast of Port Hueneme—the name recalls
a family of early residents at the spot.
Portland Canyon: see **Nelson Canyon** [LOS
ANGELES].
Port Los Angeles [LOS ANGELES]: *locality,*
2.5 miles west-northwest of present Santa
Monica city hall (lat. 34°31'20" N, long. 118°
32'15" W). Named on Calabasas (1903) 15'
quadrangle, which shows a pier about 1 mile
long there. Officials of Southern Pacific Railroad built a rail line to the place to attract
coastal trade away from San Pedro, but eventually railroad officials abandoned the enter-

prise (Gleason, p. 113-114). Postal authorities established Port Los Angeles post office
in 1897 and discontinued it in 1908 (Frickstad,
p. 79).
Port Orange: see **McFadden's Landing,** under
Newport Beach [ORANGE] (2).
Portuguese Bend [LOS ANGELES]:
(1) *embayment,* 4.5 miles west-northwest of
Point Fermin (lat. 33° 44'10" N, long.
118°21'45" W). Named on San Pedro (1964)
7.5' quadrangle. The name is from two Portuguese whaling companies that operated at the
place in the mid-nineteenth century (Fink, p.
19).
(2) *district,* 5 miles west-northwest of Point
Fermin (lat. 33°44'30" N, long. 118°22' W);
the place is above Portuguese Bend (1).
Named on San Pedro (1964) 7.5' quadrangle.
Portuguese Canyon [LOS ANGELES]: *canyon,*
1.5 miles long, opens to the sea 4.5 miles west-
northwest of Point Fermin at Portuguese Bend
(1) (lat. 33°44'15" N, long. 118°21'40" W).
Named on San Pedro (1964) and Torrance
(1964) 7.5' quadrangles.
Portuguese Point [LOS ANGELES]: *promontory,* 5 miles west-northwest of Point Fermin
along the coast (lat. 33°44'15" N, long. 118°
22'25" W); the place is 0.5 mile west of Portuguese Bend (1). Named on San Pedro (1964)
7.5' quadrangle.
Posey Canyon [LOS ANGELES]: *canyon,*
drained by a stream that flows 2.25 miles to
Piru Creek 11.5 miles south-southeast of
Gorman (lat. 34°38'45" N, long. 118°45'45"
W; near W cor. sec. 2, T 6 N, R 20 W). Named
on Black Mountain (1958) and Liebre Moun-
tain (1958) 7.5' quadrangles.
Posita Canyon: see **Palo Comado Canyon**
[LOS ANGELES-VENTURA].
Potato Mountain [LOS ANGELES]: *peak,* 8.5
miles north-northeast of Pomona city hall (lat.
34°09'55" N, long. 117°41'30" W; near S line
sec. 14, T 1 N, R 8 W). Altitude 3422 feet.
Named on Mount Baldy (1954) 7.5' quad-
rangle.
Pothole: see **The Pothole** [VENTURA].
Pot Hole Harbor: see **Empire Landing** [LOS
ANGELES].
Potholes: see **The Potholes** [LOS ANGELES].
Pothole Spring [VENTURA]: *spring,* nearly 6
miles southeast of Cobblestone Mountain (lat.
34°32'30" N, long. 118°48'20" W; near S line
sec. 6, T 5 N, R 18 W); the spring is 0.5 mile
north-northwest of The Pothole. Named on
Cobblestone Mountain (1958) 7.5' quad-
rangle.
Potrero: see **Hidden Valley** [VENTURA].
Potrero Canyon [LOS ANGELES]: *canyon,*
7.25 miles long, opens into the valley of Santa
Clara River 8.5 miles west of Newhall (lat.
34°24'10" N, long. 118°40'25" W). Named
on Newhall (1952) and Val Verde (1952) 7.5'
quadrangles. Called Larres Canyon on Los
Angeles County (1935) map.

Potrero Canyon: see **Castaic Junction** [LOS ANGELES].

Potrero Chico [LOS ANGELES]: *land grant,* 3.5 miles southwest of El Monte city hall along Rio Hondo south of Potrero Grande grant. Named on El Monte (1953) 7.5' quadrangle. According to Cowan (p. 62-63), Antonio Valenzuela received the land in 1843, and Ramon Valenzuela and others claimed it. According to Perez (p. 82), who listed the grant under the name "Potrero de la Mission Vieja de San Gabriel," Juan Alvitre and Antonio Valenzuela were the grantees in 1844, and they were the patentees for 83.46 acres in 1923.

Potrero de Felipe Lugo [LOS ANGELES]: *land grant,* 2 miles south of El Monte city hall along San Gabriel River. Named on El Monte (1953) 7.5' quadrangle. Teodoro Romero and others received the land in 1845; Jorge Morillo claimed 2042 acres patented in 1871 (Cowan, p. 63).

Potrero de la Mission Vieja de San Gabriel: see **Potrero Chico** [LOS ANGELES].

Potrero Grande [LOS ANGELES]. *land grant,* southwest of downtown El Monte. Named on El Monte (1953) 7.5' quadrangle. Manuel Antonio received 1 league in 1845; J. Matias Sanchez claimed 4432 acres patented in 1859 (Cowan, p. 63).

Potrero John Creek [VENTURA]: *stream,* flows nearly 4 miles to Sespe Creek 5.25 miles north-northeast of Wheeler Springs (lat. 34°35'05" N, long. 119°16' W; sec. 25, T 6 N, R 23 W). Named on Wheeler Springs (1943) 7.5' quadrangle.

Potrero los Pinos [ORANGE]: *land grant,* 4 miles south of Trabuco Peak. Named on Alberhill (1954) 7.5' quadrangle.

Potrero Seco [VENTURA]: *valley,* 8 miles west of Reyes Peak (lat. 34°38'10" N, long. 119°25'20" W). Named on Rancho Nuevo Creek (1943) 7.5' quadrangle.

Potrero Valley [VENTURA]: *valley,* 3.5 miles southwest of Newbury Park (lat. 34°09'25" N, long. 118°57'45" W). Named on Newbury Park (1951) 7.5' quadrangle.

Potrero Valley Creek [LOS ANGELES-VENTURA]: *stream,* heads in Ventura County and flows 12 miles to Malibu Lake 7.5 miles north-northeast of Point Dume in Los Angeles County (lat. 34°06'20" N, long. 118°45'50" W; near SE cor. sec. 4, T 1 S, R 18 W). Named on Thousand Oaks (1952) 7.5' quadrangle.

Pots Valley: see **Valley of Ollas** [LOS ANGELES].

Pound Cake Hill: see **Signal Hill** [LOS ANGELES] (1).

Poverty Canyon [VENTURA]: *canyon,* drained by a stream that flows 1.25 miles to Casitas Valley 6 miles south of White Ledge Peak (lat. 34°23'05" N, long. 119°23'50" W; sec. 33, T 4 N, R 24 W). Named on White Ledge Peak (1952) 7.5' quadrangle.

Powder Canyon [LOS ANGELES]: *canyon,* 1.5 miles long, 2.5 miles north-northeast of La Habra [ORANGE] (lat. 33°57'50" N, long. 117°50'30" W). Named on La Habra (1964) 7.5' quadrangle.

Prairie Fork [LOS ANGELES]: *stream,* heads just inside San Bernardino County and flows 4.5 miles to San Gabriel River nearly 6 miles northwest of Mount San Antonio (lat. 34°20'35" N, long. 117°43'25" W; sec. 16, T 3 N, R 8 W). Named on Mount San Antonio (1955) 7.5' quadrangle.

Pratt Canyon [LOS ANGELES]: *canyon,* drained by a stream that flows 1.5 miles to an unnamed canyon 3.5 miles north-northwest of Burnt Peak (lat. 34°43'35" N, long. 118°36'25" W; at E line sec. 6, T 7 N, R 16 W). Named on Burnt Peak (1958) 7.5' quadrangle.

Precipicio Canyon: see **Eaton Canyon** [LOS ANGELES].

Precipicio Peak: see **Occidental Peak** [LOS ANGELES].

Price Canyon [LOS ANGELES]: *canyon,* drained by a stream that flows 2 miles to Fairmont Reservoir 2 miles north of the village of Lake Hughes (lat. 34°42'15" N, long. 118°26'15" W; near S line sec. 11, T 7 N, R 15 W). Named on Lake Hughes (1957) 7.5' quadrangle. Los Angeles County (1935) map has the name "Hughes Canyon" for a feature that branches east from Price Canyon just above Fairmont Reservoir.

Prima Deshecha Cañada [ORANGE]: *canyon,* drained by a stream that flows 5 miles to the sea 4.25 miles south-southeast of San Juan Capistrano (lat. 33°26'25" N, long. 117°38'40" W). Named on Dana Point (1949) and San Clemente (1968) 7.5' quadrangles. On Capistrano (1902) 30' quadrangle, the name applies to the stream in the canyon. The feature is the first difficult canyon to cross on the road south from San Juan Capistrano mission—*Prima Deshecha Cañada* means "First Rough Canyon" in Spanish (Meadows, p. 112-113).

Prince Barranca [VENTURA]: *gully,* extends for 0.5 mile from the mouth of Hall Canyon 1.5 miles east of downtown Ventura (lat. 34°16'45" N, long. 119°15'45" W). Named on Ventura (1951) 7.5' quadrangle. The name commemorates Francis Munroe Prince, an early settler; the feature also had the name "Cunnane Barranca" for Dr. Cunnane, who owned property there (Ricard).

Prospect Bar: see **Eldoradoville Campground** [LOS ANGELES].

Prospect Canyon [LOS ANGELES]: *canyon,* drained by a stream that flows 1.5 miles to Elizabeth Lake Canyon 2.25 miles north-northeast of Warm Springs Mountain (lat. 34°37'20" N, long. 118°33'20" W). Named on Burnt Peak (1958) and Warm Springs Mountain (1958) 7.5' quadrangles.

Prospect Park [LOS ANGELES]: *locality,* 4.5 miles northwest of present Los Angeles city hall (lat. 34°05'45" N, long. 118°17'55" W). Named on Santa Monica (1902) 15' quadrangle. Postal authorities established Prospect Park post office in 1888 and discontinued it in 1912 (Salley, p. 178).

Prospero Tract [LOS ANGELES]: *land grant,* at San Marino. Named on El Monte (1953) and Mount Wilson (1953) 7.5' quadrangles. Antonio Valenzuela and Prospero Valenzuela received the land in 1843; Ramon Valenzuela and others claimed 24 acres patented in 1875 (Cowan, p. 31; Cowan listed the grant under the designation "Cuati, (or) Prospero").

Providencia [LOS ANGELES]: *land grant,* extends from southwest of downtown Burbank to Cahuenga Peak. Named on Burbank (1953) 7.5' quadrangle. Vicente de la Osa was the grantee in 1843; David W. Alexander and Francis Mellus were the petentees for 4064 acres in 1872 (Perez, p. 83).

Puckett Canyon: see **Vasquez Canyon** [LOS ANGELES].

Puddingstone Reservoir [LOS ANGELES]: *lake,* nearly 4 miles northwest of Pomona city hall in San Jose Hills (lat. 34°05'15" N, long. 117°48'20" W). Named on San Dimas (1954) 7.5' quadrangle.

Pueblo de Los Angeles: see **Los Angeles** [LOS ANGELES].

Puente: see **La Puente** [LOS ANGELES] (2).

Puente Creek [LOS ANGELES]: *stream,* flows 5.5 miles to San Jose Creek 4.5 miles southsouthwest of Baldwin Park city hall (lat. 34° 01'30" N, long. 117°58'45" W); the stream is on La Puente grant. Named on Baldwin Park (1966) 7.5' quadrangle.

Puente Hills [LOS ANGELES-ORANGE]: *range,* north of Whittier and La Habra between San Gabriel River and Brea Canyon in Los Angeles, Orange, and San Bernardino Counties. Named on Los Angeles (1975), San Bernardino (1957), and Santa Ana (1959) 1°x 2° quadrangles. Baldwin Park (1953) 7.5' quadrangle also has the name "Puente Hills" for a small range located just east of downtown La Puente and separated from the main Puente Hills by San Jose Creek. Parke's (1854-1855) map has the name "Sierra de Santa Ana" for present Puente Hills and present Santa Ana Mountains combined. English (p. 5) applied the name "Puente Hills" to "The whole group of hills lying between the towns of Pomona, Whittier, and Corona and a small area directly south of the town of Puente," and noted that "the name should preferably be used for the group of hills lying between Santa Ana and San Gabriel rivers." English (p. 5) noted also that "The part of the Puente Hills directly north of the city of Whittier and east to La Habra Canyon" is called Whittier Hills. Poland and others' (1956) map has the name "Whittier Narrows" for the place that both San

Gabriel River and Rio Hondo pass the west end of Puente Hills.

Puente Junction [LOS ANGELES]: *locality,* 5 miles south of Baldwin Park city hall along Union Pacific Railroad (lat. 34°00'50" N, long. 117°57'35" W). Named on Baldwin Park (1966) 7.5' quadrangle. Called Puente Sta. on Puente (1927) 6' quadrangle.

Puente Largo [LOS ANGELES]: *locality,* 1 mile west-northwest of Azusa city hall along Pacific Electric Railroad (lat. 34°08'20" N, long. 117°55'30" W). Named on Azusa (1953) 7.5' quadrangle.

Puente Station: see **Puente Junction** [LOS ANGELES].

Puerco Beach [LOS ANGELES]: *beach,* 2 miles west of Malibu Point along the coast (lat. 34°01'50" N, long. 118°43'05" W); the beach is mainly east of the mouth of Puerco Canyon. Named on Malibu Beach (1951) 7.5' quadrangle.

Puerco Canyon [LOS ANGELES]: *canyon,* drained by a stream that flows 2.25 miles to the sea 2.5 miles west of Malibu Point (lat. 34° 01'55" N, long. 118°43'25" W). Named on Malibu Beach (1951) 7.5' quadrangle.

Pulga Canyon [LOS ANGELES]: *canyon,* drained by a stream that flows nearly 3 miles to the sea 3.5 miles west-northwest of Santa Monica city hall (lat. 34°02'20" N, long. 118°32'35" W). Named on Topanga (1952) 7.5' quadrangle. Called Las Pulgas Canyon on Los Angeles County (1935) map.

Punchbowl Canyon [LOS ANGELES]: *canyon,* drained by a stream that flows 3.5 miles to Big Rock Creek 2 miles south-southeast of Valyermo (lat. 34°25'20" N, long. 117°50'15" W; sec. 20, T 4 N, R 9 W); part of the canyon is in Devils Punchbowl. Named on Valyermo (1958) 7.5' quadrangle. On Los Angeles County (1935) map, the stream in the canyon is called Punchbowl Creek.

Punchbowl Creek: see **Punchbowl Canyon** [LOS ANGELES].

Punta [VENTURA]: *settlement,* 4.5 miles northwest of Pitas Point (lat. 34°21'50" N, long. 119°26'50" W; on S line sec. 1, T 3 N, R 25 W); the place is 0.5 mile north-northwest of Punta Gorda. Named on Pitas Point (1950) 7.5' quadrangle. Called Punta Gorda on Ventura (1904) 15' quadrangle. Postal authorities established Punta Gorda post office in 1888 and discontinued it in 1916 (Frickstad, p. 219).

Punta de Arbolada: see **Dana Point** [ORANGE].

Punta de la Conversion: see **Point Mugu** [VENTURA].

Punta de Rio Dulce: see **Point Mugu** [VENTURA].

Punta Gorda [VENTURA]: *promontory,* 4 miles northwest of Pitas Point (lat. 34°21'20" N, long. 119°26'30" W; near W line sec. 7, T 3 N, R 24 W). Named on Pitas Point (1950) 7.5' quadrangle. United States Board on Geographic Names (1961b, p. 10) rejected the form "Point Gorda" for the name.

Punta Gorda: see **Punta** [VENTURA].

Puzzle Canyon [LOS ANGELES]: *canyon,* drained by a stream that flows nearly 3 miles to lowlands 4.25 miles north of Big Pines (lat. 34°26'30" N, long. 117°40'35" W; near SE cor. sec. 11, T 4 N, R 8 W). Named on Mescal Creek (1956) 7.5' quadrangle.

Pyramid Cove [LOS ANGELES]: *embayment,* 2 miles west of Pyramid Head at the southeast end of San Clement Island (lat. 32° 49'20" N, long. 118°23' W). Named on San Clemente Island South (1943) 7.5' quadrangle. Called Smugglers Cove on Smith's (1898) map.

Pyramid Head [LOS ANGELES]: *promontory,* at the southeast end of San Clement Island (lat. 32°49'15" N, long. 118°20'55" W). Named on San Clemente Island South (1943) 7.5' quadrangle. The name is from the resemblance of the promontory to a pyramid (Doran, 1980, p. 52). United States Board on Geographic Names (1978c, p. 3) approved the name "Balanced Rock" for a feature situated 0.5 mile southwest of Pyramid Head (lat. 32°48'58" N, long. 118°21'15" W), and rejected the names "Whitewashed Rock" and "White Washed Rock" for it.

Pyramid Lake [LOS ANGELES]: *lake,* behind a dam on Piru Creek 11 miles south-southeast of Gorman in Piru Gorge (lat. 34°38'35" N, long. 118°45'45" W; sec. 2, T 6 N, R 18 W); Pyramid Rock is just south of the dam. Named on Black Mountain (1958, photorevised 1974) 7.5' quadrangle.

Pyramid Rock [LOS ANGELES]: *relief feature,* 11.5 miles south-southeast of Gorman in Piru Gorge (lag. 34°38'30" N, long. 118°45'50" W; sec. 2, T 6 N, R 18 W). Named on Black Mountain (1958) 7.5' quadrangle.

– Q –

Quail [LOS ANGELES]: *locality,* nearly 6 miles east-southeast of Gorman at the northwest edge of present Quail Lake (lat. 34°46'20" N, long. 118°45'05" W; near SE cor. sec. 14, T 8 N, R 18 W). Named on Tejon (1903) 30' quadrangle. Postal authorities established Quail post office in 1898 and discontinued it in 1902; the name was from large coveys of quail at the place (Salley, p. 179).

Quail Canyon: see **Peters Canyon** [ORANGE].

Quail Lake [LOS ANGELES]: *lake,* 1600 feet long, 6 miles east-southeast of Gorman (lat. 34°46'20" N, long. 118°45'05" W). Named on La Liebra Ranch (1965) and Lebec (1958) 7.5' quadrangles. Quail (1938) 6' quadrangle shows the feature as an intermittent lake. The Spaniards called it La Laguna Seca (Latta, p. 31), and later it had the name "Crane Lake" (Suter, p. 20).

Quail Lake Inn [LOS ANGELES]: *locality,* 4.5 miles east-southeast of Gorman (lat. 34°46'35" N, long. 118°46'25" W); the place is 1.25 miles northwest of Quail Lake. Named on Lebec (1945) 7.5' quadrangle.

Quail Spring [LOS ANGELES]: *spring,* 10.5 miles east of Soledad (lat. 34°24' N, long. 118°16'45" W; sec. 30, T 4 N, R 13 W). Named on Agua Dulce (1960) 7.5' quadrangle.

Quarry Canyon [LOS ANGELES]: *canyon,* drained by a stream that flows 1 mile to Santa Ynez Canyon 6.5 miles northwest of Santa Monica city hall (lat. 34°05'05" N, long. 118°34' W). Named on Topanga (1952) 7.5' quadrangle.

Quarry Spring [LOS ANGELES]: *spring,* about 13 miles south-southeast of Gorman in Cherry Canyon (1) (lat. 34°37'35" N, long. 118°44'15" W; sec. 12, T 6 N, R 18 W). Named on Liebre Mountain (1958) 7.5' quadrangle.

Quarterway House: see **Little Santa Anita Canyon** [LOS ANGELES].

Quartz Hill [LOS ANGELES]:
(1) *ridge,* west-trending, 1.5 miles long, 5 miles southwest of downtown Lancaster (lat. 34°38'45" N, long. 118°12'15" W; at and near SE cor. sec. 36, T 7 N, R 13 W). Named on Lancaster West (1958) 7.5' quadrangle.
(2) *town,* 6 miles southwest of Lancaster (lat. 34°38'45" N, long. 118°13'05" W); the town is at and near Quartz Hill (1). Named on Lancaster West (1958) 7.5' quadrangle. Postal authorities established Quartz Hill post office in 1948 (Salley, p. 179).

Quatal Canyon [VENTURA]: *canyon,* drained by a stream that heads in Kern County and flows 14 miles through Ventura County to Santa Barbara County 16 miles northwest of Reyes Peak (lat. 34° 49' N, long. 119°26'30" W; near S line sec. 33, T 9 N, R 24 W). Named on Apache Canyon (1943) and Cuyama Peak (1943) 7.5' quadrangles.

Queen City: see **Emerald Bay** [LOS ANGELES].

Queensway Bay: see **Los Angeles River** [LOS ANGELES].

Quigley Canyon [LOS ANGELES]: *canyon,* 1.25 miles long, 1.5 miles east of Newhall (lat. 34°23'20" N, long. 118°30' W). Named on Mint Canyon (1960) and Newhall (1952) 7.5' quadrangles.

– R –

Rabbit Lake: see **Elizabeth Lake** [LOS ANGELES] (1).

Rabbit Canyon: see **Limestone Canyon** [ORANGE]; **Peters Canyon** [ORANGE].

Rabbit Peak [LOS ANGELES]: *peak,* nearly 4 miles west-southwest of Pacifico Mountain (lat. 34°21'25" N, long. 118°05'40" W). Altitude 5307 feet. Named on Chilao Flat (1959) 7.5' quadrangle.

Rabbitt Canyon: see **Oak Spring Canyon** [LOS ANGELES] (1).

Radford Canyon [LOS ANGELES]: *canyon*, drained by a stream that flows 1 mile to Berry Canyon 5 miles southeast of Van Nuys (lat. 34°07'55" N, long. 118°22'50" W). Named on Burbank (1953) and Van Nuys (1953) 7.5' quadrangles.

Radium Sulphur Spring: see **Colegrove** [LOS ANGELES].

Raggio: see **Drinkwater Canyon** [LOS ANGELES].

Railroad Canyon [LOS ANGELES]: *canyon*, less than 1 mile long 4.25 miles south-south-east of Del Sur (lat. 34°37'50" N, long. 118°15'45" W; on S line sec. 4, T 6 N, R 13 W). Named on Del Sur (1958) 7.5' quadrangle.

Railroad Canyon: see **Newhall** [LOS ANGELES].

Ramera Canyon [LOS ANGELES]: *canyon*, drained by a stream that flows 4.25 miles to the sea nearly 2 miles northeast of Point Dume (lat. 34°01'10" N, long. 118°47'10" W). Named on Point Dume (1951) 7.5' quadrangle.

Ramona [LOS ANGELES]: *locality*, 6 miles east of present Los Angeles city hall (lat. 34°04'30" N, long. 118°08'30" W). Named on Pasadena (1900) 15' quadrangle. Postal authorities established Ramona post office in 1887 and discontinued it in 1895 (Frickstad, p. 80).

Ramona Acres: see **Monterey Park** [LOS ANGELES].

Ramona Canyon [VENTURA]: *canyon*, drained by a stream that flows less than 1 mile to Holser Canyon 4 miles east-northeast of Piru (lat. 34°26'20" N, long. 118°43'50" W; near SE cor. sec. 11, T 4 N, R 18 W). Named on Val Verde (1952) 7.5' quadrangle.

Ramona Park [LOS ANGELES]: *district*, 7.25 miles east of Los Angeles city hall (lat. 34°04'15" N, long. 118°07'20" W). Named on Alhambra (1926) 6' quadrangle.

Ram Point: see **Arrow Point** [LOS ANGELES].

Ranchito [LOS ANGELES]: *locality*, 3 miles west-northwest of present Whittier city hall (lat. 33°59'15" N, long. 118°05'05" W). Named on Downey (1902) 15' quadrangle. Postal authorities established Ranchito post office in 1877 and discontinued it in 1886 (Frickstad, p. 80).

Rancho Los Amigos: see **County Farm Station** [LOS ANGELES].

Rancho Nuevo Creek [VENTURA]: *stream*, heads in Santa Barbara County and flows 5 miles in Ventura County to Cuyama River 7.5 miles northwest of Reyes Peak (lat. 34°42'15" N, long. 119°22'55" W). Named on Rancho Nuevo Creek (1943) 7.5' quadrangle. United States Board on Geographic Names (1950a, p. 1) rejected the name "Bear Creek" for the stream, or for its upper part.

Rancho Santa Clarita [LOS ANGELES]: *town*, 4 miles north of Newhall (lat. 34°26'30" N, long. 118°32' W). Named on Newhall (1952) 7.5' quadrangle. A small placer-mining camp of the 1890's known as Ratsburg was situated at the junction of San Francisquito Canyon and Bouquet Canyon in present Rancho Santa Clarita (Robinson, J.W., 1973, p. 19).

Randolph: see **Brea** [ORANGE].

Randolph Canyon: see **Elderberry Canyon** [LOS ANGELES].

Rankin Peak [LOS ANGELES]: *peak*, 6.5 miles northwest of Azusa city hall (lat. 34°12'30" N, long. 117°58'25" W; on N line sec. 6, T 1 N, R 10 W). Named on Azusa (1966) 7.5' quadrangle. The name commemorates the Reverend Edward Payson Rankin of Monrovia (United States Board on Geographic Names, 1949, p. 4).

Rathke: see **Camp Rathke**, under **Santiago Reservoir** [ORANGE].

Ratsburg: see **Rancho Santa Clarita** [LOS ANGELES].

Rattlesnake Canyon [LOS ANGELES]:
(1) *canyon*, drained by a stream that flows 3.25 miles to East Fork Fish Canyon (1) 3.5 miles west-northwest of Warm Springs Mountain (lat. 34°36'55" N, long. 118°37'10" W). Named on Burnt Peak (1958) and Warm Springs Mountain (1958) 7.5' quadrangles.
(2) *canyon*, drained by a stream that flows 1 mile to San Gabriel River 6 miles east-southeast of Crystal Lake (lat. 34°16'40" N, long. 117°45'10" W); the canyon heads at Rattlesnake Peak. Named on Crystal Lake (1958) 7.5' quadrangle.
(3) *canyon*, drained by a stream that flows 2 miles to Pacoima Canyon 7.25 miles north of Sunland (lat. 34°21'55" N, long. 118°18'45" W; near N line sec. 11, T 3 N, R 14 E). Named on Agua Dulce (1960) and Sunland (1953) 7.5' quadrangles.

Rattlesnake Canyon [ORANGE]: *canyon*, drained by a stream that flows 2.5 miles to lowlands 7.5 miles north-northwest of El Toro (lat. 33°43'40" N, long. 117°44'40" W). Named on El Toro (1950) 7.5' quadrangle.

Rattlesnake Canyon: see **Shoemaker Canyon** [LOS ANGELES] (2).

Rattlesnake Canyon Wash [ORANGE]: *stream*, flows 3.25 miles from the mouth of Rattlesnake Canyon to Peters Canyon Wash 5 miles east-southeast of Santa Ana city hall (lat. 33°43'05" N, long. 117°47'20" W). Named on El Toro (1968) and Tustin (1965) 7.5' quadrangles.

Rattlesnake Island: see **Terminal Island** [LOS ANGELES] (1).

Rattlesnake Peak [LOS ANGELES]: *peak*, 5 miles southeast of Crystal Lake (lat. 34°16'20" N, long. 117°46'35" W). Altitude 5826 feet. Named on Crystal Lake (1958) 7.5' quadrangle.

Rattlesnake Peak [ORANGE]: *peak*, 5 miles

east-northeast of Orange city hall (lat. 33°49' N, long. 117°46'15" W). Altitude 772 feet. Named on Orange (1964) 7.5' quadrangle.

Rattlesnake Reservoir [ORANGE]: *lake,* nearly 0.5 mile long, behind a dam at the mouth of Rattlesnake Canyon 7.5 miles north-northwest of El Toro (lat. 33°43'45" N, long. 117°44'15" W). Named on El Toro (1968) 7.5' quadrangle.

Rattlesnake Spring [LOS ANGELES]: *spring,* 3.25 miles east-northeast of Waterman Mountain (lat. 34°21'35" N, long. 117°53'10" W; near W line sec. 12, T 3 N, R 10 W). Named on Waterman Mountain (1959) 7.5' quadrangle.

Rattlesnake Terminal Island: see **Terminal Island** [LOS ANGELES] (1).

Ravena City: see **Ravenna** [LOS ANGELES].

Ravenna [LOS ANGELES]: *locality,* 2.5 miles south-southwest of Acton along Southern Pacific Railroad in Soledad Canyon (lat. 34° 26'20" N, long. 118°13'25" W; near S line sec. 10, T 4 N, R 13 W). Named on Acton (1959) 7.5' quadrangle. Postal authorities established Ravena City post office in 1868, discontinued it in 1871, reestablished it with the name "Ravena" in 1875, changed the name to Ravenna in 1876, discontinued it in 1877, reestablished it in 1878, and discontinued it in 1895 (Salley, p. 181). A mining town called Soledad sprang up at the place in 1862, but because of confusion with the town of Soledad in Monterey County, the community was renamed Ravenna for Don Manuel Ravenna, president of Soledad Gold, Silver and Copper Mining Company; the railroad listed both the names "Ravenna" and "Soledad City" at the place (Robinson, J.W., 1973, p. 21).

Raymer [LOS ANGELES]: *locality,* 2.25 miles north-northwest of Van Nuys along Southern Pacific Railroad (lat. 34°12'50" N, long. 118°27'45" W). Named on Van Nuys (1953) 7.5' quadrangle.

Raymond [LOS ANGELES]: *locality,* 1.5 miles south of present Pasadena city hall along Los Angeles Terminal Railroad (lat. 34° 07'30" N, long. 118°09' W). Named on Pasadena (1900) 15' quadrangle.

Raymond Hill [LOS ANGELES]: *district,* 7 miles northeast of Los Angeles city hall in South Pasadena (lat. 34°07'20" N, long. 118° 08'50" W). Named on Los Angeles (1953) 7.5' quadrangle.

Real Canyon [VENTURA]: *canyon,* drained by a stream that flows 1 mile to the valley of Santa Clara River 0.5 mile west-northwest of Piru (lat. 34°25' N, long. 118°48'05" W; sec. 19, T 4 N, R 18 W). Named on Piru (1952) 7.5' quadrangle. The Real family lived in the canyon in 1874 (Ricard).

Real Wash [VENTURA]: *stream,* flows 1.5 miles from the mouth of Real Canyon to Santa Clara River 1.25 miles south-southwest of Piru (lat. 34°23'50" N, long. 118°48'05" W; sec. 30, T 4 N, R 18 W). Named on Piru (1952) 7.5' quadrangle.

Reasoner Canyon [VENTURA]: *canyon,* drained by a stream that flows 4 miles to Lake Piru 4.5 miles north-northeast of Piru (lat. 34°28'45" N, long. 118°46' W; sec. 33, T 5 N, R 18 W). Named on Cobblestone Mountain (1958) and Piru (1952, photorevised 1969) 7.5' quadrangles. On Camulos (1903) 30' quadrangle, the name applies to present Dominguez Canyon. The Reasoner family lived in the canyon (Ricard).

Recreation Point [ORANGE]: *promontory,* 0.5 mile west-southwest of Laguna Beach city hall along the coast (lat. 33°32'35" N, long. 117°47'30" W). Named on Laguna Beach (1965) 7.5' quadrangle.

Red Box Gap [LOS ANGELES]: *pass,* 9.5 miles south-southwest of Pacifico Mountain (lat. 34°15'30" N, long. 118°06'15" W). Named on Chilao Flat (1959) 7.5' quadrangle. The name is from a fire box painted red that forest rangers placed at the site about 1908 (Robinson, J.W., 1977, p. 158-159).

Red Box Station [LOS ANGELES]: *locality,* 9.5 miles south-southwest of Pacifico Mountain (lat. 34°15'30" N, long. 118°06'15" W); the place is at Red Box Gap. Named on Chilao Flat (1959) 7.5' quadrangle.

Redcastle: see **Sepulveda** [LOS ANGELES] (2).

Red Fox Canyon [LOS ANGELES]: *canyon,* drained by a stream that flows 1.5 miles to Elizabeth Lake Canyon 4.25 miles southeast of Burnt Peak (lat. 34°37'50" N, long. 118°32' W). Named on Burnt Peak (1958) and Warm Springs Mountain (1958) 7.5' quadrangles.

Red Hill [ORANGE]: *hill,* 4.25 miles east of Santa Ana city hall (lat. 33°45' N, long. 117°47'30" W). Altitude 345 feet. Named on Orange (1964) and Tustin (1965) 7.5' quadrangles. In the early days the feature was a landmark called Cerro Colorado for its red color given by cinnabar, the quicksilver ore; it also was called Cerrito de las Ranas for its proximity to Cienega de las Ranas (Meadows, p. 51, 118).

Redman [LOS ANGELES]: *locality,* 17 miles north of Littlerock (lat. 34°45'50" N, long. 117°58'05" W; at SW cor. sec. 20, T 8 N, R 10 W). Named on Redman (1973) 7.5' quadrangle. Thompson's (1921) map shows Casa Desierto P.O. situated 3 miles east of Redman school at present Redman. Postal authorities established Redman post office in 1908, moved it 3 miles east in 1914 when they changed the name to Casa Desierto, and discontinued it in 1922; the name "Redman" was for the developer of the site (Salley, p. 39, 182).

Redman Canyon: see **Nelson Canyon** [LOS ANGELES].

Red Mountain [LOS ANGELES]: *peak,* 3.25 miles east of Warm Springs Mountain (lat. 34°35'10" N, long. 118°31'25" W). Named on Warm Springs Mountain (1958) 7.5' quadrangle.

Red Mountain [VENTURA]: *ridge,* generally

east-trending, 3.5 miles long, 5.5 miles north-northwest of Ventura (lat. 34°21' N, long. 119°20'30" W). Named on Ventura (1951) 7.5' quadrangle.

Redondo: see **Redondo Beach** [LOS ANGELES].

Redondo Beach [LOS ANGELES]: *city,* 12 miles west-northwest of Long Beach city hall (lat. 33°50'35" N, long. 118°23'20" W). Named on Inglewood (1952), Torrance (1964), and Venice (1950) 7.5' quadrangles. Called Redondo on Redondo (1896) 15' quadrangle. Postal authorities established Redondo Beach post office in 1889, changed the name to Redondo in 1895, and changed it back to Redondo Beach in 1909 (Salley, p. 183). The city incorporated in 1892.

Redondo Junction [LOS ANGELES]: *locality,* 2.5 miles south-southeast of Los Angeles city hall along Atchison, Topeka and Santa Fe Railroad (lat. 34°01' N, long. 118°13'30" W). Named on Los Angeles (1953) 7.5' quadrangle. Called Ballona Junction on Pasadena (1900) 15' quadrangle.

Red Reef Canyon [VENTURA]: *canyon,* drained by a stream that flows 2.5 miles to Sespe Creek 14 miles east-northeast of Wheeler Springs (lat. 34°33'50" N, long. 119°03'10" W; near SE cor. sec. 36, T 6 N, R 21 W). Named on Topatopa Mountains (1943) 7.5' quadrangle.

Redrock Canyon [LOS ANGELES]:
(1) *canyon,* drained by a stream that flows 3.5 miles to Castaic Creek 16 miles southeast of Gorman (lat. 34°37'30" N, long. 118° 39'30" W; at W line sec. 11, T 6 N, R 17 W); the canyon heads at Redrock Mountain. Named on Liebre Mountain (1958) 7.5' quadrangle.
(2) *canyon,* drained by a stream that flows less than 1 mile to Spencer Canyon 5 miles north of Burnt Peak (lat. 34°44'15" N, long. 118°34'55" W; sec. 33, T 8 N, R 16 W). Named on Burnt Peak (1958) 7.5' quadrangle.
(3) *canyon,* drained by a stream that flows 1.5 miles to Topanga Canyon 6 miles north-east of Malibu Point (lat. 34°06'20" N, long. 118°37'40" W; sec. 2, T 1 S, R 17 W). Named on Malibu Beach (1951) 7.5' quadrangle.

Redrock Creek [VENTURA]: *stream,* flows 4.25 miles to Tar Creek 5.25 miles southeast of Devils Heart Peak (lat. 34°30' N, long. 118° 54' W; near W line sec. 20, T 5 N, R 19 W). Named on Devils Heart Peak (1943) 7.5' quadrangle.

Redrock Mountain [LOS ANGELES]: *ridge,* north- to west-trending, 2.5 miles long, 13 miles southeast of Gorman (lat. 34°39'30" N, long. 118°38'20" W). Named on Liebre Mountain (1958) 7.5' quadrangle. On Tejon (1903) 30' quadrangle, the name "Redrock Mt." applies to a peak located at the south end of the ridge, and on Red Mountain (1936) 6' quadrangle, the name applies to a peak situated about 1 mile farther west.

Red Rover Canyon [LOS ANGELES]: *canyon,* 3 miles northwest of Acton (lat. 34°29'50" N, long. 118°13'25" W; sec. 22, 27, T 5 N, R 13 W). Named on Ravena (1934, reprinted 1949) 6' quadrangle.

Redwing Lake [LOS ANGELES]: *lake,* 800 feet long, 3.5 miles north of downtown Sunland in a flood control basin (lat. 34°15'50" N, long. 118°22'25" W). Named on Sunland (1966) 7.5' quadrangle.

Reed Reservoir [ORANGE]: *water feature,* 1.5 miles east-southeast of San Juan Capistrano (lat. 33°29'35" N, long. 117°38'15" W; sec. 8, T 8 S, R 7 W). Named on Dana Point (1968) 7.5' quadrangle.

Reed Spring [LOS ANGELES]: *spring,* 3.25 miles north of Crystal Lake (lat. 34°22' N, long. 117°50'50" W; at N line sec. 8, T 3 N, R 9 W). Named on Crystal Lake (1958) 7.5' quadrangle.

Reef Point [ORANGE]: *promontory,* 2.25 miles west-northwest of Laguna Beach city hall along the coast (lat. 33°33'25" N, long. 117°49'10" W). Named on Laguna Beach (1965) 7.5' quadrangle.

Reeves Creek [VENTURA]: *stream,* flows 5.25 miles to Thatcher Creek 3 miles east of the town of Ojai (lat. 34°26'55" N, long. 119° 11'25" W). Named on Ojai (1952) 7.5' quadrangle.

Relis del Codo: see **Point Vicente** [LOS ANGELES].

Remolacha: see **Talbert** [ORANGE].

Rendalia [LOS ANGELES]: *locality,* 6 miles southeast of South Gate city hall along Pacific Electric Railroad (lat. 33°53'25" N, long. 118°08' W). Named on South Gate (1952) 7.5' quadrangle.

Repollo: see **Talbert** [ORANGE].

Reseda [LOS ANGELES]: *district,* 3.5 miles east of the center of Canoga Park in Los Angeles (lat. 34°12'05" N, long. 118°32'05" W). Named on Canoga Park (1952) 7.5' quadrangle. On Calabasas (1903) 15' quadrangle, the name "Reseda" applies to a place along Southern Pacific Railroad where Reseda (1928) 6' quadrangle has the name "Reseda Siding" and Canoga Park (1952) 7.5' quadrangle has the name "Tarzana Siding." Calabasas (1903) 15' quadrangle also shows a place called Marion located 1.5 miles north of Reseda. Postal authorities established Reseda post office in 1922 (Frickstad, p. 80). The name "Reseda" originally was applied to a station on a Southern Pacific Railroad line built from Burbank to Chatsworth about 1895; after 1920 the name was transferred to a station of Pacific Electric Railroad known previously as Marion (Gudde, 1949, p. 284).

Reseda Siding: see **Tarzana Siding** [LOS ANGELES].

Reservation Point [LOS ANGELES]: *promontory,* 2 miles northeast of Point Fermin (lat. 33°43'20" N, long. 118°16' W). Named on San

Pedro (1964) 7.5' quadrangle. Reservation Point received its name in 1915 when the Treasury Department established a quarantine station there (Gudde, 1949, p. 284). Stevenson's (1884) map shows Dead Man Is. connected to the southwest end of Rattlesnake Is. (present Terminal Island) by a breakwater. The entrance to Los Angeles harbor originally lay between present Terminal Island and Dead Man's Island, but in 1872 a breakwater was built to connect the two islands with the hope that this structure would cause a new channel to be scoured out elsewhere; with the aid of dredging a new channel was made, and in 1928 this channel was widened by removal of the island and by deposit of its material along the breakwater, an operation that formed present Reservation Point (Gleason, p. 113-116). United States Board on Geographic Names (1933, p. 639) rejected the names "Deaman Island" and "Deadmans Island" for Reservation Point. The name "Deadman's Island" is from burials made at the site, including burial of six United States Marines killed in battle with the Mexicans in 1846—the place also was known as La Isla del Muerto (Gleason, p. 114-116).

Reservoir Canyon [ORANGE]: *canyon,* 1 mile long, 1.5 miles south-southeast of San Juan Capistrano (lat. 33°28'40" N, long. 117°39'20" W). Named on Dana Point (1968) 7.5' quadrangle.

Reservoir Hill [LOS ANGELES]: *peak,* 10 miles south-southeast of Gorman (lat. 34°39'40" N, long. 118°43'30" W). Named on Liebre Mountain (1958) 7.5' quadrangle, which shows a small reservoir on the feature.

Reservoir Ravine: see **Chavez Ravine** [LOS ANGELES].

Reservoir Summit [LOS ANGELES]: *pass,* 10 miles south-southeast of Gorman (lat. 34°39'45" N, long. 118°43'40" W); the pass is 1000 feet northwest of Reservoir Hill. Named on Liebre Mountain (1958) 7.5' quadrangle.

Resort Point [LOS ANGELES]: *promontory,* 5.5 miles south-southwest of Redondo Beach city hall along the coast (lat. 33°46' N, long. 118°25'25" W). Named on Redondo Beach (1951) 7.5' quadrangle.

Revolon Slough [VENTURA]: *stream,* flows 7 miles to Calleguas Creek 6.5 miles south-southwest of Camarillo (lat. 34°07'40" N, long. 119°04'35" W). Named on Camarillo (1950) 7.5' quadrangle. The Revolon family farmed near the stream in the 1870's (Ricard).

Reyes Creek [VENTURA]: *stream,* flows 6 miles to Cuyama River 5 miles north-northwest of Reyes Peak (lat. 34°41'40" N, long. 119° 19' W; near N line sec. 21, T 7 N, R 23 W); the stream heads near Reyes Peak. Named on Reyes Peak (1943) 7.5' quadrangle. C.W. Whipple (p. 148) referred to Ray's Creek.

Reyes Peak [VENTURA]: *peak,* 24 miles north of Ventura on Pine Mountain (lat. 34°37'50" N, long. 119°16'50" W; near NE cor. sec. 11, T 6 N, R 23 W). Altitude 7510 feet. Named on Reyes Peak (1943) 7.5' quadrangle. The name commemorates Jacinto Damien Reyes, who was a forest ranger in the neighborhood for more than 30 years (Hanna, p. 253).

Reynier Canyon [LOS ANGELES]: *canyon,* less than 1 mile long, opens into Sand Canyon (2) 3 miles southeast of Solemint (lat. 34° 23'10" N, long. 118°25'05" W; sec. 35, T 4 N, R 15 W). Named on Mint Canyon (1960) 7.5' quadrangle.

Ribbon Beach [LOS ANGELES]: *beach,* nearly 1 mile southwest of Silver Peak on the south side of Santa Catalina Island (lat. 33° 27' N, long. 118°34'40" W); the beach is less than 1 mile north-northwest of Ribbon Rock. Named on Santa Catalina West (1943) 7.5' quadrangle.

Ribbon Rock [LOS ANGELES]: *ridge,* west-southwest-trending, 0.5 miles long, 1.25 miles south of Silver Peak on the south side of Santa Catalina Island (lat. 33°26'30" N, long. 118°34'15" W). Named on Santa Catalina West (1943) 7.5' quadrangle. The feature is a wall of dark rock with a vein of quartz that is visible from a distance of many miles at sea (United States Coast and Geodetic Survey, p. 107).

Rice Canyon [LOS ANGELES]: *canyon,* drained by a stream that flows 2.25 miles to Gavin Canyon 2.25 miles south-southwest of Newhall (lat. 34°20'45" N, long. 118°32'30" W; near N line sec. 15, T 3 N, R 16 W). Named on Oat Mountain (1952) 7.5' quadrangle.

Rice Canyon [VENTURA]: *canyon,* 1 mile long, opens into Ojai Valley 3 miles west-northwest of the town of Ojai (lat. 34°27'30" N, long. 119°17'40" W). Named on Matilija (1952) 7.5' quadrangle.

Richardson Canyon [LOS ANGELES]: *canyon,* drained by a stream that flows 1.5 miles to Oakdale Canyon (1) 11 miles east-southeast of Gorman (lat. 34°44' N, long. 118°37'35" W; sec. 36, T 8 N, R 17 W). Named on Liebre Mountain (1958) 7.5' quadrangle.

Richardson Canyon [VENTURA]: *canyon,* drained by a stream that flows 1.5 miles to the valley of Santa Clara River 1 mile southeast of downtown Santa Paula (lat. 34°20'40" N, long. 119°02'45" W). Named on Santa Paula (1951) 7.5' quadrangle. The name is for a pioneer family that owned the place (Ricard).

Richfields: see **Atwood** [ORANGE].

Richland: see **Orange** [ORANGE].

Ridge Crest Picnic Ground [LOS ANGELES]: *locality,* 3 miles east-northeast of Waterman Mountain (lat. 34°21'10" N, long. 117°53'15" W; at NW cor. sec. 13, T 3 N, R 10 W). Named on Waterman Mountain (1959) 7.5' quadrangle.

Ridge View: see **Saugus** [LOS ANGELES].

Rim Rock Canyon [ORANGE]: *canyon,* drained by a stream that flows 1.25 miles to Bluebird Canyon 1 mile southeast of Laguna Beach city hall (lat. 33°32'05" N, long. 117°46'05" W; sec, 25, T 7 S, R 9 W). Named on Laguna Beach (1965) 7.5' quadrangle. The name once applied also to present Bluebird Canyon, but now it is restricted (Meadows, p. 119).

Rincon Beach [VENTURA]: *beach,* center 2 miles northwest of Pitas Point along the coast (near lat. 34°20'15" N, long. 119°24'30" W). Named on Pitas Point (1950) 7.5' quadrangle.

Rincon Canyon [LOS ANGELES]: *canyon,* drained by a stream that flows 1 mile to the canyon of West Fork San Gabriel River 7 miles north of Glendora city hall (lat. 34°14'10" N, long. 117°51'35" W; near N line sec. 30, T 2 N, R 9 W). Named on Glendora (1953) 7.5' quadrangle.

Rincon Creek [VENTURA]: *stream,* flows 9.5 miles, mainly along Ventura-Santa Barbara county line, to the sea 12.5 miles west-northwest of Ventura (lat. 34°22'25" N, long. 119°28'35" W); the mouth of the stream is at Rincon Point. Named on Pitas Point (1950) and White Ledge Peak (1952) 7.5' quadrangles. On Ventura (1904) 15' quadrangle, present Catharina Creek is called East Fork Rincon Creek.

Rincon de la Brea [LOS ANGELES-ORANGE]: *land grant,* at and near Brea Canyon. Named on La Habra (1952), San Dimas (1954), and Yorba Linda (1950) 7.5' quadrangles. Gil Ibarra received 1 league in 1841 and claimed 4453 acres patented in 1864; the grant first was called Cañada de la Brea (Cowan, p. 20).

Rincon de la Brea: see **Brea Canyon** [LOS ANGELES-ORANGE].

Rincon de Los Bueys [LOS ANGELES]: *land grant,* south of Beverly Hills. Named on Beverly Hills (1950) and Hollywood (1953) 7.5' quadrangles. Bernardo Higuera received three-fifths of a league in 1821 and 1843; Francisco Higuera and others claimed 3128 acres patented in 1872 (Cowan, p. 21).

Rincon de San Pasqual: see **San Pasqual** [LOS ANGELES].

Rincon Mountain [VENTURA]: *peak,* 4.25 miles north-northwest of Pitas Point (lat. 34°22'20" N, long. 119°25'15" W); the peak is 3.25 miles east of Rincon Point. Altitude 2161 feet. Named on Pitas Point (1950) 7.5' quadrangle. Called Mt. Hoar on Peckham's (1866) map.

Rincon Point [VENTURA]: *promontory,* 6.25 miles northwest of Pitas Point along the coast (lat. 34°22'20" N, long. 119°28'35" W); the feature is on El Rincon grant at the mouth of Rincon Creek. Named on Pitas Point (1950) and White Ledge Peak (1952) 7.5' quadrangles.

Rio de la Santa Clara: see **Santa Clara River** [VENTURA].

Rio del Dulcissimo Nombre de Jesus del Temblores: see **Santa Ana River** [ORANGE].

Rio del Llano: see **Big Rock Creek** [LOS ANGELES]; **Big Rock Wash** [LOS ANGELES].

Rio de los Angeles: see **Los Angeles River** [LOS ANGELES].

Rio de Porciuncula: see **Los Angeles River** [LOS ANGELES].

Rio de San Gabriel: see **San Gabriel River** [LOS ANGELES-ORANGE].

Rio de Santa Ana: see **Santa Ana River** [ORANGE].

Rio de Santa Clara [VENTURA]: *land grant,* at and near Oxnard and Port Hueneme. Named on Camarillo (1950), Oxnard (1949), and Point Mugu (1949) 7.5' quadrangles. Valentin Cota received the land in 1837 and claimed 44,883 acres patented in 1872 (Cowan, p. 92).

Rio Hondo [LOS ANGELES]:
(1) *stream,* flows 17 miles to Los Angeles River 2.25 miles southeast of South Gate city hall (lat. 33°56'05" N, long. 118°10'25" W). Named on El Monte (1953), South Gate (1952), and Whittier (1949) 7.5' quadrangles. Called Lexington Wash near El Monte on Pasadena (1900) 15' quadrangle—El Monte had the early name "Lexington." San Gabriel River followed the course of present Rio Hondo until the flood of 1867, when it took a new course and the former course took the name "Rio Hondo" (Gudde, 1949, p. 152).
(2) *locality,* 5.25 miles west of present Whittier city hall along Pacific Electric Railroad (lat. 33°58'40" N, long. 118°07'20" W). Named on Bell (1936) 6' quadrangle.

Rio Piru: see **Piru Creek** [VENTURA].

Rio San Bernadino: see **Santa Ana River** [ORANGE].

Rio San Buenaventura: see **Ventura River** [VENTURA].

Rio San Gabriel: see **San Gabriel River** [LOS ANGELES].

Rio Santa Ana: see **Santa Ana River** [ORANGE].

Rio Santa Anna: see **Santa Ana River** [ORANGE].

Rio Santa Maria: see **Cuyama River** [VENTURA].

Rio Simi: see **Calleguas Creek** [VENTURA].

Ritter Canyon [LOS ANGELES]: *canyon,* drained by a stream that flows 2.25 miles to Leona Valley (1) 7 miles west of Palmdale (lat. 34°36' N, long. 118°14'30" W; near N line sec. 22, T 6 N, R 13 W). Named on Ritter Ridge (1958) 7.5' quadrangle.

Ritter Ridge [LOS ANGELES]: *ridge,* east-southeast-trending, 3.25 miles long, 5.5 miles west-northwest of Palmdale (lat. 34°36'15" N, long. 118°12'30" W). Named on Ritter Ridge (1958) 7.5' quadrangle.

Rivera: see **Pico Rivera** [LOS ANGELES]; **Riviera** [LOS ANGELES].

Rivera Canyon [LOS ANGELES]: *canyon,*

drained by a stream that flows 1.25 miles to
lowlands 17 miles east of Gorman (lat.
34°45'25" N, long. 118°32'55" W; sec. 26, T
8 N, R 16 W). Named on Burnt Peak (1958)
and Neenach School (1965) 7.5' quadrangles.
Riverdale: see **Glendale** [LOS ANGELES].
Riviera [LOS ANGELES]: *district,* 6 miles west
of Beverly Hills city hall in Los Angels (lat.
34°03'30" N, long. 118°30' W). Named on
Beverly Hills (1950) and Topanga (1952) 7.5'
quadrangles. Called Rivera on Sawtell (1934)
6' quadrangle.
Robbers Cave: see **Fremont Canyon** [OR-
ANGE].
Robbers Peak [ORANGE]: *peak,* 6 miles east-
northeast of Orange city hall (lat. 33°49'40"
N, long. 117°45'25" W). Altitude 1152 feet.
Named on Orange (1964) 7.5' quadrangle.
Bulldozers destroyed the feature in 1973
(Sleeper, 1976, p. 165).
Robbers' Roost: see **Vasquez Rocks** [LOS
ANGELES].
Robbs Gulch [LOS ANGELES]: *canyon,*
drained by a stream that flows less than 1 mile
to San Gabriel Reservoir 6 miles north of
Glendora city hall (lat. 34°13'15" N, long.
117°51'10" W). Named on Glendora (1966)
7.5' quadrangle.
Roberts: see **Burbank** [LOS ANGELES].
Roberts Camp [LOS ANGELES]: *locality,* 3
miles east-southeast of Mount Wilson in Santa
Anita Canyon (lat. 34°12' N, long. 118°01'05"
W; sec. 3, T 1 N, R 11 W). Named on Mount
Wilson (1953) 7.5' quadrangle. Postal authorities established Roberts Camp post office in
1922 and discontinued it in 1933 (Frickstad,
p. 80). Otto L. Roberts settled at the place in
1911 and started a resort there in 1912
(Robinson, J.W., 1977, p. 133).
Roberts Canyon [LOS ANGELES]: *canyon,*
drained by a stream that flows 5.5 miles to
lowlands 2 miles north of Azusa city hall (lat.
34°09'45" N, long. 117°54'20" W; near NW
cor. sec. 23, T 1 N, R 10 W). Named on Azusa
(1953) 7.5' quadrangle. Called Rogers Canyon on Los Angeles County (1935) map. The
name "Roberts Canyon" commemorates H.C.
Roberts, a settler of 1856 (Gudde, 1949, p.
288).
Roberts Canyon: see **Williams Canyon** [LOS
ANGELES] (1).
Robinson Canyon [LOS ANGELES]: *canyon,*
1.5 miles long, 9 miles east-southeast of
Gorman (lat. 34°44' N, long. 118°40' W;
mainly in sec. 34, T 8 N, R 17 W). Named on
Liebre Mountain (1958) 7.5' quadrangle.
Roblar: see **Simi Valley** [VENTURA] (2).
Rocamp [ORANGE]: *locality,* 1.25 miles west-
northwest of Huntington Beach civic center
along Pacific Electric Railroad (lat. 33°40'10"
N, long. 118°01'05" W). Named on Seal
Beach (1950) 7.5' quadrangle.
Rock [VENTURA]: *locality,* 4.5 miles north of
Ventura along Southern Pacific Railroad (lat.

34°20'45" N, long. 119°17'50" W). Named
on Ventura (1904) 15' quadrangle.
Rockbank: see **Piru** [VENTURA].
Rockbound Canyon [LOS ANGELES]: *canyon,* drained by a stream that flows less than
2 miles to Soldier Creek 1.5 miles south-
southeast of Crystal Lake (lat. 34°17'50" N,
long. 117°50'05" W). Named on Crystal Lake
(1958) 7.5' quadrangle.
Rock Creek [LOS ANGELES]: *stream,* diverges
from Big Rock Wash and flows 9 miles to end
8.5 miles north-northeast of Littlerock (lat.
34°38'15" N, long. 117°56' W; at W line sec.
3, T 6 N, R 10 W). Named on Alpine Butte
(1957), Littlerock (1957), and Lovejoy Buttes
(1957) 7.5' quadrangles.
Rock Creek [VENTURA]: *stream,* flows 2.5
miles to Sheep Creek 14 miles east-northeast
of Reyes Peak (lat. 34°40'25" N, long.
119°02'35" W; sec. 30, T 7 N, R 20 W).
Named on Lockwood Valley (1943) 7.5' quad-
rangle.
Rock Creek: see **Big Rock Creek** [LOS AN-
GELES]; **Little Rock Creek** [LOS ANGE-
LES].
Rock Creek Wash: see **Big Rock Wash** [LOS
ANGELES].
Rock Springs: see **Big Rock Springs** [LOS
ANGELES].
Rock Wash: see **Big Rock Wash** [LOS ANGE-
LES].
Rocky Buttes [LOS ANGELES]: *peaks,* 11
miles northeast of Littlerock (lat. 34°38'45"
N, long. 117°52'15" W; on and near S line
sec. 31, T 7 N, R 9 W). Named on Alpine
Butte (1957) and Hi Vista (1957) 7.5' quad-
rangles.
Rocky Flat [VENTURA]: *area,* 6.5 miles north
of Ventura along Ventura River at the site of
present Casitas Springs (lat. 34°22'05" N,
long. 119°18'30" W). Named on Ventura
(1904) 15' quadrangle.
Rocky Peak [LOS ANGELES-VENTURA]:
peak, 1.5 miles north of Santa Susana pass
on Los Angeles-Ventura county line (lat.
34°17'30" N, long. 118°38'10" W). Altitude
2714 feet. Named on Santa Susana (1951) 7.5'
quadrangle.
Rocky Point: see **Newport Bay** [ORANGE];
Palos Verdes Point [LOS ANGELES].
Rodeo Canyon: see **Brea Canyon** [LOS AN-
GELES-ORANGE].
Rodeo de las Aguas: see **San Antonio or Rodeo de Las Agues** [LOS ANGELES].
Rodeo Flat [VENTURA]: *area,* 4.5 miles north
of Piru (lat. 34°28'45" N, long. 118°48'30"
W; sec. 31, T 5 N, R 18 W). Named on Piru
(1952) 7.5' quadrangle.
Rodeo Spring [VENTURA]: *spring,* 4.25 miles
north of Piru (lat. 34° 28'30" N, long.
118°48'30" W; sec. 31, T 5 N, R 18 W); the
feature is near Rodeo Flat. Named on Piru
(1952) 7.5' quadrangle.
Rogers Camp [LOS ANGELES]: *locality,* 17

miles southeast of Gorman in Fish Canyon (1) (lat. 34°38'05" N, long. 118°37'35" W). Named on Liebre Mountain (1958) 7.5' quadrangle.

Rogers Canyon: see **Roberts Canyon** [LOS ANGELES].

Rogers Creek [LOS ANGELES]: *stream,* flows 2.5 miles to Amargosa Creek nearly 2 miles east-southeast of the village of Leona Valley (lat. 34°36'20" N, long. 118°15'30" W; sec. 16, T 6 N, R 13 W). Named on Sleepy Valley (1958) 7.5' quadrangle.

Roger Young Village [LOS ANGELES]: *locality,* 2.5 miles south-southeast of Burbank city hall (lat. 34°09'05" N, long. 118°16'50" W). Named on Burbank (1953) 7.5' quadrangle.

Rolling Hills [LOS ANGELES]: *town,* 5.5 miles south of Torrance city hall in Palos Verdes Hills (lat. 33°45'45" N, long. 118°21' W). Named on San Pedro (1964) and Torrance (1964) 7.5' quadrangles. Postal authorities established Rolling Hills post office in 1937, discontinued it in 1942, and reestablished it in 1949 (Salley, p. 188). The town incorporated in 1957.

Rolling Hills Estates [LOS ANGELES]: *town,* 3.5 miles south-southwest of Torrance city hall in Palos Verdes Hills (lat. 33°47'15" N, long. 118°21'45" W). Named on Redondo Beach (1963) and Torrance (1964) 7.5' quadrangles. Postal authorities established Rolling Hills Estates post office in 1964 as a branch of Palos Verdes Peninsula post office, which they had established in 1962 in Palos Verdes Hills (Salley, p. 166, 188). Rolling Hills Estates incorporated in 1957.

Romero Canyon [LOS ANGELES]: *canyon,* drained by a stream that flows 3.5 miles to Halsey Canyon 9.5 miles northwest of Newhall (lat. 34°27'50" N, long. 118°39'30" W). Named on Val Verde (1952) and Whitaker Peak (1958) 7.5' quadrangles.

Roosevelt [LOS ANGELES]:

(1) *locality,* 7.5 miles east-northeast of Lancaster (lat. 34°43'10" N, long. 118°00'20" W; around NE cor. sec. 11, T 7 N, R 11 W). Named on Lancaster East (1958) 7.5' quadrangle. Postal authorities established Roosevelt Corner post office 9 miles east of Lancaster post office in 1966; the name was from Roosevelt school at the place (Salley, p. 188).

(2) *district,* 2.5 miles northeast of Torrance city hall (lat. 33°51'50" N, long. 118°18'15" W). Named on Torrance (1964) 7.5' quadrangle.

Roosevelt: see **Long Beach** [LOS ANGELES]; **Munz Canyon** [LOS ANGELES].

Roosevelt Corner: see **Roosevelt** [LOS ANGELES] (1).

Rosamond Dry Lake: see **Rosamond Lake** [LOS ANGELES].

Rosamond Lake [LOS ANGELES]: *dry lake,* about 5 miles long, 10 miles north-northeast of Lancaster on Los Angeles-Kern county line

(lat. 34°50' N, long. 118°04' W). Named on Rosamond Lake (1973) 7.5' quadrangle. Called Rosamond Dry Lake on Rosamond (1943) 15' quadrangle. Rosamond Lake (1973) 7.5' quadrangle has the designation "Air Force Flight Test Center, Edwards Air Force Base" at the dry lake. Defense Department officials named the air force base in 1949 to honor Captain Glenn W. Edwards, a pilot killed in 1948 while testing a jet plane— previously the place was called Muroc Dry Lake Center (Hanna, p. 95).

Roscoe: see **Sun Valley** [LOS ANGELES] (1).

Rose Canyon [ORANGE]: *canyon,* drained by a stream that flows 2 miles to Arroyo Trabuco 4.5 miles southwest of Santiago Peak (lat. 33°39'35" N, long. 117°35'05" W; near S line sec. 11, T 6 S, R 7 W). Named on Santiago Peak (1954) 7.5' quadrangle. The feature was called Hick's Canyon on some early maps for Jim Hickey, who kept bees there beginning in 1875; later it was called Wild Rose Canyon, and then Rose Canyon after 1886 (Sleeper, 1976, p. 166).

Rosecrans [LOS ANGELES]: *locality,* 5.5 miles southeast of present Inglewood city hall along a railroad (lat. 33°53'55" N, long. 118° 17'30" W). Named on Redondo (1896) 15' quadrangle. Postal authorities established Rosecrans post office in 1888, discontinued it in 1890, reestablished it in 1951, and discontinued it in 1962; the name commemorates Union General William S. Rosecrans of Civil War fame (Salley, p. 189).

Rosecrans Hills [LOS ANGELES]: *ridge,* north-northwest-trending, about 8 miles long, center 3.5 miles southeast of Inglewood city hall (lat. 33°56' N, long. 118°18'15" W). Named on Inglewood (1964) 7.5' quadrangle.

Rose Creek [VENTURA]: *stream,* flows 1.5 miles to Snowy Creek 4.25 miles northeast of McDonald Peak (lat. 34°40'25" N, long. 118°52'50" W; sec. 27, T 7 N, R 19 W). Named on McDonald Peak (1958) 7.5' quadrangle.

Rose Gulch [LOS ANGELES]: *canyon,* drained by a stream that flows 1 mile to Iron Fork nearly 6 miles west of Mount San Antonio (lat. 34°18'05" N, long. 117°44'50" W). Named on Mount San Antonio (1955) 7.5' quadrangle.

Rose Hill [LOS ANGELES]: *district,* 3.5 miles east-northeast of Los Angeles city hall (lat. 34°04'50" N, long. 118°11'35" W). Named on Alhambra (1926) 6' quadrangle.

Rosemead [LOS ANGELES]: *city,* 2.5 miles west-northwest of El Monte city hall (lat. 34°04'50" N, long. 118°04'20" W). Named on El Monte (1953) 7.5' quadrangle. Postal authorities established Rosemead post office in 1924 (Salley, p. 189), and the city incorporated in 1959. The name first applied in the 1870's to Leonard J. Rose's horse farm (Gudde, 1949, p. 290).

Rosenita: see **Camp Rosenita** [LOS ANGELES].
Rose Valley Creek [VENTURA]: *stream*, flows 3.5 miles to Howard Creek 5.5 miles northeast of Wheeler Springs (lat. 34°33'05" N, long. 119°12'30" W; sec. 5, T 5 N, R 22 W). Named on Lion Canyon (1943) 7.5' quadrangle.
Rose Valley Falls [VENTURA]: *waterfall*, 6.5 miles east-northeast of Wheeler Springs along Rose Valley Creek (lat. 34°31'35" N, long. 119°10'40" W; at E line sec. 9, T 5 N, R 22 W). Named on Lion Canyon (1943) 7.5' quadrangle.
Rossmoor [ORANGE]: *town*, 7 miles southwest of Buena Park civic center (lat. 33°47'10" N, long. 118°04'45" W). Named on Los Alamitos (1964) 7.5' quadrangle. Postal authorities established Rossmoor post office in 1962; the name is from Ross W. Cortese, who built the community (Salley, p. 189).
Ross Mountain [LOS ANGELES]: *peak*, 5.25 miles east of Crystal Lake (lat. 34°19'30" N, long. 117°45'20" W). Altitude 7402 feet. Named on Crystal Lake (1958) 7.5' quadrangle.
Round Canyon [ORANGE]: *canyon*, 3 miles long, opens into lowlands 4.5 miles north-northwest of El Toro (lat. 33°41'25" N, long. 117°42'30" W). Named on El Toro (1968) 7.5' quadrangle. Called Bee Canyon on Corona (1902) 30' quadrangle, where present nearby Bee Canyon is unnamed.
Round Mountain [VENTURA]: *hill*, 4 miles south-southwest of Camarillo (lat. 34°09'45" N, long. 119°03'20" W). Altitude 554 feet. Named on Camarillo (1950) 7.5' quadrangle.
Round Spring Canyon [VENTURA]: *canyon*, drained by a stream that flows 8 miles to Cuyama River 8 miles northwest of Reyes Peak (lat. 34°42'50" N, long. 119°22'55" W). Named on Apache Canyon (1943) and Reyes Peak (1943) 7.5' quadrangles.
Roundtop [LOS ANGELES]: *peak*, nearly 3 miles southwest of Pacifico Mountain (lat. 34°21'10" N, long. 118°04' W; near N line sec. 1, T 3 N, R 11 W). Altitude 6316 feet. Named on Chilao Flat (1959) 7.5' quadrangle.
Rowell Canyon: see **Hickey Canyon** [ORANGE].
Rowher Canyon [LOS ANGELES]: *canyon*, drained by a stream that flows 4 miles to Mint Canyon (1) 12.5 miles south-southeast of village of Lake Hughes (lat. 34°30'10" N, long. 118°22'45" W; near E line sec. 19, T 5 N, R 14 W). Named on Green Valley (1958) and Sleepy Valley (1958) 7.5' quadrangles.
Rowland [LOS ANGELES]: *locality*, 6 miles south-southeast of Baldwin Park city hall along Union Pacific Railroad (lat. 34°00'05" N, long. 117°55'45" W). Named on Baldwin Park (1953) 7.5' quadrangle. Postal authorities established Rowland post office in 1903 and discontinued it in 1904; the name was for Bernard F. Rowland, first postmaster (Salley,

p. 190). California Mining Bureau's (1917) map shows a place called Fallon located 2 miles east of Rowland along the railroad.
Rowland Heights [LOS ANGELES]: *city*, 4 miles northeast of La Habra [ORANGE] (lat. 33°58'30" N, long. 117°54'15" W). Named on La Habra (1964) 7.5' quadrangle. Postal authorities established Rowland Heights post office in 1963 (Salley, p. 190).
Rowland Siding [LOS ANGELES]: *locality*, 5.5 miles south-southeast of present Baldwin Park city hall along Southern Pacific Railroad (lat. 34°00'30" N, long. 117°55'45" W). Named on Pomona (1904) 15' quadrangle.
Rowley Canyon [LOS ANGELES]: *canyon*, 1.25 miles long, 2 miles east-northeast of Sunland (1) (lat. 34°16' N, long. 118°16'45" W; mainly at S line sec. 7, T 2 N, R 13 W). Named on Sunland (1953) 7.5' quadrangle.
Royball Spring [LOS ANGELES]: *spring*, 12.5 miles south-southeast of Gorman (lat. 34°37'45" N, long. 118°45'25" W). Named on Black Mountain (1958) 7.5' quadrangle.
Rubio Canyon [LOS ANGELES]:
(1) *canyon*, 2.25 miles long, opens into lowlands 3 miles west-southwest of Mount Wilson (1) (lat. 34°11'50" N, long. 118°07'20" W; sec. 3, T 1 N, R 12 W). Named on Mount Wilson (1953) 7.5' quadrangle. The name commemorates Jesus Rubio Maron, who came to the place in 1867 and built a cabin near the mouth of the canyon (Robinson, J.W., 1977, p. 101).
(2) *locality*, 3.5 miles west-southwest of Mount Wilson (1) along Pacific Electric Railroad (lat. 34°12'20" N, long. 118°07' W); the place is in Rubio Canyon (1). Named on Mount Lowe (1939) 6' quadrangle.
Rubio Wash [LOS ANGELES]: *stream*, flows 5 miles to Rio Hondo 2.25 miles west of El Monte city hall (lat. 34°03'20" N, long. 118°04' W). Named on El Monte (1953) 7.5' quadrangle.
Ruby Canyon [LOS ANGELES]:
(1) *canyon*, drained by a stream that flows 3 miles to Piru Creek 15 miles south-southeast of Gorman (lat. 34°34'35" N, long. 118°46'30" W). Named on Cobblestone Mountain (1958) and Whitaker Peak (1958) 7.5' quadrangles. Called Whitaker Canyon on Los Angeles County (1935) map.
(2) *canyon*, drained by a stream that flows 4 miles to Elizabeth Lake Canyon 1.5 miles east-northeast of Warm Springs Mountain (lat. 34°36'10" N, long. 118°33'15" W). Named on Green Valley (1958) and Warm Springs Mountain (1958) 7.5' quadrangles.
(3) *canyon*, 1 mile long, 6 miles west-north-west of Azusa city hall (lat. 34°10'20" N, long. 118°00' W; sec. 14, T 1 N, R 11 W). Named on Azusa (1953) 7.5' quadrangle.
Ruby Spring [LOS ANGELES]: *spring*, 4.25 miles east of Warm Springs Mountain (lat. 34°35'40" N, long. 118°30'10" W); the spring

is in Ruby Canyon (2). Named on Warm Springs Mountain (1958) 7.5' quadrangle.

Runkle Canyon [VENTURA]: *canyon*, 3.25 miles long, opens into Simi Valley (1) 6 miles west of Santa Susana Pass (lat. 34°15'40" N, long. 118°44'15" W; sec. 14, T 2 N, R 18 W). Named on Calabasas (1952) and Santa Susana (1951) 7.5' quadrangles.

Runkle Reservoir [VENTURA]: *lake*, 750 feet long, 5 miles west-southwest of Santa Susana Pass (lat. 34°14'35" N, long. 118°43'50" W); the lake is in Runkle Canyon. Named on Calabasas (1952) 7.5' quadrangle.

Runnymead: see **Tarzana** [LOS ANGELES].

Rush Canyon [LOS ANGELES]: *canyon*, drained by a stream that flows 1.25 miles to Mint Canyon 12.5 miles south-southeast of the village of Lake Hughes (lat. 34°30' N, long. 118°22'50" W; near E line sec. 19, T 5 N, R 14 W). Named on Green Valley (1958) 7.5' quadrangle.

Rush Creek [LOS ANGELES]: *stream*, flows about 1.25 miles to West Fork San Gabriel River 1.5 miles north-northeast of Mount Wilson (1) (lat. 34°14'45" N, long. 118°02'50" W; near E line sec. 20, T 2 N, R 11 W). Named on Mount Wilson (1953) 7.5' quadrangle.

Russ [LOS ANGELES]: *locality*, 8 miles east of Solemint along Southern Pacific Railroad (lat. 34°26'25" N, long. 118°18'50" W; near S line sec. 11, T 4 N, R 14 W). Named on Agua Dulce (1960) 7.5' quadrangle. Called Russ Siding on San Fernando (1900) 15' quadrangle.

Russell's Lake: see **Malibu Lake** [LOS ANGELES].

Russell Valley [LOS ANGELES-VENTURA]: *valley*, 5.5 miles west of Agoura on Los Angeles-Ventura county line (lat. 34°08'55" N, long. 118°49' W). Named on Thousand Oaks (1952) 7.5' quadrangle. The name commemorates A.D. Russell and H.M. Russell, who bought land in the neighborhood in 1881 (Ricard). The town of Westlake Village now occupies much of the valley. Postal authorities established Westlake Village post office 4 miles south of Thousand Oaks post office in 1966 and discontinued it in 1972 (Salley, p. 237). Westlake Village incorporated in 1981.

Russ Siding: see **Russ** [LOS ANGELES].

Rustic Canyon [LOS ANGELES]: *canyon*, drained by a stream that flows 8 miles to the sea 2 miles west-northwest of Santa Monica city hall (lat. 34°01'40" N, long. 118°31'05" W). Named on Topanga (1952) 7.5' quadrangle.

– S –

Saddleback: see **Old Saddleback**, under **Santiago Peak** [ORANGE].

Saddleback Buttes [LOS ANGELES]: *ridge*, north-northeast-trending, 2 miles long, 15 miles northeast of Littlerock (lat. 34°40'30" N, long. 117°48' W; in and near sec. 23, 26, T 7 N, R 9 W). Named on Hi Vista (1957) 7.5' quadrangle.

Saddle Peak [LOS ANGELES]: *ridge*, generally northeast-trending, 0.5 mile long, 3.5 miles north-northeast of Malibu Point (lat. 34°04'35" N, long. 118°39'15" W; near SW cor. sec. 15, T 1 S, R 17 W). Named on Malibu Beach (1951) 7.5' quadrangle.

Saddle Rock [LOS ANGELES]: *peak*, 6.5 miles north-northwest of Point Dume (lat. 34°05'40" N, long. 118°49'45" W; near W line sec. 12, T 1 S, R 19 W). Named on Point Dume (1951) 7.5' quadrangle.

Saddle Rock Lodge [LOS ANGELES]: *locality*, nearly 7 miles north of Dume Point (present Point Dume) (lat. 34°05'55" N, long. 118° 49' W); the place is less than 1 mile east-northeast of present Saddle Rock. Named on Dume Point (1932) 6' quadrangle.

Saint Helens Spur [LOS ANGELES]: *locality*, 5 miles south-southwest of El Monte city hall along Union Pacific Railroad (lat. 34°00'20" N, long. 118°03'45" W); the place is on Paso de Bartolo grant. Named on El Monte (1953) 7.5' quadrangle. Called Bartolo on El Monte (1966) 7.5' quadrangle.

Saint Johns: see **Mint Canyon** [LOS ANGELES] (2).

Salinas: see **Lake Salinas**, under **Salt Pond** [LOS ANGELES].

Sally: see **Mount Sally** [LOS ANGELES].

Salta Verde Point [LOS ANGELES]: *promontory*, nearly 4 miles south of Mount Banning on the south side of Santa Catalina Island (lat. 33°19' N, long. 118°25'15" W). Named on Santa Catalina South (1943) 7.5' quadrangle.

Salt Canyon [LOS ANGELES-VENTURA]: *canyon*, drained by a stream that heads in Los Angeles County and flows 6 miles to Santa Clara River 9.5 miles west of Newhall just inside Ventura County (lat. 34°23'55" N, long. 118°42'15" W). Named on Santa Susana (1951) and Val Verde (1952) 7.5' quadrangles. Called Salt Creek Canyon on Santa Susana (1943) 15' quadrangle. East Fork branches east 3 miles above the mouth of the main canyon; it is 2 miles long and is named on Santa Susana (1951) and Val Verde (1952) 7.5' quadrangles. Present East Fork is called No. Fork on Los Angeles County (1935) map, which shows a So. Fork farther upstream.

Salt Creek [LOS ANGELES]: *stream*, flows 7 miles to Castaic Creek 13 miles southeast of Gorman (lat. 34°38'15" N, long. 118°40'10" W; sec. 3, T 6 N, R 17 W). Named on Liebre Mountain (1958) 7.5' quadrangle. The name is from salt pools situated near the head of the stream (Preston, 1890a, p. 204).

Salt Creek [ORANGE]: *stream*, flows 4 miles to the sea nearly 4 miles west-southwest of San Juan Capistrano (lat. 33°28'55" N, long. 117°43'25" W). Named on Dana Point (1968) and San Juan Capistrano (1968) 7.5' quadrangles. Old maps have the names "Arroyo Salada" and "Cañada Niguel" for the feature (Meadows, p. 121). According to Preston (1890a, p. 210), Mexican shepherds obtained rock salt near the head of the stream.

Salt Creek Canyon: see **Salt Canyon** [LOS ANGELES].

Salt Marsh Canyon [VENTURA]: *canyon,* drained by a stream that flows 3.5 miles to Adams Canyon 6.25 miles west-southwest of Santa Paula Peak (lat. 34°23'35" N, long. 119°06'10" W). Named on Ojai (1952) and Santa Paula Peak (1951) 7.5' quadrangles. United States Board on Geographic Names (1969b, p. 5) approved the form "Saltmarsh Canyon" for the name, which commemorates John Saltmarsh (Goodyear, 1888, p. 108).

Salt Pond [LOS ANGELES]: *lake,* 1500 feet long, less than 0.5 mile north-northwest of present Redondo Beach city hall (lat. 33°51' N, long. 118°23'45" W). Named on Redondo (1896) 15' quadrangle. Called Las Salinas on Hall's (1887) map. Preston (1890b, p. 281) called the feature Lake Salinas. Indians obtained salt from the lake; in the 1850's Johnson and Allanson built a works that produced 450 tons of salt by evaporation in 1879 (Grenier, p. 175).

San Antonio [LOS ANGELES]: *land grant,* extends from Lynwood to Montebello. Named on El Monte (1953), Los Angeles (1953), South Gate (1952), and Whittier (1951) 7.5' quadrangles. Antonio Maria Lugo received the land in 1810, 1823, 1827, and 1838; Lugo claimed 29,513 acres patented in 1866 (Cowan, p. 71-72).

San Antonio: see **Mount San Antonio** [LOS ANGELES]; **Yorba** [ORANGE].

San Antonio Canyon [LOS ANGELES]: *canyon,* heads in San Bernardino County and extends for about 6 miles in Los Angeles County and along Los Angeles-San Bernardino county line to open into lowlands 8.5 miles north-northeast of Pomona city hall (lat. 34°09'30" N, long. 117°40'45" W; sec. 23, 24, T 1 N, R 8 W). Named on Mount Baldy (1954) 7.5' quadrangle.

San Antonio Creek [VENTURA]: *stream,* flows 14 miles to Ventura River 6 miles southwest of the town of Ojai (lat. 34°22'50" N, long. 119°18'25" W). Named on Matilija (1952) and Ojai (1952) 7.5' quadrangles.

San Antonio or Rodeo de las Aguas [LOS ANGELES]: *land grant,* at Beverly Hills. Named on Beverly Hills (1950) and Hollywood (1953) 7.5' quadrangles. Maria Rita Valdes received the land in 1841 and claimed 4449 acres patented in 1871 (Cowan, p. 69).

San Antonio Peak: see **Mount San Antonio** [LOS ANGELES].

San Antonio Ridge [LOS ANGELES]: *ridge,* generally west-trending, 5 miles long, center 2.5 miles west of Mount San Antonio (lat. 34°

17'30" N, long. 117°41'20" W); Mount San Antonio is at the east end. Named on Mount San Antonio (1955) 7.5' quadrangle.

San Antonio Wash [LOS ANGELES]: *stream* and *dry wash,* extends for 9 miles from the mouth of San Antonio Canyon along and near Los Angeles-San Bernardino county line to enter San Bernardino County 2.25 miles southeast of Pomona city hall (lat. 34°02'25" N, long. 117°43'30" W). Named on Mount Baldy (1954) and Ontario (1954) 7.5' quadrangles.

San Bernardino Mountains: see **San Gabriel Mountains** [LOS ANGELES].

San Bernardino Range: see **San Gabriel Mountains** [LOS ANGELES].

San Buenaventura: see **Ventura** [VENTURA].

San Buenaventura Plain: see **Santa Clara River** [VENTURA].

San Buenaventura River: see **Ventura River** [VENTURA].

San Cayetano: see **Sespe** [VENTURA] (1).

San Cayetano Mountain [VENTURA]: *peak,* 5 miles northwest of Fillmore (lat. 34°26'20" N, long. 118°58'50" W; near S line sec. 9, T 4 N, R 20 W). Named on Fillmore (1951) 7.5' quadrangle. Called San Cayetano Pk. on Los Angeles County (1935) map. Goodyear (1888, p. 112) referred to Mount San Cayatana. The name is from the alternate name "San Cayetano" for Sespe grant (Gudde, 1949, p. 300).

San Clemente [ORANGE]: *city,* 30 miles southeast of Santa Ana along the coast (lat. 33°25'40" N, long. 117°36'30" W). Named on Dana Point (1968) and San Clemente (1968) 7.5' quadrangles. Postal authorities established San Clemente post office in 1926 (Frickstad, p. 117), and the city incorporated in 1928. Ole Hanson founded the community in 1925 (Meadows, p. 121).

San Clemente Island [LOS ANGELES]: *island,* 21 miles long, 55 miles south of Point Fermin (lat. 32°54' N, long. 118°29' W). Named on Long Beach (1957) 1°x 2° quadrangles. Vizcaino named the island in 1602 for Saint Clement, third Pope and Bishop of Rome (Gudde, 1949, p. 300). United States Board on Geographic Names (1933, p. 664) rejected the form "San Clements Island" for the name.

Sand Beach: see **Newport Beach** [ORANGE].

Sandberg [LOS ANGELES]: *locality,* 8.5 miles east-southeast of Gorman (lat. 34°44'25" N, long. 118°42'30" W; near NW cor. sec. 32, T 8 N, R 17 W). Named on Liebre Mountain (1958) 7.5' quadrangle. Postal authorities established Sandberg post office in 1918 and discontinued it in 1944 (Salley, p. 193). The name is for Herman Sandberg, who operated a tavern at the place (Hanna, p. 270).

Sand Canyon [LOS ANGELES]:
(1) *canyon,* drained by a stream that flows 0.5 mile to Kings Canyon 3 miles northeast of Burnt Peak (lat. 34°42'45" N, long.

118°32'05" W; near W line sec. 12, T 7 N, R 16 W). Named on Burnt Peak (1958) 7.5' quadrangle.
(2) *canyon,* drained by a stream that flows 8 miles to Santa Clara River nearly 2 miles east of Solemint (lat. 34°25'15" N, long. 118° 25'25" W; sec. 23, T 4 N, R 15 W). Named on Agua Dulce (1960), Mint Canyon (1960), San Fernando (1953), and Sunland (1953) 7.5' quadrangles. Los Angeles County (1935) map shows a feature called Live Oak Spring Canyon that opens into Sand Canyon from the southeast about 2 miles east-southeast of Solemint (at S line sec. 23, T 4 N, R 15 W).

Sand Canyon Reservoir [ORANGE]: *lake,* 0.5 mile long, behind a dam at the head of Sand Canyon Wash 8 miles south-southeast of Santa Ana city hall (lat. 33°38'50" N, long. 117°47'45" W). Named on Tustin (1965) 7.5' quadrangle.

Sand Canyon Wash [ORANGE]: *stream,* flows 3 miles to San Diego Creek 6.25 miles south-southeast of Santa Ana city hall (lat. 33°39'30" N, long. 117°50'30" W); the feature heads at Sand Canyon Reservoir. Named on Tustin (1965) 7.5' quadrangle.

San Diego Creek [ORANGE]: *stream,* flows 13 miles to Upper Newport Bay nearly 7 miles south of Santa Ana city hall (lat. 33°38'55" N, long. 117°52'25" W). Named on El Toro (1968) and Tustin (1965) 7.5' quadrangles. The old road to San Diego followed the stream for several miles (Meadows, p. 121).

San Dimas [LOS ANGELES]: *town,* 5 miles northwest of Pomona city hall (lat. 34°06'30" N, long. 117°48'30" W). Named on Glendora (1966) and San Dimas (1966) 7.5' quadrangles. Postal authorities established San Dimas post office in 1888 (Frickstad, p. 80), and the town incorporated in 1960. The site first was called Mud Springs (Robinson, J.W., 1983, p. 49).

San Dimas Canyon [LOS ANGELES]: *canyon,* drained by a stream that flows 6.5 miles to lowlands 5 miles east of Glendora city hall (lat. 34°08'40" N, long. 117°46'30" W; sec. 25, T 1 N, R 9 W). Named on Glendora (1953) and Mount Baldy (1954) 7.5' quadrangles. East Fork branches east 3.5 miles above the mouth of the main canyon; it is 5 miles long and is named on Glendora (1966) and Mount Baldy (1954) 7.5' quadrangles. West Fork branches northwest less than 2 miles above the mouth of the main canyon; it is nearly 3 miles long and is named on Glendora (1966) 7.5' quadrangle.

San Dimas Junction: see **Lone Hill** [LOS ANGELES].

San Dimas Peak: see **Johnstone Peak** [LOS ANGELES].

San Dimas Reservoir [LOS ANGELES]: *lake,* behind a dam 5.25 miles east-northeast of Glendora city hall (lat. 34°09'15" N, long. 117°46'15" W; sec. 24, T 1 N, R 9 W); the

lake is in San Dimas Canyon. Named on Glendora (1966) 7.5' quadrangle.

San Dimas Wash [LOS ANGELES]: *stream* and *dry wash,* extends for 9 miles from the mouth of San Dimas Canyon to Big Daulton Wash 2.5 miles east-northeast of Baldwin Park city hall (lat. 34° 06' N, long. 117°55'05" W; sec. 10, T 1 S, R 10 W). Named on Baldwin Park (1966), Glendora (1953), and San Dimas (1954) 7.5' quadrangles.

Sandrock Creek [LOS ANGELES]: *stream,* flows 2.5 miles to Big Rock Creek 0.5 miles north-northwest of Valyermo (lat. 34°27'15" N, long. 117°51'20" W); the stream goes past Sandrocks. Named on Valyermo (1958) 7.5' quadrangle.

Sand Rock Peak [LOS ANGELES]: *peak,* 4.5 miles west-southwest of Newhall (lat. 34°22'05" N, long. 118°36'20" W; near SW cor. sec. 6, T 3 N, R 16 W). Altitude 2511 feet. Named on Oat Mountain (1952) 7.5' quadrangle. Pico (1940) 6' quadrangle has the form "Sandrock Pk" for the name.

Sandrocks [LOS ANGELES]: *relief feature,* about 1 mile south-southwest of Valyermo (lat. 34°25'50" N, long. 117°51'50" W; sec. 18, T 4 N, R 9 W). Named on Valyermo (1958) 7.5' quadrangle.

Sandstone Camp [VENTURA]: *locality,* 8 miles north-northwest of Wheeler Springs along Adobe Creek (lat. 34°36'35" N, long. 119° 21'55" W; near W line sec. 18, T 6 N, R 23 W). Named on Wheeler Springs (1943) 7.5' quadrangle.

Sandstone Peak [VENTURA]: *peak,* 1 mile west-northwest of Triunfo Pass (lat. 34°07'15" N, long. 118°55'50" W; near S line sec. 36, T 1 N, R 20 W). Altitude 3111 feet. Named on Triunfo Pass (1950) 7.5' quadrangle.

Sandy Point: see **Laguna Point** [VENTURA].

San Emigdio Mesa [VENTURA]: *area,* 12 miles north of Reyes Peak (lat. 34°48'15" N, long. 119°14'30" W). Named on Apache Canyon (1943) and Sawmill Mountain (1943) 7.5' quadrangles.

San Fernando [LOS ANGELES]: *town,* 22 miles northwest of Los Angeles city hall (lat. 34°16'55" N, long. 118°16'25" W). Named on San Fernando (1953) 7.5' quadrangle; which shows San Fernando mission near the edge of the town. Called Fernando on Fernando (1900) 15' quadrangle. Postal authorities established San Fernando post office in 1873, discontinued it for a time in 1876, moved it and changed the name to Fernando in 1892, and changed the name back to San Fernando in 1905 (Salley, p. 74, 194). Jeronimo Lopez started a stage station, called Lopez Station, 1.5 miles west of present San Fernando; the place reportedly had a post office in 1869 (Salley, p. 126). Water of a reservoir now covers the site (Latta, p. 57).

San Fernando Bay: see **Santa Monica Bay** [LOS ANGELES].

151

San Fernando Mountains: see San Gabriel Mountains [LOS ANGELES].

San Fernando Pass [LOS ANGELES]: *pass,* 2.5 miles south-southeast of Newhall (lat. 34°20'45" N, long. 118°30'35" W; sec. 13, T 3 N, R 16 W). Named on Oat Mountain (1952) 7.5' quadrangle. Called Fernando Pass on Camulos (1903) 30' quadrangle. Oat Mountain (1952) 7.5' quadrangle has the name "Fremont Pass" for a pass situated just east of San Fernando Pass (lat. 34°20'40" N, long. 118°30'25" W). Fremont traversed the highlands between Santa Clara River and San Fernando Valley in 1847, and his route there became known as Fremont Pass; General E.F. Beale had his men cut a trench 50 feet deep in the pass to ease the way for vehicles crossing it—this feature became known as Beale's Cut (Hoover, Rensch, and Rensch, p. 167). The cut, which also was called San Fernando Pass, was the main route north from Los Angeles until the early 1900's; a tunnel replaced the road through the pass in 1910, and a new road in present San Fernando Pass replaced the tunnel in 1939 (Barras, p. 22). A place called Hart's Ranch, later Lyon's Station, was situated 8 miles from San Fernando and north of Beale's Cut; it was an important stop on the stage line before the railroad came (Ormsby, p. 117; Barras, p. 22)—the place also was called Petroliopolis (Marcou, p. 161). Postal authorities established Petroliopolis post office in 1867 and discontinued it in 1871 (Salley, p. 170). They established Lyon's Station post office in 1874, changed the name to Andrews' Station in 1875, and discontinued it in 1879 (Frickstad, p. 77; Salley, p. 7). Lyon's Station was named for Sanford Lyons and Cyrus Lyons, who ran the stopping place in the 1850's and 1860's (Grenier, p. 311). Andrews Station post office was named for Andrew J. Krasyynski, first postmaster (Salley, p. 7).

San Fernando Plain: see San Fernando Valley [LOS ANGELES].

San Fernando Reservoir [LOS ANGELES]: *lake,* 1.5 miles long, 2.25 miles west-northwest of downtown San Fernando (lat. 34°17'30" N, long. 118°28'35" W). Named on San Fernando (1953) 7.5' quadrangle. San Fernando (1966) 7.5' quadrangle shows an unnamed debris basin at the place. Los Angeles County (1935) map shows two lakes, called San Fernando Reservoirs, there.

San Fernando Reservoir: see Upper San Fernando Reservoir [LOS ANGELES].

San Fernando Valley [LOS ANGELES]: *valley,* between San Gabriel Mountains and Santa Monica Mountains. Named on Los Angeles (1975) 1°x 2° quadrangle. Called San Fernando Plain on Parke's (1854-1855) map. Crespi called the feature El Valle de Santa Catalina de Bononia de los Encinos when he was there with Portola in 1769 (Hanna, p. 272).

San Francisco [LOS ANGELES-VENTURA]: *land grant,* along Santa Clara River between Newhall and Piru on Los Angeles-Ventura county line, mainly in Los Angeles County. Named on Newhall (1952), Oat Mountain (1952), Piru (1952), and Val Verde (1952) 7.5' quadrangles. Antonio del Valle received 8 leagues in 1839; Jacoba Felix and others claimed 48,612 acres patented in 1875 (Cowan, p. 76).

San Francisquito [LOS ANGELES]: *land grant,* at El Monte. Named on Baldwin Park (1953) and El Monte (1953) 7.5' quadrangles. Henry Dalton received 2 leagues in 1845 and claimed 8894 acres patented in 1867 (Cowan, p. 77).

San Francisquito Canyon [LOS ANGELES]: *canyon,* drained by a stream that flows 21 miles to Santa Clara River 4 miles northwest of Newhall (lat. 34°25'35" N, long. 118°34'30" W). Named on Green Valley (1958), Lake Hughes (1957), Newhall (1952), and Warm Springs Mountain (1958) 7.5' quadrangles. Barras (p. 17) noted the alternate name "Canada de Alamos" used for the canyon in 1851, and mentioned (p. 22) that a way station called Moor's or Holdansville was situated at the mouth of the canyon in 1860. Goddard's (1857) map has the name "S. Francisquito Pass" along present San Francisquito Canyon, and Whitney (p. 195-196) noted that San Francisquito Pass follows the canyon to Lake Elizabeth. Blake (p. 57) noted that "The ascent from the valley of Lake Elizabeth to the summit-level of the pass is short." Baker's (1911) map shows Turner Pass near Elizabeth Lake, and Antisell (p. 87) noted the alternate name "Turner's Pass" for San Francisquito Pass.

San Francisquito Pass: see San Francisquito Canyon [LOS ANGELES].

San Gabriel [LOS ANGELES]: *city,* 5 miles west-northwest of El Monte city hall (lat. 34°05'45" N, long. 118°06'25" W). Named on El Monte (1953) 7.5' quadrangle, which shows San Gabriel mission in the city. Postal authorities established San Gabriel post office in 1854 (Frickstad, p. 81), and the city incorporated in 1913. They established Garvalia post office 2.5 miles south of San Gabriel post office in 1898 and discontinued it in 1902; the name was for Richard Garvey, who started a community of small farms and homes at the place (Salley, p. 83).

San Gabriel: see East San Gabriel [LOS ANGELES]; North San Gabriel [LOS ANGELES]; South San Gabriel [LOS ANGELES].

San Gabriel Canyon [LOS ANGELES]: *canyon,* 9 miles long, along San Gabriel River above a point nearly 2 miles north of Azusa city hall (lat. 34°09'35" N, long. 117°54'20" W; at W line sec. 23, T 1 N, R 10 W). Named on Azusa (1953) and Glendora (1953) 7.5' quadrangles. The feature was called Azusa Canon in the 1840's (Robinson, J.W., 1983, p. 15).

San Gabriel Mountains [LOS ANGELES]: *range,* south of Mojave Desert and east of Soledad Canyon; extends east into San Bernardino County. Named on Los Angeles (1975) and San Bernardino (1966) 1°x 2° quadrangles. Goddard's (1857) map shows present San Gabriel Mountains as part of a much lager feature called San Bernardino Range. On Stevenson's (1884) map, the westernmost end of present San Gabriel Mountains and the east end of present Santa Susana Mountains together are called San Fernando Mountains; on the same map, present San Gabriel Mountains farther east near Little Tujunga Cañon is called Tujunga Mts., and the range still farther the east is called San Bernardino Range. Garces used the name "La Sierra de San Gabriel" in 1776 for the range north of San Gabriel mission (Robinson, J.W., 1983, p. 14). Azusa (1928) 6' quadrangle has the name "Sierra Madre" for present San Gabriel Mountains north of Monrovia and Azusa (3), but Azusa (1939) 6' quadrangle has the name "San Gabriel Mountains" there. United States Board on Geographic Names (1933, p. 666) rejected the names "San Bernardino Mountains," "Sierra Madre," and "Sierra San Gabriel" for present San Gabriel Mountains.

San Gabriel Peak [LOS ANGELES]: *peak,* 2.5 miles west-northwest of Mount Wilson (1) (lat. 34°14'35" N, long. 118°05'50" W). Altitude 6161 feet. Named on Mount Wilson (1953) 7.5' quadrangle. Members of the Wheeler Survey named the peak in 1875 for its apparent domination of the watershed of West Fork San Gabriel River; previously the feature was known as Observatory Peak because Professor T.S.C. Lowe had planned to built an astronomical observatory on it (Robinson, J.W., 1977, p. 154-155).

San Gabriel Reservoir [LOS ANGELES]: *lake,* behind a dam nearly 5 miles north of Glendora city hall (lat. 34°12'15" N, long. 117°51'25" W; sec. 6, T 1 N, R 9 W); the lake is along San Gabriel River. Named on Glendora (1953) 7.5' quadrangle.

San Gabriel River [LOS ANGELES-OR-ANGE]: *stream,* heads in Los Angeles County and flows 60 miles, partly at Los Angeles-Orange county line, to the sea 5 miles east-southeast of Long Beach city hall (lat. 33°44'35" N, long. 118°06'50" W). Named on Azusa (1953), Baldwin Park (1966), Crystal Lake (1958), El Monte (1953), Glendora (1953), Los Alamitos (1950), Mount San Antonio (1955), Seal Beach (1950), and Whittier (1949) 7.5' quadrangles. Called Rio de S. Gabriel on Parke's (1854-1855) map, and R. San Gabriel on Eddy's (1854) map, which shows the stream as a tributary of R. de los Angeles. Stevenson's (1884) map shows San Gabriel Riv. dividing below about the mouth of San Jose Creek; the eastern stream

below the split is called New San Gabriel Riv. (present San Gabriel River), and the westernmost stream below the split is called Old San Gabriel Riv. (present Rio Hondo)— on the map this stream joins Los Angeles Riv, and below this junction Los Angeles River also is called Old San Gabriel Riv. Present San Gabriel River first was called El Rio de los Temblores (Thompson and West, p. 20). Before the flood of 1867 and 1868, water of San Gabriel River reached San Pedro Bay, but during that flood it cut a new course from the west end of Puente Hills to the sea at Alamitos Bay; this new course was known as New River (Poland and others, p. 35). Present San Gabriel River is called East Fork San Gabriel River on Camp Bonita (1940) and Camp Rincon (1940) 6' quadrangles, and on Glendora (1953) 7.5' quadrangle, but United States Board on Geographic Names (1962, p. 16) rejected this name for the stream. A mining place called Crab Hollow Diggings was situated at the headwaters of East Fork in the 1850's (Gudde, 1975, p. 87). West Fork enters the main stream from the west 6.5 miles north of Glendora city hall; it is 19 miles long and is named on Azusa (1953), Chilao Flat (1959), Glendora (1953), and Mount Wilson (1953) 7.5' quadrangles. North Fork, which is formed by the confluence of Coldbrook Creek and Soldier Creek, enters West Fork 2 miles upstream from the mouth of West Fork; it is 4.5 miles long and is named on Crystal Lake (1958) and Glendora (1953) 7.5' quadrangles. United States Board on Geographic Names (1962, p. 16) rejected the name "North Fork San Gabriel River" for present Soldier Creek. The stream in present Shortcut Canyon is called Trail Fork San Gabriel R. on Tujunga (1900) 15' quadrangle. The watercourse below the mouth of San Gabriel Canyon is called San Gabriel Wash on Pomona (1904) 15' quadrangle.

San Gabriel Wash: see **San Gabriel River** [LOS ANGELES-ORANGE].

San Guillermo Creek [VENTURA]: *stream,* flows 6.25 miles to Lockwood Creek 13 miles northeast of Reyes Peak (lat. 34°43'55" N, long. 119°05'15" W; near S line sec. 34, T 8 N, R 21 W); the stream heads at San Guillermo Mountain. Named on Lockwood Valley (1943) 7.5' quadrangle.

San Guillermo Mountain [VENTURA]: *peak,* 9 miles east-northeast of Reyes Peak (lat. 34°41'45" N, long. 119°08'50" W; sec. 18, T 7 N, R 21 W). Altitude 6602 feet. Named on San Guillermo (1943) 7.5' quadrangle.

San Joaquin [ORANGE]: *land grant,* mainly between Upper Newport Bay and Laguna Canyon in and near San Joaquin Hills. Named on El Toro (1950), Laguna Beach (1949), Newport Beach (1951), San Juan Capistrano (1949), and Tustin (1950) 7.5' quadrangles. Jose Sepulveda received 11 leagues in 1842 and claimed 48,803 acres patented in 1867 (Cowan, p. 79).

San Joaquin Bay: see Newport Bay [ORANGE].

San Joaquin Hills [ORANGE]: range, between Upper Newport Bay and Laguna Canyon (center near lat. 33°37'30" N, long. 117° 48' W); the range is on San Joaquin grant. Named on Laguna Beach (1965) and Tustin (1965) 7.5' quadrangles. Called Lomarias de la Costa on a diseño of San Joaquin grant made in the 1840's (Becker, 1969), and called Sierra San Juan on Goddard's (1857) map.

San Joaquin Reservoir [ORANGE]: lake, 0.5 mile long, 6 miles northwest of Laguna Beach city hall (lat. 33°37' N, long. 117°50'30" W); the feature is in San Joaquin Hills on San Joaquin grant. Named on Laguna Beach (1965) 7.5' quadrangle.

San Joaquin Swamp: see Cienega de las Ranas, under Upper Newport Bay [ORANGE].

Sanjon Barranca [VENTURA]: canyon, 1.5 miles long, opens into lowlands in downtown Ventura (lat. 34°16'50" N, long. 119°16'40" W). Named on Ventura (1951) 7.5' quadrangle. The feature also had the names "Cemetery Barranca" and "Graveyard Barranca" because it is next to a cemetery (Ricard).

Sanjon de Agua con Alisos: see Ballona Creek [LOS ANGELES].

San Jose Canyon: see Castaic Junction [LOS ANGELES].

San Jose Creek: see South San Jose Creek [LOS ANGELES].

San Jose de Gracia de Simi: see Simi [LOS ANGELES-VENTURA].

San Juan: see Capistrano Beach [ORANGE].

San Juan Anchorage [ORANGE]: anchorage, 3.5 miles southwest of San Juan Capistrano off Dana Cove (lat. 33°27'25" N, long. 117°42' W). Named on Dana Point (1949) 7.5' quadrangle. United States Coast and Geodetic Survey (p. 96) called the feature San Juan Capistrano Anchorage.

San-Juan-by-the-Sea: see Capistrano Beach [ORANGE]; Serra [ORANGE].

San Juan Cajon de Santa Ana [ORANGE]: land grant, around Fullerton, Anaheim, and Placentia. Named on Anaheim (1950), La Habra (1952), Orange (1950), and Yorba Linda (1950) 7.5' quadrangles. Juan P. Ontiveros received the land in 1837 and claimed 35,971 acres patented in 1877 (Cowan, p. 82).

San Juan Campground: see Lower San Juan Campground [ORANGE].

San Juan Canyon [ORANGE]: canyon, drained by a stream that flows 2 miles to Salt Creek 2.5 miles west of San Juan Capistrano (lat. 33°30'30" N, long. 117°42'20" W; sec. 3, T 8 S, R 8 W). Named on San Juan Capistrano (1968) 7.5' quadrangle.

San Juan Canyon: see San Juan Creek [ORANGE].

San Juan Capistrano [ORANGE]: town, 23 miles southeast of Santa Ana (lat. 33°30'05" N, long. 117°39'45" W). Named on Cañada Gobernadora (1968), Dana Point (1968), San Clemente (1968), and San Juan Capistrano (1968) 7.5' quadrangles. Called Capistrano on Corona (1902) 30' quadrangle. Postal authorities established Capistrano post office in 1867 and changed the name to San Juan Capistrano in 1905 (Salley, p. 195). The community incorporated in 1961. The town name is from San Juan Capistrano mission, founded at the place in 1776; before that the site was called Santa Maria Magdalena, a name given by members of the Portola expedition in 1769 (Hanna, p. 278). A spring called Aguagito was situated 0.8 mile north of the mission and provided good drinking water (Meadows, p. 19).

San Juan Capistrano Anchorage: see San Juan Anchorage [ORANGE].

San Juan Capistrano Hot Springs: see San Juan Hot Springs [ORANGE].

San Juan Capistrano Point: see Dana Point [ORANGE] (1).

San Juan Creek [ORANGE]: stream, heads in Riverside County and flows 20 miles in Orange County to the sea 3 miles south-southwest of San Juan Capistrano (lat. 33°27'45" N, long. 117°41' W). Named on Cañada Gobernadora (1968), Dana Point (1968), San Juan Capistrano (1968), and Sitton Peak (1954) 7.5' quadrangles. The upper part of the canyon of the stream is called San Juan Canyon on Cañada Gobernadora (1968) and Sitton Peak (1954) 7.5' quadrangles; the whole canyon is called San Juan Canyon on Corona (1902) 30' quadrangle. Before construction of San Juan Capistrano mission, the canyon was known as Arroyo de la Quema because members of the Portola expedition observed Indians burning vegetation there to scare out small game—Arroyo de la Quema means "Creek of the Burned" in Spanish; Costanso in his account of the Portola expedition called it Canada del Incendio (Meadows, p. 22, 49). Cañada Gobernadora (1968) 7.5' quadrangle shows the site of Mission Vieja along San Juan Creek at the mouth of Cañada Gobernadora, and Cañada Gobernadora (1949) quadrangle has the term "Old Mission Site" at the place. San Juan Canyon had the name "Mission Vieja Valley" on the first official map of Orange County made in 1889 (Meadows, p. 101).

San Juan Hill [ORANGE]: peak, 12 miles northeast of Santa Ana on Orange-San Bernardino county line (lat. 33°54'50" N, long. 117° 44'15" W; sec. 17, T 3 S, R 8 W). Altitude 1781 feet. Named on Prado Dam (1967) 7.5' quadrangle.

San Juan Hot Springs [ORANGE]: village, 15 miles northeast of San Juan Capistrano (lat. 33°35'30" N, long. 117°30'30" W); the place is in San Juan Canyon less than 0.5 mile northeast of the mouth of Hot Spring Canyon. Named on Cañada Gobernadora (1968) 7.5' quadrangle. Corona (1902) 30' quadrangle shows a water feature called San Juan Hot Spring at the mouth of Hot Spring Canyon. The spring was called Agua Caliente de San Juan in the early days (Meadows, p. 17). Waring (p. 48-49) called the feature San Juan Capistrano Hot Springs, and noted that it consists of two main springs, four minor ones, and several marshy patches; the water was as hot as 124° Fahrenheit and was used first by Indians, and then about 1885 buildings were constructed and the place became a resort for campers and for the ailing. Postal authorities established Talega post office at the site in 1895 and discontinued it in 1896 (Frickstad, p. 118; Meadows, p. 133).

San Juan Point: see **Dana Point** [ORANGE] (1).

San Juan Rocks [ORANGE]: *rocks,* about 4.25 miles southwest of San Juan Capistrano, and 300 feet to 1200 feet offshore at Dana Point (1) (lat. 33°27'30" N, long. 117°42'55" W). Named on Dana Point (1968) 7.5' quadrangle. Capistrano (1902) 30' quadrangle shows San Juan Rock. United States Coast and Geodetic Survey (p. 96) described San Juan Rock as 10 feet high, about 50 feet in extent, and 340 yards south of the highest point on the cliff at Dana Point (1).

San Mateo Point [ORANGE]: *promontory,* 3 miles south-southeast of San Clemente civic center along the coast on Orange-San Diego county line (lat. 33°23'15" N, long. 117°35'45" W; sec. 15, T 9 S, T 7 W); the feature is just west of the mouth of San Mateo Creek in San Diego County. Named on San Clemente (1968) 7.5' quadrangle.

San Mateo Rocks [ORANGE]: *rocks,* 1.5 miles south-southwest of San Clemente civic center, and 0.5 mile offshore (lat. 33°24'15" N, long. 117°37' W); the rocks are 1.5 miles northwest of San Mateo Point. Named on San Clemente (1968) 7.5' quadrangle.

San Miguel [VENTURA]: *land grant,* between the mouth of Santa Clara River and downtown Ventura. Named on Oxnard (1949), Saticoy (1951), and Ventura (1951) 7.5' quadrangles. Raimundo Olivas and Felipe Lorenzana received the land in 1841 and claimed 4694 acres patented in 1873 (Cowan, p. 85—Cowan gave the alternate name "Los Cerritos" for the grant; Perez, p. 94).

San Nicolas Canyon: see **Nicholas Canyon** [LOS ANGELES].

San Nicolas Island [VENTURA]: *island,* 9.5 miles long, 36 miles south of Ventura (lat. 33°14'45" N, long. 119°30'30" W). Named on San Nicolas Island (1943) quadrangle. The crew of Vizcaino's launch *Tres Reyes* named the island on December 6, 1602, the day of the saint (Wagner, p. 412). Vedder's (1963) map names several features on the island:

Vizcaino Point, located at the extreme west end (lat. 33°16'40" N, long. 119°34'40" W); Thousand Springs, located along the north coast nearly 3 miles east-northeast of Vizcaino Point (lat. 33°17' N, long. 119°31'45" W); Corral Harbor, located on the north coast 3.5 miles east of Vizcaino Point (lat. 33°16'40" N, long. 119°30'55" W); Army Camp Beach, located on the north coast 5 miles east of Vizcaino Point (lat. 33°15'55" N, long. 119°29'40" W); Seal Beach, located on the south coast 4 miles southeast of Vizcaino Point (lat. 33°13'55" N, long. 119°32'15" W); Jackson Hill, located 5 miles east-southeast of Vizcaino Point (lat. 33°14'25" N, long. 119°30'15" W); Coast Guard Beach, located 1.5 miles west-northwest of the east tip of the island (lat. 33°14'25" N, long. 119°26'35" W); and Jehemy Beach, located on the side of the east tip (lat. 33°13'35" N, long. 119°25' W). These names, for the most part, are from local usage of military personnel on the island (J.G. Vedder, personal communication, 1986).

San Olene Canyon [LOS ANGELES]: *canyon,* drained by a stream that flows 1 mile to Santa Anita Canyon 3 miles southeast of Mount Wilson (1) (lat. 34°11'50" N, long. 118°01'10" W; sec. 3, T 1 N, R 11 W). Named on Mount Wilson (1953) 7.5' quadrangle. J.W. Robinson (1977, p. 123) referred to Santa Oline Creek, named for Miss Oline Newall, one of a group of hikers who had lunch at the place in 1896.

San Padro: see **San Pedro** [LOS ANGELES] (2).

San Pasqual [LOS ANGELES]: *land grant,* at and near Pasadena. Named on El Monte (1953), Los Angeles (1953), Mount Wilson (1953), and Pasadena (1953) 7.5' quadrangles. Manuel Garfias received 3.5 leagues in 1843 and claimed 13,694 acres patented in 1863; Benjamin D. Wilson claimed 709 acres patented in 1881 (Cowan, p. 86; Cowan listed the grant under the designation "Rincon de San Pasqual (or Pascual)").

San Pedro [LOS ANGELES]:

(1) *land grant,* mainly between Wilmington, Compton, and Redondo Beach. Named on Inglewood (1952), Long Beach (1949), Redondo Beach (1963), San Pedro (1964), South Gate (1952), and Torrance (1964) 7.5' quadrangles. Juan Jose Dominguez received the land before 1784; Manuel Dominguez received it in 1839 and claimed 43,119 acres patented in 1858 (Cowan, p. 86; Perez, p. 95).

(2) *district,* 2 miles north of Point Fermin in Los Angeles (lat. 33° 44'10" N, long. 118°17'45" W). Named on San Pedro (1964) 7.5' quadrangle. Postal authorities established San Padro post office in 1854, discontinued it in 1864, and reestablished it with the name "San Pedro" in 1882 (Salley, p. 196). The place developed at what was called Sepulveda's Landing, and later called Timm's Point (Hoover, Rensch, and Rensch, p. 154).

The Sepulveda brothers built a crude dock and landing there in 1835, and sold it to August Timms in 1852; Timms' name was applied to the landing as well as to a nearby promontory, Timms' Point, which previously was known as San Pedro Point (Grenier, p. 183-184). Arnold and Arnold's (1902) map has the name "Crawfish George's" for a locality situated along the coast just southwest of Timms Point.

San Pedro: see **Camp San Pedro**, under **Wilmington** [LOS ANGELES]; **East San Pedro** [LOS ANGELES]; **New San Pedro**, under **Wilmington** [LOS ANGELES].

San Pedro Bay [LOS ANGELES-ORANGE]: *embayment,* extends from San Pedro [LOS ANGELES] to Seal Beach [ORANGE]. Named on Long Beach (1949), Los Alamitos (1950), San Pedro (1964), and Seal Beach (1950) 7.5' quadrangles. Called Bay of S. Pedro on Parke's (1854-1855) map. Cabrillo named the feature Bahia de los Fumos in 1542 for the smoke from fires that the Indians set to drive out small game; Vizcaino renamed it Ensenada de San Andres to record the saint on whose day he was there, but he was mistaken on the days of the Catholic calendar; Cabrera Buena named it Bahia de San Pedro in 1784 for Saint Peter, Bishop of Alexandria (Gleason, p. 103-104). Davidson (p. 194) believed that the name "Bahia de los Fumos" of Cabrillo referred to present Santa Monica Bay.

San Pedro Canyon [LOS ANGELES]: *canyon,* drained by a stream that flows 2 miles to near 2.5 miles north of Point Fermin in San Pedro (lat. 33°44'20" N, long. 118°18'10" W); the canyon heads at San Pedro Hill. Named on San Pedro (1964) 7.5' quadrangle.

San Pedro Channel [LOS ANGELES]: *water feature,* between Santa Catalina Island and the mainland at Palos Verdes Hills. Named on Long Beach (1957) 1°x 2° quadrangle. United States Board on Geographic Names (1961a, p. 19) rejected the name "Catalina Channel" for the feature.

San Pedro Hill [LOS ANGELES]: *peak,* 3.5 miles northwest of Point Fermin (lat. 33°44'45" N, long. 118°20'05" W). Named on San Pedro (1964) 7.5' quadrangle.

San Pedro Hills: see **Palos Verdes Hills** [LOS ANGELES].

San Pedro Point: see **Timms Point**, under **San Pedro** [LOS ANGELES] (2).

San Rafael [LOS ANGELES]: *land grant,* between Arroyo Seco and Los Angeles River around Glendale. Named on Burbank (1953), Hollywood (1953), Los Angeles (1953), and Pasadena (1953) 7.5' quadrangles. Jose Maria Verdugo received the land in 1784; Julio Verdugo and others claimed 36,403 acres patented in 1882 (Cowan, p. 87; Cowan gave the alternate name "La Zanja" for the grant). Perez (p. 95) gave the date 1798 for the grant to Jose M. Verdugo. Gudde (1949, p. 312)

noted that the grant also was called Hahaonuput and Arroyo Hondo.

San Rafael: see **Paso de Bartolo** [LOS ANGELES].

San Rafael Hills [LOS ANGELES]: *range,* 3.5 miles northwest of Pasadena city hall between Arroyo Seco and Verdugo Wash (lat. 34°10'30" N, long. 118°12' W); the range is on San Rafael grant. Named on Pasadena (1953) 7.5' quadrangle.

San Rafael Peak [VENTURA]: *peak,* 16 miles east of Reyes Peak (lat. 34°37'25" N, long. 119°00'05" W; sec. 9, T 6 N, R 20 W). Altitude 6666 feet. Named on Devils Heart Peak (1943), Lockwood Valley (1943), and Topatopa Mountains (1943) 7.5' quadrangles.

Santa Ana [ORANGE]: *city,* near the center of the north part of Orange County (lat. 33°44'50" N, long. 117°52' W). Named on Anaheim (1965), Newport Beach (1965), Orange (1964), and Tustin (1965) 7.5' quadrangles. Postal authorities established Santa Ana post office in 1870 (Frickstad, p. 117), and the city incorporated in 1886. William H. Spurgeon founded the place in 1869 (Guinn, p. 192). Meadows listed places along Pacific Electric Railroad at Santa Ana: Acelga, a flag stop located 4.25 miles southwest of Santa Ana city hall (p, 17); Buaro, a flag stop located 3 miles west-northwest of the city hall (p. 31); Duena, a flag stop located 3.25 miles west-northwest of the city hall (p. 58); and West Orange, a station located 2.25 miles northwest of the city hall (p. 139).

Santa Ana [VENTURA]: *land grant,* around Lake Casitas. Named on Matilija (1952), Pitas Point (1950), Ventura (1951), and White Ledge Peak (1952) 7.5' quadrangles. Crisogono Ayala and others received the land in 1837; they claimed 21,522 acres patented in 1870 (Cowan, p. 89-90).

Santa Ana: see **Olive** [ORANGE]; **South Santa Ana** [ORANGE].

Santa Ana Abajo: see **Olive** [ORANGE].

Santa Ana Army Air Base: see **Fairview** [ORANGE].

Santa Ana Arriba: see **Olive** [ORANGE].

Santa Ana Canyon [ORANGE]: *canyon,* 7.5 miles long, mainly in Orange County, but extends east into Riverside County and San Bernardino County; along Santa Ana River above a point 6 miles northeast of Orange city hall (lat. 33°51'30" N, long. 117°47' W). Named on Black Star Canyon (1967), Orange (1964), and Prado Dam (1967) 7.5' quadrangles.

Santa Ana Creek [VENTURA]: *stream,* formed by the confluence of North Fork and West Fork, flows 3.5 miles to Lake Casitas 6 miles west-southwest of the town of Ojai (lat. 34°24'35" N, long. 119°20'15" W); the stream is partly on Santa Ana grant. Named on Matilija (1952, photorevised 1967) 7.5' quadrangle. North Fork is 2.25 miles long and is named on Matilija (1952) 7.5' quadrangle

West Fork is 4.5 miles long and is named on Matilija (1952) and White Ledge Peak (1952) 7.5' quadrangles.

Santa Ana Gardens [ORANGE]: *locality*, 7 miles northeast of present Huntington Beach civic center (lat. 33°43'35" N, long. 117° 54' W). Named on Newport Beach (1951) 7.5' quadrangle.

Santa Ana Heights [ORANGE]: *district*, 6 miles east of Huntington Beach civic center (lat. 33°39'15" N, long. 117°53'45" W). Named on Newport Beach (1965) 7.5' quadrangle.

Santa Ana Mountains [ORANGE]: *range*, extends southeast for about 20 miles along Orange-Riverside county line from Santa Ana River to a point southeast of the head of Trabuco Canyon. Named on Santa Ana (1959) 1°x 2° quadrangle. Called Sierra Santiago on Goddard's (1857) map. On Parke's (1854-1855) map, the name "Sierra de Santa Ana" applies to present Santa Ana Mountains and to present Puente Hills together. Whitney (p. 175) used the form "Santa Anna Range" for the name. Hanna (p. 287) noted use of the name "Sierra del Trabuco" for the south part of the range. Meadows (p. 133) pointed out that some people who live east of the feature call it Temescal Range.

Santa Ana Peak: see **Santiago Peak** [ORANGE].

Santa Ana River [ORANGE]: *stream*, enters Orange County from Riverside County and flows 28 miles in Orange County to the sea 3.25 miles southeast of Huntington Beach civic center (lat. 33°37'45" N, long. 117°57'25" W). Named on Anaheim (1965), Black Star Canyon (1967), Newport Beach (1965), Orange (1964), and Prado Dam (1967) 7.5' quadrangles. Called Rio S. Bernadino on Gibbes' (1852) map, called Rio Santa Anna on Williamson's (1853b) map, called R. Sta. Anna on Eddy's (1854) map, called Rio de Sta. Ana on Parke's (1854-1855) map, called Santa Anna R. on Goddard's (1857) map, and called Rio Santa Anna on Rogers and Johnston's (1857) map. Crespi named the stream Rio del Dulcissimo Nombre de Jesus del Temblores when members of the Portola expedition felt a severe earthquake while they were camped along the stream in 1769—*Rio del Dulcissimo Nombre de Jesus del Temblores* means "River of the Sweetest Name of Jesus of the Earthquakes" in Spanish; the soldiers of the expedition called the feature Rio Santa Ana because it seemed to come from Santa Ana Mountains (Meadows, p. 119, 124). Before a flood in 1825, Santa Ana River reached the sea several miles northwest of its present mouth (Poland and others, p. 35). Before the river was confined to its modern course, it entered the west end of Newport Bay; backwater from the stream formed a shallow lake of bitter water west of the river that was 2 miles long and 0.5 mile wide—this feature was called Amarus Lake or Bitterwater Lake (Meadows, p. 20). The lake extended west from a headland called Bitter Point that is 0.5 mile east-northeast of the present mouth of Santa Ana River—a dike built in 1920 from Bitter Point to the sea prevents the river from discharging into Newport Bay (Meadows, p. 27).

Santa Ana Valley [VENTURA]: *valley*, 5.25 miles west-southwest of Ojai (lat. 34°25'15" N, long. 119°20'25" W); the valley is along Santa Ana Creek. Named on Matilija (1952) 7.5' quadrangle. Water of Lake Casitas now covers part of the feature.

Santa Anita [LOS ANGELES]:

(1) *land grant*, at and near Arcadia and Sierra Madre. Named on Azusa (1953), El Monte (1953), and Mount Wilson (1953) 7.5' quadrangles. Hugo Perfecto Reid received 3 leagues in 1841 and 1846; Henry Dalton claimed 13,319 acres patented in 1866 (Cowan, p. 90). Perez (p. 97) gave 1845 as the date of the grant to Reid.

(2) *locality*, 5.25 miles south of Mount Wilson (1) along Atchison, Topeka and Santa Fe Railroad (lat. 34°08'50" N, long. 118°03'20" W); the place is on Santa Anita grant. Named on Pasadena (1900) 15' quadrangle. Postal authorities established Santa Anita post office in 1886, discontinued it in 1910, reestablished it in 1914, and discontinued it in 1940 (Frickstad, p. 81).

Santa Anita Canyon [LOS ANGELES]: *canyon*, 5.25 miles long, opens into lowlands 4.25 miles south-southeast of Mount Wilson (1) (lat. 34°10'15" N, long. 118°01'15" W; sec. 15, T 1 N, R 11 W). Named on Mount Wilson (1953) 7.5' quadrangle. East Fork branches east 3 miles above the mouth of the main canyon; it is 2.5 miles long and is named on Azusa (1953) and Mount Wilson (1953) 7.5' quadrangles. North Fork branches north 3.25 miles above the mouth of the main canyon; it is nearly 1.5 miles long and is named on Mount Wilson (1953) 7.5' quadrangle. On Pasadena (1900) 15' quadrangle, the name "Santa Antia Canyon" applies to present North Fork, and present Santa Anita Canyon above the junction is called West Fork.

Santa Antia Canyon: see **Little Santa Anita Canyon** [LOS ANGELES].

Santa Anita Falls: see **Sturtevant Falls** [LOS ANGELES].

Santa Anita Wash [LOS ANGELES]: *stream*, extends for 5.25 miles to Rio Hondo 2.25 miles north-northwest of El Monte city hall (lat. 34°06'10" N, long. 118°00'50" W); the feature heads at the mouth of Santa Anita Canyon. Named on El Monte (1953) and Mount Wilson (1953) 7.5' quadrangles.

Santa Anna Range: see **Santa Ana Mountains** [ORANGE].

Santa Anna River: see **Santa Ana River** [ORANGE].

Santa Barbara Channel [VENTURA]: *water feature,* between the coast and Anacapa Island, and between the coast and islands of Santa Barbara County. Named on Los Angeles (1975) 1°x 2° quadrangle. Vizcaino gave the name "Canal de Santa Barbara" to the feature when he sailed through it on December 4, 1602, the day of the saint (Wagner, p. 118, 413). The islands on the south side of Santa Barbara Channel—Anacapa in Ventura County, and Santa Cruz, Santa Rosa, and San Miguel in Santa Barbara County—are called Santa Barbara Islands; they are part of the larger group—including San Clemente and Santa Catalina in Los Angeles County, San Nicholas in Ventura County, and Santa Barbara in Santa Barbara County—that is called the Channel Islands (United States Coast and Geodetic Survey, p. 106).

Santa Barbara Islands: see **Santa Barbara Channel** [VENTURA].

Santa Barbara Mountains: see **Santa Ynez Mountains** [VENTURA].

Santa Catalina Island [LOS ANGELES]: *island,* 21 miles long, 21 miles south-southwest of Point Fermin across San Pedro Channel (lat. 33°24' N, long. 118°25' W). Named on Long Beach (1957) 1°x 2° quadrangle. Cabrillo discovered the island in 1542, and believed that he had found two islands that he named La Vitoria and San Salvador for his two ships; Vizcaino sighted the island on the eve of Saint Catherine's Day in 1603 and named it Santa Catalina (Hanna, p. 288; Hoover, Rensch, and Rensch, p. 146).

Santa Clara del Norte [VENTURA]: *land grant,* south of Saticoy. Named on Camarillo (1950), Oxnard (1949), Santa Paula (1951), and Saticoy (1951) 7.5' quadrangles. Juan Sanchez received the land in 1837 and claimed 13,989 acres patented in 1869 (Cowan, p. 91).

Santa Clara Plain: see **Santa Clara River** [VENTURA].

Santa Clara River [LOS ANGELES-VENTURA]: *stream,* heads in Los Angeles County and flows 68 miles to the sea 5.25 miles westnorthwest of Oxnard in Ventura County (lat. 34°14' N, long. 119° 15'55" W). Named on Agua Dulce (1960), Fillmore (1951), Mint Canyon (1960), Moorpark (1951), Newhall (1952), Oxnard (1949), Piru (1952), Santa Paula (1951), Saticoy (1951), and Val Verde (1952) 7.5' quadrangles. Called Rio de la Sta. Clara on Parke's (1854-1855) map, which has the name "Sta. Clara Plain" for lowlands near the mouth of the river. Whitney (p, 124-125) called the same lowlands San Buenaventura or Santa Clara Plain, and (p. 121) used the name "Santa Clara Valley" for the valley of the stream. Members of the Portola expedition gave the name "Cañada de Santa Clara" to the valley of the river when they reached the place on August 12, 1769, the day of the

saint (Wagner, p. 414). South Fork, formed by the confluence of the streams in Lyon Canyon and Gavin Canyon, enters from the southeast 3 miles north-northwest of Newhall (lat. 34°25'30" N, long. 118°33'30" W); it is 4.5 miles long and is named on Newhall (1952) 7.5' quadrangle.

Santa Clara Valley: see **Santa Clara River** [LOS ANGELES-VENTURA].

Santa Felicia Canyon [LOS ANGELES-VENTURA]: *canyon,* drained by a stream that heads in Los Angeles County and flows 5 miles to Lake Piru 5.5 miles northeast of Piru in Ventura County (lat. 34° 28'30" N, long. 118°43'55" W). Named on Val Verde (1952, photorevised 1969) and Whitaker Peak (1958) 7.5' quadrangles. Called Santa Feliciana Canyon on Los Angeles County (1935) map, which also names three tributaries: Fine Gold Canyon, which branches from main canyon about 5.5 miles south-southeast of Whitaker Peak; Well Canyon, which branches from the main canyon less than 1 mile downstream from the mouth of Fine Gold Canyon; and Temescal Canyon, which branches from the main canyon less than 1 mile downstream from the mouth of Well Canyon on Temescal grant.

Santa Feliciana Canyon: see **Santa Felicia Canyon** [LOS ANGELES-VENTURA].

Santa Fe Springs [LOS ANGELES]: *town,* 3.5 miles southwest of Whittier city hall (lat. 33°56'50" N, long. 118°05'05" W). Named on Whittier (1965) 7.5' quadrangle. Downey (1902) 15' quadrangle shows a place called Fulton Wells located along Southern Pacific Railroad in present Santa Fe Springs (lat. 33°56'30" N, long. 118° 04'50" W), a community called Santa Fe Springs situated 0.5 mile to the east (lat. 33°56'25" N, long. 118°04'20" W), and a place called Santa Fe Springs Sta. located along Atchison, Topeka and Santa Fe Railroad 0.5 mile east-northwest of the community of Santa Fe Springs (lat. 33°56'35" N, long. 118°03'45" W). Postal authorities established Sulphur Wells post office—with James E. Fulton as the first postmaster—in 1878, changed the name to Fulton Wells in 1879, and changed the name to Santa Fe Springs in 1888; the name "Santa Fe Springs" was from Atchison, Topeka and Santa Fe Railroad (Salley, p. 82, 197, 215). The town incorporated in 1957. Dr. J.E. Fulton put down three wells at the place in the 1870's and obtained sulphur water which he used at a resort called Santa Fe Springs or Fulton Wells (Waring, p. 282).

Santa Gertrudes [LOS ANGELES]: *land grant,* at and near Downey and Santa Fe Springs. Named on La Habra (1952), South Gate (1952), and Whittier (1951) 7.5' quadrangles. Josefa Cota de Nieto received 5 leagues in 1833 and 1834; Antonio Maria Nieto received the land in 1845; James P. McFarland and John

G. Downey claimed 17,602 acres patented in 1870; Tomás Sanches Colima claimed 3696 acres patented in 1877 (Cowan, p. 92).

Santa Inez Range: see **Santa Ynez Mountains** [VENTURA].

Santa Margarita Canyon [LOS ANGELES]: *canyon,* drained by a stream that flows 2 miles to Escondido Canyon 12 miles east-northeast of Solemint (lat. 34°28'40" N, long. 118°15'45" W; sec. 32, T 5 N, R 13 W). Named on Agua Dulce (1960) 7.5' quadrangle.

Santa Maria Creek [LOS ANGELES]: *stream,* flows 1.5 miles to Garapita Creek 9 miles northwest of Santa Monica city hall (lat. 34°07'05" N, long. 118°35'05" W; at N line sec. 5, T 1 S, R 16 W). Named on Canoga Park (1952) and Topanga (1952) 7.5' quadrangles.

Santa Maria Magdalena: see **San Juan Capistrano** [ORANGE].

Santa Maria River: see **Cuyama River** [VENTURA].

Santa Monica [LOS ANGELES]: *city,* 14 miles west of Los Angeles city hall (lat. 34°00'40" N, long. 18°29'25" W); the city is partly on San Vicente y Santa Monica grant. Named on Beverly Hills (1950), Topanga (1952), and Venice (1950) 7.5' quadrangles. Postal authorities established Santa Monica post office in 1875 (Frickstad, p. 81), and the city incorporated in 1886.

Santa Monica see **San Vicente y Santa Monica** [LOS ANGELES]; **South Santa Monica** [LOS ANGELES].

Santa Monica Bay [LOS ANGELES]: *embayment,* extends east from Point Dume past Santa Monica to Redondo Beach. Named on Beverly Hills (1950), Malibu Beach (1951), Point Dume (1951), Topanga (1952), and Venice (1950) 7.5' quadrangles. Called S. Fernando B. on Sage's (1846) map.

Santa Monica Canyon [LOS ANGELES]: *canyon,* drained by a stream that flows nearly 3 miles to Rustic Canyon 2 miles west-north-west of Santa Monica city hall (lat. 34°01'45" N, long. 118° 30'55" W). Named on Beverly Hills (1950) and Topanga (1952) 7.5' quadrangles. The canyon divides at the head to form Mandeville Canyon and Sullivan Canyon.

Santa Monica Mountains [LOS ANGELES-VENTURA]: *range,* on Los Angeles-Ventura county line; extends east for about 42 miles from Point Mugu to Los Angeles River. Named on Los Angeles (1975) 1°x 2° quadrangle. Called Sierra de la Monica on Parke's (1854-1855) map. Antisell (p. 76) referred to the Sierra Monica, Whitney (p. 168) mentioned Sierra Santa Monica, and Marcou (p. 159) described Sierra de Santa Monica. Preston (1890a, p. 189, 207) called the feature both Santa Monica Range and Sierra Santa Monica.

Santa Monica Range: see **Santa Monica**

Mountains [LOS ANGELES-VENTURA].

Santa Paula [VENTURA]: *town,* 14 miles east-northeast of Ventura (lat. 34°21'15" N, long. 119°03'30" W); the town is on Santa Paula y Saticoy grant near the mouth of Santa Paula Creek. Named on Santa Paula (1951) and Santa Paula Peak (1951) 7.5' quadrangles. Postal authorities established Santa Paula post office in 1874 (Frickstad, p. 219), and the town incorporated in 1902. They established Elisio post office 6 miles west of Santa Paula in Wheeler Canyon in 1893 and discontinued it in 1900 (Salley, p. 67). Ricard listed a place called Blanchards located 1 mile west of Santa Paula along Southern Pacific Railroad; the name recalls Nathan Weston Blanchard, who founded Santa Paula.

Santa Paula Canyon [VENTURA]: *canyon,* 9 miles long, along Santa Paula Creek above a point 4.5 miles west-southwest of Santa Paula Peak (lat. 34°25'25" N, long. 119°05'05" W). Named on Santa Paula Peak (1951) and Topatopa Mountains (1943) 7.5' quadrangles. The feature first was called Mupu Cañon (Goodyear, 1888, p. 105). East Fork branches east nearly 3 miles west of Santa Paula Peak; it is 3.25 miles long and is named on Santa Paula Peak (1951) 7.5' quadrangle.

Santa Paula Creek [VENTURA]: *stream,* flows 15 miles to Santa Clara River 0.5 mile east-southeast of downtown Santa Paula (lat. 34°20'55" N, long. 119°02'55" W); the stream drains Santa Paula Canyon. Named on Santa Paula (1951) and Santa Paula Peak (1951) 7.5' quadrangles. Called Arroyo del Mupu on the diseño of Sespe grant in 1833 (Becker, 1964).

Santa Paula Peak [VENTURA]: *peak,* 7 miles north-northeast of Santa Paula (lat. 34°26'25" N, long. 119°00'30" W; near SE cor. sec. 7, T 4 N, R 20 W). Altitude 4957 feet. Named on Santa Paula Peak (1951) 7.5' quadrangle.

Santa Paula Ridge [VENTURA]: *ridge,* west-trending, 4.5 miles long, center 2.25 miles west of Santa Paula Peak (lat. 34°26'10" N, long. 119°02'45" W); Santa Paula Peak is at the east end of the ridge. Named on Santa Paula Peak (1951) 7.5' quadrangle.

Santa Paula Sulphur Springs: see **Sulphur Springs** [VENTURA].

Santa Paula y Saticoy [VENTURA]: *land grant,* along the valley of Santa Clara River from near Ventura to Santa Paula. Named on Oxnard (1949), Santa Paula (1951), Santa Paula Peak (1951), Saticoy (1951), and Ventura (1951) 7.5' quadrangles. Manuel Jimeno Casarin received 4 leagues in 1843; J.P. Davidson claimed 17,773 acres patented in 1872 (Cowan, p. 94).

Santa Rosa Valley [VENTURA]: *valley,* 4 miles north-northwest of Newbury Park (lat. 34°14'15" N, long. 118°55'45" W). Named on Newbury Park (1951) 7.5' quadrangle.

Santa Susana: see **Simi Valley** [VENTURA] (2).

159

Santa Susana Canyon: see Santa Susana Pass [VENTURA].
Santa Susana Knolls [VENTURA]: *settlement,* 2 miles west-southwest of Santa Susana Pass (lat. 34°15'40" N, long. 118°40' W; mainly in sec. 16, T 2 N, R 17 W). Named on Santa Susana (1951) 7.5' quadrangle. Called Mortimer Park on Santa Susana (1943) 15' quadrangle.
Santa Susana Mountains [LOS ANGELES-VENTURA]: *range,* west of Newhall between Santa Clara River and San Fernando Valley; mainly in Los Angeles County, but extends west into Ventura County. Named on Los Angeles (1975) 1°x 2° quadrangle. Called Sierra De La St. Susana on Parke's (1854-1855) map. Antisell (p. 75) mentioned both Sierra Santa Susana and Sierra Susanna. Williamson (p. 29) referred to Susannah range. Whitney (p. 120) called the feature Sierra Santa Susanna, and noted that it also is known as Scorpion Hills.
Santa Susana Pass [LOS ANGELES-VENTURA]: *pass,* nearly 10 miles southwest of Newhall on Los Angeles-Ventura county line (lat. 34°16'05" N, long. 118°37'55" W; at W line sec 11, T 2 N, R 17 W); the feature is east of Simi Valley [VENTURA] (1). Named on Santa Susana (1951) 7.5' quadrangle. Called Simi Pass on Parke's (1854-1855) map. Los Angeles County (1935) map has the name "Santa Susana Cany." for the canyon west of the pass.
Santa Susana Pass Wash [LOS ANGELES]: *stream,* flows 7.5 miles to Browns Canyon Wash less than 2 miles north of the center of Canoga Park (lat. 34°13'40" N, long. 118°35'30" W); the stream heads at Santa Susana Pass. Named on Canoga Park (1952) and Oat Mountain (1952) 7.5' quadrangles.
Santa Ynez Canyon [LOS ANGELES]: *canyon,* 5.5 miles long, opens to the sea 4 miles west-northwest of Santa Monica city hall (lat. 34°02'15" N, long. 118°33'15" W). Named on Topanga (1952) 7.5' quadrangle.
Santa Ynez Lake [LOS ANGELES]: *lake,* 275 feet long, 4 miles west-northwest of Santa Monica city hall (lat. 34°02'35" N, long. 118°33'05" W). Named on Topanga (1952) 7.5' quadrangle.
Santa Ynez Mountains [VENTURA]: *range,* mainly in Santa Barbara County, but extends east into Ventura County as far as Ventura River 4 miles northwest of the town of Ojai. Named on Matilija (1952) and White Ledge Peak (1952) 7.5' quadrangles. Called Sierra de la Santa Inez on Parke's (1854-1855) map. Blake (p. 137) called the feature Santa Inez range, Antisell (p. 65) called it Santa Barbara Mountains, and Whitney (p. 111) called it Sierra Santa Iñez.
Santa Ysabel [ORANGE]: *locality,* 6.5 miles east of present Buena Park civic center along Atchison, Topeka and Santa Fe Railroad (lat.

33°52' N, long. 117°53'05" W; sec. 36, T 3 S, R 10 W). Named on Anaheim (1950) 7.5' quadrangle.
Santiago Canyon [LOS ANGELES]: *canyon,* drained by a stream that flows 7.5 miles to Little Rock Creek 6 miles north of Pacifico Mountain (lat. 34°28'05" N, long. 118°01'10" W). Named on Pacifico Mountain (1959) 7.5' quadrangle.
Santiago Canyon: see Santiago Creek [ORANGE].
Santiago City: see Modjeska Reservoir [ORANGE].
Santiago Creek [ORANGE]: *stream* and *dry wash,* extends for 27 miles to Santa Ana River 9 miles southeast of Buena Park civic center (lat. 33°46'10" N, long. 117°53'20" W; sec. 2, T 5 S, R 10 W). Named on Anaheim (1965), Black Star Canyon (1967), El Toro (1968), and Orange (1964) 7.5' quadrangles. Corona (1942) 15' quadrangle has the name "Santiago Canyon" for the canyon of the stream, and Santiago Peak (1954) 7.5' quadrangle has this name for the canyon, but leaves the stream unnamed. On Corona (1902) 30' quadrangle, the name "Santiago Canyon" applies to the upper part of the canyon of Santiago Creek. Members of the Portola expedition named the stream for Saint James in 1769 (Meadows, p. 22).
Santiago de Santa Ana [ORANGE]: *land grant,* at Orange, Santa Ana, and Newport Beach. Named on Anaheim (1950), Black Star Canyon (1950), Newport Beach (1951), Orange (1950), Prado Dam (1950), and Tustin (1950) 7.5' quadrangles. Antonio Yorba received 11 leagues in 1810 and his heirs claimed 78,941 acres patented in 1883 (Cowan, p. 90).
Santiago Northwest Peak: see Modjeska Peak [ORANGE].
Santiago Peak [ORANGE]: *peak,* 20 miles east of Santa Ana on Orange-Riverside county line (lat. 33°42'40" N, long. 117°32' W). Named on Santiago Peak (1954) 7.5' quadrangle, which shows the alternate name "Old Saddleback" for the feature. United States Board on Geographic Names (1961b, p. 15) rejected the names "Old Saddleback," "Temescal Peak," and "Trabuco Peak" for it. The name "Old Saddleback" properly applies to two peaks together, Santiago Peak and Mojeska Peak, and to the ridge between them (Stephenson, p. 3-4). Whitney (p. 177) climbed Santiago peak in 1861 and named it Mount Downey to honor J.G. Downey, then governor of California. Bowers (p. 399) called the feature Saddleback or Santa Ana Peak.
Santiago Reservoir [ORANGE]: *lake,* behind a dam 6 miles southwest of Sierra Peak (lat. 33°47'10" N, long. 117°43'30" W); the lake is along on Santiago Creek . Named on Black Star Canyon (1967) 7.5' quadrangle. Called Irvine Lake on Black Star Canyon (1950) 7.5' quadrangle. The dam that forms the lake is at a place called Sycamore Flat for the sycamore

trees there (Meadows, p. 133). During World War II, the army had a post called Camp Rathke situated in Santiago Canyon below the lake at a county park (Sleeper, 1976, p. 194).

San Vicente Mountain [LOS ANGELES]: *peak,* 7 miles southwest of the center of Canoga Park (lat. 34°07'45" N, long. 118°30'45" W); the peak is on San Vicente y Santa Monica grant. Altitude 1961 feet. Named on Canoga Park (1952) 7.5' quadrangle.

San Vicente y Santa Monica [LOS ANGELES]: *land grant,* extends from Santa Monica to Topanga Canyon. Named on Beverly Hills (1950), Canoga Park (1952), Topanga (1952), and Van Nuys (1953) 7.5' quadrangles. Francisco Sepulveda received the land in 1828, 1839, and 1846; Ramona Sepulveda claimed 30,260 acres patented in 1881; Boca de Santa Monica grant was made from the original San Vicente grant in 1839 (Cowan, p. 89).

Sargent Canyon: see **Hay Canyon** [LOS ANGELES].

Saticoy [VENTURA]: *town,* 7.5 miles east of Ventura (lat. 34°17' N, long. 119°08'50" W); the town is on Santa Paula y Saticoy grant. Named on Saticoy (1951) 7.5' quadrangle. Postal authorities established Saticoy post office in 1873 and discontinued it for a time in 1892 (Salley, p. 198). The name is of Indian origin (Kroeber, p. 56). The name "Saticoy" first applied to present West Saticoy, but in 1887 the name was transferred to the present community, which is along the railroad (Ricard). Postal authorities established Las Posas post office 6 miles southeast of Saticoy in 1892 and discontinued it in 1897—the name was from Las Posas grant (Salley, p. 118).

Saticoy: see **Santa Paula y Saticoy** [VENTURA]; **West Saticoy** [VENTURA].

Saucer Branch [LOS ANGELES]: *canyon,* drained by a stream that flows 1.25 miles to Millard Canyon 5 miles north of Pasadena city hall (lat. 34°13'10" N, long. 118°08'10" W). Named on Pasadena (1953) 7.5' quadrangle.

Saugus [LOS ANGELES]: *town,* 2 miles northnorthwest of downtown Newhall (lat. 34°24'40" N, long. 118°32'20" W). Named on Newhall (1952) 7.5' quadrangle. Camulos (1903) 30' quadrangle has both the names "Saugus" and "Surrey" at the site. Postal authorities established Surrey post office in 1891 and changed the name to Saugus in 1915; the town was called Saugus after 1877, but the post office retained the old name for years (Salley, p. 216). The railroad station at the site first was called Newhall, for Henry M. Newhall, but when this name was transferred to present Newhall in 1878, the place was renamed Saugus for Newhall's birthplace in Massachusetts (Gudde, 1949, p. 321). Postal authorities established Alolia post office 18 miles northwest of Saugus on the old ridge route from Los Angeles to Bakersfield in

1916, changed the name to Ridge View the same year, and discontinued it in 1918 (Salley, p. 5, 185). Postal authorities established Carey post office 5 miles north of Saugus (sec. 34, T 5 N, R 16 W) in 1927 and discontinued in 1928; the name was for Western movie star Harry Carey, on whose ranch the post office was situated (Salley, p. 37).

Sausal Redondo [LOS ANGELES]: *land grant,* mainly between Redondo Beach and Inglewood. Named on Inglewood (1952), Redondo Beach (1951), Torrance (1964), and Venice (1950) 7.5' quadrangles. Antonio Ignacio Avila received 5 leagues in 1822, 1837, and 1846; he claimed 22,459 acres patented in 1875 (Cowan, p. 96; Cowan used the form "Sauzal Redondo" for the name).

Savage Creek [LOS ANGELES]: *stream,* flows 1 mile to end 0.5 mile east of Whittier city hall (lat. 33°58'20" N, long. 118°01'30" W). Named on Whittier (1965) 7.5' quadrangle.

Savannah [LOS ANGELES]: *locality,* 1.5 miles west-northwest of El Monte along Southern Pacific Railroad (lat. 34°05' N, long. 118°03'30" W). Named on Pasadena (1900) 15' quadrangle. Postal authorities established Savannah post office in 1876 and discontinued it in 1900 (Frickstad, p. 81). United States Board on Geographic Names (1933, p. 674) rejected the form "Savanna" for the name.

Sawmill Campground [LOS ANGELES]: *locality,* 1.25 miles north of Burnt Peak (lat. 34°42'05" N, long. 118°34'15" W); the place is on Sawmill Mountain. Named on Burnt Peak (1958) 7.5' quadrangle.

Sawmill Canyon [LOS ANGELES]:
(1) *canyon,* less than 1 mile long, nearly 2 miles north of Burnt Peak (lat. 34°42'30" N, long. 118°34'20" W; near E line sec. 9, T 7 N, R 16 W); the canyon is on the north side of Sawmill Mountain. Named on Burnt Peak (1958) 7.5' quadrangle.
(2) *canyon,* drained by a stream that flows nearly 1 mile to Swarthout Valley 6 miles north-northwest of Mount San Antonio (lat. 34°22'20" N, long. 117°40'45" W; sec. 2, T 3 N, R 8 W). Named on Mount San Antonio (1955) 7.5' quadrangle.

Sawmill Mountain [LOS ANGELES]: *ridge,* generally west-trending, 8 miles long, center 3 miles east of Burnt Peak (lat. 34°41'10" N, long. 118°31'15" W). Named on Burnt Peak (1958) and Lake Hughes (1957) 7.5' quadrangles.

Sawmill Mountain [VENTURA]: *peak,* 14 miles north-northeast of Reyes Peak on Ventura-Kern county line (lat. 34°48'50" N, long. 119°10' W; on N line sec. 1, T 8 N, R 22 W). Named on Sawmill Mountain (1943) 7.5' quadrangle.

Sawpit Canyon [LOS ANGELES]: *canyon,* drained by a stream that flows 5 miles to lowlands 5.5 miles west-northwest of Azusa city hall (lat. 34°09'45" N, long. 117°59'30" W).

Named on Azusa (1953) 7.5' quadrangle. The name is from a sawpit located near the mouth of the canyon; the sawpit appeared old when the first settlers discovered it in the 1870's (Robinson, J.W., 1983, p. 15, 73).

Sawpit Wash [LOS ANGELES]: *stream* and *dry wash*, extends for 5 miles from the mouth of Sawpit Canyon to Rio Hondo 2.5 miles north-northeast of present El Monte city hall (lat. 34°06'40" N, long. 118°00'15" W). Named on Azusa (1953), Baldwin Park (1953), and El Monte (1953) 7.5' quadrangles.

Sawtelle: see **West Los Angeles** [LOS ANGELES].

Sawtooth Mountain [LOS ANGELES]: *ridge*, east-trending, 3 miles long, 2 miles southeast of Burnt Peak (lat. 34°39'40" N, long. 118°33'05" W). Named on Burnt Peak (1958) 7.5' quadrangle.

Saxonia Park [LOS ANGELES]: *locality*, 1 mile east-northeast of downtown Newhall (lat. 34°23'20" N, long. 118°30'45" W). Named on Newhall (1952) 7.5' quadrangle.

Scenega: see **Fillmore** [VENTURA].

Scheideck: see **Scheideck Camp** [VENTURA].

Scheideck Camp [VENTURA]: *locality*, 4 miles north-northwest of Reyes Peak along Reyes Creek (lat. 34°40'55" N, long. 119°18'30" W; at E line sec. 22, T 7 N, R 23 W). Named on Reyes Peak (1943) 7.5' quadrangle. California Division of Highways' (1934) map shows a place called Scheideck located 4 miles north of Reyes Peak and 1.25 miles east-northeast of the site of Scheideck Camp. Postal authorities established Scheideck post office in 1921 and discontinued it in 1935; the name was for Martin Scheideck, first postmaster and operator of a vacation camp (Salley, p. 199).

Scholl Canyon [LOS ANGELES]: *canyon*, nearly 3 miles long, opens into Sycamore Canyon (2) 5 miles west of Pasadena city hall (lat. 34°09'05" N, long. 118°13'40" W). Named on Pasadena (1953) 7.5' quadrangle.

Schoolhouse Canyon [LOS ANGELES]: *canyon*, 1.5 miles long, opens into lowlands 3 miles north-northwest of downtown San Fernando (lat. 34°19'30" N, long. 118°27'30" W; near S line sec. 21, T 3 N, R 15 W). Named on San Fernando (1953) 7.5' quadrangle. Sylmar (1935) 6' quadrangle has the form "School House Canyon" for the name. San Fernando (1966) 7.5' quadrangle shows Schoolhouse Debris Basin at the mouth of the canyon.

Schoolhouse Canyon [VENTURA]: *canyon*, drained by a stream that flows 2.25 miles to Russell Valley 1.25 miles southeast of Thousand Oaks (lat. 34°09'35" N, long. 118°49'05" W). Named on Thousand Oaks (1952) 7.5' quadrangle.

Schoolhouse Debris Basin: see **Schoolhouse Canyon** [LOS ANGELES].

Schumacher Point [LOS ANGELES]: *relief feature*, 3.5 miles north of Burnt Peak (lat. 34°44'

N, long. 118°34'10" W; near SW cor. sec. 34, T 8 N, R 16 W). Named on Burnt Peak (1958) 7.5' quadrangle.

Schwartz Canyon [LOS ANGELES]: *canyon*, drained by a stream that flows less than 1 mile to Tujunga Valley 2 miles west-northwest of Sunland (lat. 34°16'30" N, long. 118°20'35" W; at W line sec. 10, T 2 N, R 14 W). Named on Sunland (1953) 7.5' quadrangle.

Scorpion Hills: see **Santa Susana Mountains** [LOS ANGELES-VENTURA].

Scott Canyon [LOS ANGELES]: *canyon*, 0.5 mile long, 3.5 miles west-northwest of Azusa city hall (lat. 34°08'55" N, long. 117°57'45" W). Named on Azusa (1953) 7.5' quadrangle.

Scott's Camp: see **Camp Bonita** [LOS ANGELES].

Scully Hill [ORANGE]: *peak*, 4.25 miles southeast of San Juan Hill on Orange-San Bernardino county line (lat. 33°52'40" N, long. 117°40'40" W). Named on Prado Dam (1967) 7.5' quadrangle. The name commemorates Thomas J. Scully, a pioneer school teacher who lived near the feature; a promontory along Santa Ana River south of the peak is called Scully Point (Meadows, p. 126).

Scully Point: see **Scully Hill** [ORANGE].

Seabright [LOS ANGELES]: *locality*, 1.5 miles northwest of present Long Beach city hall (lat. 33°47' N, long. 118°12'40" W). Named on Downey (1902) 15' quadrangle.

Sea Cliff [VENTURA]: *locality*, 2.5 miles northwest of Pitas Point along Southern Pacific Railroad (lat. 34°20'40" N, long. 119°25' W; sec. 17, T 3 N, R 24 W). Named on Pitas Point (1950) 7.5' quadrangle. Diller and others' (1915) map has the form "Seaclift" for the name.

Seal Beach [ORANGE]: *city*, 8 miles northwest of Huntington Beach civic center (lat. 33°44'30" N, long. 118°06'15" W). Named on Los Alamitos (1964) and Seal Beach (1965) 7.5' quadrangles. Postal authorities established Bay City post office in 1904 and changed the name to Seal Beach in 1914 (Frickstad, p. 116). The city incorporated in 1915. Philip A. Stanton and I.A. Lothian purchased land and laid out a townsite called Bay City at the place in 1903; the name was changed to Seal Beach because of the abundance of harbor seals at the spot (Meadows, p. 126).

Seal Beach: see **San Nicolas Island** [VENTURA].

Seal Cove [LOS ANGELES]: *embayment*, 10 miles south-southeast of Northwest Harbor on the west side of San Clemente Island (lat. 32°54'15" N, long. 118°31'50" W). Named on San Clemente Island Central (1943) 7.5' quadrangle. Called Seal Hbr. on Smith's (1898) map.

Seal Garden: see **Graham** [LOS ANGELES].

Seal Harbor: see **Seal Cove** [LOS ANGELES].

Seal Rocks [LOS ANGELES]: *rocks*, 2.5 miles

south-southeast of Avalon near the southeast end of Santa Catalina Island (lat. 33°18'25" N, long. 118°18'20" W). Named on Santa Catalina East (1950) 7.5' quadrangle.

Seco Canyon: see **Williams Canyon** [ORANGE].

Segunda Deshecha Cañada [ORANGE]: *canyon*, drained by a stream that flows 5.25 miles to the sea 1.5 miles west of San Clemente civic center (lat. 33°25'55" N, long. 117°38'05" W; sec. 32, T 8 S, R 7 W); the canyon is less than 1 mile southeast of Prima Deshecha Cañada. Named on San Clemente (1968) 7.5' quadrangle. The feature is the second difficult canyon to cross on the road south from the San Juan Capistrano mission—*Segunda Deshecha Cañada* means "Second Rough Canyon" in Spanish (Meadows, p. 126).

Seminole: see **Seminole Hot Springs** [LOS ANGELES].

Seminole Hot Springs [LOS ANGELES]: *locality*, 7.5 miles north of Point Dume in La Sierra Canyon (lat. 34°06'30" N, long. 118°47'25" W; sec. 5, T 1 S, R 18 W). Named on Point Dume (1951) quadrangle, which shows Cornell school near the place. Called Cornell on Triunfo Pass (1921) 15' quadrangle. Seminole (1932) 6' quadrangle shows both Seminole and Cornell P.O. at the site. Postal authorities established Cornell post office in 1912 (Salley, p. 50). Water from an oil test well, reportedly about 3000 feet deep, is used for health-bathing and swimming at the place (Berkstresser, p.A-7).

Senior Canyon: see **Señor Canyon** [VENTURA].

Sennet Canyon [LOS ANGELES]: *canyon*, drained by a stream that flows 1.5 miles to Los Angeles River 2.25 miles south-southwest of Burbank city hall (lat. 34°09'10" N, long. 118°19'30" W). Named on Burbank (1953) 7.5' quadrangle.

Señora de Altagracia: see **El Conejo** [LOS ANGELES-VENTURA].

Señor Canyon [VENTURA]: *canyon*, 3.5 miles long, along San Antonio Creek above a point 4 miles northeast of the town of Ojai (lat. 34°28'15" N, long. 119°11'55" W; sec. 32, T 5 N, R 22 W). Named on Ojai (1952) 7.5' quadrangle. United States Board on Geographic Names (1968a, p. 9) approved name "Senior Canyon" for the feature.

Sentinel Rock [LOS ANGELES]: *rock*, 3 miles west of Mount Banning, and 550 feet off the west side of Santa Catalina Island (lat. 33°22'20" N, long. 118°29'10" W). Named on Santa Catalina South (1943) 7.5' quadrangle.

Sentous [LOS ANGELES]: *locality*, 7.5 miles west-southwest of Los Angeles city hall along Southern Pacific Railroad (lat. 34°01'35" N, long. 118°22'10" W). Named on Hollywood (1966) 7.5' quadrangle.

Sepulveda [LOS ANGELES]:

(1) *district*, 3.25 miles north-northwest of Van Nuys in Los Angeles (lat. 34°13'40" N, long. 118°28' W). Named on Van Nuys (1953) 7.5' quadrangle. Called Mission Acres on Pacoima (1927) 6' quadrangle. Postal authorities established Mission Acres post office in 1926 and changed the name to Sepulveda in 1927 (Salley, p. 142).

(2) *locality*, 2 miles southeast of Burbank city hall along Southern Pacific Railroad (lat. 34°09'45" N, long. 118°17' W). Named on Burbank (1953) 7.5' quadrangle. Called Redcastle on Santa Monica (1902) 15' quadrangle. Postal authorities established Redcastle post office in 1895 and discontinued it the same year (Frickstad, p. 80).

Sepulveda Canyon [LOS ANGELES]:

(1) *canyon*, 4 miles long, 5 miles west-northwest of Beverly Hills city hall (lat. 34°06' N, long. 118°28'40" W). Named on Beverly Hills (1950) 7.5' quadrangle. The name is for Francisco Sepulveda, who received San Vicente y Santa Monica grant (Gudde, 1949, p. 325).

(2) *canyon*, nearly 2 miles long, 4.5 miles south of Torrance city hall (lat. 33°46'25" N, long. 118°21'05" W). Named on Torrance (1964) 7.5' quadrangle.

Sepulveda Channel [LOS ANGELES]: *water feature*, joins Ballona Creek 7 miles north of Manhattan Beach city hall (lat. 33°59'35" N, long. 118°24'25" W). Named on Venice (1964) 7.5' quadrangle.

Sepulveda's Landing: see **San Pedro** [LOS ANGELES] (2).

Sequit Point [LOS ANGELES]: *promontory*, 8 miles west-northwest of Point Dume along the coast (lat. 34°02'35" N, long. 118°56'10" W); the feature is on Topanga Malibu Sequit grant. Named on Triunfo Pass (1950) 7.5' quadrangle.

Serra [ORANGE]: *locality*, 2.5 miles southsouthwest of San Juan Capistrano along Atchison, Topeka and Santa Fe Railroad at Capistrano Beach (lat. 33°28' N, long. 117°40'45" W). Named on Dana Point (1968) 7.5' quadrangle. The place first was called San Juan-by-the-Sea (Meadows, p. 126-127). California Mining Bureau's (1917) map shows a place called Mateo located along the railroad about 3 miles southeast of Serra.

Serra: see **Capistrano Beach** [ORANGE].

Serrano Canyon [VENTURA]: *canyon*, drained by a stream that flows 3.5 miles to Big Sycamore Canyon nearly 3 miles east of Point Mugu (lat. 34°05'25" N, long. 119°00'40" W). Named on Point Mugu (1949) and Triunfo Pass (1950) 7.5' quadrangles.

Serrano Creek [ORANGE]: *stream*, flows nearly 5 miles to San Diego Creek 2.5 miles west-northwest of El Toro (lat. 33°38'10" N, long. 117°44' W). Named on El Toro (1968) 7.5' quadrangle. The stream was called Agua del Toro in the early days (Meadows, p. 18). Stevenson's (1884) map shows Cañada del Toro.

Sespe [VENTURA]:
(1) *land grant,* along the valley of Santa Clara River near Fillmore. The river divides the grant into two parts: Sespe No. 1, south of the river, is named on Fillmore (1951), Moorpark (1951), and Santa Paula (1951) 7.5' quadrangles; Sespe No. 2, north of the river, is named on Fillmore (1951), Moorpark (1951), Piru (1952), Santa Paula (1951), and Santa Paula Peak (1951) 7.5' quadrangles. Carlos Antonio Carrillo received 2 leagues in 1833; T.W. Moore and others claimed 6 leagues and received 8881 acres patented in 1872 (Cowan, p. 97; Cowan gave the alternate name "San Cayetano" for the grant). The name "Sespe " is of Indian origin (Kroeber, p. 57).
(2) *locality,* 1.5 miles west-northwest of Fillmore (lat. 34°24'40" N, long. 118°56' W); the place is along Sespe Creek. Named on Piru (1921) 15' quadrangle.
(3) *locality,* 2.25 miles west of Fillmore along Southern Pacific Railroad (lat. 34°24' N, long. 118°57' W; sec. 26, T 4 N, R 20 W). Named on Fillmore (1951) 7.5' quadrangle. Called Sespe Sta. on Piru (1921) 15' quadrangle. Postal authorities established Sespe post office in 1894 and discontinued it in 1932 (Frickstad, p. 219).
Sespe Creek [VENTURA]: *stream,* flows 58 miles to Santa Clara River 2.5 miles west-southwest of Fillmore (lat. 34°22'55" N, long. 118°57'05" W; near SW cor. sec. 35, T 4 N, R 20 W). Named on Devils Heart Peak (1943), Fillmore (1951), Lion Canyon (1943), Old Man Mountain (1943), Topatopa Mountains (1943), and Wheeler Springs (1943) 7.5' quadrangles. Called Sespe R. on Goddard's (1857) map. Rothrock (p. 209) called the stream Sespo Creek, and C.W. Whipple (p. 148) called it Cespe Creek. West Fork enters from the west 2.5 miles south-southeast of Devils Heart Peak; it is 6.25 miles long and is named on Devils Heart Peak (1943) and Topatopa Mountains (1943) 7.5' quadrangles.
Sespe Creek: see Little Sespe Creek [VENTURA].
Sespe Gorge [VENTURA]: *narrows,* 5.25 miles north-northeast of Wheeler Springs (lat. 34°34'45" N, long. 119°15'25" W; near W line sec. 30, T 6 N, R 22 W); the feature is along Sespe Creek. Named on Wheeler Springs (1943) 7.5' quadrangle.
Sespe Hot Springs [VENTURA]: *spring,* 3.5 miles north-northwest of Devils Heart Peak in Hot Springs Canyon (lat. 34°35'40" N, long. 118°59'50" W). Named on Devils Heart Peak (1943) 7.5' quadrangle.
Sespe Station: see Sespe [VENTURA] (3).
Sespe Village [VENTURA]: *locality,* nearly 3 miles west-southwest of Fillmore (lat. 34°23'10" N, long. 118°57'20" W; at E line sec. 34, T 4 N, R 20 W); the place is near the mouth of Sespe Creek. Named on Fillmore (1951) 7.5' quadrangle.

Seven Pines Forest Camp [VENTURA]: *locality,* 2.5 miles northeast of McDonald Peak along Snowy Creek (lat. 34°39'25" N, long. 118°54'25" W; near W line sec. 33, T 7 N, R 19 W). Named on McDonald Peak (1958) 7.5' quadrangle.
Sewart Mountain [VENTURA]: *peak,* 2 miles east-northeast of McDonald Peak (lat. 34°38'25" N, long. 118°54'20" W; near W line sec. 4, T 6 N, R 19 W). Altitude 6825 feet. Named on McDonald Peak (1958) 7.5' quadrangle. Called Stewart Pk. on California Mining Bureau's (1917) map.
Sexton Canyon [VENTURA]: *canyon,* drained by a stream that flows 4.25 miles to the valley of Santa Clara River 4 miles west of Saticoy (lat. 34°17'05" N, long. 119°13' W). Named on Saticoy (1951) 7.5' quadrangle.
Seymour Creek [VENTURA]: *stream,* flows 8 miles to Lockwood Creek 15 miles east-northeast of Reyes Peak (lat. 34°44' N, long. 119°02'25" W; near S line sec. 31, T 8 N, R 20 W). Named on Cuddy Valley (1943) and Lockwood Valley (1943) 7.5' quadrangles. Dr. Stephen Bowers named the stream in the late 1880's for Louisa Seymour, a friend of his (Ricard).
Shady Canyon [ORANGE]: *canyon,* 2.25 miles long, opens into an unnamed canyon nearly 9 miles south-southeast of Santa Ana city hall (lat. 33°38' N, long. 117°47'45" W). Named on Laguna Beach (1965) and Tustin (1965) 7.5' quadrangles. The upper part of the feature is called Cañada de la Madra on a map of 1841 (Meadows, p. 127).
Shady Oaks Camp [LOS ANGELES]: *locality,* 7.5 miles north-northeast of Glendora city hall along San Gabriel River (lat. 34°14'05" N, long. 117°48'20" W; near NE cor. sec. 27, T 2 N, R 9 W). Named on Glendora (1966) 7.5 quadrangle. Tony Galleta bought the place in the early 1950's and named it Shady Oaks; it also was called Follows Camp West (Robinson, J.W, 1983, p. 96-97).
Shake Campground: see Lower Shake Campground [LOS ANGELES]; Upper Shake Campground [LOS ANGELES].
Shake Canyon [LOS ANGELES]: *canyon,* drained by a stream that flows 2 miles to Pine Canyon (3) 3.25 miles east-northeast of Burnt Peak (lat. 34°42'05" N, long. 118°31'25" W; near N line sec. 13, T 7 N, R 16 W). Named on Burnt Peak (1958) 7.5' quadrangle.
Shan Canyon: see Tick Canyon [LOS ANGELES].
Shangri La: see Lake Shangri La [LOS ANGELES].
Shark Island: see Linda Isle [ORANGE].
Sharps Canyon [LOS ANGELES]: *canyon,* drained by a stream that flows 1 mile to Morris Reservoir 3.25 miles north of Glendora city hall (lat. 34°11' N, long. 117°51'55" W; sec. 7, T 1 N, R 9 W). Named on Glendora (1966) 7.5' quadrangle.

Sharps Canyon [LOS ANGELES-VENTURA]: *canyon,* drained by a stream that heads in Los Angeles County and flows nearly 3 miles to Piru Creek 17 miles south-southeast of Gorman just inside Ventura County (lat. 34°32'15" N, long. 118°45'30" W; sec. 10, T 5 N, R 18 E). Named on Cobblestone Mountain (1958) and Whitaker Peak (1958) 7.5' quadrangles. Los Angeles County (1935) map shows a feature called Kester Canyon that opens into the canyon of Piru Creek just above the mouth of Sharps Canyon.

Shatto: see **Avalon** [LOS ANGELES].

Shaw Canyon: see **Bitter Canyon** [LOS ANGELES].

Shay Canyon [LOS ANGELES]: *canyon,* 0.5 mile long, 3.25 miles east of Glendora city hall (lat. 34°07'50" N, long. 117°48'20" W; sec. 34, T 1 N, R 9 W). Named on Glendora (1953) 7.5' quadrangle.

Sheas Lodge [LOS ANGELES]: *locality,* 6 miles west of Del Sur (lat. 34°41'50" N, long. 118°23'40" W; on W line sec. 17, T 5 N, R 14 W). Named on Lake (1937) 6' quadrangle. Lake Hughes (1957) 7.5' quadrangle shows Sheas Castle at the site.

Sheep Camp Spring [LOS ANGELES]: *spring,* 0.25 mile north-northwest of Pacifico Mountain (lat. 34°23'10" N, long. 118°02'10" W). Named on Pacifico Mountain (1959) 7.5' quadrangle. Alder Creek (1941) 6' quadrangle has the form "Sheepcamp Spring" for the name.

Sheep Corral Canyon [LOS ANGELES]: *canyon,* drained by a stream that flows 1.25 miles to Verdugo Wash 4 miles northeast of Burbank city hall (lat. 34°13'40" N, long. 118°15'40" W). Named on Burbank (1966) 7.5' quadrangle.

Sheep Creek [VENTURA]: *stream,* flows 3.5 miles to Piru Creek 14 miles east-northeast of Reyes Peak (lat. 34°40'20" N, long. 119°02'10" W; sec. 30, T 7 N, R 20 W). Named on Lockwood Valley (1943) 7.5' quadrangle.

Sheep Hills [ORANGE]: *range,* 5.5 miles northwest of San Juan Capistrano (lat. 33°33'15" N, long. 117°43'50" W). Named on San Juan Capistrano (1968) 7.5' quadrangle.

Shell Beach: see **Huntington Beach** [ORANGE].

Sherer Canyon [LOS ANGELES]: *canyon,* drained by a stream that flows less than 1 mile to Hillcrest Canyon 2.5 miles east of Burbank city hall (lat. 34°10'40" N, long. 118°15'50" W). Named on Burbank (1953) 7.5' quadrangle.

Sherman [LOS ANGELES]: *locality,* 1.25 miles northeast of present Beverly Hills city hall (lat. 34°05'05" N, long. 118°22'55" W). Named on Hollywood (1926) 6' quadrangle. Postal authorities established Shermanton post office in 1896, changed the name to Sherman in 1899, and changed it to West in 1928; the name "Shermanton" was for General M.H.

Sherman, railroad builder and land developer (Salley, p. 203).

Sherman Junction [LOS ANGELES]: *locality,* 1.5 miles east of Beverly Hills city hall along Pacific Electric Railroad (lat. 34°04'15" N, long. 118°22'30" W). Named on Beverly Hills (1950) 7.5' quadrangle.

Sherman Oaks [LOS ANGELES]: *district,* 2.25 miles south of the center of Van Nuys in Los Angeles (lat. 34°09' N, long. 118°26'50" W). Named on Van Nuys (1953) 7.5' quadrangle. Postal authorities established Sherman Oaks post office in 1931 (Salley, p. 203).

Shermanton: see **Sherman** [LOS ANGELES].

Sherman Way: see **North Sherman Way** [LOS ANGELES].

Sherwood Lake: see **Lake Sherwood** [VENTURA].

Shields Canyon [LOS ANGELES]: *canyon,* less than 1 mile long, nearly 9 miles northwest of Pasadena city hall (lat. 34°14'50" N, long. 118°14'15" W; on E line sec. 21, T 2 N, R 13 W). Named on Condor Peak (1959) and Pasadena (1953) 7.5' quadrangles.

Shields Canyon: see **Shiells Canyon** [VENTURA].

Shiells Canyon [VENTURA]: *canyon,* drained by a stream that flows 1.5 miles to the valley of Santa Clara River 2.25 miles southeast of Fillmore (lat. 34°22'50" N, long. 118°52'45" W). Named on Fillmore (1951), Moorpark (1951), and Simi (1951) 7.5' quadrangles. Called Shields Canyon on Camulos (1903) 30' quadrangle. The name "Shiells" commemorates brothers William Shiells and James Shiells (Ricard).

Shifting Sands [LOS ANGELES]: *area,* 1 mile south-southwest of Northwest Harbor on San Clemente Island (lat. 33°01' N, long. 118°35'30" W). Named on San Clemente Island North (1943) 7.5' quadrangle.

Ship Rock [LOS ANGELES]: *rock,* 7 miles north-northwest of Mount Banning, and 1.25 miles off the north side of Santa Catalina Island (lat. 33°27'50" N, long. 118°29'30" W). Named on Santa Catalina North (1950) 7.5' quadrangle. United States Board on Geographic Names (1936a, p. 23) rejected the name "Bird Rock" for the feature. According to Gleason (p. 34), early navigators often mistook the rock for a vessel.

Shirley [ORANGE]: *locality,* 3 miles south-southwest of present Buena Park civic center along Pacific Electric Railroad (lat. 33°49'30" N, long. 118°01'25" W; sec. 15, T 4 S, R 11 W). Named on Los Alamitos (1950) 7.5' quadrangle.

Shoemaker [LOS ANGELES]: *locality,* 1.25 miles east-southeast of present Valyermo (lat. 34°25'50" N, long. 117°50'10" W). Named on Rock Creek (1903) 15' quadrangle. Postal authorities established Shoemaker post office in 1901, moved it 1.5 miles west in 1909, and moved it 1 mile northwest when they changed the name to Valyermo in 1910; the name

"Shoemaker" was for Abram H. Shoemaker, first postmaster (Salley, p. 203). Johnson's (1911) map shows a place called Tilghman located 3.5 miles north of Shoemaker.

Shoemaker Canyon [LOS ANGELES]: (1) *canyon,* drained by a stream that flows 2.5 miles to the canyon of Big Rock Creek 1.25 miles southeast of Valyermo (lat. 34°25'55" N, long. 117°50'05" W; at E line sec. 17, T 4 N, R 9 W); the mouth of the canyon is near the site of Shoemaker. Named on Valyermo (1958) 7.5' quadrangle.
(2) *canyon,* drained by a stream that flows nearly 1 mile to San Gabriel River 6.5 miles southeast of Crystal Lake (lat. 34°15'20" N, long. 117°45'30" W). Named on Crystal Lake (1958) 7.5' quadrangle. Called Rattlesnake Canyon on Rock Creek (1903) 15' quadrangle, but United States Board on Geographic Names (1962, p. 16) rejected the names "Rattlesnake Canyon" and "Little Rattlesnake Canyon" for the feature. The name "Shoemaker" commemorates Alonzo Schoemaker, who owned land above the canyon (Robinson, J.W., 1983, p. 35).

Shorb [LOS ANGELES]: *locality,* 6 miles east-northeast of present Los Angeles city hall along Southern Pacific Railroad (lat. 34°04'45" N, long. 118°08'50" W). Named on Pasadena (1900) 15' quadrangle. Postal authorities established Shorb post office in 1895 and discontinued it in 1909; the name was for J. De Barth Shorb, a businessman (Salley, p. 203). California Mining Bureau's (1917) map shows a place called Dolgeville located about 1 mile north of Shorb along the railroad. Postal authorities established Dolgeville post office in 1904, changed the name to West Alhambra in 1911, and discontinued it in 1920; the name was for Alfred Dolge, who built a factory for the manufacture of felt at the site (Salley, p. 60, 237).

Shore Acres: see **Manhattan Beach** [LOS ANGELES].

Shortcut Canyon [LOS ANGELES]: *canyon,* drained by a stream that flows 2.25 miles to West Fork San Gabriel River nearly 3 miles north-northeast of Mount Wilson (1) (lat. 34°14'50" N, long. 118° 02'55" W; near E line sec. 20, T 2 N, R 11 W). Named on Chilao Flat (1959) and Mount Wilson (1953) 7.5' quadrangles. The stream in the canyon has the name "Trail Fork San Gabriel R." on Tujunga (1900) 15' quadrangle.

Shortcut Picnic Grounds [LOS ANGELES]: *locality,* 7.5 miles south of Pacifico Mountain (lat. 34°16'25" N, long. 118°02'20" W; sec. 9, T 2 N, R 11 W); the place is near the head of Shortcut Canyon. Named on Chilao Flat (1959) 7.5' quadrangle.

Shoulder Lake: see **Lake Palmdale** [LOS ANGELES].

Shrewsbury Canyon: see **Harding Canyon** [ORANGE].

Shrewsbury Spring [ORANGE]: *spring,* 4

miles west-northwest of Santiago Peak (lat. 33°44' N, long. 117°35'45" W; sec. 15, T 5 S, R 7 W). Named on Santiago Peak (1954) 7.5' quadrangle. The name is for Sam Shrewsbury, an early resident of Santiago Canyon (Meadows, p. 128).

Shuler Canyon [LOS ANGELES]: *canyon,* less than 1 mile long, 3.25 miles east of Glendora (lat. 34°08' N, long. 117°48'25" W; sec. 34, T 1 N, R 9 W). Named on Glendora (1953) 7.5' quadrangle.

Shuler Creek: see **East Branch**, under **Big Dalton Wash** [LOS ANGELES].

Sierra: see **Camp Sierra** [LOS ANGELES].

Sierra Canyon: see **Fremont Canyon** [ORANGE].

Sierra de la Monica: see **Santa Monica Mountains** [LOS ANGELES-VENTURA].

Sierra de la Santa Inez: see **Santa Ynez Mountains** [VENTURA].

Sierra de Liebre: see **Liebre Mountain** [LOS ANGELES].

Sierra de los Berdugos: see **Verdugo Mountains** [LOS ANGELES].

Sierra del Trabuco: see **Santa Ana Mountains** [ORANGE].

Sierra de Santa Ana: see **Santa Ana Mountains** [ORANGE].

Sierra de Santa Monica: see **Santa Monica Mountains** [LOS ANGELES-VENTURA].

Sierra Liebra: see **Liebre Mountain** [LOS ANGELES].

Sierra Madre [LOS ANGELES]: *town,* 4 miles south of Mount Wilson (1) (lat. 34°09'45" N, long. 118°03'10" W). Named on Mount Wilson (1953) 7.5' quadrangle. Postal authorities established Sierra Madre post office in 1882 (Frickstad, p. 81), and the town incorporated in 1907. The name recalls Sierra Madre Villa, one of the earliest resorts in Los Angeles County and nucleus of the present town (Hanna, p. 305).

Sierra Madre: see **San Gabriel Mountains** [LOS ANGELES].

Sierra Madre Canyon Park: see **Carter's Camp**, under **Little Santa Anita Canyon** [LOS ANGELES].

Sierra Monica: see **Santa Monica Mountains** [LOS ANGELES-VENTURA].

Sierra Peak [ORANGE]: *peak,* 14 miles east-northeast of Santa Ana on Orange-Riverside county line (lat. 33°51' N, long. 117°39'10" W; sec. 6, T 4 S, R 7 W). Altitude 3045 feet. Named on Black Star Canyon (1967) 7.5' quadrangle.

Sierra Pelona [LOS ANGELES]: *range,* west-to southwest-trending, 18 miles long, east of Bouquet Canyon and north of Mint Canyon. Named on Green Valley (1958), Ritter Ridge (1958), and Sleepy Valley (1958) 7.5' quadrangles. Called Sierra Pelona Ridge on Los Angeles County (1935) map.

Sierra Pelona Ridge: see **Sierra Pelona** [LOS ANGELES].

Sierra Pelona Valley [LOS ANGELES]: *valley,* 7 miles south of the village of Leona Valley (lat. 34°30'45" N, long. 118°18'30" W); the valley is south of Sierra Pelona. Named on Agua Dulce (1960) and Sleepy Valley (1958) 7.5' quadrangles.

Sierra San Gabriel: see **San Gabriel Mountains** [LOS ANGELES].

Sierra San Juan: see **San Joaquin Hills** [ORANGE].

Sierra Santa Iñez: see **Santa Ynez Mountains** [VENTURA].

Sierra Santa Monica: see **Santa Monica Mountains** [LOS ANGELES-VENTURA].

Sierra Santa Susana: see **Santa Susana Mountains** [LOS ANGELES-VENTURA].

Sierra Santiago: see **Santa Ana Mountains** [ORANGE].

Sierra Susana: see **Santa Susana Mountains** [VENTURA].

Sierra Vista [LOS ANGELES]: *district,* 5.5 miles east-northeast of present Los Angeles city hall (lat. 34°05'40" N, long. 118°09'25" W). Named on Alhambra (1926) 6' quadrangle.

Signal Hill [LOS ANGELES]:
(1) *peak,* 2.5 miles northeast of Long Beach city hall (lat. 33°48' N, long. 118°09'45" W). Named on Long Beach (1949) 7.5' quadrangle. Called Los Cerritos on Downey (1902) 15' quadrangle—the peak is on the boundary of Los Cerritos grant. The feature was known as Los Cerritos in Spanish times, but it was called Signal Hill after members of the Coast Survey put a signal there (Gudde, 1949, p. 332). It also was called Pound Cake Hill (Hanna, p. 306).
(2) *town,* 3 miles north-northeast of Long Beach city hall (lat. 33° 48'20" N, long. 118°10' W); Signal Hill (1) is at the town. Named on Long Beach (1949) 7.5' quadrangle. Postal authorities established Signal Hill post office in 1926, discontinued it in 1950, and reestablished it in 1956 (Salley, p. 204). The town incorporated in 1924.
(3) *locality,* 2.25 miles north-northeast of present Long Beach city hall along Los Angeles Terminal Railroad (lat. 33°48' N, long. 118°10'50" W). Named on Downey (1902) 15' quadrangle.

Signal Peak [ORANGE]: *peak,* 4.5 miles northnorthwest of Laguna Beach city hall (lat. 33°36'20" N, long. 117°48'40" W). Named on Laguna Beach (1965) 7.5' quadrangle. The feature was used as a signal point for early surveys in Orange County (Meadows, p. 129).

Signal Point: see **Mount Wilson** [LOS ANGELES] (1).

Silver Acres [ORANGE]: *locality,* 7 miles northnortheast of present Huntington Beach civic center (lat. 33°45' N, long. 117°56'15" W). Named on Anaheim (1950) and Newport Beach (1951) 7.5' quadrangles.

Silverado [ORANGE]: *locality,* 9 miles north-

northeast of El Toro (lat. 33°44'45" N, long. 117°38' W); the place is in Silverado Canyon. Named on El Toro (1968) 7.5' quadrangle. Postal authorities established Silverado post office in 1878, discontinued it in 1883, reestablished it in 1906, discontinued it in 1907, and reestablished it in 1931 (Salley, p. 204). J.W. Clark laid out a townsite called Silverado after a reported silver strike in Santa Ana Mountains in 1877 (Meadows, p, 129).

Silverado Canyon [ORANGE]: *canyon,* drained by a stream that flows 9 miles to Santiago Creek 6.5 miles south of Sierra Peak (lat. 33°45'30" N, long. 117°40'45" W). Named on Corona South (1967), El Toro (1968), and Santiago Peak (1954) 7.5' quadrangles. The feature first was called Cañada de la Madera for the trees there that provided lumber in the early days (Meadows, p. 49). The name "Silverado Canyon" came after Hank Smith and William Curry discovered silver in the canyon in 1877 (Hoover, Rensch, and Rensch, p. 264). Black Star Canyon (1950) 7.5' quadrangle has the name "Silverado Creek" for the stream in the canyon. After Ramon Mesquida discovered coal in the canyon in 1878, a mining town called Carbondale sprang up 1.5 miles above the mouth of the canyon; Tom Harris supervised the mine, and the community was known as Harrisburg before Carbondale post office opened (Hoover, Rensch, and Rensch, p. 264; Meadows, p. 50). Postal authorities established Carbondale post office in 1881 and discontinued it in 1884 (Salley, p. 37).

Silverado Creek: see **Silverado Canyon** [ORANGE].

Silver Canyon [LOS ANGELES]: *canyon,* drained by a stream that flows nearly 3 miles to the sea 4.25 miles southeast of Mount Banning on Santa Catalina Island (lat. 33°19'15" N, long. 118°23'20" W). Named on Santa Catalina East (1950) and Santa Catalina South (1943) 7.5' quadrangles.

Silver Canyon Landing [LOS ANGELES]: *locality,* 4.25 miles southeast of Mount Banning on the south side of Santa Catalina Island (lat. 33°19'15" N, long. 118°23'20" W); the place is at the mouth of Silver Canyon. Named on Santa Catalina South (1943) 7.5' quadrangle. Smith's (1897) map has the name "Silver C." (the "C" presumably for "Cove") at the site.

Silver Cove: see **Silver Canyon Landing** [LOS ANGELES].

Silver Creek [LOS ANGELES]: *stream,* flows 1 mile to Big Tujunga Canyon 3.5 miles south of Condor Peak (lat. 34°16'35" N, long. 118°12'50" W; sec. 11, T 2 N, R 13 W). Named on Condor Peak (1959) 7.5' quadrangle.

Silver Hill: see **Silver Peak** [LOS ANGELES].

Silver Lake: see **Silver Lake Reservoir** [LOS ANGELES].

Silver Lake Heights [LOS ANGELES]: *district,* 3.5 miles north-northwest of Los Angeles city

DURHAM'S PLACE-NAMES

hall (lat. 34°06'10" N, long. 118°15'20" W); the place is east of Silver Lake Reservoir. Named on Glendale (1928) 6' quadrangle.

Silver Lake Reservoir [LOS ANGELES]: *lake,* 4400 feet long, 3.25 miles north-northwest of Los Angeles city hall (lat. 34°05'50" N, long. 118°15'45" W). Named on Hollywood (1953) 7.5' quadrangle. Called Silver Lake on Los Angeles (1928) 6' quadrangle.

Silver Mountain [LOS ANGELES]: *peak,* 4.5 miles north of Azusa city hall (lat. 34°11'50" N, long. 117°53'20" W; on E line sec. 2, T 1 N, R 10 W). Altitude 3391 feet. Named on Azusa (1953) 7.5' quadrangle. Mines near the peak produced silver in the 1880's (Robinson, J.W., 1983, p. 30).

Silver Peak [LOS ANGELES]: *peak,* 16 miles northwest of Avalon on Santa Catalina Island (lat. 33°27'35" N, long. 118°34'05" W). Named on Santa Catalina West (1943) 7.5' quadrangle. Doran (1980, p. 66) associated the name with the discovery of silver-bearing galena; the feature also was called Silver Hill.

Silver Strand [VENTURA]: *town,* nearly 4 miles south-southwest of Oxnard near the coast (lat. 34°09'05" N, long. 119°13' W). Named on Oxnard (1949) 7.5' quadrangle.

Simi [LOS ANGELES-VENTURA]: *land grant,* at and around Simi Valley (1) on Los Angeles-Ventura county line. Named on Calabasas (1952), Moorpark (1951), Newbury Park (1951), Santa Susana (1951), Simi (1951), Thousand Oaks (1952), and Val Verde (1952) 7.5' quadrangles. Francisco Javier Pico, Miguel Pico, and Patricio Pico received 14 leagues in 1795 and 1821; Manuel Pico and Patricio Pico received the grant in 1842; Jose de la Guerra y Noriega claimed 113,009 acres patented in 1865 (Cowan, p. 98; Cowan listed the grant under the name "San Jose de Gracia de Simi"). The name "Simi" is of Indian origin (Kroeber, p. 58).

Simi: see **Simi Valley** [VENTURA] (2).

Simi Hills [VENTURA]: *range,* 7 miles northeast of Thousand Oaks (lat. 34°13'30" N, long. 118°44'50" W); the range is south of Simi Valley (1). Named on Calabasas (1952), Santa Susana (1951), and Thousand Oaks (1952) 7.5' quadrangles.

Simiopolis: see **Simi Valley** [VENTURA] (2).

Simi Pass: see **Santa Susana Pass** [LOS ANGELES-VENTURA].

Simi Peak [VENTURA]: *peak,* 4 miles northeast of Thousand Oaks (lat. 34°12'15" N, long. 118°46'50" W; near NE cor. sec. 5, T 1 N, R 18 W); the feature is in Simi Hills. Altitude 2403 feet. Named on Thousand Oaks (1952) 7.5' quadrangle.

Simi Station [VENTURA]: *locality,* 6 miles east of Moorpark along Southern Pacific Railroad in the present city of Simi Valley (lat. 34°16'30" N, long. 118°46'35" W; at W line sec. 9, T 2 N, R 18 W). Named on Simi (1951) 7.5' quadrangle.

Simi Valley [VENTURA]:
(1) *valley,* west of Santa Susana Pass (center near lat. 34°16'30" N, long. 118°44'30" W). Named on Santa Susana (1951), Simi (1951), and Thousand Oaks (1952) 7.5' quadrangles.
(2) *city,* 32 miles east of Ventura in Simi Valley (1) (lat. 34°16'15" N, long. 118°43'15" W). Named on Los Angeles (1975) 1°x 2° quadrangle. The communities of Simi, Santa Susana, and Community Center combined in 1969 as the incorporated city of Simi Valley. The former community of Simi was in the east part of Simi Valley (1) (lat. 34°16'10" N, long. 118°46'50" W; at E line sec. 8, T 2 N, R 18 W) and is named on Simi (1951) 7.5' quadrangle. The former community of Santa Susana was in the west part of Simi Valley (1) (lat. 34°16'20" N, long. 118°42'30" W; on E line sec. 12, T 2 N, R 18 W) and is named on Santa Susana (1951) 7.5' quadrangle. The town of Community Center began about 1924 when schools and a church were established midway between the communities of Santa Susana and Simi (Ricard). Community Center was situated near the center of Simi Valley (1) (lat. 34°16'15" N, long. 118°44'10" W; sec. 11, T 2 N, R 18 W) and is named on Santa Susana (1951) 7.5' quadrangle—it is called Simi Valley Community on Santa Susana (1943) 15' quadrangle. Postal authorities established Simiopolis post office in 1889, changed the name to Simi the same year, and changed it to Simi Valley in 1971 (Salley, p. 205). They established Santa Susana post office in 1904 and it became a station of Simi Valley post office in 1971 (Salley, p. 198). They established Roblar post office 5 miles east of Simi post office in 1894 and discontinued it the same year (Salley, p. 187).

Simi Valley: see **Little Simi Valley** [VENTURA].

Simi Valley Community: see **Community Center**, under **Simi Valley** [VENTURA] (2).

Simon Canyon: see **Elderberry Canyon** [LOS ANGELES].

Simons [LOS ANGELES]: *locality,* 4.5 miles east-northeast of South Gate city hall along Atchison, Topeka and Santa Fe Railroad (lat. 33°59'15" N, long. 118°07'55" W). Named on South Gate (1952) 7.5' quadrangle. The name is from Walter Simons, who started a brickyard at the place in 1905 (Gudde, 1949, p. 333). Postal authorities established Simons post office in 1908 and discontinued it in 1934 (Salley, p. 205).

Singing Pines: see **Camp Singing Pines** [LOS ANGELES].

Singing Springs [LOS ANGELES]: *locality,* 5.25 miles east of Condor Peak along Mill Creek (lat. 34°19'15" N, long. 118°07'40" W). Named on Condor Peak (1959) 7.5' quadrangle.

Sinks: see **The Sinks** [ORANGE].

Siphon Reservoir [ORANGE]: *lake,* 1800 feet

168

long, 6 miles northwest of El Toro (lat. 33°42'40" N, long. 117°43'45" W). Named on El Toro (1968) 7.5' quadrangle.

Sisar Canyon [VENTURA]: *canyon*, 4.25 miles long, along Sisar Creek above a point 6.25 miles east of the town of Ojai (lat. 34°26'40" N, long. 119°08' W; sec. 12, T 4 N, R 22 W). Named on Ojai (1952) and Santa Paula Peak (1951) 7.5' quadrangles. The name is of Indian origin (Kroeber, p. 58).

Sisar Creek [VENTURA]: *stream*, flows 7.5 miles to Santa Paula Creek 4.25 miles west of Santa Paula Peak (lat. 34°25'35" N, long. 119°05'25" W). Named on Ojai (1952) and Santa Paula Peak (1951) 7.5' quadrangles.

Sister Elsie Peak: see **Mount Lukens** [LOS ANGELES].

Skeleton Canyon [VENTURA]: *canyon*, 2.5 miles long, opens into Russell Valley at Thousand Oaks (lat. 34°10'05" N, long. 118°49'30" W). Named on Thousand Oaks (1952) 7.5' quadrangle.

Slaughter Canyon [LOS ANGELES]: *canyon*, drained by a stream that flows 1 mile to Gold Canyon 5.5 miles north-northeast of Sunland (lat. 34°20'15" N, long. 118°17'10" W). Named on Sunland (1953) 7.5' quadrangle.

Slauson [LOS ANGELES]: *locality*, 4.25 miles east-northeast of present Inglewood city hall along Atchison, Topeka and Santa Fe Railroad (lat. 33°59'15" N, long. 118°17' W). Named on Redondo (1896) 15' quadrangle.

Slauson: see **Camp Slauson** [LOS ANGELES].

Sleeper Canyon [LOS ANGELES]: *canyon*, drained by a stream that flows 1 mile to Malibu Creek nearly 4 miles north-northwest of Malibu Point (lat. 34°04'55" N, long. 118°42'20" W; sec. 18, T 1 S, R 17 W). Named on Malibu Beach (1951) 7.5' quadrangle.

Sleepy Valley [LOS ANGELES]: *settlement*, 8.5 miles south-southwest of the village of Leona Valley in Mint Canyon (1) (lat. 34°30'35" N, long. 118°21'50" W; at NE cor. sec. 20, T 5 N, R 14 W). Named on Sleepy Valley (1958) 7.5' quadrangle.

Sloan Canyon [LOS ANGELES]: *canyon*, drained by a stream that flows 2.5 miles to Halsey Canyon 9 miles northwest of Newhall (lat. 34°27'45" N, long. 118°39'10" W; sec. 3, T 4 N, R 17 W). Named on Val Verde (1952) 7.5' quadrangle.

Smeltzer [ORANGE]: *locality*, 4.5 miles north of Huntington Beach civic center along Southern Pacific Railroad (lat. 33°43'45" N, long. 117°59'50" W; at N line sec. 23, T 5 S, R 11 W). Named on Newport Beach (1965) 7.5' quadrangle. Postal authorities established Smeltzer post office 2 miles south of Westminister post office in 1900 and discontinued it the same year; the name was for Daniel E. Smeltzer, first postmaster (Salley, p. 206)—Mr. Smeltzer introduced the raising of celery to the region in 1894, and the railroad siding at a packing house was named for him (Meadows, p. 130). Santa Ana (1942) 15' quadrangle shows a place called Sugar located along the railroad 0.5 mile north of Smeltzer.

Smith Canyon [LOS ANGELES]: *canyon*, drained by a stream that flows 2.25 miles to Romero Canyon 9.5 miles northwest of Newhall (lat. 34°28'20" N, long. 118°39'30" W). Named on Santa Susana (1943) 15' quadrangle.

Smith Canyon [VENTURA]: *canyon*, drained by a stream that flows 2 miles to the valley of Santa Clara River 1.5 miles south of Piru (lat. 34°23'30" N, long. 118°47'30" W; sec. 32, T 4 N, R 18 W). Named on Piru (1952) 7.5' quadrangle.

Smith Fork [VENTURA]: *stream*, flows 2.5 miles to Piru Creek 6.25 miles northeast of McDonald Peak (lat. 34°42'10" N, long. 118°52' W; sec. 14, T 7 N, R 19 W). Named on Black Mountain (1958) and McDonald Peak (1958) 7.5' quadrangles.

Smith Mountain [LOS ANGELES]: *peak*, nearly 3 miles south-southwest of Crystal Lake (lat. 34°16'55" N, long. 117°51'45" W). Altitude 5111 feet. Named on Crystal Lake (1958) 7.5' quadrangle. Gudde (1949, p. 335) used the form "Mount Smith" for the name.

Smugglers Cove: see **Pyramid Cove** [LOS ANGELES].

Snail Canyon [VENTURA]: *canyon*, drained by a stream that flows 4.5 miles to the canyon of Cuyama River 5 miles northwest of Reyes Peak (lat. 34°41'15" N, long. 119°20'15" W; sec. 20, T 7 N, R 23 W). Named on Reyes Peak (1943) 7.5' quadrangle.

Snover Canyon [LOS ANGELES]: *canyon*, 0.5 mile long, 7.25 miles northwest of Pasadena city hall (lat. 34°14' N, long. 118°13' W; sec. 26, 27, T 2 N, R 13 W). Named on Pasadena (1953) 7.5' quadrangle.

Snow Canyon [VENTURA]: *canyon*, drained by a stream that flows 2.25 miles to the valley of Santa Clara River 2.25 miles west-northwest of Fillmore (lat. 34°25'10" N, long. 118°56'45" W; sec. 23, T 4 N, R 20 W). Named on Fillmore (1951) 7.5' quadrangle.

Snowslide Canyon [LOS ANGELES]: *canyon*, drained by a stream that flows 1 mile to Pine Flats 1 mile northeast of Crystal Lake (lat. 34°19'45" N, long. 117°49'50" W). Named on Crystal Lake (1958) 7.5' quadrangle.

Snow Spring [LOS ANGELES]: *spring*, 1.25 miles north of Crystal Lake (lat. 34°20'20" N, long. 117°51'05" W). Named on Crystal Lake (1958) 7.5' quadrangle.

Snowy Creek [VENTURA]: *stream*, flows 7.5 miles to Piru Creek 6.25 miles northeast of McDonald Peak (lat. 34°41'35" N, long. 118°51'40" W; near S line sec. 14, T 7 N, R 19 W). Named on Black Mountain (1958) and McDonald Peak (1958) 7.5' quadrangles.

Snowy Forest Camp [VENTURA]: *locality*, 3 miles northeast of McDonald Peak (lat. 34°39'45" N, long. 118°54'15" W; near N line sec. 33, T 7 N, R 19 W); the place is along

Snowy Creek. Named on McDonald Peak (1958) 7.5' quadrangle.

Snowy Peak [VENTURA]: *peak,* 3 miles east-northeast of McDonald Peak (lat. 34°39' N, long. 118°53'15" W; near SW cor. sec. 34, T 7 N, R 19 W). Altitude 6559 feet. Named on McDonald Peak (1958) 7.5' quadrangle.

Solamint: see Solemint [LOS ANGELES].

Solano Ravine: see Chavez Ravine [LOS ANGELES].

Sold Canyon [LOS ANGELES]: *canyon,* drained by a stream that flows 1 mile to Pacoima Canyon 8 miles north-northeast of Sunland (lat. 34°22' N, long. 118°15'15" W). Named on Condor Peak (1959) and Sunland (1953) 7.5' quadrangles.

Soldier Creek [LOS ANGELES]: *stream,* flows 3 miles to join Coldbrook Creek and form North Fork San Gabriel River 2 miles south of Crystal Lake (lat. 34°17'25" N, long. 117°50'20" W). Named on Crystal Lake (1958) 7.5' quadrangle. United States Board on Geographic Names (1962, p. 16) rejected the name "North Fork San Gabriel River" for the stream.

Soldiers Home: see West Los Angeles [LOS ANGELES].

Soledad: see Ravenna [LOS ANGELES].

Soledad Campground [LOS ANGELES]: *locality,* 8.5 miles east of Solemint (lat. 34°26'25" N, long. 118°18'25" W; near E line sec. 11, T 4 N, R 14 W); the place is in Soledad Canyon. Named on Agua Dulce (1960) 7.5' quadrangle.

Soledad Canyon [LOS ANGELES]: *canyon,* 32 miles long, along Santa Clara River above a point 2.5 miles north of Newhall (lat. 34°25'30" N, long. 118°32'15" W). Named on Acton (1959), Agua Dulce (1960), Mint Canyon (1960), Newhall (1952), and Pacifico Mountain (1959) 7.5' quadrangles.

Soledad City: see Ravenna [LOS ANGELES].

Soledad Pass [LOS ANGELES]: *pass,* 5.5 miles south of Palmdale at Vincent (lat. 34°30' N, long. 118°06'55" W; sec. 22, 23, T 5 N, R 12 W); the pass is approached from the southwest by way of Soledad Canyon, but it is not at the head of that canyon. Named on Pacifico Mountain (1959) and Palmdale (1958) 7.5' quadrangles. Called Williamson's Pass on Blake's (1857) map, and called La Soledad Pass on Gray's (1873) map. Williamson (p. 30) called the feature New Pass.

Soledad Sulphur Springs [LOS ANGELES]: *locality,* 6 miles east of Solemint (lat. 34°26' N, long. 118°21'35" W; at W line sec. 16, T 4 N, R 14 W). Named on Lang (1933) 6' quadrangle.

Solemint [LOS ANGELES]: *town,* 9 miles north of San Fernando (lat. 34°25' N, long. 118°27'15" W; sec. 21, T 4 N, R 15 W); the place is at the junction of Soledad Canyon and Mint Canyon. Named on Mint Canyon (1960) 7.5' quadrangle. Called Solamint on Hum-

phreys (1932) 6' quadrangle. San Fernando (1900) 15' quadrangle has the name "Thompson" at the site. Los Angeles County (1935) map names four branches of Soledad Canyon near Solemint: Whites Canyon, which opens into Soledad Canyon from the northeast about 1 mile northwest of Solemint (sec. 17, T 4 N, R 15 W); Irwin Canyon, which opens into Soledad Canyon from the south about 1.5 miles west of Solemint (sec. 20, T 4 N, R 15 W); Suracco Canyon, which opens into Soledad Canyon from the south about 1 mile southwest of Solemint (near SE cor. sec. 20, T 4 N, R 15 W); and Nadeau Canyon, which opens into Soledad Canyon from the south 0.5 mile south-southwest of Solemint (at N line sec. 28, T 4 N, R 15 W).

Solromar [VENTURA]: *locality,* 5 miles south-southwest of Triunfo Pass along the coast (lat. 34°03' N, long. 118°57'15" W; on W line sec. 26, T 1 S, R 20 W). Named on Triunfo Pass (1950) 7.5' quadrangle. Postal authorities established Solromar post office in 1944 and discontinued it in 1956 (Salley, p. 207). The name was coined from *sol, oro,* and *mar*— the Spanish words for "sun," "gold," and "sea"—to suggest a golden sunset on the sea (Gudde, 1949, p. 338).

Solstice Canyon [LOS ANGELES]: *canyon,* drained by a stream that flows 4.5 miles to the sea 3.5 miles west of Malibu Point (lat. 34° 01'55" N, long. 118°44'30" W). Named on Malibu Beach (1951) and Point Dume (1951) 7.5' quadrangles.

Sombrero Canyon [LOS ANGELES]: *canyon,* 2 miles long, opens into lowlands 3.5 miles north-northwest of downtown San Fernando (lat. 34°19'45" N, long. 118°28'05" W near E line sec. 20, T 3 N, R 15 W). Named on San Fernando (1953) 7.5' quadrangle. West Fork branches northwest near the mouth of the main canyon; it is 1.25 miles long and is named on San Fernando (1966) 7.5' quadrangle.

Somerset: see Bellflower [LOS ANGELES].

Somis [VENTURA]: *town,* 7 miles west-southwest of Moorpark (lat. 34°15'25" N, long. 118°59'45" W). Named on Moorpark (1951) 7.5' quadrangle. Postal authorities established Somis post office in 1893 (Frickstad, p. 219). The name is of Indian origin (Kroeber, p. 59).

Sonome Canyon [LOS ANGELES-ORANGE]: *canyon,* drained by a stream that heads in Los Angeles County and flows 2.25 miles to Carbon Canyon 2.5 miles north-northeast of Yorba Linda in Orange County (lat. 33°55'40" N, long. 117°48' W; near W line sec. 11, T 3 S, R 9 W). Named on Yorba Linda (1950) 7.5' quadrangle.

Sopers Hot Springs [VENTURA]: *locality,* 4 miles northwest of Ojai (lat. 34°28'55" N, long. 119°17'25" W). Named on Ventura (1941) 15' quadrangle. Matilija (1952) 7.5' quadrangle shows Sopers ranch at or near the site.

Soquel Canyon [ORANGE]: *canyon,* drained by a stream that heads in San Bernardino County and flows 2.5 miles in Orange County to Carbon Canyon 2.5 miles north-northeast of Yorba Linda (lat. 33° 55'25" N, long. 117°48' W; at W line sec. 11, T 3 S, R 9 W). Named on Yorba Linda (1950) 7.5' quadrangle. Called Clapp Canon on Watts' (1898-1899) map.

Soto Street Junction [LOS ANGELES]: *locality,* nearly 3 miles south-southeast of Los Angeles city hall along Union Pacific Railroad (lat. 34°01'05" N, long. 118°13'05" W). Named on Los Angeles (1966) 7.5' quadrangle. Lankershim Ranch Land and Water Company's (1888) map shows a place called De Soto Heights located just east of downtown Los Angeles near present Soto Street Junction.

South Anaheim [ORANGE]: *locality,* 7 miles southeast of Buena Park civic center along Southern Pacific Railroad (lat. 33°48'30" N, long. 117°54' W; sec. 23, T 4 S, R 10 W). Named on Anaheim (1965) 7.5' quadrangle. Called Tustin Junction on Anaheim (1950) 7.5' quadrangle

South Clearwatrer: see Paramount [LOS ANGELES].

South El Monte [LOS ANGELES]: *town,* 2 miles southwest of El Monte city hall (lat. 34°03'10" N, long. 118°03'15" W). Named on El Monte (1966) 7.5' quadrangle. Postal authorities established South El Monte post office in 1958 (Salley, p. 208), and the town incorporated the same year.

South Fork Campground [LOS ANGELES]: *locality,* 4 miles south-southeast of Valyermo (lat. 34°23'40" N, long. 117°49'10" W; near NE cor. sec. 33, T 4 N, R 9 W); the place is along South Fork Big Rock Creek. Named on Valyermo (1958) 7.5' quadrangle.

South Gable Promontory: see Mount Harvard [LOS ANGELES].

South Gate [LOS ANGELES]: *city,* 12 miles north of Long Beach city hall (lat. 33°57'20" N, long. 118°12'15" W). Named on South Gate (1952) 7.5' quadrangle. Postal authorities established South Gate post office in 1923 (Salley, p. 209), and the city incorporated the same year. The place was named in 1918 from South Gate Gardens of Cudahy ranch, opened to the public in 1917 (Gudde, 1949, p. 340).

South Hills [LOS ANGELES]: *range,* 7 miles northwest of Pomona city hall (lat. 34°07'15" N, long. 117°50'45" W). Named on Glendora (1953) and San Dimas (1954) 7.5' quadrangles.

South Laguna [ORANGE]: *town,* 4.5 miles west of San Juan Capistrano (lat. 33°30' N, long. 117°44'30" W); the place is southeast of Laguna Beach along the coast. Named on Dana Point (1968) and San Juan Capistrano (1968) 7.5' quadrangles. Postal authorities established Three Arches post office in 1933 and changed

the name to South Laguna in 1934 (Frickstad, p. 118). The Whiting Company and Blanch L. Dolph started a subdivision at the place in 1927 (Meadows, p. 134).

South Long Canyon [LOS ANGELES]: *canyon,* drained by a stream that flows 2 miles to lowlands 5.5 miles northeast of Burnt Peak (lat. 34°44' N, long. 118°30'15" W; sec. 31, T 8 N, R 15 W); the canyon is less than 1 mile south of North Long Canyon. Named on Burnt Peak (1958) 7.5' quadrangle.

South Los Angeles [LOS ANGELES]: (1) *district,* 3.5 miles south-southwest of present Los Angeles city hall (lat. 34°00'10" N, long. 118°15'20" W). Named on Santa Monica (1902) 15' quadrangle. Postal authorities established South Los Angeles post office in 1891 and discontinued it in 1897 (Frickstad, p. 81).
(2) *locality,* 5 miles east-southeast of Inglewood city hall along Southern Pacific Railroad (lat. 33°55'40" N, long. 118°16'35" W). Named on Inglewood (1964, photorevised 1981) 7.5' quadrangle.

South Mountain [VENTURA]: *ridge,* generally southwest-trending, 9.5 miles long, center 2.25 miles south of Santa Paula (lat. 34°19'15" N, long. 119°03'30" W). Named on Moorpark (1951) and Santa Paula (1951) 7.5' quadrangles.

South Mount Hawkins [LOS ANGELES]: *peak,* 2 miles east-southeast of Crystal Lake (lat. 34°18'40" N, long. 117°48'35" W); the peak is 2 miles south of Mount Hawkins. Altitude 7783 feet. Named on Crystal Lake (1958) 7.5' quadrangle.

South Pasadena [LOS ANGELES]: *city,* 7 miles northeast of Los Angeles city hall (lat. 34°06'55" N, long. 118°09'05" W); the city is south of Pasadena. Named on Los Angeles (1953) 7.5' quadrangle. Postal authorities established Hermosa post office in 1882 and changed the name to South Pasadena in 1884 (Salley, p. 96). The city incorporated in 1888. The name "Hermosa" was from Hermosa Vista Hotel, where Hermosa post office was located (Hanna, p. 312).

South Portal: see South Portal Canyon [LOS ANGELES].

South Portal Campground [LOS ANGELES]: *locality,* 3.5 miles south of the village of Lake Hughes (lat. 34°37'20" N, long. 118° 26'30" W); the place is in South Portal Canyon. Named on Green Valley (1958) 7.5' quadrangle.

South Portal Canyon [LOS ANGELES]: *canyon,* drained by a stream that flows 3.5 miles to San Francisquito Canyon 4.5 miles south of the village of Lake Hughes (lat. 34°36'35" N, long. 118°26'15" W). Named on Green Valley (1958) and Lake Hughes (1957) 7.5' quadrangles. Called Bear Canyon on Elizabeth Lake (1917) 30' quadrangle. Johnson'a (1911) map shows an inhabited place called

South Portal situated in the canyon near the south end of a tunnel along the aqueduct that brings Owens Valley water from Inyo County to Los Angeles.

South San Gabriel [LOS ANGELES]: *town,* 4 miles west of El Monte city hall (lat. 34°03'45" N, long. 118°05'55" W); the town is south of San Gabriel. Named on El Monte (1953) 7.5' quadrangle, which gives the alternate name "Garvey" for the place. Postal authorities established Garvey Avenue post office in 1925, changed the name to Gavey in 1930, and discontinued it in 1952 (Salley, p. 83). They established South San Gabriel post office in 1938, discontinued it in 1948, and reestablished it in 1949 (Salley, p. 209). The name "Garvey" commemorates Richard Garvey, who started a subdivision of small farms and homesites at present South San Gabriel (Hanna, p. 118).

South San Jose Creek [LOS ANGELES]: *stream,* flows 2.5 miles to San Jose Creek nearly 5 miles west-southwest of Pomona city hall (lat. 34°01'40" N, long. 117°49'45" W). Named on San Dimas (1966) 7.5' quadrangle. Called San Jose Creek on San Dimas (1954) 7.5' quadrangle, but United States Board on Geographic Names (1967b, p. 5) rejected this name.

South Santa Ana [ORANGE]: *locality,* 2.5 miles south of Santa Ana city hall along Southern Pacific Railroad (lat. 33°42'40" N, long. 117°52'05" W). Named on Tustin (1965) 7.5' quadrangle.

South Santa Monica [LOS ANGELES]: *locality,* 8.5 miles north-northwest of present Manhattan Beach city hall along Atchison, Topeka and Santa Fe Railroad (lat. 34°00' N, long. 118°29' W). Named on Redondo (1896) 15' quadrangle.

South Tapo Canyon: see **Tapo Canyon** [VENTURA] (1).

South Tule Canyon [LOS ANGELES]: *canyon,* drained by a stream that flows 2.5 miles to Tule Canyon 4.5 miles east-northeast of Warm Springs Mountain (lat. 34°36'40" N, long. 118°30'05" W). Named on Green Valley (1958) and Warm Springs Mountain (1958) 7.5' quadrangles.

Southwest Village [LOS ANGELES]: *locality,* nearly 2 miles east-northeast of Torrance city hall (lat. 33°50'45" N, long. 118°18'35" W). Named on Torrance (1964) 7.5' quadrangle.

South Whittier [LOS ANGELES]: *district,* 1 mile south-southwest of present Whittier city hall (lat. 33°57'35" N, long. 118°02'30" W). Named on Whittier (1949) 7.5' quadrangle. Postal authorities established South Whittier post office in 1964 (Salley, p. 209).

South Whittier Heights [LOS ANGELES]: *district,* 3.5 miles south of present Whittier city hall (lat. 33°55'15" N, long. 118°01'30" W). Named on Whittier (1949) 7.5' quadrangle.

Spade Canyon [LOS ANGELES]: *canyon,* drained by a stream that flows 2.5 miles to

Rowher Canyon 8 miles south-southwest of the village of Leona Valley (lat. 34°31' N, long. 118°21'45" W; near E line sec. 17, T 5 N, R 14 W). Named on Sleepy Valley (1958) 7.5' quadrangle. On Los Angeles County (1935) map, the name "Spade Canyon" applies to present Spade Spring Canyon.

Spade Spring Canyon [LOS ANGELES]: *canyon,* drained by a stream that flows 4.5 miles to Mint Canyon 8 miles south-southwest of the village of Leona Valley (lat. 34°30'40" N, long. 118°21'25" W; at S line sec. 16, T 5 N, R 14 W). Named on Sleepy Valley (1958) 7.5' quadrangle. Called Spring Canyon on Bouquet Reservoir (1937) 6' quadrangle, but United States Board on Geographic Names (1959, p. 7) rejected this name for the feature. Called Spade Canyon on Los Angeles County (1935) map.

Spadra [LOS ANGELES]:
(1) *locality,* 3.25 miles west of Pomona city hall along Southern Pacific Railroad (lat. 34°03'05" N, long. 117°48'30" W). Named on San Dimas (1954) 7.5' quadrangle. Postal authorities established Spadra post office in 1868, discontinued it for a time in 1875, and discontinued it finally in 1955 (Salley, p. 210). Billy Rubotton built a tavern at the place in 1866 and applied for a post office named from his former home at Spadra Bluff, Arkansas (Anonymous, 1976, p. 13-14). The railroad station at the place took the name in 1874 (Gudde, 1949, p. 340).
(2) *locality,* nearly 3 miles west of Pomona city hall along Union Pacific Railroad (lat. 34°03'10" N, long. 117°48' W). Named on San Dimas (1966) 7.5' quadrangle.

Spanish Canyon [LOS ANGELES]: *canyon,* drained by a stream that flows 2 miles to Sawpit Canyon 5.5 miles west-northwest of Azusa city hall (lat. 34°10'05" N, long. 117°59'25" W; sec. 13, T 1 N, R 11 W). Named on Azusa (1953) 7.5' quadrangle.

Spanishtown [LOS ANGELES]: *locality,* 2.25 miles north-northwest of present South Gate city hall (lat. 33°59'30" N, long. 118°14'20" W). Named on Downey (1902) 15' quadrangle.

Sparr Heights [LOS ANGELES]: *locality,* 5.5 miles northwest of Pasadena city hall (lat. 34°11'45" N, long. 118°13'30" W). Named on Glendale (1928) 6' quadrangle.

Spencer Canyon [LOS ANGELES]: *canyon,* 2.5 miles long, opens into lowlands 15 miles east of Gorman (lat. 34°45'35" N, long. 118°34'30" W; at N line sec. 28, T 8 N, R 16 W). Named on Burnt Peak (1958) and Neenach School (1965) 7.5' quadrangles. Manzana (1938) 6' quadrangle shows Spencer ranch in the canyon.

Spinks Canyon [LOS ANGELES]: *canyon,* drained by a stream that flows 1.25 miles to Scott Canyon 3.5 miles west-northwest of Azusa city hall (lat. 34°08'55" N, long.

117°57'45" W). Named on Azusa (1953) 7.5' quadrangle.

Spouting Caves [LOS ANGELES]: *caves,* 5.5 miles north-northwest of Mount Banning along the north side of Santa Catalina Island (lat. 33°26'40" N, long. 118°28'30" W). Named on Santa Catalina North (1950) 7.5' quadrangle.

Spring Camp [LOS ANGELES]: *locality,* 7 miles northwest of Azusa city hall (lat. 34°12'50" N, long. 117°58'40" W; at E line sec. 36, T 2 N, R 11 W). Named on Azusa (1953) 7.5' quadrangle. The camp, which appears to date from the early 1900's, is named from an ever-flowing spring there (Owens, p. 53).

Spring Canyon [LOS ANGELES]:
(1) *canyon,* drained by a stream that flows 1 mile to Kings Canyon 3.5 miles northeast of Burnt Peak (lat. 34°43'05" N, long. 118°31'55" W; sec. 12, T 7 N, R 16 W). Named on Burnt Peak (1958) 7.5' quadrangle.
(2) *canyon,* drained by a stream that flows 2.5 miles to Tapie Canyon 4.5 miles east-northeast of Solemint (lat. 34°26'10" N, long. 118°22'35" W; near NW cor. sec. 17, T 4 N, R 14 W). Named on Agua Dulce (1960) 7.5' quadrangle.
(3) *canyon,* less than 0.5 mile long, about 3 miles east of Glendora city hall (lat. 34°07'50" N, long. 117°48'45" W; sec. 34, T 1 N, R 9 W). Named on Glendora (1953) 7.5' quadrangle.
(4) *canyon,* 0.5 mile long, 3.5 miles south-southeast of Burbank city hall (lat. 34°07'55" N, long. 118°17'35" W). Named on Burbank (1953) 7.5' quadrangle.

Spring Canyon [ORANGE]: *canyon,* drained by a stream that flows 0.5 mile to Williams Canyon 7.5 miles north-northeast of El Toro (lat. 33°43'45" N, long. 117°38'40" W; at S line sec. 18, T 5 S, R 7 W). Named on El Toro (1968) 7.5' quadrangle.

Spring Canyon: see **Spade Spring Canyon** [LOS ANGELES]; **Spring Creek** [LOS ANGELES].

Spring Canyon Creek [VENTURA]: *stream,* flows 2.5 miles to Tar Creek 6.5 miles north of Fillmore (lat. 34°29'40" N, long. 118°53'40" W; near N line sec. 29, T 5 N, R 19 W). Named on Devils Heart Peak (1943) and Fillmore (1951) 7.5' quadrangles. Called North Fork Tar Cr. on Tejon (1903) 30' quadrangle, but United States Board on Geographic Names (1990, p. 11) rejected this name for the feature.

Spring Creek [LOS ANGELES]: *stream,* flows nearly 2 miles to Pacoima Canyon 7.25 miles north of Sunland (lat. 34°21'55" N, long. 118°18'30" W; at NE cor. sec. 11, T 3 N, R 14 W). Named on Agua Dulce (1960) and Sunland (1953) 7.5' quadrangles. The canyon of the stream is called Spring Canyon on Los Angeles County (1935) map.

Spring Hill [LOS ANGELES]: *relief feature,* nearly 12 miles north-northeast of Pomona city hall (lat. 34°12'35" N, long. 117°40'05" W; sec. 36, T 2 N, R 8 W). Named on Mount Baldy (1954) 7.5' quadrangle.

Spring Landing [LOS ANGELES]: *locality,* nearly 1 mile southwest of Silver Peak on the south side of Santa Catalina Island (lat. 33° 27'05" N, long. 118°34'50" W). Named on Santa Catalina West (1943) 7.5' quadrangle.

Springs: see **Sulphur Springs** [VENTURA].

Springs Canyon: see **Little Springs Canyon** [LOS ANGELES].

Springville [VENTURA]: *locality,* 3.25 miles west of downtown Camarillo (lat. 34°13'15" N, long. 119°05'25" W). Named on Camarillo (1950) 7.5' quadrangle. Postal authorities established Springville post office in 1875 and discontinued it in 1903 (Frickstad, p. 219).

Spruce Canyon [LOS ANGELES]: *canyon,* drained by a stream that flows 1.25 miles to San Antonio Canyon 10 miles north-northeast of Pomona city hall (lat. 34°11'15" N, long. 117°40'30" W; sec. 12, T 1 N, R 8 W). Named on Mount Baldy (1954) 7.5' quadrangle.

Spruce Canyon [ORANGE]: *canyon,* drained by a stream that flows less than 1 mile to Silverado Canyon 4.25 miles southeast of Pleasants Peak (lat. 33°45'05" N, long. 117°33'05" W. Named on Corona South (1967) and Santiago Peak (1954) 7.5' quadrangles.

Spruce Draw [LOS ANGELES]: *canyon,* drained by a stream that flows 0.5 mile to South Portal Canyon 2.5 miles southeast of the village of Lake Hughes (lat. 34°38'50" N, long. 118°25'05" W; near S line sec. 36, T 7 N, R 15 W). Named on Lake Hughes (1957) 7.5' quadrangle.

Spruce Grove Campground [LOS ANGELES]: *locality,* nearly 2 miles east of Mount Wilson (1) in Santa Anita Canyon (lat. 34°13'15" N, long. 118°01'45" W; near NW cor. sec. 34, T 2 N, R 11 W). Named on Mount Wilson (1966) 7.5' quadrangle.

Spunky Canyon [LOS ANGELES]: *canyon,* drained by a stream that flows nearly 3 miles to Bouquet Reservoir 6.5 miles south-southeast of the village of Lake Hughes (lat. 34°35'35" N, long. 118°22'55" W; sec. 20, T 6 N, R 14 W). Named on Green Valley (1958) and Sleepy Valley (1958) 7.5' quadrangles.

Spunky Canyon Campground [LOS ANGELES]: *locality,* 5.25 miles south-southeast of the village of Lake Hughes (lat. 34°36'35" N, long. 118°23'25" W; near W line sec. 17, T 6 N, R 14 W); the place is nearly 1 mile northwest of Spunky Canyon. Named on Green Valley (1958) 7.5' quadrangle.

Square Top: see **Mount Markham** [LOS ANGELES].

Squatters Country: see **Fountain Valley** [ORANGE].

Squaw Camp: see **Camp Singing Pines** [LOS ANGELES].

Squaw Canyon [LOS ANGELES]: *canyon,* drained by a stream that flows 3.5 miles to South Fork Little Rock Creek 8.5 miles southwest of Valyermo (lat. 34°22'35" N, long. 117°58'25" W; near W line sec. 6, T 3 N, R 10 W). Named on Juniper Hills (1959) and Waterman Mountain (1959) 7.5' quadrangles.

Squaw Flat [VENTURA]: *area,* 4.5 miles east of Devils Heart Peak (lat. 34°32'20" N, long. 118°53'45" W). Named on Devils Heart Peak (1943) 7.5' quadrangle.

Squaw Spring [VENTURA]: *spring,* 4.5 miles east of Devils Heart Peak (lat. 34°32'10" N, long. 118°53'50" W); the spring is at Squaw Flat. Named on Devils Heart Peak (1943) 7.5' quadrangle.

Squirrel Inn [LOS ANGELES]: *locality,* 2 miles south-southeast of Crystal Lake along North Fork San Gabriel River (lat. 34°17'30" N, long. 117°50'30" W; near N line sec. 5, T 2 N, R 9 W). Named on Rock Creek (1903) 15' quadrangle.

Stanton [ORANGE]: *town,* 4 miles south of Buena Park civic center (lat. 33°48'10" N, long. 117°59'45" W). Named on Anaheim (1965) and Los Alamitos (1964) 7.5' quadrangles. Postal authorities established Stanton post office in 1912 and discontinued it for a time in 1921 (Frickstad, p. 118). The town incorporated in 1956. California Mining Bureau's (1909b) map shows a place called Benedict at the site. The crossing of Pacific Electric Railroad and Southern Pacific Railroad at the place was called Benedict; Philip A Stanon laid out a subdivision called Benedict there in 1905, and later the community of Stanton was named for him (Meadows, p. 26, 131). A flag stop along Pacific Electric Railroad called Vignola was situated less than 1 mile east-southeast of present Stanton city hall (Meadows, p. 137).

Star Bay [LOS ANGELES]: *embayment,* 1.25 miles west of Silver Peak on the south side of Santa Catalina Island (lat. 33°27'40" N, long. 118°35'20" W). Named on Santa Catalina West (1943) 7.5' quadrangle.

Stauffer [VENTURA]: *locality,* 15 miles northeast of Reyes Peak in Lockwood Valley (lat. 34°45'15" N, long. 119°03'55" W; on E line sec. 26, T 8 N, R 21 W). Named on Cuddy Valley (1943) 7.5' quadrangle. Postal authorities established Stauffer post office in 1905, discontinued it in 1933, reestablished it in 1937, and discontinued it in 1942 (Frickstad, p. 219). The name was for John Stauffer, who with Thomas Thorkildsen formed Frazier Borate Company and had the company camp and store at the place (Bailey, p. 63).

Stearn: see **Yorba Linda** [ORANGE].

Steep Hill Canyon [LOS ANGELES]: *canyon,* drained by a stream that flows 1.25 miles to the sea 4 miles northwest of Point Dume (lat. 34°02'10" N, long. 118°51'30" W). Named on Point Dume (1951) 7.5' quadrangle.

Steil's Camp: see **Martins Camp** [LOS ANGELES]; **Mount Harvard** [LOS ANGELES].

Steiner Canyon [LOS ANGELES]: *canyon,* drained by a stream that flows less than 1 mile to Pine Canyon (3) 3 miles west-northwest of the village of Lake Hughes (lat. 34°41'35" N, long. 118°29'30" W; sec. 17, T 7 N, R 15 W). Named on Lake Hughes (1957) 7.5' quadrangle.

Sterling: see **Camp Sterling** [LOS ANGELES].

Stevens Canyon: see **Halsey Canyon** [LOS ANGELES].

Stewart: see **Brea** [ORANGE]:

Stewart Canyon [VENTURA]: *canyon,* drained by a stream that flows nearly 3 miles to Ojai Valley 1.25 miles north-northwest of downtown Ojai (lat. 34°27'40" N, long. 119°15'10" W; near N line sec. 2, T 4 N, R 23 W). Named on Matilija (1952) 7.5' quadrangle.

Stewart Peak: see **Sewart Mountain** [VENTURA].

Stingleys Hot Springs: see **Vickers Hot Springs** [VENTURA].

Stockton Canyon: see **Canton Canyon** [LOS ANGELES-VENTURA].

Stokes Canyon [LOS ANGELES]: *canyon,* drained by a stream that flows 4.25 miles to Las Virgenes Creek 5 miles north-northwest of Malibu Point (lat. 34°05'45" N, long. 118°43' W; sec. 12, T 1 S, R 18 W). Named on Malibu Beach (1951) 7.5' quadrangle. Los Angeles County (1935) map shows a feature called Hoagland Cany. that opens into Stokes Canyon from the north 1.5 miles northeast of the mouth of Stokes Canyon (at W line sec. 5, T 1 S, R 17 W).

Stone Cabin Flat [LOS ANGELES]: *area,* 5.5 miles north-northwest of Azusa city hall (lat. 34°12'20" N, long. 117°56'45" W; near NE cor. sec. 5, T 21 N, R 10 W). Named on Azusa (1966) 7.5' quadrangle. Azusa (1953) 7.5' quadrangle shows a feature called Stone Cabin at the site. The name is from the cabin that Hardy Harris and several school boys built in 1911 using boulders from the bed of the nearby stream (Robinson, J.W., 1983, p. 78).

Stone Canyon [LOS ANGELES]:
(1) *canyon,* drained by a stream that flows 1.25 miles to Big Tujunga Canyon 2.5 miles southsouthwest of Condor Peak (lat. 34°17'35" N, long. 118°14'10" W; at W line sec. 3, T 2 N, R 13 W). Named on Condor Peak (1959) 7.5' quadrangle.
(2) *canyon,* 3 miles long, 3.5 miles west-northwest of Beverly Hills city hall (lat. 34°06' N, long. 118°27'15" W). Named on Beverly Hills (1950) 7.5' quadrangle.

Stone Canyon Reservoir [LOS ANGELES]: *lake,* nearly 1 mile long, behind a dam 4 miles northwest of Beverly Hills city hall (lat. 34°06'15" N, long. 118°27'05" W); the lake is in Stone Canyon (2). Named on Beverly Hills (1950) 7.5' quadrangle.

Stone Canyon Reservoir: see **Upper Stone Canyon Reservoir** [LOS ANGELES].

Stone Corral Creek [VENTURA]: *stream,* flows nearly 4 miles to Sespe Creek 2 miles east-northeast of Devils Heart Peak (lat. 34° 33'25" N, long. 118°56'35" W). Named on Devils Heart Peak (1943) 7.5' quadrangle. Tejon (1903) 30' quadrangle shows a feature called Stone Corral located along upper reaches of the stream.

Stonehurst [LOS ANGELES]: *district,* 3.5 miles west-southwest of Sunland (lat. 34°15' N, long. 118°22'15" W). Named on Burbank (1953) and Sunland (1953) 7.5' quadrangles.

Stoneman [LOS ANGELES]: *locality,* 5.5 miles west-northwest of El Monte city hall along Southern Pacific Railroad (lat. 34°05'20" N, long. 118°07'15" W). Named on El Monte (1953) 7.5' quadrangle.

Stone Quarry Hills: see **Chavez Ravine** [LOS ANGELES].

Stony Gulch: see **Camp Hi-Hill** [LOS ANGELES].

Stony Point [LOS ANGELES]:
(1) *hill,* 1 mile north of Chatsworth (lat. 34°16'15" N, long. 118°36'10" W; near W line sec. 7, T 2 N, R 16 W). Named on Oat Mountain (1952) 7.5' quadrangle.
(2) *promontory,* 1.25 miles northeast of Silver Peak on the north side of Santa Catalina Island (lat. 33°28'30" N, long. 118°33'20" W). Named on Santa Catalina West (1943) 7.5' quadrangle.

Stony Point: see **Arrow Point** [LOS ANGELES].

Story Canyon [LOS ANGELES]: *canyon,* 0.5 mile long, 1.5 miles northeast of Burbank city hall (lat. 34°11'45" N, long. 118°17'20" W). Named on Burbank (1953) 7.5' quadrangle.

Stough Canyon [LOS ANGELES]: *canyon,* 1.5 miles long, 2 miles north of Burbank city hall (lat. 34°12'30" N, long. 118°18'10" W). Named on Burbank (1953) 7.5' quadrangle.

Strathearn [VENTURA]: *locality,* 4.5 miles east of Moorpark along Southern Pacific Railroad (lat. 34°16'50" N, long. 118°47'45" W; near SE cor. sec. 6, T 2 N, R 18 W). Named on Simi (1951) 7.5' quadrangle. The name is for the Strathearn family, owners of part of Simi grant (Ricard).

Strawberry Park [LOS ANGELES]: *district,* 5.25 miles southeast of Inglewood city hall (lat. 33°54' N, long. 118°18' W). Named on Inglewood (1952) 7.5' quadrangle. Redondo (1896) 15' quadrangle has the name for a place located along a railroad in or near the district.

Strawberry Peak [LOS ANGELES]: *peak,* 8.5 miles south-southwest of Pacifico Mountain (lat. 34°17' N, long. 118°07'10" W). Altitude 6164 feet. Named on Chilao Flat (1959) 7.5' quadrangle. The name, given in the 1880's, is from the shape of the peak (Robinson, J.W., 1977, p. 155).

Strayns Canyon [LOS ANGELES]: *canyon,*

drained by a stream that flows 2.25 miles to West Fork San Gabriel River 1.5 miles north of Mount Wilson (lat. 34°14'55" N, long. 118°03'30" W; sec. 20, T 2 N, R 11 W). Named on Mount Wilson (1953) 7.5' quadrangle.

Stringtown: see **Bardsdale** [VENTURA].

Studebaker [LOS ANGELES]: *locality,* 5.5 miles southwest of present Whittier city hall (lat. 33°55'25" N, long. 118°06'20" W). Named on Whittier (1949) 7.5' quadrangle. On Downey (1902) 15' quadrangle, the name refers to a place along Southern Pacific Railroad.

Studio City [LOS ANGELES]: *district,* 4 miles southeast of the center of Van Nuys in Los Angeles (lat. 34°08'50" N, long. 118°23'45" W). Named on Van Nuys (1953) 7.5' quadrangle. Postal authorities established Studio City post office in 1928; the name is from Republic movie studio (Salley, p. 214).

Sturtevant Camp [LOS ANGELES]: *locality,* 1.5 miles east of Mount Wilson (1) in Santa Anita Canyon (lat. 34°13'20" N, long. 118°02'05" W; near N line sec. 33, T 2 N, R 11 W). Named on Mount Wilson (1953) 7.5' quadrangle. The name commemorates William M. Sturtevant, who opened the resort in 1893; the Methodist Church bought the place in 1945 and operated it as a religious retreat called Camp Sturtevant (Robinson, J.W., 1977, p. 119, 125).

Sturtevant Falls [LOS ANGELES]: *waterfall,* 2.5 miles east-southeast of Mount Wilson (1) in Santa Anita Canyon (lat. 34°12'40" N, long. 118°01'05" W; sec. 34, T 2 N, R 11 W). Named on Mount Wilson (1953) 7.5' quadrangle. The feature first was called Santa Anita Falls (Owens, p. 1).

Sucrosa [VENTURA]: *locality,* 2.5 miles west-southwest of Camarillo along Southern Pacific Railroad (lat. 34°11'40" N, long. 119° 04'20" W). Named on Hueneme (1904) 15' quadrangle.

Sugar: see **Smeltzer** [ORANGE].

Sugarloaf [LOS ANGELES]: *peak,* nearly 4 miles east-northeast of downtown San Fernando (lat. 34°18'40" N, long. 118°23' W; sec. 30, T 3 N, R 14 W). Named on San Fernando (1966) 7.5' quadrangle.

Sugarloaf [ORANGE]: *peak,* 5.25 miles south of Trabuco Peak (lat. 33°37'35" N, long. 117°28'50" W; near W line sec. 23, T 6 S, R 6 W). Altitude 3227 feet. Named on Alberhill (1954) 7.5' quadrangle.

Sugarloaf Peak: see **Pleasants Peak** [ORANGE].

Sugarloaf Point [ORANGE]: *promontory,* 2 miles south-southeast of Laguna Beach city hall along the coast (lat. 33°31'10" N, long. 117°45'45" W; on E line sec. 36, T 7 S, R 9 W). Named on Laguna Beach (1965) 7.5' quadrangle.

Sugarloaf Point: see **Casino Point** [LOS ANGELES].

Sullivan Canyon [LOS ANGELES]: *canyon,* drained by a stream that flows 5.25 miles to Santa Monica Canyon 5.5 miles west of Beverly Hills city hall (lat. 34°03'40" N, long. 118°29'40" W). Named on Beverly Hills (1950), Canoga Park (1952), and Topanga (1952) 7.5' quadrangles.

Sullivans Beach [LOS ANGELES]: *beach,* 2.5 miles east of Silver Peak on the north side of Santa Catalina Island (lat. 33°27'40" N, long. 118°31'15" W). Named on Santa Catalina West (1943) 7.5' quadrangle.

Sulphur Canyon [LOS ANGELES]: *canyon,* drained by a stream that flows 2 miles to Las Llajas Canyon [LOS ANGELES-VENTURA] 7.5 miles west-southwest of Newhall (lat. 34°19'40" N, long. 118°38'20" W). Named on Oat Mountain (1952) and Santa Susana (1951) 7.5' quadrangles

Sulphur Canyon [VENTURA]: *canyon,* drained by a stream that flows 3 miles to Cañada Larga 8 miles northwest of Saticoy (lat. 34°22'05" N, long. 119°14'15" W); the canyon heads on Sulphur Mountain (1). Named on Ojai (1952) and Saticoy (1951) 7.5' quadrangles.

Sulphur Canyon: see **Balcom Canyon** [VENTURA].

Sulphur Creek [ORANGE]: *stream,* flows 4.5 miles to Aliso Creek 4.5 miles northwest of San Juan Capistrano (lat. 33°33' N, long. 117°43'05" W). Named on San Juan Capistrano (1968) 7.5' quadrangle. Santiago Peak (1943) 15' quadrangle has the name "Arroyo Salada" for the canyon of the upper part of the stream, and Corona (1902) 30' quadrangle has the name "Canada Salada" for it.

Sulphur Creek [VENTURA]:

(1) *stream,* flows 3 miles to Agua Blanca Creek 4.5 miles southeast of Cobblestone Mountain (lat. 34°33'05" N, long. 118°49'25" W). Named on Cobblestone Mountain (1958) 7.5' quadrangle.

(2) *stream,* flows 1 mile to Rincon Creek 5 miles south-southwest of White Ledge Peak (lat. 34°24'35" N, long. 119°26'40" W; sec. 24, T 4 N, R 25 W). Named on White Ledge Peak (1952) 7.5' quadrangle.

Sulphur Creek Reservoir [ORANGE]: *lake,* 0.5 mile long, behind a dam 4.25 miles northwest of San Juan Capistrano (lat. 33°33' N, long. 117°42'25" W); the lake is along Sulphur Creek. Named on San Juan Capistrano (1968) 7.5' quadrangle.

Sulphur Mountain [VENTURA]:

(1) *ridge,* generally west-trending, 13 miles long, extends from Santa Paula Creek to Ventura River, mainly south of Ojai Valley and Upper Ojai Valley (center near lat. 34°24'45" N, long. 119°11'30" W). Named on Matilija (1952), Ojai (1952), and Santa Paula Peak (1951) 7.5' quadrangles. Goodyear (1888, p. 109) noted that the feature "is well named on account of the numerous sulphur springs on all sides of it."

(2) *peak,* 3.5 miles west of Piru (lat. 34°25' N, long. 118°51'15" W; sec. 22, T 4 N, R 19 W). Altitude 2130 feet. Named on Piru (1952) 7.5' quadrangle.

Sulphur Mountain Spring: see **Sulphur Springs** [VENTURA].

Sulphur Peak [VENTURA]: *peak,* 3.5 miles east-southeast of Devils Heart Peak (lat. 34°31'05" N, long. 118°55'30" W). Altitude 4528 feet. Named on Devils Heart Peak (1943) 7.5' quadrangle.

Sulphur Ravine: see **Chavez Ravine** [LOS ANGELES].

Sulphur Spring [LOS ANGELES]: *spring,* 3.5 miles northwest of Waterman Mountain (lat. 34°22' N, long. 117°59'10" W; near N line sec. 12, T 3 N, R 11 W). Named on Waterman Mountain (1959) 7.5' quadrangle. Los Angeles County (1935) map has the plural name "Sulphur Springs" for the name.

Sulphur Spring [VENTURA]: *spring,* 2 miles northeast of Ojai (lat. 34°28'10" N, long. 119°13'15" W; sec. 31, T 5 N, R 22 W). Named on Santa Paula (1903) 15' quadrangle.

Sulphur Spring Canyon [VENTURA]: *canyon,* drained by a stream that flows 5 miles to Dry Canyon (2) 4.5 miles north of Reyes Peak (lat. 34°41'45" N, long. 119°17'10" W). Named on Apache Canyon (1943) and Reyes Peak (1943) 7.5' quadrangles.

Sulphur Springs [LOS ANGELES]: *locality,* 8 miles northwest of Newhall (lat. 34°28'40" N, long. 118°36'50" W; sec. 36, T 5 N, R 17 W). Named on Newhall (1952) 7.5' quadrangle. Castaic (1940) 6' quadrangle shows a place called Foothill Sta. near the site.

Sulphur Springs [VENTURA]: *locality,* 5 miles west of Santa Paula Peak along Sisar Creek (lat. 34°25'40" N, long. 119°05'40" W). Named on Santa Paula Peak (1951) 7.5' quadrangle. Santa Paula (1903) 15' quadrangle has the name "Sulphur Mt. Spring" for a spring at or near the place. Postal authorities established Springs post office at the site in 1909 and discontinued it in 1912 (Salley, p. 210). Crawford (p. 524) called the place Santa Paula Sulphur Springs, and Waring (p. 279) called it Sulphur Mountain Springs.

Sulphur Wells: see **Santa Fe Springs** [LOS ANGELES].

Summit [LOS ANGELES]: *locality,* 8.5 miles west-southwest of Palmdale (lat. 34°31'20" N, long. 118°14'45" W; sec. 16, T 5 N, R 13 W). Named on Ritter Ridge (1958) 7.5' quadrangle.

Summit Reservoir [LOS ANGELES]: *lake,* 350 feet long, 5.25 miles north-northwest of Mount Banning on Santa Catalina Island (lat. 33°26'15" N, long. 118°28'50" W). Named on Santa Catalina North (1950) 7.5' quadrangle.

Sun Garden Village [ORANGE]: *locality,* 6.5 miles south of present Buena Park civic center (lat. 33°46'20" N, long. 117°58'45" W; near

N line sec. 1, T 5 S, R 11 W). Named on Anaheim (1950) 7.5' quadrangle.

Sunland [LOS ANGELES]: *district,* 7 miles east of San Fernando in Los Angeles (lat. 34°15'35" N, long. 118°18'40" W). Named on Sunland (1953) 7.5' quadrangle. Postal authorities established Sunland post office in 1887 (Frickstad, p. 82).

Sunny Hills [ORANGE]: *district,* 2.25 miles south-southeast of downtown La Habra in Fullerton (lat. 33°54'05" N, long. 117° 56' W). Named on La Habra (1964) 7.5' quadrangle. Postal authorities established Sunny Hills post office in 1969 (Salley, p. 215). La Habra (1952) 7.5' quadrangle shows Sunny Hills ranch at the place, and Coyote Hills (1935) 7.5' quadrangle shows Bastanchury ranch there. Sunny Hills Ranch Company bought Bastanchury ranch and subdivided it in 1940 (Gudde, 1949, p. 347). Pacific Electric Railroad had a station called Bastanchury that was named for Domingo Bastanchury, who owned 6000 acres of land north of Fullerton (Meadows, p. 24).

Sunnyside [LOS ANGELES]: *locality,* 4 miles east-southeast of present Inglewood city hall along a railroad (lat. 33°56'35" N, long. 118°17'30" W). Named on Redondo (1896) 15' quadrangle.

Sunny Slope [LOS ANGELES]: *locality,* 6.5 miles south of Mount Wilson (1) along Southern Pacific Railroad (lat. 34°07'30" N, long. 118°05'05" W). Named on Pasadena (1900) 15' quadrangle. The name is from Leonard J. Rose's Sunny Slope farm (Gudde, 1949, p. 347).

Sunrise [LOS ANGELES]: *locality,* 1.5 miles south of Lancaster along Southern Pacific Railroad (lat. 34°40'25" N, long. 118°07'55" W). Named on Lancaster West (1958) 7.5' quadrangle.

Sunset: see **Westwood** [LOS ANGELES].

Sunset Bay: see **Huntington Harbor** [ORANGE] (1).

Sunset Beach [ORANGE]: *town,* 5.5 miles northwest of Huntington Beach civic center along the coast (lat. 33°43' N, long. 118°04'05" W). Named on Seal Beach (1965) 7.5' quadrangle. Postal authorities established Sunset Beach post office in 1905, discontinued it in 1924, and reestablished it in 1925 (Frickstad, p. 118).

Sunset Canyon [LOS ANGELES]: *canyon,* 2 miles long, 2 miles northeast of Burbank city hall (lat. 34°12'15" N, long. 118°17'05" W). Named on Burbank (1953) 7.5' quadrangle.

Sunset Hills: see **Ivanhoe** [LOS ANGELES] (1).

Sunset Peak [LOS ANGELES]: *peak,* 12 miles north-northeast of Pomona city hall (lat. 34°13' N, long. 117°41'20" W). Altitude 5796 feet. Named on Mount Baldy (1954) 7.5' quadrangle.

Sunshine: see **Norwalk** [LOS ANGELES].

Sunshine Acres [LOS ANGELES]: *district,* nearly 3 miles south of present Whittier city

hall (lat. 33°55'25" N, long. 118°02'45" W). Named on Whittier (1949) 7.5' quadrangle.

Sunshine Canyon: see **Tunnel** [LOS ANGELES].

Sun Valley [LOS ANGELES]:
(1) *district,* 4.25 miles northwest of Burbank city hall in Los Angeles (lat. 34°13'05" N, long. 118°22'05" W). Named on Burbank (1953) and Van Nuys (1953) 7.5' quadrangles. Called Roscoe on Santa Monica (1902) 15' quadrangle. Postal authorities established Roscoe post office in 1924 and changed the name to Sun Valley in 1948; the name "Roscoe" was for a brakeman for Southern Pacific Railroad (Salley, p. 188). Residents of the place chose the name "Sun Valley" by popular vote in 1948 to replace the name "Roscoe" (Hanna, p. 320).
(2) *locality,* 5 miles northeast of Van Nuys along Southern Pacific Railroad (lat. 34°13'35" N, long. 118°22'40" W); the place is north of Sun Valley (1). Named on Van Nuys (1953) 7.5' quadrangle. Called Monte Vista on Santa Monica (1902) 15' quadrangle.

Suracco Canyon: see **Solemint** [LOS ANGELES].

Surfside [ORANGE]: *district,* 6.5 miles northwest of Huntington Beach city hall along the coast in Seal Beach (lat. 33°43'40" N, long. 118°04'55" W). Named on Seal Beach (1965) 7.5' quadrangle. Postal authorities established Surfside post office in 1943 (Frickstad, p. 118).

Surprise City: see **Falls Canyon** [ORANGE].

Surrey: see **Saugus** [LOS ANGELES].

Susanna Canyon [LOS ANGELES]: *canyon,* drained by a stream that flows nearly 3 miles to San Gabriel River 7.5 miles north-northeast of Glendora city hall (lat. 34°14'15" N, long. 117°49'05" W). Named on Crystal Lake (1958) and Glendora (1953) 7.5' quadrangles. East Fork branches northeast 0.5 mile upstream from the mouth of the main canyon; it is 1.25 miles long and is named on Glendora (1953) 7.5' quadrangle.

Susannah Range: see **Santa Susana Range** [LOS ANGELES-VENTURA].

Sutton Canyon [LOS ANGELES]: *canyon,* drained by a stream that flows 1.25 miles to Pickens Canyon 8 miles northwest of Pasadena city hall (lat. 34°14'35" N, long. 118°13'20" W; near E line sec. 22, T 2 N, R 13 W). Named on Condor Peak (1959) and Pasadena (1953) 7.5' quadrangles. Called East Fork [Pickens Canyon] on Los Angeles County (1935) map.

Swain Canyon [LOS ANGELES]: *canyon,* drained by a stream that flows 1.25 miles to the sea 2.5 miles north-northwest of Avalon on Santa Catalina Island (lat. 33°22'30" N, long. 118°21'10" W). Named on Santa Catalina East (1950) 7.5' quadrangle.

Swain's Landing: see **Whites Landing** [LOS ANGELES].

Swarthout: see **Big Pines** [LOS ANGELES].
Swarthout Valley [LOS ANGELES]: *valley,*
5.25 miles north of Mount San Antonio on
Los Angeles-San Bernardino county line (lat.
34°22' N, long. 117°39' W). Named on Mount
San Antonio (1955) 7.5' quadrangle. C.W.
Whipple (p. 148) referred to Swarthows
Cañon. The name commemorates Nathan
Swarthout and Truman Swarthout, brothers
who settled in the valley about 1851
(Robinson, J.W., 1983, p. 196).
Swartout: see **Big Pines** [LOS ANGELES].
Swinnerton Camp: see **Little Jimmy Spring**
[LOS ANGELES].
Switzer Camp [LOS ANGELES]: *locality,* 6
miles southeast of Condor Peak along Arroyo
Seco (lat. 34°15'30" N, long. 118°09'15" W).
Named on Condor Peak (1959) 7.5' quad-
rangle. Called Switzers Camp on Mount Lowe
(1939) 6' quadrangle. Perry Switzer built a
trail to the place in 1884 and opened Switzer's
Camp, the first tourist resort in San Gabriel
Mountains; after a forest fire destroyed the
camp in 1896, Lloyd B. Austin took over the
site in 1912 and built a mountain hostelry first
called Camp Losadena, but renamed Switzer-
land (Robinson, J.W., 1977, p. 108, 110-111).
Switzer Campground: see **Lower Switzer
Campground** [LOS ANGELES]; **Upper
Switzer Campground** [LOS ANGELES].
Switzer-land: see **Switzer Camp** [LOS ANGE-
LES].
Switzer Station [LOS ANGELES]: *locality,* 6
miles southeast of Condor Peak along Arroyo
Seco (lat. 34°16' N, long. 118°08'35" W).
Named on Condor Peak (1959) 7.5' quadrangle.
Sycamore Campground [LOS ANGELES]: *locality,* 7 miles west-southwest of Valyermo
along Little Rock Creek (lat. 34°25'05" N,
long. 117°58'20" W; sec. 19, T 4 N, R 10 W).
Named on Juniper Hills (1959) 7.5' quadrangle.
Sycamore Canyon [LOS ANGELES]:
(1) *canyon,* drained by a stream that flows
nearly 2 miles to San Dimas Wash 4 miles
east of Glendora city hall (lat. 34°07'35" N,
long. 117°47'35" W; sec. 35, T 1 N, R 9 W).
Named on Glendora (1953) 7.5' quadrangle.
(2) *canyon,* 3.5 miles long, 4 miles west-northwest of Pasadena city hall (lat. 34°10' N, long.
118°12'20" W). Named on Pasadena (1953)
7.5' quadrangle.
(3) *canyon,* drained by a stream that flows 1.5
miles to Sawpit Canyon 5 miles northwest of
Azusa city hall (lat. 34°10'45" N, long.
117°58'20" W; near N line sec. 18, T 1 N, R
10 W). Named on Azusa (1953) 7.5' quadrangle.
(4) *canyon,* less than 1 mile long, 4.25 miles
southwest of El Monte city hall (lat. 34°02'10"
N, long. 118°05'20" W). Named on El Monte
(1966) 7.5' quadrangle.
(5) *canyon,* drained by a stream that flows 3.5

miles to lowlands along San Gabriel River 4.5
miles south-southwest of El Monte city hall
(lat. 34°00'40" N, long. 118°03'15" W).
Named on El Monte (1953) 7.5' quadrangle.
Watts' (1898-1899) map shows a feature
called Dark Canyon that opens into Sycamore
Canyon from the east near the west end of
Puente Hills. Berkstresser (p. A-7) listed a
place called Cal-Baden Mineral Spring located in Sycamore Canyon (5) near the canyon mouth (lat. 34°00'12" N, long.
118°02'55"W).
Sycamore Canyon [VENTURA]:
(1) *canyon,* drained by a stream that flows 1.5
miles to Alder Creek 4.25 miles north-northeast of Devils Heart Peak (lat. 34°36'05" N,
long. 118°56'30" W; near W line sec. 19, T 6
N, R 19 W). Named on Devils Heart Peak
(1943) 7.5' quadrangle.
(2) *canyon,* drained by a stream that flows 2
miles to an unnamed canyon 6 miles north-
northeast of Thousand Oaks (lat. 34°15'05"
N, long. 118°48'10" W). Named on Thousand
Oaks (1952) 7.5' quadrangle.
Sycamore Canyon: see **Big Sycamore Canyon**
[VENTURA]; **Elderberry Canyon** [LOS
ANGELES]; **Little Sycamore Canyon**
[VENTURA]; **Meier Canyon** [VENTURA].
Sycamore Creek [VENTURA]:
(1) *stream,* flows 3 miles to Sespe Creek 14
miles east-northeast of Wheeler Springs (lat.
34°34' N, long. 119°03' W; at E line sec. 36,
T 6 N, R 21 W). Named on Topatopa Moun-
tains (1943) 7.5' quadrangle.
(2) *stream,* flows 2.5 miles to Lion Creek 4.5
miles east of the town of Ojai in Upper Ojai
Valley (lat. 34°26'10" N, long. 119°09'45" W).
Named on Ojai (1952) 7.5' quadrangle.
Sycamore Flat [LOS ANGELES]:
(1) *area,* 2 miles south-southeast of Crystal
Lake along North Fork San Gabriel River (lat.
34°17'20" N, long. 117°50'25" W; sec. 5, T 2
N, R 9 W). Named on Rock Creek (1903) 15'
quadrangle.
(2) *area,* 4 miles east-northeast of Glendora city
hall (lat. 34°09'05" N, long. 117°47'35" W; at
S line sec. 23, T 1 N, R 9 W). Named on
Glendora (1953) 7.5' quadrangle. The name
is from Sycamore Canyon (1), which is lo-
cated below the area (Robinson, J.W., 1983,
p. 118).
Sycamore Flat: see **Santiago Reservoir** [OR-
ANGE].
Sycamore Flat Campground [LOS ANGE-
LES]: *locality,* 2.5 miles southeast of
Valyermo along Big Rock Creek (lat.
34°24'45" N, long. 117°49'25" W; sec. 21, T
4 N, R 9 W). Named on Valyermo (1958) 7.5'
quadrangle.
Sycamore Flats: see **Coldbrook Camp** [LOS
ANGELES].
Sycamore Lake: see **Crystal Lake** [LOS AN-
GELES].
Sycamore Park [LOS ANGELES]: *locality,* 4

miles north-northeast of present Los Angeles city hall along Los Angeles Terminal Railroad (lat. 34°05'50" N, long. 118°12'15" W). Named on Pasadena (1900) 15' quadrangle.

Sylmar [LOS ANGELES]: *district,* 2.5 miles northwest of downtown San Fernando in Los Angeles (lat. 34°18'35" N, long. 118°28'20" W). Named on San Fernando (1953) 7.5' quadrangle.

Sylvia Park [LOS ANGELES]: *locality,* 9 miles northwest of Santa Monica city hall (lat. 34°06'50" N, long. 118°34'55" W; sec. 5, T 1 S, R 16 W). Named on Topanga (1952) 7.5' quadrangle.

– T –

Table Mountain [LOS ANGELES]: *ridge,* west-northwest-trending, 2.5 miles long, center less than 1 mile east-northeast of Big Pine (lat. 34°22'55" N, long. 117°40'40" W). Named on Mescal Creek (1956) 7.5' quadrangle.

Table Mountain: see **Mount Markham** [LOS ANGELES].

Table Mountain Campground [LOS ANGELES]: *locality,* 0.5 mile north of Big Pines (lat. 34°23'15" N, long. 117°41'20" W); the place is on Table Mountain. Named on Mescal Creek (1956) 7.5' quadrangle.

Table Rock [LOS ANGELES]: *relief feature,* 11 miles south-southeast of the village of Lake Hughes in Texas Canyon (lat. 34°31'25" N, long. 118°23'15" W; near N line sec. 18, T 5 N, R 14 W). Named on Green Valley (1958) 7.5' quadrangle.

Tacobi Creek [LOS ANGELES]: *stream,* flows 3 miles to Leffingwell Creek nearly 3 miles south-southeast of present Whittier city hall (lat. 33°56'10" N, long. 118°00'35" W). Named on La Habra (1952) and Whittier (1949) 7.5' quadrangles.

Tahunga Canyon: see **Big Tujunga Canyon** [LOS ANGELES].

Tajauta [LOS ANGELES]: *land grant,* near Watts. Named on Inglewood (1964) and South Gate (1952) 7.5' quadrangles. Called Tajuata on Inglewood (1952) 7.5' quadrangle. Anastasio Avila received 1 league in 1843; Enrique Avila claimed 3560 acres patented in 1873 (Cowan, p. 101).

Tajunga Canyon: see **Big Tujunga Canyon** [LOS ANGELES].

Talamantes: see **Andrade Corner** [LOS ANGELES].

Talbert [ORANGE]: *locality,* 3.5 miles northeast of present Huntington Beach civic center (lat. 33°42'05" N, long. 117°57'45" W; on N line sec. 31, T 5 S, R 10 W). Named on Newport Beach (1951) 7.5' quadrangle. Postal authorities established Talbert post office in 1899 and discontinued it in 1907 (Frickstad, p. 118). The Talbert family bought land at the place in 1896 and established a small trading

center (Meadows, p. 133). Pacific Electric Railroad had a flag stop called Remolacha located 1.5 miles south of Talbert, and a flag stop called Repollo located about 2 miles east of Talbot (Meadows, p. 118, 119).

Talega: see **San Juan Hot Springs** [ORANGE].

Talega Canyon [ORANGE]: *canyon,* drained by a stream that heads in Riverside County and flows 6 miles back and forth across Orange-San Diego county line to Christianitos Creek nearly 3 miles northeast of San Clemente civic center (lat. 33° 27'05" N, long. 117°34'10" W; sec. 25, T 8 S, R 7 W). Named on Margarita Peak (1968), San Clemente (1968), and Sitton Peak (1954) 7.5' quadrangles.

Tanbark Creek: see **Tanbark Flats** [LOS ANGELES].

Tanbark Flats [LOS ANGELES]: *locality,* 7.5 miles northeast of Glendora city hall near the head of San Dimas Canyon (lat. 34°12'15" N, long. 117°45'35" W; sec. 6, T 1 N, R 8 W). Named on Glendora (1953) 7.5' quadrangle. On Glendora (1966) 7.5' quadrangle, the name "Tanbark Creek" applies to the stream in San Dimas Canyon at and near Tanbark Flats.

Tapia Canyon [LOS ANGELES]: *canyon,* drained by a stream that flows 4 miles to Castaic Canyon nearly 8 miles northwest of Newhall (lat. 34°28'40" N, long. 118°36'25" W; at E line sec. 36, T 5 N, R 17 W). Named on Newhall (1952) 7.5' quadrangle.

Tapie Canyon [LOS ANGELES]: *canyon,* drained by a stream that flows nearly 3 miles to Santa Clara River 4.25 miles east-northeast of Solemint (lat. 34°25'55" N, long. 118°23' W; sec. 18, T 4 N, R 14 W). Named on Agua Dulce (1960) 7.5' quadrangle. Called Vorhees Canyon on Los Angeles County (1935) map.

Tapo Canyon [VENTURA]:
(1) *canyon,* drained by a stream that flows nearly 4 miles to Simi Valley (1) 5.5 miles west-northwest of Santa Susana Pass (lat. 34° 18' N, long. 118°43'05" W; sec. 36, T 3 N, R 18 W). Named on Santa Susana (1951) 7.5' quadrangle. Tapo Canyon (1) and Tapo Canyon (2) head on opposite sides of the pass located between Santa Susana Mountains and Oak Ridge. The upper part of Tapo Canyon (1) is called Hog Canyon on Santa Susana (1943) 15' quadrangle, and the lower part is called South Tapo Canyon on that map. The name "Tapo" is of Indian origin (Kroeber, p. 61).
(2) *canyon,* drained by a stream that flows 3 miles to the valley of Santa Clara River 4.5 miles east-southeast of Piru (lat. 34°23'35" N, long. 118°53'15" W). Named on Santa Susana (1951) and Val Verde (1952) 7.5' quadrangles.

Tar Creek [VENTURA]: *stream,* flows 5.5 miles to Sespe Creek 6.5 miles north-north-west of Fillmore (lat. 34°29'25" N, long. 118°56'30" W). Named on Fillmore (1951) and Piru (1952) 7.5' quadrangles. Present

Spring Canyon Creek is called North Fork Tar Cr. on Tejon (1903) 30' quadrangle, but United States Board on Geographic Names (1990, p. 11) rejected this designation for the stream.

Tarzana [LOS ANGELES]: *district*, 3.25 miles southeast of the center of Canoga Park in Los Angeles (lat. 34°10'20" N, long. 118° 33' W). Named on Canoga Park (1952) 7.5' quadrangle. Postal authorities established Tarzana post office in 1930 at a place first called Runnymead (Salley, p. 218). The name "Tarzana" is from Edgar Rice Burroughs' estate at the place; Burroughs named the estate for his fictional character "Tarzan" (Gudde, 1949, p. 354).

Tarzana Siding [LOS ANGELES]: *locality*, 4 miles east-southeast of Canoga Park along Southern Pacific Railroad (lat. 34°10'50" N, long, 118°32' W); the place is 1 mile northeast of Tarzana. Named on Canoga Park (1952) 7.5' quadrangle. Called Reseda on Camulos (1903) 30' quadrangle, and called Reseda Siding on Reseda (1928) 6' quadrangle.

Taylor Campground [LOS ANGELES]: *locality*, 3 miles south of Warm Springs Mountain in Elizabeth Lake Canyon (lat. 34°33' N, long. 118°34'35" W; sec. 5, T 5 N, R 16 W). Named on Warm Springs Mountain (1958) 7.5' quadrangle.

Taylor Junction [LOS ANGELES]: *locality*, 1.5 miles east-northeast of Los Angeles city hall along Southern Pacific Railroad (lat. 34° 03'45" N, long. 118°13'15" W). Named on Los Angeles (1966) 7.5' quadrangle.

Teddy's Outpost: see **Oakwilde** [LOS ANGELES].

Tehachapi Mountains [LOS ANGELES]: *range*, mainly in Kern County, but extends southwest into Los Angeles County northeast of Gorman (lat. 34°49' N, long. 118°48'30" W). Named on Los Angeles (1975) 1°x 2° quadrangle.

Tejon Pass [LOS ANGELES]: *pass*, 1.5 miles west-northwest of Gorman (lat. 34°48'05" N, long. 118°52'30" W; at N line sec. 10, T 8 N, R 19 W). Named on Frazier Mountain (1958) and Lebec (1958) 7.5' quadrangles. Called Holland Summit on Lebec (1945) 7.5' quadrangle. The feature first was known as Fort Tejon Pass, for the fort in Kern County, and later as Tejon Pass; the name "Tejon Pass" earlier applied to a feature in Kern County (Gudde, 1949, p. 356).

Telegraph Canyon [ORANGE]: *canyon*, drained by a stream that heads in San Bernardino County and flows nearly 5 miles in Orange County to Carbon Canyon 2.25 miles north-northwest of Yorba Linda (lat. 33°55'10" N, long. 117°49'35" W; near S line sec. 9, T 3 S, R 9 W). Named on Prado Dam (1950) and Yorba Linda (1950) 7.5' quadrangles. Watts' (1898-1899) map has the designation "Latrango or Telegraph Canon" for

the feature. The name "Telegraph Canyon" is from a telegraph line in the canyon (Meadows, p. 133).

Tell's Landing: see **Playa del Rey** [LOS ANGELES].

Temescal [LOS ANGELES-VENTURA]: *land grant*, northeast of Piru on Los Angeles-Ventura county line. Named on Piru (1952), Val Verde (1952), and Whitaker Peak (1958) 7.5' quadrangles. Francisco Lopez R. de la Custa received 3 leagues in 1843 and claimed 13,339 acres patented in 1871 (Cowan, p. 101-102).

Temescal Canyon [LOS ANGELES]: *canyon*, drained by a stream that flows nearly 5.5 miles to the sea 3 miles west-northwest of Santa Monica city hall (lat. 34°02'05" N, long. 118°32'05" W). Named on Topanga (1952) 7.5' quadrangle.

Temescal Canyon: see **Santa Felicia Canyon** [LOS ANGELES-VENTURA].

Temescal Peak: see **Santiago Peak** [ORANGE].

Temescal Range: see **Santa Ana Mountains** [ORANGE].

Temple: see **Temple City** [LOS ANGELES].

Temple City [LOS ANGELES]: *city*, 3 miles north-northwest of El Monte city hall (lat. 34°06'30" N, long. 118°03'25" W). Named on El Monte (1953) 7.5' quadrangle. Called Temple on Sierra Madre (1928) 6' quadrangle. Postal authorities established Temple post office in 1924 and changed the name to Temple City in 1928 (Frickstad, p. 82). The city incorporated in 1960. Walter Paul Temple founded the community in 1922 (Hanna, p. 327).

Temple Hill [ORANGE]: *ridge*, south-trending, 1.25 miles long, 1.5 miles east-northeast of Laguna Beach city hall (lat. 33°33' N, long. 117°45'15" W; sec. 19, T 7 S, R 8 W). Named on Laguna Beach (1965) 7.5' quadrangle.

Ten Sycamore Flat [VENTURA]: *area*, 15 miles east-northeast of Wheeler Springs (lat. 34°34'15" N, long. 119°02'40" W; sec. 31, T 6 N, R 20 W). Named on Topatopa Mountains (1943) 7.5' quadrangle.

Tentrock Canyon [LOS ANGELES]: *canyon*, drained by a stream that flows 4.5 miles to lowlands 10 miles east of Gorman (lat. 34° 46'30" N, long. 118°40'30" W; near SW cor sec. 15, T 8 N, R 17 W). Named on La Liebre Ranch (1965) and Liebre Mountain (1958) 7.5' quadrangles.

Teresita Pines: see **Camp Teresita Pines** [LOS ANGELES].

Terminal: see **Terminal Island** [LOS ANGELES] (2).

Terminal Island [LOS ANGELES]:
(1) *island*, 2 miles long, 3 miles west-southwest of Long Beach city hall (lat. 33°45'30" N, long. 118°14'30" W). Named on Long Beach (1949), San Pedro (1964), and Torrance (1964) 7.5' quadrangles. Called Rattle Snake Is. on Lankershim Ranch Land and Water

Company's (1888) map, and called Rattle-snake I. on Mendenhall's (1908) map, but United States Board on Geographic Names (1933, p. 750) rejected the names "Rattlesnake Island" and "Rattlesnake Terminal Island" for the feature. The Spaniards called the it La Isla de la Culebra de Cascabel because it was infested with rattlesnakes—*La Isla de la Culebra de Cascabel* means "The Island of the Snake of the Rattle" in Spanish; after Terminal Railroad Company bought the place in 1891, the name was changed to Terminal Island and it became a popular summer resort (Gleason, p. 116, 118).
(2) *locality,* nearly 4 miles west-southwest of Long Beach city hall along Union Pacific Railroad (lat. 33°45'10" N, long. 118°15'20" W); the place is on Terminal Island (1). Named on Wilmington (1925) 6' quadrangle. Called Terminal on California Mining Bureau's (1917) map. Postal authorities established Terminal post office in 1898, changed the name to Terminal Island in 1924, and discontinued it in 1943 (Frickstad, p. 82).
Ternez [VENTURA]: *locality,* 3 miles west-southwest of Moorpark along Southern Pacific Railroad (lat. 34°16'15" N, long. 118°56'15" W). Named on Piru (1921) 15' quadrangle. Called Ternez Siding on Camulos (1903) 30' quadrangle, and called Tarnez on Los Angeles County (1955) map.
Texas Canyon [LOS ANGELES]: *canyon,* drained by a stream that flows 8 miles to Bouquet Canyon 5.25 miles north of Solemint (lat. 34°29'30" N, long. 118°27'35" W; sec. 28, T 5 N, R 15 W). Named on Green Valley (1958), Mint Canyon (1960), and Sleepy Valley (1958) 7.5' quadrangles.
Thatcher Creek [VENTURA]: *stream,* flows 6.5 miles to San Antonio Creek less than 1 mile east-southeast of downtown Ojai (lat. 34°26'35" N, long. 119°13'50" W). Named on Ojai (1952) 7.5' quadrangle.
The Eyrie: see **Steil's Camp,** under **Mount Harvard** [LOS ANGELES].
The Hogback: see **Mount Harvard** [LOS ANGELES].
The Isthmus [LOS ANGELES]: *relief feature,* 0.5 miles southwest of Northwest Harbor on San Clemente Island (lat. 33°01'30" N, long. 118°35'25" W). Named on San Clemente Island North (1943) 7.5' quadrangle.
Thenard [LOS ANGELES]: *locality,* 3 miles west-northwest of Long Beach city hall along Southern Pacific Railroad (lat. 33°47'15" N, long. 118°14'30" W). Named on Long Beach (1949) 7.5' quadrangle. Called Thenard Junc. on Downey (1902) 15' quadrangle.
Thenard Junction: see **Thenard** [LOS ANGELES].
The Narrows [LOS ANGELES]:
(1) *narrows,* 4.5 miles east-northeast of Condor Peak in Big Tujunga Canyon (lat. 34°18'35" N, long. 118°08'30" W). Named

on Chilao Flat (1959) and Condor Peak (1959) 7.5' quadrangles.
(2) *narrows,* 5.5 miles west of Mount Antonio along San Gabriel River (lat. 34°17'35" N, long. 117°44'30" W). Named on Mount San Antonio (1955) 7.5' quadrangle.
The Narrows [ORANGE]: *relief feature,* constricted part of Upper Newport Bay 6.5 miles east-southeast of Huntington Beach city hall (lat. 33°38'15" N, long. 117°53'15" W). Named on Newport Beach (1965) 7.5' quadrangle.
The Oaks [LOS ANGELES]: *locality,* 8 miles south-southwest of the village of Leona Valley in Mint Canyon (lat. 34°30'40" N, long. 118°21'15" W; at N line sec. 21, T 5 N, R 14 W). Named on Sleepy Valley (1958) 7.5' quadrangle.
The Old Trading Post: see **Little Santa Anita Canyon** [LOS ANGELES].
The Pines Camp Ground [VENTURA]: *locality,* 5.5 miles east-northeast of the town of Ojai (lat. 34°29'05" N, long. 119°09'30" W; sec. 26, T 5 N, R 22 W). Named on Ojai (1952) 7.5' quadrangle.
The Pinnacle [LOS ANGELES]: *peak,* 6.5 miles north-northwest of Sunland (lat. 34°20'55" N, long. 118°20'35" W; near NE cor. sec. 16, T 3 N, R 14 W). Altitude 3836 feet. Named on Sunland (1966) 7.5' quadrangle.
The Pothole [VENTURA]: *relief feature,* closed depression 6.25 miles southeast of Cobblestone Mountain (lat. 34°32' N, long. 118° 48'10" W; sec. 7, T 5 N, R 18 W). Named on Cobblestone Mountain (1958) 7.5' quadrangle. Called The Potholes on California Mining Bureau's (1917) map.
The Potholes [LOS ANGELES]: *water feature,* 4 miles east of Burnt Peak along upper reaches of Fish Creek (lat. 34°40'25" N, long. 118°30'15" W; on S line sec. 19, T 7 N, R 15 W). Named on Burnt Peak (1958) 7.5' quadrangle.
The Sinks [ORANGE]: *relief feature,* 6.25 miles north-northeast of El Toro near the head of Agua Chinon Wash (lat. 33°42'55" N, long. 117°39'55" W). Named on El Toro (1968) 7.5' quadrangle.
Thompson: see **Mint Canyon** [LOS ANGELES] (2); **Solemint** [LOS ANGELES].
Thompson Creek: see **Thompson Wash** [LOS ANGELES].
Thompson Flat [LOS ANGELES]: *area,* 12.5 miles north of Pomona city hall (lat. 34°14'05" N, long. 117°43'35" W). Named on Mount Baldy (1954) 7.5' quadrangle, which shows Thompson ranch by the place.
Thompsonville: see **Huntington Beach** [ORANGE].
Thompson Wash [LOS ANGELES]: *stream,* flows 4 miles to end in lowlands 2.5 miles north of Pomona city hall (lat. 34°05'45" N, long. 117°45'20" W). Named on Ontario (1954) and San Dimas (1954) 7.5' quad-

181

rangles. On Mount Baldy (1954) 7.5' quadrangle, the name "Thompson Creek" applies
to the upper part of present Thompson Wash.
Thorn Meadows [VENTURA]: *area,* 9.5 miles
east of Reyes Peak (lat. 34°37'55" N, long.
119°06'40" W; at N line sec. 9, T 6 N, R 21
W). Named on Lockwood Valley (1943) 7.5'
quadrangle. Mount Pinos (1903) 30' quadrangle shows marsh in the area.
Thorn Point [VENTURA]: *peak,* 9 miles east
of Reyes Peak (lat. 34° 36'20" N, long.
119°07'35" W; near S line sec. 17, T 6 N, R
21 W). Altitude 6935 feet. Named on Lion
Canyon (1943) 7.5' quadrangle.
Thousand Oaks [VENTURA]: *city,* 20 miles
east of Oxnard (lat. 34° 10'15" N, long.
118°50'15" W). Named on Thousand Oaks
(1952) 7.5' quadrangle. Called Thousand
Oaks Community on Triunfo Pass (1940) 15'
quadrangle. Postal authorities established
Thousand Oaks post office in 1938 (Frickstad,
p. 219), and the city incorporated in 1964.
Thousand Springs: see **San Nicolas Island**
[VENTURA].
Thrall: see **Will Thrall Peak** [LOS ANGELES].
Three Arch Bay [ORANGE]: *locality,* 4 miles
west of San Juan Capistrano along the coast
(lat. 33°29'30" N, long. 117°43'30" W).
Named on Dana Point (1968) 7.5' quadrangle.
The name is from three natural arches at the
place (Gudde, 1949, p. 361).
Three Arches: see **South Laguna** [ORANGE].
Threemile House [LOS ANGELES]: *locality,*
3.25 miles north of present Los Angeles city
hall along Los Angeles Terminal Railroad (lat.
34°06'05" N, long. 118°14'20" W). Named
on Pasadena (1900) 15' quadrangle.
Threepoint: see **Three Points** [LOS ANGELES]
(1).
Three Points [LOS ANGELES]:
(1) *locality,* 4 miles north-northwest of Burnt
Peak at the mouth of Oakgrove Canyon (lat.
34°44'05" N, long. 118°35'50" W; sec. 32, T
8 N, R 16 W). Named on Burnt Peak (1958)
7.5' quadrangle. Called Threepoint on
Manzana (1938) 6' quadrangle, but United
States Board on Geographic Names (1960a,
p. 18) rejected the forms "Threepoint" and
"Three Point" for the name. Los Angeles
County (1935) map shows a place called
Voltaire located about 1 mile southeast of
Three Points. Postal authorities established
Voltair post office in 1912 and discontinued
it in 1922 (Frickstad, p. 83).
(2) *locality,* 2.5 miles west of Waterman Mountain (lat. 34°20'35" N, long. 117°58'55"W;
sec. 13, T 3 N, R 11 W). Named on Waterman
Mountain (1959) 7.5' quadrangle.
3 Sister Buttes: see **Three Sisters** [LOS AN-
GELES].
Three Sisters [LOS ANGELES]: *peaks,* three,
1.5 miles southeast of Black Butte (lat.
34°32'15" N, long. 117°42'15" W; sec. 10, T
5 N, R 8 W). Named on El Mirage (1956)

7.5' quadrangle. Called 3 Sister Buttes on Los
Angeles County (1935) map.
Throop Mountain: see **Throop Peak** [LOS
ANGELES].
Throop Peak [LOS ANGELES]: *peak,* 3.5 miles
northeast of Crystal Lake (lat. 34°21' N, long.
117°47'55" W). Altitude 9138 feet. Named on
Crystal Lake (1958) 7.5' quadrangle. United
States Board on Geographic Names (1962, p.
17) rejected the names "North Baldy Peak"
and "Throop Mountain" for the feature, and
noted that the name "Throop" commemorates
Amos G. Throop, who in 1891 founded
Throop University, a forerunner of Califor-
nia Institute of Technolgy. Students from the
school climbed the peak and named it in 1916;
previously the feature was called Dougherty
Peak for A.A. Dougherty of Coldbrook Camp
(Robinson, J.W., 1983, p. 112).
Thurin [ORANGE]: *locality,* 5.5 miles east of
present Huntington Beach civic center along
Southern Pacific Railroad (lat. 33°39'15" N,
long. 117°54'15" W). Named on Newport
Beach (1935) 7.5' quadrangle.
Tick Canyon [LOS ANGELES]: *canyon,*
drained by a stream that flows 5.5 miles to
Santa Clara River nearly 4 miles east-northeast of Solemint (lat. 34°25'55" N, long.
118°23'30" W; sec. 18, T 4 N, R 14 W).
Named on Agua Dulce (1960) and Mint Can-
yon (1960) 7.5' quadrangles. Los Angeles
County (1935) map shows a feature called
Goat Canyon that opens into Tick Canyon
from the north about 2 miles above the mouth
of Tick Canyon (at E line sec. 6, T 4 N, R 14
W), and a feature called Shan Canyon that
opens into Tick Canyon from the north about
1 mile above the mouth of Tick Canyon (sec.
7, T 4 N, R 14 W).
Tico: see **Matilija** [VENTURA].
Tie Canyon [LOS ANGELES]: *canyon,* drained
by a stream that flows 1.25 miles to Aliso
Canyon (1) 2.5 miles west-northwest of
Pacifico Mountain (lat. 34°23'55" N, long.
118°04'25" W). Named on Pacifico Mountain (1959) 7.5' quadrangle.
Tierra Bonita: see **Littlerock** [LOS ANGE-
LES].
Tierra Rejada Valley [VENTURA]: *valley,* 2.5
miles southeast of Moorpark (lat. 34°15'25"
N, long. 118°51'15" W). Named on Simi
(1951) 7.5' quadrangle. Called Tierra Rejada
on Piru (1921) 15' quadrangle.
Tie Summit Station [LOS ANGELES]: *local-
ity,* 2.5 miles west-northwest of Pacifico
Mountain (lat. 34°23'25" N, long. 118°04'45"
W); the place is less than 1 mile south-south-
west of the mouth of Tie Canyon by Mill
Creek Summit. Named on Pacifico Mount-
ain (1959) 7.5' quadrangle.
Tijeras Canyon [ORANGE]: *canyon,* drained
by a stream that flows 5.25 miles to Arroyo
Trabuco 4 miles southeast of El Toro (lat. 33°
35'35" N, long. 117°37'55" W). Named on

Cañada Gobernadora (1968), San Juan Capistrano (1968), and Santiago Peak (1954) 7.5' quadrangles.

Tilghman: see Shoemaker [LOS ANGELES].

Timber Canyon [VENTURA]: *canyon,* 2.25 miles long, opens into the valley of Santa Clara River 4 miles northeast of Santa Paula (lat. 34°23'30" N, long. 119°00'45" W). Named on Santa Paula Peak (1951) 7.5' quadrangle.

Timber Creek [VENTURA]: *stream,* flows 4.5 miles to Sespe Creek 13 miles east-northeast of Wheeler Springs (lat. 34°33'25" N, long. 119°04'10" W; sec. 3, T 5 N, R 21 W). Named on Topatopa Mountains (1943) 7.5' quadrangle.

Timberville: see Newbury Park [VENTURA].

Timms Bay: scc Avalon Bay [LOS ANGELES].

Timms Cove: see Avalon Bay [LOS ANGELES].

Timm's Landing: see Avalon [LOS ANGELES].

Timms' Point: see San Pedro [LOS ANGELES] (2).

Tin Can Cabin Campground [VENTURA]: *locality,* 2.5 miles south of Cobblestone Mountain along Agua Blanca Creek (lat. 34°34'10" N, long. 118°51'40" W; sec. 35, T 6 N, R 19 W). Named on Cobblestone Mountain (1958) 7.5' quadrangle.

Tin Mine Canyon [ORANGE]: *canyon,* drained by a stream that flows nearly 0.5 mile to Riverside County 2.25 miles southeast of Serra Peak (lat. 33°49'20" N, long. 117°37'45" W; sec. 17, T 4 S, R 7 W). Named on Black Star Canyon (1967) 7.5' quadrangle.

Tinta Creek [VENTURA]: *stream,* heads in Santa Barbara County and flows 4.5 miles in Ventura County to Rancho Nuevo Creek 8 miles northwest of Reyes Peak (lat. 34°42'15" N, long. 119°23'20" W). Named on Rancho Nuevo Creek (1943) 7.5' quadrangle.

Tobanao Canyon: see Topanga Canyon [LOS ANGELES].

Tobanca Canyon: see Topanga Canyon [LOS ANGELES].

Todd: see Oxnard [VENTURA].

Todd Barranca [VENTURA]: *gully,* extends for 3 miles from the mouth of Wheeler Canyon to Santa Clara River 4.5 miles southwest of Santa Paula (lat. 34°18'10" N, long. 119°06'40" W). Named on Santa Paula (1951) and Saticoy (1951) 7.5' quadrangles. The name commemorates Marquis de LaFayette Todd, who came to Ventura in 1869 (Ricard).

Toll Canyon [LOS ANGELES]: *canyon,* less than 0.5 mile long, nearly 3 miles east of Burbank city hall (lat. 34°10'30" N, long. 118°15'40" W). Named on Burbank (1953) 7.5' quadrangle.

Toluca: see North Hollywood [LOS ANGELES].

Toluca Lake [LOS ANGELES]: *lake,* less than 0.5 mile long, 3.5 miles southwest of Burbank city hall (lat. 34°08'45" N, long. 118° 20'45"

W). Named on Burbank (1953) 7.5' quadrangle.

Tomato Spring [ORANGE]: *spring,* 5 miles north of El Toro (lat. 33° 41'45" N, long. 117°42'30" W). Named on El Toro (1968) 7.5' quadrangle. The feature first was called Aguage del Padre Gomez because Padre Gomez of the Portola expedition discovered it in 1769; the present name is from tomato plants found growing wild at the spot early in American times (Meadows, p. 18, 135).

Tomato Spring Canyon: see Agua Chinon Wash [ORANGE].

Tom Lucas Campground [LOS ANGELES]: *locality,* nearly 1.5 miles west-northwest of Condor Peak in Trail Canyon (lat. 34°19'50" N, long. 118°14'30" W). Named on Condor Peak (1959) 7.5' quadrangle. The name commemorates "Barefoot Tom" Lucas, a forest ranger who lived in Big Tujunga Canyon for more than 30 years (Robinson, J.W., 1977, p. 148-149).

Toms Canyon [VENTURA]: *canyon,* drained by a stream that flows 3.5 miles to Hopper Canyon 2.5 miles west-northwest of Piru (lat. 34°25'25" N, long. 118°50'05" W; at S line sec. 14, T 4 N, R 19 W). Named on Piru (1952) 7.5' quadrangle.

Tonner Canyon [LOS ANGELES-ORANGE]: *canyon,* drained by a stream that heads in Los Angeles County and flows 9 miles, partly in San Bernardino County but mainly in Los Angeles County, to Brea Canyon 4 miles west of La Habra in Orange County (lat. 33° 56'20" N, long. 117°52'35" W). Named on San Dimas (1954) and Yorba Linda (1950) 7.5' quadrangles. Called La Brea Canyon on La Brea (1928) 6' quadrangle, and called Brea Canyon on Watts' (1898-1899) map, where present Brea Canyon is called Canada del Rodeo.

Topanga [LOS ANGELES]: *town,* 8.5 miles north-northwest of Santa Monica city hall (lat. 34°05'45" N, long. 118°36' W; sec. 7, T 1 S, R 16 W); the place is in Topanga Canyon. Named on Topanga (1952) 7.5' quadrangle. Postal authorities established Topanga post office in 1908 (Frickstad, p. 82).

Topanga Beach [LOS ANGELES]: *town,* 5.5 miles west-northwest of Santa Monica city hall along the coast (lat. 34°02'20" N, long. 118° 34'50" W); the place is at the mouth of Topanga Canyon. Named on Topanga (1952) 7.5' quadrangle.

Topanga Canyon [LOS ANGELES]: *canyon,* drained by a stream that flows 8 miles to the sea 5.5 miles west-northwest of Santa Monica city hall (lat. 34°02'15" N, long. 118°34'55" W). Named on Canoga Park (1952) and Topanga (1952) 7.5' quadrangles. United States Board on Geographic Names (1960c, p. 19) rejected the names "Tobanao Canyon," "Tobanca Canyon," and "Topango Canyon" for the feature. Calabasas (1903) 15' quadrangle shows Garapito Creek in present Topanga Canyon above the mouth of present Old Topanga Canyon. On Malibu Beach (1951) 7.5' quadrangle, present Old Topanga Canyon is called Topanga Canyon, but on Malibu Beach (1950, photorevised 1981) 7.5' quadrangle, present Old Topanga Canyon is named properly.

Topanga Canyon: see **Old Topanga Canyon** [LOS ANGELES].

Topanga Malibu Sequit [LOS ANGELES]: *land grant,* extends along the coast from Sequit Point to Las Flores Canyon (2). Named on Malibu Beach (1951), Point Dume (1951), and Triunfo Pass (1950) 7.5' quadrangles. Jose Bartolome Tapia received the land in 1804; Matthew Keller claimed 13,316 acres patented in 1872 (Cowan, p. 104). The words "Topanga" and "Malibu" have an Indian origin, and the word "Sequit" evidently has also (Kroeber, p. 46, 57, 63). According to Perez (p. 102), Jose J. Tapia was the grantee in 1805.

Topanga Malibu Sequit Creek: see **Malibu Creek** [LOS ANGELES].

Topanga Malibu Sequit Point: see **Malibu Point** [LOS ANGELES].

Topanga Park [LOS ANGELES]: *locality,* 6 miles north-northeast of Malibu Point (lat. 34°06'20" N, long. 118°37'40" W; sec. 2, T 1 S, R 17 W); the place is in Topanga Canyon. Named on Malibu Beach (1951) 7.5' quadrangle.

Topango Canyon: see **Topanga Canyon** [LOS ANGELES].

Topatopa Bluff [VENTURA]: *escarpment,* north-northwest-trending, 1.5 miles long, 6.25 miles west-northwest of Santa Paula Peak (lat. 34°29'15" N, long. 119°06'15" W; mainly in sec. 29, T 5 N, R 21 W). Named on Santa Paula Peak (1951) 7.5' quadrangle.

Topatopa Mountains [VENTURA]: *ridge,* northeast- to east-trending, 6 miles long, center 15 miles east of Wheeler Springs (near lat. 34°32' N, long. 119°02' W); Topatopa Peak is at the east end of the ridge. Named on Devils Heart Peak (1943) and Topatopa Mountains (1943) 7.5' quadrangles. Called Topatopa Ridge on Los Angeles County (1935) map. C.W. Whipple (p. 148) used the form "Topa Topa Mountains" for the name, which is of Indian origin (Kroeber, p. 63).

Topatopa Peak [VENTURA]: *peak,* less than 1 mile west-southwest of Devils Heart Peak (lat. 34°32'20" N, long. 118°59'15" W). Altitude 6210 feet. Named on Devils Heart Peak (1943) 7.5' quadrangle.

Topatopa Ridge: see **Topatopa Mountains** [VENTURA].

Top of the World [ORANGE]: *locality,* 1.5 miles east of Laguna Beach city hall at the south end of Temple Hill (lat. 33°32'35" N, long. 117°45'10" W; near S line sec. 19, T 7 S, R 8 W). Named on Laguna Beach (1965) 7.5' quadrangle.

Torqua Spring [LOS ANGELES]: *spring,* 3.5 miles northwest of Avalon on Santa Catalina Island (lat. 33°23'05" N, long. 118° 22' W). Named on Santa Catalina East (1950) 7.5' quadrangle.

Torquemada: see **Mount Torquemada** [LOS ANGELES].

Torrance [LOS ANGELES]: *city,* 10 miles west-northwest of Long Beach city hall (lat. 33°50'15" N, long. 118°20'25" W). Named on Inglewood (1952), Redondo Beach (1951), and Torrance (1964) 7.5' quadrangles. Postal authorities established Torrance post office in 1912 (Frickstad, p. 82), and the city incorporated in 1921. The name is for Jared S. Torrance, who founded the community and named it in 1911 (Gudde, 1949, p. 366).

Torrey Canyon [VENTURA]: *canyon,* drained by a stream that flows 1.5 miles to the valley of Santa Clara River nearly 1.5 miles south of Piru (lat. 34°23'20" N, long. 118°47'45" W; at E line sec. 31, T 4 N, R 18 W). Named on Piru (1952) and Simi (1951) 7.5' quadrangles. The name commemorates Dr. John Torrey, who visited the place in 1865 while inspecting petroleum deposits (White, p. 96).

Townsend Peak [LOS ANGELES]: *peak,* 2.5 miles east-southeast of Whitaker Peak (lat. 34°33'35" N, long. 118°41'20" W; near S line sec. 33, T 6 N, R 17 W). Altitude 3184 feet. Named on Whitaker Peak (1958) 7.5' quadrangle.

Towsley Canyon [LOS ANGELES]: *canyon,* drained by a stream that flows 4 miles to Gavin Canyon 2.25 miles southwest of Newhall (lat. 34°21'30" N, long. 118°33'20" W; sec. 9, T 3 N, R 16 W). Named on Oat Mountain (1952) 7.5' quadrangle. The name commemorates Darius Towsley, a pioneer in the canyon (Reynolds, p. 13).

Toyon: see **Camp Toyon** [LOS ANGELES].

Toyon Bay: see **Willow Cove** [LOS ANGELES].

Trabuco [ORANGE]: *land grant,* along and near the upper part of Arroyo Trabuco. Named on Cañada Gobernadora (1949), El Toro (1950), San Juan Capistrano (1949), and Santiago Peak (1954) 7.5' quadrangles. Santiago Arguello and others received 5 leagues in 1841 and 1846; John Forster claimed 22,184 acres patented in 1866 (Cowan, p. 104). According to Perez (p. 102), Juan Forster was the grantee in 1846.

Trabuco: see **Trabuco Oaks** [ORANGE].

Trabuco Campground [ORANGE]: *locality,* 2.5 miles south of Santiago Peak (lat. 33°40'30" N, long. 117°31'15" W; near E line sec. 5, T 6 S, R 6 W); the place is in Trabuco Canyon. Named on Santiago Peak (1954) 7.5' quadrangle.

Trabuco Canyon [ORANGE]: *canyon,* drained by a stream that flows nearly 7 miles to lowlands 3.5 miles south-southwest of Santiago Peak (lat. 33°40'05" N, long. 117°33'45" W; sec. 12, T 6 S, R 7 W). Named on Alberhill

(1954) and Santiago Peak (1954) 7.5' quadrangles. The name recalls a blunderbuss that one of Portola's soldiers lost at the place in 1769—*trabuco* means "blunderbuss" in Spanish (Gudde, 1949, p. 367).

Trabuco Canyon: see **Trabuco Oaks** [ORANGE].

Trabuco Creek: see **Arroyo Trabuco** [ORANGE].

Trabuco Mesa: see **Plano Trabuco** [ORANGE].

Trabuco Oaks [ORANGE]: *village*, 4.5 miles southwest of Santiago Peak in Hickey Canyon (lat. 33°39'50" N, long. 117°35'20" W; at W line sec. 11, T 6 S, R 7 W). Named on Santiago Peak (1954) 7.5' quadrangle, which shows Trabuco Canyon post office at the site. Postal authorities established Trabuco Canyon post office in 1938 (Frickstad, p. 118). United States Board on Geographic Names (1970a, p. 2) approved the name "Trabuco Canyon" for the place, and gave the names "Trabuco Oaks" and "Trabuco" as variants.

Trabuco Peak [ORANGE]: *peak*, 26 miles east of Santa Ana on Orange-Riverside county line (lat. 33°42'10" N, long. 117°28'30" W; sec. 26, T 5 S, R 6 W). Named on Alberhill (1954) 7.5' quadrangle.

Trabuco Peak: see **Santiago Peak** [ORANGE].

Trail Canyon [LOS ANGELES]: *canyon*, drained by a stream that flows 5 miles to Big Tujunga Canyon 4.25 miles northeast of Sunland (lat. 34°18'10" N, long. 118°15'20" W; near E line sec. 32, T 3 N, R 13 W). Named on Condor Peak (1959) and Sunland (1953) 7.5' quadrangles. North Fork branches from the main canyon 1.5 miles west of Condor Peak; it is 9 miles long and is named on Condor Peak (1959) 7.5' quadrangle.

Trail Canyon [VENTURA]: *canyon*, drained by a stream that flows 1.5 miles to Piru Creek nearly 5 miles north-northeast of McDonald Peak (lat. 34°41'25" N, long. 118°53'30" W; near NE cor. sec. 21, T 7 N, R 19 W). Named on McDonald Peak (1958) 7.5' quadrangle.

Trailer Canyon [LOS ANGELES]: *canyon*, drained by a stream that flows 1.25 miles to Santa Ynez Canyon 6 miles northwest of Santa Monica city hall (lat. 34°04'25" N, long. 118°33'50" W). Named on Topanga (1952) 7.5' quadrangle.

Trail Fork [LOS ANGELES]: *canyon*, 2 miles long, opens into Shortcut Canyon 8 miles south of Pacifico Mountain (lat. 34°15'40" N, long. 118°02'45" W; near W line sec. 16, T 2 N, R 11 W). Named on Chilao Flat (1959) 7.5' quadrangle.

Trail Fork: see **San Gabriel River** [LOS ANGELES].

Trampas Canyon [ORANGE]: *canyon*, drained by a stream that flows 2 miles to San Juan Creek nearly 5 miles east of San Juan Capistrano (lat. 33°30'50" N, long. 117°34'55" W; near S line sec. 35, T 7 S, R 7 W). Named on Cañada Gobernadora (1968)

and San Clemente (1968) 7.5' quadrangles.

Trancas [LOS ANGELES]: *locality*, 3 miles northwest of Point Dume (lat. 34°01'50" N, long. 118°50'35" W); the place is at the mouth of Trancas Canyon. Dume Point (1932) 6' quadrangle shows a place called Malibu Trading Sta. at the site.

Trancas Beach [LOS ANGELES]: *beach*, 3 miles northwest of Point Dume along the coast (lat. 34°02' N, long. 118°51' W); the beach is at and west of the mouth of Trancas Canyon. Named on Point Dume (1951) 7.5' quadrangle. On Dume Point (1932) 6' quadrangle, the name "Trancas Beach" applies also to the beach southeast of the mouth of Trancas Canyon, where Point Dume (1951) 7.5' quadrangle has the name "Zuma Beach County Park."

Trancas Canyon [LOS ANGELES]: *canyon*, drained by a stream that flows 6 miles to the sea 3 miles northwest of Point Dume (lat. 34° 01'45" N, long. 118°50'30" W). Named on Point Dume (1951) 7.5' quadrangle.

Trego: see **Harold** [LOS ANGELES].

Tres Isleos: see **Anacapa Island** [VENTURA].

Tripas Canyon [VENTURA]: *canyon*, drained by a stream that flows 5.25 miles to Tapo Canyon (1) 6.25 miles northwest of Santa Susana Pass (lat. 34°19'30" N, long. 118°43'10" W; near S line sec. 24, T 3 N, R 18 W). Named on Santa Susana (1951) and Simi (1951) 7.5' quadrangles.

Triunfo: see **Triunfo Corner** [VENTURA].

Triunfo Canyon [LOS ANGELES]: *canyon*, extends for 10 miles along Potrero Valley Creek [LOS ANGELES-VENTURA] below Russell Valley [LOS ANGELES-VENTURA], and along Malibu Creek above a point 4 miles north-northwest of Malibu Point (lat. 34°05' N, long. 118°42'30" W; sec. 18, T 1 S, R 17 W). Named on Malibu Beach (1951), Point Dume (1951), and Thousand Oaks (1952) 7.5' quadrangles. The name recalls the designations "El triunfo del Dulcisimo Nombre de Jeses" and "El triunfo de Jesus" that Crespi gave to places in the vicinity of the canyon in 1770—*El triunmfo del Dulcisimo Nombre de Jeses* means "The triumph of the Sweet Name of Jesus" in Spanish. (Gudde, 1949, p. 369). Parke (p. 3) used the form "Triompho" for the name.

Triunfo Corner [VENTURA]: *locality*, 1.25 miles southeast of downtown Thousand Oaks (lat. 34°09'20" N, long. 118°49'20" W; sec. 24, T 1 N, R 19 W). Named on Thousand Oaks (1952) 7.5' quadrangle. Called Triunfo on Triunfo Pass (1921) 15' quadrangle. Postal authorities established Triumfo (with an "m") post office in 1915, changed the name to Triunfo in 1917, and discontinued it in 1936 (Frickstad, p. 219). They established Yerba Buena post office 3 miles west of Triumfo post office (NW quarter sec. 11, T 1 S, R 20 W) in 1916 and discontinued it in 1917 (Salley, p. 244).

Triunfo Pass [VENTURA]: *pass,* 5 miles south-southwest of Newbury Park (lat. 34°06'45" N, long. 118°55' W; near W line sec. 6, T 1 S, R 19 W). Named on Triunfo Pass (1950) 7.5' quadrangle.

Troedel Spring [LOS ANGELES]: *spring,* 2 miles north-northwest of the village of Lake Hughes (lat. 34°42' N, long. 118°27'40" W; sec. 15, T 7 N, R 15 W). Named on Lake Hughes (1957) 7.5' quadrangle.

Tropico [LOS ANGELES]: *locality,* 5 miles south-southeast of Burbank along Southern Pacific Railroad (lat. 34°07'25" N, long. 118° 15'45" W). Named on Santa Monica (1902) 15' quadrangle. Postal authorities established Tropico post office in 1888, discontinued it in 1918, and reestablished it in 1964; developers of the community coined the name (Salley, p. 225). Postal authorities established Casa Verdugo post office 3 miles north of Tropico in 1906 and discontinued it in 1918 (Salley, p. 39).

Trough Canyon [LOS ANGELES]:
(1) *canyon,* drained by a stream that flows 3.5 miles to Salt Creek 11.5 miles southeast of Gorman (lat. 34°39'05" N, long. 118°41'20" W; sec. 33, T 7 N, R 17 W). Named on Liebre Mountain (1958) 7.5' quadrangle.
(2) *canyon,* drained by a stream that flows less than 1 mile to Lobo Canyon (1) 8 miles north of Point Dume (lat. 34°07'05" N, long. 118°31' W; near S line sec. 31, T 1 N, R 18 W). Named on Point Dume (1951) 7.5' quadrangle.

Trough Canyon [VENTURA]: *canyon,* drained by a stream that flows 1 mile to Bus Canyon 6 miles northeast of Thousand Oaks (lat. 34°14'15" N, long. 118°45'55" W; near SE cor. sec. 21, T 2 N, R 18 W). Named on Thousand Oaks (1952) 7.5' quadrangle.

Trough Canyon: see **Little Trough Canyon** [LOS ANGELES].

Trout Creek [VENTURA]: *stream,* flows 4 miles to Sespe Creek 9 miles east-northeast of Wheeler Springs (lat. 34°33'35" N, long. 119°08'35" W; near NW cor. sec. 1, T 5 N, R 22 W). Named on Lion Canyon (1943) 7.5' quadrangle.

Tuhunga: see **Tujunga** [LOS ANGELES] (2).

Tujunga [LOS ANGELES]:
(1) *land grant,* at Sunland and Tujunga (2). Named on Burbank (1953) and Sunland (1953) 7.5' quadrangles. Pedro Lopez and others received 1.5 leagues in 1840; D.W. Alexander and others claimed 6661 acres patented in 1874 (Cowan, p. 105).
(2) *district,* 1.25 miles east-southeast of Sunland in Los Angeles (lat. 34°15' N, long. 118°17' W); the place is on Tujunga grant. Named on Burbank (1953) and Sunland (1953) 7.5' quadrangles. Postal authorities established Tuhunga post office in 1855, discontinued it in 1894, and reestablished it with the name Tujunga in 1916 (Salley, p. 225). California Mining Bureau's (1917) map shows a

place called Littlelands located about halfway between Sunland and La Crescenta. Postal authorities established Littlelands post office 9 miles southeast of San Fernando in 1914; they moved it and changed the name to Tujunga in 1916 (Salley, p. 123).

Tujunga Canyon: see **Big Tujunga Canyon** [LOS ANGELES]; **Little Tujunga Canyon** [LOS ANGELES].

Tujunga Creek: see **Big Tujunga Canyon** [LOS ANGELES]; **Little Tujunga Creek**, under **Little Tujunga Canyon** [LOS ANGELES].

Tujunga Mountains: see **San Gabriel Mountains** [LOS ANGELES].

Tujunga River: see **Big Tujunga Canyon** [LOS ANGELES].

Tujunga Valley [LOS ANGELES]: *valley,* 3.5 miles long, center 1.5 miles west-northwest of Sunland (lat. 34°16'05" N, long. 118° 20' W); the valley is below the mouth of Big Tujunga Canyon. Named on Sunland (1953) 7.5' quadrangle.

Tujunga Wash [LOS ANGELES]: *dry wash,* extends for 9 miles from Hansen Flood Control Basin to Los Angeles River 4.25 miles southeast of Van Nuys (lat. 34°08'45" N, long. 118°23'15" W). Named on San Fernando (1966) and Van Nuys (1953) 7.5' quadrangles. Van Nuys (1953) 7.5' quadrangle also shows a feature called Tujunga Wash Flood Control Channel, which occupies an artificial watercourse that diverges from Tujunga Wash 4.5 miles northeast of Van Nuys and extends for 7.5 miles to Los Angeles River 4.25 miles southeast of Van Nuys (lat. 34°08'45" N, long. 118°23'15" W). The Tujunga Wash Flood Control Channel of Van Nuys (1953) 7.5' quadrangle is called Tujunga Wash on Van Nuys (1966) 7.5' quadrangle, which shows Hollywood freeway following the original Tujunga Wash, which it calls Central Branch Tujunga Wash.

Tule Canyon [LOS ANGELES]: *canyon,* drained by a stream that flows 5 miles to Ruby Canyon (2) nearly 4 miles east of Warm Springs Mountain (lat. 34°35'50" N, long. 118°30'40" W. Named on Green Valley (1958), Lake Hughes (1957), and Warm Springs Mountain (1958) 7.5' quadrangles.

Tule Canyon: see **South Tule Canyon** [LOS ANGELES].

Tule Creek [VENTURA]: *stream,* flows 5.25 miles to Sespe Creek 3.5 miles north-northeast of Wheeler Spring (lat. 34°33'30" N, long. 119°16' W; at S line sec. 36, T 6 N, R 23 W). Named on Wheeler Springs (1943) 7.5' quadrangle.

Tule Ridge [LOS ANGELES]: *ridge,* southeast-trending, 4.25 miles long, 4 miles south-southwest of the village of Lake Hughes (lat. 34°37'15" N, long. 118°27'50" W); the ridge is southeast of Tule Canyon and South Tule Canyon. Named on Green Valley (1958) and Lake Hughes (1957) 7.5' quadrangles.

Tumble Inn [LOS ANGELES]: *locality,* 7 miles southeast of Gorman (lat. 34°42'30" N, long. 118°43'15" W; sec. 7, T 7 N, R 17 W). Named on Liebre Mountain (1958) 7.5' quadrangle.

Tumble Inn Campground [LOS ANGELES]: *locality,* 7 miles southeast of Gorman (lat. 34°42'55" N, long. 118°43' W; sec. 7, T 7 N, R 17 W); the place is 0.5 mile north-north-east of the site of Tumble Inn. Named on Liebre Mountain (1958) 7.5' quadrangle.

Tumbler Canyon [LOS ANGELES]: *canyon,* drained by a stream that flows 1.5 miles to Cogswell Reservoir 8.5 miles north-northwest of Azusa city hall (lat. 34°14'20" N, long. 117°58'45" W; near SE cor. sec. 24, T 2 N, R 11 W). Named on Azusa (1953) 7.5' quadrangle.

Tuna Canyon [LOS ANGELES]: *canyon,* drained by a stream that flows 3 miles to the sea 6 miles west-northwest of Santa Monica city hall (lat. 34°02'20" N, long. 118°35'20" W; at E line sec. 31, T 1 S, R 16 W); the mouth of the canyon is at Las Tunas Beach. Named on Topanga (1952) 7.5' quadrangle.

Tunnel [LOS ANGELES]: *locality,* 3.5 miles south-southeast of Newhall along Southern Pacific Railroad (lat. 34°19'45" N, long. 118°30'10" W); the place is at the south end of a railroad tunnel. Named on Oat Mountain (1952) 7.5' quadrangle. Postal authorities established Tunnel post office in 1876 and discontinued it the same year (Frickstad, p. 82). Los Angeles County (1935) map shows a feature called Sunshine Canyon that is about 2 miles long and opens into Weldon Canyon from the west less than 0.5 mile south-southeast of Tunnel.

Turkey Canyon [LOS ANGELES]: *canyon,* drained by a stream that flows nearly 3 miles to Elizabeth Lake Canyon 4.25 miles southeast of Burnt Peak (lat. 34°38'05" N, long. 118°31'45" W). Named on Burnt Peak (1958) 7.5' quadrangle.

Turnbull Canyon [LOS ANGELES]: *canyon,* drained by a stream that flows nearly 2 miles to end less than 1 mile north of present Whittier city hall (lat. 33°59'05" N, long. 118°01'55" W). Named on Whittier (1949) 7.5' quadrangle.

Turnbull Creek [LOS ANGELES]: *stream,* flows less than 1 mile from Painter Lagoon to La Canada Verde Creek 2.5 miles south of present Whittier city hall (lat. 33°56'05" N, long. 118°02'15" W). Named on Whittier (1949) 7.5' quadrangle. Whittier (1965) 7.5' quadrangle shows a drain along the course of the stream

Turner's Pass: see **San Francisquito Pass,** under **San Francisquito Canyon** [LOS ANGELES].

Turtle Canyon [VENTURA]: *canyon,* drained by a stream that flows 2.5 miles to Piru Creek 5.5 miles east-southeast of Cobblestone Mountain (lat. 34°34'05" N, long. 118°46'40"

W). Named on Cobblestone Mountain (1958) 7.5' quadrangle.

Tustin [ORANGE]: *city,* 2.5 miles east of Santa Ana city hall (lat. 33° 44'35" N, long. 117°49'25" W). Named on Orange (1964) and Tustin (1965) 7.5' quadrangles. Postal authorities established Tustin City post office in 1872 and changed the name to Tustin in 1894 (Frickstad, p. 118). The city incorporated in 1927. Columbus Tustin bought land at the place in 1868 and laid out Tustin City in 1870 (Meadows, p. 136).

Tustin City: see **Tustin** [ORANGE].

Tustin Junction: see **South Anaheim** [ORANGE].

Tuyanga Canyon: see **Big Tujunga Canyon** [LOS ANGELES].

Tweedy Canyon: see **Hughes Lake** [LOS ANGELES].

Tweedy Lake [LOS ANGELES]: *lake,* 650 feet long, 3.25 miles north of Burnt Peak (lat. 34°43'50" N, long. 118°34' W; on N line sec. 3, T 7 N, R 16 W). Named on Burnt Peak (1958) 7.5' quadrangle. The name is for Robert Tweedy, a homesteader who was the first owner of the lake (Gudde, 1969, p. 348). The feature now is called Lake Katrina (Settle, p. 36).

Twin Canyon [LOS ANGELES]: *canyon,* drained by a stream that flows less than 0.5 mile to Arroyo Seco 7 miles north-northwest of Pasadena city hall (lat. 34°14'30" N, long. 118°11' W). Named on Pasadena (1953) 7.5' quadrangle.

Twin Lakes [LOS ANGELES]: *locality,* 1.5 miles north of Chatsworth (lat. 34°16'40" N, long. 118°35'50" W; on N line sec. 7, T 2 N, R 16 W). Named on Oat Mountain (1952) 7.5' quadrangle. On Chatsworth (1940) and Zelzah (1941) 6' quadrangles, present Deer Lake Highlands is called Twin Lakes.

Twin Lakes Canyon: see **Falls Creek** [LOS ANGELES].

Twin Lakes Park: see **Deer Lake Highlands** [LOS ANGELES].

Twin Peaks [LOS ANGELES]: *peaks,* two, 1.5 miles south of Waterman Mountain (lat. 34°19' N, long. 117°55'50" W). Named on Waterman Mountain (1959) 7.5' quadrangle. Called Waterman Mountain on Rock Creek (1903) 15' quadrangle, but United States Board on Geographic Names (1939, p. 35) rejected this name for the feature.

Twin Pines Camp [VENTURA]: *locality,* 2.5 miles north-northwest of McDonald Peak (lat. 34°40'10" N, long. 118°57'05" W; sec. 25, T 7 N, R 20 W). Named on McDonald Peak (1958) 7.5' quadrangle.

Twin Points [ORANGE]: *promontory,* 1 mile west of Laguna Beach city hall along the coast (lat. 33°32'40" N, long. 117°47'55" W). Named on Laguna Beach (1965) 7.5' quadrangle.

Twin Rocks [LOS ANGELES]: *relief feature,* 4 miles northeast of Mount Banning on the north side of Santa Catalina Island (lat. 33° 25'05" N, long. 118°23'20" W). Named on Santa Catalina North (1950) 7.5' quadrangle. The feature first was called Pinnacle Rocks (Doran, 1980, p. 66).

Twin Springs Canyon [LOS ANGELES]: *canyon*, drained by a stream that flows 1 mile to Sawpit Canyon 5 miles northwest of Azusa city hall (lat. 34°11' N, long. 117°57'55" W; sec. 7, T 1 N, R 10 W). Named on Azusa (1953) 7.5' quadrangle.

Twin Valley Camp [LOS ANGELES]: *locality*, 3 miles west-northwest of Big Pines (lat. 34°23'55" N, long. 117°44'15" W). Named on Mescal Creek (1956) 7.5' quadrangle.

Twomile Point [LOS ANGELES]: *relief feature*, 8 miles north-northwest of Azusa city hall along Cogswell Reservoir (lat. 34°14'20" N, long. 117°58'25" W). Named on Azusa (1953) 7.5' quadrangle.

Two Rock Point [ORANGE]: *promontory*, 1.25 miles west of Laguna Beach city hall along the coast (lat. 33°32'45" N, long. 117°48'10" W). Named on Laguna Beach (1965) 7.5' quadrangle.

– U –

Una Lake [LOS ANGELES]: *lake*, 1100 feet long, 2 miles south of Palmdale (lat. 34°33' N, long. 118°06'40" W; near W line sec. 2, T 5 N, R 12 W); a road and railroad separate the feature from Lake Palmdale. Named on Palmdale (1958) 7.5' quadrangle.

Union Bay: see **Isthmus Cove** [LOS ANGELES].

Universal City [LOS ANGELES]: *locality*, 4 miles southwest of Burbank city hall (lat. 34°08'15" N, long. 118°21'15" W). Named on Burbank (1966) 7.5' quadrangle. Postal authorities established Universal City post office in 1915 (Frickstad, p. 83). The name is from Universal Pictures Company (Gudde, 1969, p. 350). Burbank (1966) 7.5' quadrangle shows a place called Campo de Cahunga located 1.25 miles northwest of Cahuenga Pass at Universal City. It was here that Fremont accepted the surrender of Andreas Pico in 1847; postal authorities established Cahuenga post office at or near the place in 1881, discontinued it in 1886, reestablished it in 1904, and discontinued it in 1907 (Salley, p. 31). Lankershim Ranch Land and Water Company's (1888) map shows a place called Wyneka situated just west of Cahuenga.

University [LOS ANGELES]: *district*, 3.5 miles southwest of Los Angeles city hall (lat. 34°01'05" N, long. 118°17' W); present University of Southern California campus is at the place. Named on Santa Monica (1902) 15' quadrangle.

Upper Big Tujunga Canyon: see **Big Tujunga Canyon** [LOS ANGELES].

Upper Buffalo Corral Reservoir [LOS ANGELES]: *lake*, 650 feet long, 4.25 miles northwest of Mount Banning in Little Springs Canyon on Santa Catalina Island (lat. 33°25'35" N, long. 118°28'05" W); the lake is 1 mile north of Lower Buffalo Corral Reservoir. Named on Santa Catalina North (1950) 7.5' quadrangle.

Upper Falls Public Camp [LOS ANGELES]: *locality*, about 2.5 miles east-northeast of Mount Wilson (1) in Santa Anita Canyon (lat. 34°12'55" N, long. 118°01'10" W; sec. 34, T 2 N, R 11 W); the place is 0.25 mile north of Sturtevant Falls. Named on Mount Wilson (1953) 7.5' quadrangle.

Upper Franklin Canyon Reservoir [LOS ANGELES]: *lake*, 1200 feet long, behind a dam 3.25 miles north of Beverly Hills city hall (lat. 34°07'10" N, long. 118°24'35" W; at S line sec. 36, T 1 N, R 15 W); the dam is in Franklin Canyon about 2 miles upstream from the dam that forms Franklin Canyon Reservoir. Named on Beverly Hills (1966) 7.5' quadrangle. Called Upper Res. on Beverly Hills (1950) 7.5' quadrangle.

Upper Newport Bay [ORANGE]: *bay*, 6.5 miles east of Huntington Beach civic center (lat. 33°38'30" N, long. 117°53'15" W); the feature extends inland from Newport Bay. Named on Newport Beach (1965) 7.5' quadrangle. Called Newport Bay on Newport Beach (1935) 7.5' quadrangle. In the early days, millions of tree frogs lived in a swamp in lowlands between Upper Newport Bay and Red Hill; the place was known as Cienega de las Ranas—*Cienega de las Ranas* means "Swamp of the Frogs" in Spanish—and later it was called San Joaquin Swamp or Cienega de San Joaquin for San Joaquin grant (Meadows, p. 52).

Upper Ojai Valley [VENTURA]: *valley*, 4 miles east of the town of Ojai (lat. 34°26'15" N, long. 119°10'15" W); the feature is southeast of the east end of Ojai Valley, and at a higher elevation. Named on Ojai (1952) 7.5' quadrangle.

Upper Pacifico Campground [LOS ANGELES]: *locality*, at Pacifico Mountain (lat. 34°22'55" N, long. 118°02' W). Named on Pacifico Mountain (1959) 7.5' quadrangle.

Upper San Fernando Reservoir [LOS ANGELES]: *lake*, 0.5 mile long, 3.5 miles westnorthwest of downtown San Fernando (lat. 34°18'25" N, long. 118°29'30" W). Named on San Fernando (1953) 7.5' quadrangle. Called Upper Van Norman Lake on San Fernando (1966) 7.5' quadrangle.

Upper Shake Campground [LOS ANGELES]: *locality*, 2.5 miles east-northeast of Burnt Peak (lat. 34°41'25" N, long. 118°31'45" W; near S line sec. 13, T 7 N, R 16 W); the place is in Shake Canyon 0.5 mile south-southwest of Lower Shake Campground. Named on Burnt Peak (1958) 7.5' quadrangle.

Upper Stone Canyon Reservoir [LOS ANGE-

LES]: *lake,* 0.25 miles long, behind a dam 4.5 miles northwest of Beverly Hills city hall (lat. 34°07'05" N, long. 118°27'15" W); the lake is in Stone Canyon (2) just above Stone Canyon Reservoir. Named on Beverly Hills (1966) 7.5' quadrangle.

Upper Switzer Campground [LOS ANGELES]: *locality,* 6 miles southeast of Condor Peak along Arroyo Seco (lat. 34°16' N, long. 118°08'30" W); the place is 0.25 mile east of Lower Switzer Campground. Named on Condor Peak (1959) 7.5' quadrangle.

Upper Van Norman Lake: see **Upper San Fernando Reservoir** [LOS ANGELES].

— V —

Valcrest: see **Camp Valcrest** [LOS ANGELES].
Valencia: see **Castaic Junction** [LOS ANGELES].
Valencia Siding: see **East Irvine** [ORANGE].
Valinda [LOS ANGELES]: *district,* 3 miles south-southeast of Baldwin Park city hall (lat. 34°02'40" N, long. 117°56'30" W). Named on Baldwin Park (1966) 7.5' quadrangle.
Valla [LOS ANGELES]: *locality,* nearly 2 miles southwest of Whittier city hall along Southern Pacific Railroad (lat. 33°57'30" N, long. 118°03'35" W). Named on Whittier (1965) 7.5' quadrangle. Called Valla Siding on Whittier (1949) 7.5' quadrangle, which shows the place along Pacific Electric Railroad.
Valley Forge Canyon [LOS ANGELES]: *canyon,* drained by a stream that flows 1.5 miles to West Fork San Gabriel River 9 miles southsouthwest of Pacifico Mountain (lat. 34°15'10" N, long. 118°04'20" W; near S line sec. 18, T 2 N, R 11 W). Named on Chilao Flat (1959) 7.5' quadrangle.
Valley Forge Lodge: see **Camp Kole** [LOS ANGELES].
Valley of Ollas [LOS ANGELES]: *canyon,* drained by a stream that flows less than 1 mile to the sea nearly 4 miles north of Mount Banning at Empire Landing on Santa Catalina Island (lat. 33°25'35" N, long. 118°26' W). Named on Santa Catalina North (1950) 7.5' quadrangle. Doran (1980, p. 72) gave the alternate name "Pots Valley" for the feature.
Val Verde [LOS ANGELES]: *settlement,* 9 miles west-northwest of Newhall in San Martinez Chiquito Canyon (lat. 34°26'50" N, long. 118°39'45" W; sec. 9, 10, T 4 N, R 17 W). Named on Val Verde (1952) 7.5' quadrangle, which shows Val Verde county park at the place. Castaic (1940) 6' quadrangle shows Valverde Lodge there, and has the name "Valverde Park" for the county park. Postal authorities established Val Verde Park post office in 1954, discontinued it in 1965, and reestablished it in 1966 (Salley, p. 229).
Valverde Lodge: see **Val Verde** [LOS ANGELES].

Val Verde Park: see **Val Verde** [LOS ANGELES].
Valyermo [LOS ANGELES]: *village,* 9 miles southeast of Littlerock along Big Rock Creek (lat. 34°26'40" N, long. 117°51'05" W; at W line sec. 8, T 4 N, R 9 W). Named on Valyermo (1958) 7.5' quadrangle. On Valyermo (1940) 6' quadrangle, the name "Valyermo" applies to a place located about 1 mile farther southeast (near E line sec. 17, T 4 N, R 9 W). Postal authorities established Valyermo post office in 1910, discontinued it in 1920, and reestablished in it 1930 (Frickstad, p. 83). W.C. Petchner, who owned Valyermo ranch, named the village in 1909 (Gudde, 1949, p. 376). California Mining Bureau's (1917) map shows a place called Bighorn situated about 8 miles southeast of Valyermo. Postal authorities established Bighorn post office in 1904 and discontinued it in 1908 (Frickstad, p. 71). California Division of Highways' (1934) map shows a place called Border City located 10 miles east of Valyermo at the east border of Los Angeles County (sec. 1, T 4 N, R 8 W).
Van Norman Lake: see **Upper Van Norman Lake**, under **Upper San Fernando Reservoir** [LOS ANGELES].
Van Nuys [LOS ANGELES]: *district,* 15 miles northwest of Los Angeles city hall (lat. 34°11' N, long. 118°26'45" W). Named on Van Nuys (1953) 7.5' quadrangle. Postal authorities established Van Nuys post office in 1911 (Frickstad, p. 83). The name is for I.N. Van Nuys, who came to Los Angeles County in 1870 and later helped organize San Fernando Farm and Homestead Association (Bancroft, 1890, p. 759).
Van Tassel Canyon [LOS ANGELES]: *canyon,* drained by a stream that flows 2.5 miles to lowlands 2 miles northwest of Azusa city hall (lat. 34°09'15" N, long. 117°55'55" W; sec. 21, T 1 N, R 10 W). Named on Azusa (1953) 7.5' quadrangle.
Van Tassel Ridge [LOS ANGELES]: *ridge,* generally south-southeast-trending, 2.25 miles long, center 3 miles northwest of Azusa city hall (lat. 34°10'15" N, long. 117°56'15" W); the feature is east of Van Tassel Canyon. Named on Azusa (1953) 7.5' quadrangle.
Vasquez Canyon [LOS ANGELES]: *canyon,* drained by a stream that flows 4.5 miles to the stream in Bouquet Canyon 4 miles north of Solemint (lat. 34°28'25" N, long. 118°27'55" W; near W line sec. 33, T 5 N, 15 W). Named on Green Valley (1958) and Mint Canyon (1960) 7.5' quadrangles. Los Angeles County (1935) map shows a feature called Puckett Canyon that opens into Vasquez Canyon from the east near the mouth of Vasquez Canyon.
Vasquez Creek [LOS ANGELES]: *stream,* flows 1.25 miles to Big Tujunga Canyon 3.5 miles south of Condor Peak (lat. 34°16'35" N, long. 118°12'35" W; sec. 11, T 2 N, R 13 W).

Named on Condor Peak (1959) 7.5' quadrangle. Called Vasques Cr. on Los Angeles County (1935) map.

Vasquez Rocks [LOS ANGELES]: *relief feature*, 9 miles east-northeast of Solemint (lat. 34°29'05" N, long. 118°19' W; sec. 26, T 5 N, R 14 W). Named on Agua Dulce (1960) 7.5' quadrangle. Lang (1933) 6' quadrangle has the singular form "Vasquez Rock" for the name. The feature also is called Robbers' Roost—the outlaw Tiburcio Vasquez is said to have hid there (Hoover, Rensch, and Rensch, p. 168).

Vassar Canyon [LOS ANGELES]: *canyon*, drained by a stream that flows 1 mile to Sawpit Canyon 5 miles northwest of Azusa city hall (lat. 34°10'45" N, long. 117°58'20" W; at N line sec. 18, T 1 N, R 10 W). Azusa (1953) 7.5' quadrangle.

Veeh Reservoir [ORANGE]: *lake*, 2000 feet long, 2.25 miles west of El Toro (lat. 33°37'20" N, long. 117°43'50" W; near NE cor. sec. 29, T 6 S, R 8 W). Named on El Toro (1968) and San Juan Capistrano (1968) 7.5' quadrangles.

Vegala [LOS ANGELES]: *locality*, 5 miles southeast of Los Angeles city hall along Atchison, Topeka and Santa Fe Railroad (lat. 34°00'05" N, long. 118°10'30" W). Named on Alhambra (1926) 6' quadrangle.

Vejor: see **Malibu Junction** [LOS ANGELES].

Venedo Canyon [LOS ANGELES]: *canyon*, drained by a stream that flows 1.5 miles to San Gabriel Reservoir 6.5 miles north of Glendora city hall (lat. 34°13'40" N, long. 117°50'30" W; sec. 29, T 2 N, R 9 W). Named on Glendora (1953) 7.5' quadrangle.

Venice [LOS ANGELES]: *district*, 8 miles north-northwest of Manhattan Beach city hall in Los Angeles (lat. 33°59'30" N, long. 118° 27'30" W). Named on Beverly Hills (1950) and Venice (1950) 7.5' quadrangles. Postal authorities established Venice post office in 1905 (Frickstad, p. 83). Abbot Kinney designed and built the community in 1904 with a system of canals in the style of Venice, Italy (Gudde, 1949, p. 377). It became part of Los Angeles in 1925 (Hanna, p. 343).

Venice Beach [LOS ANGELES]: *beach*, along the coast north of the mouth of Ballona Creek at Venice (lat. 33°58'45" N, long. 118° 28' W). Named on Venice (1950) 7.5' quadrangle.

Venta: see **Irvine Siding** [ORANGE].

Ven-Tu Park [VENTURA]: *settlement*, 0.5 mile south of Newbury Park (lat. 34°10'30" N, long. 118°54'30" W; sec. 18, T 1 N, R 19 W). Named on Newbury Park (1951) 7.5' quadrangle.

Ventura [VENTURA]: *city*, along the coast between the mouth of Ventura River and the mouth of Santa Clara River (lat. 34°16'45" N, long. 119°17'25" W). Named on Saticoy (1951) and Ventura (1951) 7.5' quadrangles. Ventura (1951) 7.5' quadrangle has the alter-

nate name "San Buenaventura" for the place. Postal authorities established San Buenaventura post office in 1862 and changed the name to Ventura in 1889 (Frickstad, p. 219). The community incorporated under the name "San Buenaventura" in 1866, but United States Board on Geographic Names (1933, p. 788) rejected this designation for the city. The name is from San Buenaventura mission, founded at the site in 1782 (Hoover, Rensch, and Rensch, p. 576, 577). Postal authorities established Hammell post office 21 miles east of San Buenaventura post office in 1882 and discontinued it in 1883; the name was for James Hammell, first postmaster (Salley, p. 92). Ricard listed a place called Absco located 2 miles southeast of Ventura along Southern Pacific Railroad and named from initial letters of the term "American Beet Sugar Company"—the company built a refinery at the site in 1897.

Ventura County Small Craft Harbor: see **Channel Islands Harbor**, under **Port Hueneme** [VENTURA].

Ventura Harbor: see **Ventura Keys** [VENTURA].

Ventura Keys [VENTURA]: *water feature*, small-boat harbor 2 miles southeast of downtown Ventura along the coast (lat. 34°15'25" N, long. 119°15'50" W). Named on Ventura (1951, photorevised 1967) 7.5' quadrangle. United States Board on Geographic Names (1986, p. 2) approved the name "Ventura Harbor" for the place, and rejected the name "Ventura Marina."

Ventura Marina: see **Ventura Keys** [VENTURA].

Ventura River [VENTURA]: *stream*, formed by the confluence of Matilija Creek and North Fork Matilija Creek, flows 16 miles to the sea 1 mile west-southwest of downtown Ventura (lat. 34°16'25" N, long. 119°18'25" W). Named on Matilija (1952) and Ventura (1951) 7.5' quadrangles. Called Rio San Buenaventura on Peckham's (1866) map. Whitney (p. 125) called it San Buenaventura River. On Wheeler Springs (1944) 7.5' quadrangle, present North Fork Matilija Creek is called North Fork Ventura River.

Verdi: see **Cañada Larga** [VENTURA].

Verdugo [LOS ANGELES]: *locality*, 5.5 miles west of present Pasadena city hall (lat. 34°08'25" N, long. 118°14'35" W). Named on Pasadena (1900) 15' quadrangle. Postal authorities established Verdugo post office in 1884 and discontinued it in 1902 (Frickstad, p. 83).

Verdugo: see **Glendale** [LOS ANGELES].

Verdugo Canyon [LOS ANGELES]: *canyon*, 5.5 miles west-northwest of Pasadena city hall (lat. 34°11'15" N, long. 118°13'35" W); the canyon is at the east end of Verdugo Hills along Verdugo Wash. Named on Pasadena (1966) 7.5' quadrangle. On Pasadena (1953)

7.5' quadrangle, the name applies to the canyon a little father upstream along Verdugo Wash.

Verdugo Canyon [ORANGE]: *canyon,* drained by a stream that heads in Riverside County and flows 5.5 miles to San Juan Creek 6.5 miles east-northeast of San Juan Capistrano (lat. 33°31'25" N, long. 117°33'30" W). Named on Cañada Gobernadora (1968) and Sitton Peak (1954) 7.5' quadrangles. Members of the Verdugo family lived in the canyon (Meadows, p. 137).

Verdugo Canyon: see **Aliso Canyon** [ORANGE].

Verdugo City [LOS ANGELES]: *district,* 7 miles northwest of Pasadena city hall in Glendale (lat. 34°12'45" N, long. 118°14'30" W); the district is north of Verdugo Mountains on San Rafael grant. Named on Pasadena (1953) 7.5' quadrangle. Postal authorities established Verdugo City post office in 1924 (Frickstad, p. 83). Harry Fowler laid out the community in 1925 (Gudde, 1949, p. 378). The name recalls Jose Maria Verdugo, who received San Rafael grant.

Verdugo Creek: see **Verdugo Wash** [LOS ANGELES].

Verdugo Mountains [LOS ANGELES]: *range,* 11 miles north-northwest of Los Angeles city hall between La Canada (2) and Burbank (lat. 34°13' N, long. 118°17'30" W). Named on Burbank (1953) and Pasadena (1953) 7.5' quadrangles. The feature was called Sierra de los Berdugos on a diseño in 1843 (Gudde, 1949, p. 378).

Verdugo Park [LOS ANGELES]: *locality,* 5 miles west-northwest of present Pasadena city hall (lat. 34°10'05" N, long. 118°13'45" W); the place is in Verdugo Canyon. Named on Pasadena (1900) 15' quadrangle.

Verdugo Pines: see **Camp Verdugo Pines** [LOS ANGELES].

Verdugo Wash [LOS ANGELES]: *stream,* flows 9 miles to Los Angeles River 2.5 miles southeast of Burbank city hall (lat. 34°09'15" N, long. 118°16'40" W). Named on Burbank (1966) and Pasadena (1966) 7.5' quadrangles. The upper part of the stream is called Verdugo Creek on Burbank (1953) 7.5' quadrangle.

Vermont Canyon [LOS ANGELES]: *canyon,* 1 mile long, 5.5 miles northwest of Los Angeles city hall (lat. 34°07'10" N, long. 118°17'40" W). Named on Burbank (1953) and Hollywood (1953) 7.5' quadrangles.

Vernon [LOS ANGELES]: *locality,* industrial area 3.5 miles south of Los Angeles city hall (lat. 34°00'20" N, long. 118°13'45" W). Named on Los Angeles (1953) and South Gate (1952) 7.5' quadrangles. Pasadena (1900) 15' quadrangle shows a place called Vernondale located along the railroad at present Vernon. Postal authorities established Vernondale post office in 1888 and discontinued it in 1897; they established Vernon

post office in 1926 (Salley, p. 231). Vernon incorporated in 1905. The name commemorates George R. Vernon, who settled at the place after 1871 (Gudde, 1949, p. 379).

Vernondale: see **Vernon** [LOS ANGELES].

Veteran Springs: see **Glenview** [LOS ANGELES].

Vetter Mountain [LOS ANGELES]: *peak,* nearly 6 miles south of Pacifico Mountain (lat. 34°17'50" N, long. 118°01'40" W; at SW cor. sec. 34, T 3 N, R 11 W). Altitude 5908 feet. Named on Chilao Flat (1959) 7.5' quadrangle. Called Pine Mt. on Tujunga (1900) 15' quadrangle. The name "Vetter Mountain" commemorates Victor P. Vetter, Forest Service district ranger (Gudde, 1949, p. 379).

Vicente: see **Point Vicente** [LOS ANGELES].

Vickers Hot Springs [VENTURA]: *locality,* 6 miles west-northwest of the town of Ojai along Matilija Creek (lat. 34°29'35" N, long. 119°20'10" W). Named on Ventura (1904) 15' quadrangle. Waring (p. 63) mentioned a feature called Stingleys Hot Springs located about 0.5 mile below Vickers Hot Springs on the property of S.G. Stingley.

Victoria Beach [ORANGE]: *beach,* 2.25 miles south-southeast of Laguna Beach city hall along the coast (lat. 33°31' N, long. 117°45'35" W; near W line sec. 31, T 7 S, R 8 W). Named on Laguna Beach (1965) 7.5' quadrangle. The name is from Victoria Drive, a street that leads to the beach (Meadows, p. 137).

Viejo Siding [ORANGE]: *locality,* 2 miles south-southeast of La Habra along Union Pacific Railroad (lat. 33°54'15" N, long. 117°55'35" W). Named on Coyote Hills (1935) 7.5' quadrangle.

View Park [LOS ANGELES]: *district,* 2.5 miles north-northeast of Inglewood city hall (lat. 34°00' N, long. 118°20'30" W). Named on Hollywood (1966) and Inglewood (1964) 7.5' quadrangles.

Vignola: see **Stanton** [ORANGE].

Villa Canyon [LOS ANGELES]: *canyon,* drained by a stream that flows nearly 2 miles to Castaic Valley 7.5 miles northwest of Newhall (lat. 34°28'05" N, long. 118°37' W; at S line sec. 36, T 5 N, R 17 W). Named on Newhall (1952) and Val Verde (1952) 7.5' quadrangles.

Villa Park [ORANGE]: *town,* 3 miles northeast of Orange city hall (lat. 33°48'50" N, long. 117°48'45" W). Named on Orange (1964) 7.5' quadrangle. Postal authorities established Villa Park post office in 1888, discontinued it for a time in 1900, discontinued it again in 1906, and reestablished it 1964 (Salley, p. 232). Villa Park incorporated in 1962. The original name of the community was Mountain View for the school at the place, but when postal authorities rejected this name for a post office, the name of the town was changed to Villa Park—the post office opened in a country store at Wanda (Meadows, p. 137). The Southern Pacific Railroad station that opened 0.5 mile west of Villa Park in 1888 was called Wanda (Meadows, p. 138). Corona (1902) 30' quadrangle shows Wanda located along the railroad at the site of present Villa Park, and the name "Villa Park" applies to a place situated a little farther east.

Vicente: see **Point Vicente** [LOS ANGELES].

Vincent [LOS ANGELES]: *locality,* 5.5 miles south of Palmdale along Southern Pacific Railroad at Soledad Pass (lat. 34°30' N, long. 118°06'55" W; near E line sec. 22, T 5 N, R 12 W). Named on Pacifico Mountain (1959) and Palmdale (1958) 7.5' quadrangles. Postal authorities established Vincent post office in 1892 and discontinued it in 1896 (Salley, p. 232).

Vincente: see **Point Vincente**, under **Point Vicente** [LOS ANGELES].

Vincent Gap [LOS ANGELES]: *pass,* 6.5 miles northeast of Crystal Lake (lat. 34°22'25" N, long. 117°45'10" W; sec. 6, T 3 N, R 8 W); the pass is at the head of Vincent Gulch. Named on Crystal Lake (1958) 7.5' quadrangle.

Vincent Gulch [LOS ANGELES]: *canyon,* 3 miles long, along San Gabriel River above a point 6 miles northwest of Mount San Antonio (lat. 34°20'35" N, long. 117°43'25" W; sec. 16, T 3 N, R 8 W). Named on Mount San Antonio (1955) 7.5' quadrangle. The name commemorates Charles Vincent Dougherty, alias Charles Tom Vincent, who lived a solitary life in San Gabriel Mountains from 1870 until 1926 (Robinson, J.W., 1983, p. 164).

Vine Creek [LOS ANGELES]: *stream,* flows 2.5 miles to Walnut Creek Wash (present Walnut Creek) 3.25 miles east-southeast of Baldwin Park city hall (lat. 34°03'50" N, long. 117°54'35" W). Named on Baldwin Park (1953) 7.5' quadrangle.

Vineland: see **Baldwin Park** [LOS ANGELES].

Vineyard [LOS ANGELES]: *locality,* 5.5 miles west of Los Angeles city hall (lat. 34°02'50" N, long. 118°20'05" W). Named on Hollywood (1926) 6' quadrangle.

Vinvale [LOS ANGELES]: *locality,* 2.5 miles east of South Gate city hall along Southern Pacific Railroad (lat. 33°57'10" N, long. 118° 09'45" W). Named on South Gate (1952) 7.5' quadrangle.

Violin Canyon [LOS ANGELES]: *canyon,* drained by a stream that flows 6.5 miles to Marple Canyon 7.25 miles southeast of Whitaker Peak (lat. 34°30'30" N, long. 118°37'45" W; sec. 23, T 5 N, R 17 W). Named on Whitaker Peak (1958) 7.5' quadrangle. After Juan Yuca and Estanislao Olaje played the violin for grizzly bears there, the canyon was known as La Cañada del Violin— early American settlers preserved the name as Violin Canyon (Latta, p. 173).

Violin Summit [LOS ANGELES]: *pass,* 3 miles

east of Whitaker Peak (lat. 34°33'55" N, long. 118°41'05" W; sec. 33, T 6 N, R 17 W); the pass is near the head of Violin Canyon. Named on Whitaker Peak (1958) 7.5' quadrangle.

Virgenes Creek: see **Las Virgenes Creek** [LOS ANGELES-VENTURA].

Virginia City: see **North Long Beach** [LOS ANGELES].

Virginia Colony [VENTURA]: *locality,* 1 mile east of Moorpark (lat. 34°17'15" N, long. 118°51'35" W; sec. 3, T 2 N, R 19 W). Named on Simi (1951) 7.5' quadrangle. The name is from the given name of a woman who did missionary and social work with Mexicans who lived at the place in the early 1920's (Ricard).

Vista del Mar [LOS ANGELES]: *district,* 3.25 miles north of Long Beach city hall (lat. 33°49'05" N, long. 118°11'55" W). Named on Long Beach (1949) 7.5' quadrangle.

Vista Picnic Ground [LOS ANGELES]: *locality,* 2.5 miles east-northeast of Waterman Mountain (lat. 34°20'55" N, long. 117°53'30" W; sec. 14, T 3 N, R 10 W). Named on Waterman Mountain (1959) 7.5' quadrangle.

Vizcaino: see **Mount Vizcaino**, under **Cactus Peak** [LOS ANGELES].

Vizcaino Point: see **San Nicolas Island** [VENTURA].

Vogel Canyon [LOS ANGELES]: *canyon,* drained by a stream that flows nearly 3 miles to Big Tujunga Canyon 2.5 miles south of Condor Peak (lat. 34°17'20" N, long. 118°13'35" W; sec. 3, T 2 N, R 13 W). Named on Condor Peak (1959) 7.5' quadrangle.

Vogel Flat [LOS ANGELES]: *area,* 2.5 miles south of Condor Peak in Big Tujunga Canyon (lat. 34°17'20" N, long. 118°13'35" W; sec. 3, T 2 N, R 13 W); the place is at the mouth of Vogel Canyon.. Named on Condor Peak (1959) 7.5' quadrangle.

Volfe Canyon [LOS ANGELES]: *canyon,* less than 2 miles long, joins Bell Canyon to form Big Dalton Canyon 5 miles northeast of Glendora city hall (lat. 34°10'55" N, long. 117°47'45" W; sec. 11, T 1 N, R 9 W). Named on Glendora (1953) 7.5' quadrangle.

Voltaire: see **Three Points** [LOS ANGELES] (1).

Von Schritz: see **Greenville** [ORANGE].

Vorhees Canyon: see **Tapie Canyon** [LOS ANGELES].

Vulture Field: see **Downey** [LOS ANGELES].

Vulture Crags [ORANGE]: *relief feature,* 4 miles west-southwest of Santiago Peak (lat. 33°41'35" N, long. 117°36'10" W; sec. 34, T 5 S, T 7 W). Named on Santiago Peak (1954) 7.5' quadrangle. J.E. Pleasants and Samuel Shrewsbury named the feature for California condors that frequented the place (Stephenson, p. 129).

– W –

Wadstrom [VENTURA]: *locality,* 2.5 miles north of Ventura along Southern Pacific Railroad (lat. 34°18'55" N, long. 119°17'25" W). Named on Ventura (1951) 7.5' quadrangle.

Wagon Road Canyon [VENTURA]: *canyon,* drained by a stream that flows 9 miles to Alamo Creek (2) 4.5 miles north-northeast of Reyes Peak (lat. 34°41'35" N, long. 119°15'20" W; near N line sec. 19, T 7 N, R 22 W). Named on San Guillermo (1943) 7.5' quadrangle.

Wagon Wheel Canyon [ORANGE]: *canyon,* drained by a stream that flows 2.5 miles to Cañada Gobernadora 6 miles northeast of San Juan Capistrano (lat. 33°33'35" N, long. 117°35'10" W; near W line sec. 14, T 7 S, R 7 W). Named on Cañada Gobernadora (1968) 7.5' quadrangle.

Wagon Wheels Camp: see **Fox Creek** [LOS ANGELES].

Wahoo [LOS ANGELES]: *locality,* 5 miles west-southwest of Sunland along Southern Pacific Railroad (lat. 34°14'35" N, long. 118° 23'50" W). Named on Sunland (1942) 6' quadrangle.

Walnut [LOS ANGELES]: *town,* 6.5 miles west-southwest of Pomona city hall (lat. 34°00'55" N, long. 117°51'15" W). Named on Baldwin Park (1966) and San Dimas (1966) 7.5' quadrangles. Called Lemon on Pomona (1904) 15' quadrangle. Postal authorities established Lemon post office in 1895 and changed the name to Walnut in 1908 (Frickstad, p. 76). The town incorporated in 1959.

Walnut Canyon [LOS ANGELES]: *canyon,* drained by a stream that flows 1.5 miles to the sea 1.25 miles northeast of Point Dume (lat. 34°00'50" N, long. 118°47'30" W). Named on Point Dume (1951) 7.5' quadrangle.

Walnut Canyon [ORANGE]: *canyon,* drained by a stream that flows 2.5 miles to Santa Ana Canyon 6 miles northeast of Orange city hall (lat. 33°50'50" N, long. 117°46'40" W). Named on Black Star Canyon (1950) and Orange (1964) 7.5' quadrangles. The feature also was called Cañada de la Madera (Meadows, p. 138). An inhabited place in Santa Ana Canyon near the mouth of Walnut Canyon was called Peralta—the headquarters of the Peralta family was there (Meadows, p. 110).

Walnut Canyon Reservoir [ORANGE]: *lake,* 2000 feet long, behind a dam 6.5 miles east-northeast of Orange city hall (lat. 33°50'25" N, long. 117°45'05" W); the lake is in Walnut Canyon. Named on Black Star Canyon (1967, photorevised 1988) and Orange (1964, photorevised 1981) 7.5' quadrangles.

Walnut Creek [LOS ANGELES]: *stream,* flows 14 miles to San Gabriel River 1.5 miles southeast of El Monte city hall (lat. 34°03'35" N, long. 118°00'15" W). Named on Baldwin Park

(1966), El Monte (1966), and San Dimas (1954) 7.5' quadrangles. Called Walnut Creek Wash on Baldwin Park (1953) 7.5' quadrangle, but United States Board on Geographic Names (1967b, p. 5) rejected this name for the feature

Walnut Creek Wash: see **Walnut Creek** [LOS ANGELES].

Walnut Park [LOS ANGELES]: *district,* 1.5 miles northwest of South Gate city hall (lat. 33°58'10" N, long. 118°13'15" W). Named on South Gate (1964) 7.5' quadrangle.

Walnut Siding [LOS ANGELES]: *locality,* 7 miles west-southwest of Pomona city hall, along Union Pacific Railroad (lat. 34°00'15" N, long. 117°51'10" W). Named on San Dimas (1966) 7.5' quadrangle.

Walnut Station [LOS ANGELES]: *locality,* nearly 7 miles west-southwest of present Pomona city hall along Union Pacific Railroad (lat. 34°00'15" N, long. 117°51'15" W); the place is 0.5 mile south-southeast of Walnut. Named on Covina (1927) 6' quadrangle.

Walteria [LOS ANGELES]: *district,* 2.5 miles south of Torrance city hall (lat. 33°48'05" N, long. 118°21' W). Named on Torrance (1964) 7.5' quadrangle. Postal authorities established Walteria post office in 1926 and discontinued it in 1954 (Frickstad, p. 83). The name is from Captain Walters, who built Walters hotel in the early part of the twentieth century (Gudde, 1969, p. 358).

Waltz [LOS ANGELES]: *locality,* 1.5 miles south-southeast of Newhall along Southern Pacific Railroad (lat. 34°21'35" N, long. 118°31'10" W). Named on Newhall (1933) 6' quadrangle. Called Waltz Jct. on California Division of Highways' (1934) map.

Wanda: see **Villa Park** [ORANGE].

Ward Canyon [LOS ANGELES]: *canyon,* 0.5 mile long, 9 miles northwest of Pasadena city hall (lat. 34°14'55" N, long. 118°14'50" W; sec. 21, T 2 N, R 13 W). Named on Condor Peak (1959) and Pasadena (1953) 7.5' quadrangles.

Warm Spring: see **Warm Springs Camp** [LOS ANGELES].

Warm Springs Camp [LOS ANGELES]: *locality,* 1.25 miles northeast of Warm Springs Mountain in Elizabeth Lake Canyon (lat. 34° 36'30" N, long. 118°33'35" W). Named on Warm Springs Mountain (1958) 7.5' quadrangle. Tejon (1903) 30' quadrangle shows a spring called Warm Spring at the site, and Los Angeles County (1935) map has the name "Warm Springs" there.

Warm Springs Canyon [LOS ANGELES]: *canyon,* drained by a stream that flows nearly 3 miles to Elizabeth Lake Canyon 1.5 miles northeast of Warm Springs Mountain (lat. 34°36'25" N, long. 118°33'35" W). Named on Warm Springs Mountain (1958) 7.5' quadrangle.

Warm Springs Mountain [LOS ANGELES]:

peak, 14 miles north of Newhall (lat.
34°35'45" N, long. 118°34'45" W). Altitude
4020 feet. Named on Warm Springs Mountain (1958) 7.5' quadrangle.le.
Warring Canyon [VENTURA]: *canyon,*
drained by a stream that flows 2 miles to the
valley of Santa Clara River at Piru (lat.
34°25'05" N, long. 118°47'50" W; sec. 19, T
4 N, R 18 W). Named on Piru (1952,
photorevised 1969) 7.5' quadrangle. Called
Nigger Canyon on Piru (1952) 7.5' quadrangle; United States Board on Geographic
Names (1970b, p. 3) gave this name as a variant.
Washington: see **Mount Washington** [LOS
ANGELES].
Wason Barranca [VENTURA]: *gully,* extends
for 2.25 miles from the mouth of Peppertree
Canyon to Santa Clara River 0.5 mile east-
southeast of Saticoy (lat. 34°16'55" N, long.
119°08'20" W). Named on Saticoy (1951) 7.5'
quadrangle. The name commemorates Milton
Wason, who was the first county judge of
Ventura County (Ricard).
Water Canyon [LOS ANGELES]: *canyon,*
drained by a stream that flows 1 mile to Morris Reservoir 3.5 miles north-northeast of
Azusa city hall (lat. 34°11' N, long.
117°52'40" W; sec. 12, T 1 N, R 10 W).
Named on Azusa (1953) 7.5' quadrangle.
Waterdale: see **Oban** [LOS ANGELES].
Waterman Mountain [LOS ANGELES]: *peak,*
12 miles north-northwest of Azusa (lat.
34°20'10" N, long. 117°56'10" W). Altitude
8038 feet. Named on Waterman Mountain
(1959) 7.5' quadrangle. Called Mt. Waterman
on Los Angeles County (1935) map. Rock
Creek (1903) 15' quadrangle has the name
"Waterman Mt." for present Twin Peaks, located 1.5 miles farther south. Bob Waterman,
his wife Liz, and Perry Switzer climbed the
peak in 1889; the men named it Lady
Waterman Mountain for Liz, whom they believed was the first white woman to cross San
Gabriel Mountains, but the name became simply Mount Waterman (Robinson, J.W., 1977,
p. 191).
Water Street [LOS ANGELES]: *locality,* 2.5
miles northeast of Los Angeles city hall along
Atchison, Topeka and Santa Fe Railroad (lat.
34°05' N, long. 118°13' W). Named on Los
Angeles (1953) 7.5' quadrangle.
Waterville: see **Cypress** [ORANGE].
Watkins Creek [LOS ANGELES]: *stream,*
flows 2 miles to Holmes Creek nearly 2 miles
west-southwest of Valyermo (lat. 34°26'10"
N, long. 17°52'40" W; sec. 13, T 4 N, R 10
W). Name on Valyermo (1958) 7.5' quadrangle.
Watson [LOS ANGELES]: *locality,* 3.5 miles
northwest of Long Beach city hall along
Southern Pacific Railroad (lat. 33°48'30" N,
long. 118°14'05" W). Named on Long Beach
(1964) 7.5' quadrangle. Called Watson Cross-

ing on Downey (1902) 15' quadrangle. The
name is from Maria Dominguez de Watson,
who was allocated the part of San Pedro grant
where the place is situated (Gudde, 1949, p.
384).
Watson Crossing: see **Watson** [LOS ANGE-
LES].
Watson Junction [LOS ANGELES]: *locality,*
5.5 miles east-southeast of Torrance city hall
along Atchison Topeka and Santa Fe Railroad
(lat. 33°48' N, long. 118°15'10" W). Named
on Torrance (1964) 7.5' quadrangle.
Watts [LOS ANGELES]: *district,* 2.25 miles
west-southwest of South Gate in Los
Angeles (lat. 33°56'30" N, long. 118°14'30"
W). Named on South Gate (1952) 7.5' quadrangle. Postal authorities established Watts
post office in 1904 (Frickstad, p. 83). The
name commemorates C.H. Watts, who had a
ranch at the place; the community originally
was called Mud Town—Los Angeles annexed
the district in 1926 (Gudde, 1969, p. 359).
Way Hill [LOS ANGELES]: *ridge,* east-trending, 0.5 mile long, 4.25 miles northeast of
Pomona city hall (lat. 34°06'45" N, long. 117°
48'50" W). Named on San Dimas (1954) 7.5'
quadrangle.
Wayside Canyon [LOS ANGELES]: *canyon,*
drained by a stream that flows 3 miles to
Castaic Valley 7 miles northwest of Newhall
(lat. 34°27'55" N, long. 118°36'15" W).
Named on Newhall (1952) 7.5' quadrangle,
which shows Wayside Honor Ranch at the
mouth of the canyon.
Weakly Canyon: see **Hickey Canyon** [OR-
ANGE].
Webb Canyon [LOS ANGELES]: *canyon,*
drained by a stream that flows 1.5 miles to
Thompson Wash 4.5 miles north of Pomona
city hall (lat. 34°07'15" N, long. 117°44'15"
W; at N line sec. 5, T 1 S, R 8 W). Named on
Mount Baldy (1954) and Ontario (1954) 7.5'
quadrangles.
Webber Canyon [LOS ANGELES]: *canyon,* 0.5
mile long, 7 miles northwest of Pasadena city
hall (lat. 34°13'45" N, long. 118°12'55" W;
sec. 26, T 2 N, R 13 W). Named on Pasadena
(1953) 7.5' quadrangle.
Webbers Camp: see **Weber Camp** [LOS AN-
GELES].
Weber Camp [LOS ANGELES]: *locality,* 4.5
miles west-southwest of Mount San Antonio
in Coldwater Canyon (2) (lat. 34°15'25" N,
long. 117°42'50" W). Named on Mount San
Antonio (1955) 7.5' quadrangle. Called
Webbers Camp on Los Angeles County
(1935) map. John P. Weber founded Weber's
Camp in 1906—it lasted until 1924
(Robinson, J.W., 1983, p. 97-98).
Weeks Poultry Community: see **Winnetka**
[LOS ANGELES].
Weir Canyon [ORANGE]: *canyon,* drained by
a stream that flows 3.25 miles to Santiago
Creek 5.25 miles east-northeast of present

Orange city hall (lat. 33°48'35" N, long. 117°45'35" W). Named on Black Star Canyon (1967) and Orange (1950) 7.5' quadrangles. The feature first was called Los Bueyos Canyon for the oxen that drew carretas over the road there; the name "Weir Canyon" is from a weir built in the canyon (Meadows, p. 80, 138).

Weldon Canyon [LOS ANGELES]: *canyon,* 1.25 miles long, 3 miles south-southeast of Newhall (lat. 34°20'20" N, long. 118°30'50" W; on S line sec. 13, T 3 N, R 16 W). Named on Oat Mountain (1952) 7.5' quadrangle.

Weldon Canyon [VENTURA]: *canyon,* drained by a stream that flows 3 miles to Ventura River 4.5 miles north of Ventura (lat. 34° 20'40" N, long. 119°17'50" W); the mouth of the stream is at Weldons. Named on Ventura (1951) 7.5' quadrangle.

Weldons [VENTURA]: *locality,* 4.5 miles north of Ventura along Southern Pacific Railroad (lat. 34°20'40" N, long. 119°17'45" W); the place is on Cañada Larga o Verde grant. Named on Ventura (1951) 7.5' quadrangle. The name commemorates W.R.H. Weldon, who owned and operated Canet ranch in the 1890's (Ricard). California Division of Highways' (1934) map shows a place called Canet located 1 mile northwest of Weldons along the railroad. The name "Canet" recalls Anselme Canet, a Frenchman who settled in Ventura in 1873 and purchased part of Cañada Larga o Verde grant (Hanna, p. 54).

Well Canyon: see **Santa Felicia Canyon** [LOS ANGELES-VENTURA].

Wellington Heights [LOS ANGELES]: *district,* 3.25 miles east-southeast of Los Angeles city hall (lat. 34°02'20" N, long. 118°11'10" W). Named on Los Angeles (1953) 7.5' quadrangle.

Werner Camp [LOS ANGELES]: *locality,* 3.25 miles south-southeast of Acton in Arrastre Canyon (lat. 34°25'20" N, long. 118°10'55" W; at NW cor. sec. 19, T 4 N, R 12 W). Named on Acton (1959) 7.5' quadrangle.

West: see **Sherman** [LOS ANGELES].

West Alhambra: see **Dolgeville**, under **Shorb** [LOS ANGELES].

West Anaheim [ORANGE]: *locality,* 4.25 miles east-southeast of Buena Park civic center along Southern Pacific Railroad (lat. 33° 49'50" N, long. 117°55'55" W; sec. 16, T 4 S, R 10 W). Named on Anaheim (1965) 7.5' quadrangle. Called Loara on California Mining Bureau's (1909b) map. Postal authorities established Loara post office in 1900 and discontinued it in 1907; the name was for the wife of the first postmaster (Salley, p. 124).

West Anaheim Junction [ORANGE]: *locality,* 7.25 miles southeast of Buena Park civic center along Southern Pacific Railroad (lat. 33°47'50" N, long. 117°53'45" W; sec. 26, T 4 S, R 10 W). Named on Anaheim (1950) 7.5' quadrangle.

West Arcadia [LOS ANGELES]: *district,* in the southwest part of Arcadia (lat. 34°07'30" N, long. 118°03'15" W). Named on El Monte (1953) and Mount Wilson (1953) 7.5' quadrangles.

West Casitas Pass [VENTURA]: *pass,* 5.5 miles south of White Ledge Peak (lat. 34°23'20" N, long. 119°24'50" W; sec. 32, T 4 N, R 24 W); the feature is 2 miles west of East Casitas pass at the head of Casitas Creek. Named on White Ledge Peak (1952) 7.5' quadrangle.

Westchester [LOS ANGELES]: *district,* 5 miles north of Manhattan Beach city hall in Los Angeles (lat. 33°57'35" N, long. 118°24' W). Named on Venice (1950) 7.5' quadrangle.

West Cove [LOS ANGELES]: *embayment,* 1.5 miles south-southwest of Northwest Harbor on San Clemente Island (lat. 33°00'50" N, long. 118°35'50" W); the feature is on the west side of the island. Named on San Clemente Island North (1943) 7.5' quadrangle.

West Covina [LOS ANGELES]: *city,* 1.5 miles southeast of Baldwin Park city hall (lat. 34°04'15" N, long. 117°56'10" W). Named on Baldwin Park (1966) and San Dimas (1966) 7.5' quadrangles. Postal authorities established West Covina post office in 1954 (Salley, p. 237). The city incorporated in 1923.

West Coyote Hills [ORANGE]: *range,* extends for 3 miles east from Los Angeles-Orange county line to Brea Canyon; center 2.5 miles south of downtown La Habra (lat. 33°54' N, long. 117°57'45" W); the range is on Los Coyotes grant. Named on La Habra (1964) 7.5' quadrangle. Called Coyote Hills on La Habra (1952) 7.5' quadrangle.

West End: see **Lands End** [LOS ANGELES].

Western Anacapa: see **Anacapa Island** [VENTURA].

West Fork: see **Camp West Fork**, under **Camp Hi-Hill** [LOS ANGELES].

Westgate [LOS ANGELES]: *district,* 4.25 miles west-southwest of Beverly Hills city hall in Los Angeles (lat. 34°03'20" N, long. 118° 28'15" W). Named on Beverly Hills (1950) 7.5' quadrangle. Postal authorities established Westgate post office in 1909 and discontinued it in 1915 (Frickstad, p. 83).

Westgate Heights: see **Brentwood Heights** [LOS ANGELES].

West Glendale [LOS ANGELES]: *locality,* 1.5 miles west of Glendale city hall along Southern Pacific Railroad (lat. 34°08'55" N, long. 118°16'20" W). Named on Burbank (1953) 7.5' quadrangle. Postal authorities established West Glendale post office in 1888 and discontinued it in 1893 (Frickstad, p. 83).

West Hills: see **Canoga Park** [LOS ANGELES].

West Hollywood [LOS ANGELES]: *city,* 8 miles west-northwest of Los Angeles city hall (lat. 34°05'30" N, long. 118°22'30" W). Named on Beverly Hills (1950) and Hollywood (1953) 7.5' quadrangles.

West Lake [LOS ANGELES]: *lake,* 1200 feet

long, 2.25 miles west of present Los Angeles city hall (lat. 34°03'25" N, long. 118°16'45" W). Named on Santa Monica (1902) 15' quadrangle.

West Lake Elizabeth: see **Lake Hughes** [LOS ANGELES].

Westlake Village: see **Russell Valley** [LOS ANGELES-VENTURA].

West Liebre Gulch: see **West Fork**, under **Liebre Gulch** [LOS ANGELES].

West Los Angeles [LOS ANGELES]: *district*, 3.5 miles southwest of Beverly Hills city hall in Los Angeles (lat. 34°02'30" N, long. 118° 27'15" W). Named on Beverly Hills (1966) 7.5' quadrangle. Beverly Hills (1950) 7.5' quadrangle has the designation "Sawtelle (West Los Angeles P.O.)" at the place. Postal authorities established Sawtelle post office in 1899 and discontinued it in 1929; the named "Sawtell" was for W.E Sawtelle, owner of the site and manager of Pacific Land Company—the place also was known as Barrett (Salley, p. 199). Postal authorities established West Los Angeles post office in 1922, discontinued it in 1926 when they moved the post office to Sawtelle, and reestablished it in 1929 (Salley, p. 238). California Mining Bureau's (1909b) map shows a place called Soldiers Home located just northwest of Sawtelle. Postal authorities established Soldiers Home post office in 1889 and discontinued it in 1915 (Frickstad, p. 81).

Westminister [ORANGE]: *city*, 5.5 miles north-northeast of Huntington Beach city hall (lat. 33°44'15" N, long. 117°58'15" W). Named on Anaheim (1965), Los Alamitos (1964), Newport Beach (1965), and Seal Beach (1965) 7.5' quadrangles. Postal authorities established Westminister post office in 1874 (Frickstad, p. 118), and the city incorporated in 1957. The Reverend L.P. Weber started a colony at the place in the 1870's for people sympathetic with the principles of the Presbyterian Church as formulated in the seventeenth century by the Westminister Assembly (Gudde, 1949, p. 387).

Weston: see **Ben Weston Beach** [LOS ANGELES]; **Ben Weston Point** [LOS ANGELES].

West Orange: see **Santa Ana** [ORANGE].

West Palmdale: see **Palmdale** [LOS ANGELES].

West Pine Flat [LOS ANGELES]: *area*, less than 0.5 mile east of Crystal Lake (lat. 34°19'05" N, long. 117°50'20" W); the place is at the southwest end of Pine Flats. Named on Crystal Lake (1958) 7.5' quadrangle.

West Ravine [LOS ANGELES]: *canyon*, less than 1 mile long, 4 miles north of Pasadena city hall (lat. 34°12'20" N, long. 118° 09' W; on W line sec. 4, T 1 N, R 12 W). Named on Pasadena(1953) 7.5' quadrangle.

West Saticoy [VENTURA]: *settlement*, less than 1 mile west of Saticoy (lat. 34°17'05" N, long. 119°09'35" W). Named on Saticoy (1951) 7.5'

quadrangle. Postal authorities established West Saticoy post office in 1892 and discontinued it in 1913 (Salley, p. 238). The place first was called Saticoy, but when in 1887 the railroad was built nearly a mile to the east, a new community (present Saticoy) at the railroad took the name (Ricard).

Westward Beach [LOS ANGELES]: *beach*, extends for 1 mile along the coast northwest from Point Dume (lat. 34°00'30" N, long. 118° 48'50" W). Named on Point Dume (1951) 7.5' quadrangle. Called Zuma Beach on Dume Point (1932) 6' quadrangle.

West Whittier [LOS ANGELES]: *district*, 2 miles northwest of present Whittier city hall (lat. 33°59'25" N, long. 118°03'45" W). Named on Whittier (1949) 7.5' quadrangle. Postal authorities established West Whittier post office in 1926 and discontinued it that year (Salley, p. 238).

Westwood [LOS ANGELES]: *district*, 2 miles west-southwest of Beverly Hills city hall (lat. 34°03'25" N, long. 118°25'45" W). Named on Beverly Hills (1966) 7.5' quadrangle. Called Sunset on Lankershim Ranch Land and Water Company's (1888) map, and called Westwood Hills on Sawtelle (1934) 6' quadrangle.

Westwood Hills: see **Westwood** [LOS ANGELES].

Westwood Village [LOS ANGELES]: *locality*, nearly 2 miles west-southwest of Beverly Hills city hall (lat. 34°03'35" N, long. 118° 26'40" W). Named on Beverly Hills (1950) 7.5' quadrangle.

Whale Rock [LOS ANGELES]: *rock*, 2 miles south-southeast of Silver Peak, and 200 feet off the south side of Santa Catalina Island (lat. 33°25'55" N, long. 118°33'35" W). Named on Santa Catalina West (1943) 7.5' quadrangle.

Wheeler Canyon [VENTURA]: *canyon*, drained by a stream that flows 7 miles to the valley of Santa Clara River 3.5 miles north of Saticoy (lat. 34°20'05" N, long. 119°08'20" W). Named on Ojai (1952) and Saticoy (1951) 7.5' quadrangles. The feature was called Millhouse Canyon in the 1860's for Dr. Millhouse, who kept a boarding house for oilfield workers there (Ricard).

Wheeler Gorge [VENTURA]: *narrows*, 1 mile east of Wheeler Springs along North Fork Matilija Creek (lat. 34°30'30" N, long. 119°16'30" W; at S line sec. 15, T 5 N, R 23 W). Named on Wheeler Springs (1943) 7.5' quadrangle.

Wheeler's Cold Spring: see **Wheeler Springs** [VENTURA].

Wheeler's Hot Springs: see **Wheeler Springs** [VENTURA].

Wheeler Springs [VENTURA]: *locality*, 16 miles north of Ventura (lat. 34°30'30" N, long. 119°17'25" W; at S line sec. 16, T 5 N, R 23 W). Named on Wheeler Springs (1943) 7.5' quadrangle. Postal authorities established

Wheeler Springs post office in 1913 and discontinued it in 1962 (Salley, p. 239). Huguenin (p. 766-767) called the place Wheeler's Hot Springs, mentioned that it had been a resort since 1890, and noted that the resort owner conducted a summer camp at Wheeler's Cold Spring, located 9 miles by trail north of Wheeler's Hot Springs in the canyon of Sespe Creek.

Whisky Spring [LOS ANGELES]: *spring*, 11 miles south-southeast of the village of Lake Hughes (lat. 34°31'25" N, long. 118°22'35" W; near NW cor. sec. 17, T 5 N, R 14 W). Named on Green Valley (1958) 7.5' quadrangle.

Whitaker Canyon: see **Ruby Canyon** [LOS ANGELES] (1).

Whitaker Peak [LOS ANGELES]: *peak*, nearly 17 miles south-southeast of Gorman (lat. 34°34'20" N, long. 118°44' W; near N line sec. 36, T 6 N, R 18 W). Altitude 4148 feet. Named on Whitaker Peak (1958) 7.5' quadrangle.

Whitaker Summit [LOS ANGELES]: *pass*, 1.5 miles northeast of Whitaker Peak (lat. 34°35'15" N, long. 118°42'50" W; near NE cor. sec. 30, T 6 N, R 17 W). Named on Whitaker Peak (1958) 7.5' quadrangle.

Whiteacre Peak [VENTURA]: *peak*, 4.5 miles south of Cobblestone Mountain (lat. 34°32'30" N, long. 118°52'20" W). Altitude 5079 feet. Named on Cobblestone Mountain (1958) 7.5' quadrangle.

White Canyon [ORANGE]: *canyon*, about 0.5 mile long, opens into Silverado Canyon 9 miles north-northeast of El Toro at Silverado (lat. 33°44'45" N, long. 117°38'05" W). Named on El Toro (1968) 7.5' quadrangle.

White Cove [LOS ANGELES]: *embayment*, 4.25 miles north-northwest of Avalon on the northeast side of Santa Catalina Island (lat. 33°23'35" N, long. 118°22'05" W). Named on Santa Catalina East (1950) 7.5' quadrangle. Smith's (1897) map has the name "Whitley's Cove" for an embayment that includes present White Cove.

White Heather [LOS ANGELES]: *locality*, 7 miles south of the village of Leona Valley in Sierra Pelona Valley (lat. 34°31'10" N, long. 118°18'15" W; near W line sec. 13, T 5 N, R 14 W). Named on Sleepy Valley (1958) 7.5' quadrangle.

White Island: see **Island White** [LOS ANGELES].

White Ledge Peak [VENTURA]: *peak*, 15 miles north-northwest of Ventura (lat. 34°28'10" N, long. 119°23'30" W). Altitude 4640 feet. Named on White Ledge Peak (1952) 7.5' quadrangle.

White Mountain [VENTURA]: *ridge*, west- to southwest-trending, 3 miles long, 2 miles north-northeast of Cobblestone Mountain (lat. 34°37'55" N, long. 118°50'50" W). Named on Black Mountain (1958) and Cobblestone

Mountain (1958) 7.5' quadrangles.

White Oak Canyon [LOS ANGELES]: *canyon*, drained by a stream that flows 1 mile to Big Tujunga Canyon 2.5 miles southeast of Condor Peak (lat. 34°18' N, long. 118°11'05" W). Named on Condor Peak (1959) 7.5' quadrangle.

White Point: see **Whites Point** [LOS ANGELES].

White Rock [LOS ANGELES]: *relief feature*, 7.25 miles northwest of Pyramid Head on the northeast side of San Clemente Island (lat. 32°53'30" N, long. 118°26'25" W). Named on San Clemente Island Central (1943) 7.5' quadrangle.

White Rock: see **Bird Rock** [LOS ANGELES].

White Saddle [LOS ANGELES]: *pass*, 5.25 miles northwest of Azusa city hall (lat. 34°11'50" N, long. 117°57'25" W; near SW cor. sec. 5, T 1 N, R 10 W). Named on Azusa (1953) 7.5' quadrangle.

Whites Canyon: see **Solemint** [LOS ANGELES].

Whites Landing [LOS ANGELES]: *locality*, 4.25 miles north-northwest of Avalon on the northeast side of Santa Catalina Island (lat. 33°23'40" N, long. 118°22'10" W); the place is at White Cove. Named on Santa Catalina East (1950) 7.5' quadrangle. Called Swain's Ldg. on Smith's (1897) map.

Whites Point [LOS ANGELES]: *promontory*, 1.5 miles west-northwest of Point Fermin (lat 33°42'50" N, long. 118°19' W). Named on San Pedro (1964) 7.5' quadrangle. United States Board on Geographic Names (1983a, p. 5) approved the form "White Point" for the name.

Whites Point Hot Springs [LOS ANGELES]: *locality*, 1.5 miles west-northwest of Point Fermin (lat. 33°43' N, long. 118°19'10" W); the place is near Whites Point (present White Point). Named on San Pedro Hills (1928) 6' quadrangle.

Whitewashed Rock: see **Balanced Rock**, under **Pyramid Head** [LOS ANGELES].

Whitewater Canyon [LOS ANGELES]: *canyon*, drained by a stream that flows 0.5 mile to Pacoima Canyon 7 miles north-northwest of Sunland (lat. 34°21'20" N, long. 118°21'10" W; sec. 9, T 3 N, R 14 W). Named on Sunland (1953) 7.5' quadrangle.

Whitley's Cove: see **White Cove** [LOS ANGELES].

Whitleys Peak [LOS ANGELES]: *peak*, 3.5 miles northwest of Avalon on Santa Catalina Island (lat. 33°22'55" N, long. 118°22'05" W). Altitude 1302 feet. Named on Santa Catalina East (1950) 7.5' quadrangle.

Whitney Canyon [LOS ANGELES]: *canyon*, 3.5 miles long, opens into the canyon of Newhall Creek 2 miles southeast of Newhall (lat. 34°21'55" N, long. 118°30'15" W). Named on San Fernando (1953) 7.5' quadrangle.

Whittier [LOS ANGELES]: *city*, 17 miles north-northeast of Long Beach city hall (lat. 33°58'25" N, long. 118°02' W). Named on El Monte (1966) and Whittier (1965) 7.5' quadrangles. Postal authorities established Whittier post office in 1887 (Frickstad, p. 83), and the city incorporated in 1898. An organization of Quakers founded the place in 1887, and at the suggestion of Micajah D. Johnson named it for John Greenleaf Whitter, the Quaker poet (Gudde, 1949, p. 389).

Whittier: see **East Whittier** [LOS ANGELES]; **North Whittier Heights** [LOS ANGELES]; **South Whittier** [LOS ANGELES]; **South Whittier Heights** [LOS ANGELES]; **West Whittier** [LOS ANGELES].

Whittier Creek [LOS ANGELES]: *stream,* flows 1.5 miles to Painter Lagoon 2 miles south-southwest of present Whittier city hall (lat. 33°56'45" N, long. 118°02'45" W). Named on Whittier (1949) 7.5' quadrangle.

Whittier Hills: see **Puente Hills** [LOS ANGELES].

Whittier Junction [LOS ANGELES]: *locality,* 5 miles south-southwest of El Monte city hall along Union Pacific Railroad (lat. 34°00'15" N, long. 118°04' W). Named on El Monte (1953) 7.5' quadrangle.

Whittier Narrows: see **Puente Hills** [LOS ANGELES].

Wicham Canyon [LOS ANGELES]: *canyon,* drained by a stream that flows 1.5 miles to Pico Canyon 3.5 miles west of Newhall (lat. 34° 22'40" N, long. 118°35'40" W; near N line sec. 6, T 3 N, R 16 W). Named on Newhall (1952) and Oat Mountain (1952) 7.5' quadrangles. Called Big Moore Canyon on Pico (1940) 6' quadrangle.

Wickiup Campground [LOS ANGELES]: *locality,* 6.5 miles southwest of Pacifico Mountain in Big Tujunga Canyon (lat. 34°18'20" N, long. 118°06'30" W; sec. 35, T 3 N, R 12 W); the place is nearly 0.5 mile southwest of the mouth of Wickiup Canyon. Named on Chilao Flat (1959) 7.5' quadrangle

Wilbur Wash [LOS ANGELES]: *stream,* flows 2.25 miles to Aliso Canyon Wash 4.25 miles northeast of the center of Canoga Park (lat. 34°14'40" N, long. 118°32'35" W). Named on Canoga Park (1952) and Oat Mountain (1952) 7.5' quadrangles.

Wildasin [LOS ANGELES]: *locality,* 3.5 miles east-northeast of Inglewood city hall along Atchison, Topeka and Santa Fe Railroad (lat. 33°59'20" N, long. 118°17'50" W). Named on Inglewood (1964) 7.5' quadrangle. Called Wildeson on Redondo (1896) 15' quadrangle.

Wildcat Gulch [LOS ANGELES]: *canyon,* drained by a stream that flows 2 miles to Upper Big Tujunga Canyon nearly 6 miles southsouthwest of Pacifico Mountain (lat. 34°18'30" N, long. 118°04'45" W; near NW cor. sec. 31, T 3 N, R 11 W). Named on Chilao Flat (1959) 7.5' quadrangle.

Wildeson: see **Wildasin** [LOS ANGELES].

Wild Rose Canyon: see **Rose Canyon** [ORANGE].

Wildwood [LOS ANGELES]: *locality,* 2.5 miles south-southwest of Condor Peak in Big Tujunga Canyon (lat. 34°17'40" N, long. 118° 14'25" W; near NE cor. sec. 4, T 2 N, R 13 W). Named on Condor Peak (1959) 7.5' quadrangle.

Wildwood: see **Fernwood** [LOS ANGELES].

Wildwood Canyon [LOS ANGELES]:
(1) *canyon,* 1.5 miles long, 2 miles north-northeast of Burbank city hall (lat. 34°12'30" N, long. 118°17'30" W). Named on Burbank (1966) 7.5' quadrangle.
(2) *canyon,* 1.5 miles long, 3 miles east of Glendora city hall (lat. 34°08'20" N, long. 117°48'40" W; sec. 27, 34, T 1 N, R 9 W). Named on Glendora (1953) 7.5' quadrangle.

Wildwood Canyon: see **Newhall** [LOS ANGELES].

Wiley Canyon [LOS ANGELES]: *canyon,* drained by a stream that flows 1.25 miles to Towsley Canyon 2.25 miles southwest of Newhall (lat. 34°21'25" N, long. 118°33'25" W; sec. 9, T 3 N, R 16 W). Named on Oat Mountain (1952) 7.5' quadrangle. Henry Clay Wiley, a merchant and expressman, was a pioneer in the canyon (Reynolds, p. 13).

Wiley Canyon [VENTURA]: *canyon,* drained by a stream that flows 2 miles to the valley of Santa Clara River 3 miles southwest of Piru (lat. 34°22'55" N, long. 119°49'50" W). Named on Piru (1952) and Simi (1951) 7.5' quadrangles.

Willard Canyon [VENTURA]: *canyon,* drained by a stream that flows 1.25 miles to the valley of Santa Clara River 2 miles east of Santa Paula (lat. 34°21'10" N, long. 119°01'20" W; sec. 7, T 3 N, R 20 W). Named on Santa Paula (1951) 7.5' quadrangle.

Williams Camp: see **Williams Flat** [LOS ANGELES].

Williams Canyon [LOS ANGELES]:
(1) *canyon,* drained by a stream that flows 1.5 miles to San Gabriel River 8 miles northeast of Glendora city hall (lat. 34°14' N, long. 117°47'20" W). Named on Glendora (1953) 7.5' quadrangle. Called Roberts Canyon on Pomona (1904) 15' quadrangle.
(2) *canyon,* 0.5 mile long, 7 miles north-northeast of Pomona city hall (lat. 34°09'05" N, long. 117°42'15" W; on S line sec. 22, T 1 N, R 8 W). Named on Mount Baldy (1954) 7.5' quadrangle.

Williams Canyon [ORANGE]: *canyon,* drained by a stream that flows 3.25 miles to Santiago Creek 7.5 miles north-northeast of El Toro (lat. 33°43'40" N, long. 117°39' W). Named on El Toro (1968) and Santiago Peak (1954) 7.5' quadrangles. The name commemorates Marshall Williams, who lived in the canyon; the feature also was known as Cañada Seco and as Seco Canyon in the early days (Meadows, p. 50, 126, 139).

Williams Flat [LOS ANGELES]: *area,* 8 miles north-northeast of Glendora city hall along San Gabriel River (lat. 34°13'55" N, long. 117°47'25" W); the place is opposite the mouth of Williams Canyon (1). Named on Glendora (1953) 7.5' quadrangle. Camp Bonita (1940) 6' quadrangle shows Williams Camp near the site. Jim Williams founded Williams Camp 1.25 miles downstream from Camp Bonita in 1913 (Robinson, J.W., 1983, p. 96).

Williamson: see **Mount Williamson** [LOS ANGELES].

Williamson's Pass: see **Soledad Pass** [LOS ANGELES].

Willmore City: see **Long Beach** [LOS ANGELES].

Willowbrook [LOS ANGELES]: *district,* 3 miles south-southwest of South Gate city hall (lat. 33°55' N, long. 118°13'45" W). Named on South Gate (1952) 7.5' quadrangle. South Gate (1964) 7.5' quadrangle has the designation "Willowbrook (Willow Brook P.O.)" at the place. Postal authorities established Willowbrook post office in 1906 and changed the name to Willow Brook in 1952: the name is from willow trees that grew along a stream at the site when Pacific Electric Railroad built a station there (Salley, p. 241).

Willow Cove [LOS ANGELES]: *embayment,* 2.5 miles north-northwest of Avalon on the northeast side of Santa Catalina Island (lat. 33°22'30" N, long. 118°21'10" W). Named on Santa Catalina East (1950) 7.5' quadrangle, which shows Camp Toyon at the place. United States Board on Geographic Names (1975, p. 12) approved the name "Toyon Bay" for the feature, and approved the name "Willow Cove" for an embayment situated 0.25 mile north-northwest of present Toyon Bay (lat. 33°22'39" N, long. 118°21'18" W).

Willow Creek [LOS ANGELES]: *stream,* flows 1 mile to the sea 7.5 miles west-northwest of Point Dume (lat. 34°02'45" N, long. 118° 55'40" W). Named on Triunfo Pass (1950) 7.5' quadrangle. Los Angeles County (1935) map has the name "Little Nicholas Canyon" for the canyon of present Willow Creek—the feature is less than 1 mile west of Nicholas Canyon.

Willow Creek [VENTURA]: *stream,* flows nearly 2 miles to Lake Casitas 8 miles southwest of the town of Ojai (lat. 34°23'25" N, long. 119°21'40" W). Named on Matilija (1952, photorevised 1967) and White Ledge Peak (1952) 7.5' quadrangles.

Willow Spring [LOS ANGELES]: *spring,* 5 miles southwest of the village of Leona Valley (lat. 34°34' N, long. 118°21'10" W; sec. 34, T 6 N, R 14 W). Named on Sleepy Valley (1958) 7.5' quadrangle.

Willow Springs Canyon [LOS ANGELES]:
(1) *canyon,* drained by a stream that flows 3.5 miles to lowlands 4 miles west-northwest of Del Sur (lat. 34°42'30" N, long. 118°21'20"

W; sec. 10, T 7 N, R 14 W). Named on Del Sur (1958) and Lake Hughes (1957) 7.5' quadrangles.
(2) *canyon,* drained by a stream that flows 1.5 miles to Hauser Canyon 5.25 miles south of the village of Leona Valley (lat. 34°32'30" N, long. 118°16'10" W; near SW cor. sec. 5, T 5 N, R 13 W). Named on Sleepy Valley (1958) 7.5' quadrangle. Called Willow Springs Gulch on Red Rover (1937) 6' quadrangle, but United States Board on Geographic Names (1959, p. 8) rejected this name for the feature.

Willow Springs Gulch: see **Willow Springs Canyon** [LOS ANGELES] (2).

Willowville [LOS ANGELES]: *locality,* 2.5 miles north of Long Beach city hall along Pacific Electric Railroad (lat. 33°48'20" N, long. 118°11'15" W). Named on Long Beach (1949) 7.5' quadrangle.

Wills Canyon [VENTURA]: *canyon,* 2 miles long, opens into Ojai Valley 3 miles west of the town of Ojai (lat. 34°27' N, long. 119° 17'45" W). Named on Matilija (1952) 7.5' quadrangle.

Will Thrall Peak [LOS ANGELES]: *peak,* 5 miles south-southwest of Valyermo (lat. 34°23'05" N, long. 117°54'05" W; near SW cor. sec. 35, T 4 N, R 10 W). Named on Juniper Hills (1959) 7.5' quadrangle. The name commemorates William H. Thrall, an early conservationist (United States Board on Geographic Names, 1963, p. 15).

Wilmar [LOS ANGELES]: *district,* 2 miles south of present San Gabriel city hall (lat. 34°04'15" N, long. 118°05'10" W). Named on Alhambra (1926) and El Monte (1926) 6' quadrangles.

Wilmington [LOS ANGELES]: *district,* 6 miles southeast of Torrance city hall in Los Angeles (lat. 33°47' N, long. 118°15'40" W). Named on Long Beach (1964) and Torrance (1964) 7.5' quadrangles. Postal authorities established Wilmington post office in 1864 (Frickstad, p. 84). Los Angeles annexed the place in 1909 (Hanna, p. 356). Phineas Banning named the community after his birthplace in Delaware; until 1863 the place was known as New San Pedro or Newtown (Gudde, 1949, p. 391). Postal authorities established East Wilmington post office in 1912, discontinued it in 1918, reestablished it in 1919, and discontinued it in 1921 (Frickstad, p. 73). Redondo (1896) 15' quadrangle shows a place called Drum Barracks located less than 1 mile northeast of the center of Wilmington (lat. 33°47' N, long. 118°15'30" W). The place first was called Camp San Pedro, then Camp Drum to honor Adjutant-General Richard C. Drum, and after December 1, 1863, it was designated Drum Barracks (Hart, p. 54).

Wilmington: see **North Wilmington**, under **Carson** [LOS ANGELES].

Wilmington Lagoon [LOS ANGELES]: *water*

feature, south of Wilmington between Wilmington and present Terminal Island (lat. 33° 45'30" N, long. 118°16" W). Named on Redondo (1896) 15' quadrangle. The feature now is modified to form part of Los Angeles Harbor.

Wilshire: see **Cavin** [VENTURA].

Wilsie Canyon [VENTURA]: canyon, 4 miles long, drained by Reeves Creek above a point 4 miles east of the town of Ojai (lat. 34°27'15" N, long. 119°10'25" W; sec. 3, T 4 N, R 22 W). Named on Ojai (1952) 7.5' quadrangle.

Wilson: see **Camp Wilson**, under **Martins Camp** [LOS ANGELES]; **Mount Wilson** [LOS ANGELES].

Wilsona [LOS ANGELES]: locality, 14 miles east-northeast of Littlerock (lat. 34°36'50" N, long. 117°46'05" W; near N line sec. 18, T 6 N, R 8 W). Named on Wilsona (1935) 6' quadrangle. Postal authorities established Wilsona post office in 1917 and discontinued it in 1933; the name was for President Woodrow Wilson (Salley, p. 241).

Wilsona Gardens [LOS ANGELES]: locality, 14 miles northeast of Littlerock (lat. 34°40' N, long. 117°49'30" W; sec. 27, T 7 N, R 9 W). Named on Hi Vista (1957) 7.5' quadrangle.

Wilson Canyon [LOS ANGELES]: canyon, 2 miles long, opens into lowlands 3.25 miles north of downtown San Fernando (lat. 34°19'45" N, long. 118°26'40" W; sec. 22, T 3 N, R 15 W). Named on San Fernando (1953) 7.5' quadrangle.

Wilson Canyon Saddle [LOS ANGELES]: pass, 5 miles north of downtown San Fernando (lat. 34°21'25" N, long. 118°27'05" W; near E line sec. 9, T 3 N, R 15 W); the pass is near the head of Wilson Canyon. Named on San Fernando (1966) 7.5' quadrangle.

Wilson Cove [LOS ANGELES]: embayment, 2.5 miles southeast of Northwest Harbor on the east side of San Clemente Island (lat. 33° 30' N, long. 118°33'25" W). Named on San Clemente Island North (1943) 7.5' quadrangle.

Wilson Lake [LOS ANGELES]: intermittent lake, 2.25 miles south-southeast of present Pasadena city hall (lat. 34°07'10" N, long. 118°07'20" W). Named on Altadena (1928) 6' quadrangle.

Wilson's Cove: see **Emerald Bay** [LOS ANGELES].

Wilson's Peak: see **Mount Wilson** [LOS ANGELES] (1).

Windmill Canyon [LOS ANGELES-VENTURA]: canyon, 0.5 mile long, 2 miles east-southeast of Thousand Oaks on Los Angeles-Ventura county line (lat. 34°09'45" N, long. 118°48' W). Named on Thousand Oaks (1952) 7.5' quadrangle.

Windmill Canyon [VENTURA]: canyon, drained by a stream that flows nearly 3 miles to Gillibrand Canyon 5.5 miles northwest of

Santa Susana Pass (lat. 34°19'40" N, long. 118°41'50" W; sec. 19, T 3 N, R 17 W). Named on Santa Susana (1951) 7.5' quadrangle.

Windsor Hills [LOS ANGELES]: district, 2 miles north of Inglewood city hall (lat. 33°59'25" N, long. 118°21'10" W). Named on Inglewood (1964) 7.5' quadrangle.

Windy Gap [LOS ANGELES]: pass, 2 miles north-northeast of Crystal Lake (lat. 34°20'35" N, long. 117°49'40" W). Named on Crystal Lake (1958) 7.5' quadrangle.

Windy Spring [LOS ANGELES]: spring, 2 miles north-northeast of Crystal Lake (lat. 34°20'50" N, long. 117°50'05" W). Named on Crystal Lake (1958) 7.5' quadrangle.

Winery Canyon [LOS ANGELES]: canyon, about 1 mile long, 6.5 miles north-northwest of Pasadena city hall (lat. 34°13'45" N, long. 118°12'20" W; mainly in sec. 26, T 2 N, R 13 W). Named on Pasadena (1953) 7.5' quadrangle.

Wingfoot [LOS ANGELES]: locality, 6 miles east-northeast of Inglewood city hall along Atchison, Topeka and Santa Fe Railroad (lat. 33°59'20" N, long. 118°15'15" W). Named on Inglewood (1964) 7.5' quadrangle.

Winnetka [LOS ANGELES]: district, less than 2 miles east-northeast of the center of Canoga Park in Los Angeles (lat. 34°12'50" N, long. 118°34'10" W). Named on Canoga Park (1952) 7.5' quadrangle. Postal authorities established Winnetka post office in 1935 (Salley, p. 242). The place first was called Weeks Poultry Community (Gudde, 1969, p. 366).

Winston Peak [LOS ANGELES]: peak, 1.5 miles north of Waterman Mountain (lat. 34°21'30" N, long. 117°56'05" W; sec. 9, T 3 N, R 10 W); the peak is at the southeast end of Winston Ridge. Altitude 7502 feet. Named on Waterman Mountain (1959) 7.5' quadrangle.

Winston Ridge [LOS ANGELES]: ridge, generally west-northwest-trending, 3.5 miles long, 7.25 miles southwest of Valyermo (lat. 34°22'25" N, long. 117°56'30" W). Named on Juniper Hills (1959) and Waterman Mountain (1959) 7.5' quadrangles. The name commemorates L.C. Winston, a Pasadena businessman who froze to death on the ridge during a blizzard in 1893 (Robinson, J.W., 1977, p. 191-192).

Winston Spring [LOS ANGELES]: spring, 1 mile northwest of Waterman Mountain (lat. 34°20'50" N, long. 117°57' W; sec. 17, T 3 N, R 10 W); the spring is about 1 mile southwest of Winston Peak. Named on Waterman Mountain (1959) 7.5' quadrangle.

Winter Camp Creek: see **Winter Creek** [LOS ANGELES].

Winter Canyon [LOS ANGELES]: canyon, 1 mile long, 1.5 miles northwest of Malibu Point (lat. 34°02'35" N, long. 118°42'10" W; on S line sec. 30, T 1 S, R 17 W). Named on Malibu

Beach (1951) 7.5' quadrangle. Called Amarillo Canyon on Los Angeles County (1935) map.

Winter Creek [LOS ANGELES]: *stream,* flows 3 miles to Santa Anita Canyon 3 miles southeast of Mount Wilson (1) (lat. 34° 12' N, long. 118°01'10" W; sec. 3, T 1 N, R 11 W). Named on Mount Wilson (1953) 7.5' quadrangle. Called Winter Camp Creek on Los Angeles County (1935) map. Wilbur M. Sturtevant began work on a trail in 1895 and set up a camp, called Sturtevant's Winter Camp, which gave its name to Winter Camp Creek (Owens, p. 4-5).

Winter Gardens [LOS ANGELES]: *district,* 5 miles east-southeast of Los Angeles city hall (lat. 34°01' N, long. 118°10' W). Named on Alhambra (1926) 6' quadrangle.

Wintersburg [ORANGE]: *locality,* nearly 4 miles north of Huntington Beach civic center along Southern Pacific Railroad (lat. 33°43'05" N, long. 117°59'50" W; near S line sec. 23, T 5 S, R 11 W). Named on Newport Beach (1965) 7.5' quadrangle. The name commemorates Henry Winters, an early-day celery farmer (Meadows, p. 139).

Wire Springs Canyon [ORANGE]: *canyon,* drained by a stream that flows nearly 1 mile to Blue Mud Canyon 1.25 miles south-southeast of San Juan Hill (lat. 33°53'50" N, long. 117°44' W). Named on Prado Dam (1967) 7.5' quadrangle.

Wiseburn: see **Lairport** [LOS ANGELES].

Woersham Cañon: see **Worsham Creek** [LOS ANGELES].

Wolfskill Camp [LOS ANGELES]: *locality,* 8.5 miles north of Pomona city hall (lat. 34°10'30" N, long. 117°45'05" W); the place is in Wolfskill Canyon. Named on La Verne (1940) 6' quadrangle.

Wolfskill Canyon [LOS ANGELES]: *canyon,* drained by a stream that flows nearly 4 miles to San Dimas Canyon 7 miles east-northeast of Glendora city hall (lat. 34°10'35" N, long. 117°45'20" W; sec. 18, T 1 N, R 8 W). Named on Glendora (1953) and Mount Baldy (1954) 7.5' quadrangles. The name commemorates William Wolfskill, who settled at Los Angeles in 1836 and was a pioneer of the fruit-growing industry (Gudde, 1949, p. 392).

Wolfskill Falls [LOS ANGELES]: *waterfall,* 8.5 miles north of Pomona city hall (lat. 34°10'35" N, long. 117°44'55" W; near W line sec. 17, T 1 N, R 8 W); the feature is in Wolfskill Canyon. Named on Mount Baldy (1954) 7.5' quadrangle. J.W. Robinson (1983, p. 118) described Wolfskill Falls Camp, a resort that Albert Coulatti and his wife Marion built 100 yards downstream from Wolfskill Falls in 1923—the resort operated until 1934.

Wolfskill Falls Camp: see **Wolfskill Falls** [LOS ANGELES].

Wood Canyon [ORANGE]: *canyon,* drained by a stream that flows nearly 4 miles to Aliso

Creek 5 miles west-northwest of San Juan Capistrano (lat. 33°32'30" N, long. 117°44'10" W). Named on San Juan Capistrano (1968) 7.5' Quadrangle. The name is from oak trees in the canyon (Meadows, p. 140).

Wood Canyon [VENTURA]: *canyon,* drained by a stream that flows 3.5 miles to Big Sycamore Canyon 3.5 miles northeast of Point Mugu (lat. 34°06'40" N, long. 119°00'35" W). Named on Camarillo (1950) and Point Mugu (1949) 7.5' quadrangles.

Woodland Hills [LOS ANGELES]: *district,* 2.5 miles south of the center of Canoga Park in Los Angeles (lat. 34°09'45" N, long. 118° 36'15" W). Named on Calabasas (1952) and Canoga Park (1952) 7.5' quadrangles. Called Girard on Dry Canyon (1932) 6' quadrangle, but United States Board on Geographic Names (1950b, p. 7) rejected this name for the place. Postal authorities established Girard post office in 1923 and changed the name to Woodland Hills in 1941; the name "Girard" was for Victor Girard, who subdivided the place (Salley, p. 85).

Woodland Park [LOS ANGELES]: *district,* 8 miles northeast of Long Beach city hall (lat. 33°50'30" N, long. 118°05' W; sec. 12, T 4 S, R 12 W). Named on Los Alamitos (1950) 7.5' quadrangle.

Wood Ranch Reservoir [VENTURA]: *lake,* 1 mile long, 4.5 miles north of Thousand Oaks (lat. 34°14'15" N, long. 118°49'30" W). Named on Thousand Oaks (1950, photorevised 1981) 7.5' quadrangle.

Woods Cove [ORANGE]: *embayment,* 1.5 miles south-southeast of Laguna Beach city hall along the coast (lat. 33°31'30" N, long. 117°46'05" W). Named on Laguna Beach (1965) 7.5' quadrangle.

Woodwardia Canyon [LOS ANGELES]: *canyon,* drained by a stream that flows less than 1 mile to Dark Canyon (1) 5.25 miles south-southeast of Condor Peak (lat. 34°15'10" N, long. 118°11'30" W; near S line sec. 13, T 2 N, R 13 W). Named on Condor Peak (1959) 7.5' quadrangle.

Woolsey Canyon [LOS ANGELES-VENTURA]: *canyon,* drained by a stream that heads just inside Ventura County and flows 1.5 miles to lowlands at Chatsworth Reservoir nearly 3 miles southwest of Chatsworth in Los Angeles County (lat. 34°13'55" N, long. 118° 38'40" W). Named on Calabasas (1952) 7.5' quadrangle.

Workman [LOS ANGELES]: *locality,* nearly 3 miles southeast of South Gate city hall along Union Pacific Railroad (lat. 33°55'40" N, long. 118°10'05" W). Named on South Gate (1952) 7.5' quadrangle. Postal authorities established Workman post office in 1878, discontinued it the same year, reestablished it in 1892, discontinued it in 1893, reestablished it in 1898, discontinued it in 1904, reestablished it in 1911, and discontinued it in 1913;

the name was for William Workman, a pioneer of 1841 (Salley, p. 243).

Workman Hill [LOS ANGELES]: *peak,* 2.25 miles east-northeast of present Whittier city hall (lat. 33°59'30" N, long. 118°00'05" W); the feature is near La Puente grant. Altitude 1387 feet. Named on La Habra (1952) and Whittier (1949) 7.5' quadrangles. The name is for William Workman, who was one of the recipients of La Puente grant (Gudde, 1949, p. 393).

Worsham Creek [LOS ANGELES]: *stream,* flows less than 2 miles to end 0.5 mile east of present Whittier city hall (lat. 33°58'20" N, long. 118°01'30" W). Named on Whittier (1949) 7.5' quadrangle. Watts' (1898-1899) map has the name "Woersham Cañon" for the canyon of the stream.

Woyden [LOS ANGELES]: *locality,* 2.5 miles southeast of El Monte along Southern Pacific Railroad (lat. 34°03'05" N, long. 118°00'10" W). Named on Pasadena (1900) 15' quadrangle.

Wright Canyon: see **Mint Canyon** [LOS ANGELES] (1).

Wrigley Reservoir [LOS ANGELES]: *lake,* 500 feet long, 1.5 miles west-northwest of Avalon on Santa Catalina Island (lat. 33°21'10" N, long. 118°21'05" W). Named on Santa Catalina East (1950) 7.5' quadrangle.

Wyatt [LOS ANGELES]: *locality,* 6 miles northeast of present Los Angeles city hall along Los Angeles Terminal Railroad (lat. 34° 07' N, long. 118°10' W). Named on Pasadena (1900) 15' quadrangle.

Wyneka: see **Cahuenga**, under **Universal City** [LOS ANGELES].

Wynema: see **Port Hueneme** [VENTURA].

– X - Y –

Xalisco: see **Huntington Beach** [ORANGE].

Yaeger Mesa [ORANGE]: *relief feature,* 1.5 miles south-southwest of Trabuco Peak (lat. 33°40'50" N, long. 117°29'15" W; near NE cor. sec. 3, T 6 S, R 6 W). Named on Alberhill (1954) 7.5' quadrangle. The name commemorates Jacob Yaeger, who came to the neighborhood in 1899 and settled at the upper end of Trabuco Canyon (Meadows, p. 140).

Ybarra Canyon [LOS ANGELES]:
(1) *canyon,* drained by a stream that flows 2.5 miles to Devil Canyon 2.5 miles north-northwest of Chatsworth (lat. 34°17'35" N, long. 118°36'50" W; at S line sec. 36, T 3 N, R 17 W). Named on Oat Mountain (1952) 7.5' quadrangle. On Santa Susana (1903) 15' quadrangle, the upper part of present Devil Canyon is called Ybarra Canyon, and part of present Ybarra Canyon is unnamed.
(2) *canyon,* drained by a stream that flows nearly 3 miles to Big Tujunga Canyon 2.5 miles southwest of Condor Peak (lat. 34°17'50" N, long. 118°14'45" W; sec. 33, T

3 N, R 13 W). Named on Condor Peak (1959) 7.5' quadrangle, which shows Ybarra ranch located near the mouth of the canyon.

Yellow Creek: see **Pole Creek** [VENTURA].

Yerba Buena: see **Triunfo Corner** [VENTURA].

Yerba Buena Ridge [LOS ANGELES]: *ridge,* southwest-trending, 2.25 miles long, 5.5 miles north-northeast of Sunland (lat. 34° 20' N, long. 118°16'45" W). Named on Sunland (1966) 7.5' quadrangle.

Yerba Buena Spring [LOS ANGELES]: *spring,* 6 miles north-northeast of Sunland (lat. 34°20'25" N, long. 118°16'15" W); the spring is near the northeast end of Yerba Buena Ridge. Named on Sunland (1953) 7.5' quadrangle.

Yorba [ORANGE]: *locality,* 6 miles north-northeast of Orange city hall along Atchison, Topeka and Santa Fe Railroad (lat. 33°51'55" N, long. 117°48'30" W). Named on Orange (1950) 7.5' quadrangle. Postal authorities established Yorba post office in 1880, discontinued it in 1881, reestablished it in 1888, discontinued it in 1900, reestablished it in 1902, and discontinued it in 1905—the place also was known as San Antonio (Salley, p. 245).

Yorba Linda [ORANGE]: *city,* 10 miles northnortheast of Santa Ana (lat. 33°53'20" N, long. 117°48'45" W). Named on Orange (1964, photorevised 1981) and Yorba Linda (1964) 7.5' quadrangles. Postal authorities established Yorba Linda post office in 1912 (Frickstad, p. 118), and the city incorporated in 1967. The place began in 1909 as a station along Pacific Electric Railroad (Meadows, p. 141). A flag stop called Casa Loma was located along the same railroad 1 mile northwest of Yorba Linda; a station called Stearn, named for Jacob Stearn, a landowner there, was situated along the railroad 1.4 miles southeast of Yorba Linda (Meadows, p. 51, 131).

Yorba Linda Reservoir [ORANGE]: *lake,* 0.5 mile long, 1 mile south of Yorba Linda (lat. 33°52'30" N, long. 117°48'40" W). Named on Orange (1950) and Yorba Linda (1950) 7.5' quadrangles.

Young: see **Roger Young Village** [LOS ANGELES].

Young Canyon [LOS ANGELES]: *canyon,* drained by a stream that flows 2.5 miles to Santa Clara River 11.5 miles east of Solemint (lat. 34°26'25" N, long. 118°15'45" W; near S line sec. 8, T 4 N, R 13 W). Named on Agua Dulce (1960) 7.5' quadrangle.

– Z –

Zachau Canyon [LOS ANGELES]: *canyon,* 1.25 miles long, 2 miles east-northeast of Sunland (lat. 34°16'20" N, long. 118°16'45" W; sec. 7, T 2 N, R 13 W). Named on Sunland (1953) 7.5' quadrangle.

Zelzah: see **Northridge** [LOS ANGELES].
Zion: see **Mount Zion** [LOS ANGELES].
Zuma Beach: see **Westward Beach** [LOS ANGELES].
Zuma Canyon [LOS ANGELES]: *canyon,* drained by a stream that flows 7 miles to the sea 1.25 miles northwest of Point Dume (lat. 34°00'50" N, long. 118°49'15" W). Named on Point Dume (1951) 7.5' quadrangle. Called Dume Canyon on Camulos (1903) 30' quadrangle, but United States Board on Geographic Names (1961b, p. 18) rejected the names "Dume Canyon" and "Zuma Valley" for the feature.
Zuma Valley: see **Zuma Canyon** [LOS ANGELES].

REFERENCES CITED

BOOKS AND ARTICLES

Anonymous. 1950. "A run into the country." *Westways,* v.42, no.12, p. 32-33.

_____1976. *Pomona centennial history.* Pomona, California: Pomona Centennial-Bicentennial Committee, 198 p.

Antisell, Thomas. 1856. "Geological report." *Reports of explorations and surveys, to ascertain the most practicable and economical route for a railroad from the Mississippi River to the Pacific Ocean.* Volume VII, Part II. (33d Cong., 2d Sess., Sen. Ex. Doc. No. 78.) Washington: Beverley Tucker, Printer, 204 p.

Arnold, Delos, and Arnold, Ralph. 1902. "The marine Pliocene and Pleistocene stratigraphy of the coast of southern California." *The Journal of Geology,* v. 10, no. 2, p. 117-138.

Bailey, Richard C. 1962. *Explorations in Kern.* Bakersfield, California: Kern County Historical Society, 81 p.

Baker, Charles Laurence. 1911. "Notes on the later Cenozoic history of the Mohave Desert region in southeastern California." *University of California Publications, Bulletin of the Department of Geology,* v. 6, no. 15, p. 333-383.

Bancroft, Hubert Howe. 1888. *History of California, Volume VI, 1848-1859.* San Francisco: The History Company, Publishers, 787 p.

_____1890. *History of California, Volume VII, 1860-1890.* San Francisco: The History Company, Publishers, 826 p.

Barras, Judy. 1976. *The long road to Tehachapi.* Tehachapi, California: (Author), 231 p.

Becker, Robert H. 1964. *Diseños of California ranchos.* San Francisco: The Book Club of California, (no pagination).

_____1969. *Designs on the land.* San Francisco: The Book Club of California, (no pagination).

Bell, Horace. 1930. *On the old West Coast.* New York: William Morrow & Co., 336 p.

Berkstresser, C.F., Jr. 1968. *Data for springs in the Southern Coast, Transverse, and Peninsular Ranges of California.* (United States Geological Survey, Water Resources Division, Open-file report.) Menlo Park, California, 21 p. + appendices.

Blake, William P. 1857. "Geological report." *Reports of explorations and surveys, to ascertain the most practicable and economical route for a railroad from the Mississippi River to the Pacific Ocean,* Volume V, Part II. (33d Cong., 2d Sess., Sen. Ex. Doc. No. 78.) Washington: Beverly Tucker, Printer, 370 p.

Bowers, Stephen. 1890. "Orange County." *Tenth annual report of the State Mineralogist, for the year ending December 1, 1890.* Sacramento: California State Mining Bureau, p. 399-409.

Bunje, Emil T.H., and Kean, James C. 1983. *Pre-Marshall gold in California. Volume II.* Sacramento, California: Historic California Press, 70 p.

Burnham, Frederick R. 1927. "The remarks of Major Frederick R. Burnham." *Annual Publications.* Los Angeles, California: Historical Society of Southern California, p. 334-352.

California Division of Highways. 1934. *California highway transportation survey, 1934.* Sacramento: Department of Public Works, Division of Highways, 130 p. + appendices.

Carpenter, Virginia L. 1977. *Placentia, A pleasant place.* Santa Ana, California: Friis-Pioneer Press, 285 p.

Cowan, Robert G. 1956. *Ranchos of California.* Fresno, California: Academy Library Guild, 151 p.

Coy, Owen C. 1923. *California county boundaries.* Berkeley: California Historical Survey Commission, 335 p.

Crawford, J.J. 1896. "Report of the State Mineralogist." *Thirteenth report (Third Biennial) of the State Mineralogist for the two years ending September 15, 1896.* Sacramento: California State Mining Bureau, p. 10-646.

Davidson, George. 1887. "An examination of some of the early voyages of discovery and exploration on the northwest coast of America, from 1539 to 1603." *Report of the Superintendent of the U.S. Coast and Geodetic Survey, showing progress of the work during the fiscal year ending with June, 1886.* Appendix No. 7. Washington: Government Printing Office, p. 155-247.

Diller, J.S., and others. 1915. *Guidebook of the Western United States, Part D. The Shasta Route and Coast Line.* (United States Geological Survey Bulletin 614.) Washington: Government Printing Office, 142 p.

Doran, Adelaide LeMert. 1963. *The ranch that was Robbins'.* Los Angeles: (Author), 211 p.

_____1980. *Pieces of eight Channel Islands, A bibliographical guide and source book.* Glendale, California: The Arthur H. Clark Company, 340 p.

Eldridge, George Homans, and Arnold, Ralph. 1907. *The Santa Clara Valley, Puente Hills, and Los Angeles oil districts, southern California.* (Unites States Geological Survey Bulletin 309.) Washington: Government Printing Office, 266 p.

English, Walter A. 1926. *Geology and oil resources of the Puente Hills region, southern California.* (United States Geological Survey Bulletin 768.) Washington: Government Printing Office, 110 p.

Evans, George W.B. 1945. *Mexican gold trail, The journal of a forty-niner.* (Edited by Glenn S. Dumke.) San Marino, California: The Huntington Library, 340 p.

Fairbanks, Harold W. 1894. "Geology of northern Ventura, Santa Barbara, San Luis Obispo, Monterey, and San Benito Counties." *Twelfth report of the State Mineralogist, (Second Biennial,) two years ending September 15, 1894.* Sacramento: California State Mining Bureau, p. 493-526.

Femling, Jean. 1984. *Great piers of California.* Santa Barbara, California: Capra Press, 137 p.

Fink, Augusta. 1966. *Time and the terraced land.* Berkeley, California: Howell-North Books, 136 p.

Franks, Kenny A., and Lambert, Paul F. 1985. *Early California oil.* College Station: Texas A & M University Press, 243 p.

Frazer, Robert W. 1965. *Forts of the West.* Norman: University of Oklahoma Press, 246 p.

Frickstad, Walter N. 1955. *A century of California post offices, 1848 to 1954.* Oakland, California: Philatelic Research Society, 395 p.

Gagnon, Dennis R. 1981. *Exploring the Santa Barbara backcountry.* Santa Cruz: Western Tanager Press, 151 p.

Garner, Bess Adams. 1939. *Windows in an old adobe.* Claremont, California: Sauders Press, 246 p.

Gay, Thomas E., Jr., and Hoffman, Samuel R. 1954. "Mines and mineral deposits of Los Angeles County, California." *California Journal of Mines and Geology,* v. 50, nos. 3 and 4, p. 467-709.

Gleason, Duncan. 1958. *The islands and ports of California.* New York: The Devin-Adair Company, 201 p.

Goodyear, W.A. 1888. "Petroleum, asphaltum, and natural gas." *Seventh annual report of the State Mineralogist, for the year ending October 1, 1887.* Sacramento: California State Mining Bureau, p. 63-114.

Grenier, Judson A. 1978. *A guide to historic places in Los Angeles County.* Dubuque, Iowa: Kedall/Hunt Publishing Company, 324 p.

Gudde, Erwin G. 1949. *California place names.* Berkeley and Los Angeles: University of California Press, 431 p.

_____1969. *California place names.* Berkeley and Los Angeles: University of California Press, 416 p.

_____1975. *California gold camps.* Berkeley, Los Angeles, London: University of California Press, 467 p.

Guinn, J.M. 1902. *Historical and biographical record of Southern California.* Chicago: Chapman Publishing Company, 1019 p,

Hanna, Phil Townsend. 1951. *The dictionary of California land names.* Los Angeles: The Automobile Club of Southern California, 392 p.

Harrington, Marie. 1978. "California's pioneer oil town." *Desert,* v. 41, no. 10, p. 38-40.

Hart, Herbert M. 1965. *Old forts of the Far West.* New York: Bonanza Books, 192 p.

Hess, Frank L. 1910. *A reconnaissance of the gypsum deposits of California.* (United States Geological Survey Bulletin 413.) Washington: Government Printing Office, 36 p.

Hine, Robert V. 1983. *California's utopian colonies.* Berkeley, Los Angeles, London: University of California Press, 209 p.

Hoover, Mildred Brooke, Rensch, Hero Eugene, and Rensch, Ethel Grace. 1966. *Historic spots in California.* (Third edition, revised by William N. Abeloe.) Stanford, California: Stanford University Press, 642 p.

Huguenin, Emile. 1919. "Ventura County." *Report XV of the State Mineralogist.* Sacramento: California State Mining Bureau, p. 751-769.

Jackson, Sheldon G. 1977. *A British ranchero in old California.* Glendale and Azusa, California: Arthur H. Clark Company and Azusa Pacific College, 265 p.

Johnson, Harry R. 1911. *Water resources of Antelope Valley, California.* (United States Geological Survey Water-Supply Paper 278.) Washington: Government Printing Office, 92 p.

Kroeber, A.L. 1916. "California place names of Indian origin." *University of California Publications in American Archæology and Ethnology,* v. 12, no. 2, p. 31-69.

Latta, Frank F. 1976. *Saga of Rancho El Tejón.* Santa Cruz, California: Bear State Books, 293 p.

Marcou, Jules. 1876. "Report on the geology of a portion of southern California." *Annual report upon the geographical surveys west of the one hudredth meridian, in California, Nevada, Utah, Colorado, Wyoming, New Mexico, Arizona, and Montana.* (Appendix JJ of *The Annual Report of the Chief of Engineers for 1876.*) Washington: Government Printing Office, p. 158-172.

Meadows, Don. 1966. *Historic place names in Orange County.* Balboa Island, California: Paisano Press, Inc., 141 p.

Mendenhall, Walter C. 1908. *Ground waters and irrigation enterprises in the Foothill belt, southern California.* (United States Geological Survey Water-Supply Paper 219.) Washington: Government Printing Office, 180 p.

Merrill, Frederick J.H. 1919. "Los Angeles County, Orange County, Riverside County." *Report XV of the State Mineralogist.* Sacramento: California State Mining Bureau, p. 461-589.

Ormsby, Waterman L. 1968. *The Butterfield*

Overland mail. San Marino, California: The Huntington Library, 179 p.

Outland, Charles F. 1963. *Man-made disaster, The story of St. Francis Dam.* Glendale, California: The Arthur H. Clark Company, 249 p.

_____1969. *Mines, murders, and grizzlies, Tales of California's Ventura back country.* (No place): Ventura County Historical Society and The Ward Ritchie Press, 134 p.

Owens, Glen. 1981. *The heritage of the Big Santa Anita.* (No place): Big Santa Anita Historical Society, 105 p.

Parke, John G. 1857. "General report." *Reports of explorations and surveys, to ascertain the most practicable and economical route for a railroad from the Mississippi River to the Pacific Ocean.* Volume VII, part I. (33d. Cong., 2d Sess., Sen. Ex. Doc. No. 78.) Washington: Beverley Tucker, Printer, 42 p.

Peckham, S.F. 1882. (Prepared in 1866.) "Examination of the bituminous substances occurring in southern California." *The Coast Ranges.* (Geological Survey of California, Geology, Volume II, Appendix F; the complete Volume II was not published.) Cambridge, Massachusetts: John Wilson & Son, University Press, p. 49-90.

Perez, Crisostomo N. 1996. *Land grants in Alta California.* Rancho Cordova, California: Landmark Enterprises, 264 p.

Poland, J.F., and others. 1956. *Ground-water geology of the coastal zone, Long Beach-Santa Ana area, California.* (United States Geological Survey Water-Supply Paper 1109.) Washington: Government Printing Office, 162 p.

Poland, J.F., Garrett, A.A., and Sinnott, Allen. 1959. *Geology, hydrology, and chemical character of ground waters in the Torrance-Santa Monica area, California.* (United States Geological Survey Water-Supply Paper 1461.) Washington: Government Printing Office, 425 p.

Preston, E.B. 1890a. "Los Angeles County." *Ninth annual report of the State Mineralogist, for the year ending December 1, 1889.* Sacramento: California State Mining Bureau, p. 189-210.

_____1890b. "Los Angeles County." *Tenth annual report of the State Mineralogist, for the year ending December 1, 1890.* Sacramento: California State Mining Bureau, p. 277-298.

Reynolds, Gerald G. 1985. *Pico Canyon chronicles, The story of California's pioneer oil field.* Newhall, California: Santa Clara Valley Historical Society, 46 p.

Ricard, Herbert F. 1972. "Place names of Ventura County." *Ventura County Historical Society Quarterly,* v. 17, no. 2, (no pagination).

Robinson, John W. 1973. *Mines of the San Gabriels.* Glendale, California: La Siesta Press, 71 p.

_____1977. *The San Gabriels, Southern California mountain country.* San Marino, California: Golden West Books, 214 p.

_____1983. *The San Gabriels II, The mountains from Monrovia Canyon to Lytle Creek.* Arcadia, California: Big Santa Anita Historical Society, 224 p.

Robinson, W.W. 1966. *Maps of Los Angeles from Ord's Survey of 1849 to the end of the Boom of the Eighties.* Los Angeles: Dawson's Bookshop, 87 p.

Rothrock, J.T. 1876. "Report upon the operations of a special natural-history party and main field-party No. 1, California section, field-season of 1875." *Annual report upon the geographical surveys west of the one hudredth meridian, in California, Nevada, Utah, Colorado, Wyoming, New Mexico Arizona, and Montana.* (Appendix JJ of *The Annual Report of the Chief of Engineers for 1876.*) Washington: Government Printing Office, p. 202-213.

Salley, H.E. 1977. *History of California post offices, 1849-1976.* La Mesa, California: Postal History Associates, Inc., 300 p.

Sampson, R.J. 1937. "Mineral resources of Los Angeles County." *California Journal of Mines and Geology,* v. 33, no. 3, p. 173-213.

Settle, Glen A. 1963. *Here roamed the antelope.* Rosamond, California: The Kern-Antelope Historical Society, Inc., 64 p.

Sleeper, Jim. 1968. "Trabuco tin faces axe." *Mineral Information Service,* v. 21, no. 11, p. 164-167.

_____1976. *A Boys' book of bear stories (Not for boys). A grizzly introduction to the Santa Ana Mountains.* Trabuco Canyon, California: California Classics, 212 p.

Smith, William Sidney Tangier. 1897. "The geology of Santa Catalina Island." *Proceedings of the California Academy of Sciences* (third series), v. 1, no. 1, p. 1-71.

_____1898. "A geological sketch of San Clemente Island." *Eighteenth annual report of the United States Geological Survey, 1896-97.* Part II. Washington: Government Printing Office, p. 450-496.

Stephenson, Terry E. 1948. *The shadows of Old Saddleback.* (No place): The Fine Arts Press, 207 p.

Storms, W.H. 1893. "Los Angeles County." *Eleventh report of the State Mineralogist, (First Biennial,) Two years ending September 15, 1892.* Sacramento: California State Mining Bureau, p. 243-248.

Suter, Coral. 1993. "Riding high on the old Ridge Route." *The Californians,* v. 10, no. 5, p. 18-31.

Thompson, David G. 1921. *Routes to desert watering places in the Mohave Desert region, California.* (United States Geological Survey Water-Supply Paper 490-B.) Washington: Government Printing Office, p. 87-269.

_____1929. *The Mohave Desert region, California.* (United States Geological Survey Water-Supply Paper 578.) Washington: Government

Printing Office, 759 p.

Thompson and West. 1880. *History of Los Angeles County, California.* Oakland, California: Thompson & West, 192 p.

Trask, John B. 1856 *Report on the geology of northern and southern California.* (Sen. Sess. of 1856, Doc. No. 14.) Sacramento: State Printer, 66 p.

Tucker, W. Burling. 1925. "Los Angeles field division (Orange County)." *Mining in California,* v. 21, no. 1, p. 58-71.

United States Board on Geographic Names (under name "United States Geographic Board"). 1933. *Sixth report of the United States Geographic Board, 1890-1932.* Washington: Government Printing Office, 834 p.

_____(under name "United States Geographic Board"). 1934. *Decisions of the United States Geographic Board, No. 34—Decisions June 1933-March 1934.* Washington: Government Printing Office, 20 p.

_____(under name "United States Board on Geographical Names"). 1936a. *Decisions of the United States Board on Geographical Names, Decisions rendered between July 1, 1934, and June 30, 1935.* Washington: Government Printing Office, 26 p.

_____(under name "United States Board on Geographical Names"). 1936b. *Decisions of the United States Board on Geographical Names, Decisions rendered between July 1, 1935, and June 30, 1936.* Washington: Government Printing Office, 44 p.

_____(under name "United States Board on Geographical Names"). 1938. *Decisions of the United States Board on Geographical Names, Decisions rendered between July 1, 1937, and June 30, 1938.* Washington: Government Printing Office, 62 p.

_____(under name "United States Board on Geographical Names"). 1939. *Decisions of the United States Board on Geographical Names, Decisions rendered between July 1, 1938, and June 30, 1939.* Washington: Government Printing Office, 41 p.

_____(under name "United States Board on Geographical Names"). 1940. *Decisions of the United States Board on Geographical Names, Decisions rendered between July 1, 1939, and June 30, 1940.* Washington: Government Printing Office, 46 p.

_____(under name "United States Board on Geographical Names"). 1943. *Decisions rendered between July 1, 1941, and June 30, 1943.* Washington: Department of the Interior, 104 p.

_____1949. *Decision lists nos. 4907, 4908, 4909, July, August, September, 1949.* Washington: Department of the Interior, 24 p.

_____1950a. *Decision lists nos. 4910, 4911, 4912, October, November, December, 1949.* Washington: Department of the Interior, 10 p.

_____1950b. *Decisions on names in the United States and Alaska rendered during April, May, and June 1950.* (Decision list no. 5006.) Washington: Department of the Interior, 47 p.

_____1954. *Decisions on names in the United States, Alaska and Puerto Rico, Decisions rendered from July 1950 to May 1954.* (Decision list no. 5401.) Washington: Department of the Interior, 115 p.

_____1959. *Decisions on names in the United States, Decisions rendered from January, 1959 through April, 1959.* (Decision list no. 5902.) Washington: Department of the Interior, 49 p.

_____1960a. *Decisions on names in the United States and Puerto Rico, Decisions rendered in May, June, July, and August, 1959.* (Decision list no. 5903.) Washington: Department of the Interior, 79 p.

_____1960b. *Decisions on names in the United States, Decisions rendered from September 1959 through December 1959.* (Decision list no. 5904.) Washington: Department of the Interior, 68 p.

_____1960c. *Decisions on names in the United States, Puerto Rico and the Virgin Islands, Decisions rendered from January through April 1960.* (Decision list no. 6001.) Washington: Department of the Interior, 79 p.

_____1960d. *Decisions on names in the United States and the Virgin Islands, Decisions rendered from May 1960 through August 1960.* (Decision list no. 6002.) Washington: Department of the Interior, 77 p.

_____1961a. *Decisions on names in the United States, Decisions rendered from September through December 1960.* (Decision list no. 6003.) Washington: Department of the Interior, 73 p.

_____1961b. *Decisions on names in the United States, Decisions rendered from May through August 1961.* (Decision list no. 6102.) Washington: Department of the Interior, 73 p.

_____1962. *Decisions on names in the United States, Decisions rendered from September through December 1961.* (Decision list no. 6103.) Washington: Department of the Interior, 81 p.

_____1963. *Decisions on geographic names in the United States, May through August 1963.* (Decision list no. 6302.) Washington: Department of the Interior, 81 p.

_____1965a. *Decisions on geographic names in the United States, January through March 1965.* (Decision list no. 6501.) Washington: Department of the Interior, 85 p.

_____1965b. *Decisions on geographic names in the United States, April through June 1965.* (Decision list no. 6502.) Washington: Department of the Interior, 39 p.

_____1965c. *Decisions on geographic names in the United States, July through September 1965.* (Decision list no. 6503.) Washington: Department of the Interior, 74 p.

_____1967a. *Decisions on geographic names in the United States, April through June 1967.* (Decision list no. 6702.) Washington: Department of the Interior, 26 p.

_____1967b. *Decisions on geographic names in the United States, July through September 1967.* (Decision list no. 6703.) Washington: Department of the Interior, 29 p.

_____1968a. *Decisions on geographic names in the United States, January through March 1968.* (Decision list no. 6801). Washington: Department of the Interior, 51 p.

_____1968b. *Decisions on geographic names in the United States, April through June 1968.* (Decision list no. 6802.) Washington: Department of the Interior, 42 p.

_____1969a. *Decisions on geographic names in the United States, October through December 1968.* (Decision list no. 6804.) Washington: Department of the Interior, 33 p.

_____1969b. *Decisions on geographic names in the United States, January through March 1969.* (Decision list no. 6901.) Washington: Department of the Interior, 31 p.

_____1970a. *Decisions on geographic names in the United States, January through March 1970.* (Decision list no. 7001.) Washington: Department of the Interior, 31 p.

_____1970b. *Decisions on geographic names in the United States, April through June 1970.* (Decision list. no. 7002.) Washington: Department of the Interior, 20 p.

_____1973. *Decisions on geographic names in the United States, July through September 1973.* (Decision list no. 7303.) Washington: Department of the Interior, 14 p.

_____1975. *Decisions on geographic names in the United States, January through March 1975.* (Decision list no. 7501.) Washington: Department of the Interior, 36 p.

_____1976a. *Decisions on geographic names in the United States, October through December 1975.* (Decision list no. 7504.) Washington: Department of the Interior, 45 p.

_____1976b. *Decisions on geographic names in the United States, July through September 1976.* (Decision list no. 7603.) Washington: Department of the Interior, 25 p.

_____1978a. *Decisions on geographic names in the United States, October through December 1977.* (Decision list no. 7704.) Washington: Department of the Interior, 29 p.

_____1978b. *Decisions on geographic names in the United States, January through March 1978.* (Decision list no. 7801.) Washington: Department of the Interior, 18 p.

_____1978c. *Decisions on geographic names in the United States, April through June 1978.* (Decision list no. 7802.) Washington: Department of the Interior, 30 p.

_____1979. *Decisions on geographic names in the United States, April through June 1979.* (Decision list no. 7902.) Washington: Department of the Interior, 33 p.

_____1983a. *Decisions on geographic names in the United States, July through September 1982.* (Decision list no. 8203.) Washington: Department of the Interior, 25 p.

_____1983b. *Decisions on geographic names in the United States, January through March 1983.* (Decision list no. 8301.) Washington: Department of the Interior, 33 p.

_____1986. *Decisions on geographic names in the United States, January through March 1986.* (Decision list no. 8601.) Washington: Department of the Interior, 13 p.

_____1990. *Decisions on geographic names in the United States.* (Decision list 1990.) Washington: Department of the Interior, 35 p.

_____1992. *Decisions on geographic names in the United States.* (Decision list 1992.) Washington: Department of the Interior, 21 p.

United States Coast and Geodetic Survey. 1963. *United States Coast Pilot 7, Pacific Coast, California, Oregon, Washington, and Hawaii.* (Ninth edition.) Washington: United States Government Printing Office, 336 p.

Vancouver, George. 1953. *Vancouver in California, 1792-1794.* (The original account edited and annotated by Marguerite Eyer Wilbur.) Los Angeles: Glen Dawson, 274 p.

Van Kampen, Carol. 1977. "From Dairy Valley to Chino: An example of urbanization in southern California's dairy land." *The California Geographer,* v. 17, p. 39-48.

Vedder, J.G., and Norris, Robert M. 1963. *Geology of San Nicolas Island.* (United States Geological Survey Professional Paper 369.) Washington: Government Printing Office, 65 p.

Wagner, Henry R. 1968. *The cartography of the Northwest Coast of America to the year 1800.* (One-volume reprint of 1937 edition.) Amsterdam: N. Israel, 543 p.

Warner, J.J., Hayes, Benjamin, and Widney, J.P. 1876. *An historical sketch of Los Angeles County, California.* Los Angeles: Louis Lewis & Co., 159 p.

Waring, Gerald A. 1915. *Springs of California.* (United States Geological Survey Water-Supply Paper 338.) Washington: Government Printing Office, 410 p.

Watts, W.L. 1901. *Oil and gas yielding formations of California.* (California State Mining Bureau Bulletin No. 19.) Sacramento: California State Mining Bureau, 236 p.

Whipple, A.W. 1856. "Itinerary." *Reports of explorations and surveys, to ascertain the most practicable and economical route for a railroad from the Mississippi River to the Pacific Ocean.* Volume III, Part I. (33d Cong., 2d Sess, Sen. Ex. Doc. No. 78.) Washington: Beverley Tucker Printer, 136 p.

Whipple, C.W. 1876. "Executive report of Lieutenant C.W. Whipple, Ordnance Corps, on the operations of special party, California section, field-season of 1875." *Annual report upon the geographical surveys west of the one hundredth meridian, in California, Nevada, Utah,*

Colorado,Wyoming, New Mexico, Arizona, and Montana. (Appendix JJ of *The Annual Report of the Chief of Engineers for 1876.*) Washington: Government Printing Office, p. 147-150.

White, Gerald T. 1968. *Scientists in conflict, The beginnings of the oil industry in California.* San Marino, California: The Huntington Library, 272 p.

Whiting, J.S., and Whiting, Richard J. 1960. *Forts of the State of California.* (Authors), 90 p.

Whitney, J.D. 1865. *Report of progress and synopsis of the field-work from 1860 to 1864.* (Geological Survey of California, Geology, Volume I.) Published by authority of the Legislature of California, 498 p.

Williamson, R.S. 1855. "Report." *Reports of explorations and surveys, to ascertain the most practicable and economical route for a railroad from the Mississippi River to the Pacific Ocean.* Volume V, part I. (33d Cong., 2d Sess., Sen. Ex. Doc. No. 78.) Washington: Beverley Tucker, Printer, 43 p.

Yates, Lorenzo Z. 1890. "Stray notes on the geology of the Channel Islands." *Ninth annual report of the State Mineralogist, for the year ending December 1, 1889.* Sacramento: California State Mining Bureau, p. 171-174.

MISCELLANEOUS MAPS

Arnold and Arnold. 1902. "Sketch map of San Pedro and vicinity." (*In* Arnold and Arnold, p. 119.)

Baker. 1911. (Untitled map. Plate 34 *in* Baker.)

Blake. 1857. "Geological map of a part of the State of California explored in 1855 by Lieut. R.S. Williamson, U.S. Top. Engr." (*Accompanies* Blake.)

California Division of Highways. 1934. (Appendix "A" *of* California Division of Highways.)

California Mining Bureau. 1909a. "Santa Barbara and Ventura Counties." (*In* California Mining Bureau Bulletin 56.)

_____1909b. "Los Angeles and Orange Counties." (*In* California Mining Bureau Bulletin 56.)

_____1917. (Untitled map *in* California Mining Bureau Bulletin 74, p. 174.)

Diller and others. 1915. "Geologic and topographic map of the Coast Route from Los Angeles, California, to San Francisco, California." (*In* Diller and others.)

Eddy. 1854. "Approved and declared to be the official map of the State of California by an act of the Legislature passed March 25th 1853." Compiled by W.M. Eddy, State Surveyor General. Published for R.A. Eddy, Marysville, California, by J.H. Colton, New York.

Eldridge and Arnold, 1907. "Geologic map of the Santa Clara Valley and adjacent oil fields, Ventura and Los Angels Counties, California." (Plate I *in* Eldridge and Arnold).

Gibbes. 1852. "A new map of California." By Charles Drayton Gibbes, from his own and other recent surveys and explorations. Published by C.D. Gibbes, Stockton, Cal.

Goddard. 1857. "Britton & Rey's map of the State of California." By George H. Goddard.

Gray. 1873. "Gray's Atlas, New rail road and county map of the States of Oregon, California and Nevada." Compiled and drawn by Frank A. Gray. Published by O.W. Gray. Philadelphia.

Hall. 1887. "Plan of Redondo Beach, Los Angeles County, California." Designed and drawn under the direction of Wm. Ham Hall, consulting civil engineer. (Reproduced *in* Robinson, W.W., map 76.)

Hanson. 1868. "Map of the 35 acre tracts of the Los Angeles City lands, Hancocks survey, situate on the southern slope of the Stone Quarry Hills." Surveyed in August 1868 by Geo. Hansen, County Surv., assisted by Captain Wm. Moore and August Ashbrand. (Reproduced *in* Harlow, 1976).

Johnson. 1911. "Reconnaissance hydrographic map of Antelope Valley region, California." (Plate VI *in* Johnson.)

Lankershim Ranch Land and Water Company. 1888. (Untitled map reproduced *in* Robinson, W.W., map 91.)

Los Angeles County. 1935. "Map of Los Angeles County, California." Prepared by The Department of Forester and Firewarden, County of Los Angeles. (Printed 1935; 1947 edition.) (Used as base map for Plates 5 and 6 *in* Gay and Hoffman.)

Mendenhall. 1908. "Map showing the artesian areas and hydrographic contours in the valley of southern California." (Plate III *in* Mendenhall, 1908.)

Parke. 1854-1855. "Map No. 1, San Francisco Bay to the plains of Los Angeles." From explorations and surveys made by Lieut. John C. Parke. Constructed and drawn by H. Custer. (In *Reports of explorations and surveys, to ascertain the most practicable and economical route for a railroad from the Mississippi River to the Pacific Ocean.* Volume XI. 1861.)

Peckham. 1866. "Topographical sketch of a portion of the oil region of southern California." (Plate B *in* Peckham,)

Poland and others. 1956. "Map of the Long Beach-Santa Ana area, California, showing landform elements and generalized locations on base of principal fresh-water body." (Plate 1 *in* Poland and others.)

Rogers and Johnston. 1857. "State of California." By Prof. H.D. Rogers & A. Keith Johnston.

Sage. 1846. "Map of Oregon, California, New Mexico, N.W. Texas, & the proposed Territory of Ne-Bras-ka." By Rufus B. Sage.

Smith. 1897. "Geological map of Santa Catalina Island." (Plate I *in* Smith , 1897.)

_____1898. "Geological map of San Clemente

Island." (Plate LXXXIV *in* Smith, 1898.)
Stevenson. 1884. "Map of the county of Los
Angeles, California." By H.J. Stevenson, U.S.
Dept. Surveyor. (Reproduced *in* Robinson,
W.W.)
Thompson. 1921. "Relief map of part of Mohave
Desert region, California, showing desert
watering places." (Plates IX, X *in* Thompson,
1921.)
Vedder. 1963. "Geologic map and sections of San
Nicolas Island, California." (Plate 3 *in* Vedder
and Norris.)
Watts. 1898-1899. "Geological relief map of the
Puente Hills, California." (Fig. 1 *in* Watts.)
Williamson. 1853a. "Map of passes in the Si-
erra Nevada from Walker's Pass to the Coast
Range." By Lieut. R.S. Williamson, Topl.

Engr., assisted by Lieut. J.G. Parke, Topl.
Engr., and Mr. Isaac Williams Smith, Civ.
Engr. (In *Reports of explorations and surveys,
to ascertain the most practicable and economical route for a railroad from the Mississippi River to the Pacific Ocean.* Volume XI.
1861).

_____1853b. "General map of explorations and
surveys in California." By Lieut. R.S.
Williamson, Topl. Engr., assisted by Lieut.
J.G. Parke, Topl. Engr., and Mr. Isaac William Smith, Civ. Engr. (In *Reports of explorations and surveys, to ascertain the most practicable and economical route for a railroad
from the Mississippi River to the Pacific
Ocean.* Volume XI. 1861).

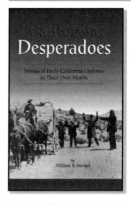

ABOUT THE AUTHOR

Many years ago in connection with his more than three-decade-long career as a geologist with the United States Geological Survey, David L. Durham often needed to know the whereabouts of some obscure or vanished place in California. He searched for a suitable gazetteer to help him locate these features but found no such volume. To meet his needs he began compiling his own gazetteer for part of the state and, as his interests expanded, so did his gazetteer.

For the first twelve years of his retirement, Mr. Durham compiled information for the gazetteer nearly full-time. Eventually he extended coverage to all of California. The definitive gazetteer of California, *California's Geographic Names: A Gazetteer of Historic and Modern Names of the State* is the result. The Durham's Place-Names of California series, of which this volume is one, contains the same information as *California's Geographic Names* but in thirteen regional divisions.

Mr. Durham was born in California, served as an infantryman in France and Germany during World War II and holds a Bachelor of Science degree from the California Institute of Technology. He and his wife Nancy have two grown children.

CALIFORNIA'S GEOGRAPHIC NAMES
A Gazetteer of Historic and Modern Names of the State

Compiled by David L. Durham

"The quantity and value of the information included in this work are simply staggering...a boon to historians, genealogists and outdoor folk of all kinds."
— Robert C. Berlo, Secretary of the California Map Society

"I am impressed! California's Geographic Names *is the new standard."*
— Robert J. Chandler, Wells Fargo Historian

The definitive gazetteer of California.

Hardcover • 1,680pp • 8½" x 11"
Bibliography • Index
ISBN 1-884995-14-4

Available from bookstores, on-line bookstores or
by calling 1-800-497-4909